# Zits®

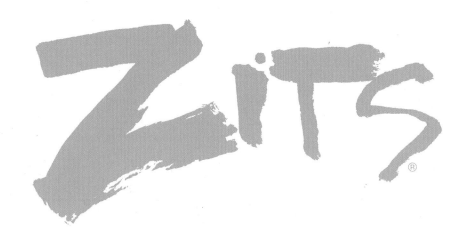

# Peace, Love & Wi-Fi

**Also By Jerry Scott and Jim Borgman**

*Zits: Sketchbook 1*
*Growth Spurt: Zits Sketchbook 2*
*Don't Roll Your Eyes at Me, Young Man!: Zits Sketchbook 3*
*Are We an "Us"?: Zits Sketchbook 4*
*Zits Unzipped: Zits Sketchbook 5*
*Busted!: Zits Sketchbook 6*
*Road Trip: Zits Sketchbook 7*
*Teenage Tales: Zits Sketchbook No. 8*
*Thrashed: Zits Sketchbook No. 9*
*Pimp My Lunch: Zits Sketchbook No. 10*
*Are We Out of the Driveway Yet?: Zits Sketchbook No. 11*
*Rude, Crude, and Tattooed: Zits Sketchbook No. 12*
*Jeremy and Mom*
*Pierced*
*Lust and Other Uses for Spare Hormones*
*Jeremy & Dad*
*You're Making That Face Again*
*Drive!*
*Triple Shot, Double Pump, No Whip Zits*
*Zits en Concert*

**Treasuries**

*Humongous Zits*
*Big Honkin' Zits*
*Zits: Supersized*
*Random Zits*
*Crack of Noon*
*Alternative Zits*
*My Bad*
*Sunday Brunch*

**Gift Book**

*A Zits Guide to Living with Your Teenager*

# Peace, Love & Wi-Fi

A ZITS® Treasury by Jerry Scott and Jim Borgman

**Andrews McMeel Publishing**

Kansas City · Sydney · London

To Sheldon Green, living proof that laughter keeps you young.
—JS

To Tom DeVoge, my brother from another mother.
—JB

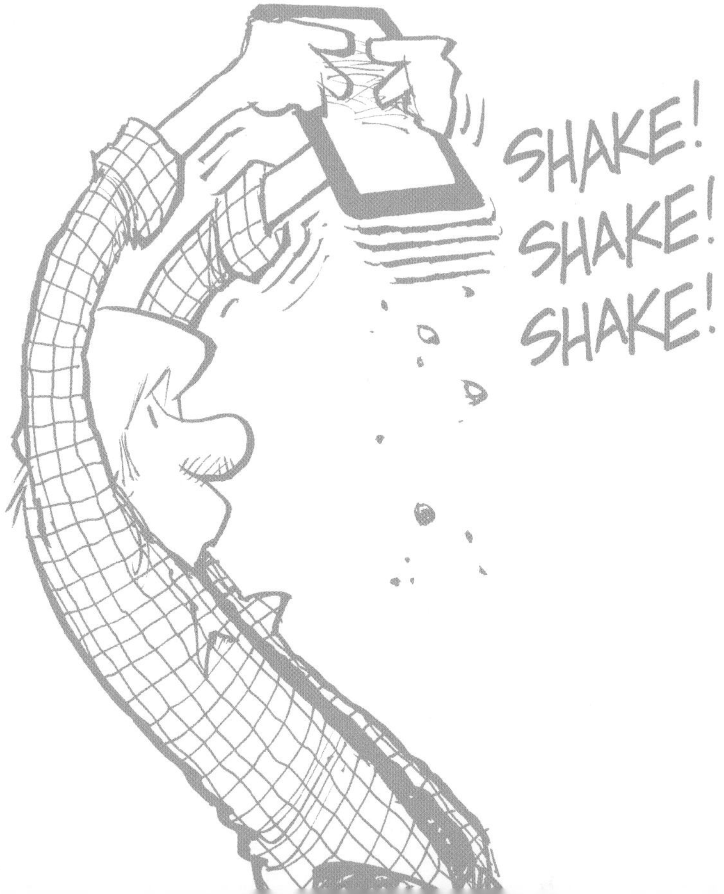
SHAKE!
SHAKE!
SHAKE!

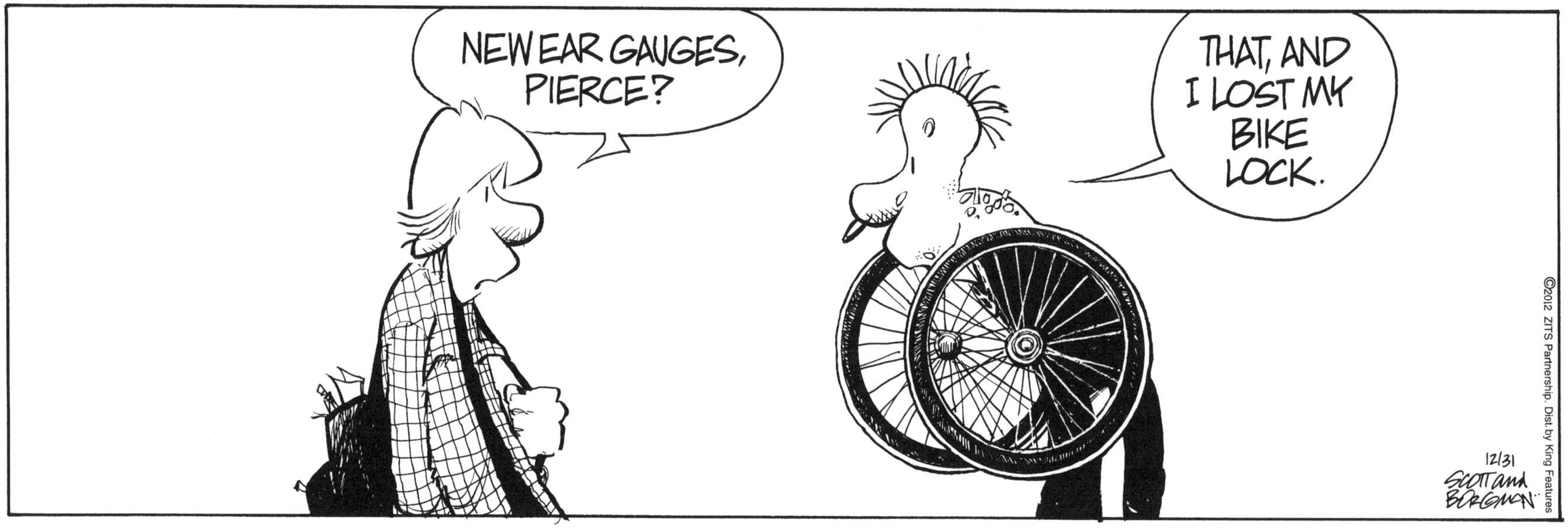
NEW EAR GAUGES, PIERCE?
THAT, AND I LOST MY BIKE LOCK.
12/31 SCOTT and BORGMAN
©2012 ZITS Partnership. Dist. by King Features

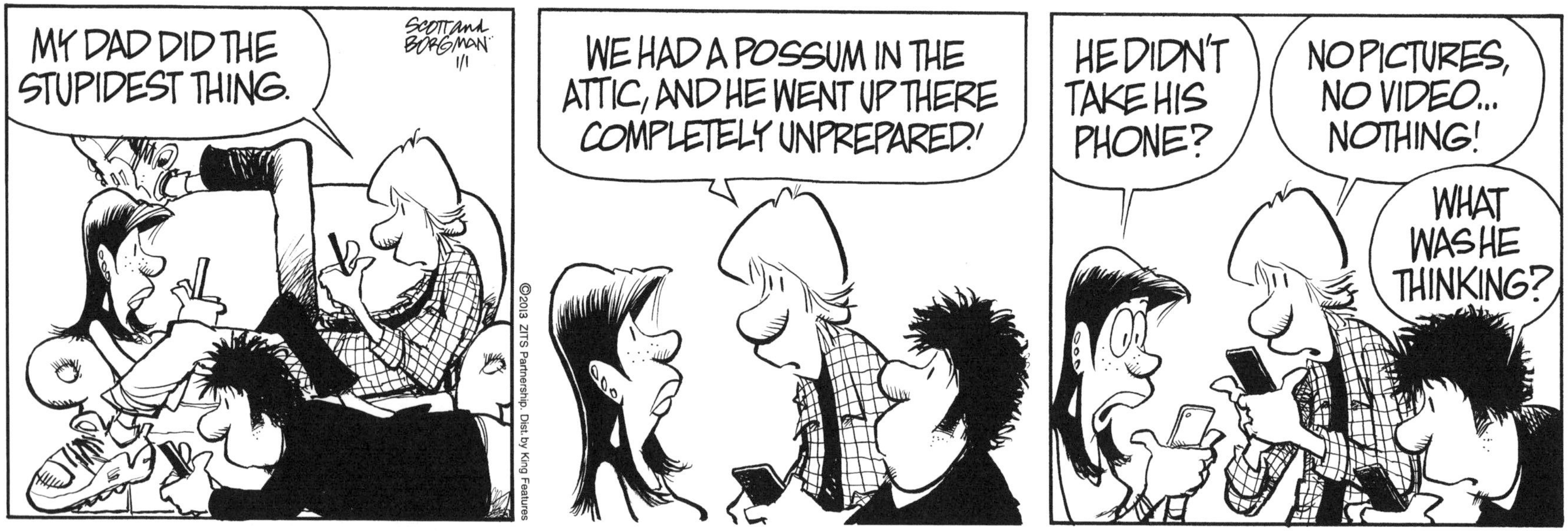
MY DAD DID THE STUPIDEST THING.
SCOTT and BORGMAN 1/1
©2013 ZITS Partnership. Dist. by King Features
WE HAD A POSSUM IN THE ATTIC, AND HE WENT UP THERE COMPLETELY UNPREPARED!
HE DIDN'T TAKE HIS PHONE?
NO PICTURES, NO VIDEO... NOTHING!
WHAT WAS HE THINKING?

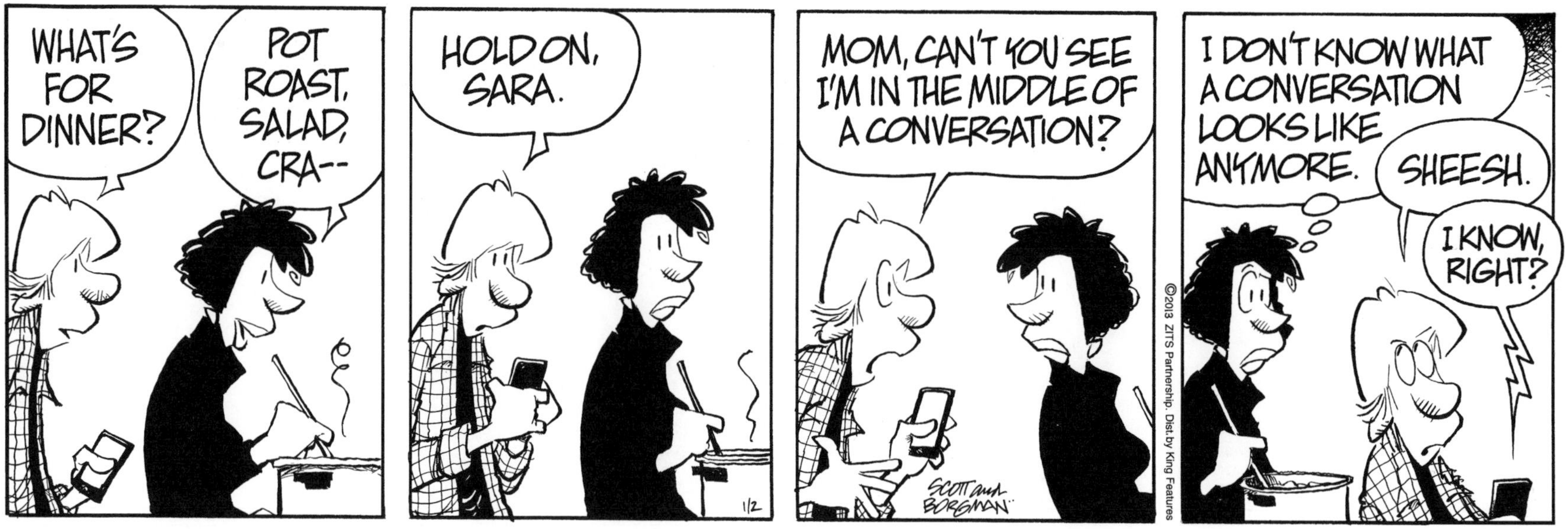
WHAT'S FOR DINNER?
POT ROAST, SALAD, CRA--
HOLD ON, SARA.
1/2
MOM, CAN'T YOU SEE I'M IN THE MIDDLE OF A CONVERSATION?
SCOTT and BORGMAN
©2013 ZITS Partnership. Dist. by King Features
I DON'T KNOW WHAT A CONVERSATION LOOKS LIKE ANYMORE.
SHEESH.
I KNOW, RIGHT?

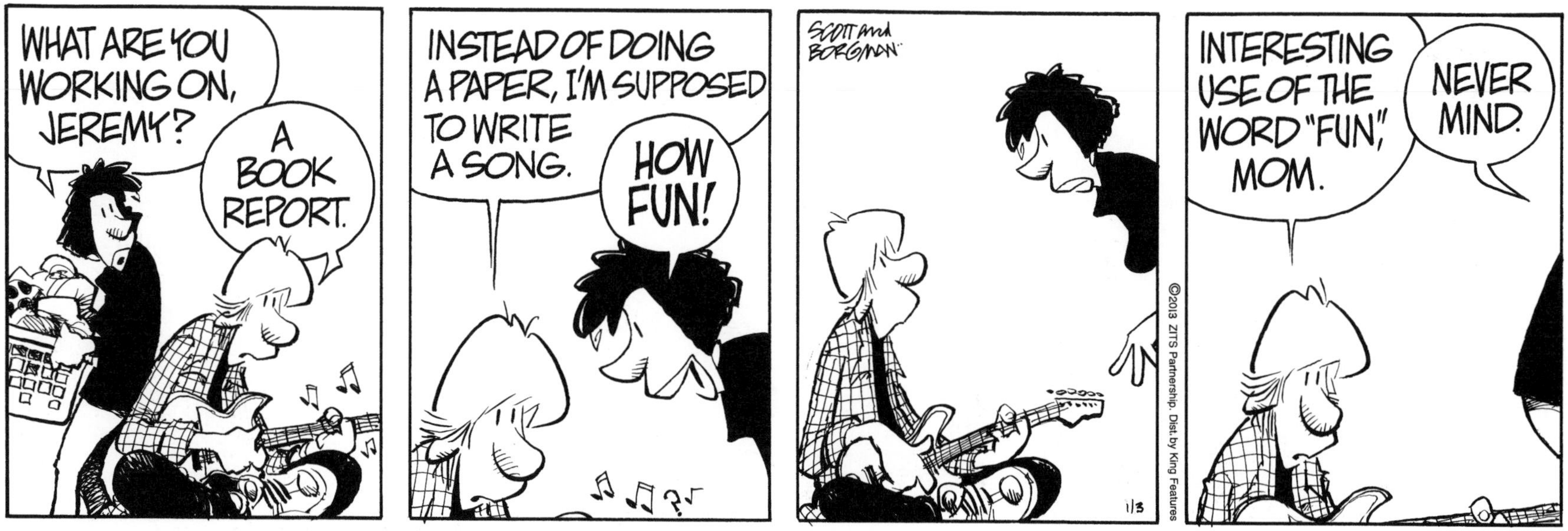
WHAT ARE YOU WORKING ON, JEREMY?
A BOOK REPORT.
INSTEAD OF DOING A PAPER, I'M SUPPOSED TO WRITE A SONG.
HOW FUN!
SCOTT and BORGMAN
1/3
©2013 ZITS Partnership. Dist. by King Features
INTERESTING USE OF THE WORD "FUN," MOM.
NEVER MIND.

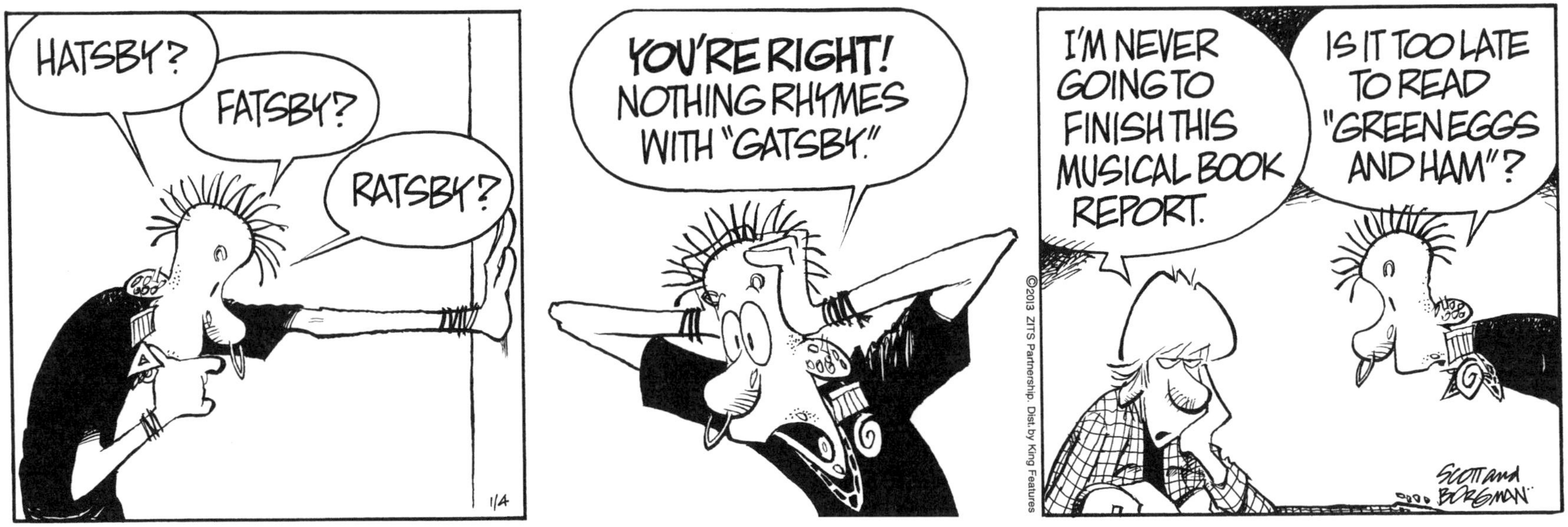
HATSBY?
FATSBY?
RATSBY?
1/4
YOU'RE RIGHT! NOTHING RHYMES WITH "GATSBY."
©2013 ZITS Partnership. Dist. by King Features
I'M NEVER GOING TO FINISH THIS MUSICAL BOOK REPORT.
IS IT TOO LATE TO READ "GREEN EGGS AND HAM"?
SCOTT AND BORGMAN

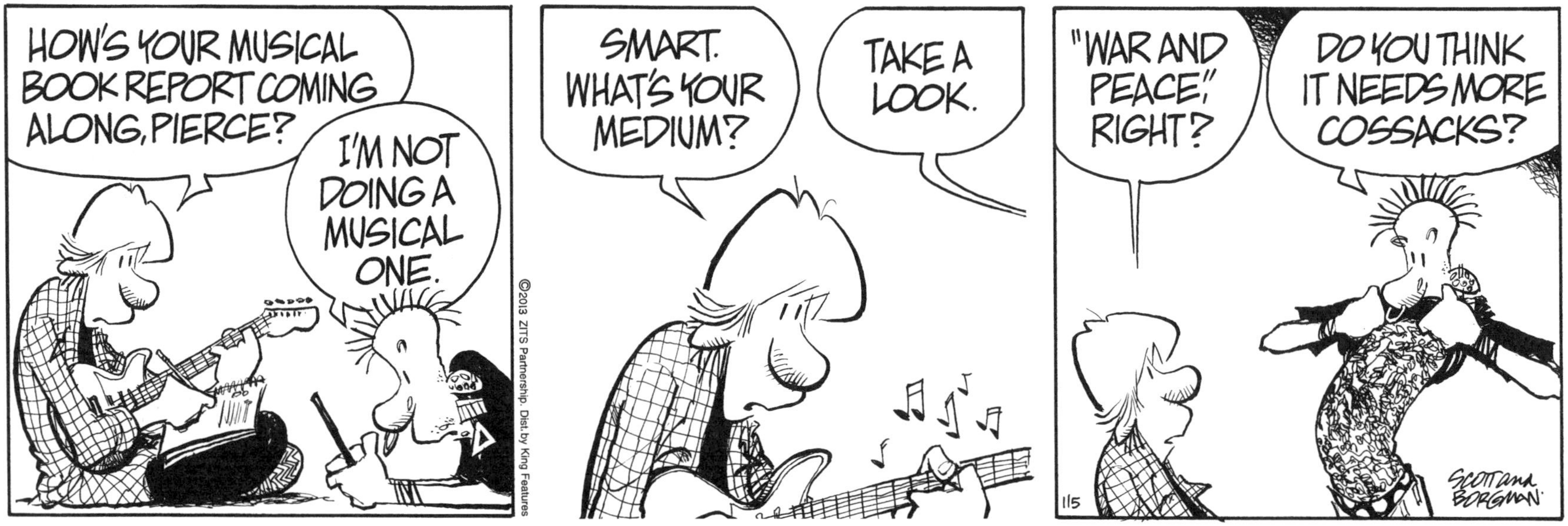
HOW'S YOUR MUSICAL BOOK REPORT COMING ALONG, PIERCE?
I'M NOT DOING A MUSICAL ONE.
©2013 ZITS Partnership. Dist. by King Features
SMART. WHAT'S YOUR MEDIUM?
TAKE A LOOK.
"WAR AND PEACE," RIGHT?
DO YOU THINK IT NEEDS MORE COSSACKS?
1/5
SCOTT AND BORGMAN

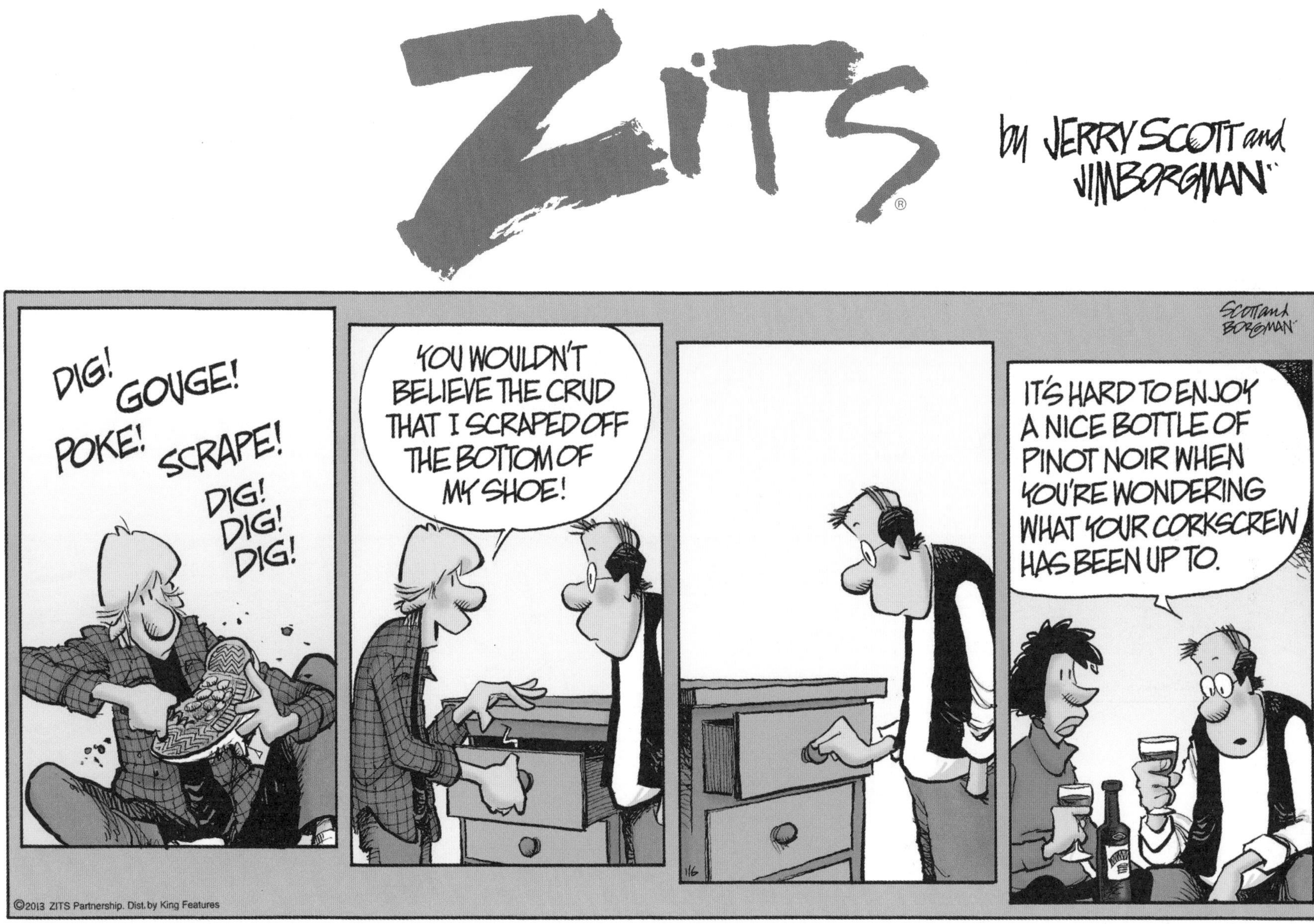
ZITS
by JERRY SCOTT and JIM BORGMAN
SCOTT and BORGMAN
DIG! GOUGE! POKE! SCRAPE! DIG! DIG! DIG!
YOU WOULDN'T BELIEVE THE CRUD THAT I SCRAPED OFF THE BOTTOM OF MY SHOE!
IT'S HARD TO ENJOY A NICE BOTTLE OF PINOT NOIR WHEN YOU'RE WONDERING WHAT YOUR CORKSCREW HAS BEEN UP TO.
©2013 ZITS Partnership. Dist. by King Features

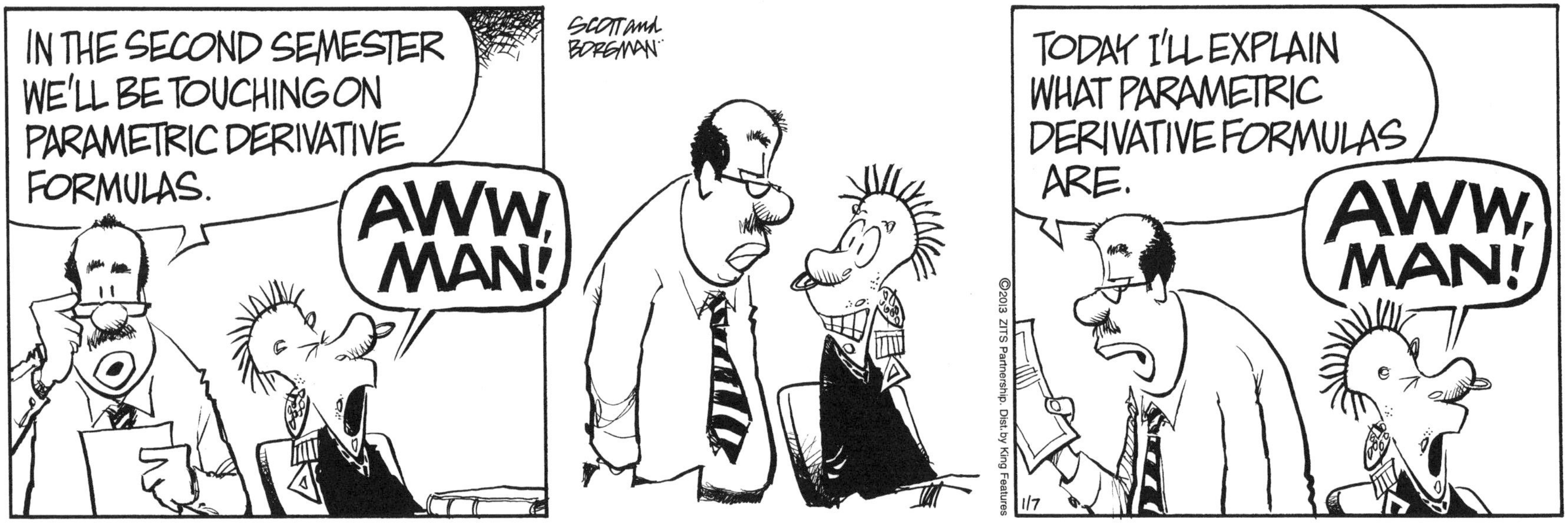
IN THE SECOND SEMESTER WE'LL BE TOUCHING ON PARAMETRIC DERIVATIVE FORMULAS.
AWW, MAN!
SCOTT and BORGMAN
TODAY I'LL EXPLAIN WHAT PARAMETRIC DERIVATIVE FORMULAS ARE.
AWW, MAN!
©2013 ZITS Partnership. Dist. by King Features
1/7

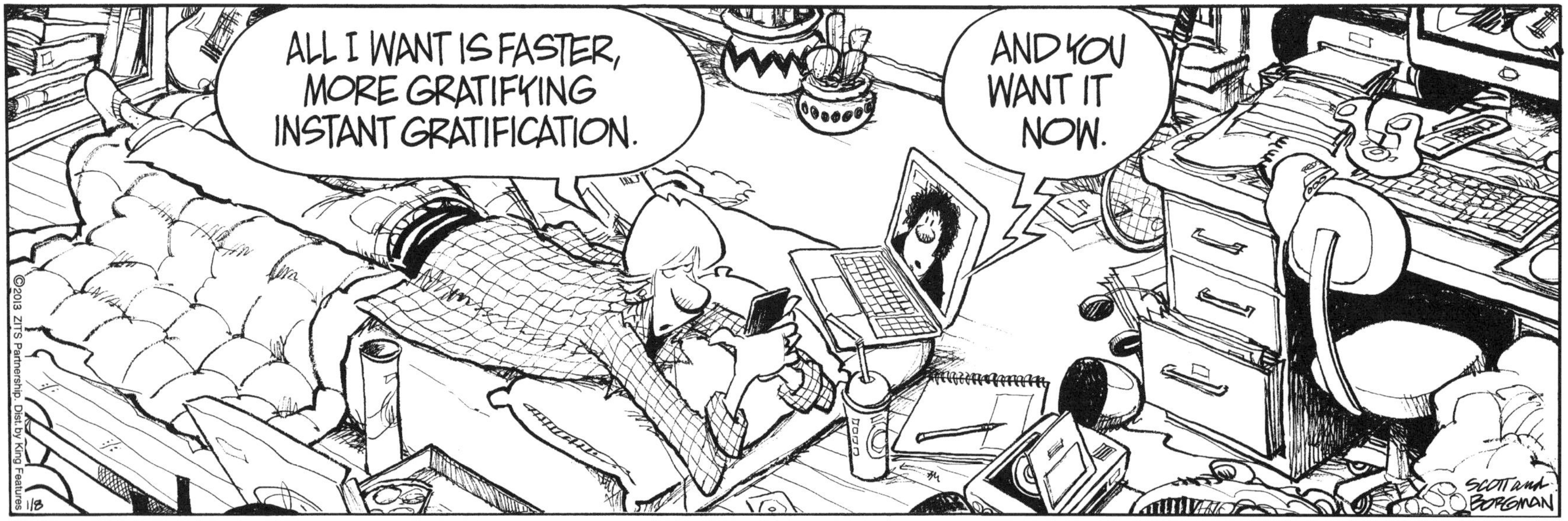
ALL I WANT IS FASTER, MORE GRATIFYING INSTANT GRATIFICATION.
AND YOU WANT IT NOW.
©2013 ZITS Partnership. Dist. by King Features
1/8
SCOTT and BORGMAN

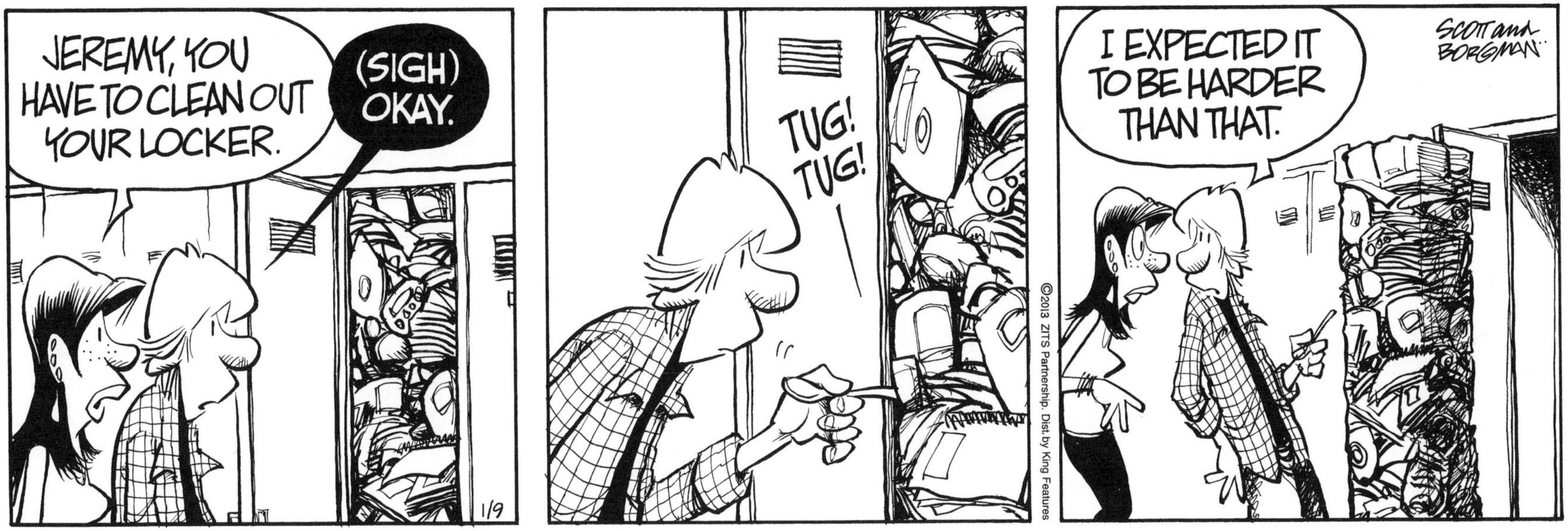
JEREMY, YOU HAVE TO CLEAN OUT YOUR LOCKER.
(SIGH) OKAY.
1/9
TUG! TUG!
©2013 ZITS Partnership. Dist. by King Features
I EXPECTED IT TO BE HARDER THAN THAT.
SCOTT AND BORGMAN

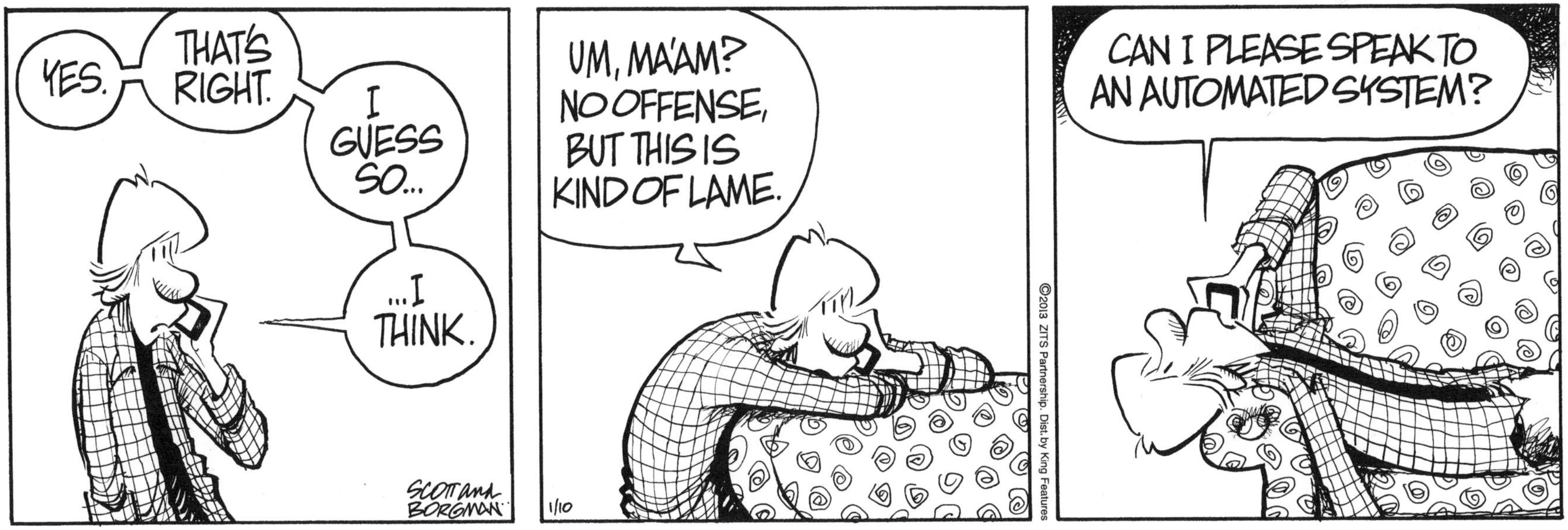
YES.
THAT'S RIGHT.
I GUESS SO...
...I THINK.
SCOTT AND BORGMAN
UM, MA'AM? NO OFFENSE, BUT THIS IS KIND OF LAME.
1/10
©2013 ZITS Partnership. Dist. by King Features
CAN I PLEASE SPEAK TO AN AUTOMATED SYSTEM?

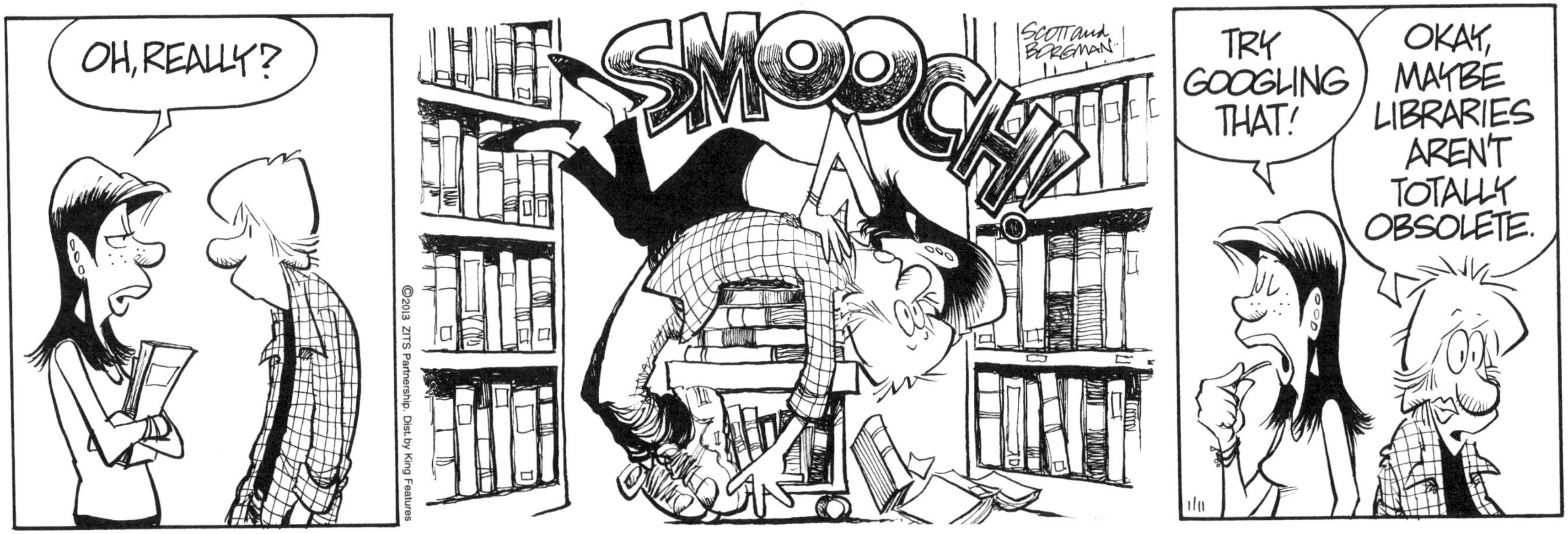
OH, REALLY?
SMOOCH!
SCOTT and BORGMAN..
©2013 ZITS Partnership. Dist. by King Features
TRY GOOGLING THAT!
OKAY, MAYBE LIBRARIES AREN'T TOTALLY OBSOLETE.
1/11

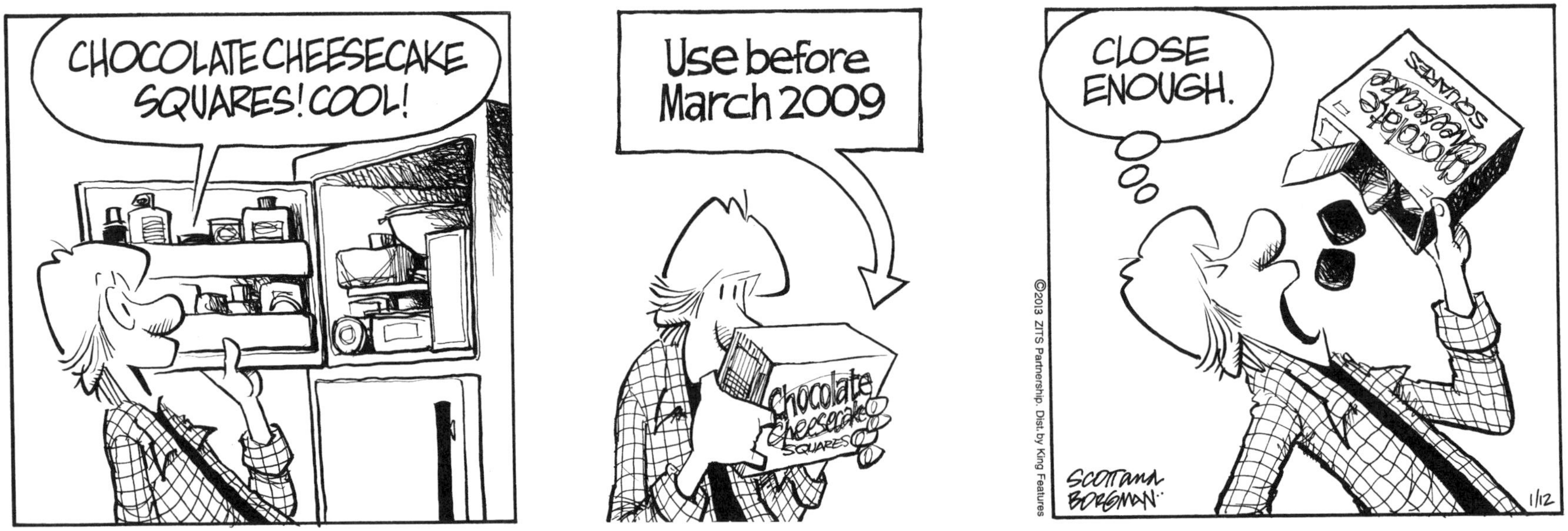
CHOCOLATE CHEESECAKE SQUARES! COOL!
Use before March 2009
Chocolate Cheesecake SQUARES
©2013 ZITS Partnership. Dist. by King Features
CLOSE ENOUGH.
SCOTT and BORGMAN..
1/12

# ZITS®

by JERRY SCOTT and JIM BORGMAN

Manicure
CALENDAR
GIFT CARD
©2013 ZITS Partnership. Dist. by King Features
MAN-ICURE
CHEW!
CHEW!
CHEW!
1/13
SCOTT and BORGMAN

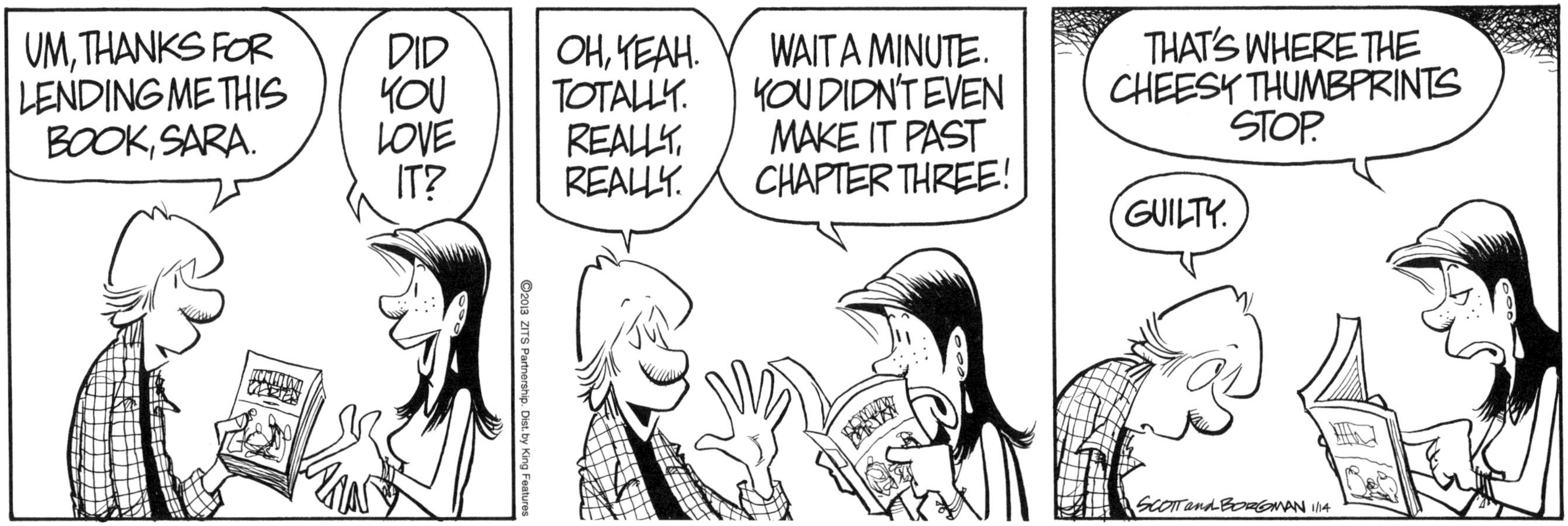
UM, THANKS FOR LENDING ME THIS BOOK, SARA.
DID YOU LOVE IT?
©2013 ZITS Partnership. Dist. by King Features
OH, YEAH. TOTALLY. REALLY, REALLY.
WAIT A MINUTE. YOU DIDN'T EVEN MAKE IT PAST CHAPTER THREE!
THAT'S WHERE THE CHEESY THUMBPRINTS STOP.
GUILTY.
SCOTT and BORGMAN 1/14

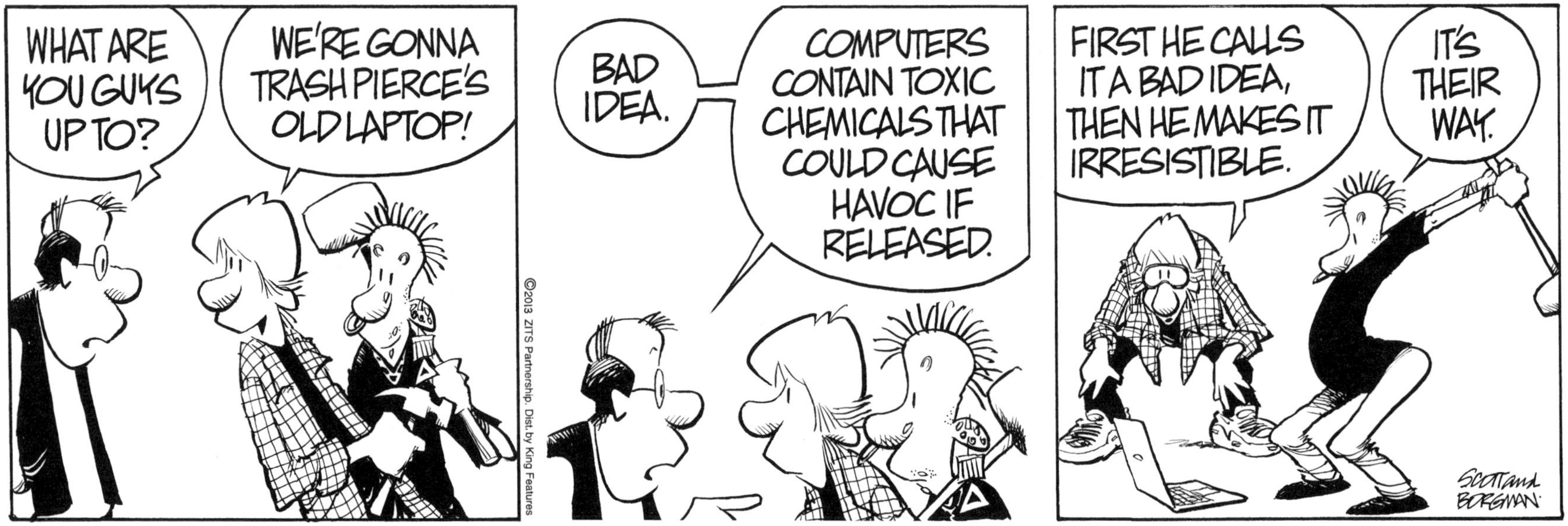
WHAT ARE YOU GUYS UP TO?
WE'RE GONNA TRASH PIERCE'S OLD LAPTOP!
©2013 ZITS Partnership. Dist. by King Features
BAD IDEA.
COMPUTERS CONTAIN TOXIC CHEMICALS THAT COULD CAUSE HAVOC IF RELEASED.
FIRST HE CALLS IT A BAD IDEA, THEN HE MAKES IT IRRESISTIBLE.
IT'S THEIR WAY.
SCOTT and BORGMAN

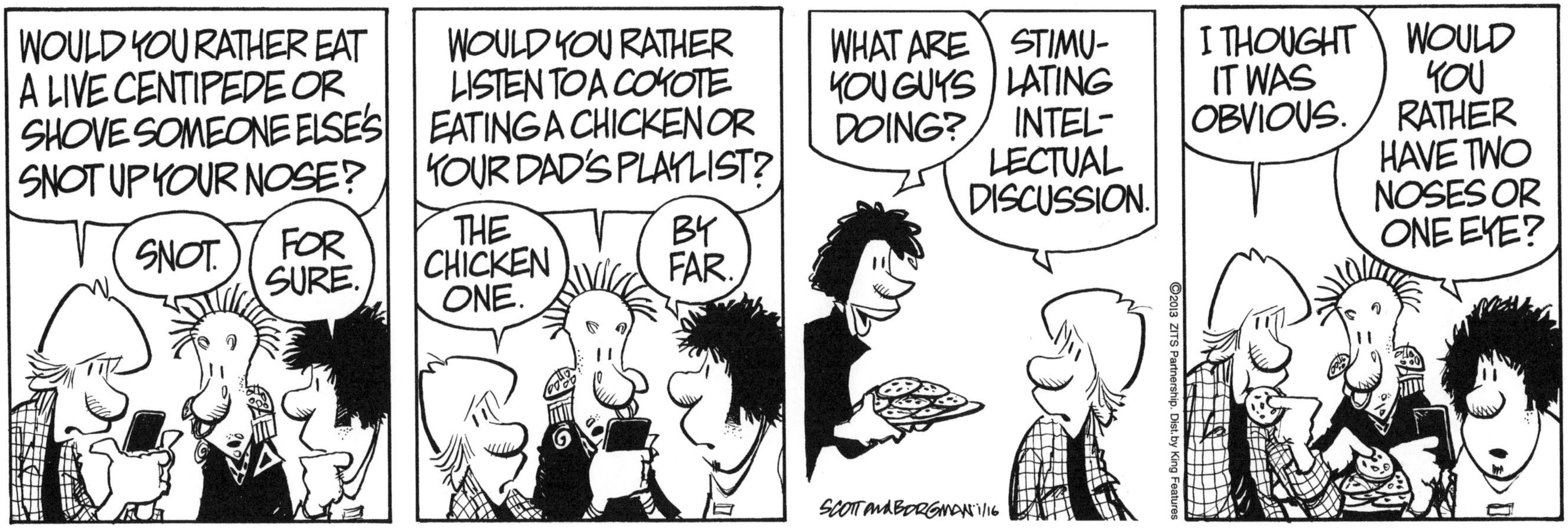
WOULD YOU RATHER EAT A LIVE CENTIPEDE OR SHOVE SOMEONE ELSE'S SNOT UP YOUR NOSE?
SNOT.
FOR SURE.
WOULD YOU RATHER LISTEN TO A COYOTE EATING A CHICKEN OR YOUR DAD'S PLAYLIST?
THE CHICKEN ONE.
BY FAR.
WHAT ARE YOU GUYS DOING?
STIMU-LATING INTEL-LECTUAL DISCUSSION.
SCOTT AND BORGMAN 1/16
©2013 ZITS Partnership. Dist. by King Features
I THOUGHT IT WAS OBVIOUS.
WOULD YOU RATHER HAVE TWO NOSES OR ONE EYE?

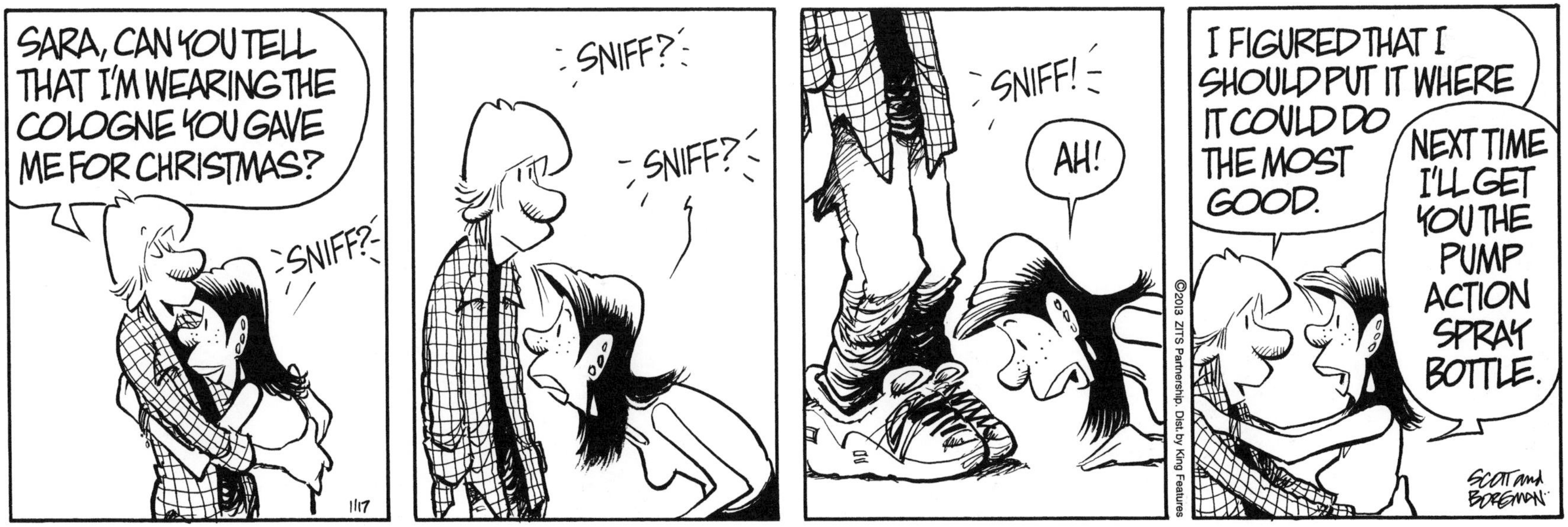
SARA, CAN YOU TELL THAT I'M WEARING THE COLOGNE YOU GAVE ME FOR CHRISTMAS?
SNIFF?
1/17
SNIFF?
SNIFF?
SNIFF!
AH!
©2013 ZITS Partnership. Dist. by King Features
I FIGURED THAT I SHOULD PUT IT WHERE IT COULD DO THE MOST GOOD.
NEXT TIME I'LL GET YOU THE PUMP ACTION SPRAY BOTTLE.
SCOTT AND BORGMAN

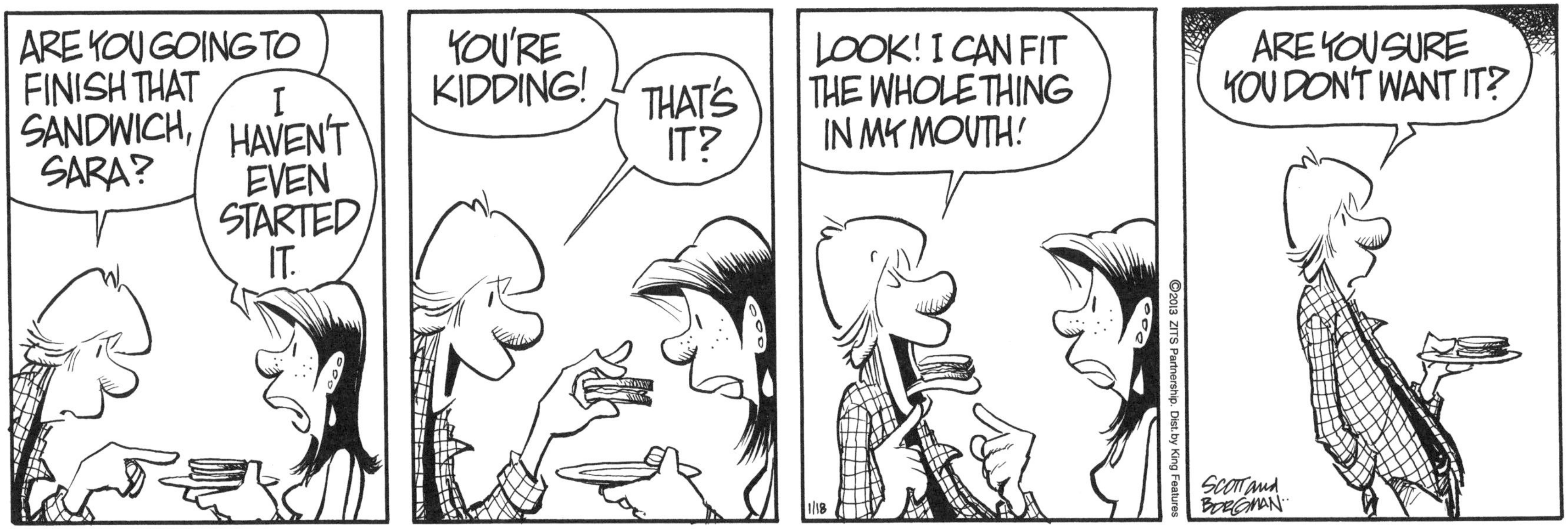
ARE YOU GOING TO FINISH THAT SANDWICH, SARA?
I HAVEN'T EVEN STARTED IT.
YOU'RE KIDDING!
THAT'S IT?
LOOK! I CAN FIT THE WHOLE THING IN MY MOUTH!
ARE YOU SURE YOU DON'T WANT IT?
1/18
©2013 ZITS Partnership. Dist. by King Features
SCOTT and BORGMAN

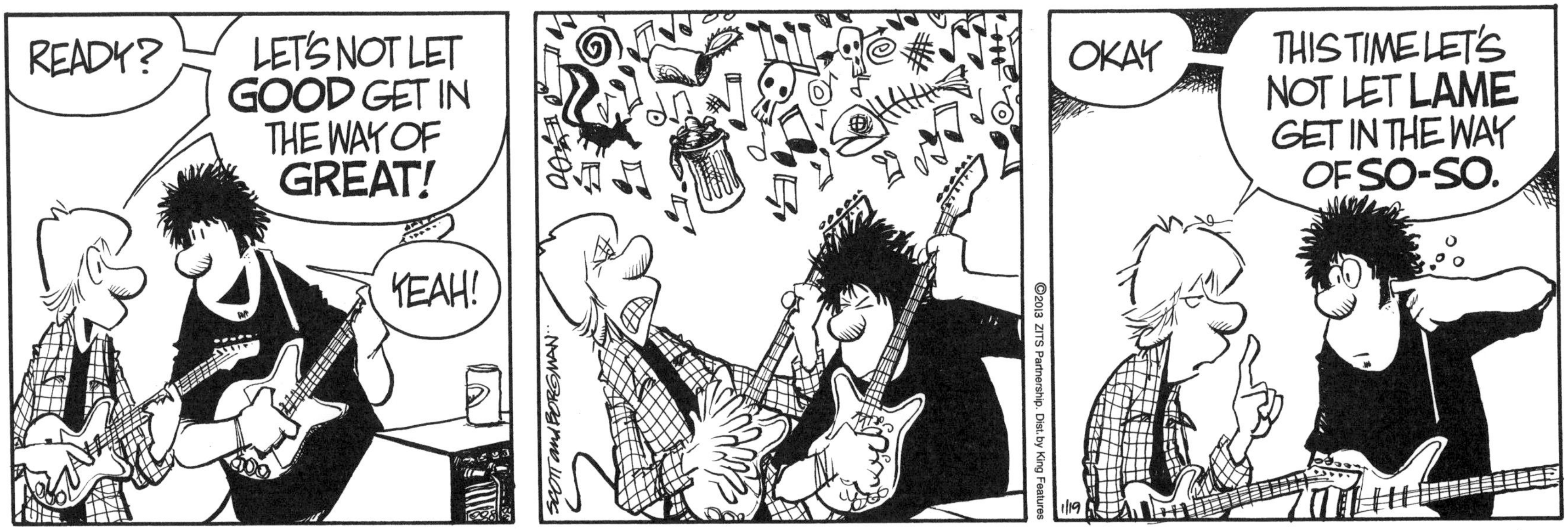
READY?
LET'S NOT LET **GOOD** GET IN THE WAY OF **GREAT!**
YEAH!
OKAY
THIS TIME LET'S NOT LET **LAME** GET IN THE WAY OF **SO-SO.**
SCOTT and BORGMAN
©2013 ZITS Partnership. Dist. by King Features
1/19

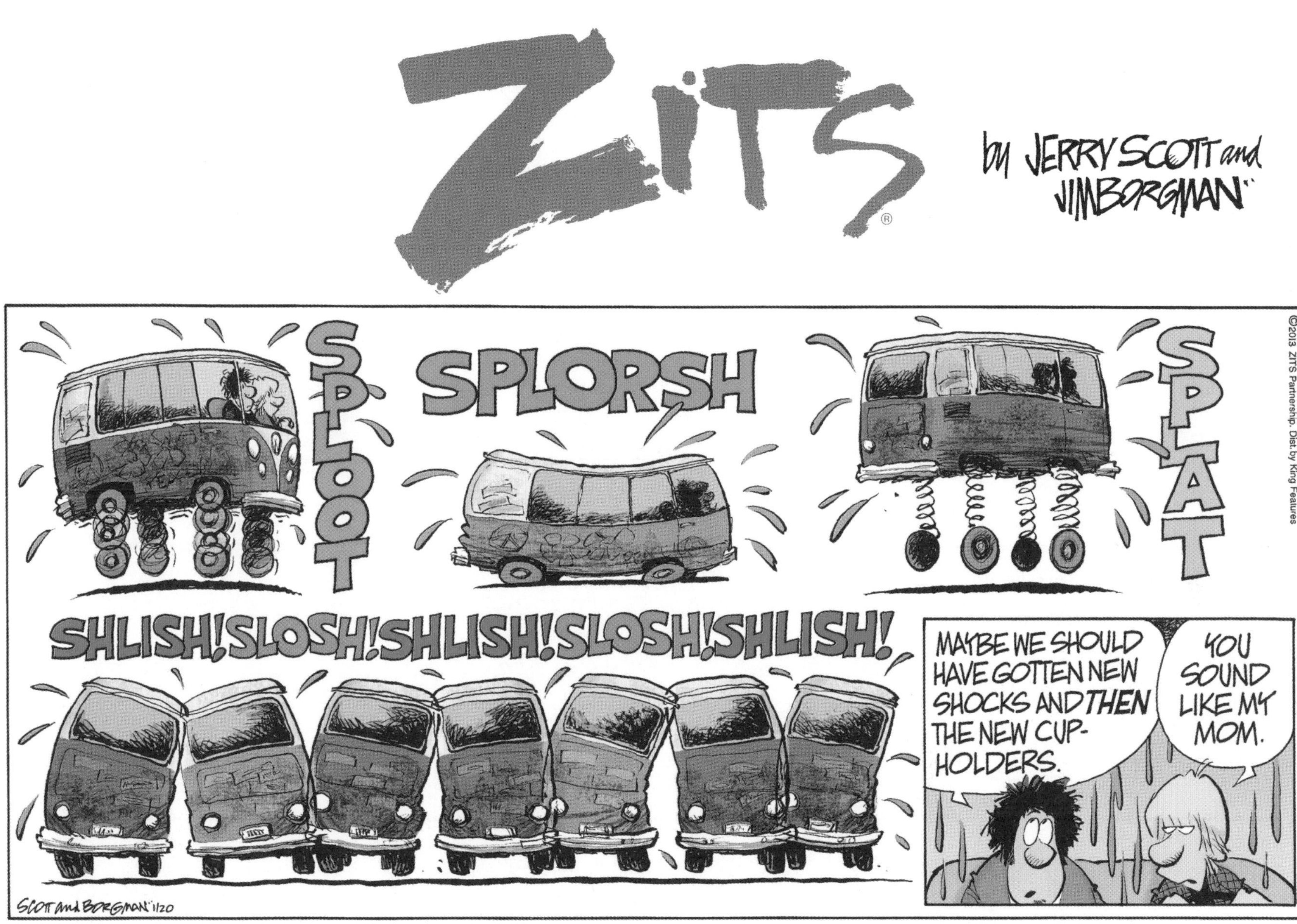

ZITS®
by JERRY SCOTT and JIM BORGMAN
SPLOOT
SPLORSH
SPLAT
©2013 ZITS Partnership. Dist. by King Features
SHLISH! SLOSH! SHLISH! SLOSH! SHLISH!
MAYBE WE SHOULD HAVE GOTTEN NEW SHOCKS AND THEN THE NEW CUP-HOLDERS.
YOU SOUND LIKE MY MOM.
SCOTT and BORGMAN 1/20

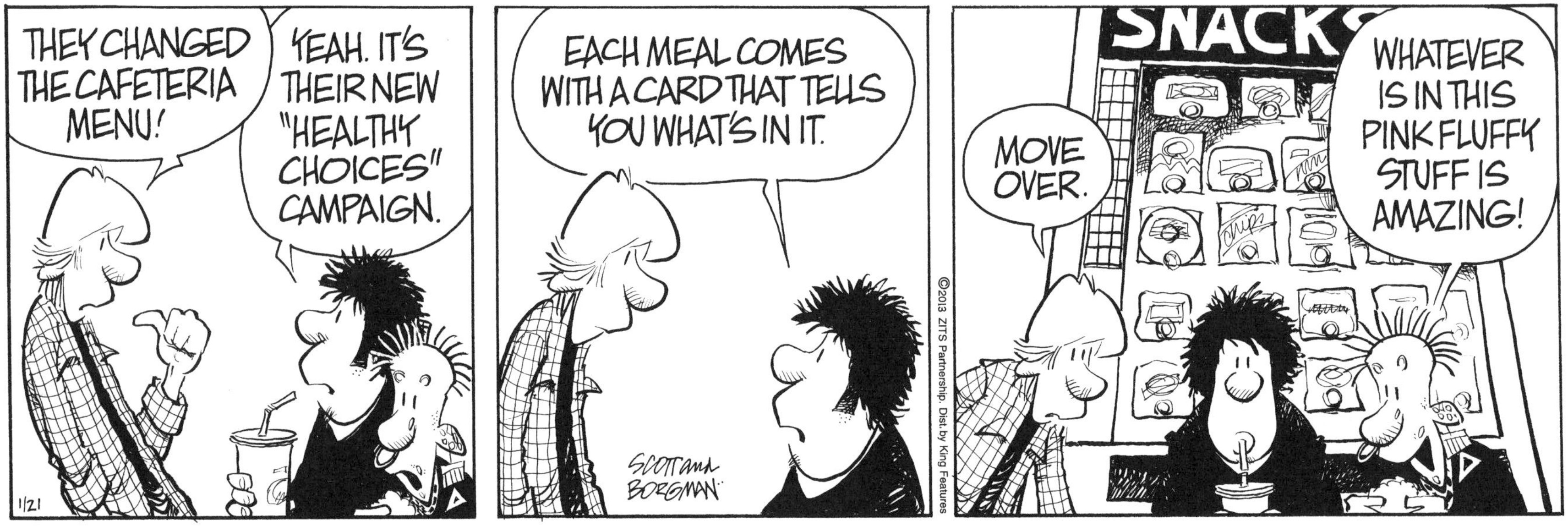

THEY CHANGED THE CAFETERIA MENU!
YEAH. IT'S THEIR NEW "HEALTHY CHOICES" CAMPAIGN.
1/21
EACH MEAL COMES WITH A CARD THAT TELLS YOU WHAT'S IN IT.
SCOTT AND BORGMAN
©2013 ZITS Partnership. Dist. by King Features
SNACKS
MOVE OVER.
WHATEVER IS IN THIS PINK FLUFFY STUFF IS AMAZING!


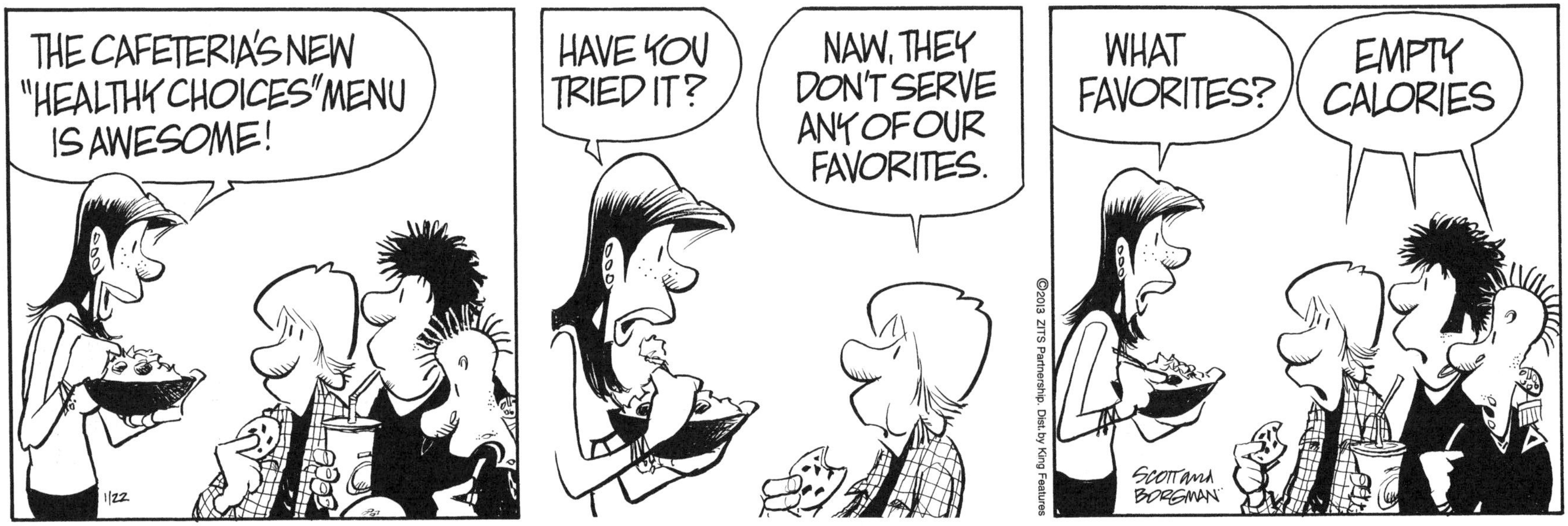

THE CAFETERIA'S NEW "HEALTHY CHOICES" MENU IS AWESOME!
1/22
HAVE YOU TRIED IT?
NAW, THEY DON'T SERVE ANY OF OUR FAVORITES.
©2013 ZITS Partnership. Dist. by King Features
WHAT FAVORITES?
EMPTY CALORIES
SCOTT AND BORGMAN

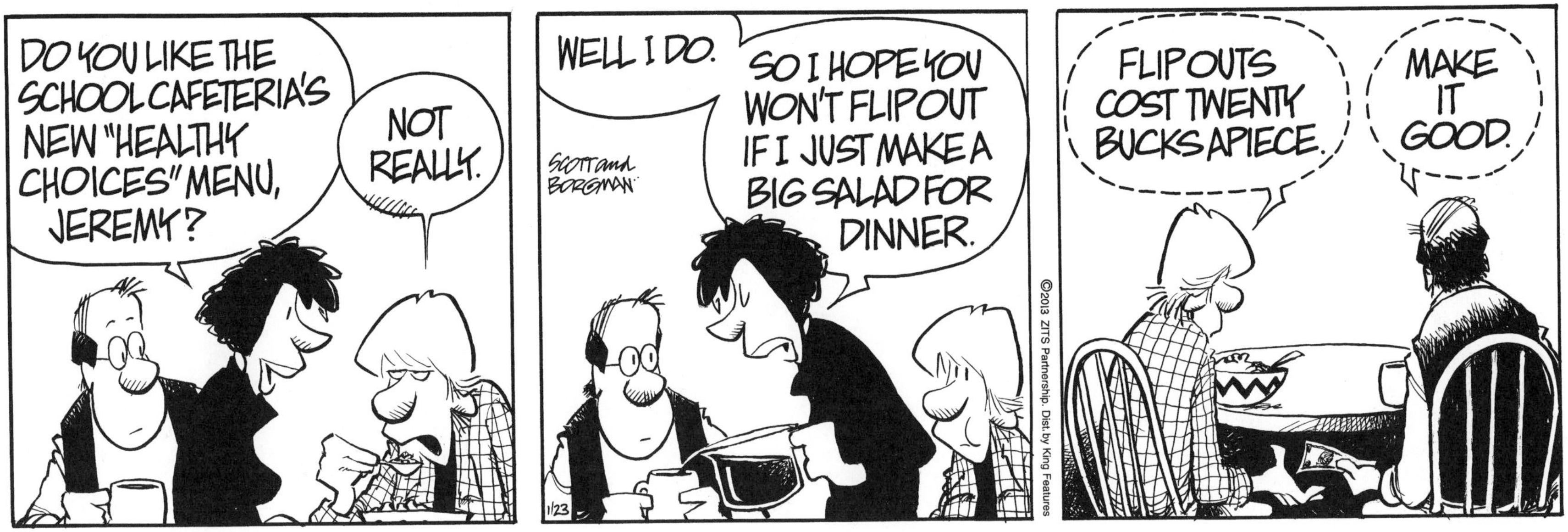
DO YOU LIKE THE SCHOOL CAFETERIA'S NEW "HEALTHY CHOICES" MENU, JEREMY?
NOT REALLY.
WELL I DO.
SO I HOPE YOU WON'T FLIP OUT IF I JUST MAKE A BIG SALAD FOR DINNER.
SCOTT AND BORGMAN
1/23
©2013 ZITS Partnership. Dist. by King Features
FLIP OUTS COST TWENTY BUCKS APIECE.
MAKE IT GOOD.

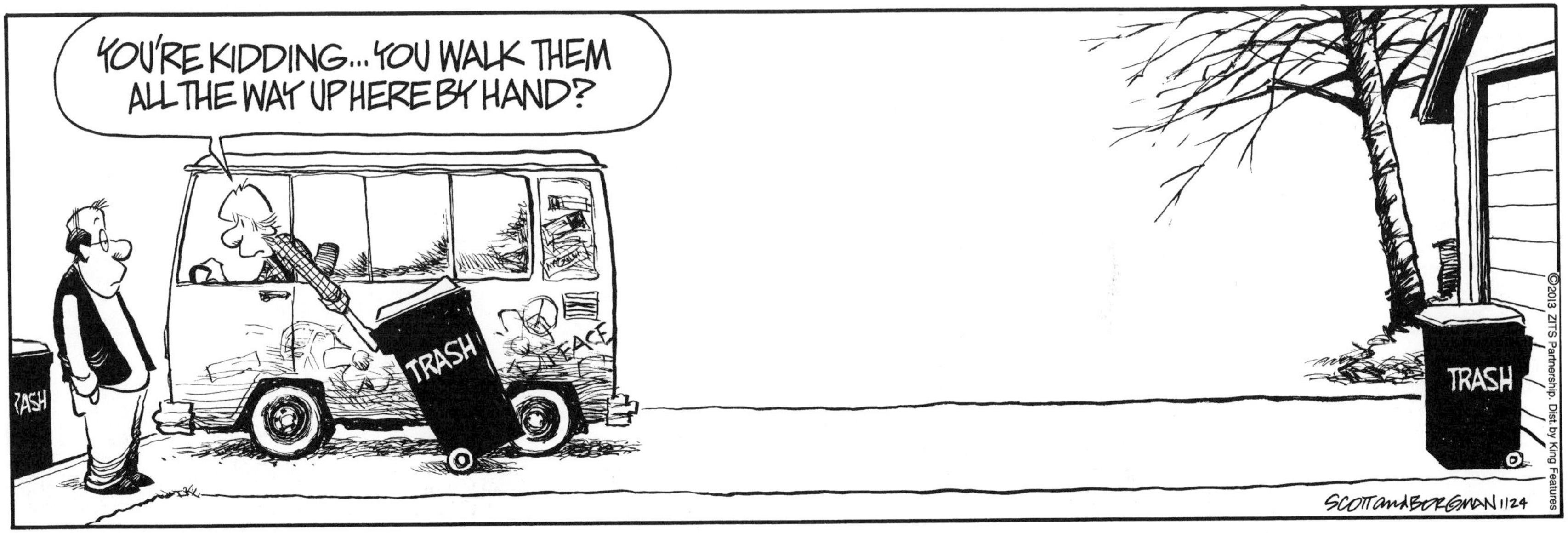
YOU'RE KIDDING... YOU WALK THEM ALL THE WAY UP HERE BY HAND?
TRASH
TRASH
PEACE
TRASH
©2013 ZITS Partnership. Dist. by King Features
SCOTT AND BORGMAN 11/24

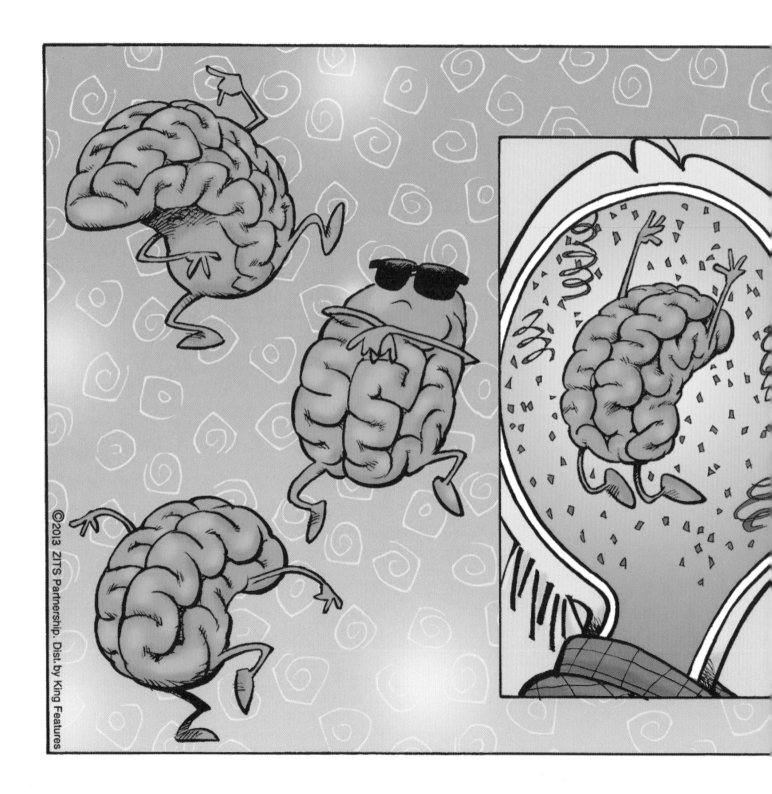

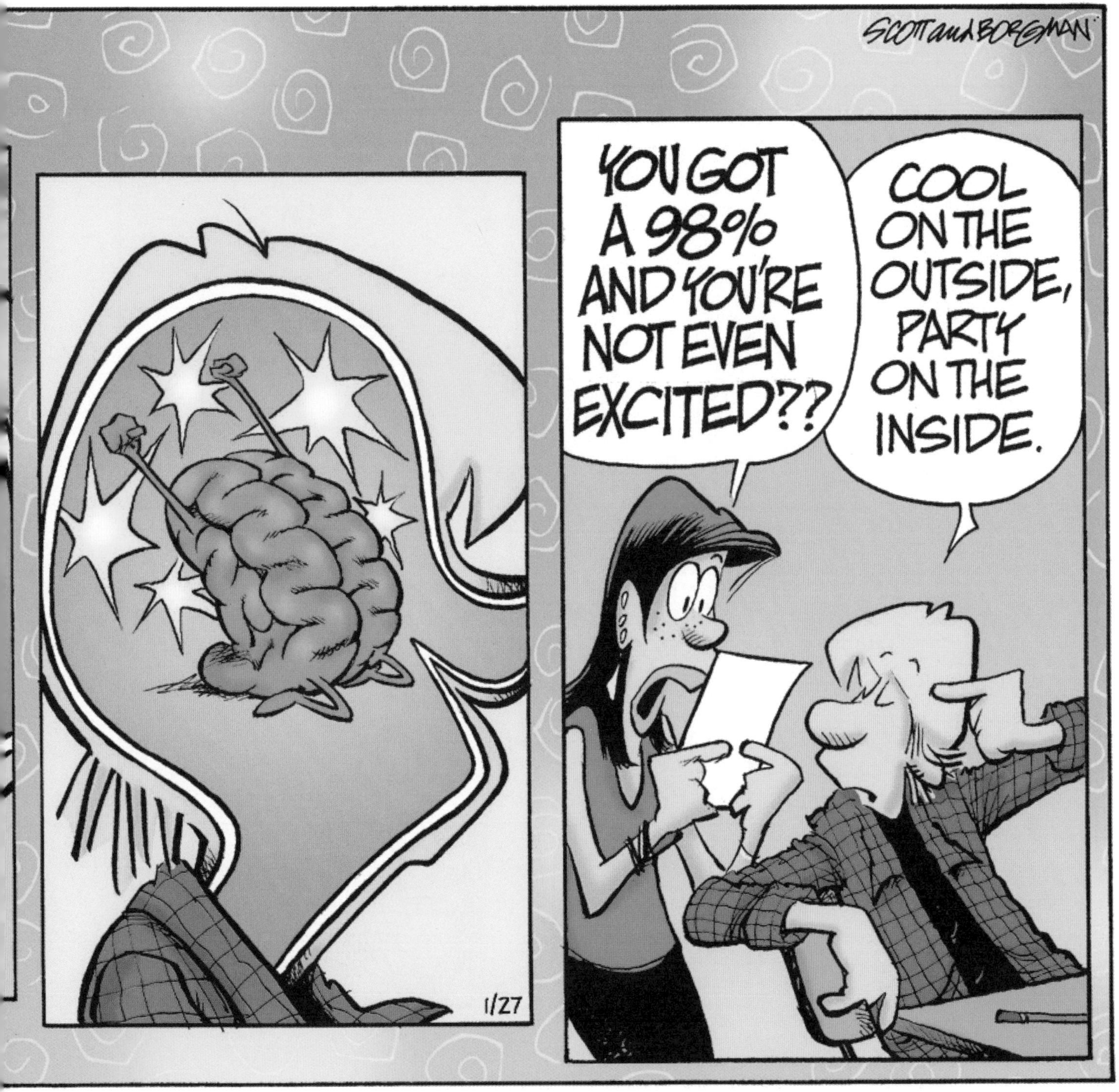
SCOTT and BORGMAN
1/27
YOU GOT A 98% AND YOU'RE NOT EVEN EXCITED??
COOL ON THE OUTSIDE, PARTY ON THE INSIDE.

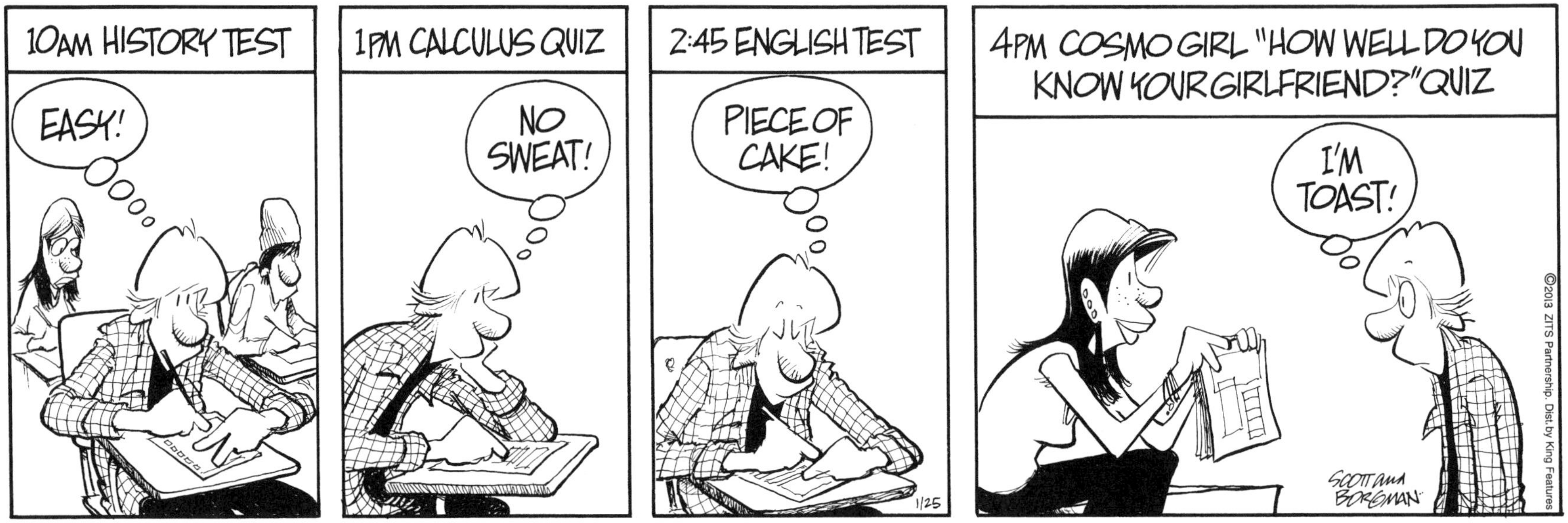
10AM HISTORY TEST
EASY!
1PM CALCULUS QUIZ
NO SWEAT!
2:45 ENGLISH TEST
PIECE OF CAKE!
1/25
4PM COSMO GIRL "HOW WELL DO YOU KNOW YOUR GIRLFRIEND?" QUIZ
I'M TOAST!
SCOTT and BORGMAN
©2013 ZITS Partnership. Dist. by King Features

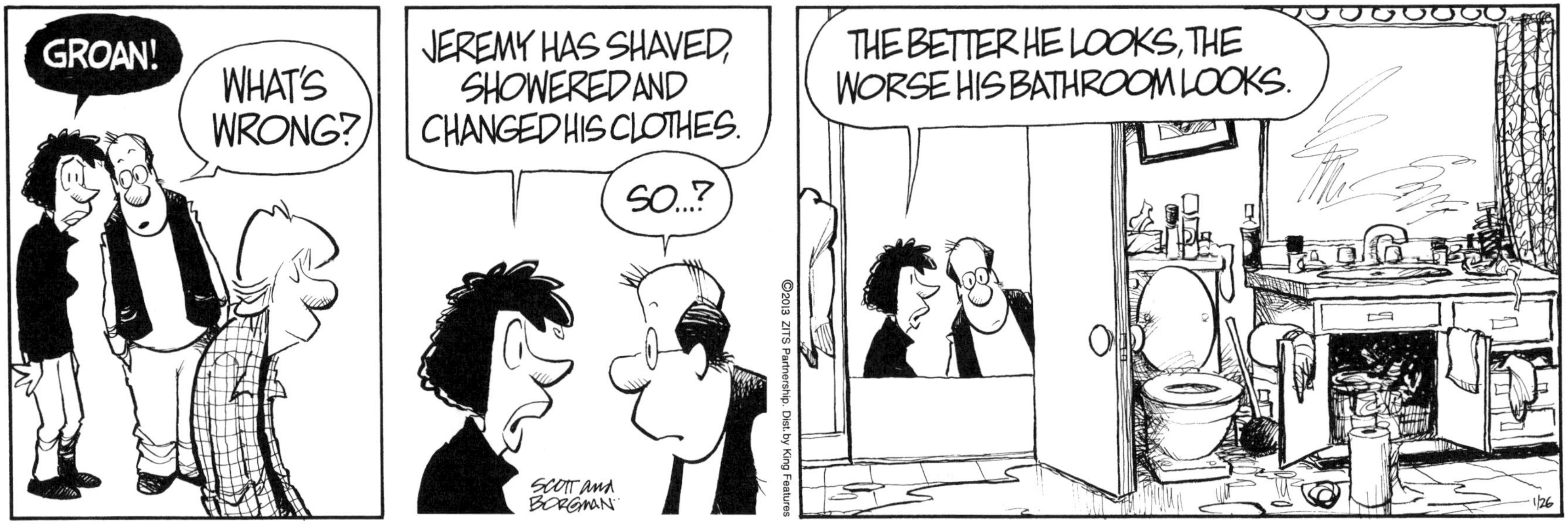
GROAN!
WHAT'S WRONG?
JEREMY HAS SHAVED, SHOWERED AND CHANGED HIS CLOTHES.
SO...?
SCOTT and BORGMAN
©2013 ZITS Partnership. Dist. by King Features
THE BETTER HE LOOKS, THE WORSE HIS BATHROOM LOOKS.
1/26

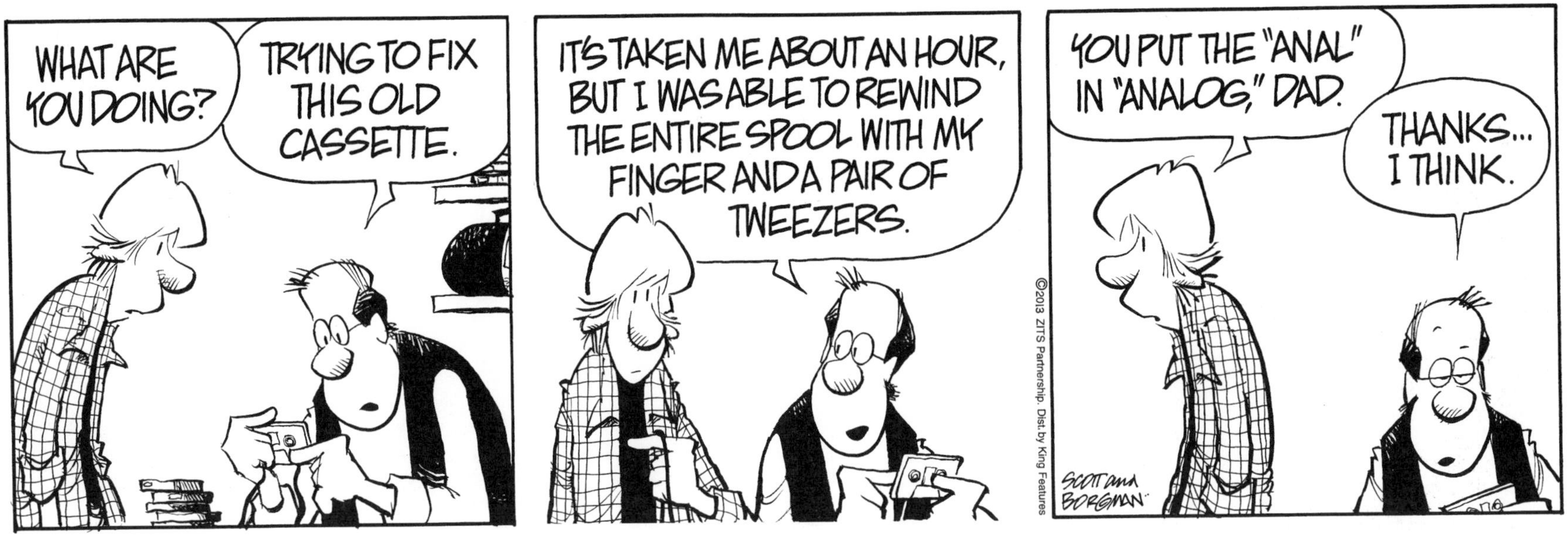
WHAT ARE YOU DOING?
TRYING TO FIX THIS OLD CASSETTE.
IT'S TAKEN ME ABOUT AN HOUR, BUT I WAS ABLE TO REWIND THE ENTIRE SPOOL WITH MY FINGER AND A PAIR OF TWEEZERS.
©2013 ZITS Partnership. Dist.by King Features
YOU PUT THE "ANAL" IN "ANALOG," DAD.
THANKS... I THINK.
SCOTT and BORGMAN

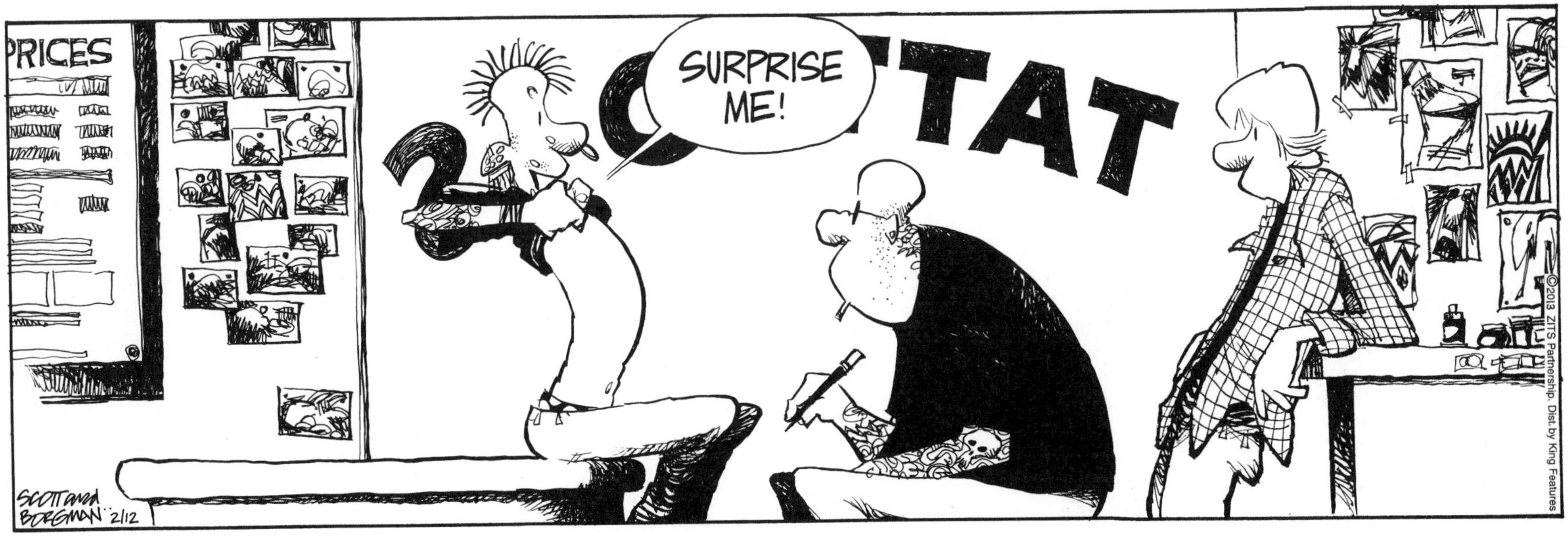
PRICES
SURPRISE ME!
TAT
©2013 ZITS Partnership. Dist.by King Features
SCOTT and BORGMAN 2/12

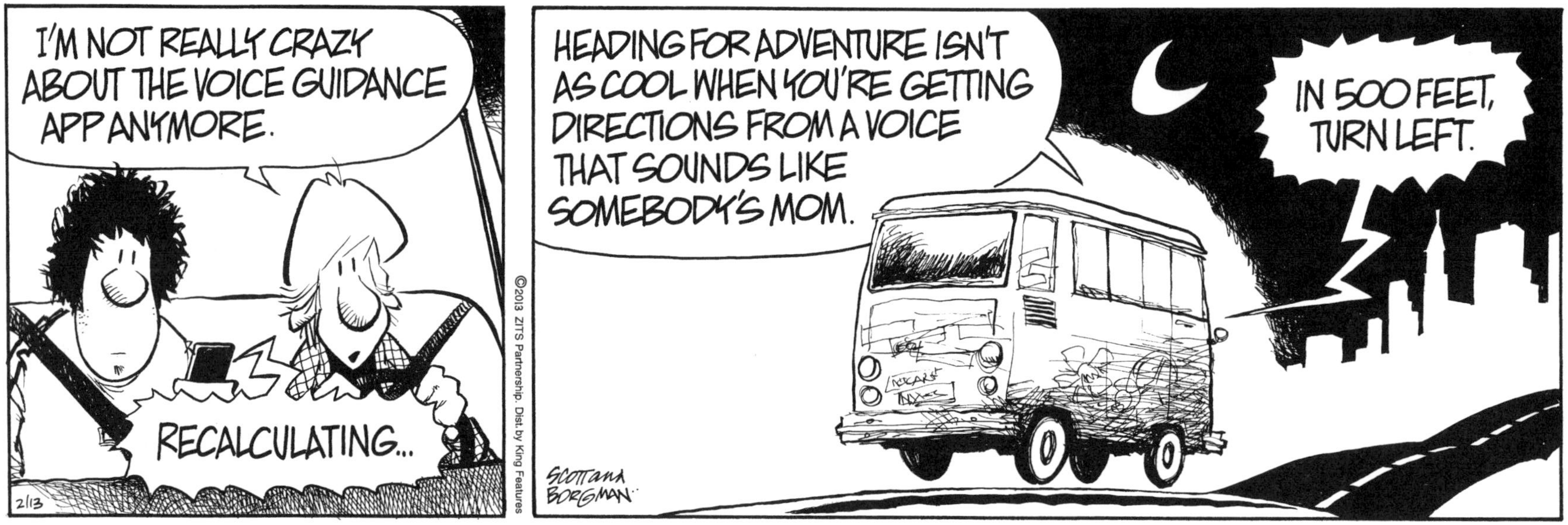
I'M NOT REALLY CRAZY ABOUT THE VOICE GUIDANCE APP ANYMORE.
RECALCULATING...
2/13
©2013 ZITS Partnership. Dist. by King Features
HEADING FOR ADVENTURE ISN'T AS COOL WHEN YOU'RE GETTING DIRECTIONS FROM A VOICE THAT SOUNDS LIKE SOMEBODY'S MOM.
IN 500 FEET, TURN LEFT.
SCOTT AND BORGMAN

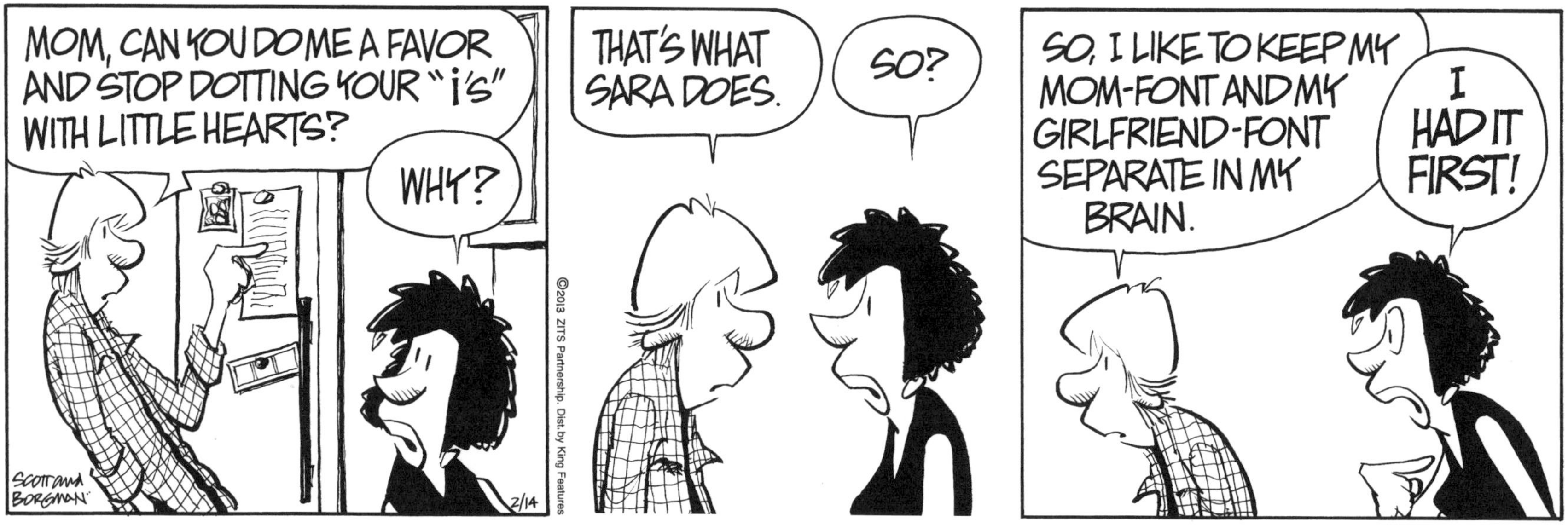
MOM, CAN YOU DO ME A FAVOR AND STOP DOTTING YOUR "i's" WITH LITTLE HEARTS?
WHY?
SCOTT AND BORGMAN
2/14
©2013 ZITS Partnership. Dist. by King Features
THAT'S WHAT SARA DOES.
SO?
SO, I LIKE TO KEEP MY MOM-FONT AND MY GIRLFRIEND-FONT SEPARATE IN MY BRAIN.
I HAD IT FIRST!

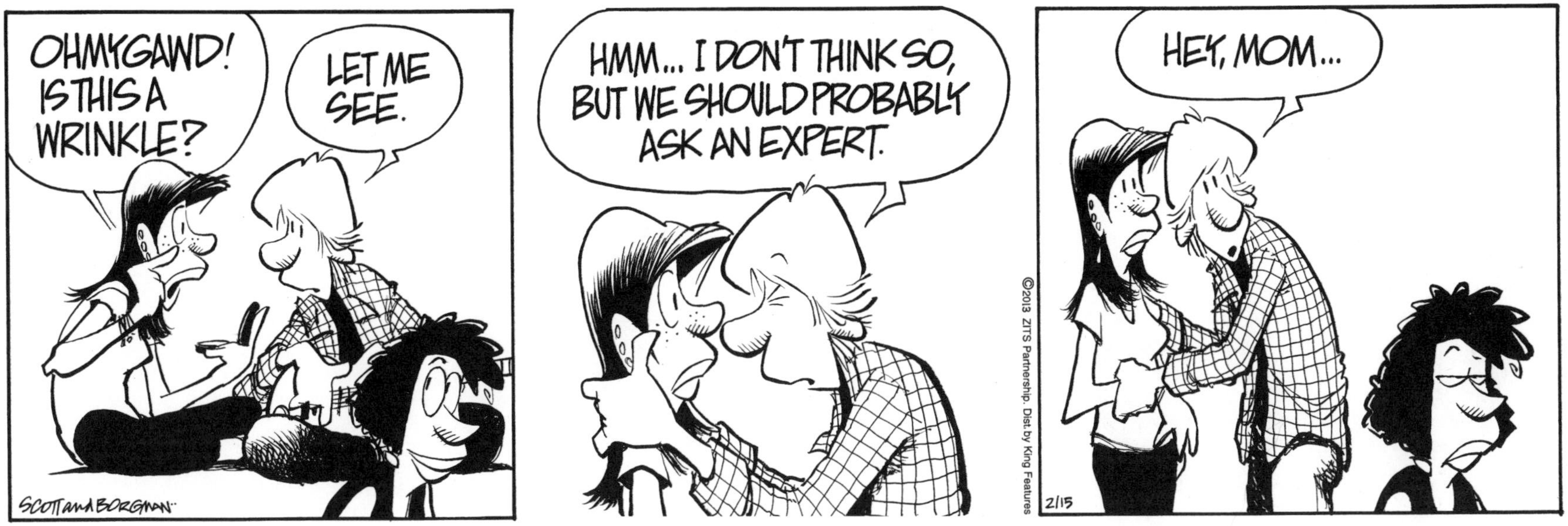
OHMYGAWD! IS THIS A WRINKLE?
LET ME SEE.
HMM... I DON'T THINK SO, BUT WE SHOULD PROBABLY ASK AN EXPERT.
HEY, MOM...
SCOTT and BORGMAN
©2013 ZITS Partnership. Dist. by King Features
2/15

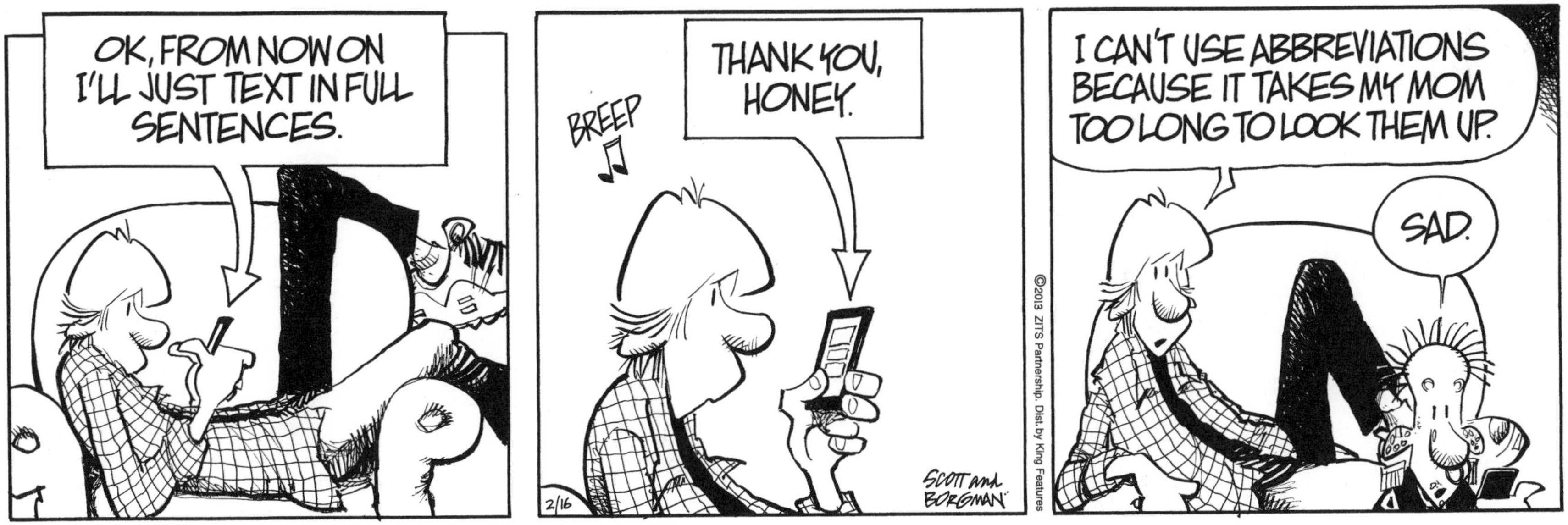
OK, FROM NOW ON I'LL JUST TEXT IN FULL SENTENCES.
BREEP
THANK YOU, HONEY.
I CAN'T USE ABBREVIATIONS BECAUSE IT TAKES MY MOM TOO LONG TO LOOK THEM UP.
SAD.
2/16
SCOTT and BORGMAN
©2013 ZITS Partnership. Dist. by King Features

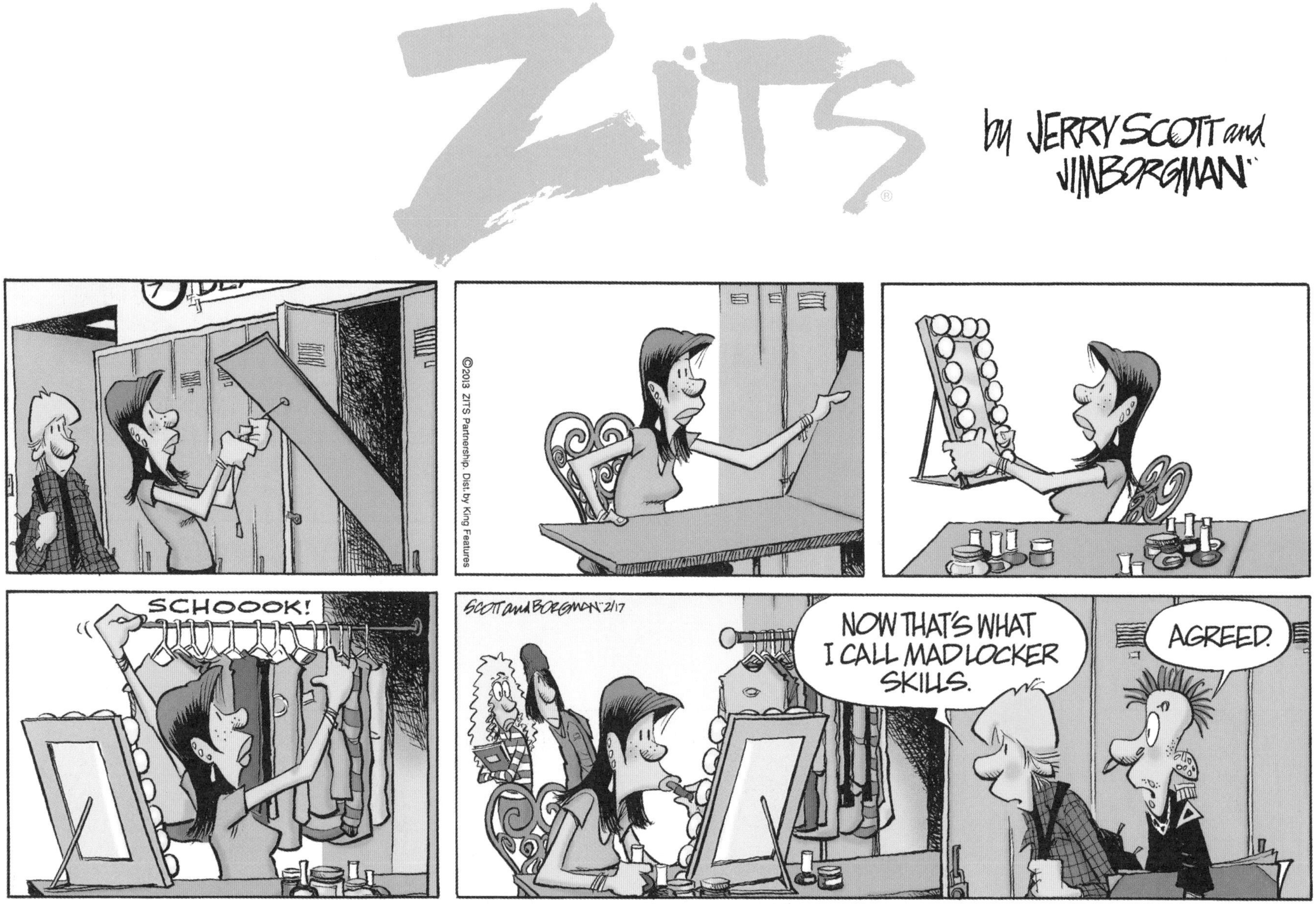
ZITS
by JERRY SCOTT and JIM BORGMAN
©2013 ZITS Partnership. Dist.by King Features
SCHOOOK!
SCOTT and BORGMAN 2/17
NOW THAT'S WHAT I CALL MAD LOCKER SKILLS.
AGREED.

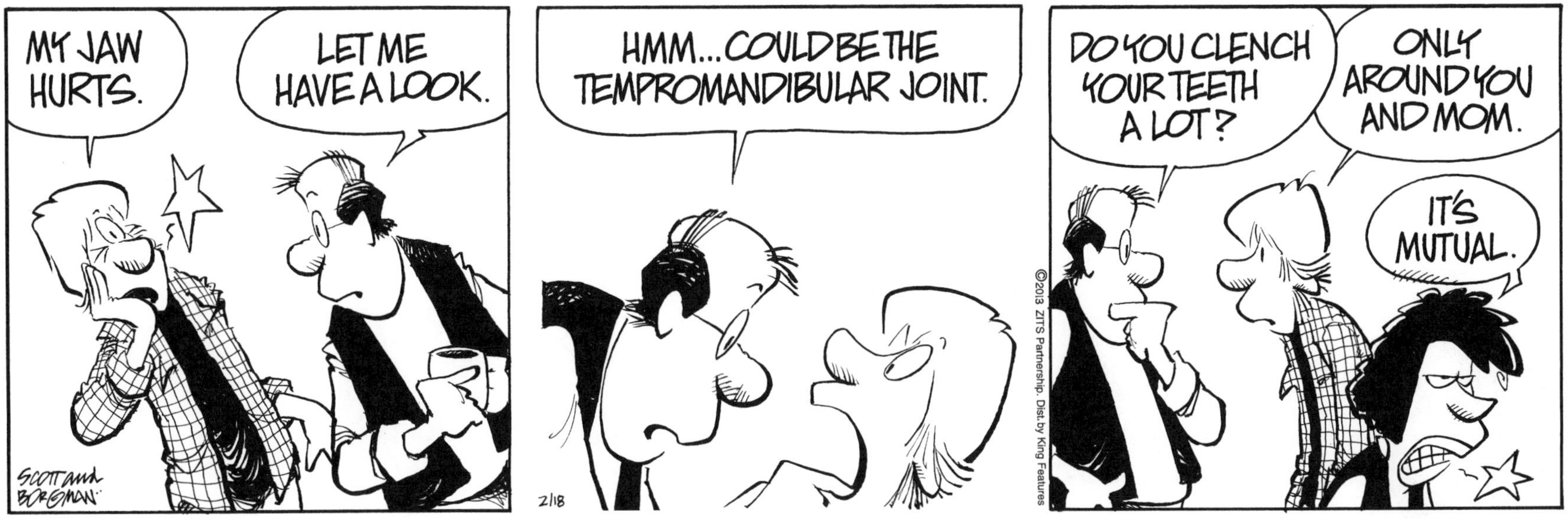
MY JAW HURTS.
LET ME HAVE A LOOK.
SCOTT and BORGMAN
HMM... COULD BE THE TEMPROMANDIBULAR JOINT.
2/18
©2013 ZITS Partnership. Dist. by King Features
DO YOU CLENCH YOUR TEETH A LOT?
ONLY AROUND YOU AND MOM.
IT'S MUTUAL.

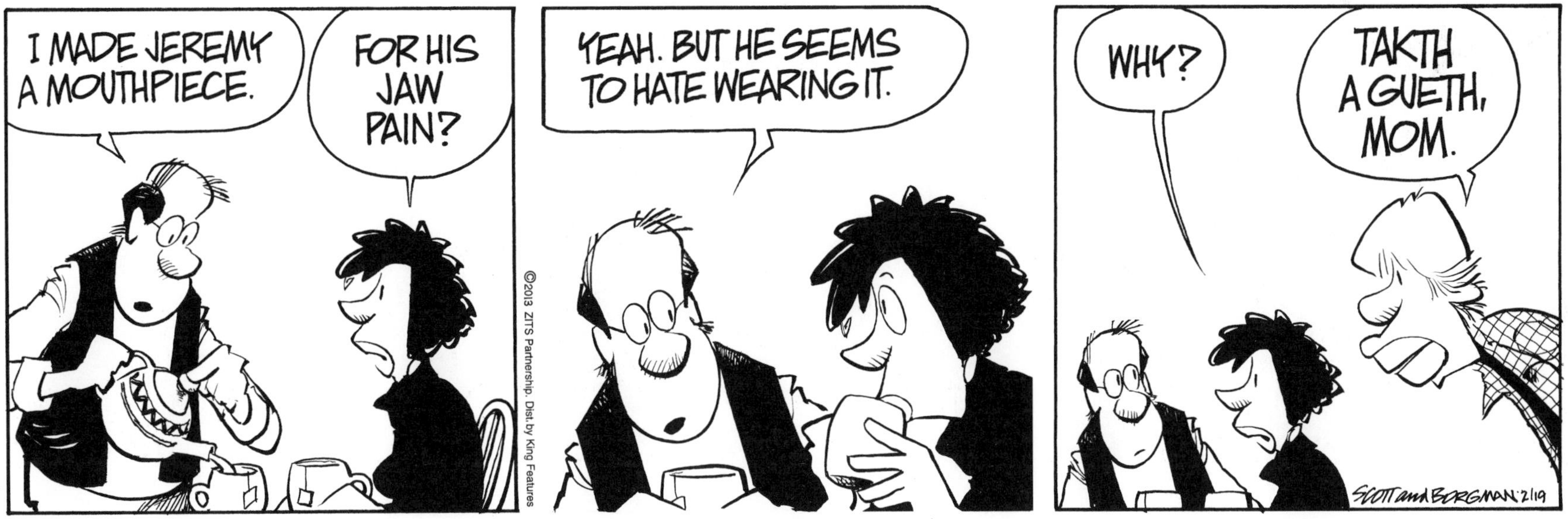
I MADE JEREMY A MOUTHPIECE.
FOR HIS JAW PAIN?
©2013 ZITS Partnership. Dist. by King Features
YEAH. BUT HE SEEMS TO HATE WEARING IT.
WHY?
TAKTH A GUETH, MOM.
SCOTT and BORGMAN 2/19

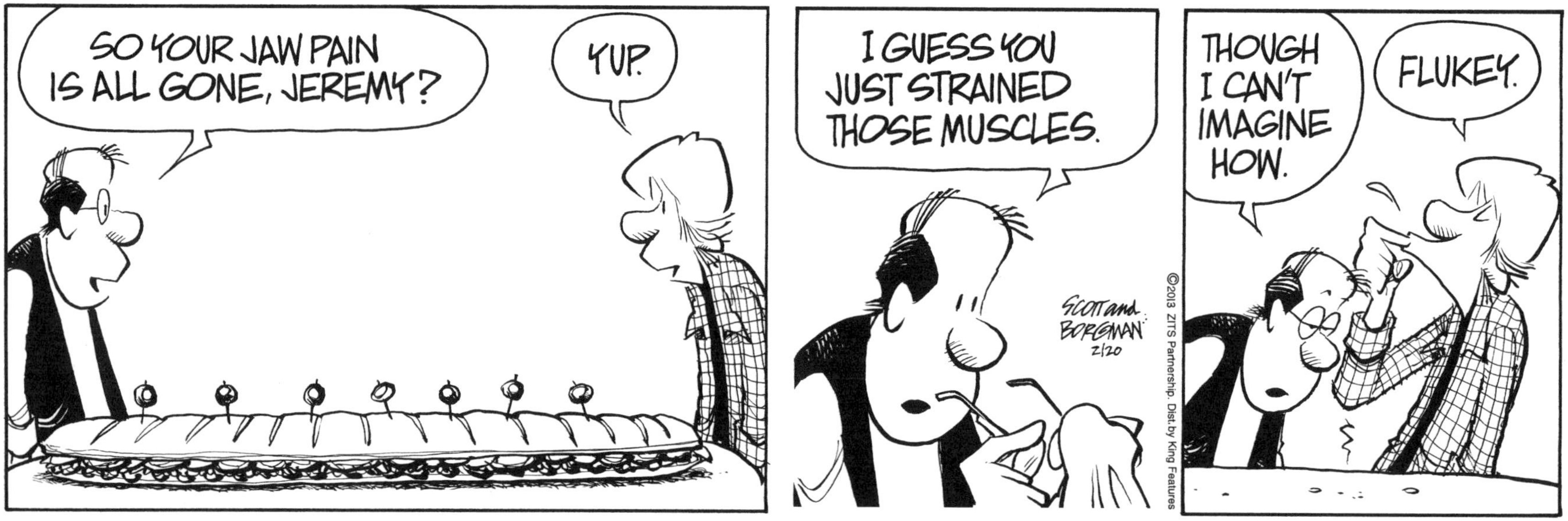
SO YOUR JAW PAIN IS ALL GONE, JEREMY?
YUP.
I GUESS YOU JUST STRAINED THOSE MUSCLES.
SCOTT and BORGMAN 2/20
©2013 ZITS Partnership. Dist. by King Features
THOUGH I CAN'T IMAGINE HOW.
FLUKEY.

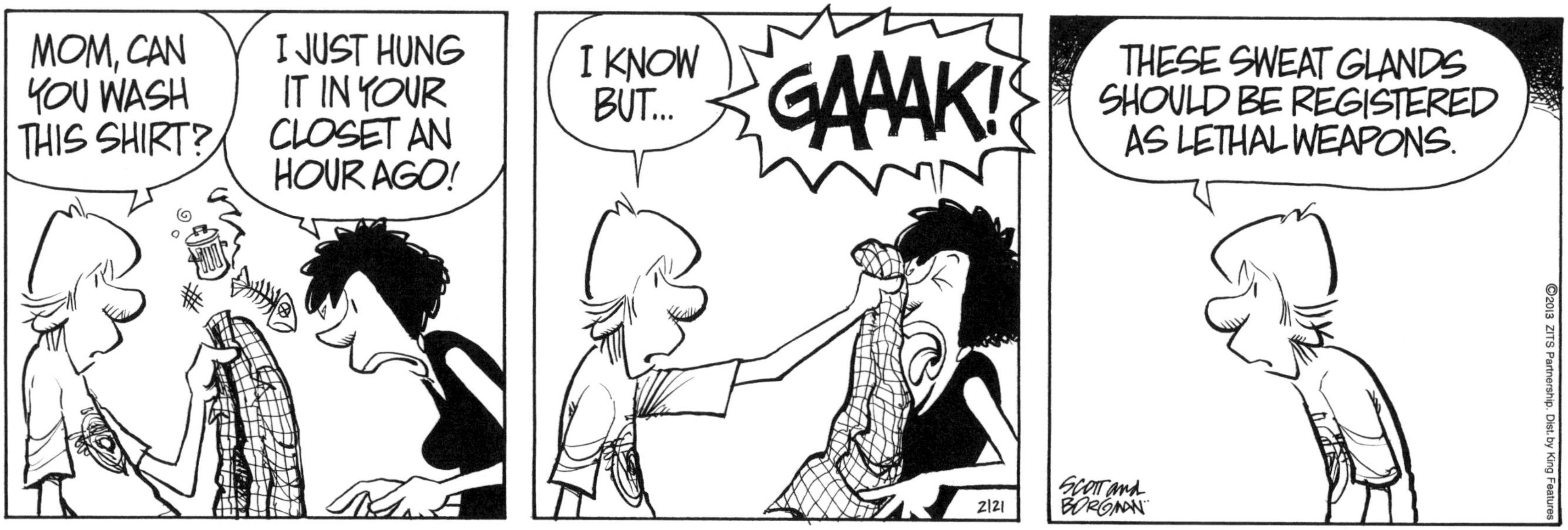
MOM, CAN YOU WASH THIS SHIRT?
I JUST HUNG IT IN YOUR CLOSET AN HOUR AGO!
I KNOW BUT...
GAAAK!
2/21
THESE SWEAT GLANDS SHOULD BE REGISTERED AS LETHAL WEAPONS.
SCOTT and BORGMAN
©2013 ZITS Partnership. Dist. by King Features

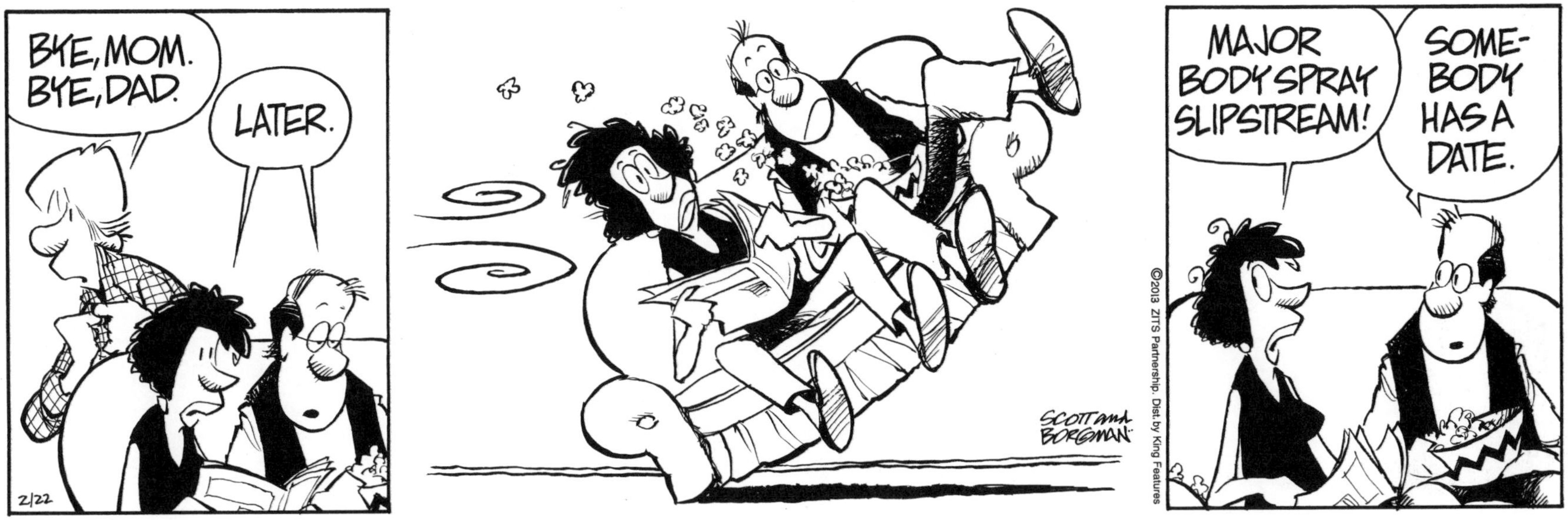
BYE, MOM. BYE, DAD.
LATER.
MAJOR BODY SPRAY SLIPSTREAM!
SOME-BODY HAS A DATE.
SCOTT and BORGMAN
©2013 ZITS Partnership. Dist. by King Features
2/22

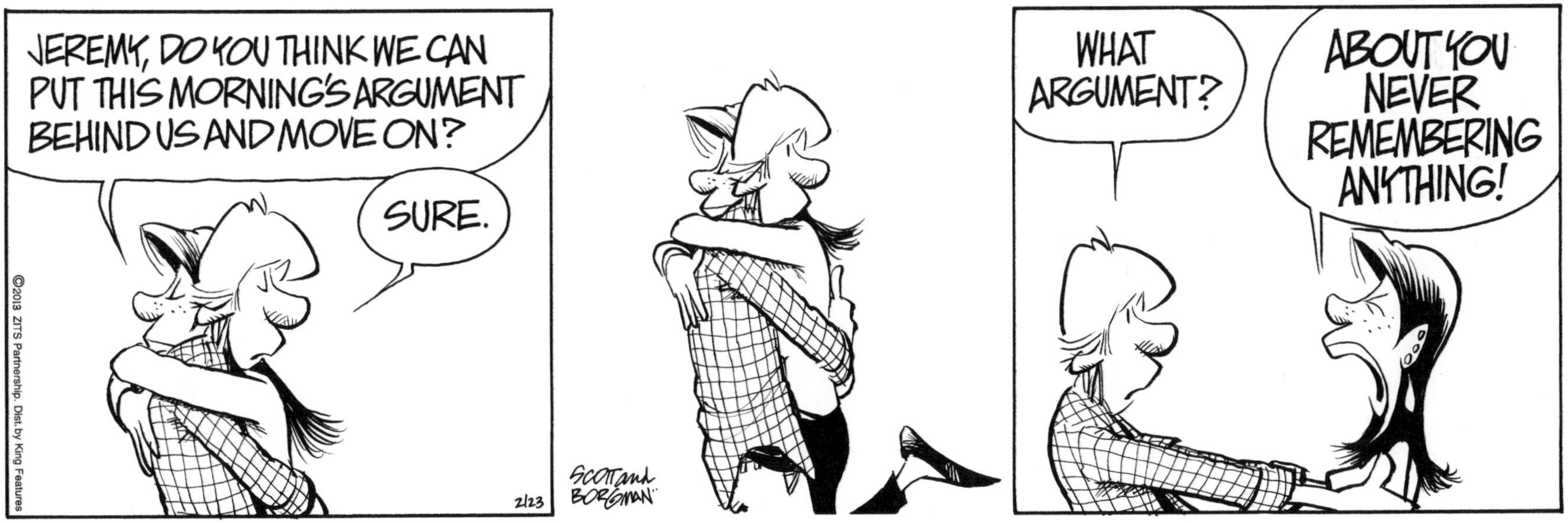
JEREMY, DO YOU THINK WE CAN PUT THIS MORNING'S ARGUMENT BEHIND US AND MOVE ON?
SURE.
WHAT ARGUMENT?
ABOUT YOU NEVER REMEMBERING ANYTHING!
SCOTT and BORGMAN
©2013 ZITS Partnership. Dist. by King Features
2/23

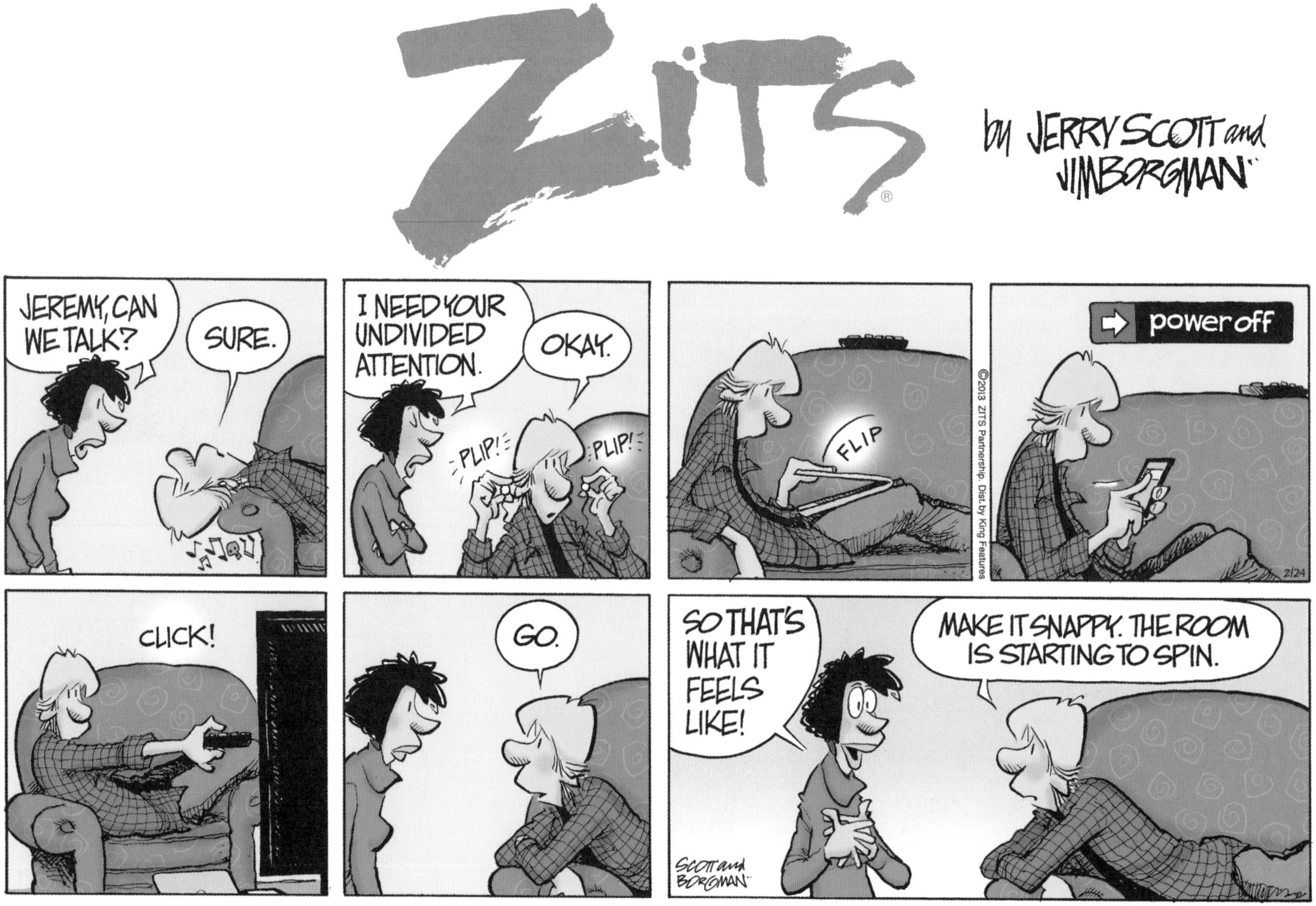
ZITS
by JERRY SCOTT and JIM BORGMAN
JEREMY, CAN WE TALK?
SURE.
I NEED YOUR UNDIVIDED ATTENTION.
OKAY.
PLIP!
PLIP!
FLIP
©2013 ZITS Partnership. Dist. by King Features
power off
CLICK!
GO.
SO THAT'S WHAT IT FEELS LIKE!
MAKE IT SNAPPY. THE ROOM IS STARTING TO SPIN.
SCOTT and BORGMAN

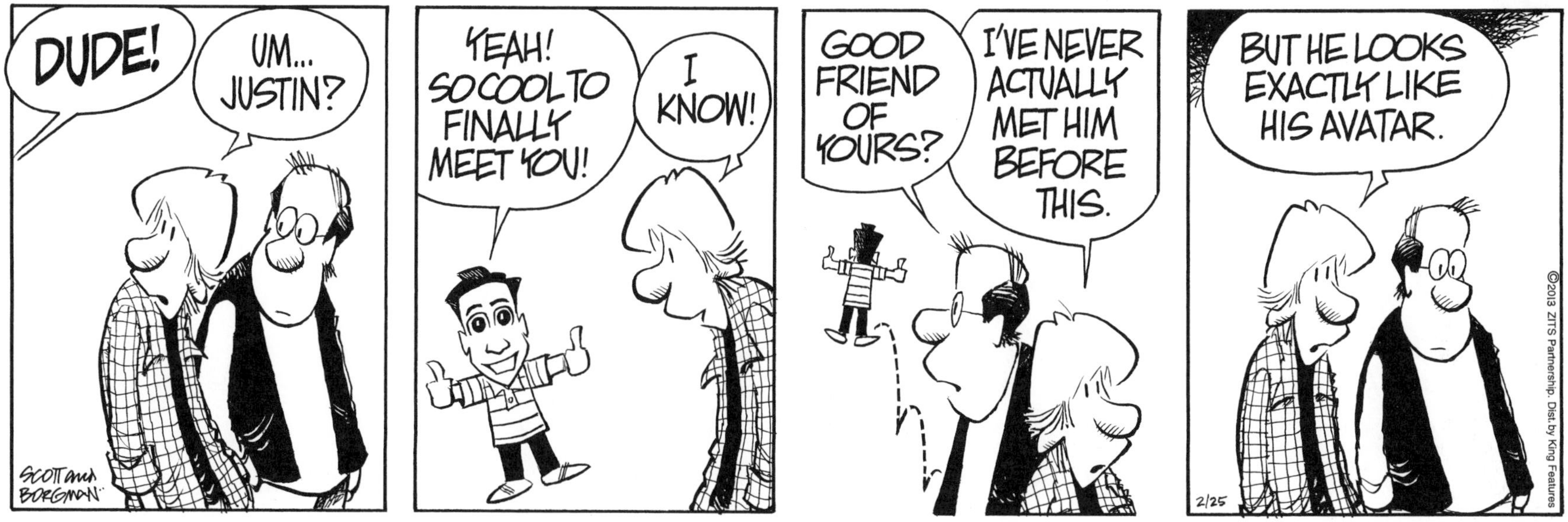
DUDE!
UM... JUSTIN?
SCOTT and BORGMAN
YEAH! SO COOL TO FINALLY MEET YOU!
I KNOW!
GOOD FRIEND OF YOURS?
I'VE NEVER ACTUALLY MET HIM BEFORE THIS.
BUT HE LOOKS EXACTLY LIKE HIS AVATAR.
2/25
©2013 ZITS Partnership. Dist. by King Features

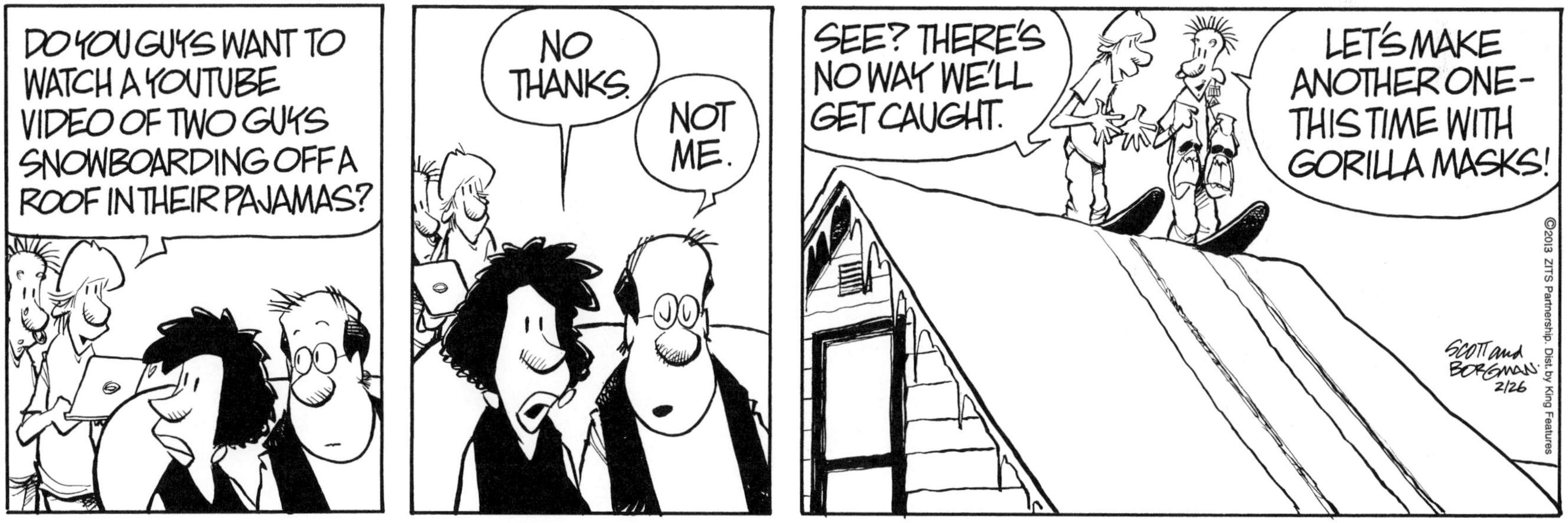
DO YOU GUYS WANT TO WATCH A YOUTUBE VIDEO OF TWO GUYS SNOWBOARDING OFF A ROOF IN THEIR PAJAMAS?
NO THANKS.
NOT ME.
SEE? THERE'S NO WAY WE'LL GET CAUGHT.
LET'S MAKE ANOTHER ONE- THIS TIME WITH GORILLA MASKS!
SCOTT and BORGMAN 2/26
©2013 ZITS Partnership. Dist. by King Features

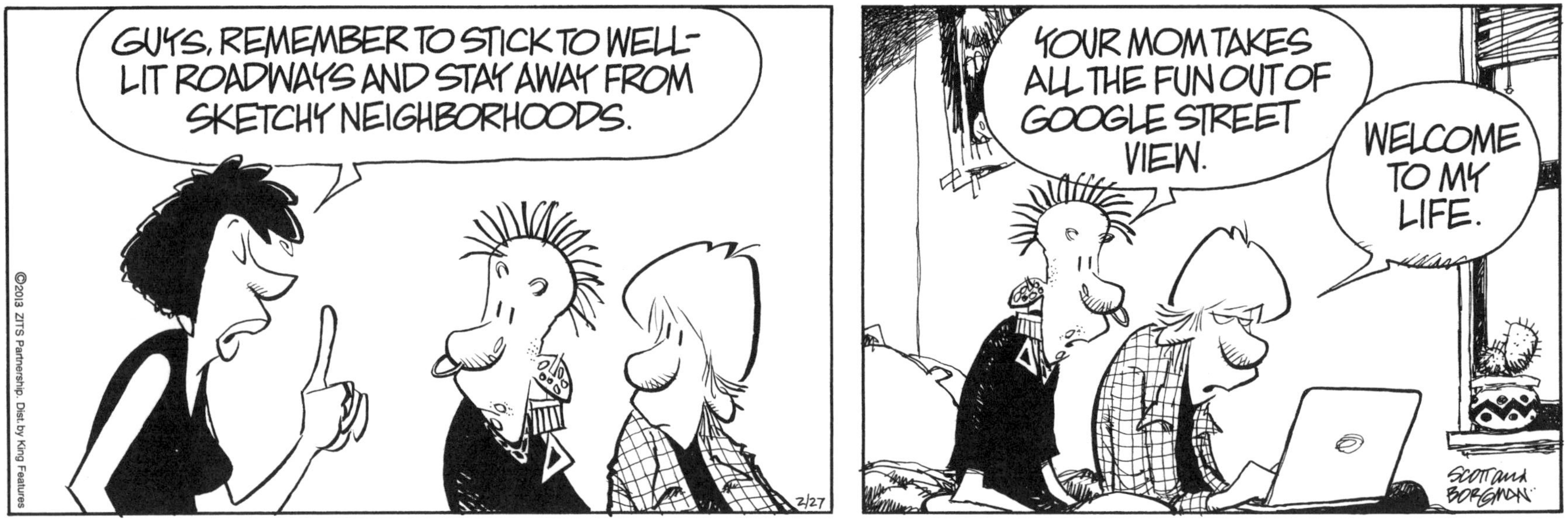
GUYS, REMEMBER TO STICK TO WELL-LIT ROADWAYS AND STAY AWAY FROM SKETCHY NEIGHBORHOODS.
YOUR MOM TAKES ALL THE FUN OUT OF GOOGLE STREET VIEW.
WELCOME TO MY LIFE.
©2013 ZITS Partnership. Dist. by King Features
2/27
SCOTT and BORGMAN

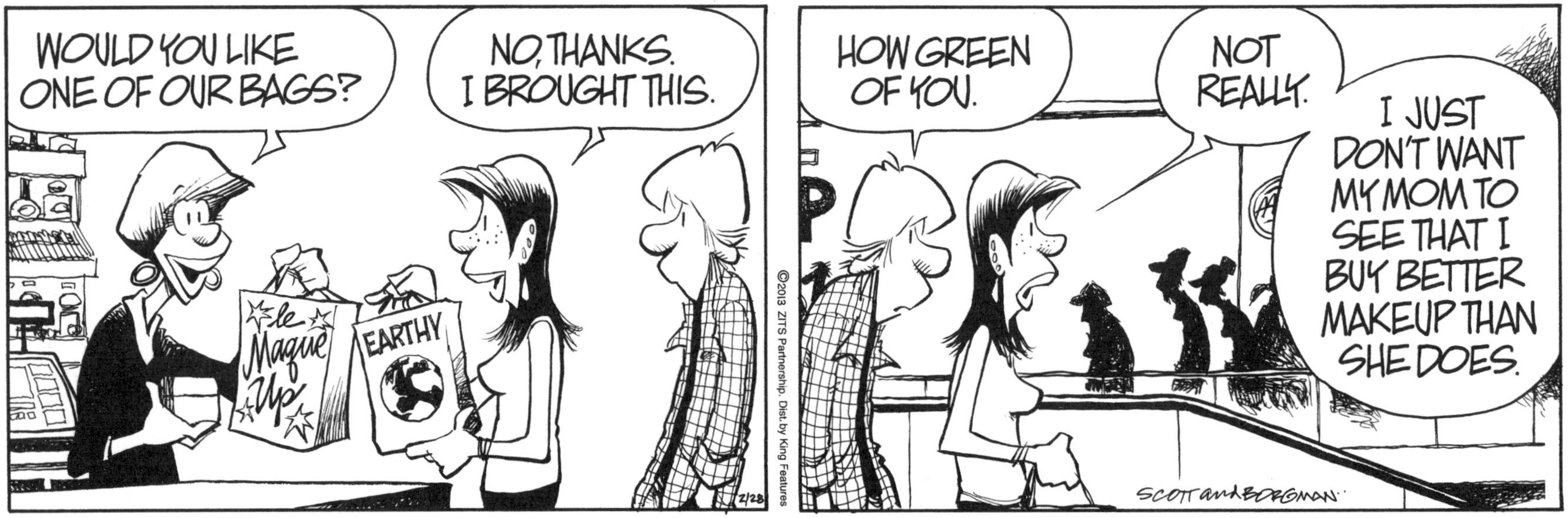
WOULD YOU LIKE ONE OF OUR BAGS?
NO, THANKS. I BROUGHT THIS.
le Maque Up
EARTHY
HOW GREEN OF YOU.
NOT REALLY.
I JUST DON'T WANT MY MOM TO SEE THAT I BUY BETTER MAKEUP THAN SHE DOES.
©2013 ZITS Partnership. Dist. by King Features
2/28
SCOTT and BORGMAN

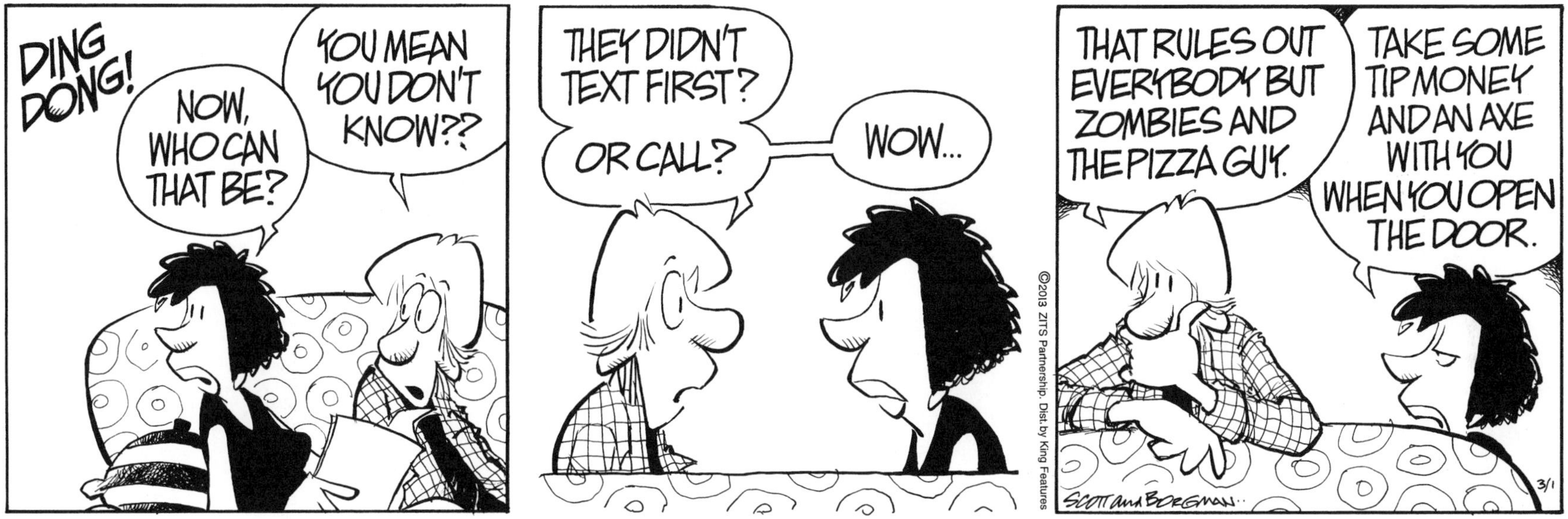
DING DONG!
NOW, WHO CAN THAT BE?
YOU MEAN YOU DON'T KNOW??
THEY DIDN'T TEXT FIRST?
OR CALL?
WOW...
THAT RULES OUT EVERYBODY BUT ZOMBIES AND THE PIZZA GUY.
TAKE SOME TIP MONEY AND AN AXE WITH YOU WHEN YOU OPEN THE DOOR.
©2013 ZITS Partnership. Dist. by King Features
SCOTT and BORGMAN
3/1

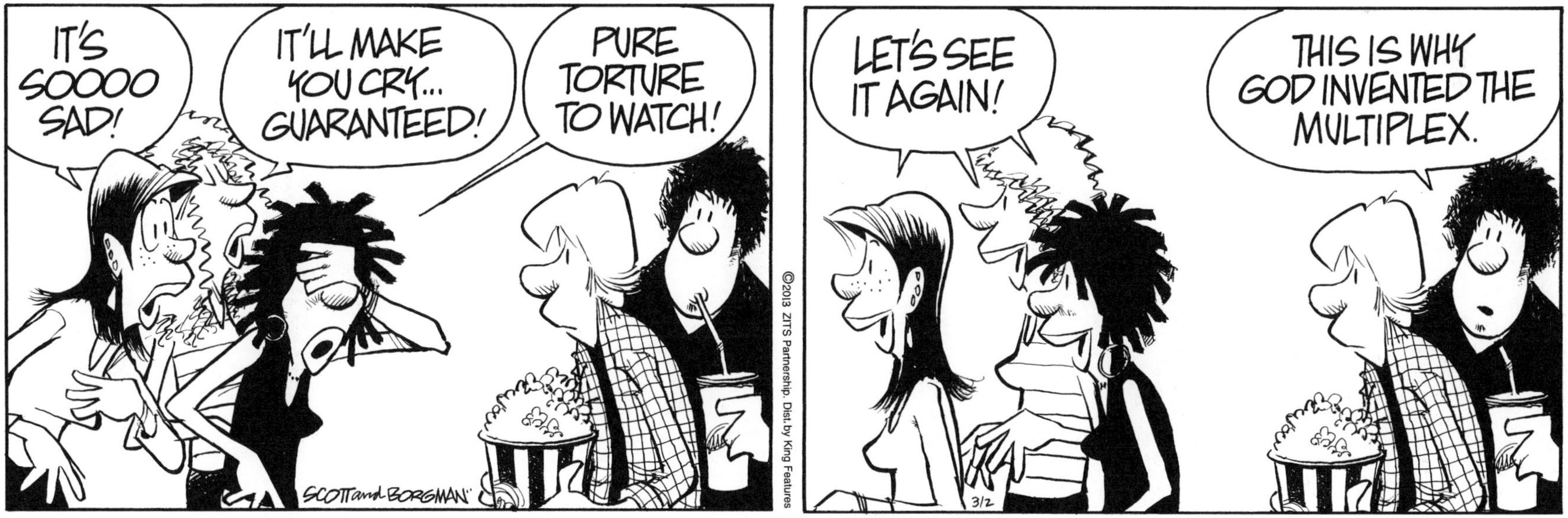
IT'S SOOOO SAD!
IT'LL MAKE YOU CRY... GUARANTEED!
PURE TORTURE TO WATCH!
©2013 ZITS Partnership. Dist. by King Features
SCOTT and BORGMAN
LET'S SEE IT AGAIN!
THIS IS WHY GOD INVENTED THE MULTIPLEX.
3/2

# ZITS

by JERRY SCOTT and JIM BORGMAN

SCOTT and BORGMAN
3/3
UP FOR A WALK, JEREMY?
IN THIS WEATHER??
©2013 ZITS Partnership. Dist. by King Features

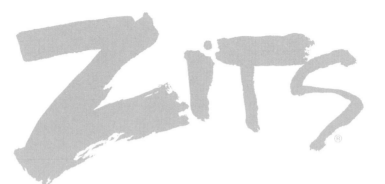

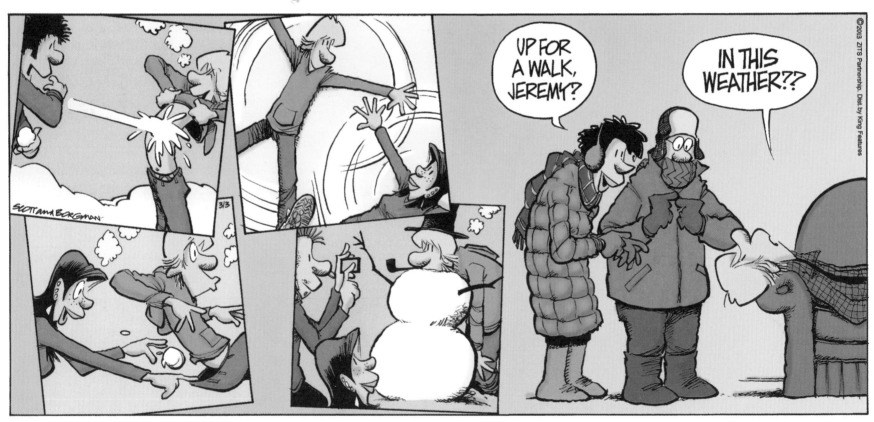

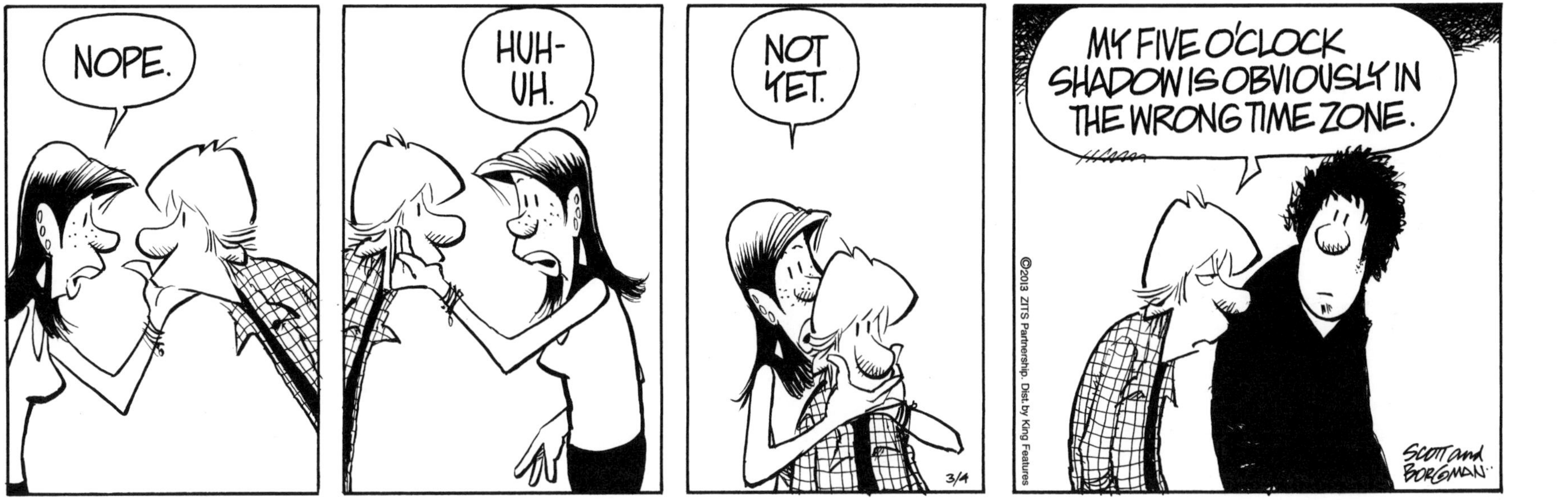
NOPE.
HUH-UH.
NOT YET.
3/4
©2013 ZITS Partnership. Dist. by King Features
MY FIVE O'CLOCK SHADOW IS OBVIOUSLY IN THE WRONG TIME ZONE.
SCOTT and BORGMAN

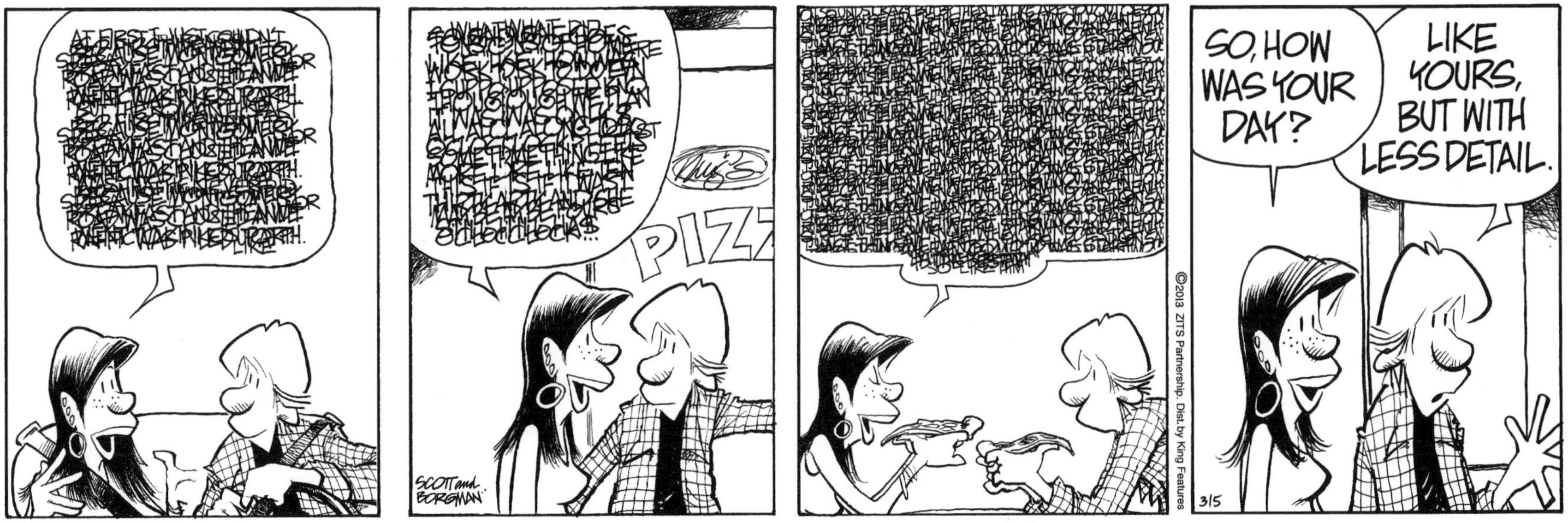
PIZZ
SCOTT and BORGMAN
©2013 ZITS Partnership. Dist. by King Features
3/5
SO, HOW WAS YOUR DAY?
LIKE YOURS, BUT WITH LESS DETAIL.

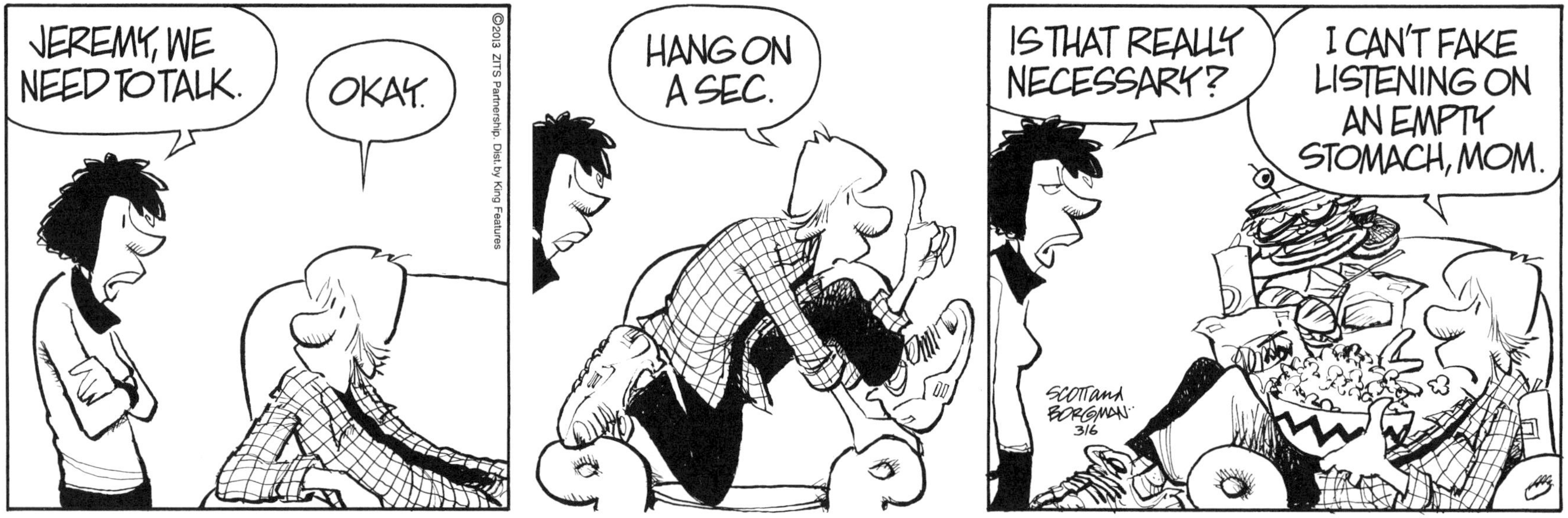
JEREMY, WE NEED TO TALK.
OKAY.
©2013 ZITS Partnership. Dist. by King Features
HANG ON A SEC.
IS THAT REALLY NECESSARY?
I CAN'T FAKE LISTENING ON AN EMPTY STOMACH, MOM.
SCOTT and BORGMAN 3/6

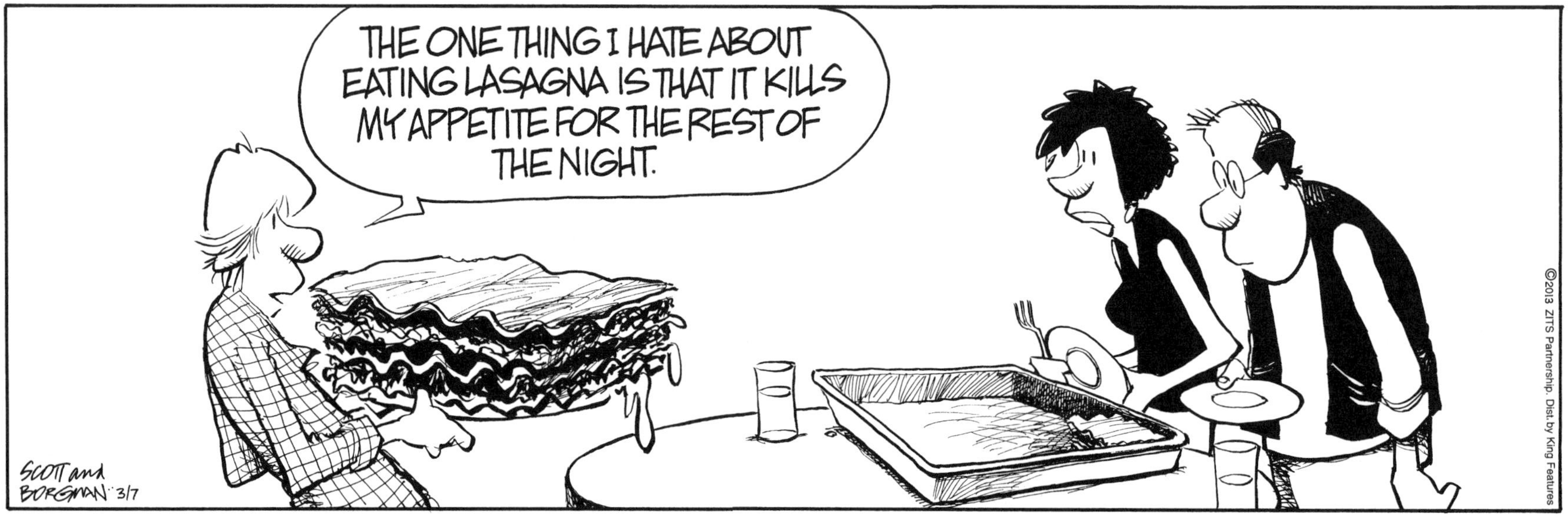
THE ONE THING I HATE ABOUT EATING LASAGNA IS THAT IT KILLS MY APPETITE FOR THE REST OF THE NIGHT.
SCOTT and BORGMAN 3/7
©2013 ZITS Partnership. Dist. by King Features

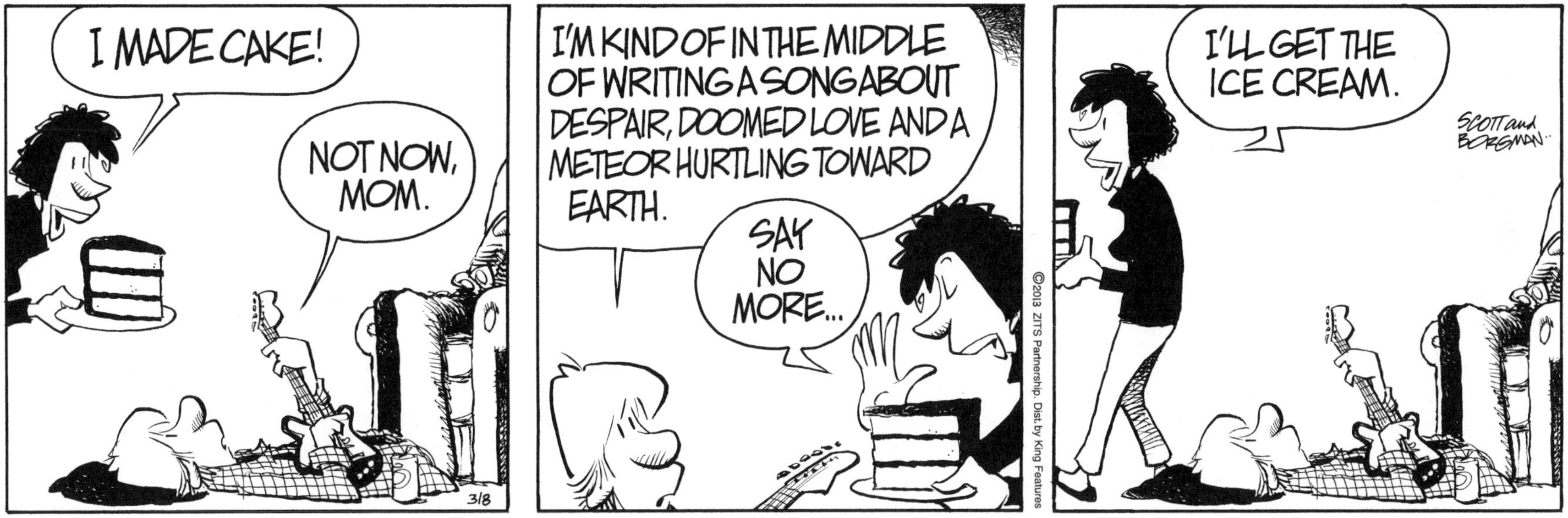
I MADE CAKE!
NOT NOW, MOM.
3/8
I'M KIND OF IN THE MIDDLE OF WRITING A SONG ABOUT DESPAIR, DOOMED LOVE AND A METEOR HURTLING TOWARD EARTH.
SAY NO MORE...
©2013 ZITS Partnership. Dist. by King Features
I'LL GET THE ICE CREAM.
SCOTT and BORGMAN

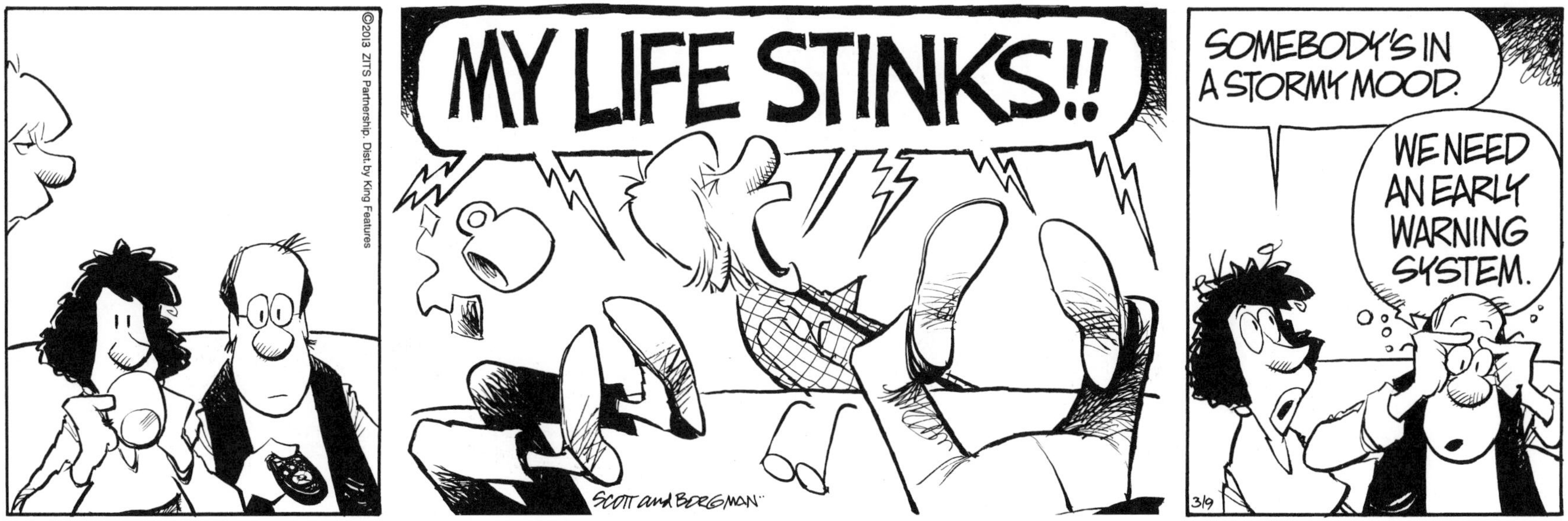
©2013 ZITS Partnership. Dist. by King Features
MY LIFE STINKS!!
SCOTT and BORGMAN
SOMEBODY'S IN A STORMY MOOD.
WE NEED AN EARLY WARNING SYSTEM.
3/9

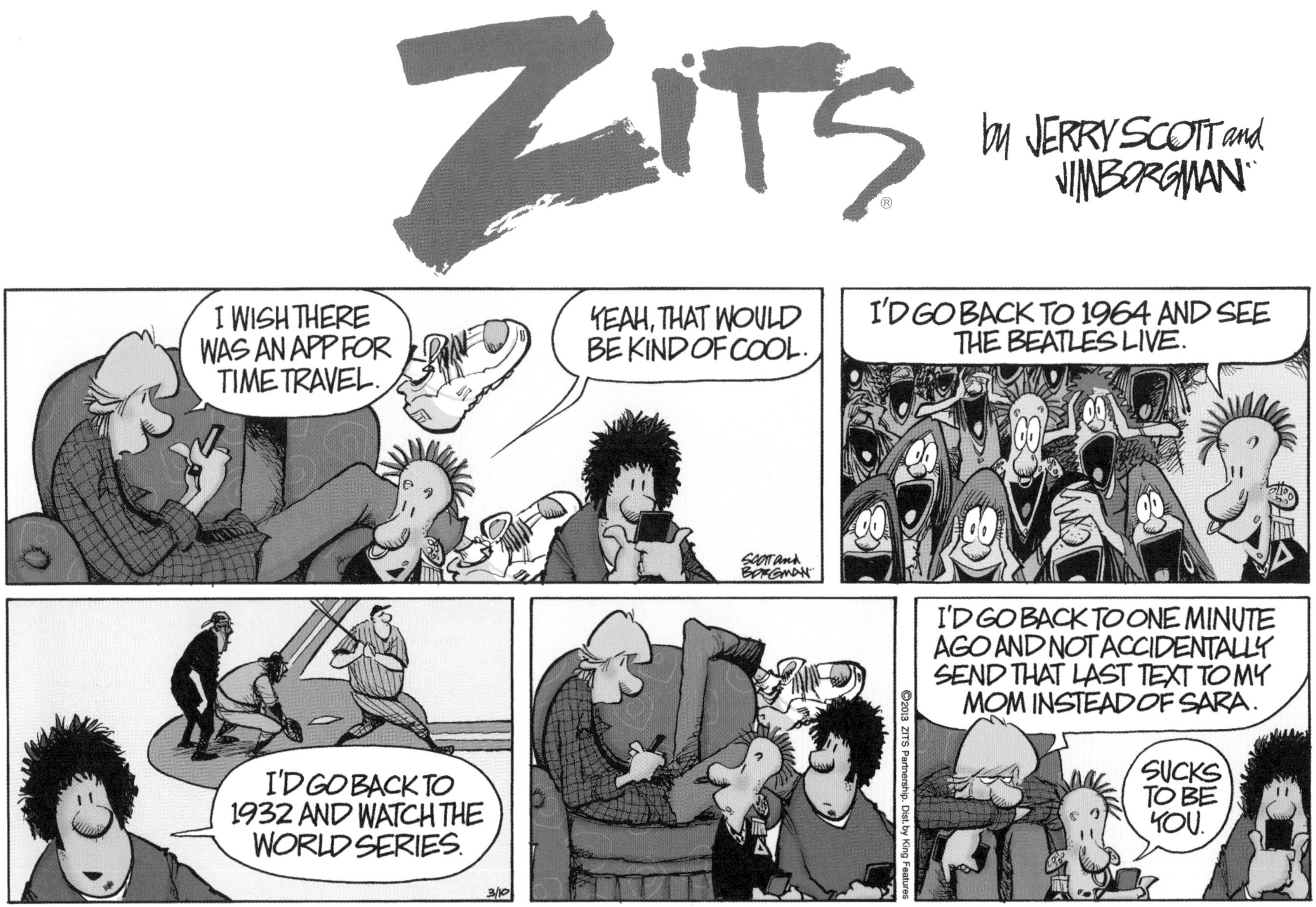
ZITS®
by JERRY SCOTT and JIM BORGMAN
I WISH THERE WAS AN APP FOR TIME TRAVEL.
YEAH, THAT WOULD BE KIND OF COOL.
SCOTT and BORGMAN
I'D GO BACK TO 1964 AND SEE THE BEATLES LIVE.
I'D GO BACK TO 1932 AND WATCH THE WORLD SERIES.
3/10
©2013 ZITS Partnership. Dist. by King Features
I'D GO BACK TO ONE MINUTE AGO AND NOT ACCIDENTALLY SEND THAT LAST TEXT TO MY MOM INSTEAD OF SARA.
SUCKS TO BE YOU.

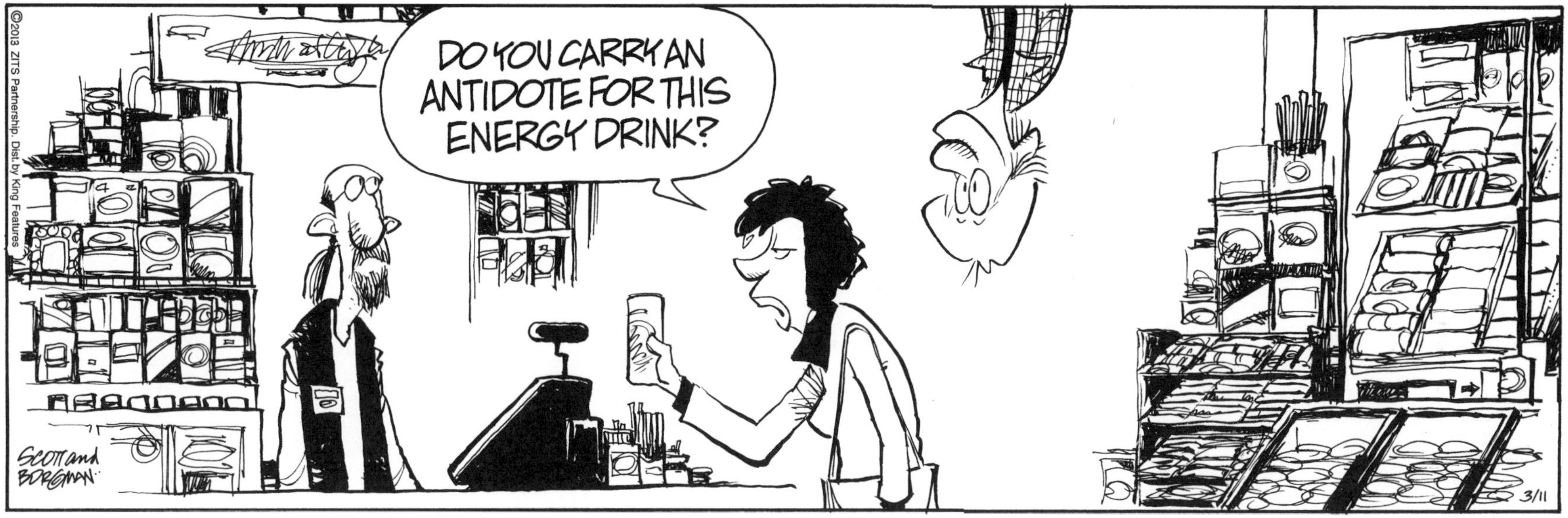
©2013 ZITS Partnership. Dist. by King Features
DO YOU CARRY AN ANTIDOTE FOR THIS ENERGY DRINK?
SCOTT and BORGMAN
3/11

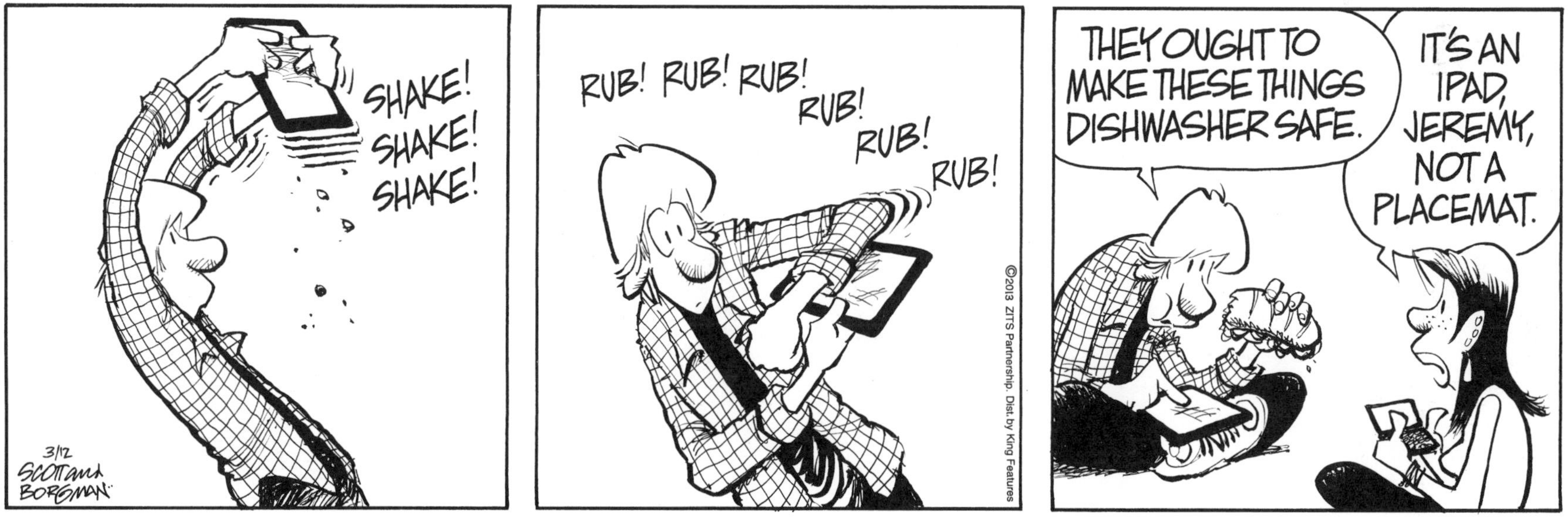
SHAKE! SHAKE! SHAKE!
3/12
SCOTT and BORGMAN
RUB! RUB! RUB! RUB! RUB! RUB!
©2013 ZITS Partnership. Dist. by King Features
THEY OUGHT TO MAKE THESE THINGS DISHWASHER SAFE.
IT'S AN IPAD, JEREMY, NOT A PLACEMAT.

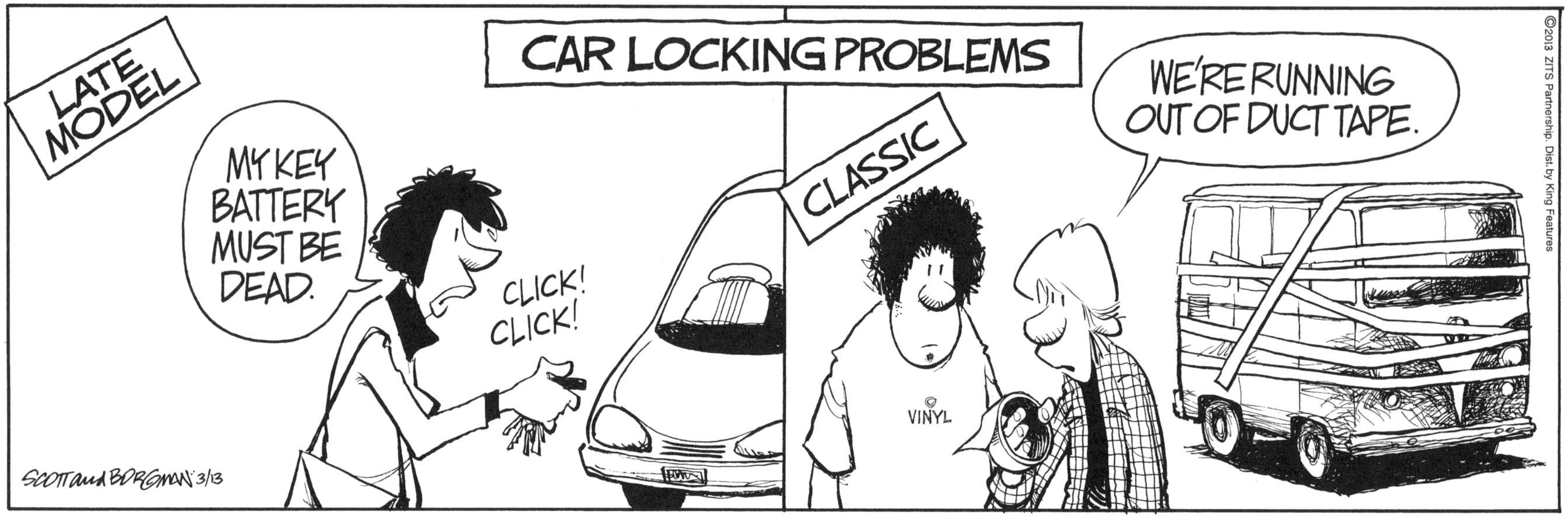
CAR LOCKING PROBLEMS
LATE MODEL
MY KEY BATTERY MUST BE DEAD.
CLICK! CLICK!
SCOTT and BORGMAN 3/13
CLASSIC
WE'RE RUNNING OUT OF DUCT TAPE.
VINYL
©2013 ZITS Partnership. Dist. by King Features

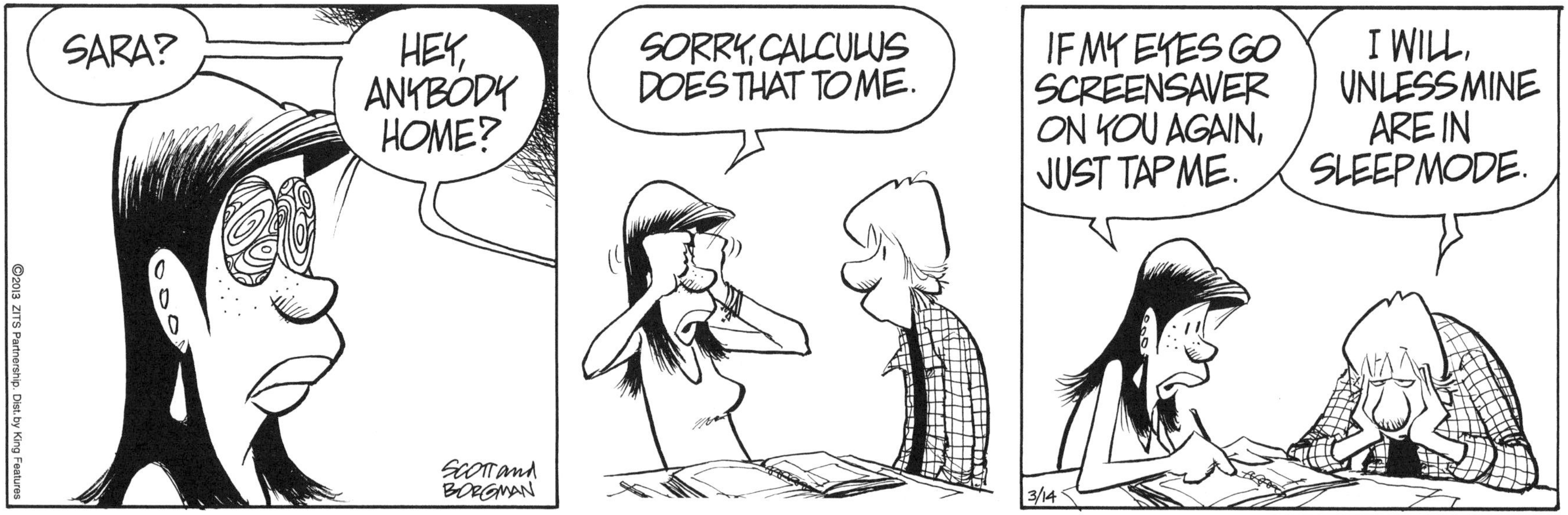
SARA?
HEY, ANYBODY HOME?
©2013 ZITS Partnership. Dist. by King Features
SCOTT and BORGMAN
SORRY, CALCULUS DOES THAT TO ME.
IF MY EYES GO SCREENSAVER ON YOU AGAIN, JUST TAP ME.
I WILL, UNLESS MINE ARE IN SLEEP MODE.
3/14

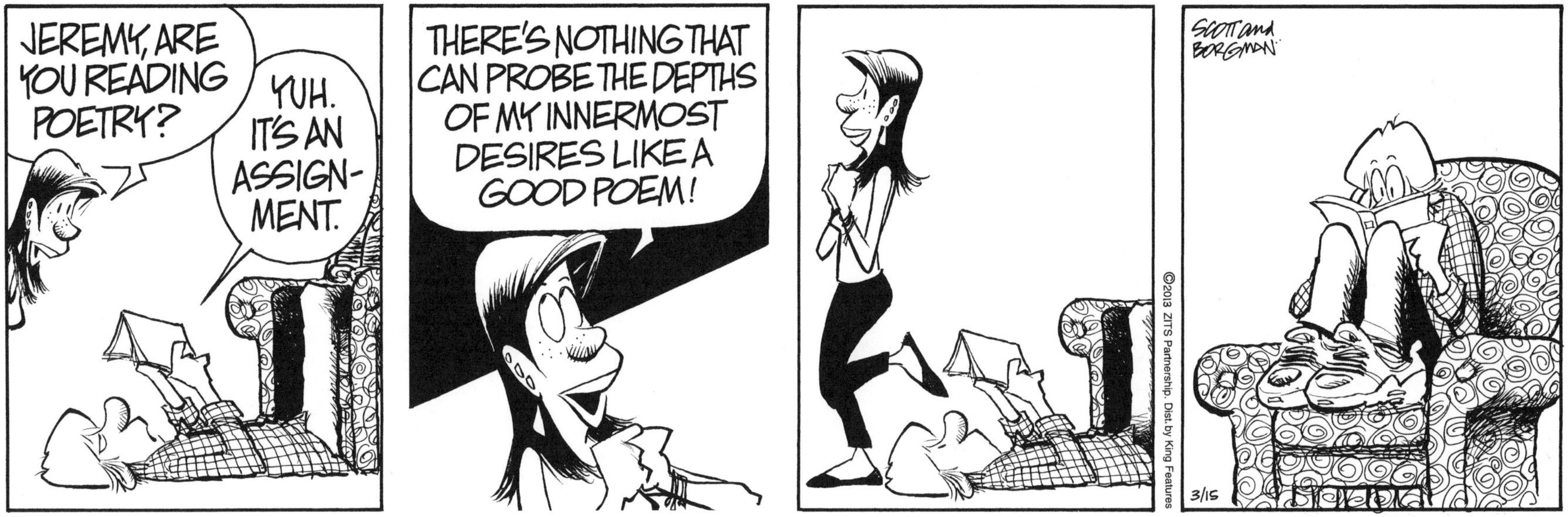
JEREMY, ARE YOU READING POETRY?
YUH. IT'S AN ASSIGN-MENT.
THERE'S NOTHING THAT CAN PROBE THE DEPTHS OF MY INNERMOST DESIRES LIKE A GOOD POEM!
SCOTT and BORGMAN
©2013 ZITS Partnership. Dist. by King Features
3/15

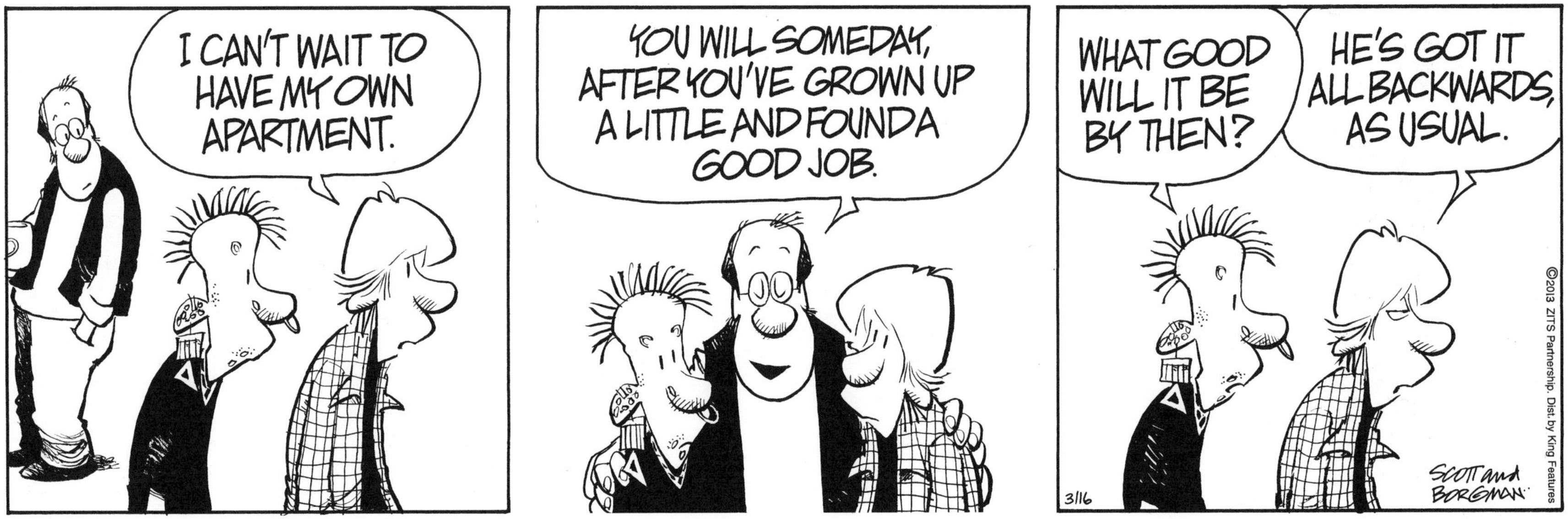
I CAN'T WAIT TO HAVE MY OWN APARTMENT.
YOU WILL SOMEDAY, AFTER YOU'VE GROWN UP A LITTLE AND FOUND A GOOD JOB.
WHAT GOOD WILL IT BE BY THEN?
HE'S GOT IT ALL BACKWARDS, AS USUAL.
3/16
SCOTT and BORGMAN
©2013 ZITS Partnership. Dist. by King Features

# ZITS®

by JERRY SCOTT and JIM BORGMAN

DO YOU EVER WONDER WHAT THE FUTURE WILL BRING, JEREMY?
I THINK WE'LL PROBABLY HAVE A BASE ON MARS.
NO, I MEAN *OUR* FUTURE.
ON MARS?
**NO!** I'M NOT TALKING ABOUT PLANETS OR ROCKETS, I'M--
OH, JUST NEVER MIND!!!
THEN, IRONICALLY, SHE SAYS, "I NEED SOME SPACE."
CURIOUS...
SCOTT and BORGMAN 3/17
©2013 ZITS Partnership. Dist. by King Features

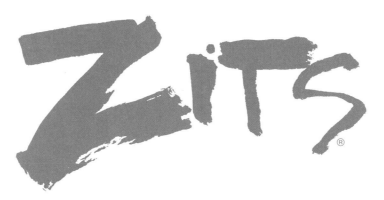

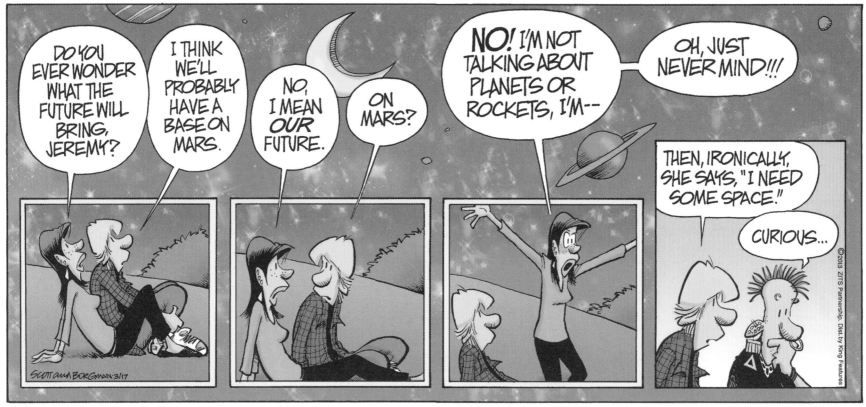

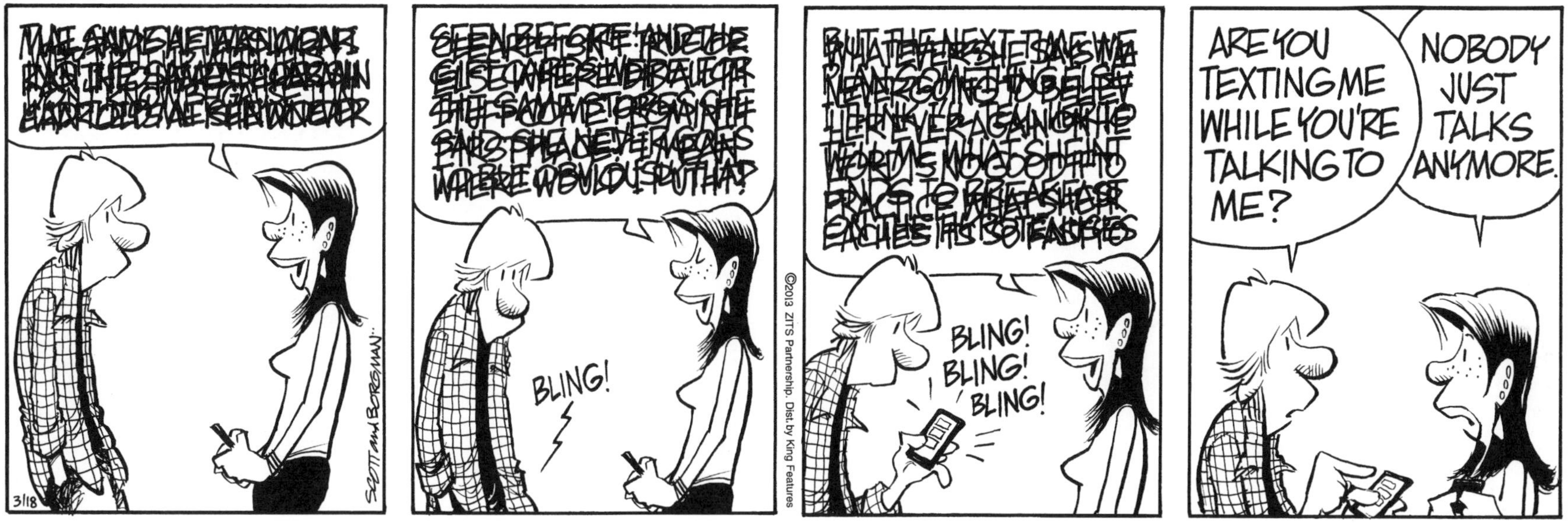
3/18
SCOTT and BORGMAN
BLING!
©2013 ZITS Partnership. Dist. by King Features
BLING! BLING! BLING!
ARE YOU TEXTING ME WHILE YOU'RE TALKING TO ME?
NOBODY JUST TALKS ANYMORE.

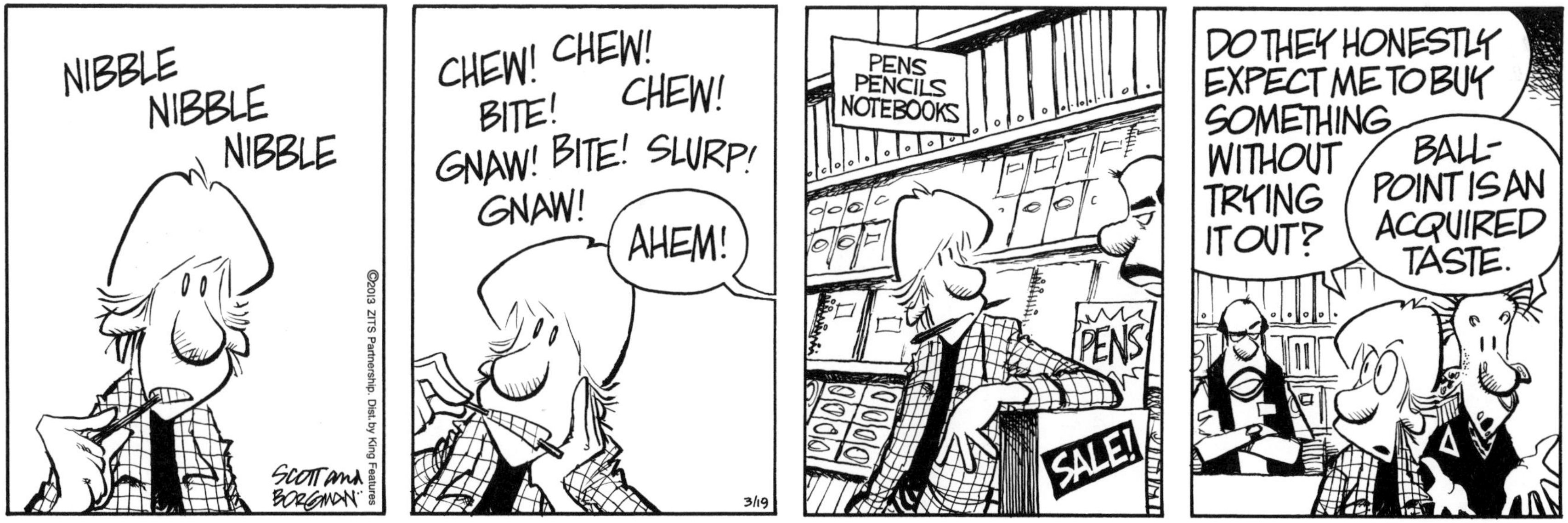
NIBBLE NIBBLE NIBBLE
©2013 ZITS Partnership. Dist. by King Features
SCOTT and BORGMAN
CHEW! CHEW! BITE! CHEW! GNAW! BITE! SLURP! GNAW!
AHEM!
3/19
PENS PENCILS NOTEBOOKS
PENS
SALE!
DO THEY HONESTLY EXPECT ME TO BUY SOMETHING WITHOUT TRYING IT OUT?
BALL-POINT IS AN ACQUIRED TASTE.

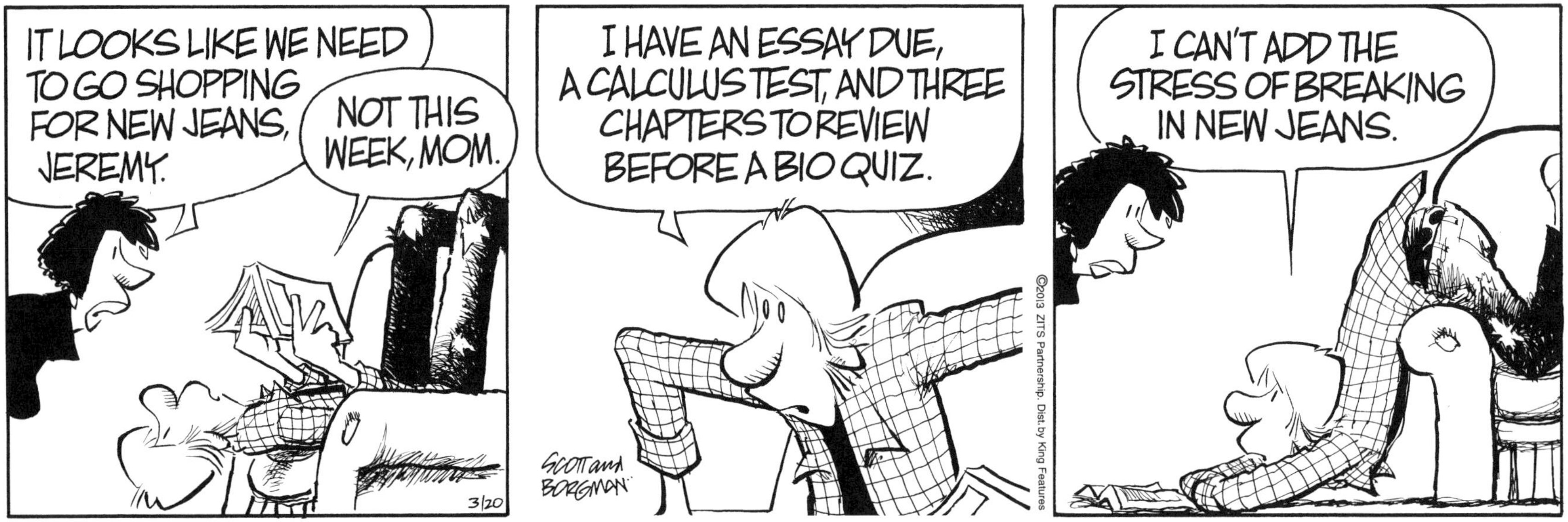
IT LOOKS LIKE WE NEED TO GO SHOPPING FOR NEW JEANS, JEREMY.
NOT THIS WEEK, MOM.
3/20
I HAVE AN ESSAY DUE, A CALCULUS TEST, AND THREE CHAPTERS TO REVIEW BEFORE A BIO QUIZ.
SCOTT and BORGMAN
©2013 ZITS Partnership. Dist. by King Features
I CAN'T ADD THE STRESS OF BREAKING IN NEW JEANS.

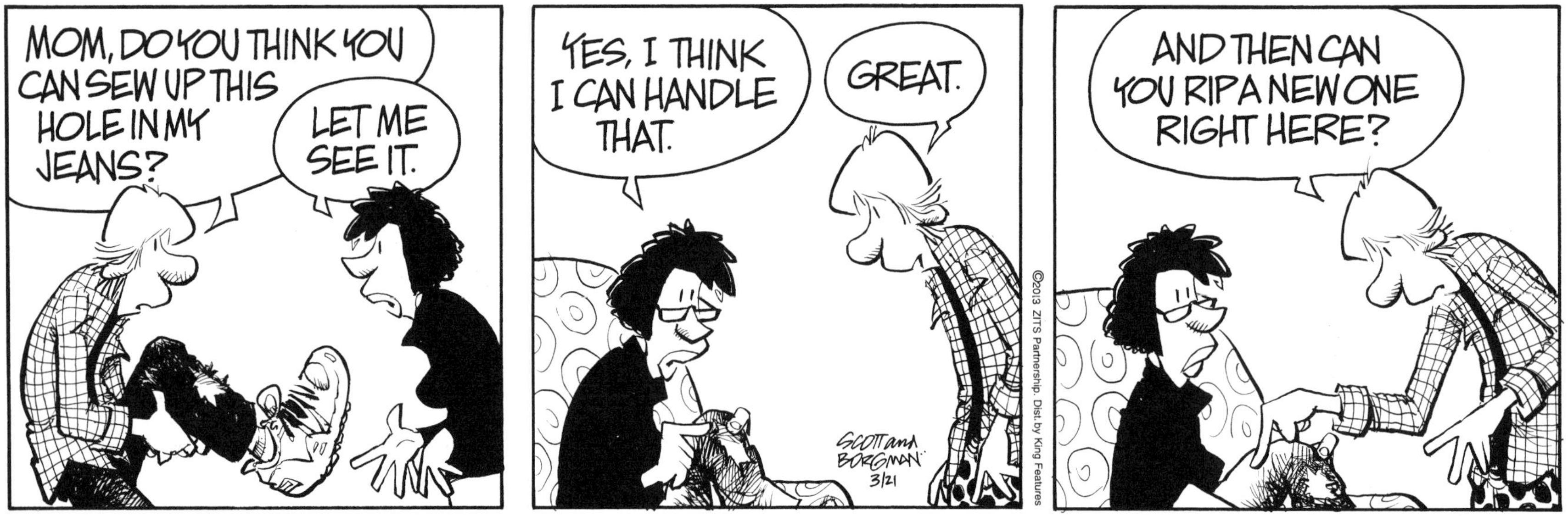
MOM, DO YOU THINK YOU CAN SEW UP THIS HOLE IN MY JEANS?
LET ME SEE IT.
YES, I THINK I CAN HANDLE THAT.
GREAT.
SCOTT and BORGMAN
3/21
©2013 ZITS Partnership. Dist. by King Features
AND THEN CAN YOU RIP A NEW ONE RIGHT HERE?

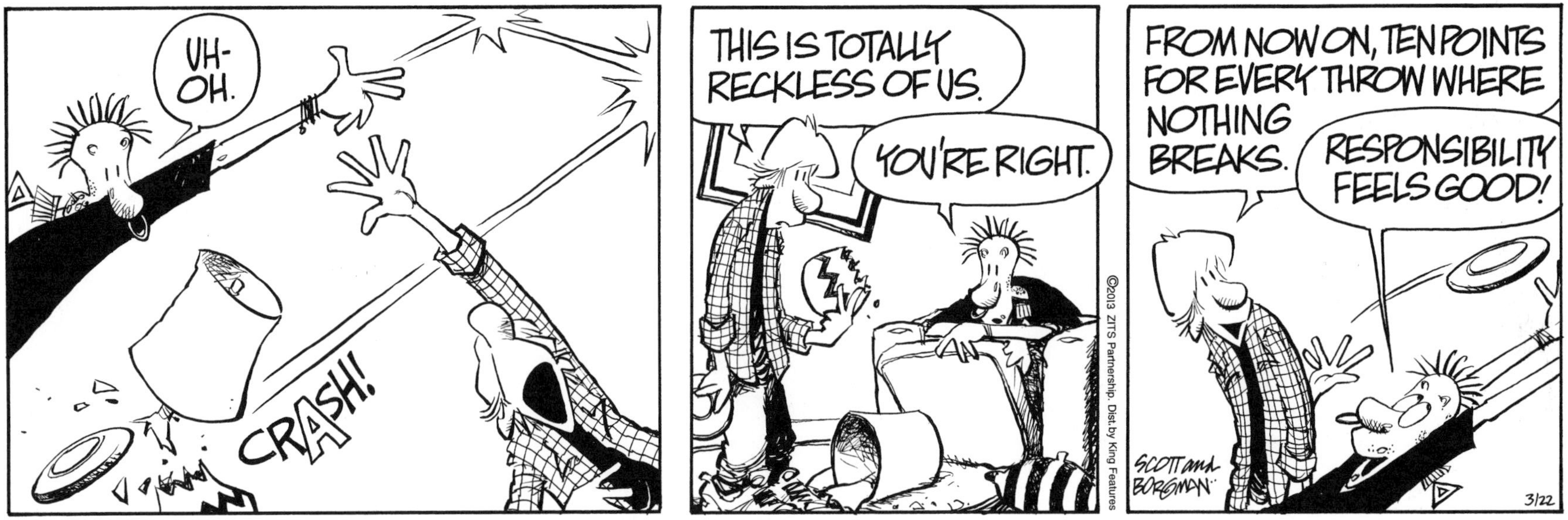
UH-OH.
CRASH!
THIS IS TOTALLY RECKLESS OF US.
YOU'RE RIGHT.
©2013 ZITS Partnership. Dist. by King Features
FROM NOW ON, TEN POINTS FOR EVERY THROW WHERE NOTHING BREAKS.
RESPONSIBILITY FEELS GOOD!
SCOTT and BORGMAN
3/22

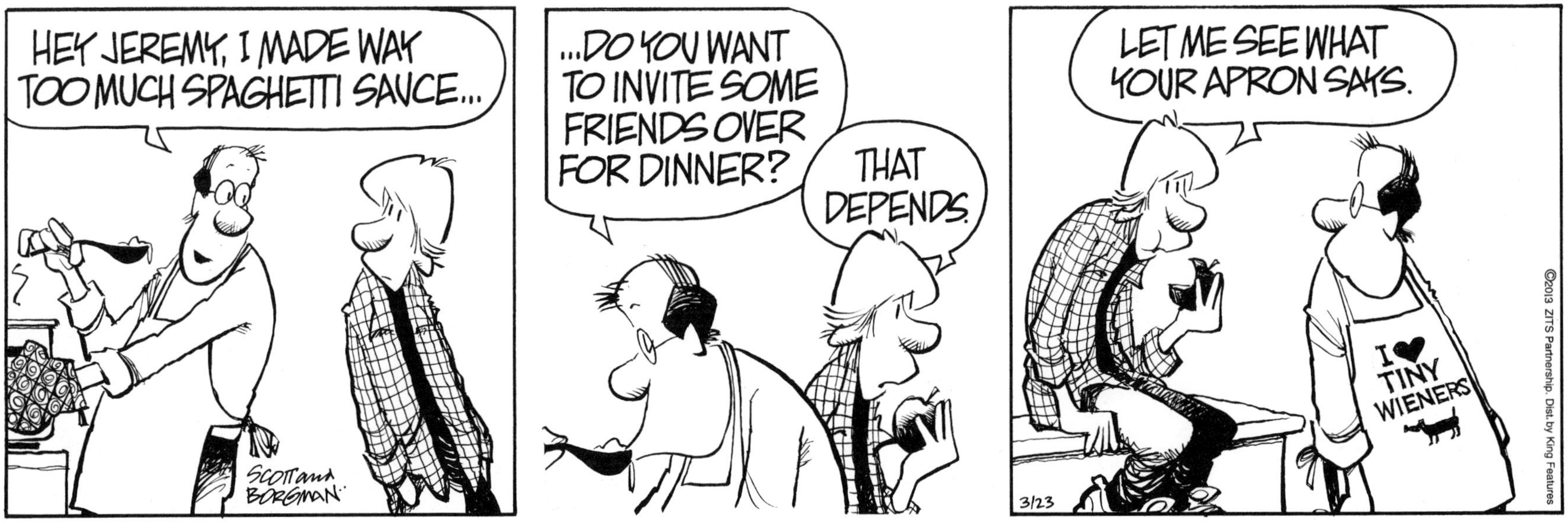
HEY JEREMY, I MADE WAY TOO MUCH SPAGHETTI SAUCE...
SCOTT and BORGMAN
...DO YOU WANT TO INVITE SOME FRIENDS OVER FOR DINNER?
THAT DEPENDS.
LET ME SEE WHAT YOUR APRON SAYS.
I ♥ TINY WIENERS
3/23
©2013 ZITS Partnership. Dist. by King Features

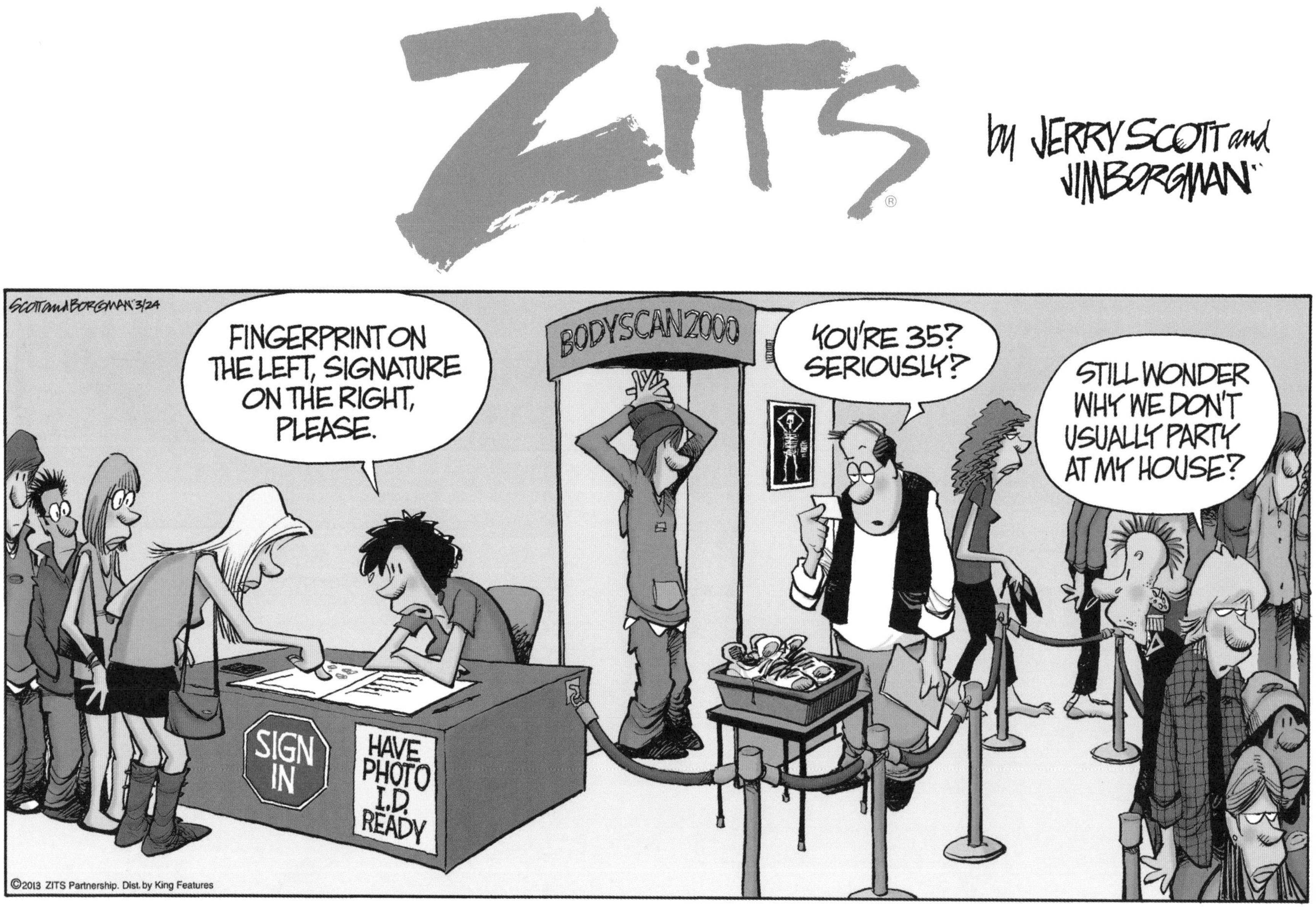
ZITS
by JERRY SCOTT and JIM BORGMAN
SCOTT and BORGMAN 3/24
FINGERPRINT ON THE LEFT, SIGNATURE ON THE RIGHT, PLEASE.
BODYSCAN2000
YOU'RE 35? SERIOUSLY?
STILL WONDER WHY WE DON'T USUALLY PARTY AT MY HOUSE?
SIGN IN
HAVE PHOTO I.D. READY
©2013 ZITS Partnership. Dist. by King Features

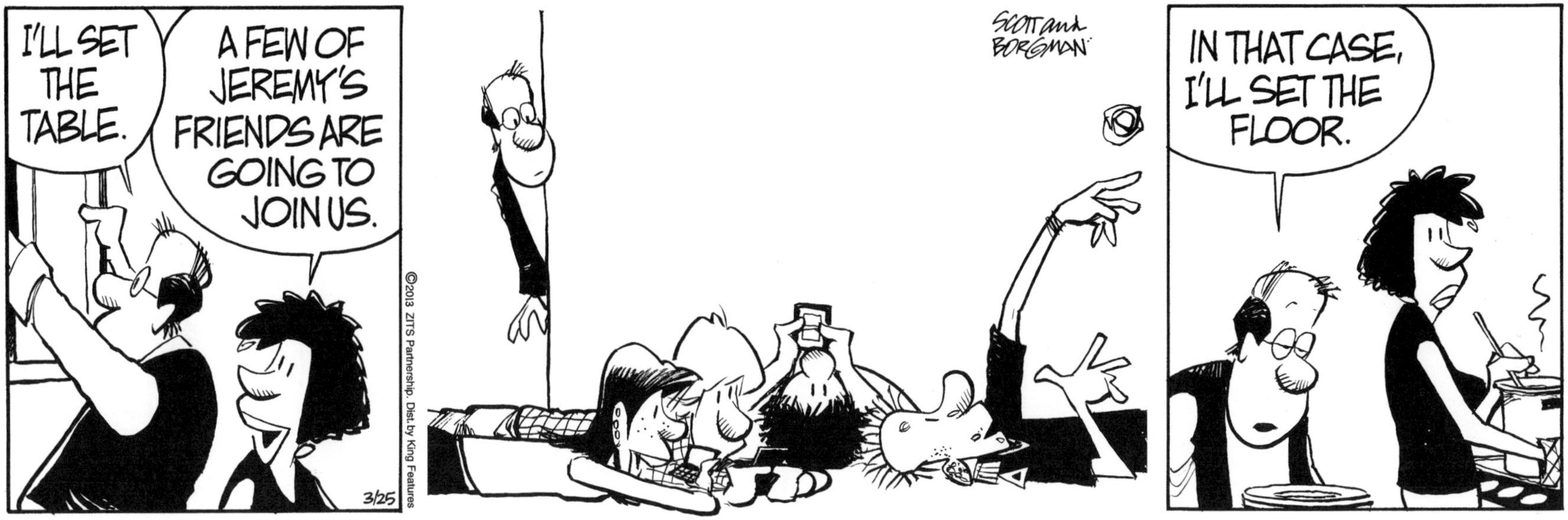
I'LL SET THE TABLE.
A FEW OF JEREMY'S FRIENDS ARE GOING TO JOIN US.
©2013 ZITS Partnership. Dist. by King Features
3/25
SCOTT and BORGMAN
IN THAT CASE, I'LL SET THE FLOOR.

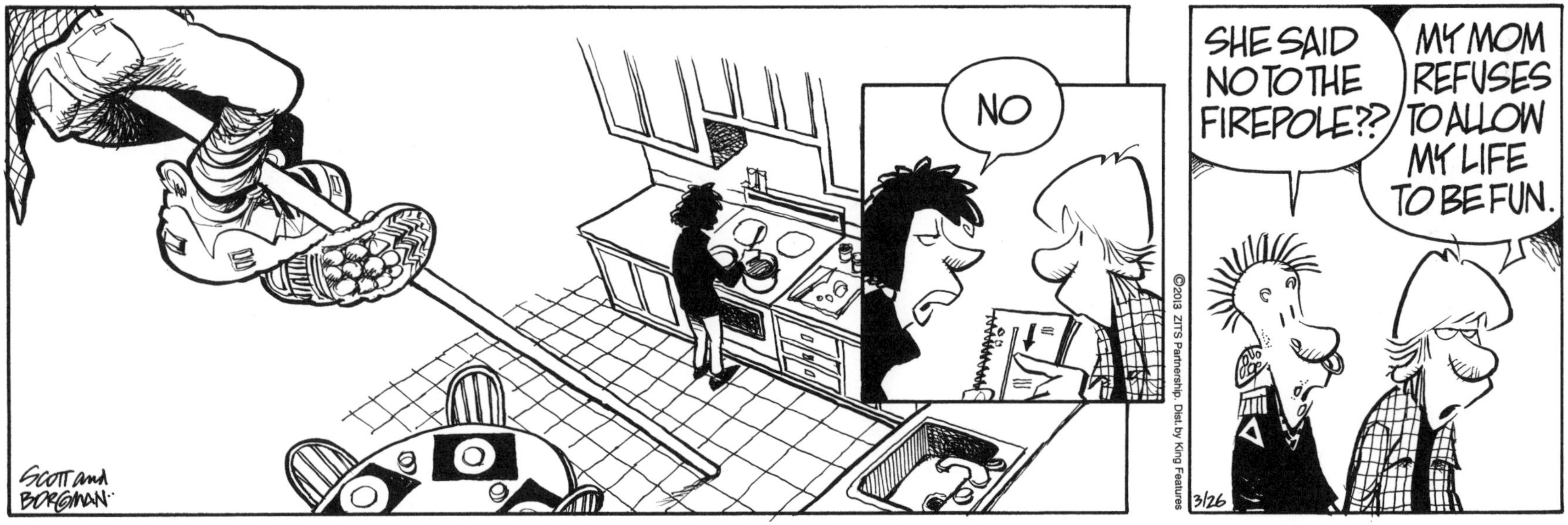
SCOTT and BORGMAN
NO
SHE SAID NO TO THE FIREPOLE??
MY MOM REFUSES TO ALLOW MY LIFE TO BE FUN.
©2013 ZITS Partnership. Dist. by King Features
3/26

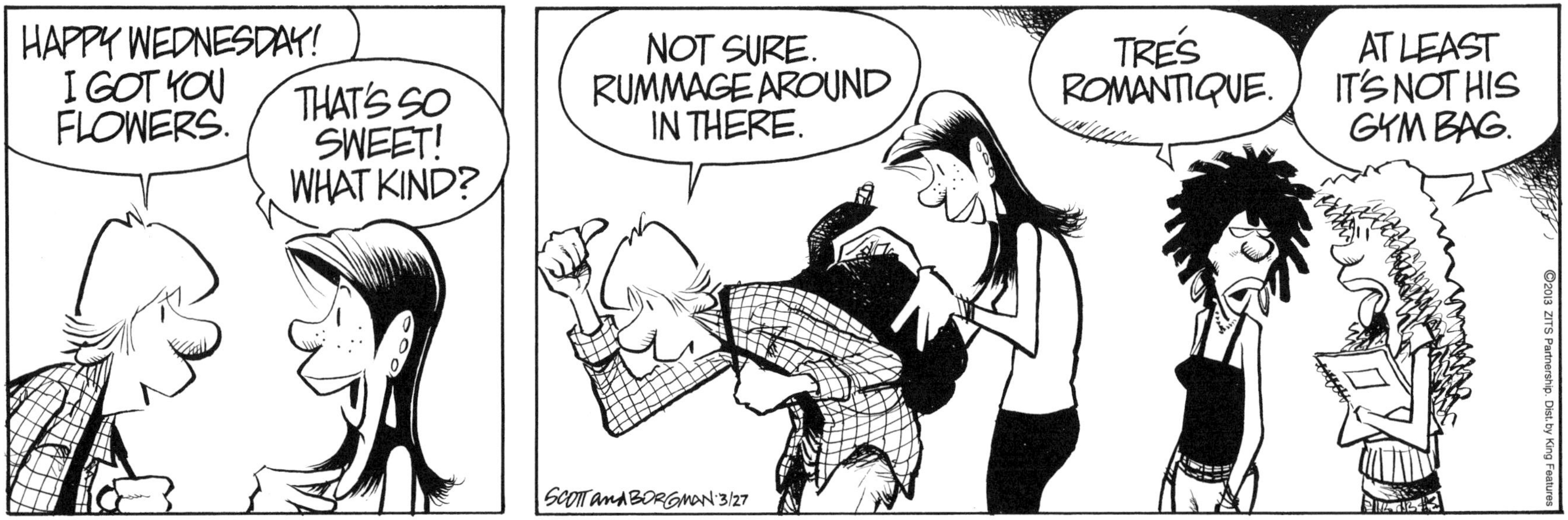
HAPPY WEDNESDAY! I GOT YOU FLOWERS.
THAT'S SO SWEET! WHAT KIND?
NOT SURE. RUMMAGE AROUND IN THERE.
TRÉS ROMANTIQUE.
AT LEAST IT'S NOT HIS GYM BAG.
SCOTT and BORGMAN 3/27
©2013 ZITS Partnership. Dist. by King Features

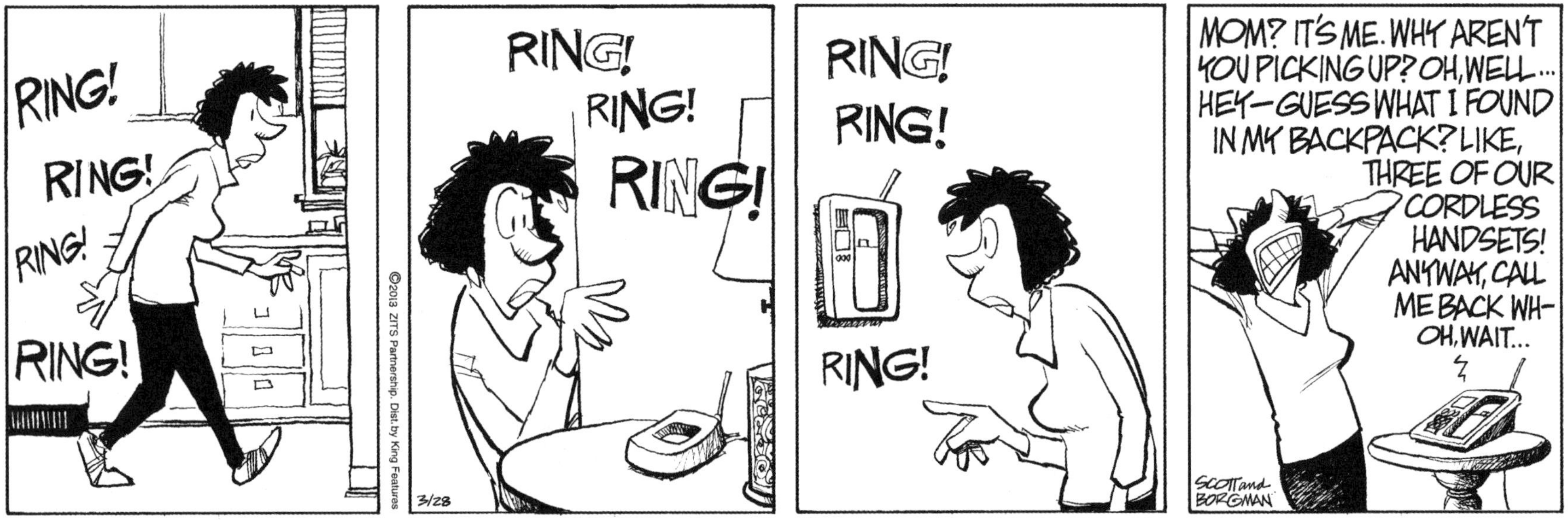
RING!
RING!
RING!
RING!
©2013 ZITS Partnership. Dist. by King Features
RING!
RING!
RING!
3/28
RING!
RING!
RING!
MOM? IT'S ME. WHY AREN'T YOU PICKING UP? OH, WELL... HEY—GUESS WHAT I FOUND IN MY BACKPACK? LIKE, THREE OF OUR CORDLESS HANDSETS! ANYWAY, CALL ME BACK WH- OH, WAIT...
SCOTT and BORGMAN

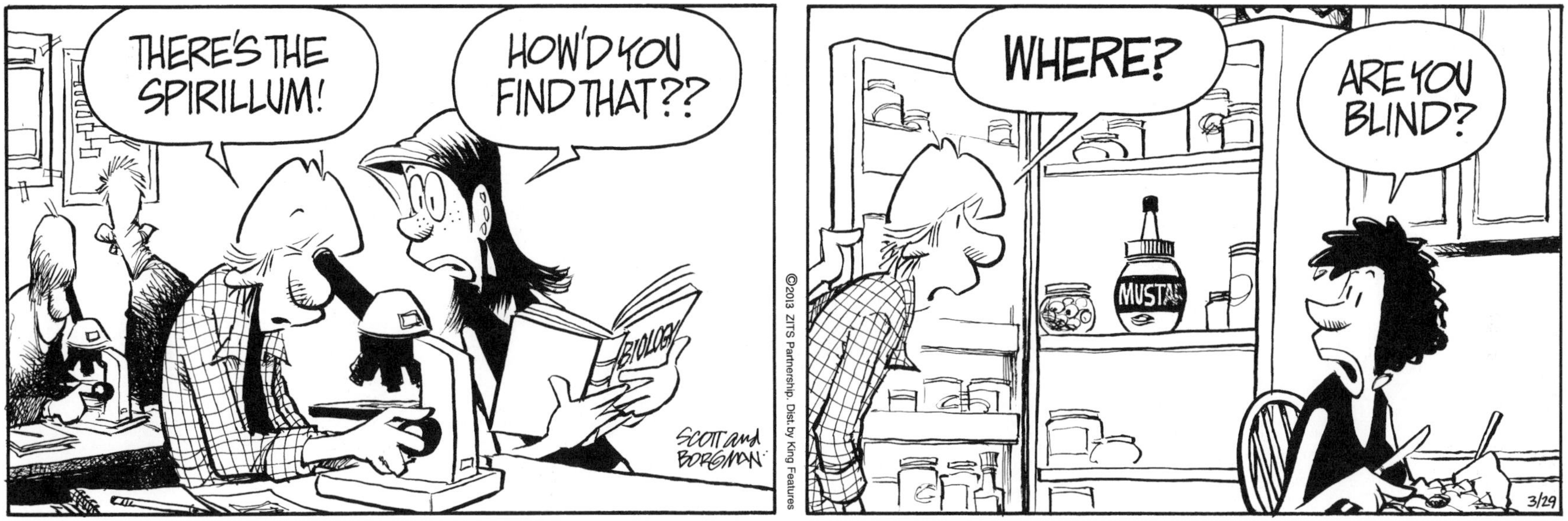
THERE'S THE SPIRILLUM!
HOW'D YOU FIND THAT??
BIOLOGY
SCOTT and BORGMAN
©2013 ZITS Partnership. Dist. by King Features
WHERE?
MUSTA
ARE YOU BLIND?
3/29

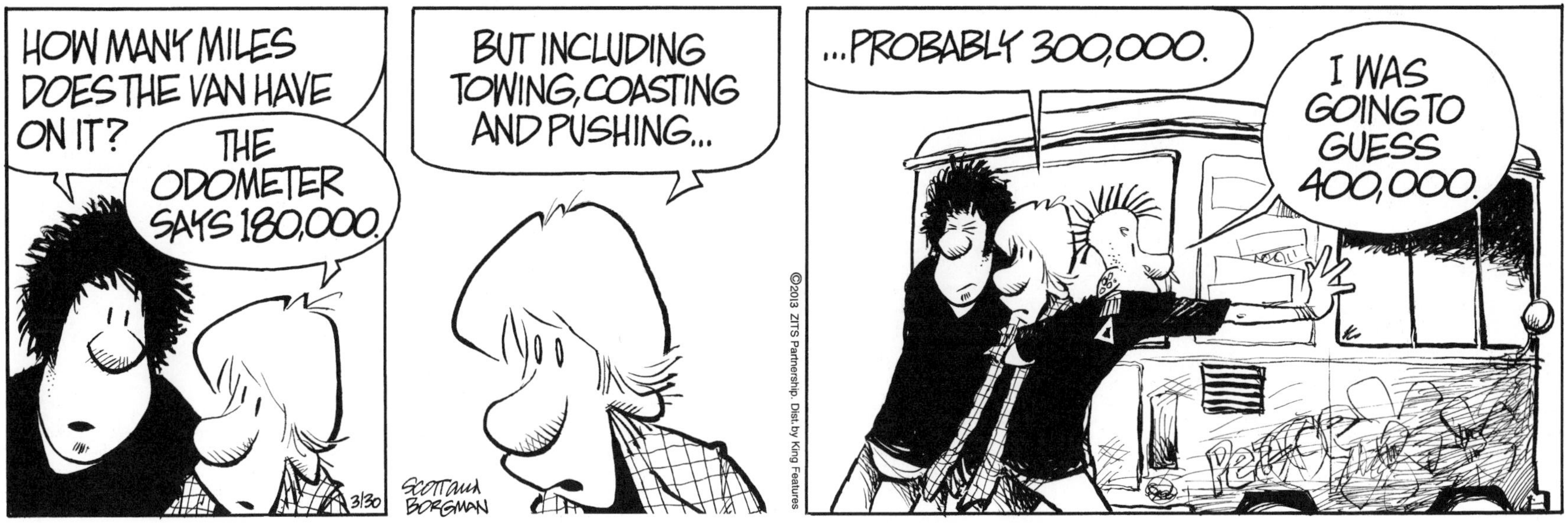
HOW MANY MILES DOES THE VAN HAVE ON IT?
THE ODOMETER SAYS 180,000.
3/30
BUT INCLUDING TOWING, COASTING AND PUSHING...
SCOTT and BORGMAN
©2013 ZITS Partnership. Dist. by King Features
...PROBABLY 300,000.
I WAS GOING TO GUESS 400,000.

ZITS®

by JERRY SCOTT and JIM BORGMAN

SCOTT and BORGMAN
SO, YEAH...
THAT WAS THE KITCHEN.
HOW NICE!
SHOW THEM THE FIREPLACE, JEREMY.
OKAY. THERE IT IS.
OOH!
OH– AND THIS IS MY DAD.
YOU HAVE A BEAUTIFUL HOME, YOUNG MAN!
IF I'D KNOWN I WAS GOING TO MEET SARA'S GRANDPARENTS, I'D HAVE PUT ON SOME PANTS.
3/31

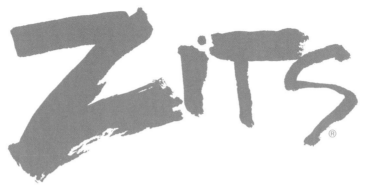

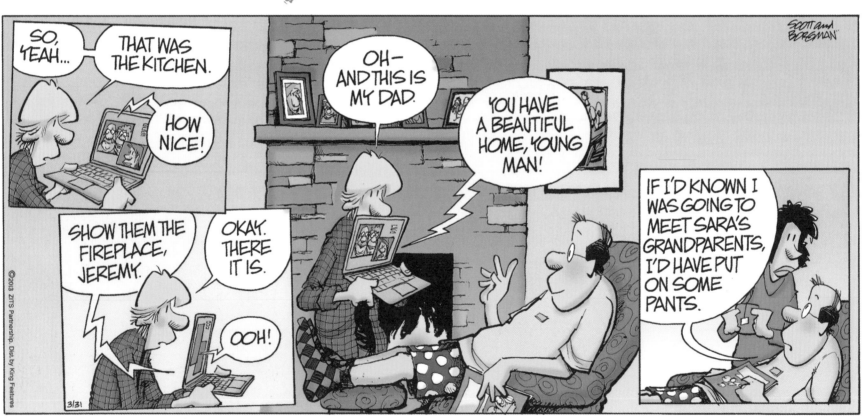

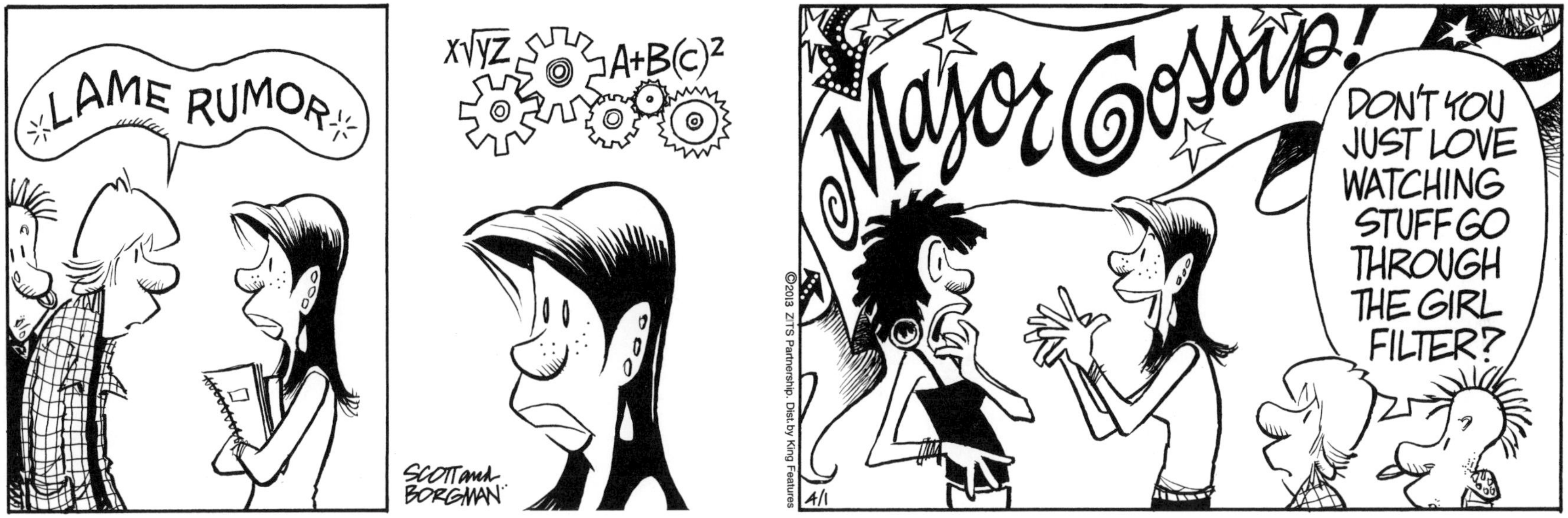
LAME RUMOR
X√YZ A+B(C)²
SCOTT and BORGMAN
Major Gossip!
DON'T YOU JUST LOVE WATCHING STUFF GO THROUGH THE GIRL FILTER?
©2013 ZITS Partnership. Dist. by King Features
4/1

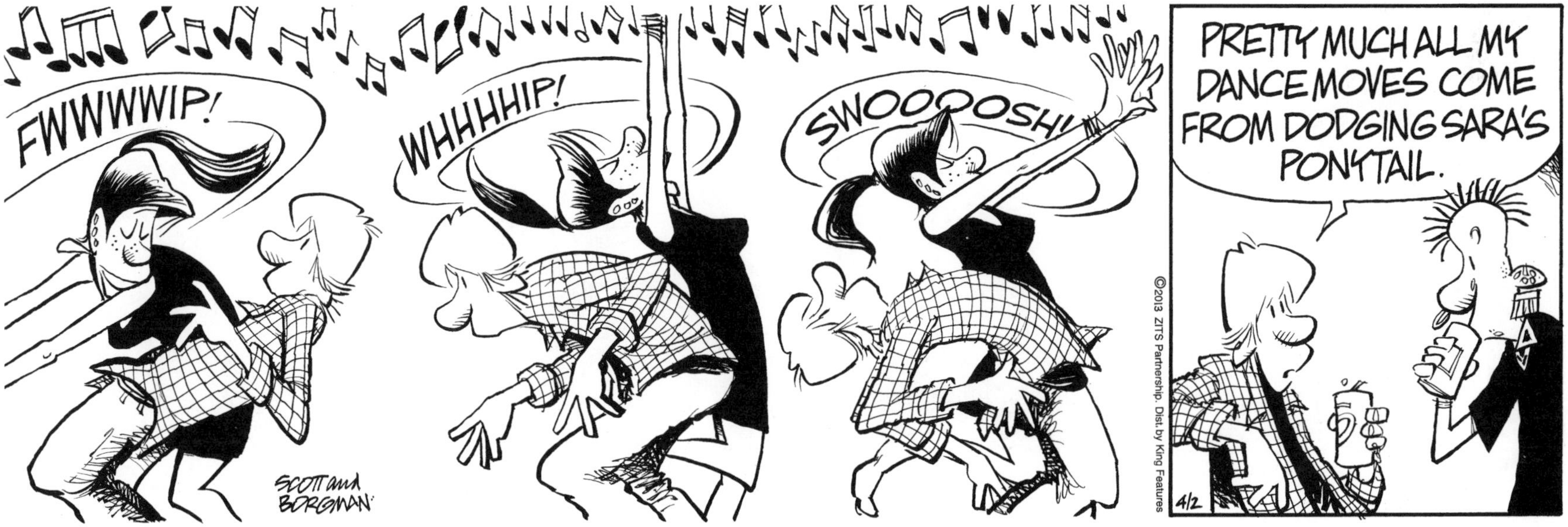
FWWWWIP!
SCOTT and BORGMAN
WHHHHIP!
SWOOOOSH!
PRETTY MUCH ALL MY DANCE MOVES COME FROM DODGING SARA'S PONYTAIL.
©2013 ZITS Partnership. Dist. by King Features
4/2

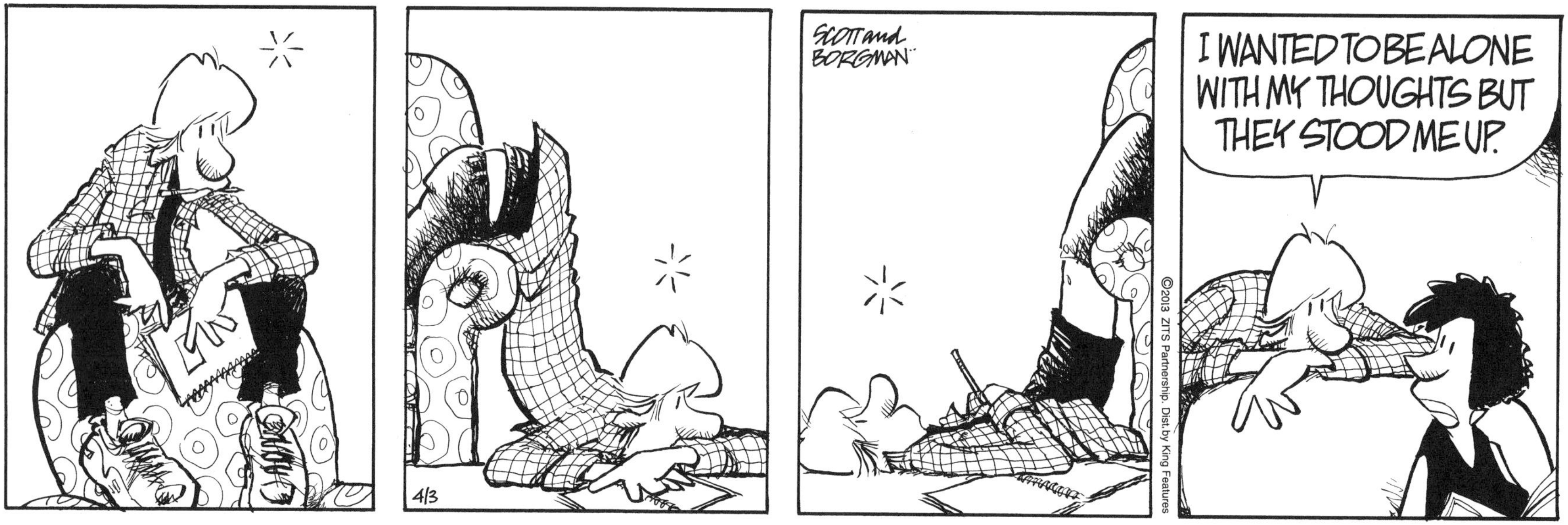
SCOTT and BORGMAN
4/3
©2013 ZITS Partnership. Dist. by King Features
I WANTED TO BE ALONE WITH MY THOUGHTS BUT THEY STOOD ME UP.

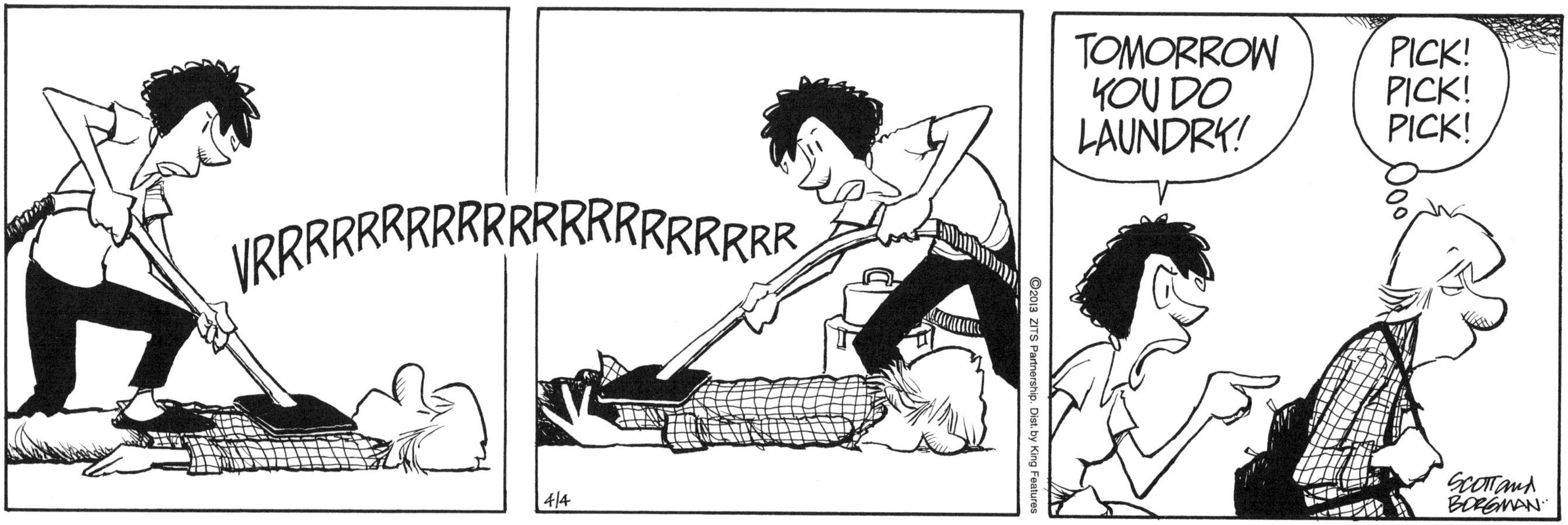
VRRRRRRRRRRRRRRRRRRRRRRRR
4/4
©2013 ZITS Partnership. Dist. by King Features
TOMORROW YOU DO LAUNDRY!
PICK! PICK! PICK!
SCOTT and BORGMAN

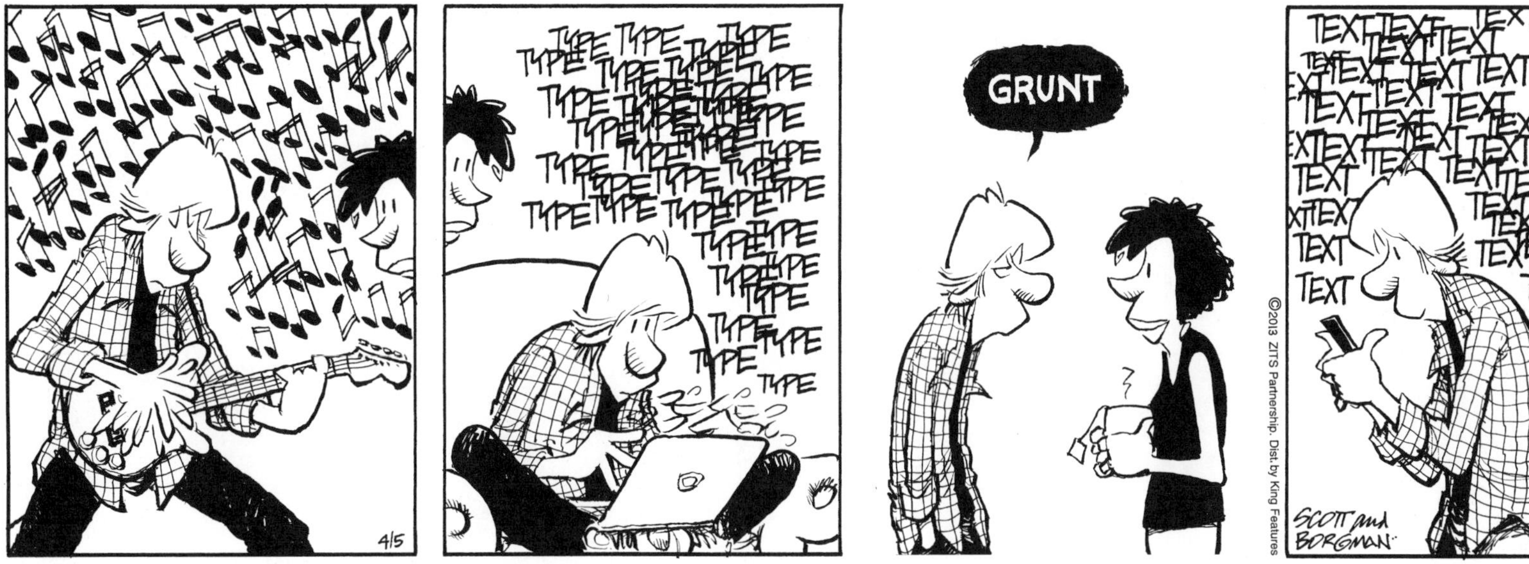
4/5
TYPE TYPE TYPE
GRUNT
©2013 ZITS Partnership. Dist. by King Features
TEXT TEXT TEXT
*SIGH*
SCOTT and BORGMAN

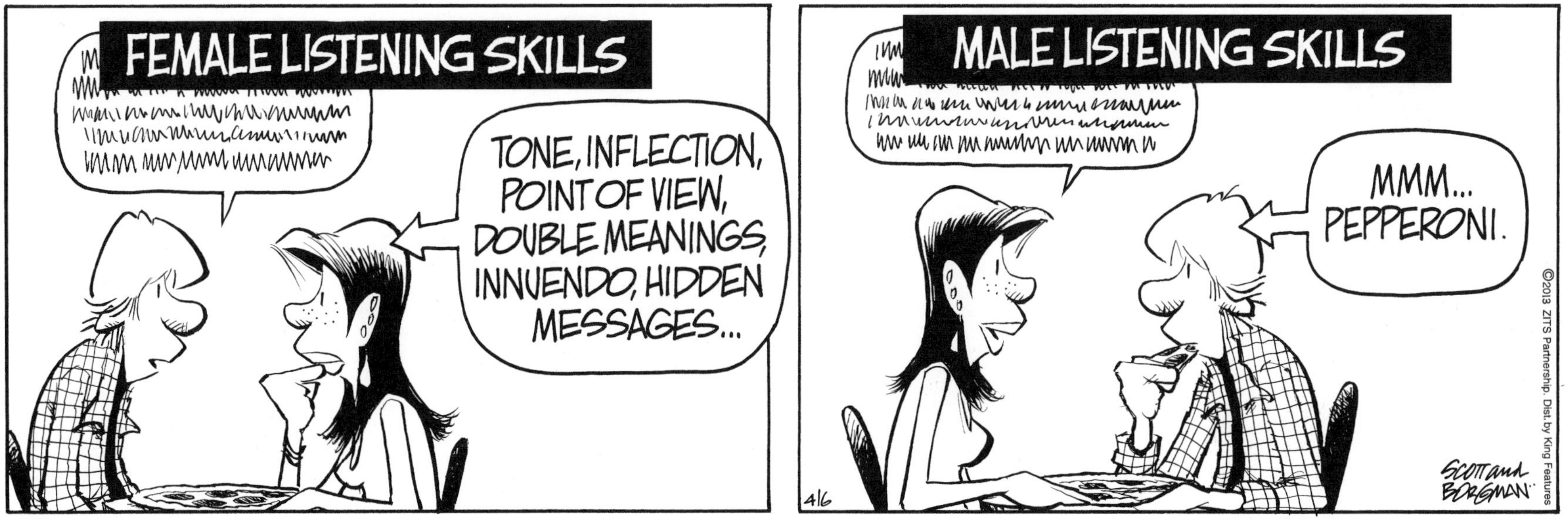
FEMALE LISTENING SKILLS
TONE, INFLECTION, POINT OF VIEW, DOUBLE MEANINGS, INNUENDO, HIDDEN MESSAGES...
MALE LISTENING SKILLS
MMM... PEPPERONI.
4/6
©2013 ZITS Partnership. Dist. by King Features
SCOTT and BORGMAN

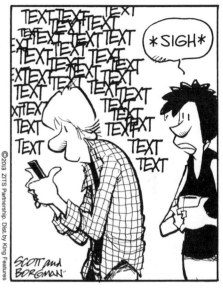

# ZITS®

by JERRY SCOTT and JIM BORGMAN

YAWN!
THIS SIDE UP
GLAD I CHECKED.
JERRY SCOTT and JIM BORGMAN 4/7
©2013 ZITS Partnership. Dist. by King Features

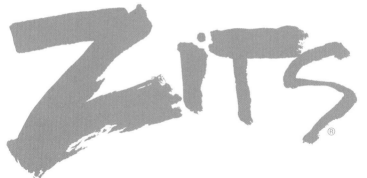

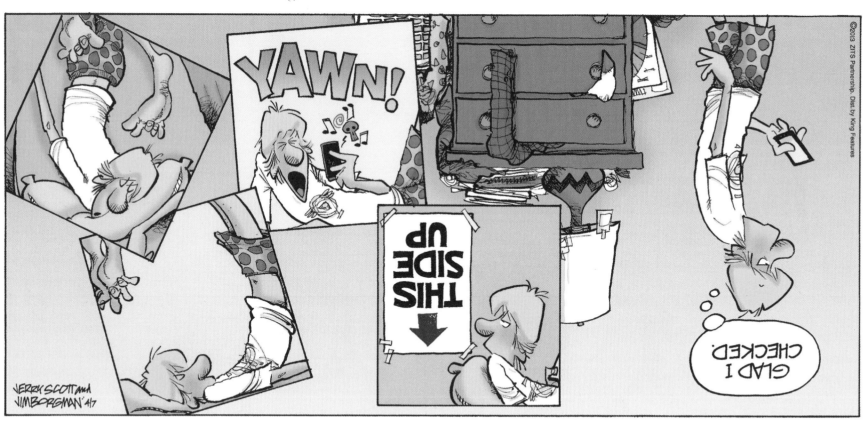

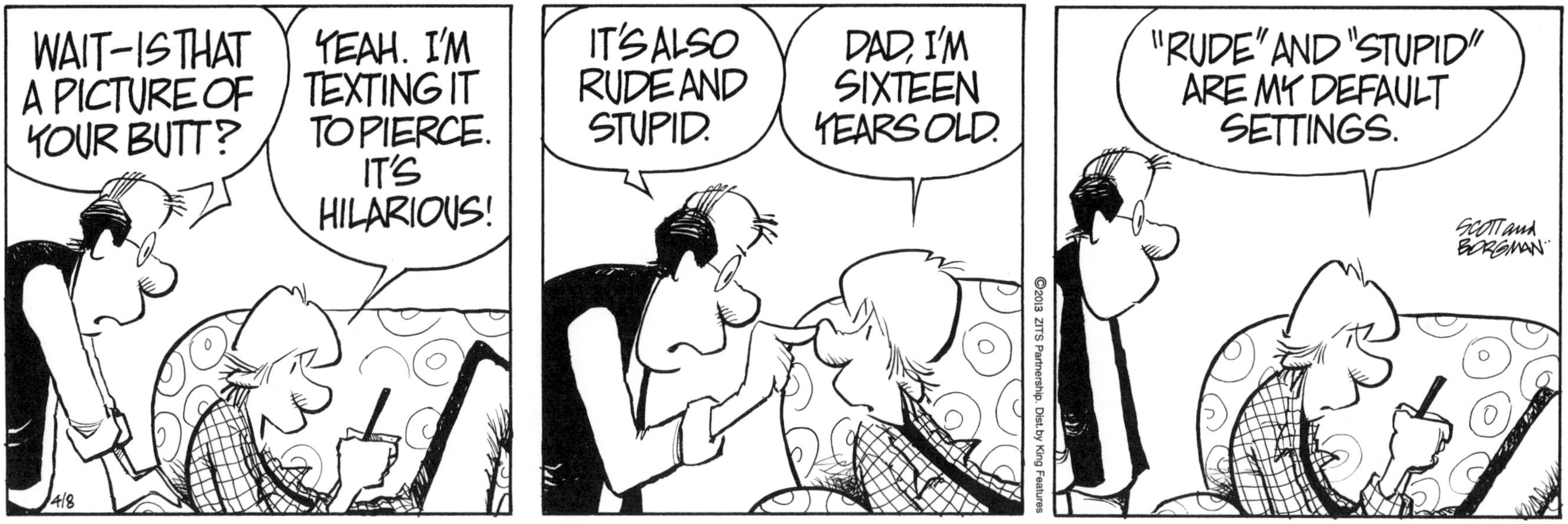
WAIT—IS THAT A PICTURE OF YOUR BUTT?
YEAH. I'M TEXTING IT TO PIERCE. IT'S HILARIOUS!
4/8
IT'S ALSO RUDE AND STUPID.
DAD, I'M SIXTEEN YEARS OLD.
©2013 ZITS Partnership. Dist. by King Features
"RUDE" AND "STUPID" ARE MY DEFAULT SETTINGS.
SCOTT and BORGMAN

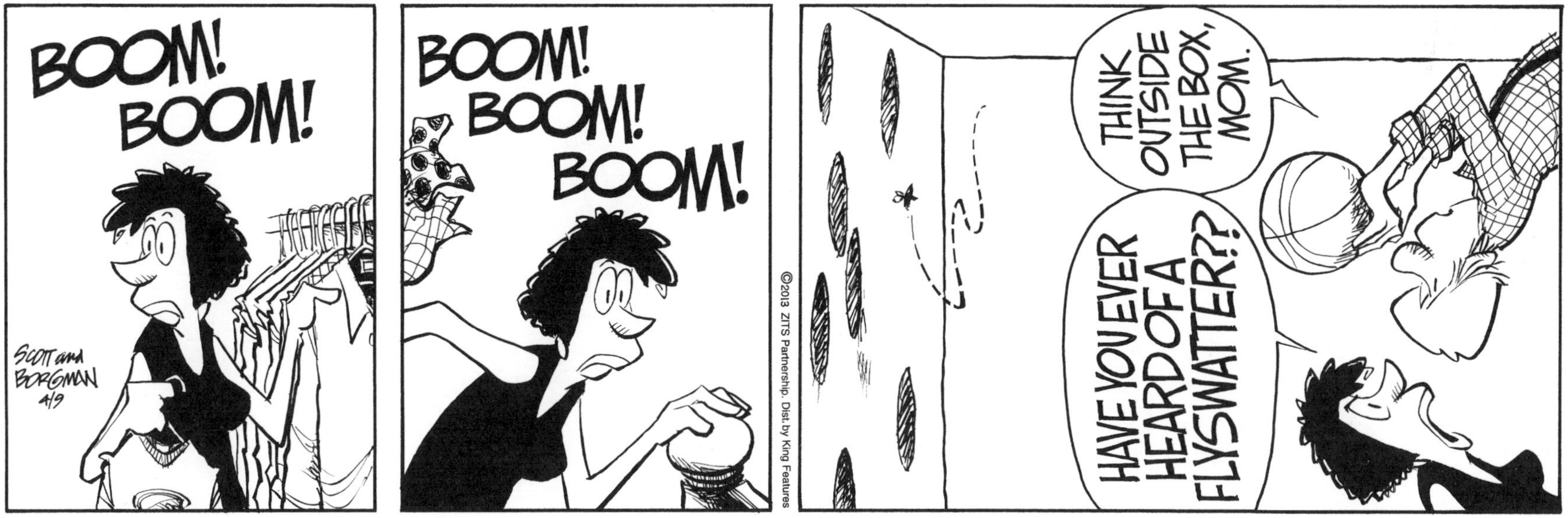
BOOM! BOOM!
SCOTT and BORGMAN 4/9
BOOM! BOOM! BOOM!
©2013 ZITS Partnership. Dist. by King Features
HAVE YOU EVER HEARD OF A FLYSWATTER??
THINK OUTSIDE THE BOX, MOM.

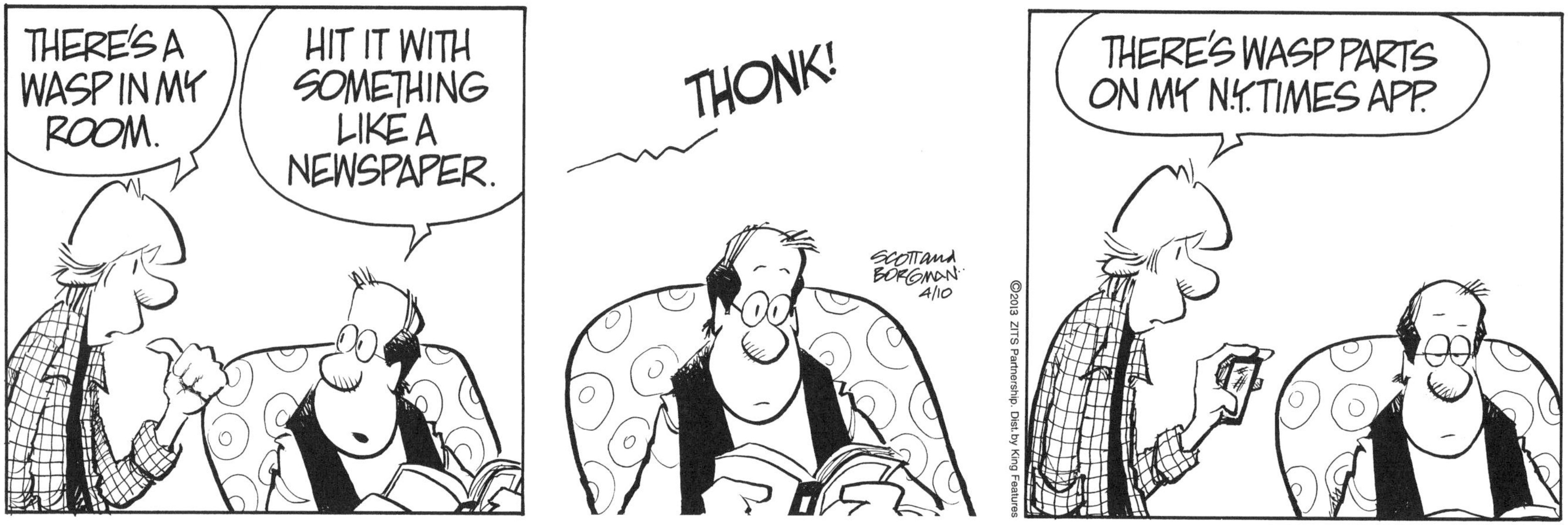
THERE'S A WASP IN MY ROOM.
HIT IT WITH SOMETHING LIKE A NEWSPAPER.
THONK!
SCOTT and BORGMAN 4/10
©2013 ZITS Partnership. Dist. by King Features
THERE'S WASP PARTS ON MY N.Y. TIMES APP.

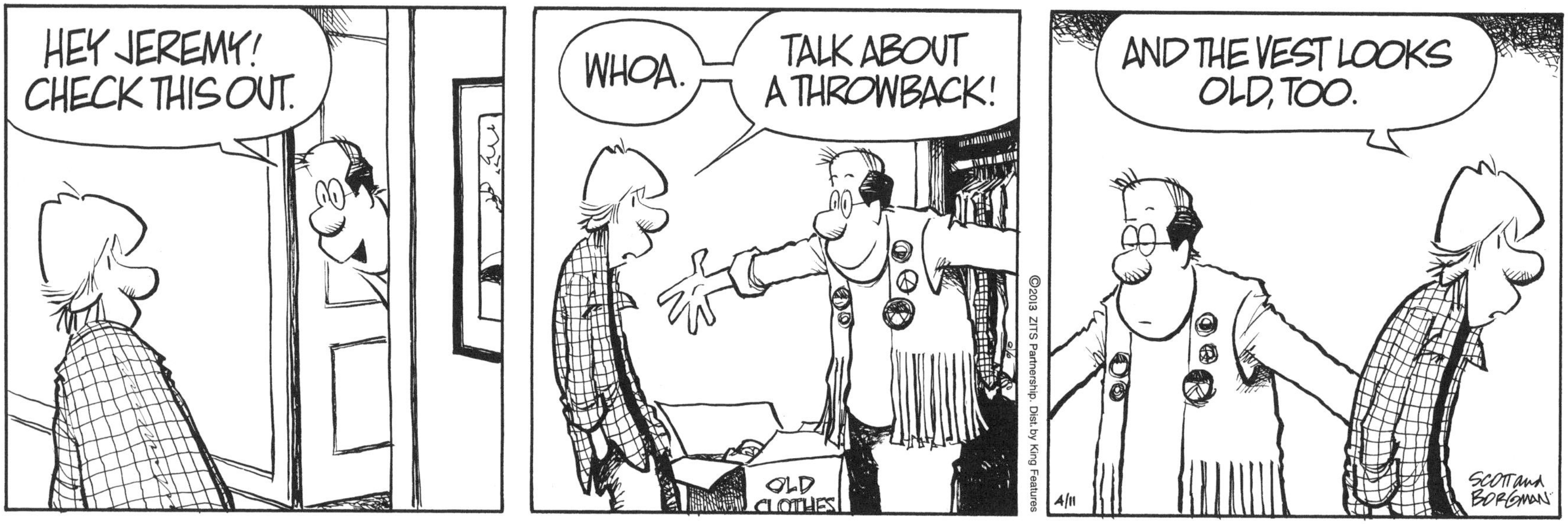
HEY JEREMY! CHECK THIS OUT.
WHOA.
TALK ABOUT A THROWBACK!
OLD CLOTHES
©2013 ZITS Partnership. Dist. by King Features
4/11
AND THE VEST LOOKS OLD, TOO.
SCOTT and BORGMAN

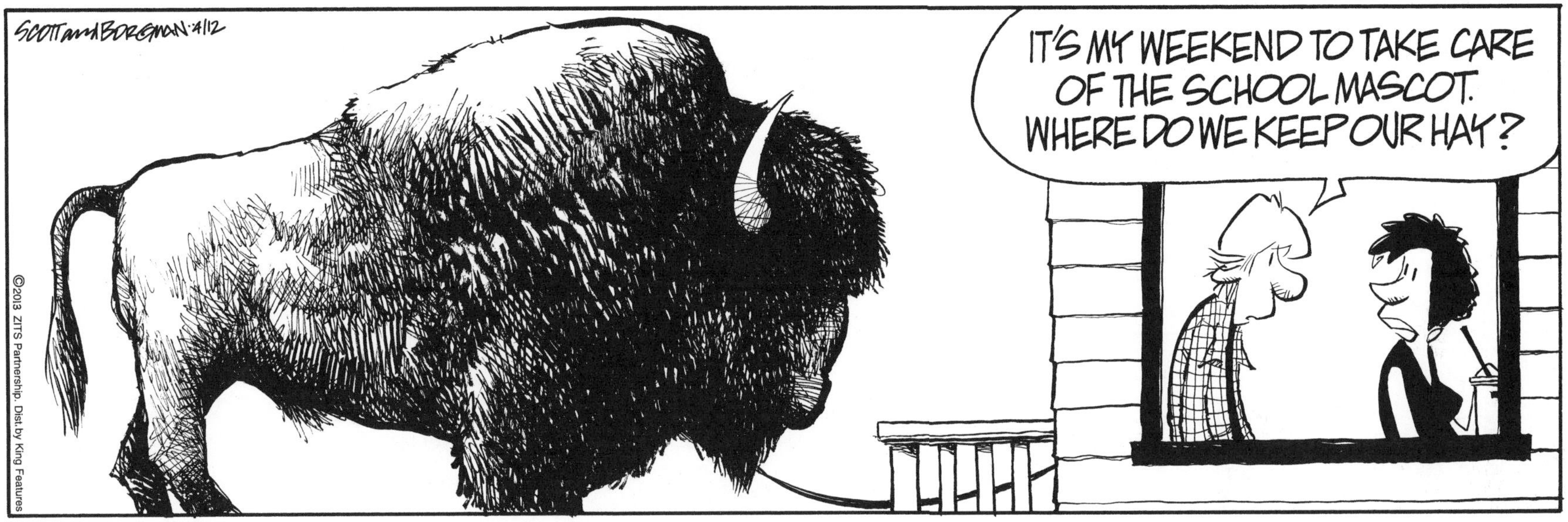
SCOTT and BORGMAN 4/12
IT'S MY WEEKEND TO TAKE CARE OF THE SCHOOL MASCOT. WHERE DO WE KEEP OUR HAY?
©2013 ZITS Partnership. Dist. by King Features

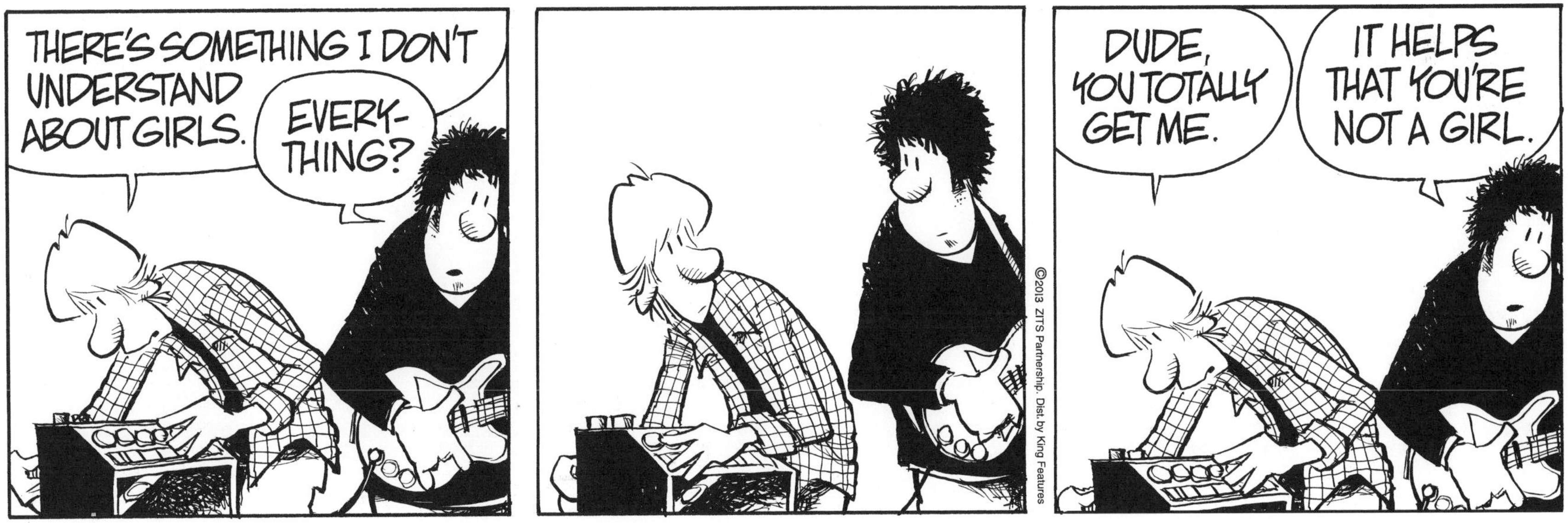
THERE'S SOMETHING I DON'T UNDERSTAND ABOUT GIRLS.
EVERY-THING?
©2013 ZITS Partnership. Dist. by King Features
DUDE, YOU TOTALLY GET ME.
IT HELPS THAT YOU'RE NOT A GIRL.

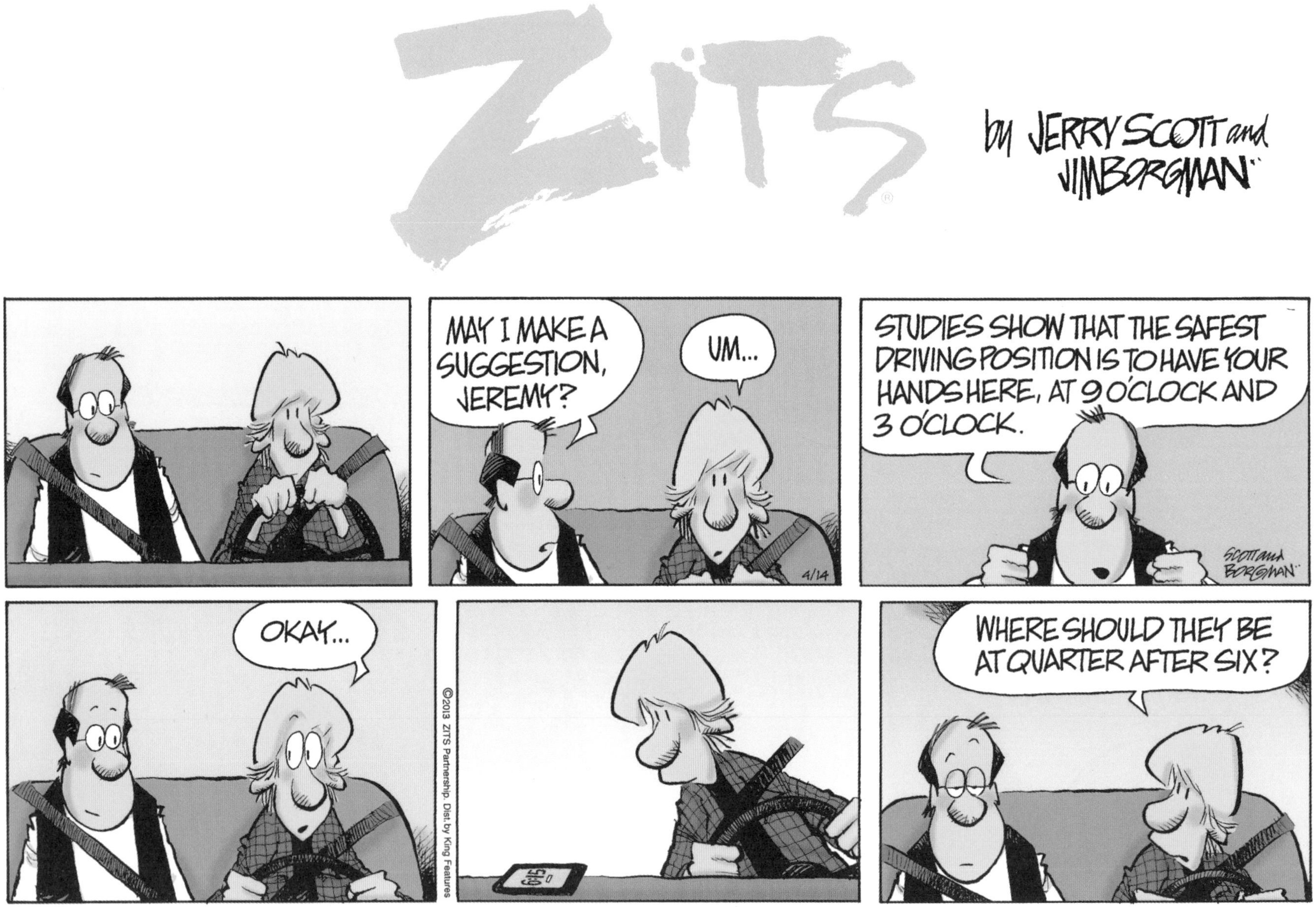
ZITS
by JERRY SCOTT and JIM BORGMAN
MAY I MAKE A SUGGESTION, JEREMY?
UM...
4/14
STUDIES SHOW THAT THE SAFEST DRIVING POSITION IS TO HAVE YOUR HANDS HERE, AT 9 O'CLOCK AND 3 O'CLOCK.
SCOTT and BORGMAN
OKAY...
©2013 ZITS Partnership. Dist. by King Features
6:15
WHERE SHOULD THEY BE AT QUARTER AFTER SIX?

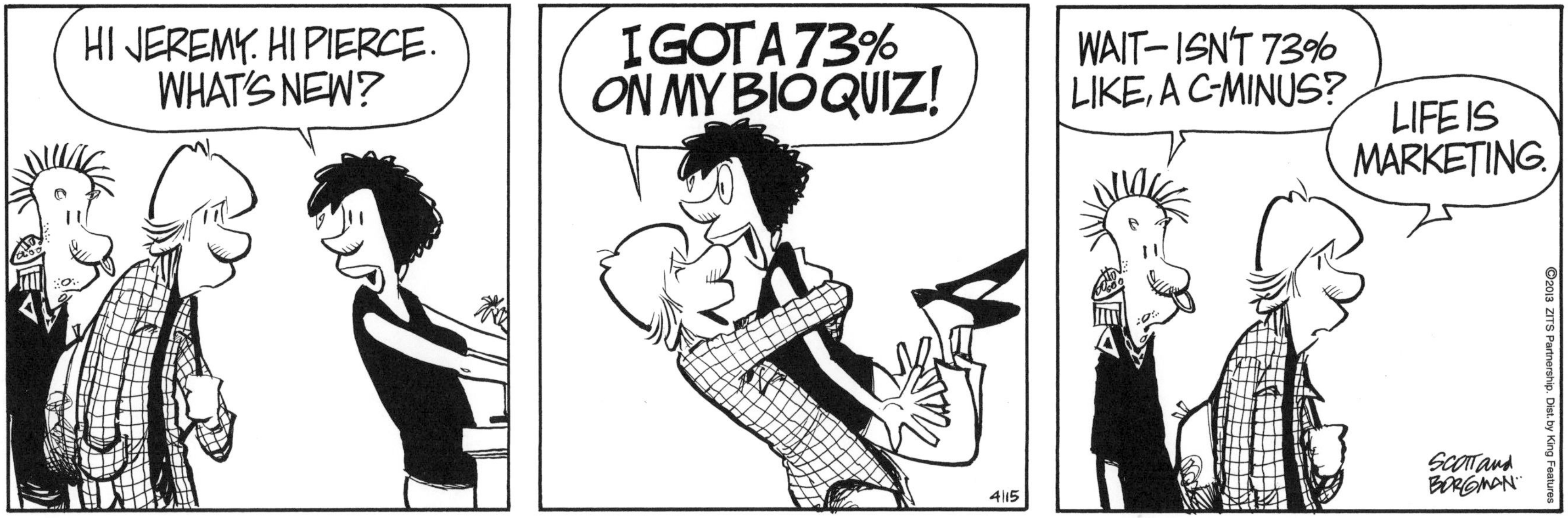
HI JEREMY. HI PIERCE. WHAT'S NEW?
I GOT A 73% ON MY BIO QUIZ!
4/15
WAIT– ISN'T 73% LIKE, A C-MINUS?
LIFE IS MARKETING.
SCOTT and BORGMAN
©2013 ZITS Partnership. Dist. by King Features

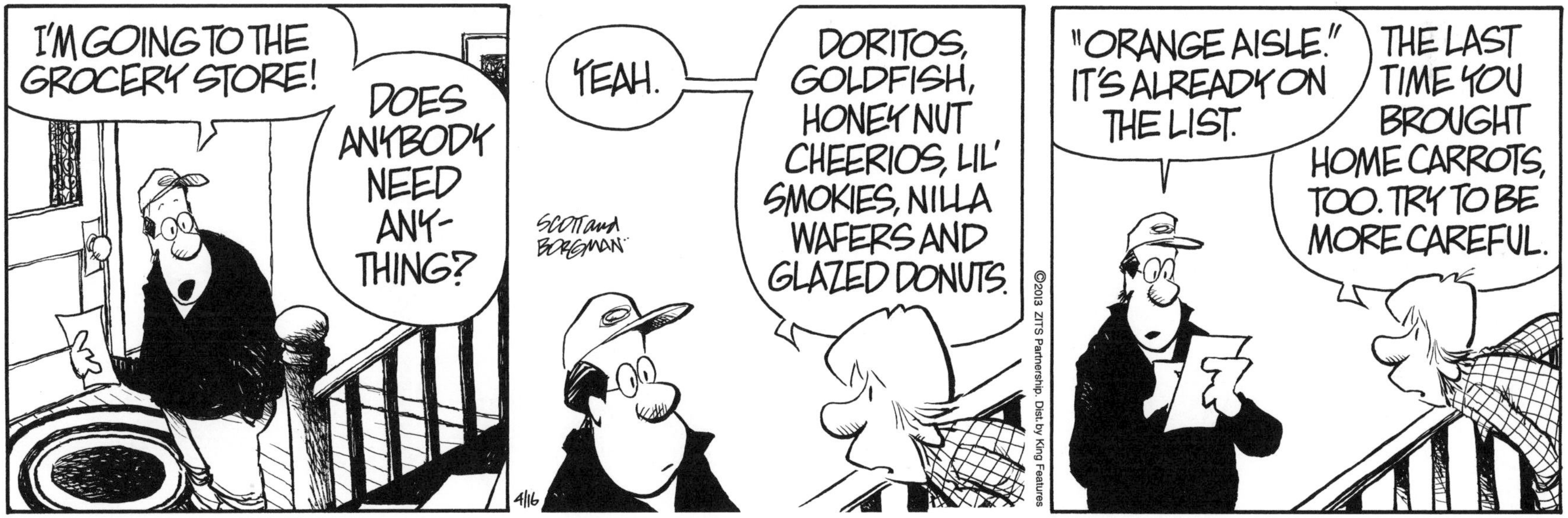
I'M GOING TO THE GROCERY STORE!
DOES ANYBODY NEED ANY-THING?
SCOTT and BORGMAN
4/16
YEAH.
DORITOS, GOLDFISH, HONEY NUT CHEERIOS, LIL' SMOKIES, NILLA WAFERS AND GLAZED DONUTS.
©2013 ZITS Partnership. Dist. by King Features
"ORANGE AISLE." IT'S ALREADY ON THE LIST.
THE LAST TIME YOU BROUGHT HOME CARROTS, TOO. TRY TO BE MORE CAREFUL.

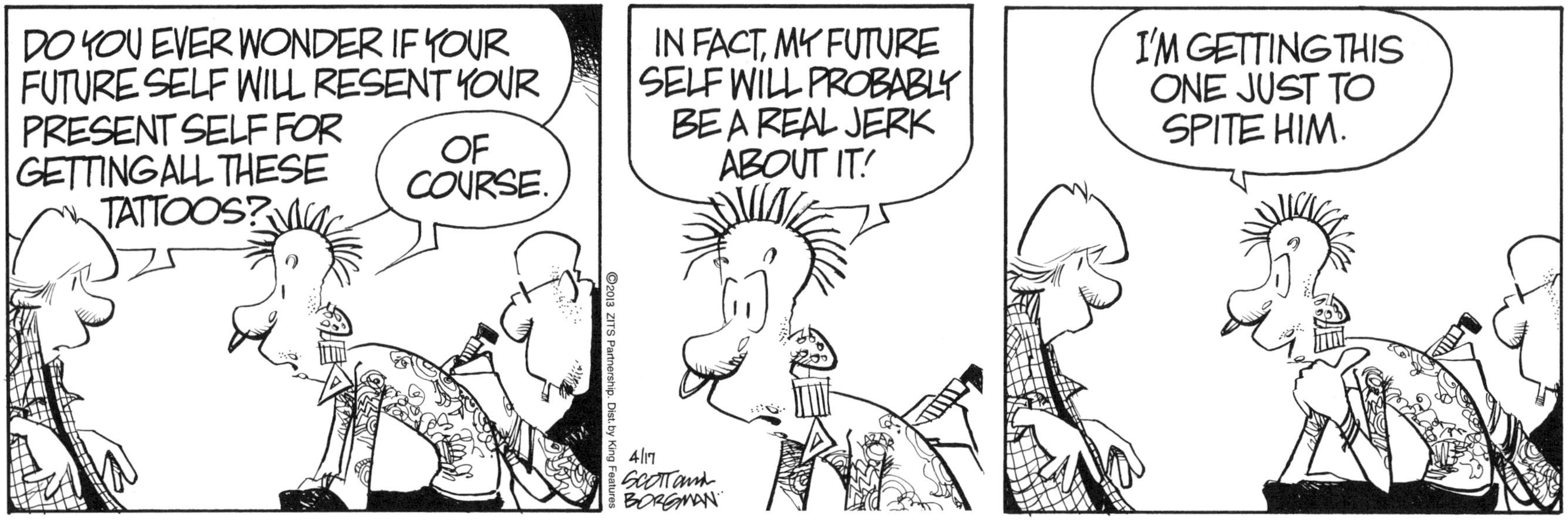
DO YOU EVER WONDER IF YOUR FUTURE SELF WILL RESENT YOUR PRESENT SELF FOR GETTING ALL THESE TATTOOS?
OF COURSE.
IN FACT, MY FUTURE SELF WILL PROBABLY BE A REAL JERK ABOUT IT!
I'M GETTING THIS ONE JUST TO SPITE HIM.
©2013 ZITS Partnership. Dist. by King Features
4/17
SCOTT and BORGMAN

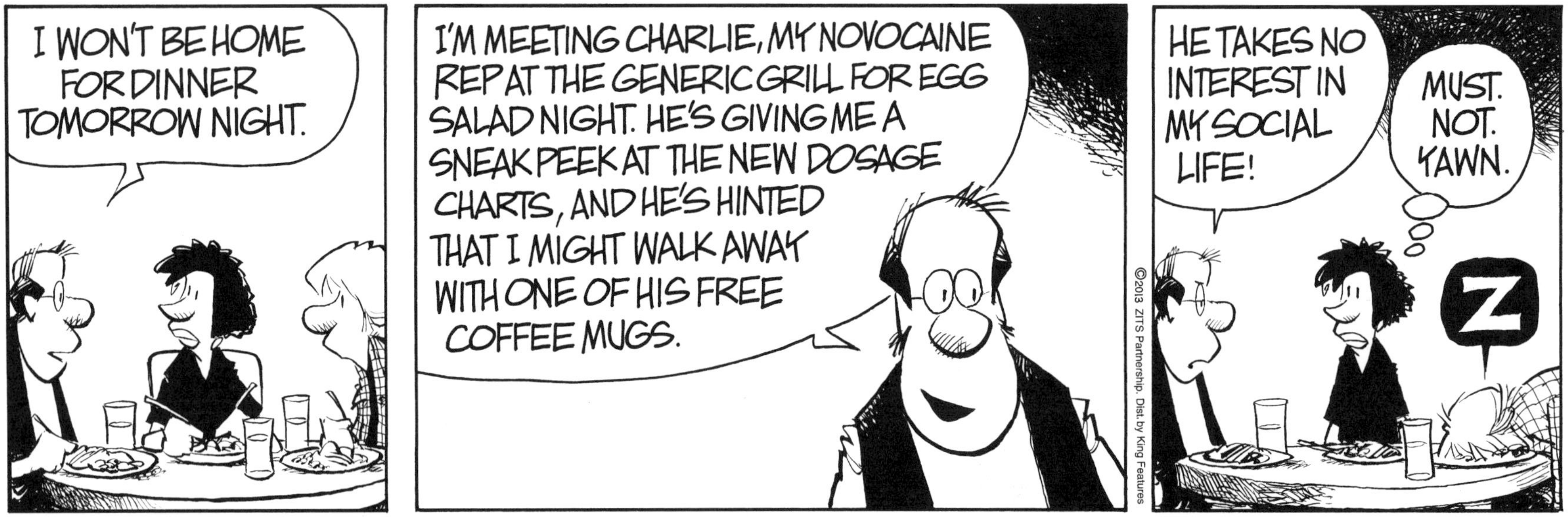
I WON'T BE HOME FOR DINNER TOMORROW NIGHT.
I'M MEETING CHARLIE, MY NOVOCAINE REP AT THE GENERIC GRILL FOR EGG SALAD NIGHT. HE'S GIVING ME A SNEAK PEEK AT THE NEW DOSAGE CHARTS, AND HE'S HINTED THAT I MIGHT WALK AWAY WITH ONE OF HIS FREE COFFEE MUGS.
HE TAKES NO INTEREST IN MY SOCIAL LIFE!
MUST. NOT. YAWN.
Z
©2013 ZITS Partnership. Dist. by King Features

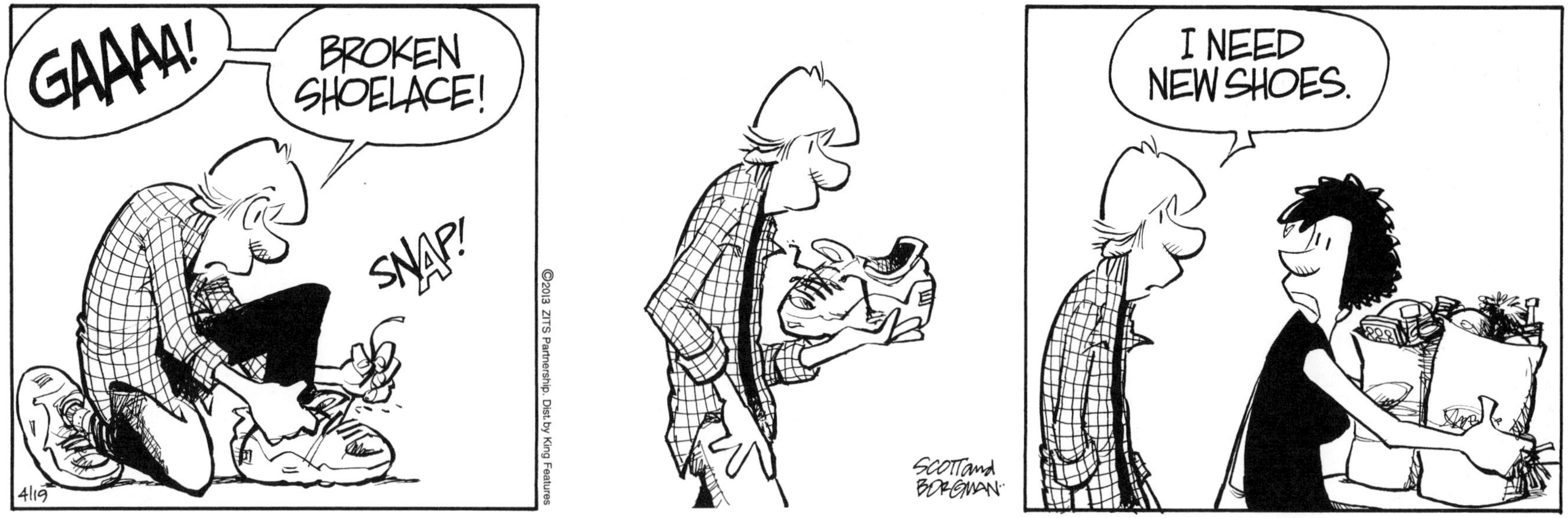
GAAAA!
BROKEN SHOELACE!
SNAP!
4/19
©2013 ZITS Partnership. Dist. by King Features
SCOTT and BORGMAN
I NEED NEW SHOES.

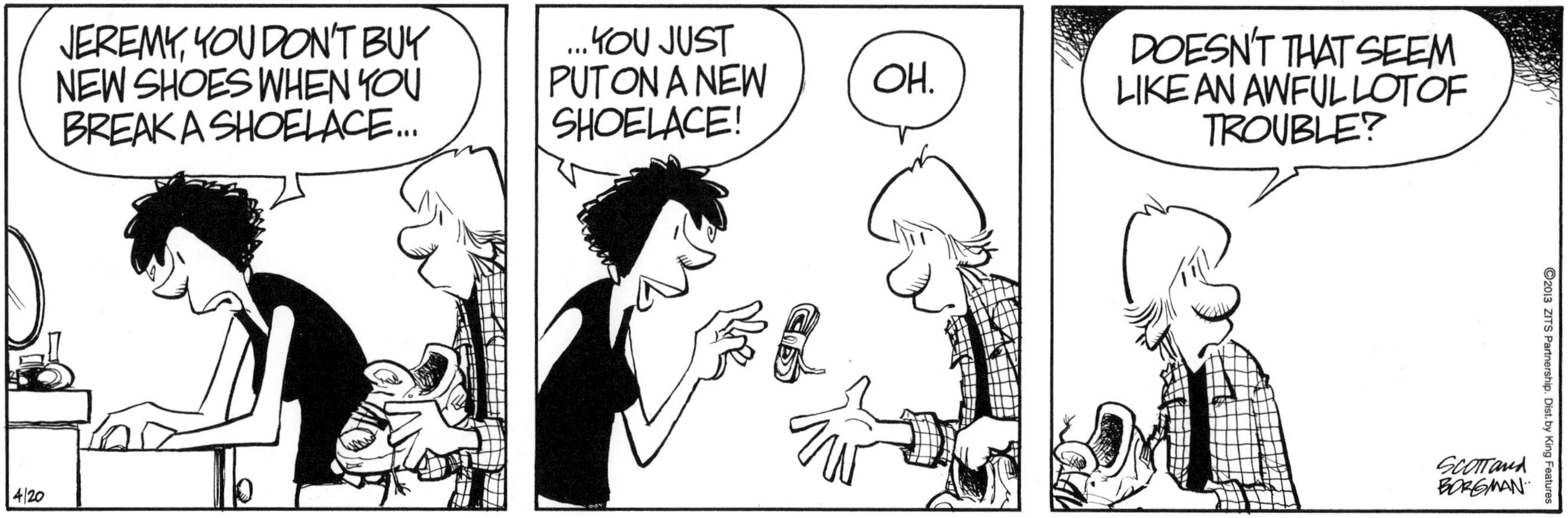
JEREMY, YOU DON'T BUY NEW SHOES WHEN YOU BREAK A SHOELACE...
4/20
...YOU JUST PUT ON A NEW SHOELACE!
OH.
DOESN'T THAT SEEM LIKE AN AWFUL LOT OF TROUBLE?
©2013 ZITS Partnership. Dist. by King Features
SCOTT and BORGMAN

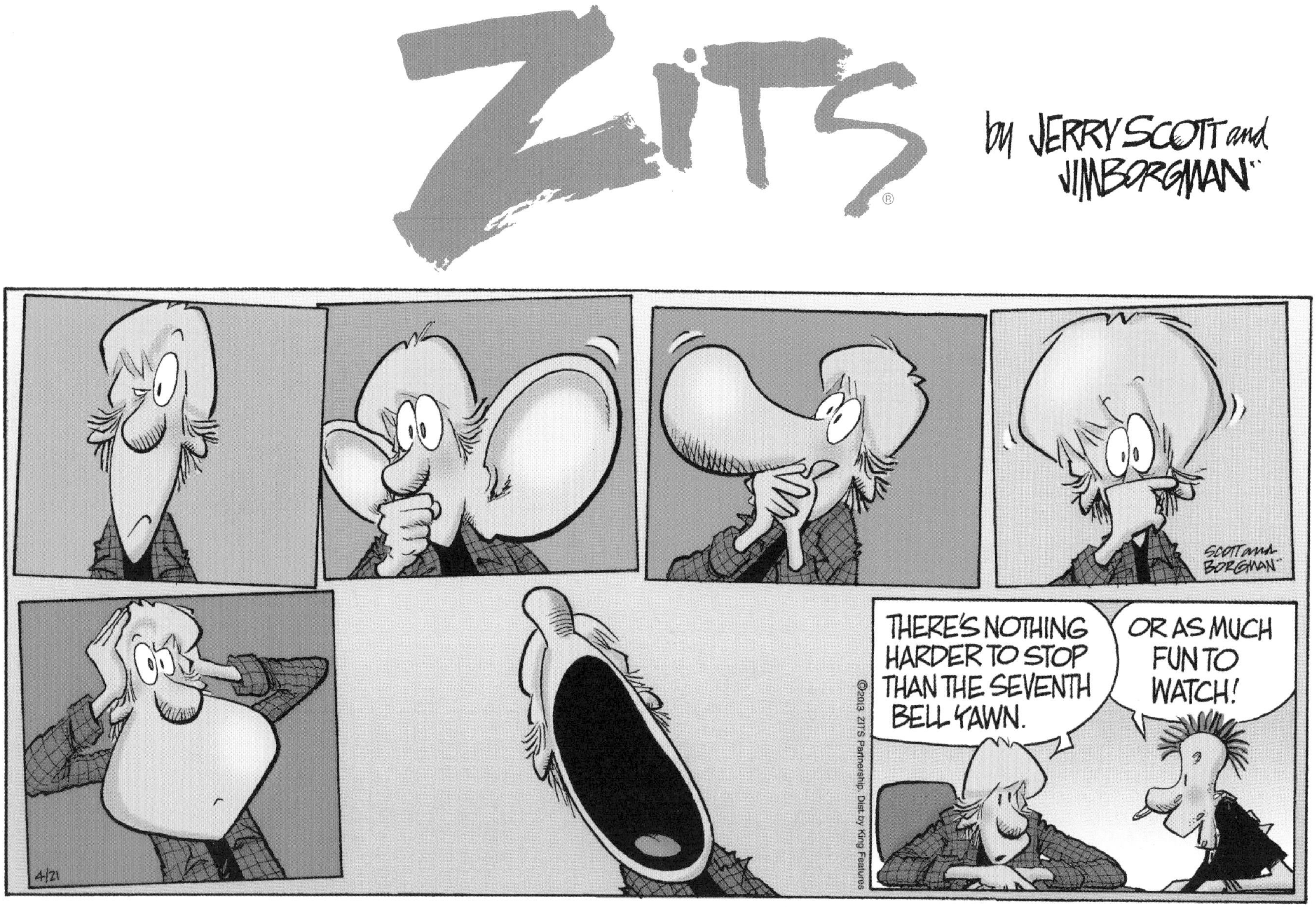
ZITS®
by JERRY SCOTT and JIM BORGMAN
SCOTT and BORGMAN
4/21
©2013 ZITS Partnership. Dist. by King Features
THERE'S NOTHING HARDER TO STOP THAN THE SEVENTH BELL YAWN.
OR AS MUCH FUN TO WATCH!

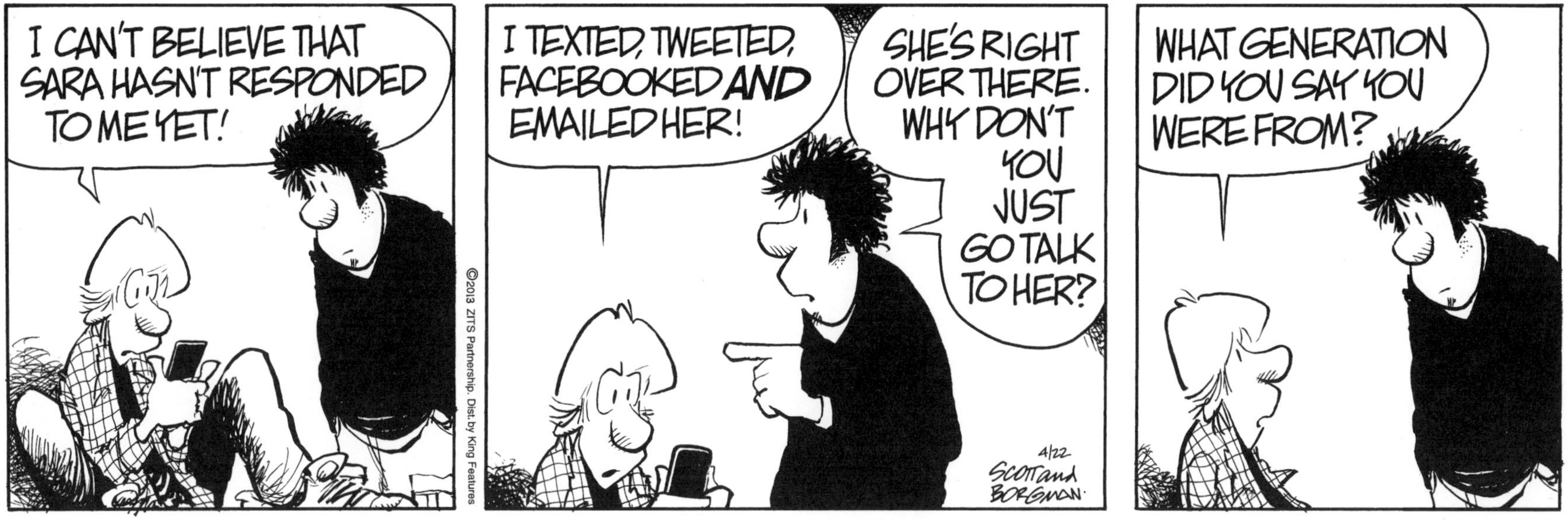
I CAN'T BELIEVE THAT SARA HASN'T RESPONDED TO ME YET!
©2013 ZITS Partnership. Dist. by King Features
I TEXTED, TWEETED, FACEBOOKED **AND** EMAILED HER!
SHE'S RIGHT OVER THERE. WHY DON'T YOU JUST GO TALK TO HER?
4/22
SCOTT and BORGMAN
WHAT GENERATION DID YOU SAY YOU WERE FROM?

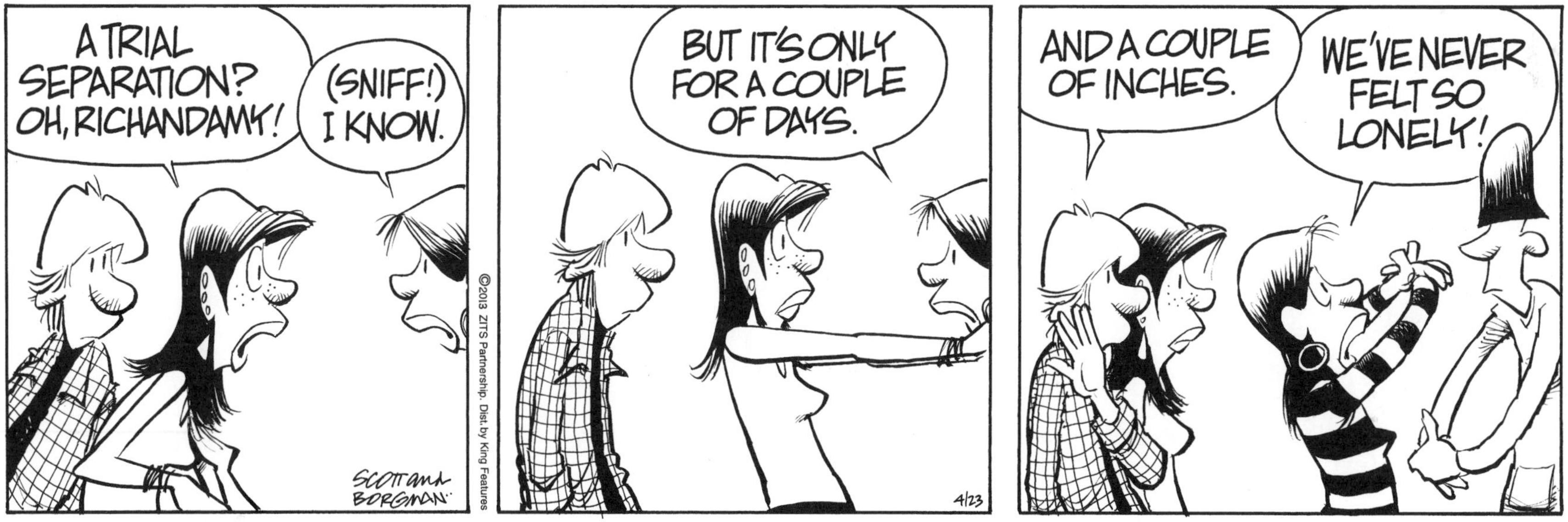
A TRIAL SEPARATION? OH, RICHANDAMY!
(SNIFF!) I KNOW.
SCOTT and BORGMAN
©2013 ZITS Partnership. Dist. by King Features
BUT IT'S ONLY FOR A COUPLE OF DAYS.
4/23
AND A COUPLE OF INCHES.
WE'VE NEVER FELT SO LONELY!

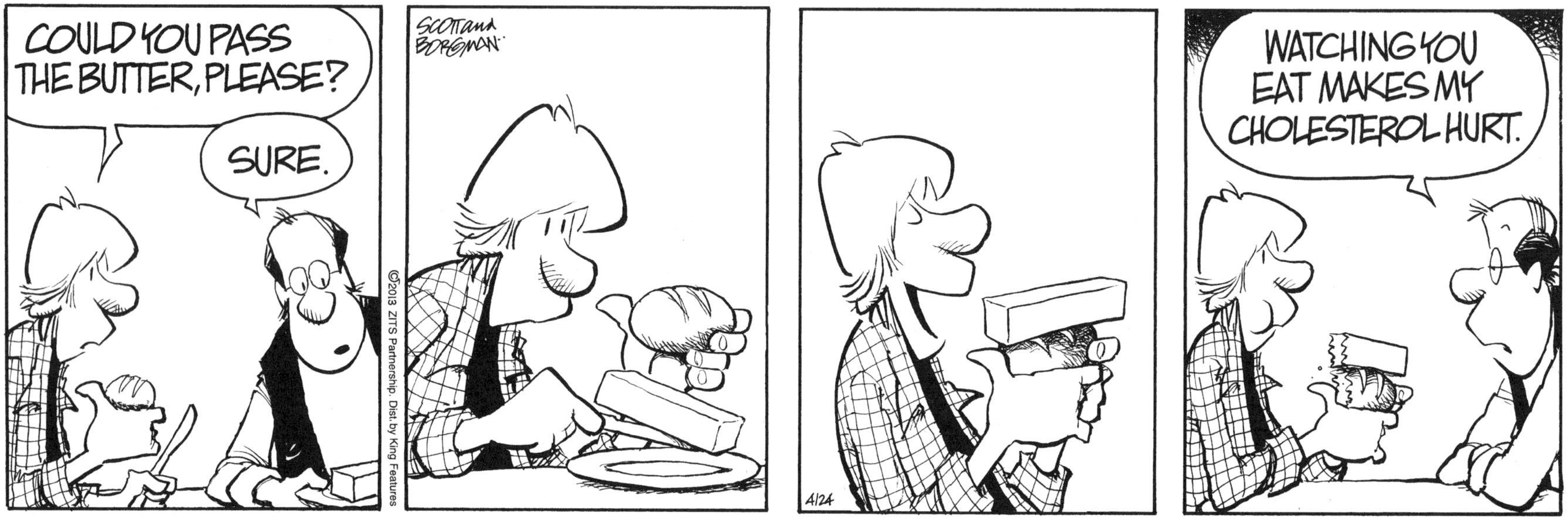
COULD YOU PASS THE BUTTER, PLEASE?
SURE.
SCOTT and BORGMAN
©2013 ZITS Partnership. Dist. by King Features
WATCHING YOU EAT MAKES MY CHOLESTEROL HURT.
4/24

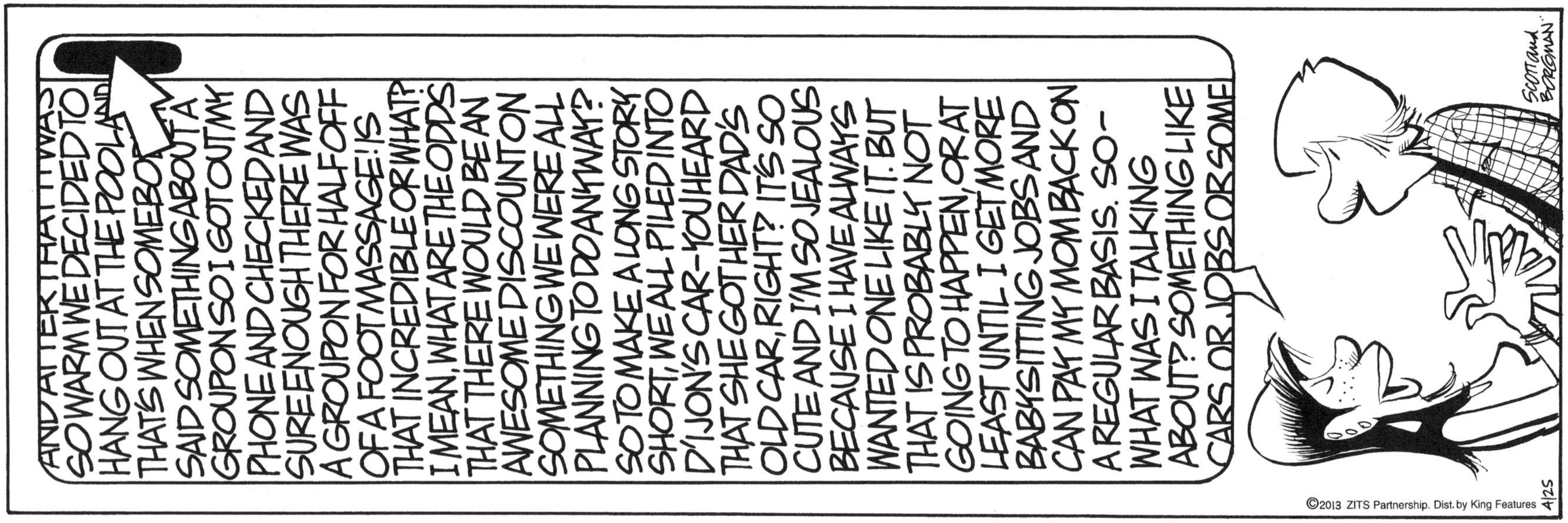
AND AFTER THAT IT WAS
SO WARM WE DECIDED TO
HANG OUT AT THE POOL
THAT'S WHEN SOMEBO
SAID SOMETHING ABOUT A
GROUPON SO I GOT OUT MY
PHONE AND CHECKED AND
SURE ENOUGH THERE WAS
A GROUPON FOR HALF OFF
OF A FOOT MASSAGE! IS
THAT INCREDIBLE OR WHAT?
I MEAN, WHAT ARE THE ODDS
THAT THERE WOULD BE AN
AWESOME DISCOUNT ON
SOMETHING WE WERE ALL
PLANNING TO DO ANYWAY?
SO TO MAKE A LONG STORY
SHORT, WE ALL PILED INTO
D'JON'S CAR—YOU HEARD
THAT SHE GOT HER DAD'S
OLD CAR, RIGHT? IT'S SO
CUTE AND I'M SO JEALOUS
BECAUSE I HAVE ALWAYS
WANTED ONE LIKE IT. BUT
THAT IS PROBABLY NOT
GOING TO HAPPEN, OR AT
LEAST UNTIL I GET MORE
BABYSITTING JOBS AND
CAN PAY MY MOM BACK ON
A REGULAR BASIS. SO—
WHAT WAS I TALKING
ABOUT? SOMETHING LIKE
CARS, OR JOBS OR SOME
SCOTT and BORGMAN
©2013 ZITS Partnership. Dist. by King Features
4/25

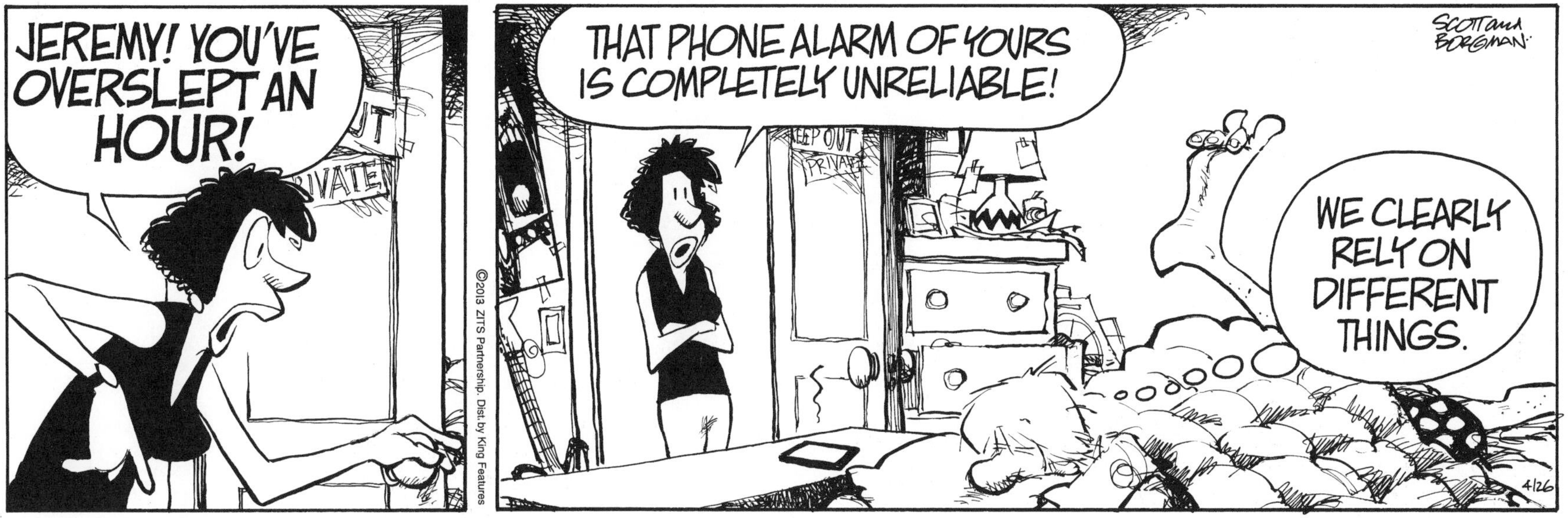
JEREMY! YOU'VE OVERSLEPT AN HOUR!
THAT PHONE ALARM OF YOURS IS COMPLETELY UNRELIABLE!
WE CLEARLY RELY ON DIFFERENT THINGS.
SCOTT and BORGMAN
©2013 ZITS Partnership. Dist. by King Features
4/26

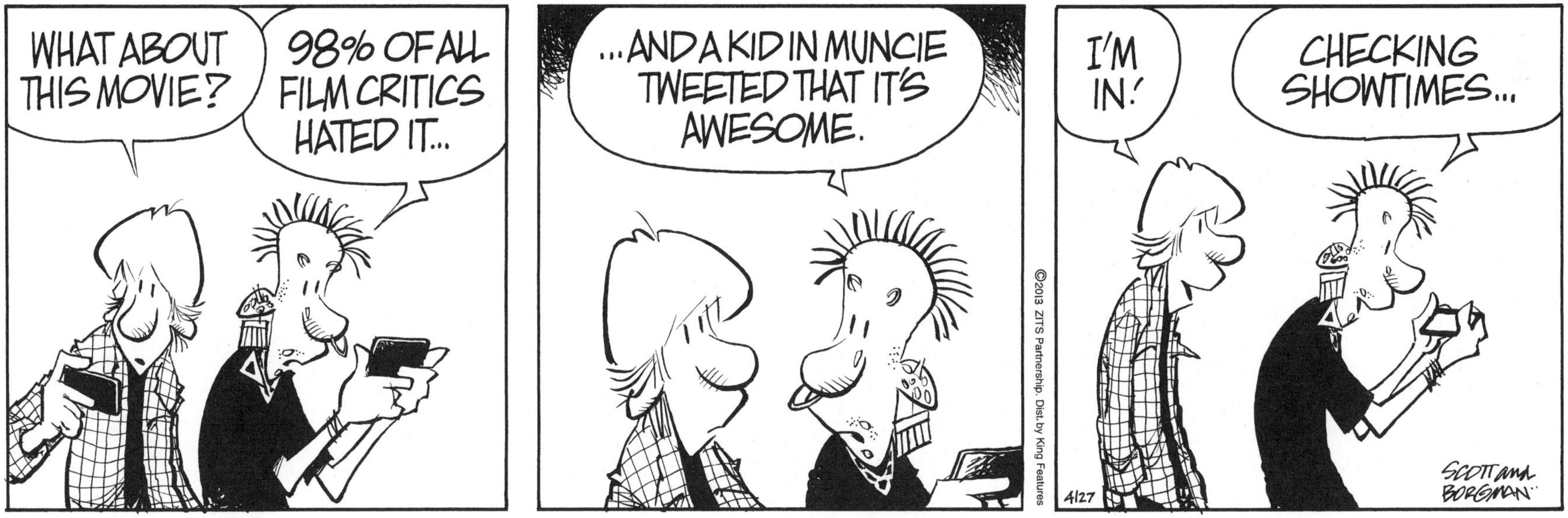
WHAT ABOUT THIS MOVIE?
98% OF ALL FILM CRITICS HATED IT...
...AND A KID IN MUNCIE TWEETED THAT IT'S AWESOME.
I'M IN!
CHECKING SHOWTIMES...
©2013 ZITS Partnership. Dist. by King Features
4/27
SCOTT and BORGMAN

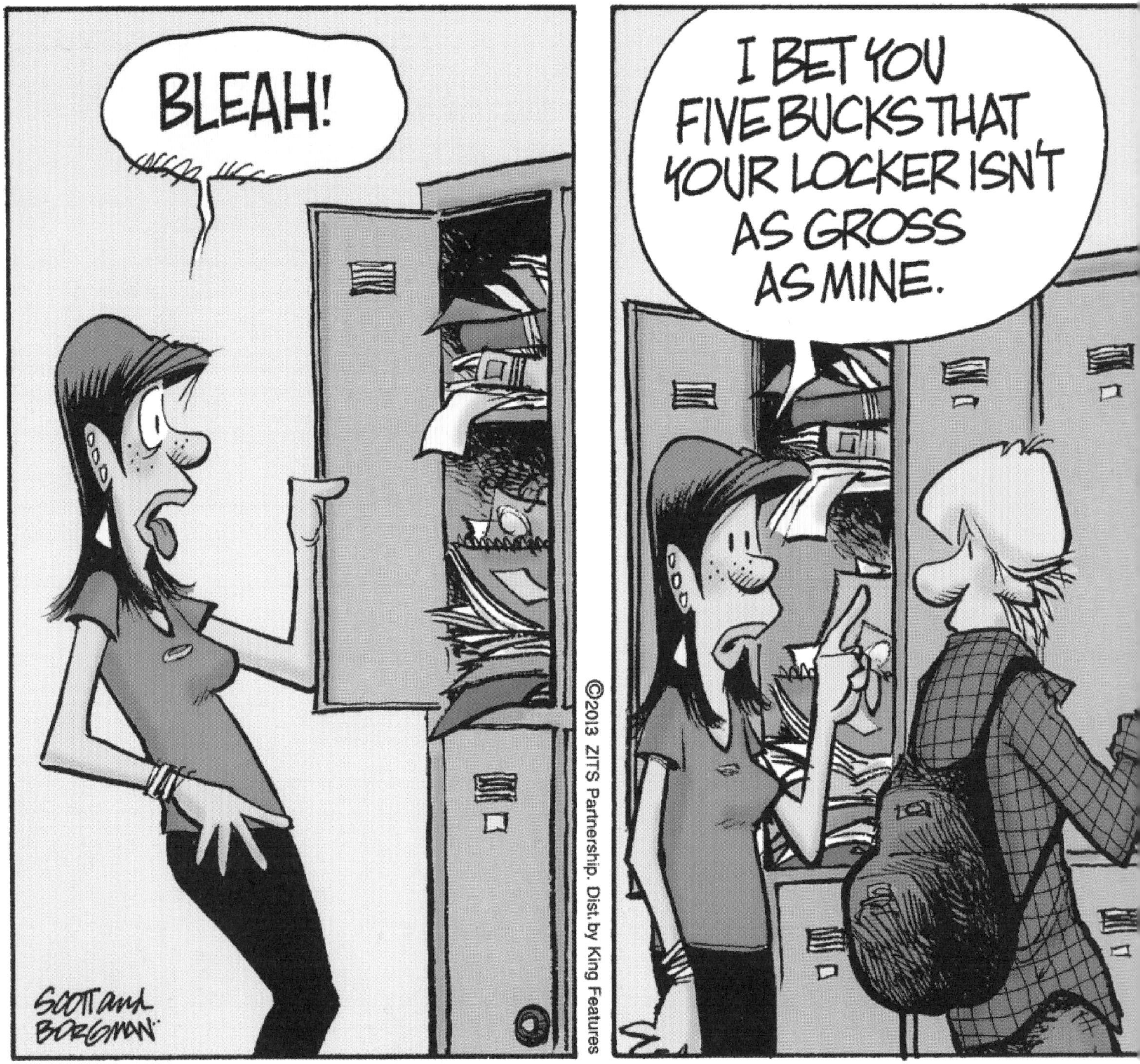
BLEAH!
I BET YOU FIVE BUCKS THAT YOUR LOCKER ISN'T AS GROSS AS MINE.
SCOTT and BORGMAN
©2013 ZITS Partnership. Dist.by King Features

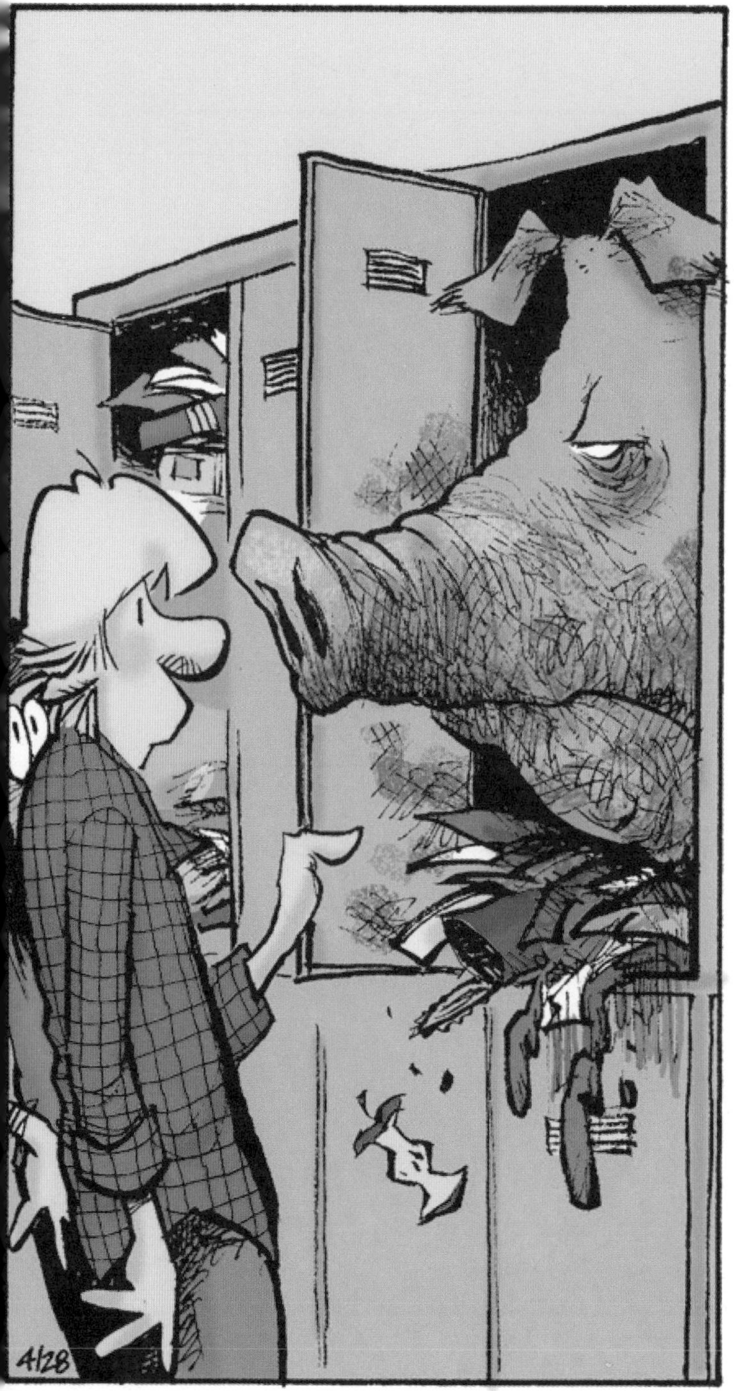

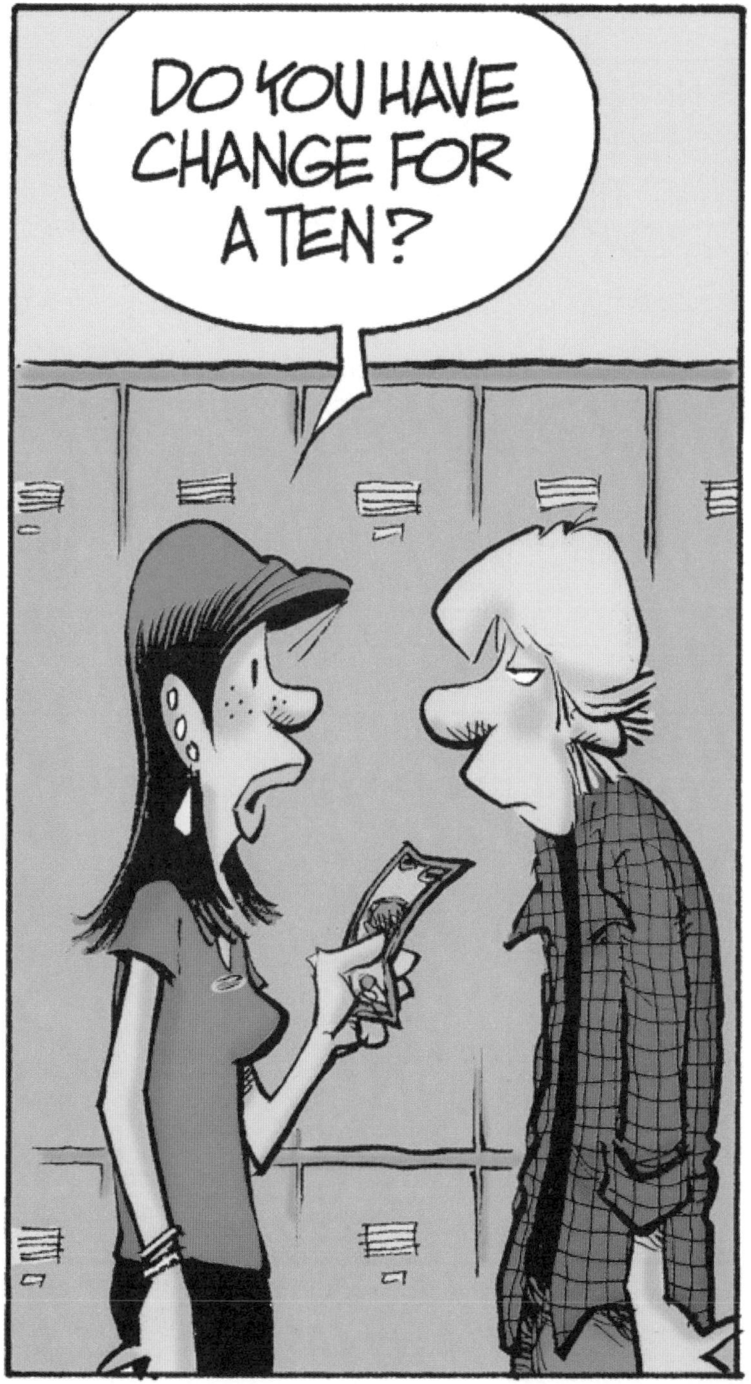
DO YOU HAVE CHANGE FOR A TEN?

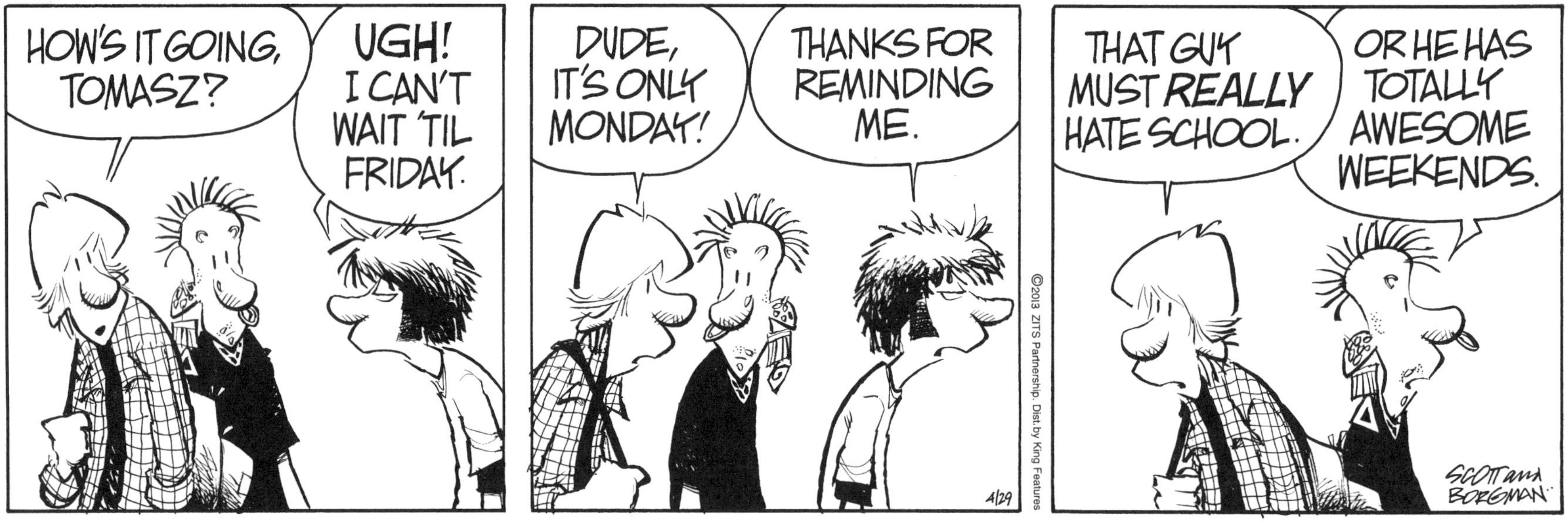
HOW'S IT GOING, TOMASZ?
UGH! I CAN'T WAIT 'TIL FRIDAY.
DUDE, IT'S ONLY MONDAY!
THANKS FOR REMINDING ME.
4/29
©2013 ZITS Partnership. Dist. by King Features
THAT GUY MUST **REALLY** HATE SCHOOL.
OR HE HAS TOTALLY AWESOME WEEKENDS.
SCOTT and BORGMAN

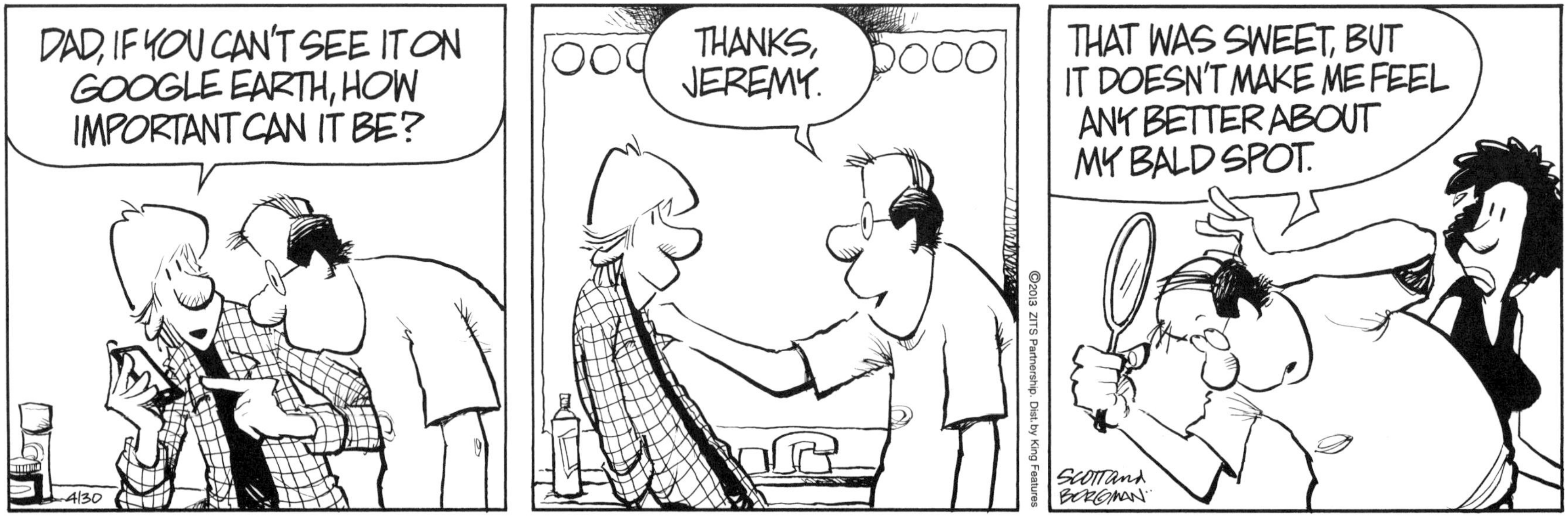
DAD, IF YOU CAN'T SEE IT ON GOOGLE EARTH, HOW IMPORTANT CAN IT BE?
4/30
THANKS, JEREMY.
©2013 ZITS Partnership. Dist. by King Features
THAT WAS SWEET, BUT IT DOESN'T MAKE ME FEEL ANY BETTER ABOUT MY BALD SPOT.
SCOTT and BORGMAN

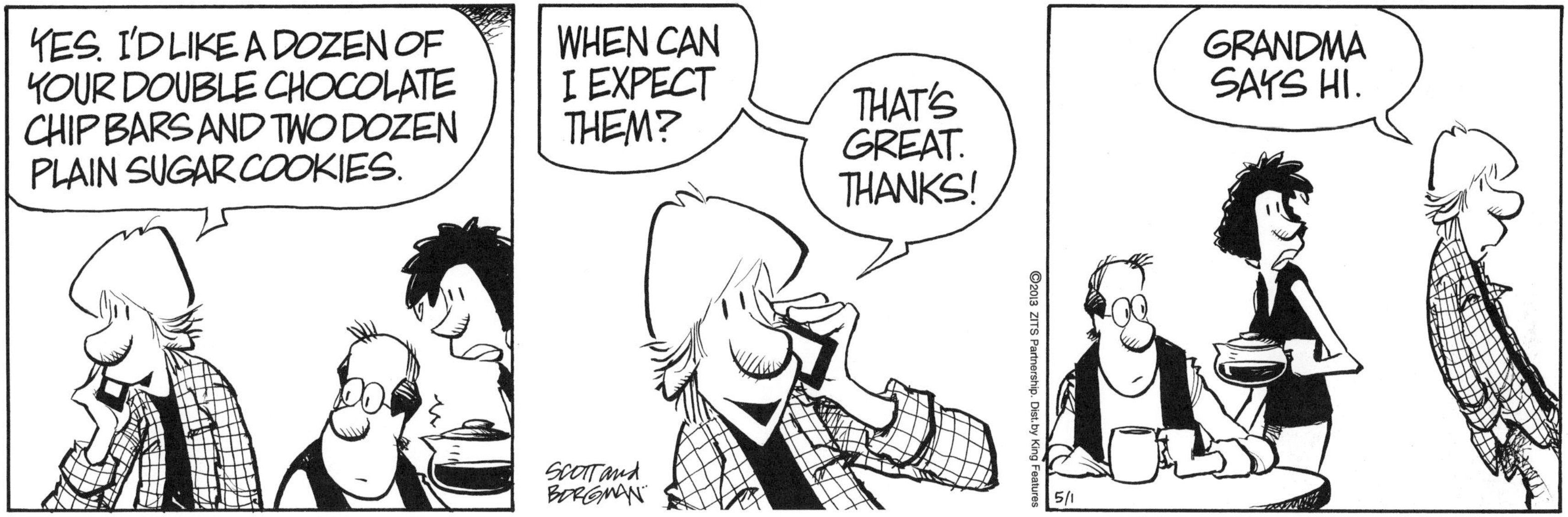
YES. I'D LIKE A DOZEN OF YOUR DOUBLE CHOCOLATE CHIP BARS AND TWO DOZEN PLAIN SUGAR COOKIES.
WHEN CAN I EXPECT THEM?
THAT'S GREAT. THANKS!
SCOTT and BORGMAN
©2013 ZITS Partnership. Dist.by King Features
GRANDMA SAYS HI.
5/1

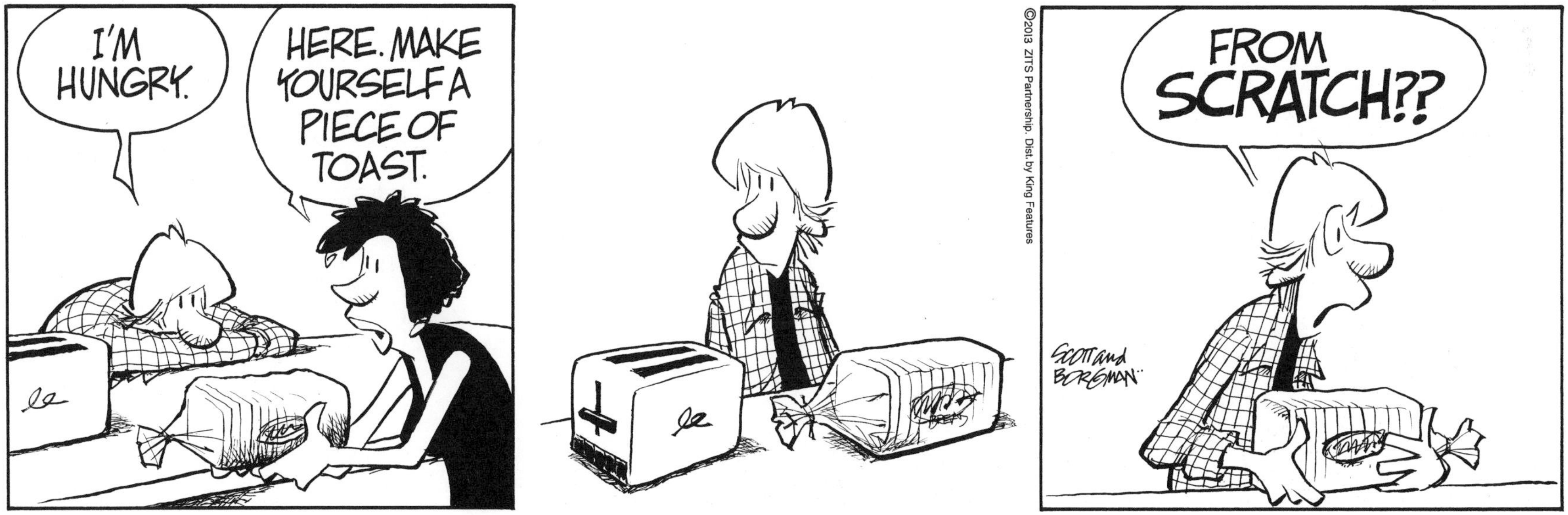
I'M HUNGRY.
HERE. MAKE YOURSELF A PIECE OF TOAST.
©2013 ZITS Partnership. Dist.by King Features
FROM SCRATCH??
SCOTT and BORGMAN

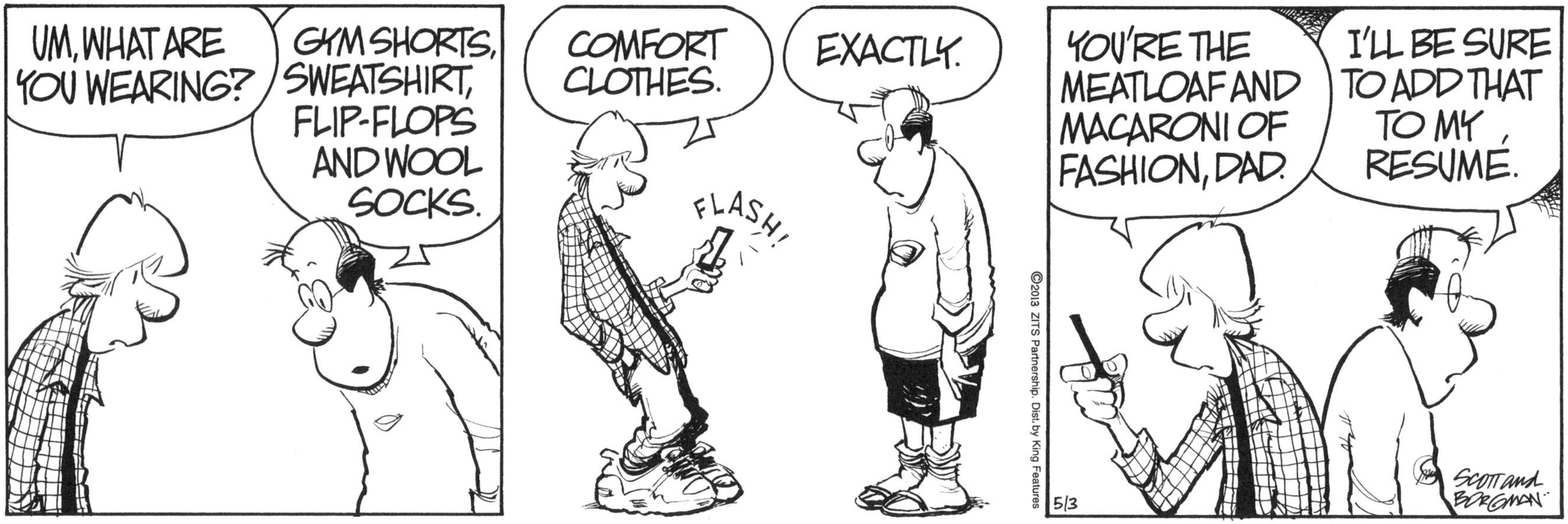
UM, WHAT ARE YOU WEARING?
GYM SHORTS, SWEATSHIRT, FLIP-FLOPS AND WOOL SOCKS.
COMFORT CLOTHES.
FLASH!
EXACTLY.
©2013 ZITS Partnership. Dist. by King Features
5/3
YOU'RE THE MEATLOAF AND MACARONI OF FASHION, DAD.
I'LL BE SURE TO ADD THAT TO MY RESUMÉ.
SCOTT and BORGMAN

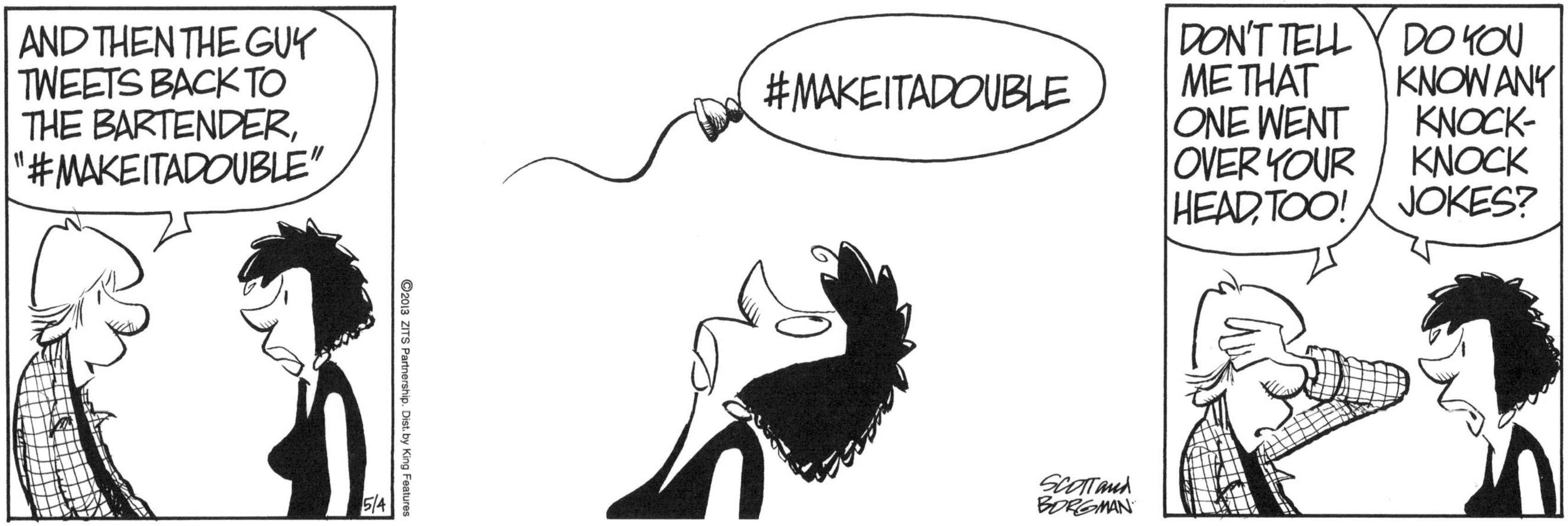
AND THEN THE GUY TWEETS BACK TO THE BARTENDER, "#MAKEITADOUBLE"
©2013 ZITS Partnership. Dist. by King Features
5/4
#MAKEITADOUBLE
SCOTT and BORGMAN
DON'T TELL ME THAT ONE WENT OVER YOUR HEAD, TOO!
DO YOU KNOW ANY KNOCK-KNOCK JOKES?

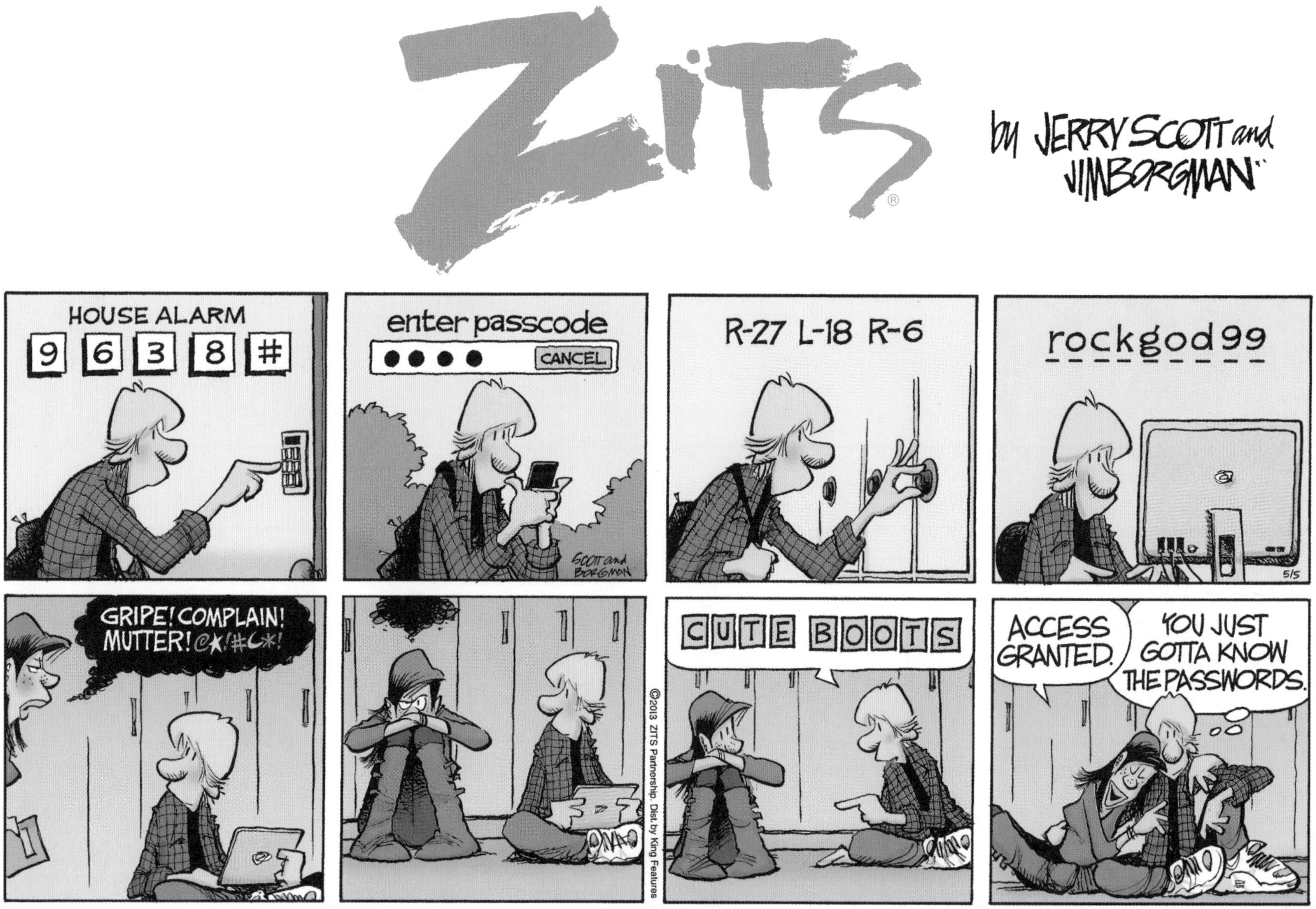
ZITS
by JERRY SCOTT and JIM BORGMAN
HOUSE ALARM
9 6 3 8 #
enter passcode
CANCEL
SCOTT and BORGMAN
R-27 L-18 R-6
rockgod99
5/5
GRIPE! COMPLAIN! MUTTER! @★!#C*!
©2013 ZITS Partnership. Dist. by King Features
CUTE BOOTS
ACCESS GRANTED.
YOU JUST GOTTA KNOW THE PASSWORDS.

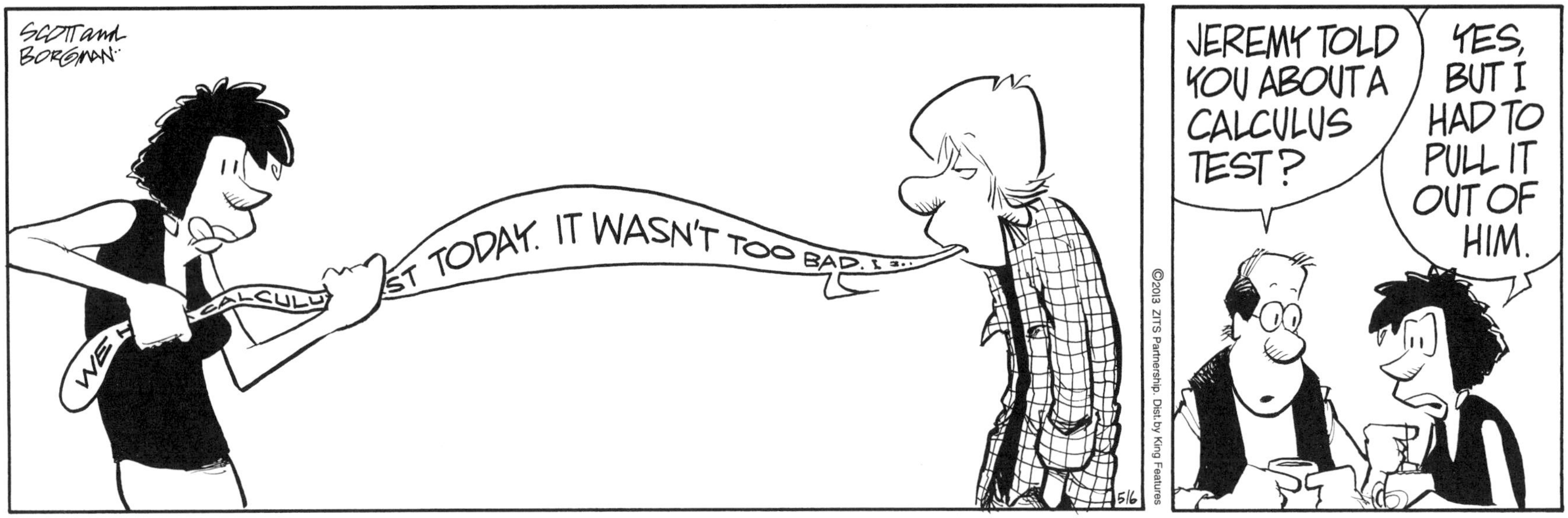
SCOTT and BORGMAN
WE H CALCULU ST TODAY. IT WASN'T TOO BAD.
5/6
©2013 ZITS Partnership. Dist. by King Features
JEREMY TOLD YOU ABOUT A CALCULUS TEST?
YES, BUT I HAD TO PULL IT OUT OF HIM.

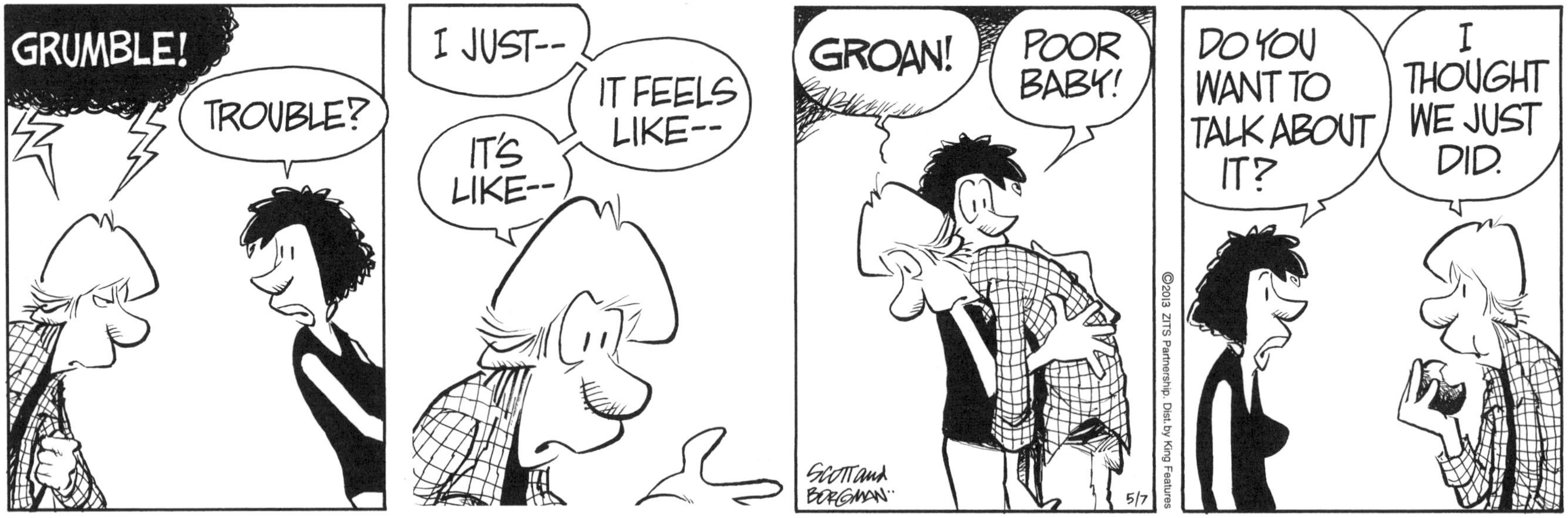
GRUMBLE!
TROUBLE?
I JUST--
IT FEELS LIKE--
IT'S LIKE--
GROAN!
POOR BABY!
SCOTT and BORGMAN
5/7
©2013 ZITS Partnership. Dist. by King Features
DO YOU WANT TO TALK ABOUT IT?
I THOUGHT WE JUST DID.

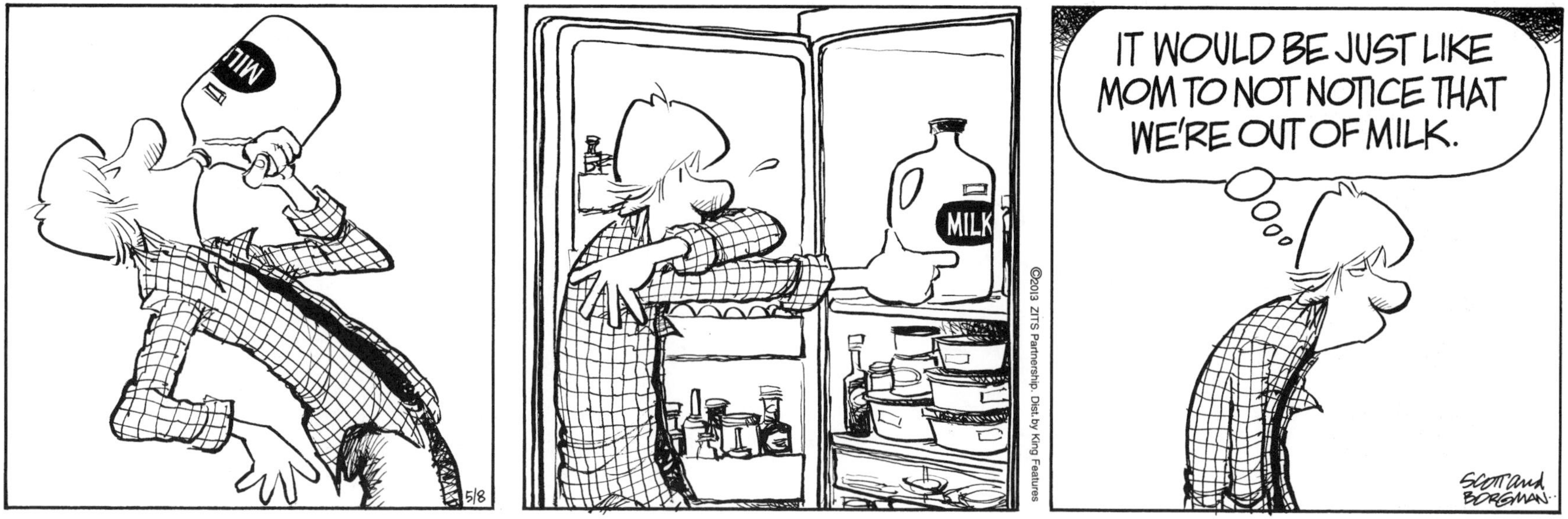
MILK
MILK
©2013 ZITS Partnership. Dist. by King Features
IT WOULD BE JUST LIKE MOM TO NOT NOTICE THAT WE'RE OUT OF MILK.
5/8
SCOTT and BORGMAN

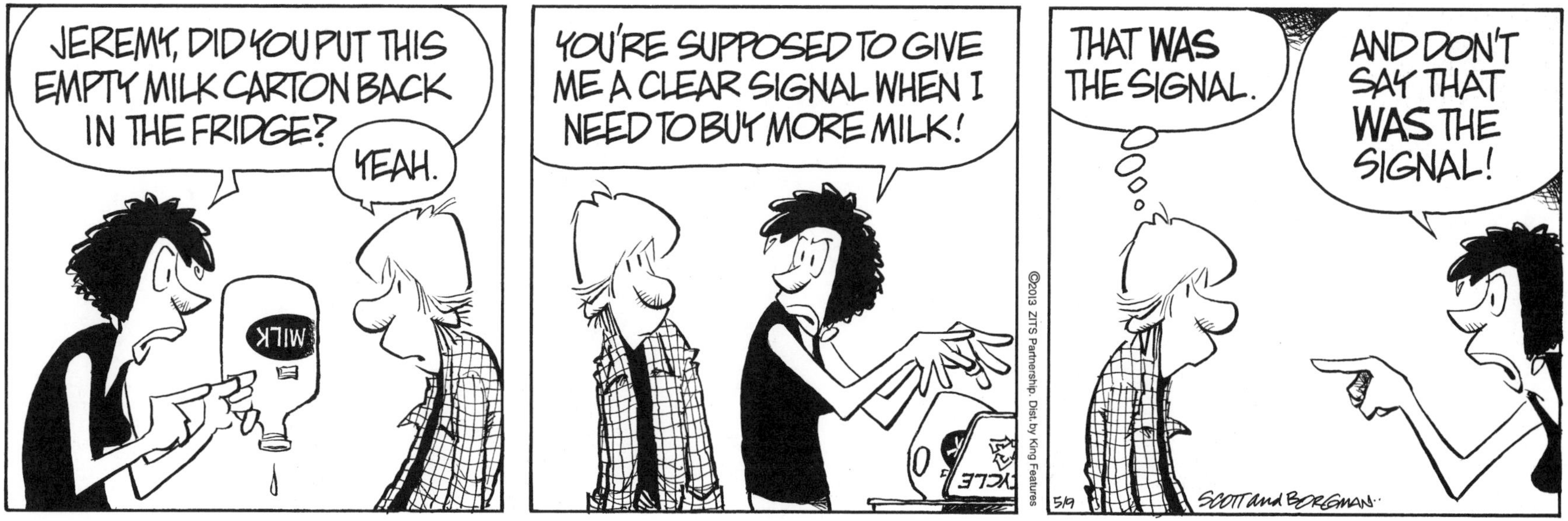
JEREMY, DID YOU PUT THIS EMPTY MILK CARTON BACK IN THE FRIDGE?
YEAH.
MILK
YOU'RE SUPPOSED TO GIVE ME A CLEAR SIGNAL WHEN I NEED TO BUY MORE MILK!
©2013 ZITS Partnership. Dist. by King Features
THAT **WAS** THE SIGNAL.
AND DON'T SAY THAT **WAS** THE SIGNAL!
5/9
SCOTT and BORGMAN

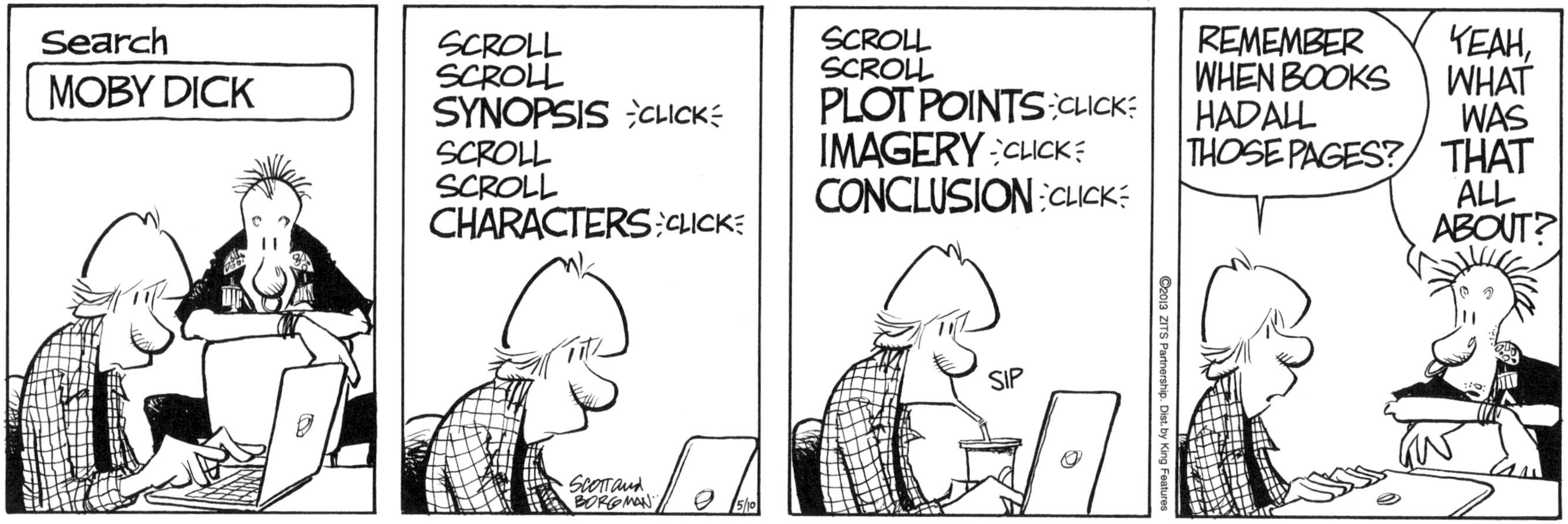
Search
MOBY DICK
SCROLL
SCROLL
SYNOPSIS CLICK
SCROLL
SCROLL
CHARACTERS CLICK
SCOTT and BORGMAN 5/10
SCROLL
SCROLL
PLOT POINTS CLICK
IMAGERY CLICK
CONCLUSION CLICK
SIP
©2013 ZITS Partnership. Dist. by King Features
REMEMBER WHEN BOOKS HAD ALL THOSE PAGES?
YEAH, WHAT WAS THAT ALL ABOUT?

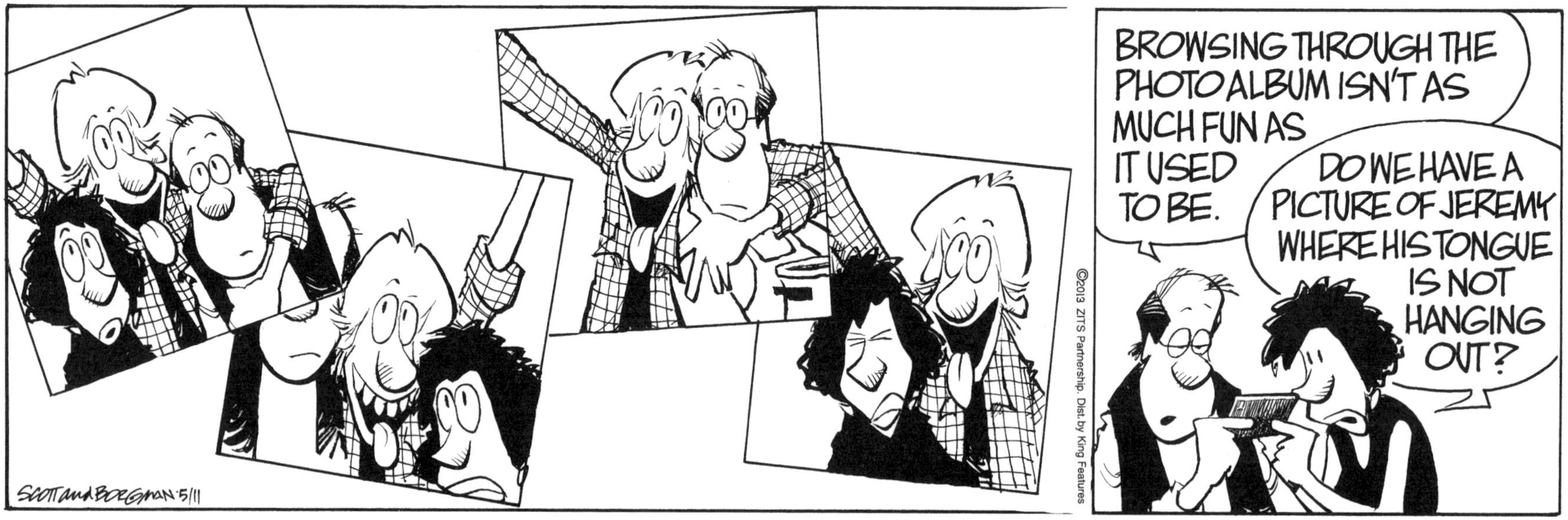
SCOTT and BORGMAN 5/11
©2013 ZITS Partnership. Dist. by King Features
BROWSING THROUGH THE PHOTO ALBUM ISN'T AS MUCH FUN AS IT USED TO BE.
DO WE HAVE A PICTURE OF JEREMY WHERE HIS TONGUE IS NOT HANGING OUT?

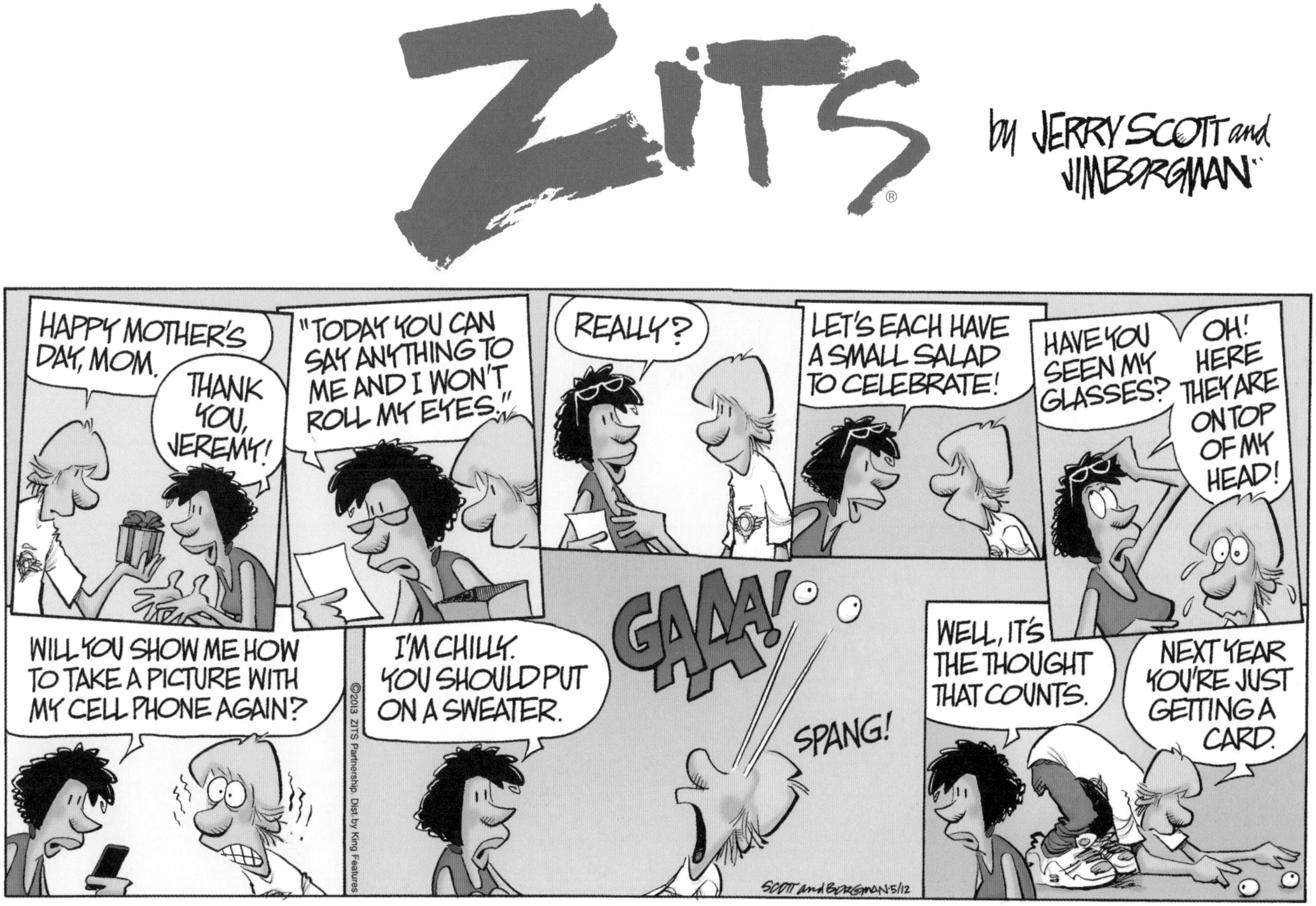
ZITS®
by JERRY SCOTT and JIM BORGMAN
HAPPY MOTHER'S DAY, MOM.
THANK YOU, JEREMY!
"TODAY YOU CAN SAY ANYTHING TO ME AND I WON'T ROLL MY EYES."
REALLY?
LET'S EACH HAVE A SMALL SALAD TO CELEBRATE!
HAVE YOU SEEN MY GLASSES?
OH! HERE THEY ARE ON TOP OF MY HEAD!
WILL YOU SHOW ME HOW TO TAKE A PICTURE WITH MY CELL PHONE AGAIN?
©2013 ZITS Partnership. Dist. by King Features
I'M CHILLY. YOU SHOULD PUT ON A SWEATER.
GAAA!
SPANG!
SCOTT and BORGMAN 5/12
WELL, IT'S THE THOUGHT THAT COUNTS.
NEXT YEAR YOU'RE JUST GETTING A CARD.

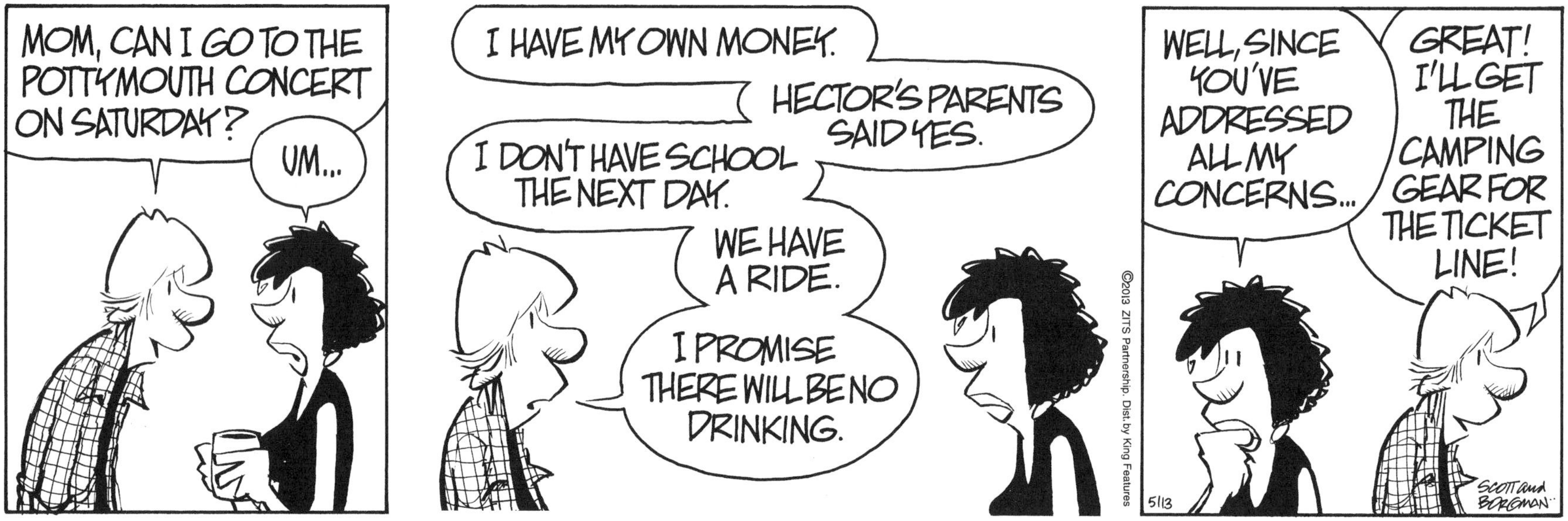
MOM, CAN I GO TO THE POTTYMOUTH CONCERT ON SATURDAY?
UM...
I HAVE MY OWN MONEY.
HECTOR'S PARENTS SAID YES.
I DON'T HAVE SCHOOL THE NEXT DAY.
WE HAVE A RIDE.
I PROMISE THERE WILL BE NO DRINKING.
©2013 ZITS Partnership. Dist. by King Features
5/13
WELL, SINCE YOU'VE ADDRESSED ALL MY CONCERNS...
GREAT! I'LL GET THE CAMPING GEAR FOR THE TICKET LINE!
SCOTT and BORGMAN

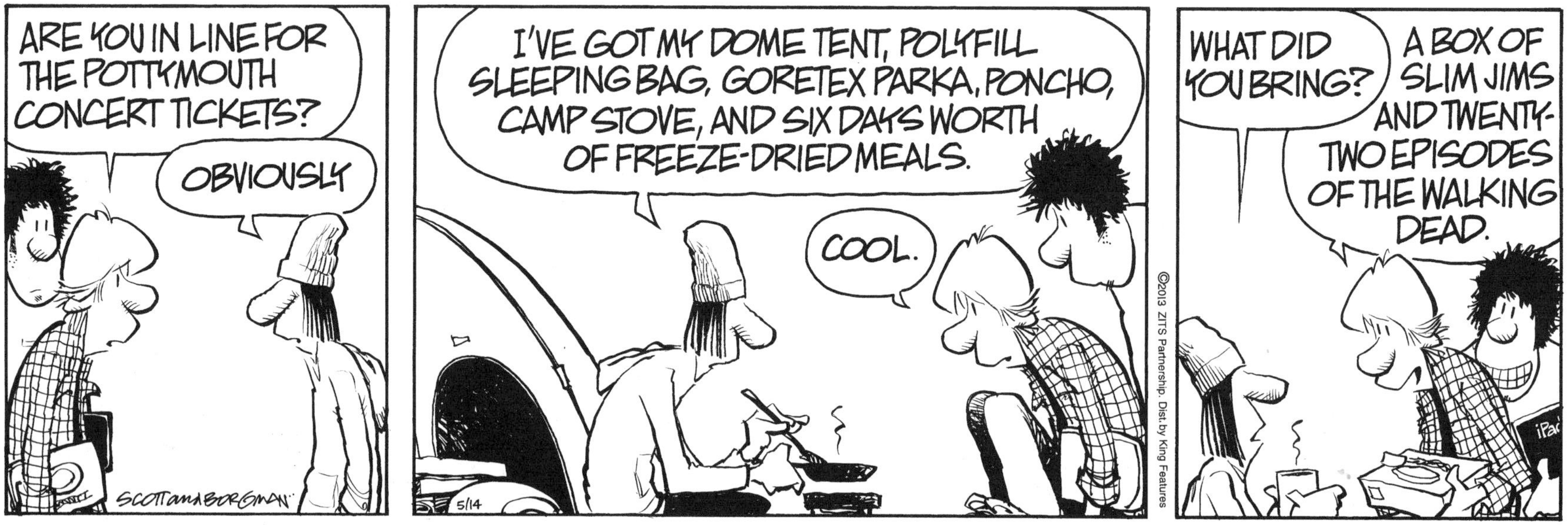
ARE YOU IN LINE FOR THE POTTYMOUTH CONCERT TICKETS?
OBVIOUSLY
SCOTT and BORGMAN
I'VE GOT MY DOME TENT, POLYFILL SLEEPING BAG, GORETEX PARKA, PONCHO, CAMP STOVE, AND SIX DAYS WORTH OF FREEZE-DRIED MEALS.
COOL.
5/14
©2013 ZITS Partnership. Dist. by King Features
WHAT DID YOU BRING?
A BOX OF SLIM JIMS AND TWENTY-TWO EPISODES OF THE WALKING DEAD.
iPad

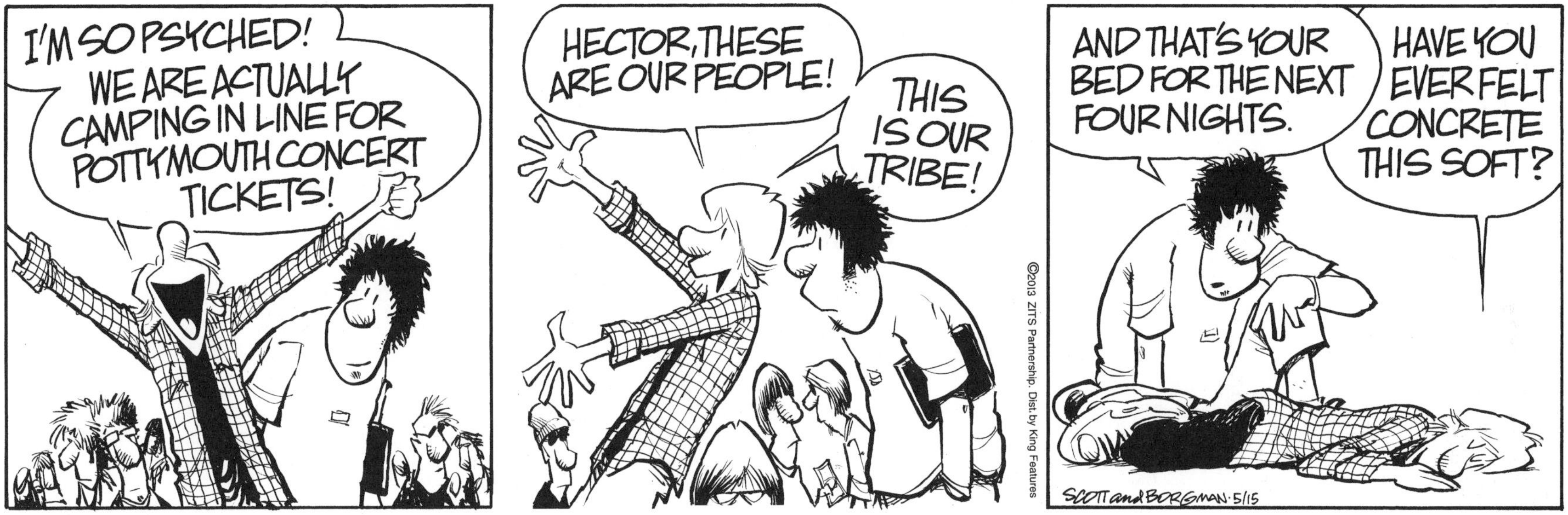
I'M SO PSYCHED! WE ARE ACTUALLY CAMPING IN LINE FOR POTTYMOUTH CONCERT TICKETS!
HECTOR, THESE ARE OUR PEOPLE!
THIS IS OUR TRIBE!
AND THAT'S YOUR BED FOR THE NEXT FOUR NIGHTS.
HAVE YOU EVER FELT CONCRETE THIS SOFT?
©2013 ZITS Partnership. Dist. by King Features
SCOTT and BORGMAN 5/15

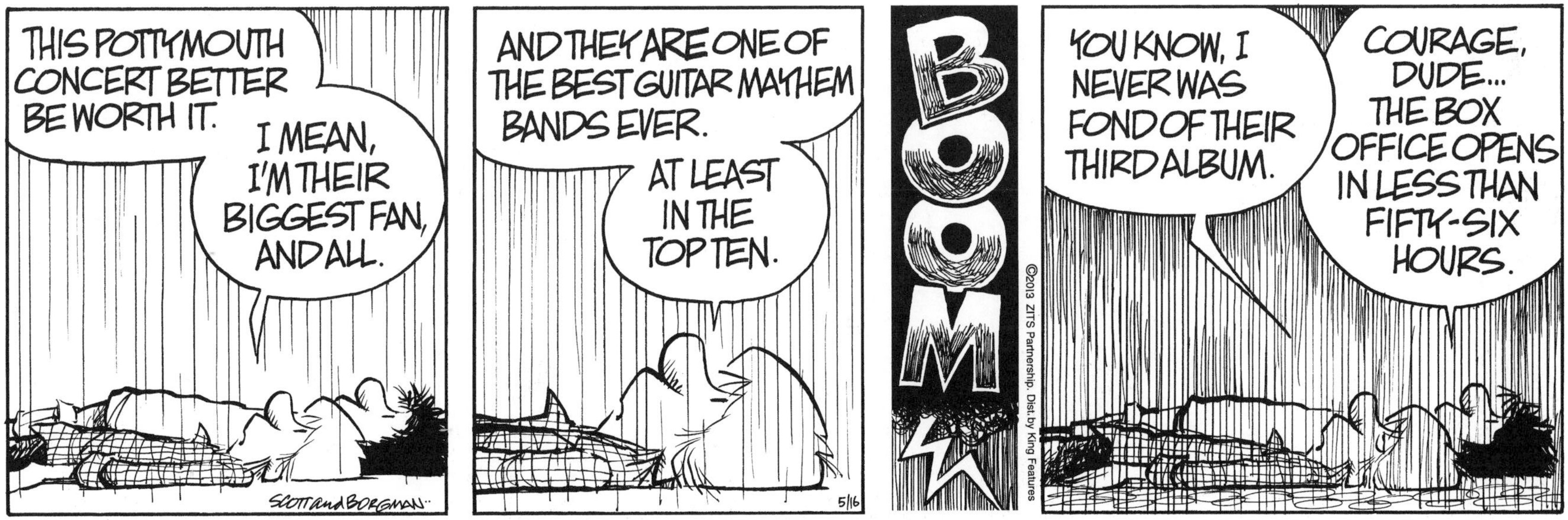
THIS POTTYMOUTH CONCERT BETTER BE WORTH IT.
I MEAN, I'M THEIR BIGGEST FAN, AND ALL.
SCOTT and BORGMAN
AND THEY ARE ONE OF THE BEST GUITAR MAYHEM BANDS EVER.
AT LEAST IN THE TOP TEN.
5/16
BOOM
©2013 ZITS Partnership. Dist. by King Features
YOU KNOW, I NEVER WAS FOND OF THEIR THIRD ALBUM.
COURAGE, DUDE... THE BOX OFFICE OPENS IN LESS THAN FIFTY-SIX HOURS.

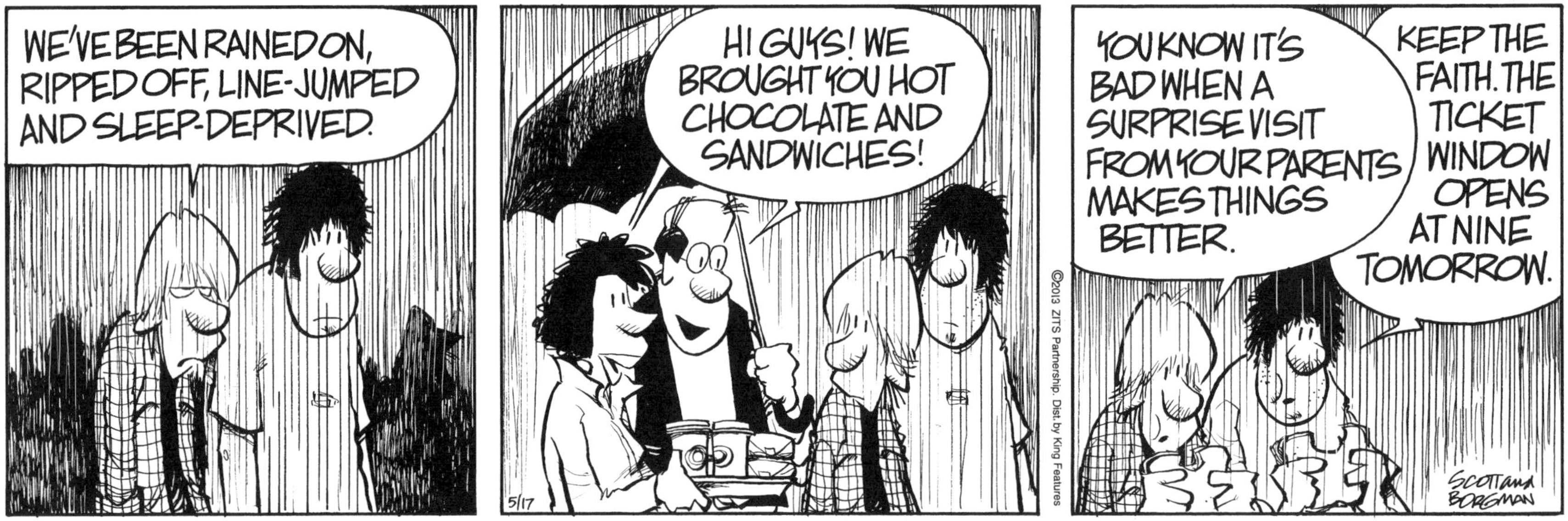
WE'VE BEEN RAINED ON, RIPPED OFF, LINE-JUMPED AND SLEEP-DEPRIVED.
HI GUYS! WE BROUGHT YOU HOT CHOCOLATE AND SANDWICHES!
YOU KNOW IT'S BAD WHEN A SURPRISE VISIT FROM YOUR PARENTS MAKES THINGS BETTER.
KEEP THE FAITH. THE TICKET WINDOW OPENS AT NINE TOMORROW.
5/17
©2013 ZITS Partnership. Dist. by King Features
SCOTT and BORGMAN

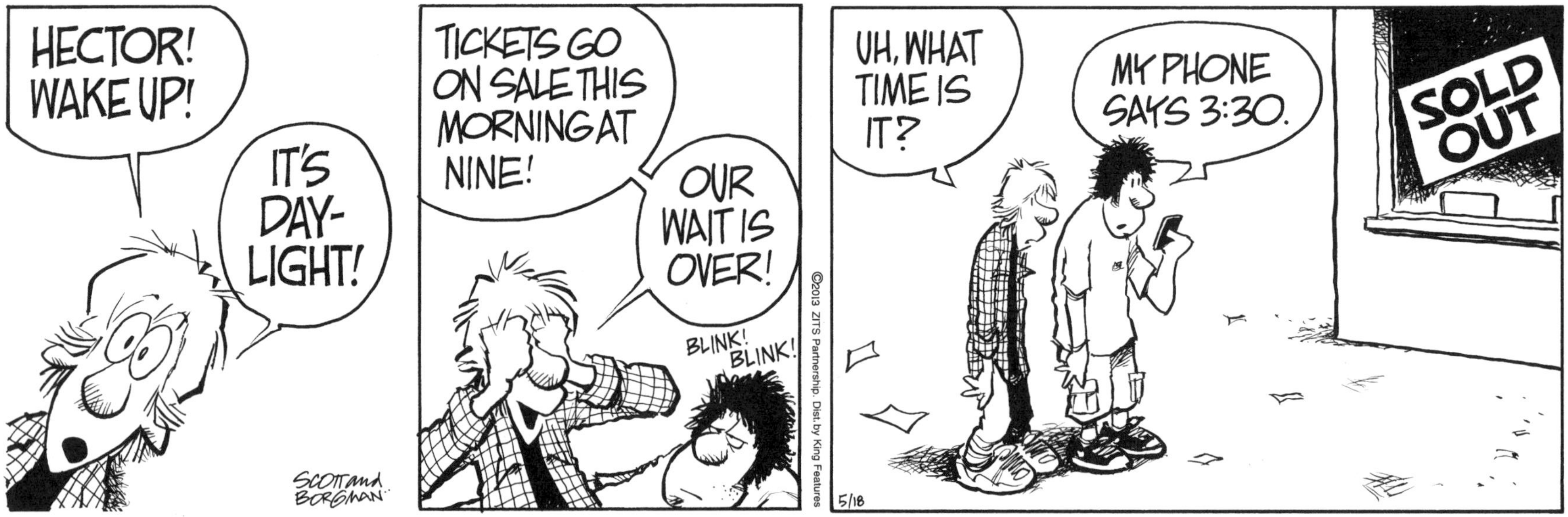
HECTOR! WAKE UP!
IT'S DAY-LIGHT!
SCOTT and BORGMAN
TICKETS GO ON SALE THIS MORNING AT NINE!
OUR WAIT IS OVER!
BLINK! BLINK!
©2013 ZITS Partnership. Dist. by King Features
UH, WHAT TIME IS IT?
MY PHONE SAYS 3:30.
SOLD OUT
5/18

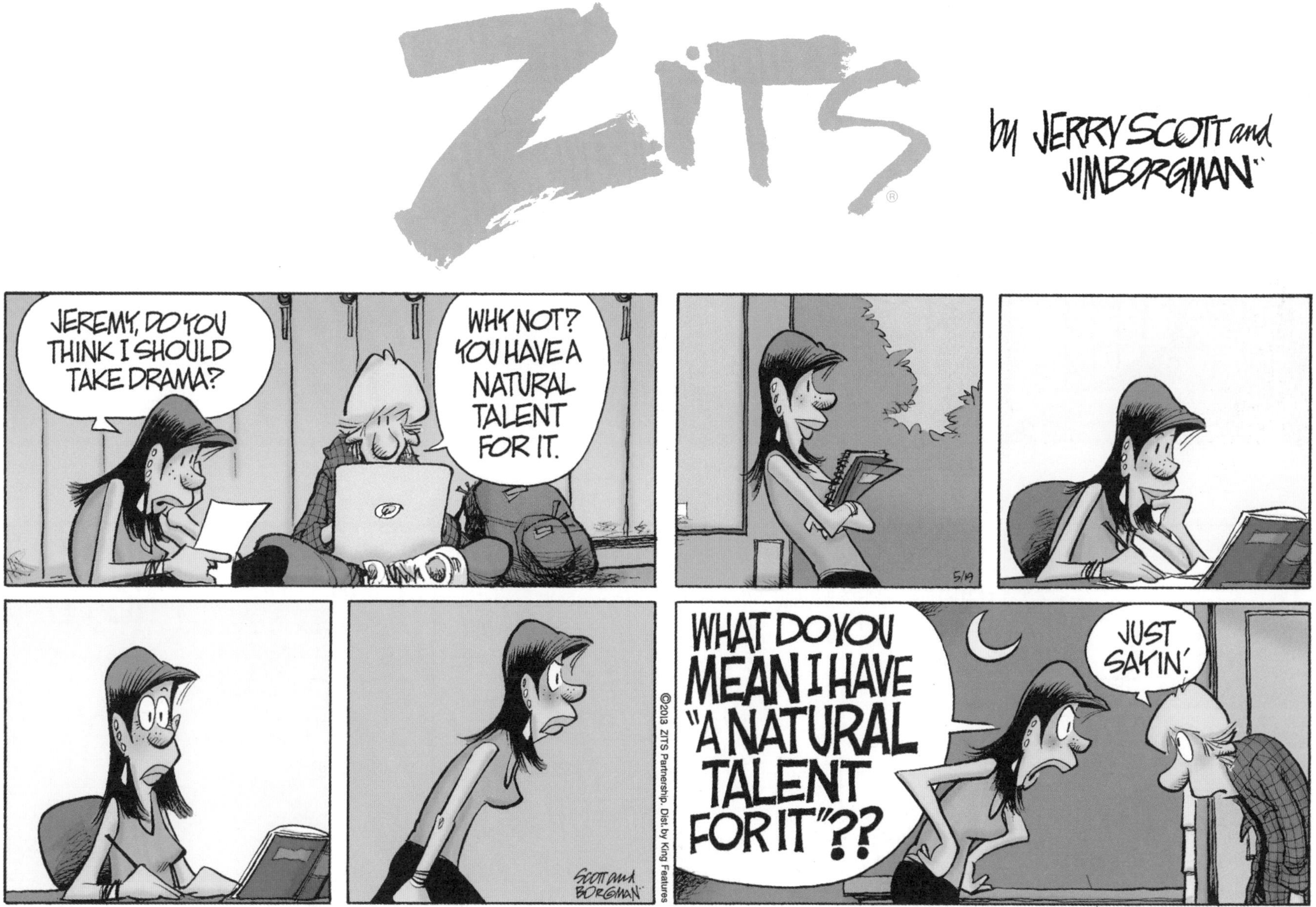
ZITS
by JERRY SCOTT and JIM BORGMAN
JEREMY, DO YOU THINK I SHOULD TAKE DRAMA?
WHY NOT? YOU HAVE A NATURAL TALENT FOR IT.
5/19
©2013 ZITS Partnership. Dist. by King Features
SCOTT and BORGMAN
WHAT DO YOU MEAN I HAVE "A NATURAL TALENT FOR IT"??
JUST SAYIN'.

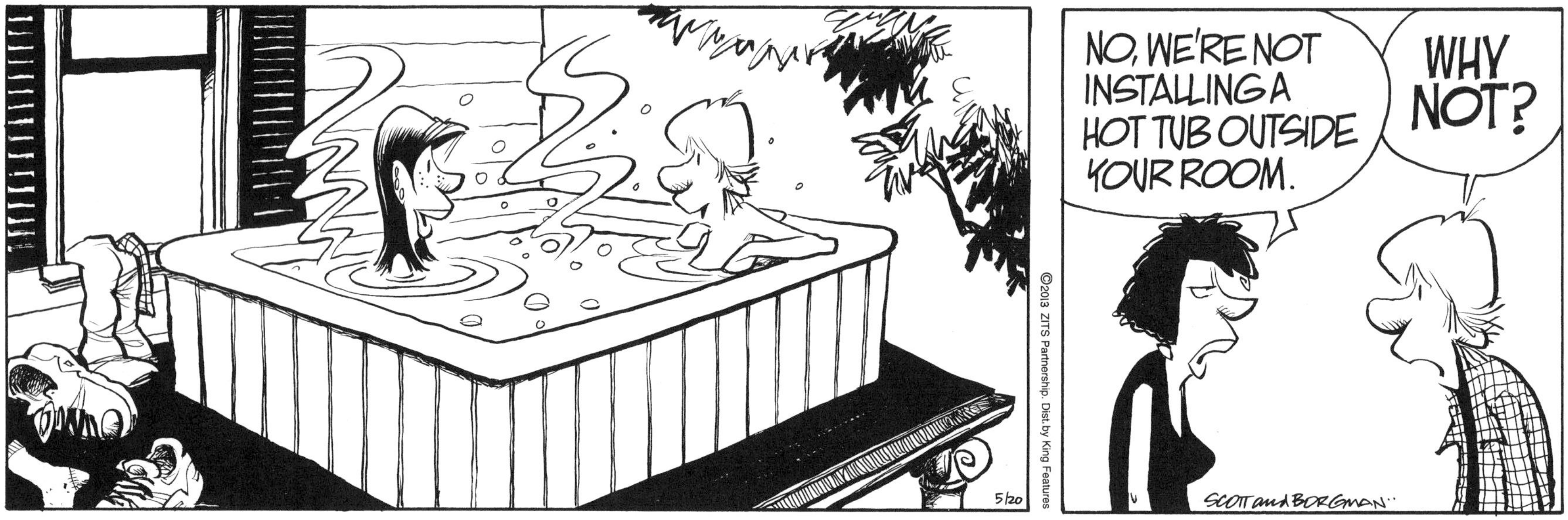

5/20
©2013 ZITS Partnership. Dist. by King Features
NO, WE'RE NOT INSTALLING A HOT TUB OUTSIDE YOUR ROOM.
WHY NOT?
SCOTT and BORGMAN


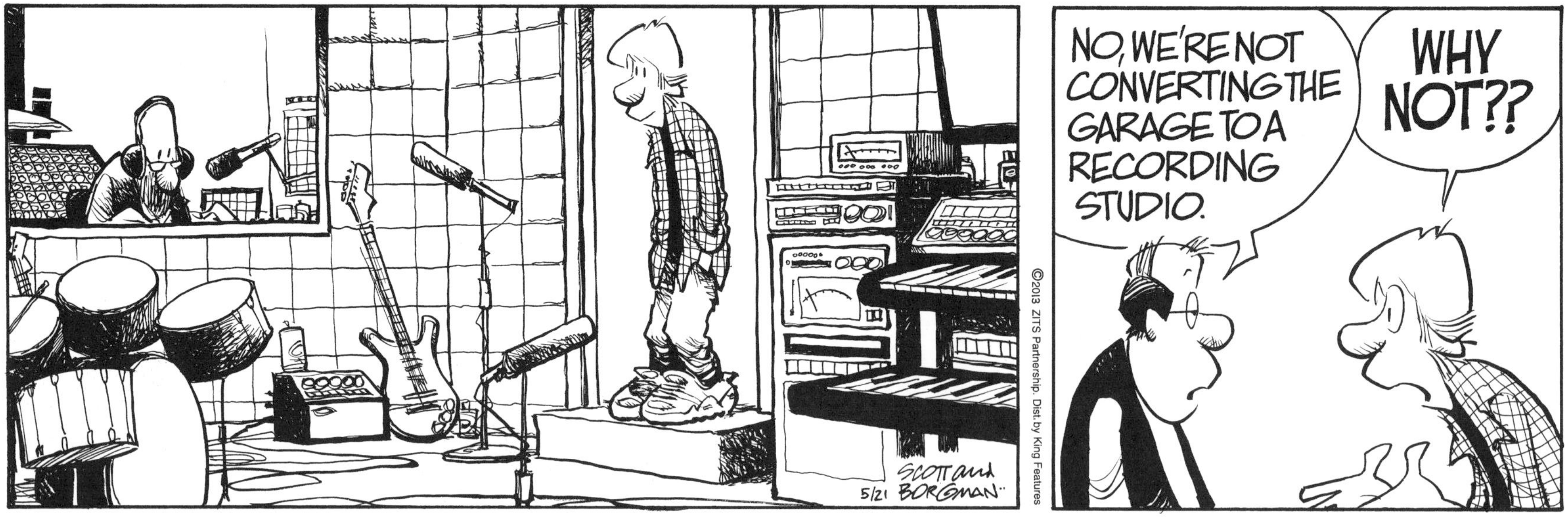

5/21
SCOTT and BORGMAN
©2013 ZITS Partnership. Dist. by King Features
NO, WE'RE NOT CONVERTING THE GARAGE TO A RECORDING STUDIO.
WHY NOT??

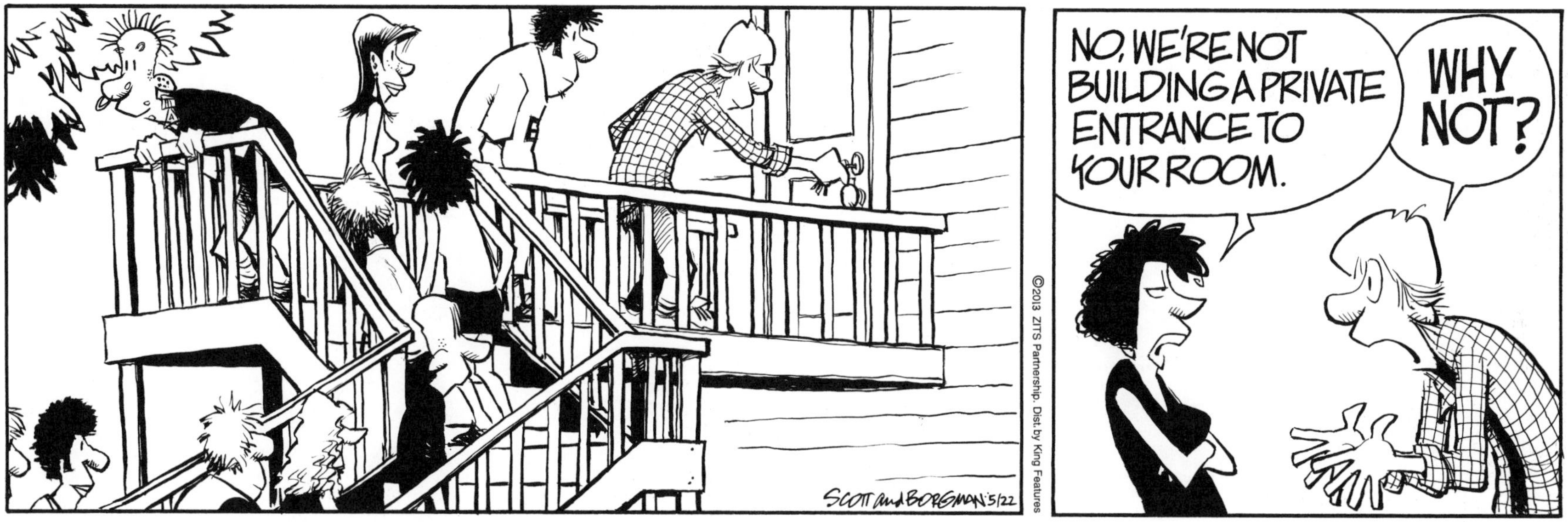
SCOTT and BORGMAN 5/22
©2013 ZITS Partnership. Dist. by King Features
NO, WE'RE NOT BUILDING A PRIVATE ENTRANCE TO YOUR ROOM.
WHY NOT?

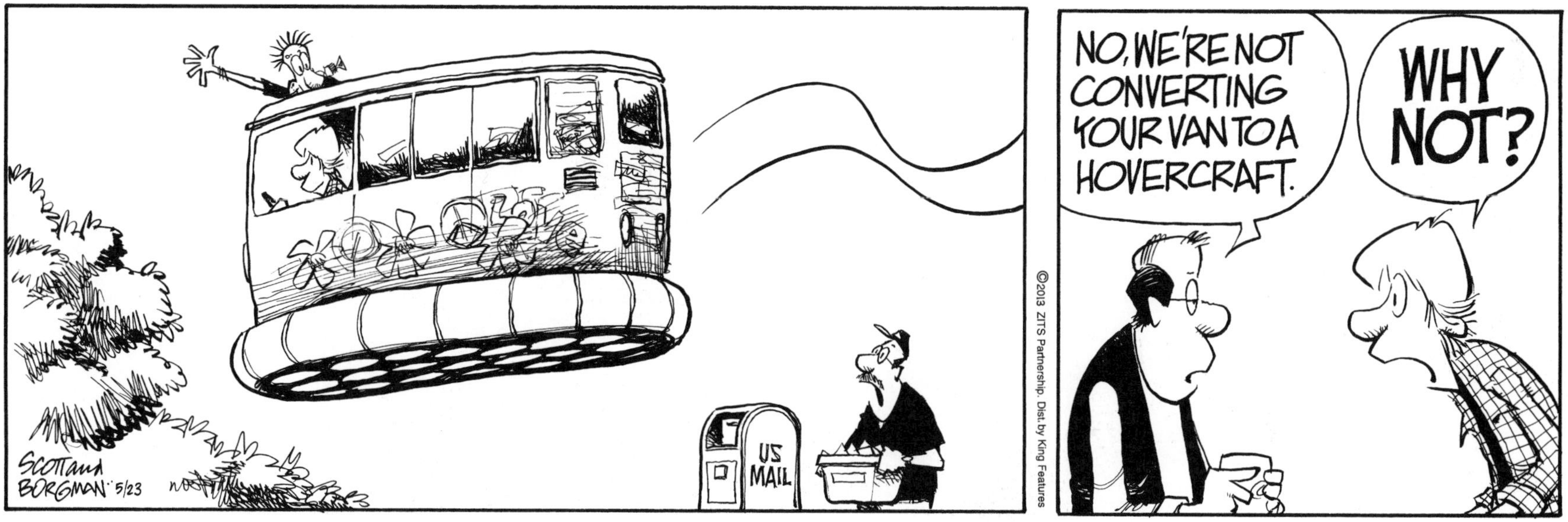
US MAIL
SCOTT and BORGMAN 5/23
©2013 ZITS Partnership. Dist. by King Features
NO, WE'RE NOT CONVERTING YOUR VAN TO A HOVERCRAFT.
WHY NOT?

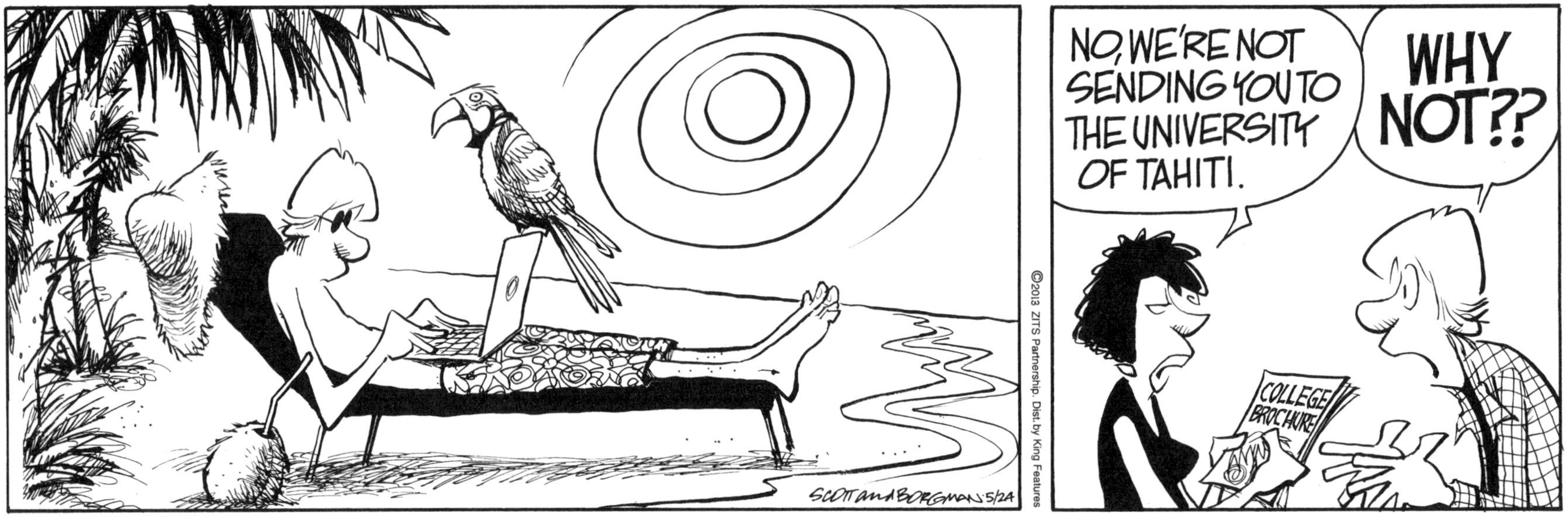
SCOTT and BORGMAN 5/24
©2013 ZITS Partnership, Dist. by King Features
NO, WE'RE NOT SENDING YOU TO THE UNIVERSITY OF TAHITI.
WHY NOT??
COLLEGE BROCHURE

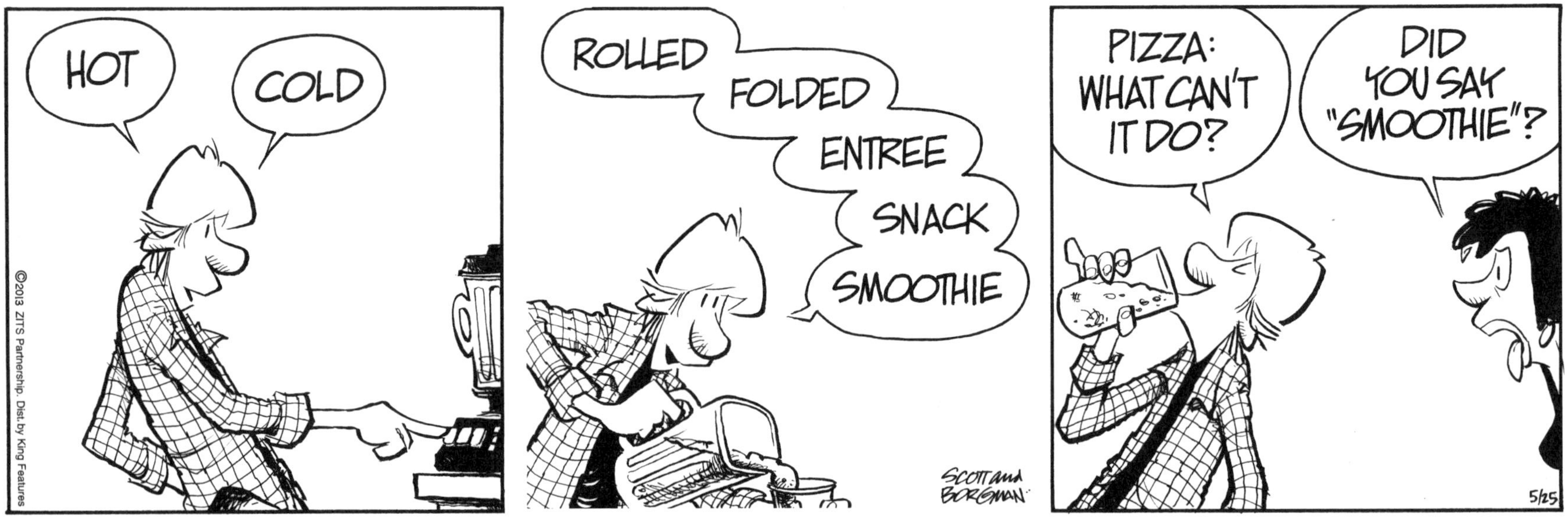
©2013 ZITS Partnership, Dist. by King Features
HOT
COLD
ROLLED
FOLDED
ENTREE
SNACK
SMOOTHIE
SCOTT and BORGMAN
PIZZA: WHAT CAN'T IT DO?
DID YOU SAY "SMOOTHIE"?
5/25

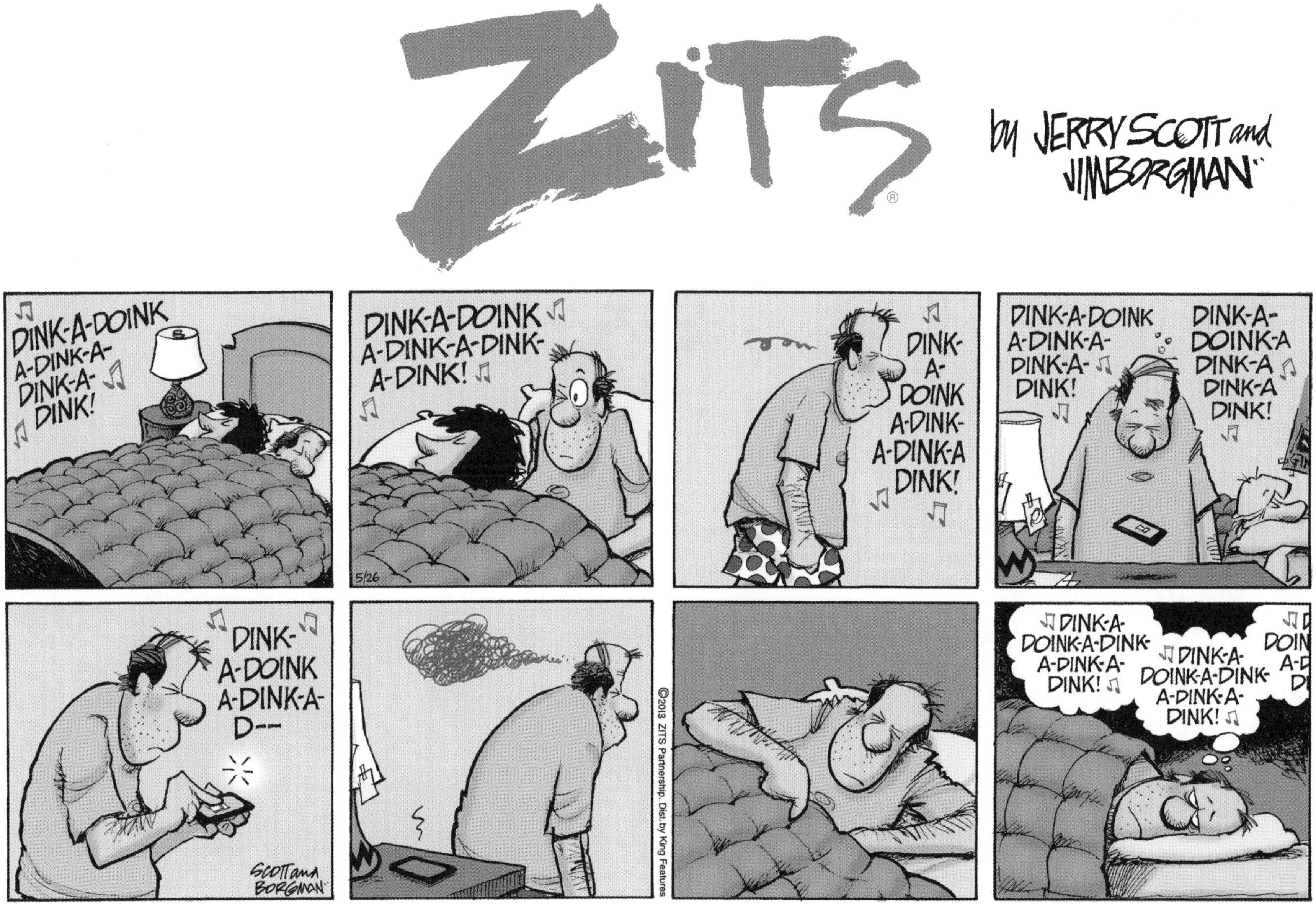
ZITS®
by JERRY SCOTT and JIM BORGMAN
DINK-A-DOINK A-DINK-A-DINK-A-DINK!
DINK-A-DOINK A-DINK-A-DINK-A-DINK!
5/26
DINK-A-DOINK A-DINK-A-DINK-A DINK!
DINK-A-DOINK A-DINK-A-DINK-A-DINK!
DINK-A-DOINK-A DINK-A DINK-A DINK!
DINK-A-DOINK A-DINK-A-D--
SCOTT and BORGMAN
©2013 ZITS Partnership. Dist. by King Features
DINK-A-DOINK-A-DINK-A-DINK-A-DINK!
DINK-A-DOINK-A-DINK-A-DINK-A-DINK!

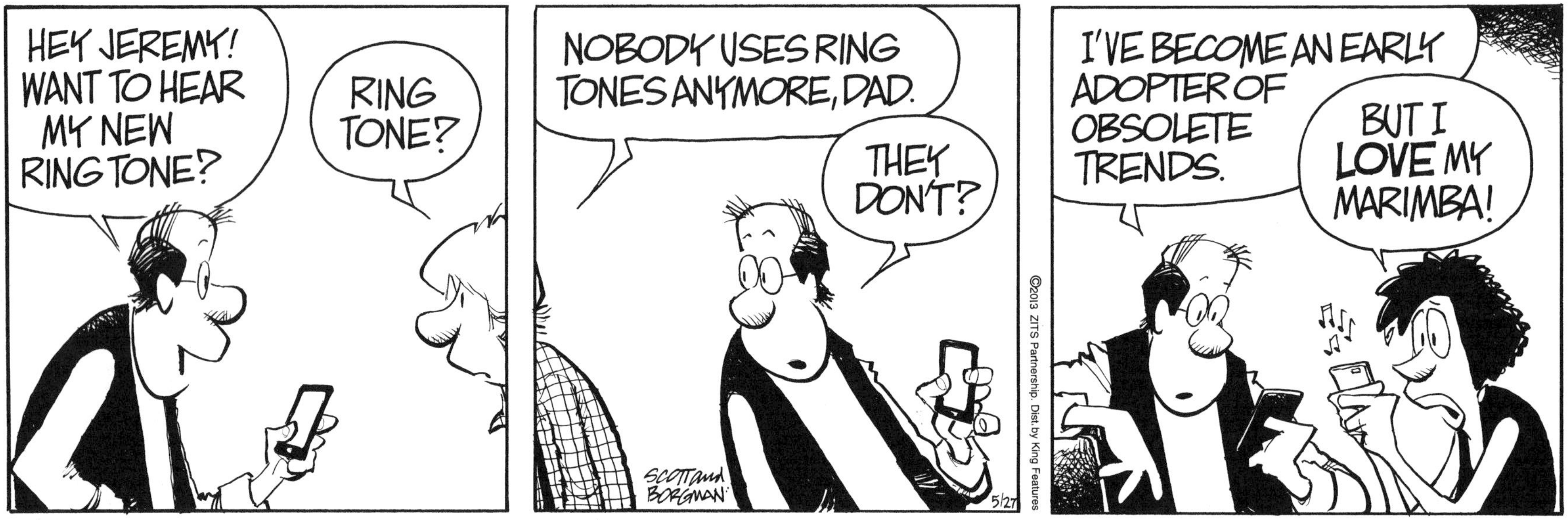
HEY JEREMY! WANT TO HEAR MY NEW RING TONE?
RING TONE?
NOBODY USES RING TONES ANYMORE, DAD.
THEY DON'T?
SCOTT and BORGMAN
5/27
©2013 ZITS Partnership. Dist. by King Features
I'VE BECOME AN EARLY ADOPTER OF OBSOLETE TRENDS.
BUT I LOVE MY MARIMBA!

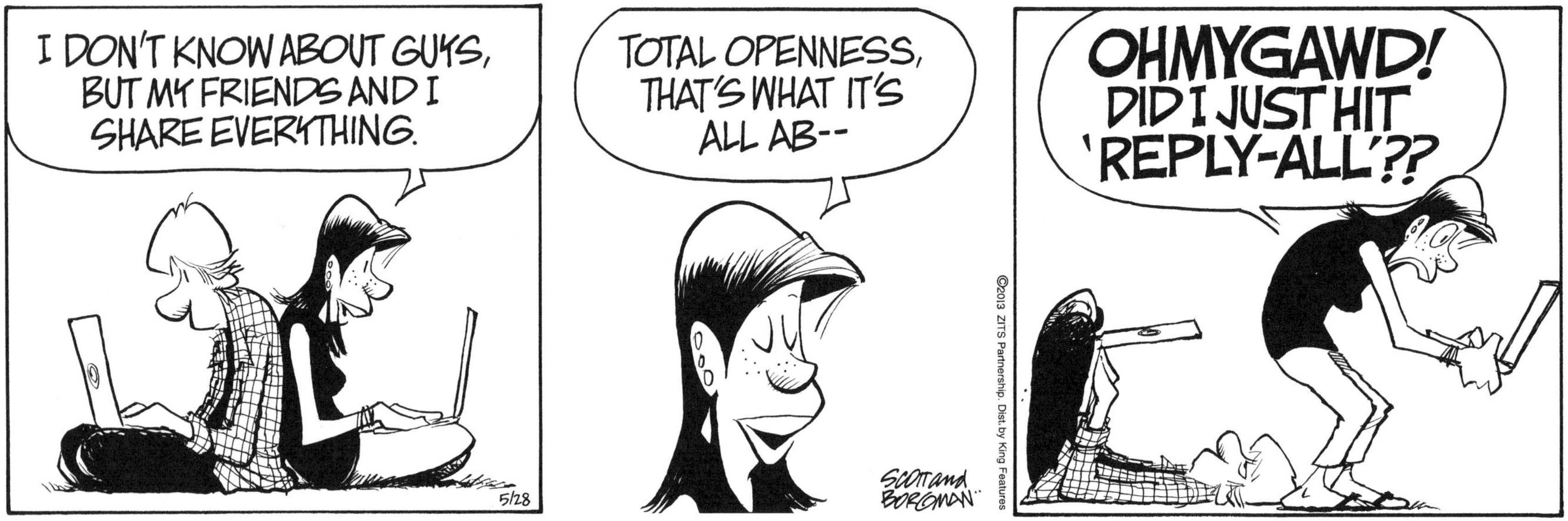
I DON'T KNOW ABOUT GUYS, BUT MY FRIENDS AND I SHARE EVERYTHING.
5/28
TOTAL OPENNESS, THAT'S WHAT IT'S ALL AB--
SCOTT and BORGMAN
©2013 ZITS Partnership. Dist. by King Features
OHMYGAWD! DID I JUST HIT 'REPLY-ALL'??

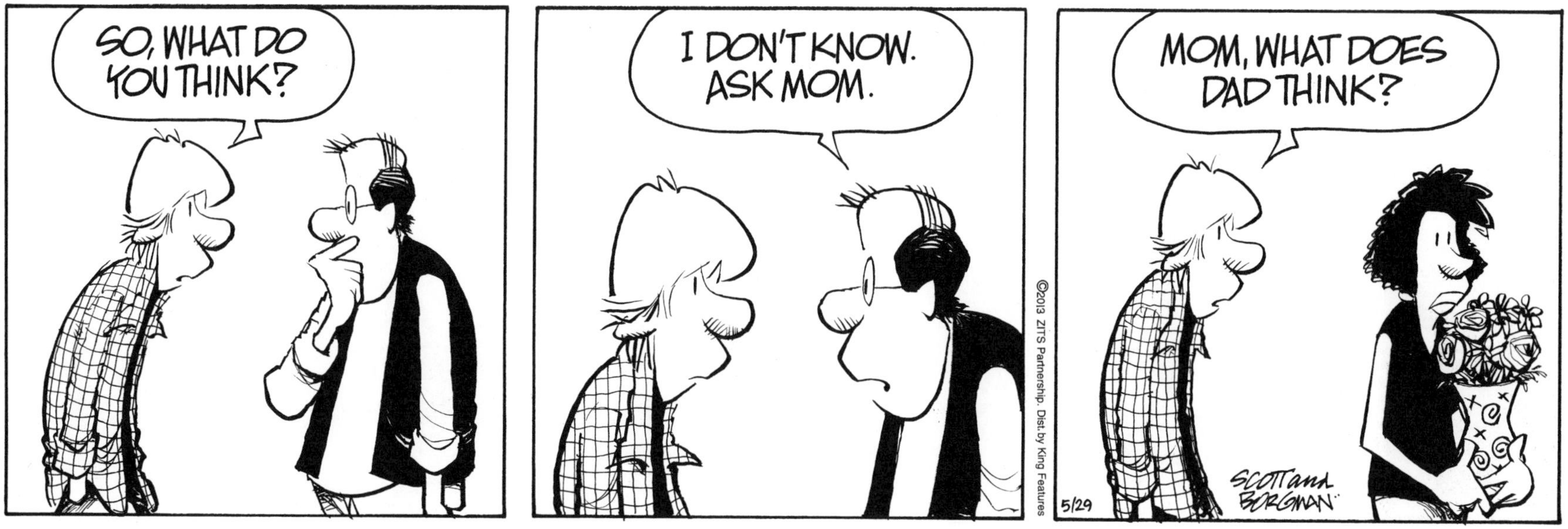
SO, WHAT DO YOU THINK?
I DON'T KNOW. ASK MOM.
MOM, WHAT DOES DAD THINK?
©2013 ZITS Partnership. Dist. by King Features
5/29
SCOTT and BORGMAN

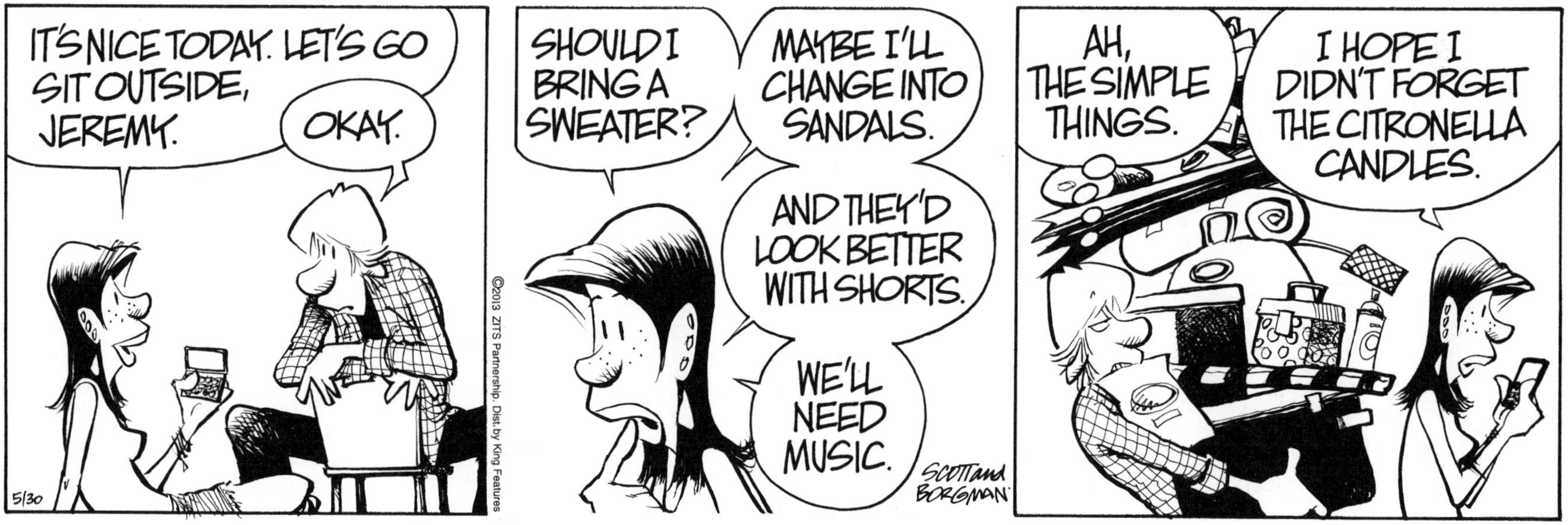
IT'S NICE TODAY. LET'S GO SIT OUTSIDE, JEREMY.
OKAY.
©2013 ZITS Partnership. Dist. by King Features
5/30
SHOULD I BRING A SWEATER?
MAYBE I'LL CHANGE INTO SANDALS.
AND THEY'D LOOK BETTER WITH SHORTS.
WE'LL NEED MUSIC.
SCOTT and BORGMAN
AH, THE SIMPLE THINGS.
I HOPE I DIDN'T FORGET THE CITRONELLA CANDLES.

OOH! AN ONLINE COUPON!

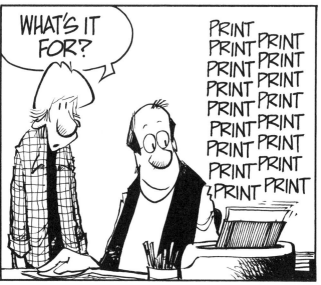

WHAT'S IT FOR?

PRINT PRINT
PRINT PRINT
PRINT PRINT
PRINT PRINT
PRINT PRINT
PRINT PRINT
PRINT PRINT
PRINT PRINT
PRINT PRINT

5/31

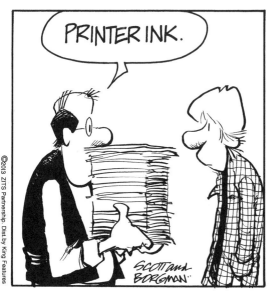

PRINTER INK.

SCOTT and BORGMAN

©2013 ZITS Partnership. Dist. by King Features

BUBBLE GUM FLAVOR

SCOTT and BORGMAN

BUBBLE GUM SCENTED

6/1

BUBBLE GUM CHUNK

I DON'T SEE A FLAVOR I LIKE.

BUBBLE GUM

©2013 ZITS Partnership. Dist. by King Features

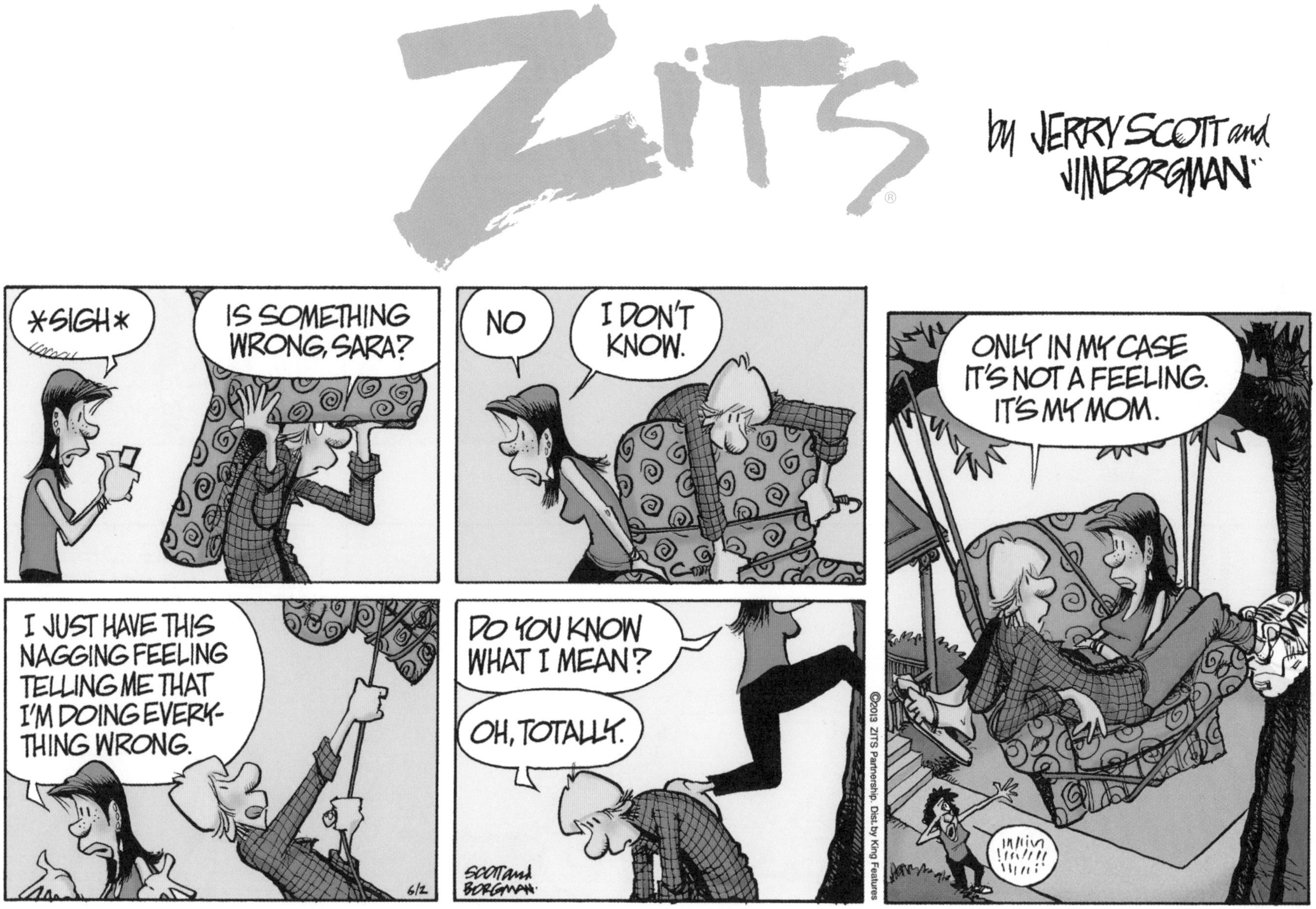
ZITS
by JERRY SCOTT and JIM BORGMAN
*SIGH*
IS SOMETHING WRONG, SARA?
NO
I DON'T KNOW.
I JUST HAVE THIS NAGGING FEELING TELLING ME THAT I'M DOING EVERYTHING WRONG.
6/2
DO YOU KNOW WHAT I MEAN?
OH, TOTALLY.
SCOTT and BORGMAN
©2013 ZITS Partnership. Dist. by King Features
ONLY IN MY CASE IT'S NOT A FEELING. IT'S MY MOM.

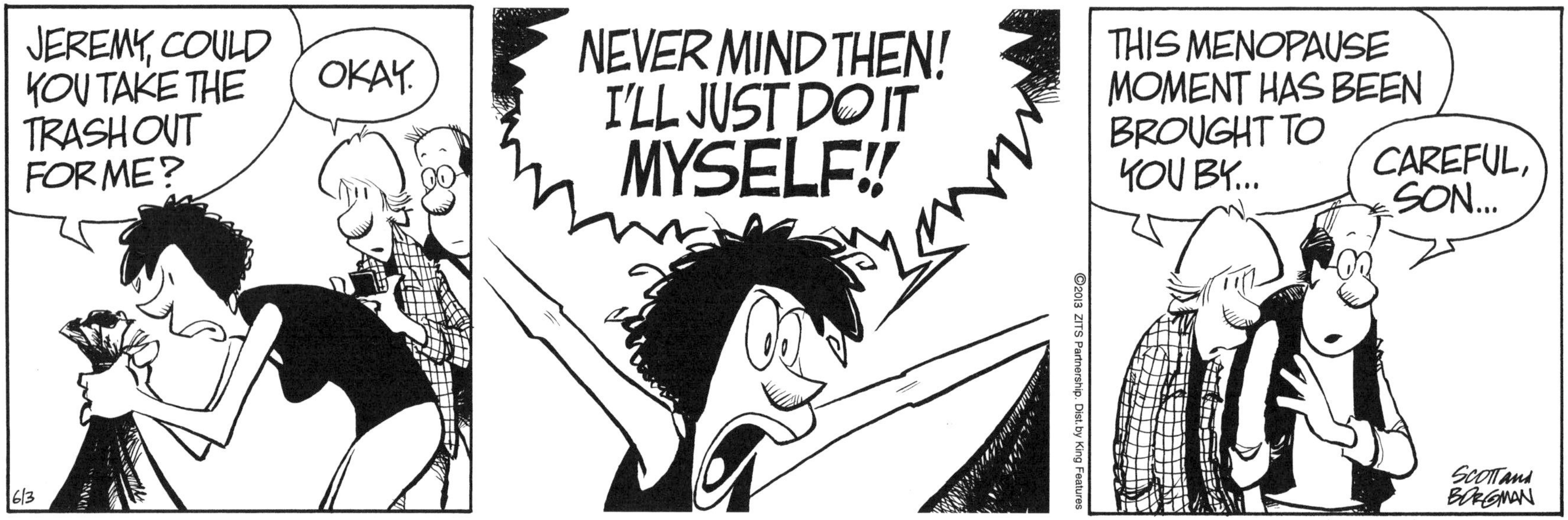
JEREMY, COULD YOU TAKE THE TRASH OUT FOR ME?
OKAY.
NEVER MIND THEN! I'LL JUST DO IT MYSELF!!
THIS MENOPAUSE MOMENT HAS BEEN BROUGHT TO YOU BY...
CAREFUL, SON...
SCOTT and BORGMAN
©2013 ZITS Partnership. Dist. by King Features
6/3

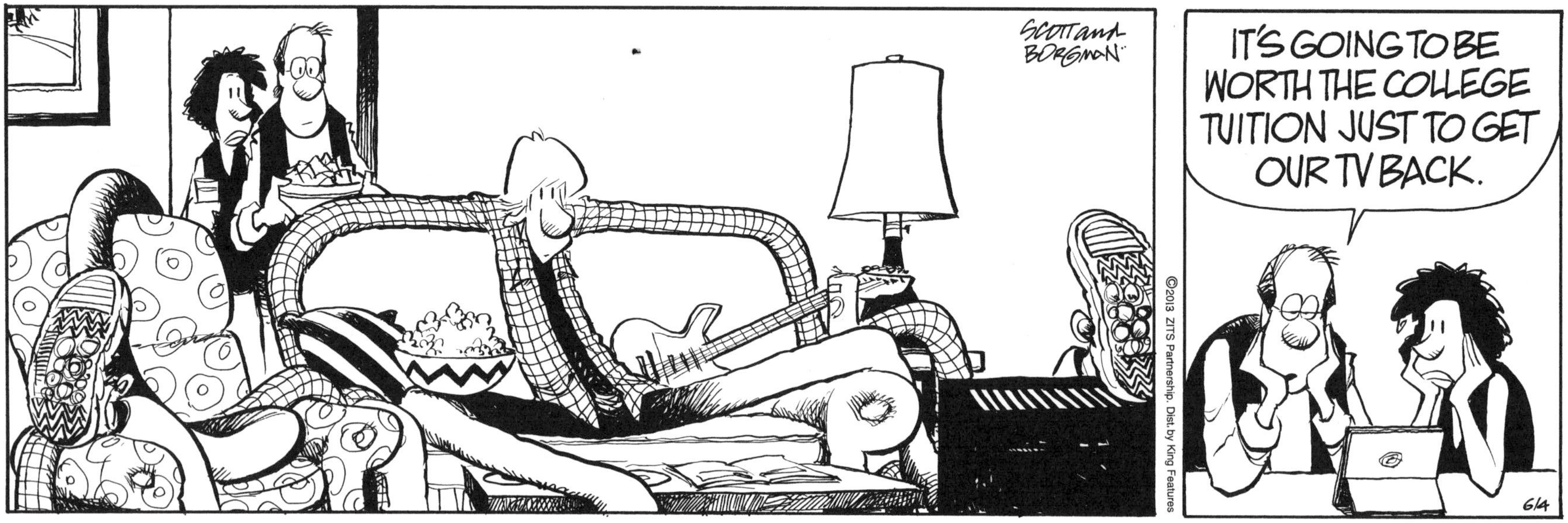
SCOTT and BORGMAN
IT'S GOING TO BE WORTH THE COLLEGE TUITION JUST TO GET OUR TV BACK.
©2013 ZITS Partnership. Dist. by King Features
6/4

JEREMY, I'D LIKE TO BOUNCE SOME IDEAS OFF YOU ABOUT YOUR SUMMER VACATION.

SCOTT and BORGMAN

6/5

...BUT I SEE THAT YOUR FATHER'S ALREADY BEEN AT IT.

YA THINK?

JOB

COLLEGE APPLICATION ESSAY VOLUNTEER START BUSINESS CAMP PAINT THE GARAGE GET A JOB MOWING TAKE A CLASS visit Grandma GUITAR LESSONS Help

WHAT'S THIS EMPTY JAR FOR, JEREMY?

IT HAD THIS HUGE HAIRY SPIDER IN IT.

I THOUGHT IT WAS DEAD, SO I TOOK THE LID OFF.

THEN THIS MORNING IT WAS GONE.

6/6

SCOTT and BORGMAN

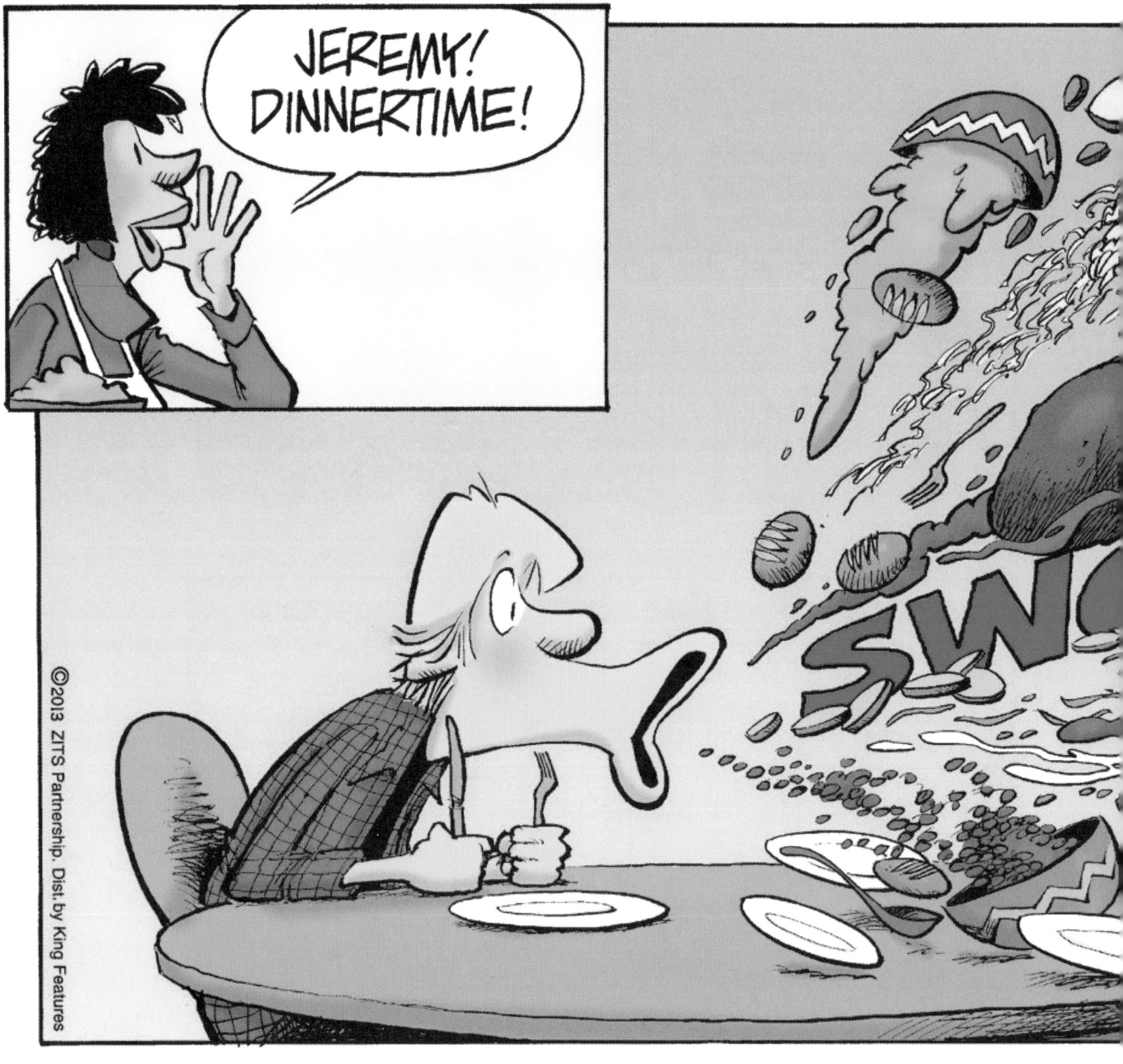
JEREMY! DINNERTIME!
©2013 ZITS Partnership. Dist. by King Features

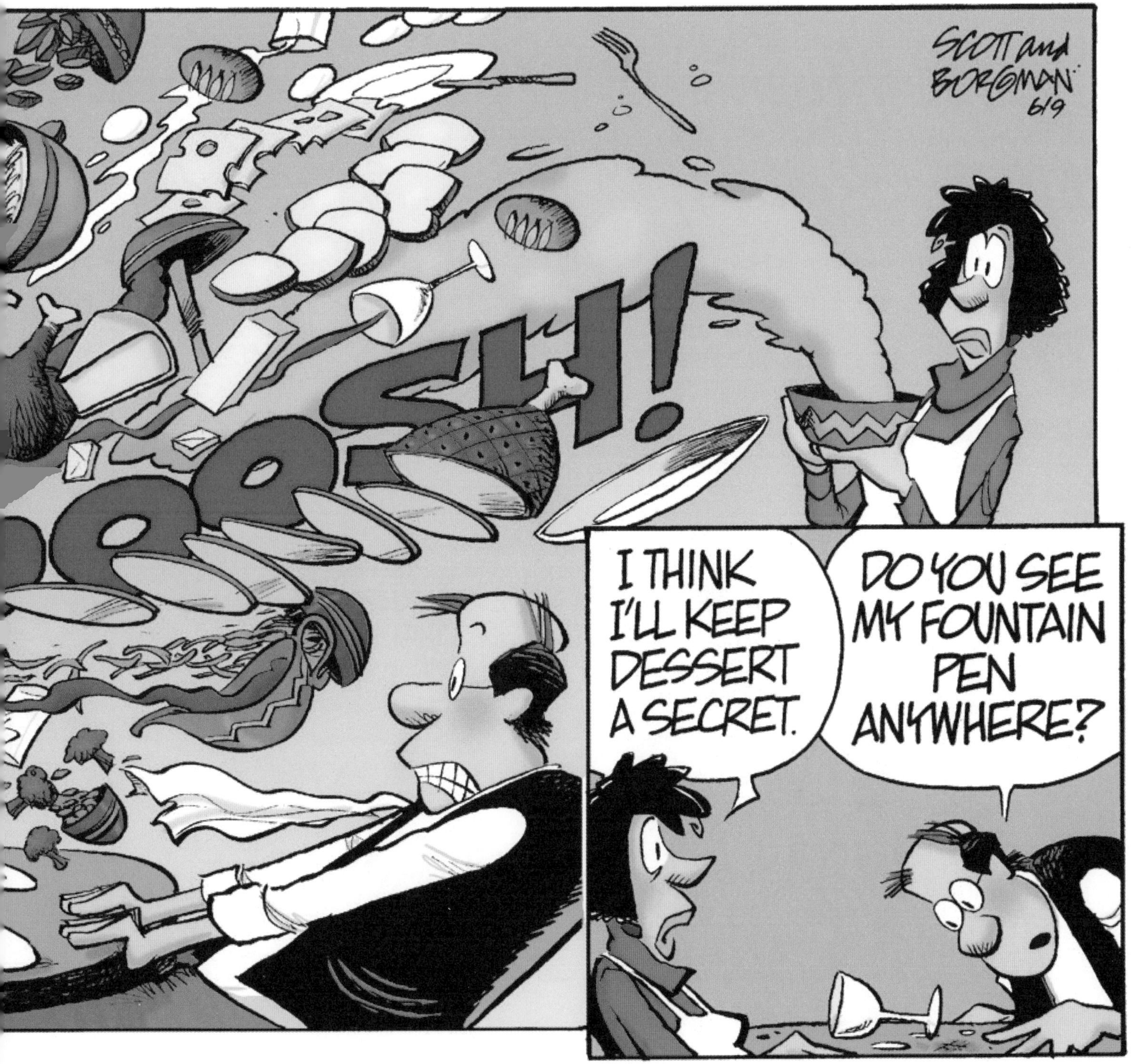
SCOTT and BORGMAN 6/9
SH!
I THINK I'LL KEEP DESSERT A SECRET.
DO YOU SEE MY FOUNTAIN PEN ANYWHERE?

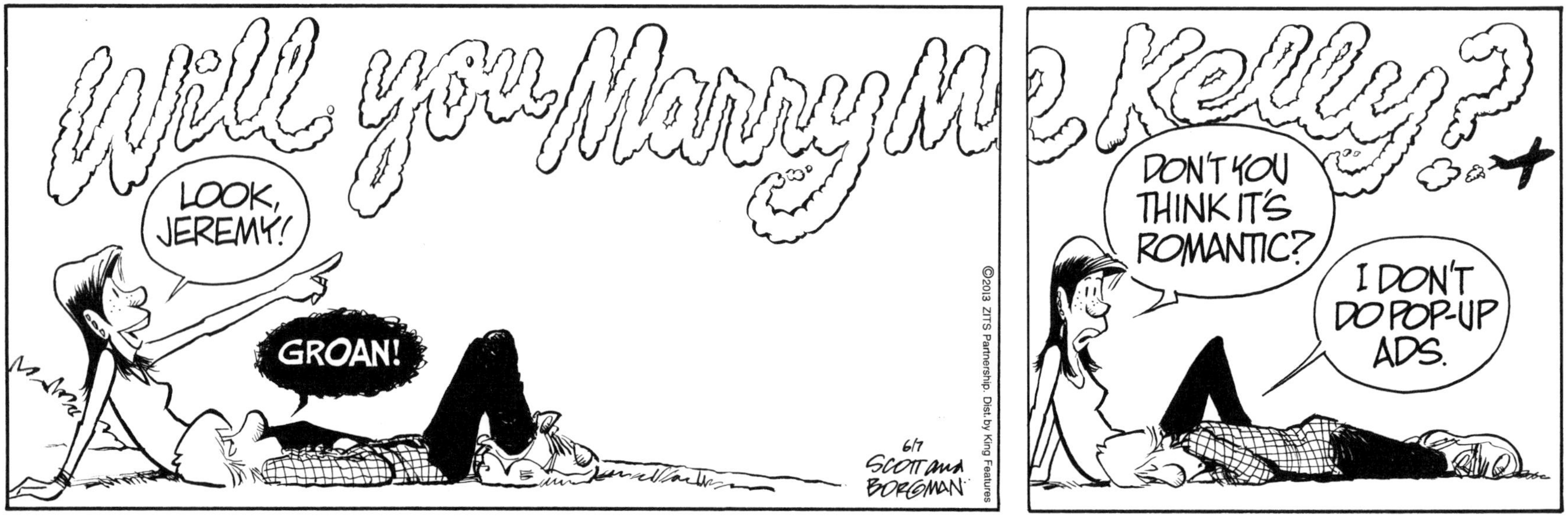
Will you Marry Me Kelly?
LOOK, JEREMY!
GROAN!
©2013 ZITS Partnership. Dist. by King Features
6/7 SCOTT and BORGMAN
DON'T YOU THINK IT'S ROMANTIC?
I DON'T DO POP-UP ADS.

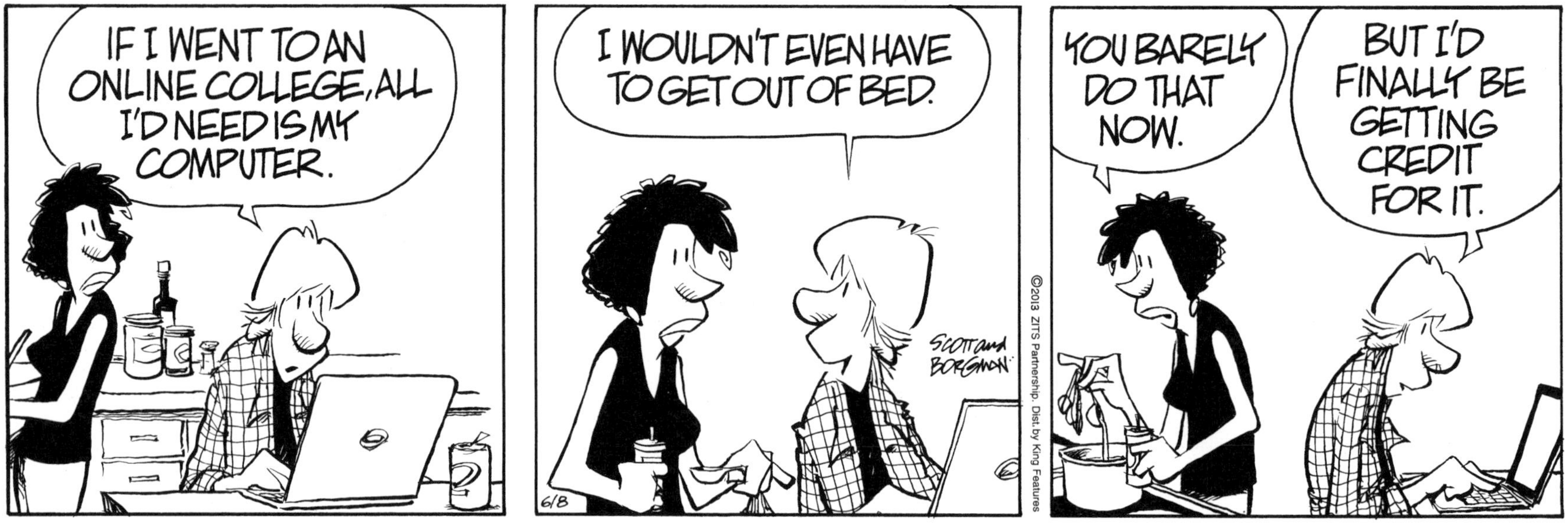
IF I WENT TO AN ONLINE COLLEGE, ALL I'D NEED IS MY COMPUTER.
I WOULDN'T EVEN HAVE TO GET OUT OF BED.
SCOTT and BORGMAN
6/8
©2013 ZITS Partnership. Dist. by King Features
YOU BARELY DO THAT NOW.
BUT I'D FINALLY BE GETTING CREDIT FOR IT.

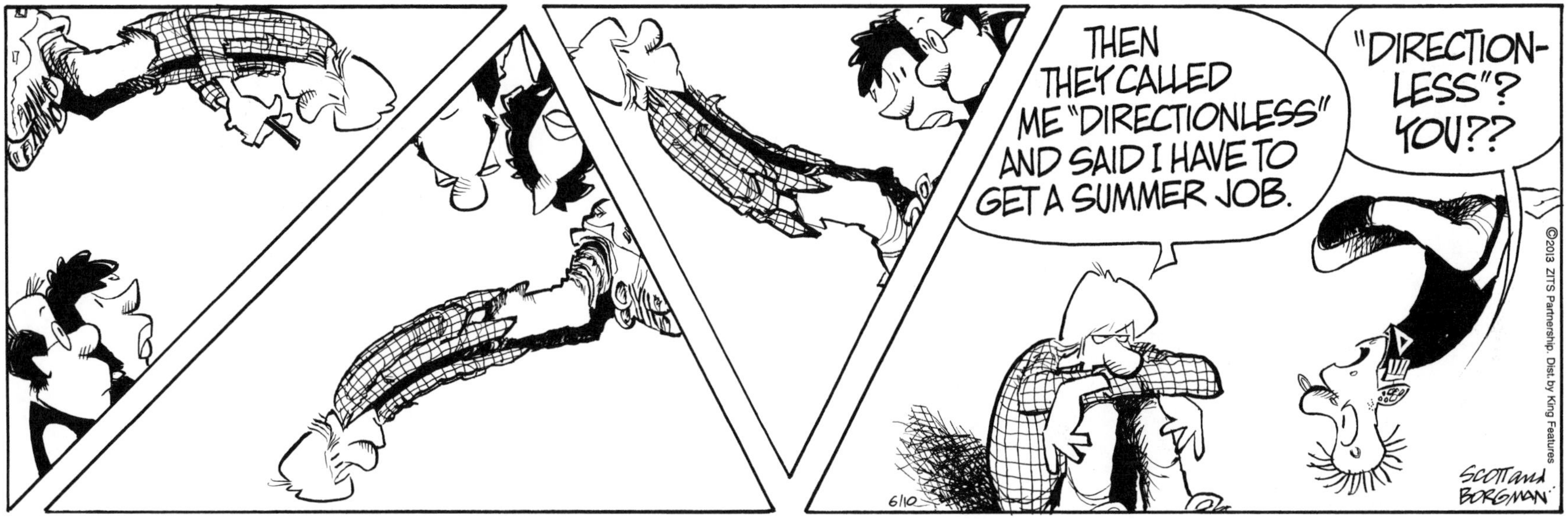
THEN THEY CALLED ME "DIRECTIONLESS" AND SAID I HAVE TO GET A SUMMER JOB.
"DIRECTION-LESS"? YOU??
©2013 ZITS Partnership. Dist. by King Features
SCOTT and BORGMAN
6/10

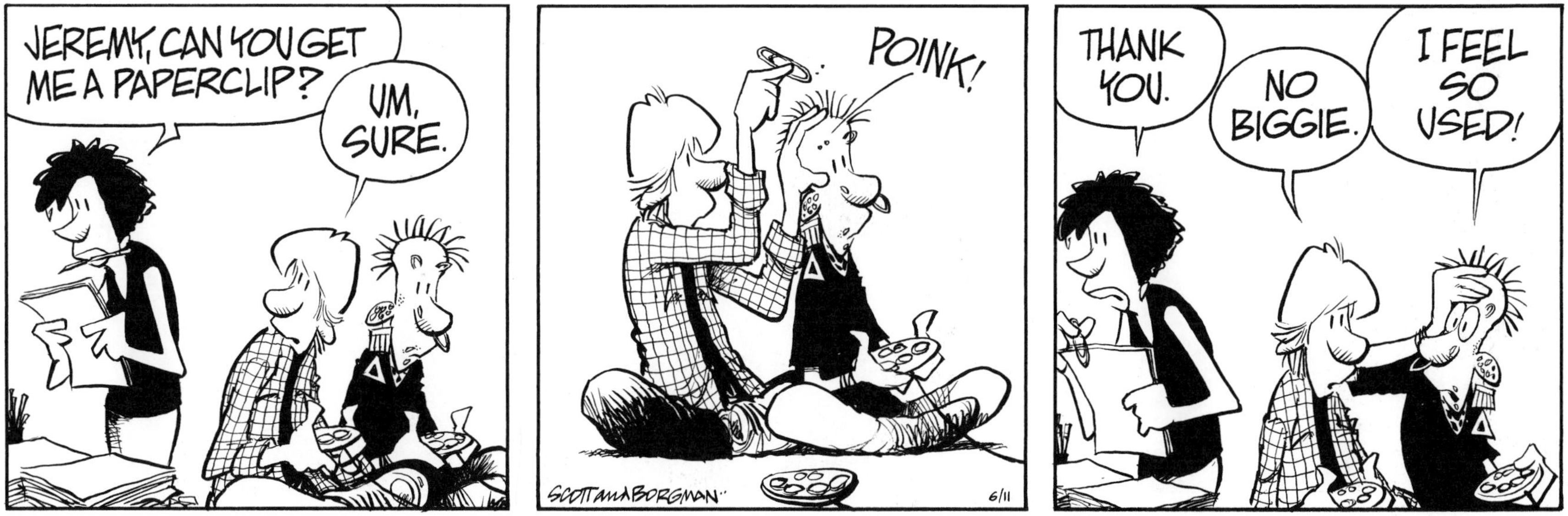
JEREMY, CAN YOU GET ME A PAPERCLIP?
UM, SURE.
POINK!
SCOTT and BORGMAN
6/11
THANK YOU.
NO BIGGIE.
I FEEL SO USED!

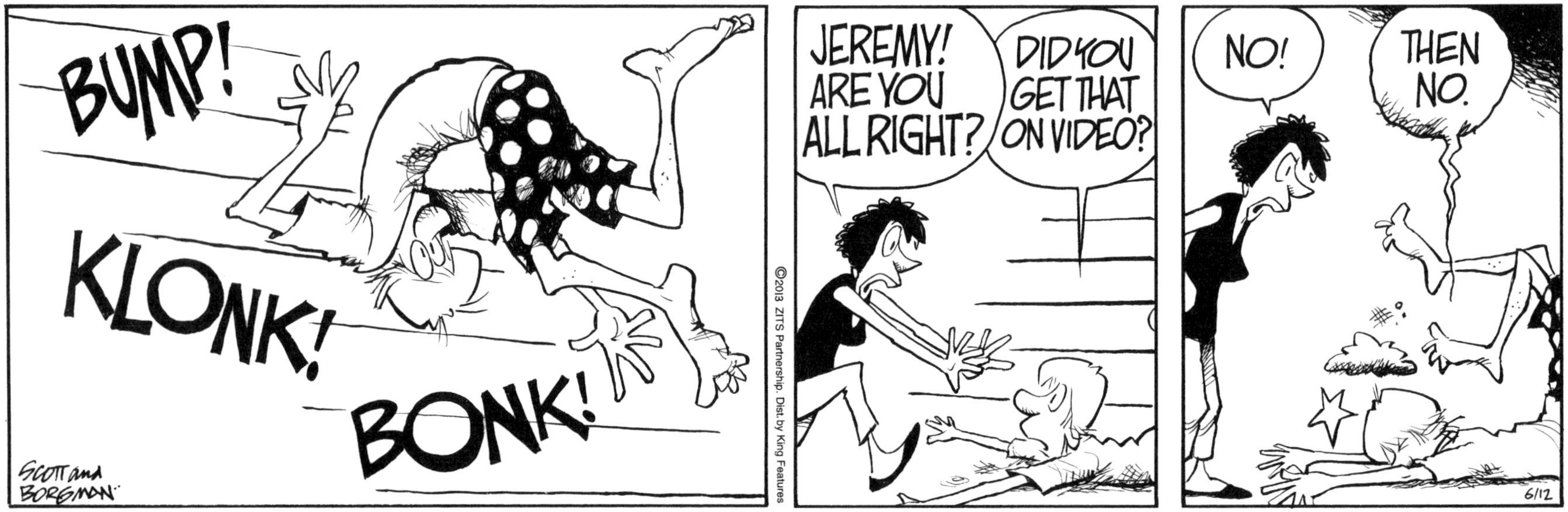
BUMP!
KLONK!
BONK!
SCOTT and BORGMAN
©2013 ZITS Partnership. Dist.by King Features
JEREMY! ARE YOU ALL RIGHT?
DID YOU GET THAT ON VIDEO?
NO!
THEN NO.
6/12

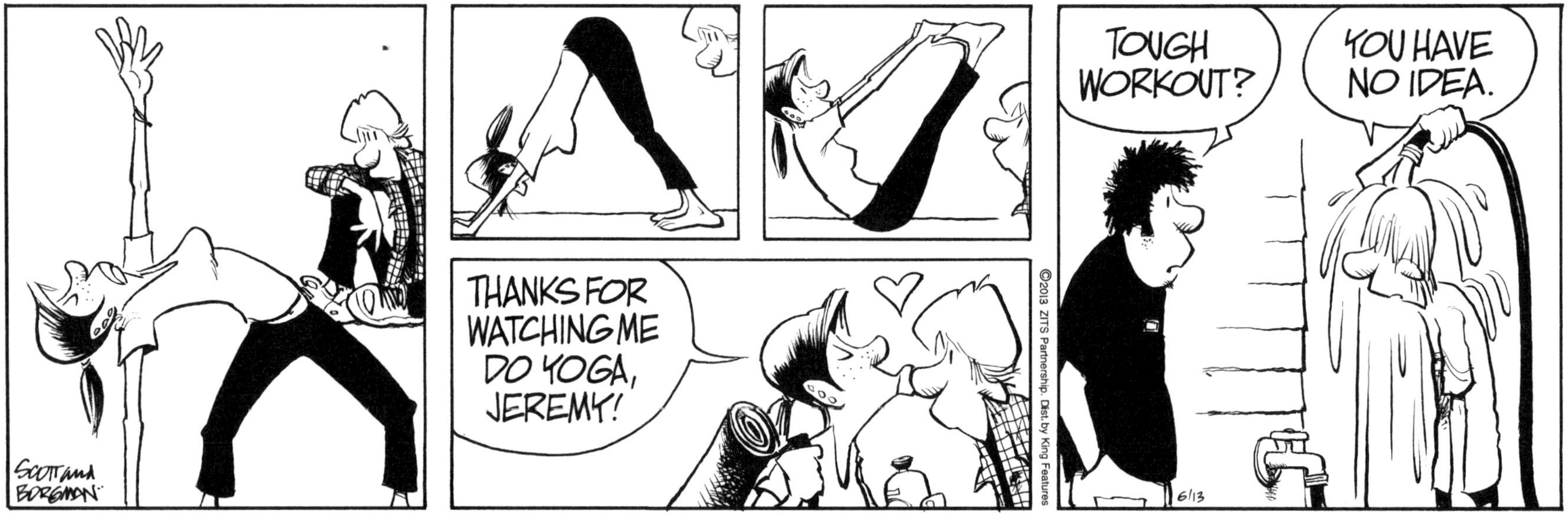
SCOTT and BORGMAN
THANKS FOR WATCHING ME DO YOGA, JEREMY!
©2013 ZITS Partnership. Dist.by King Features
TOUGH WORKOUT?
YOU HAVE NO IDEA.
6/13

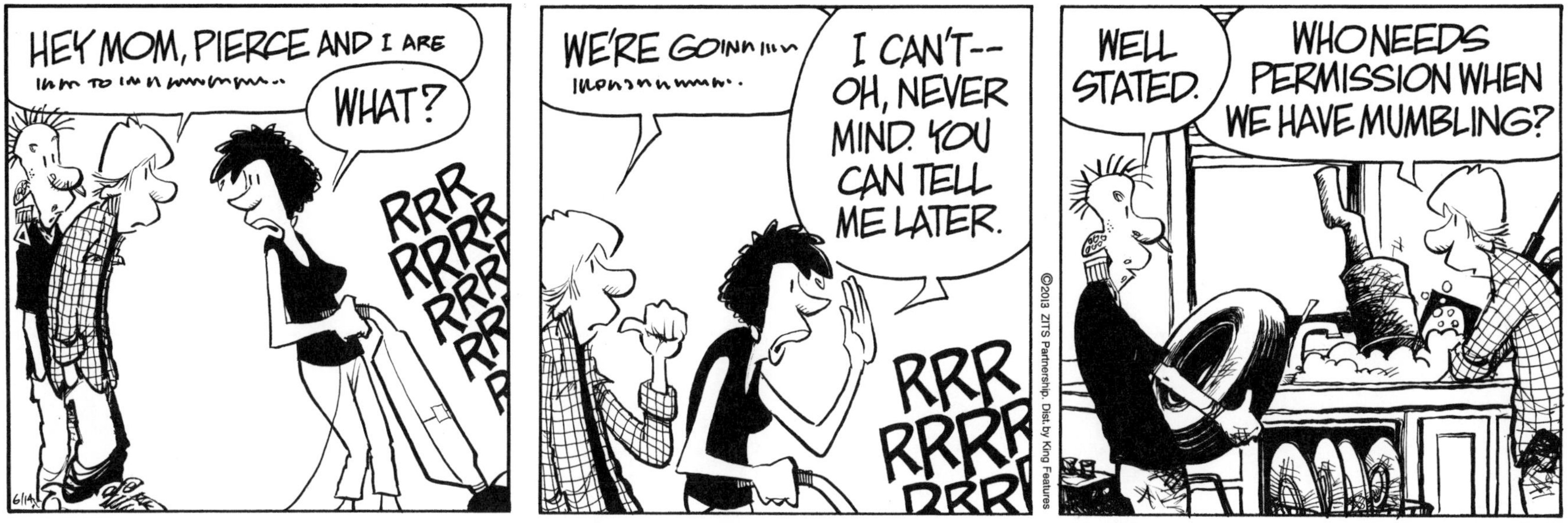

HEY MOM, PIERCE AND I ARE
WHAT?
RRR RRRR RRRR RRRR RRR R
WE'RE GOIN
I CAN'T-- OH, NEVER MIND. YOU CAN TELL ME LATER.
RRR RRRR RRR
©2013 ZITS Partnership. Dist. by King Features
WELL STATED.
WHO NEEDS PERMISSION WHEN WE HAVE MUMBLING?
6/14


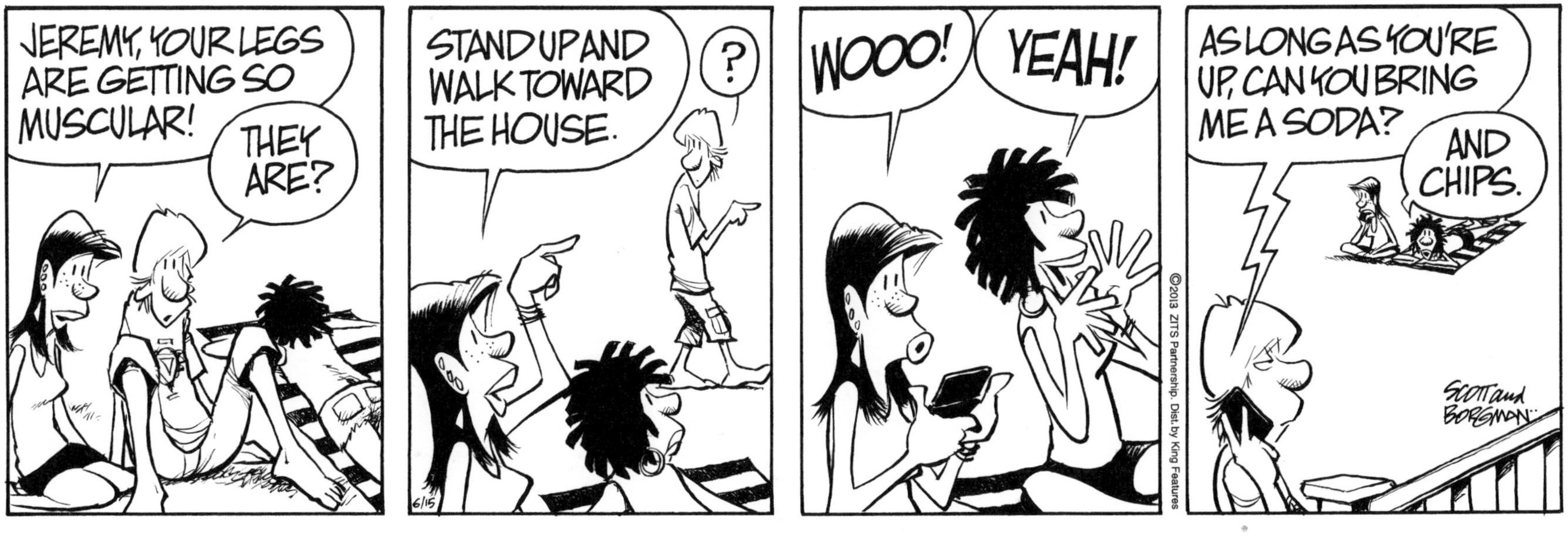

JEREMY, YOUR LEGS ARE GETTING SO MUSCULAR!
THEY ARE?
6/15
STAND UP AND WALK TOWARD THE HOUSE.
?
WOOO!
YEAH!
©2013 ZITS Partnership. Dist. by King Features
AS LONG AS YOU'RE UP, CAN YOU BRING ME A SODA?
AND CHIPS.
SCOTT and BORGMAN

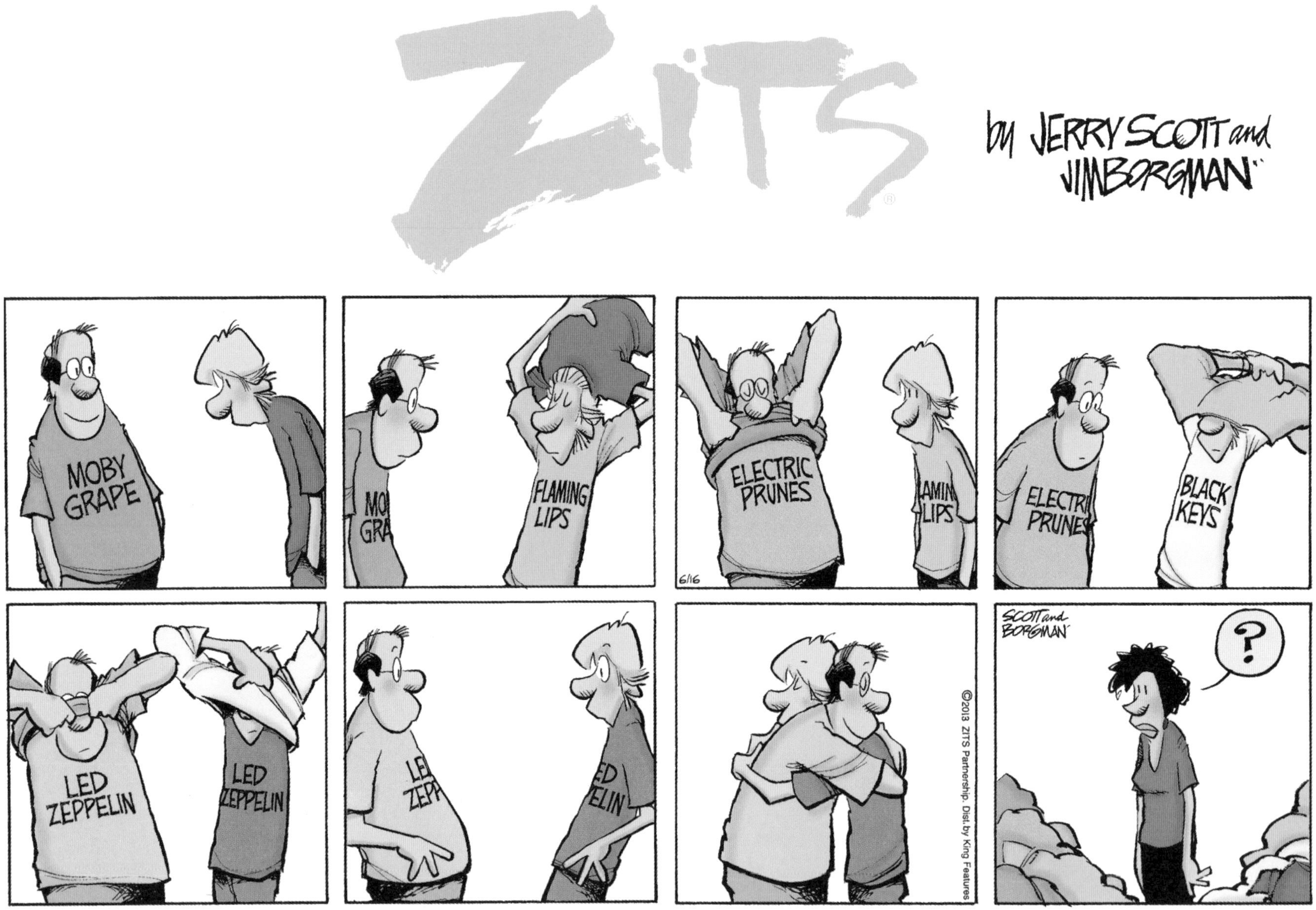
ZITS
by JERRY SCOTT and JIM BORGMAN
MOBY GRAPE
FLAMING LIPS
ELECTRIC PRUNES
6/16
BLACK KEYS
LED ZEPPELIN
LED ZEPPELIN
©2013 ZITS Partnership. Dist. by King Features
SCOTT and BORGMAN
?

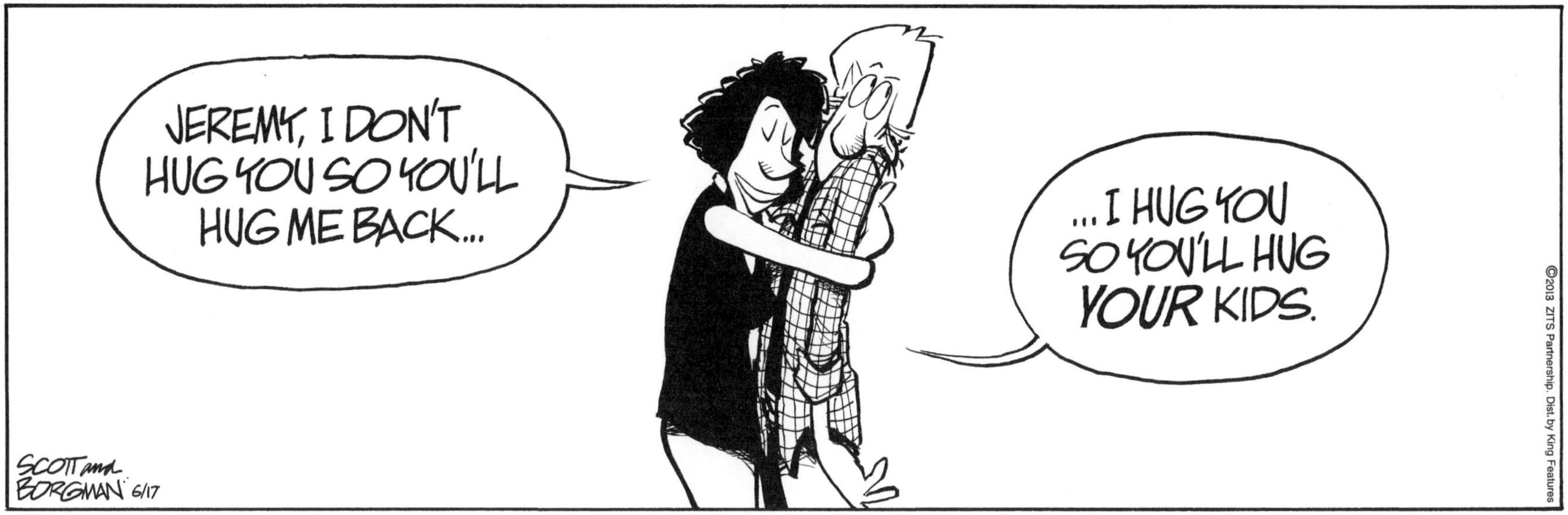
JEREMY, I DON'T HUG YOU SO YOU'LL HUG ME BACK...
...I HUG YOU SO YOU'LL HUG YOUR KIDS.
SCOTT and BORGMAN 6/17
©2013 ZITS Partnership. Dist. by King Features

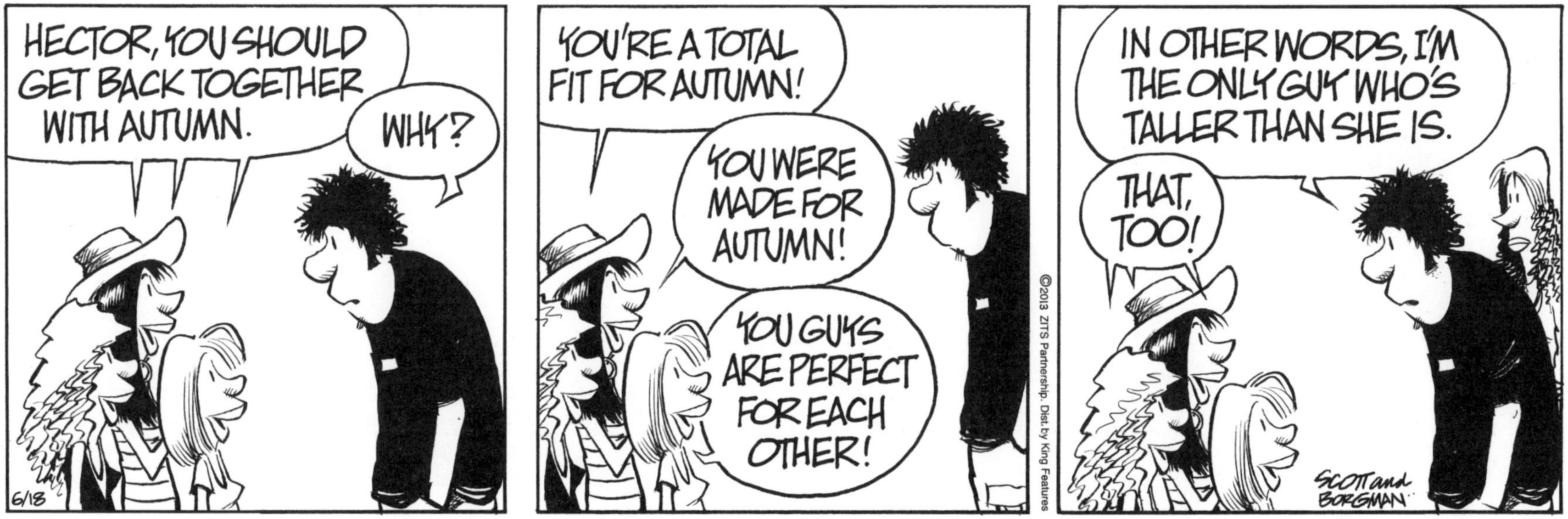
HECTOR, YOU SHOULD GET BACK TOGETHER WITH AUTUMN.
WHY?
6/18
YOU'RE A TOTAL FIT FOR AUTUMN!
YOU WERE MADE FOR AUTUMN!
YOU GUYS ARE PERFECT FOR EACH OTHER!
©2013 ZITS Partnership. Dist. by King Features
IN OTHER WORDS, I'M THE ONLY GUY WHO'S TALLER THAN SHE IS.
THAT, TOO!
SCOTT and BORGMAN

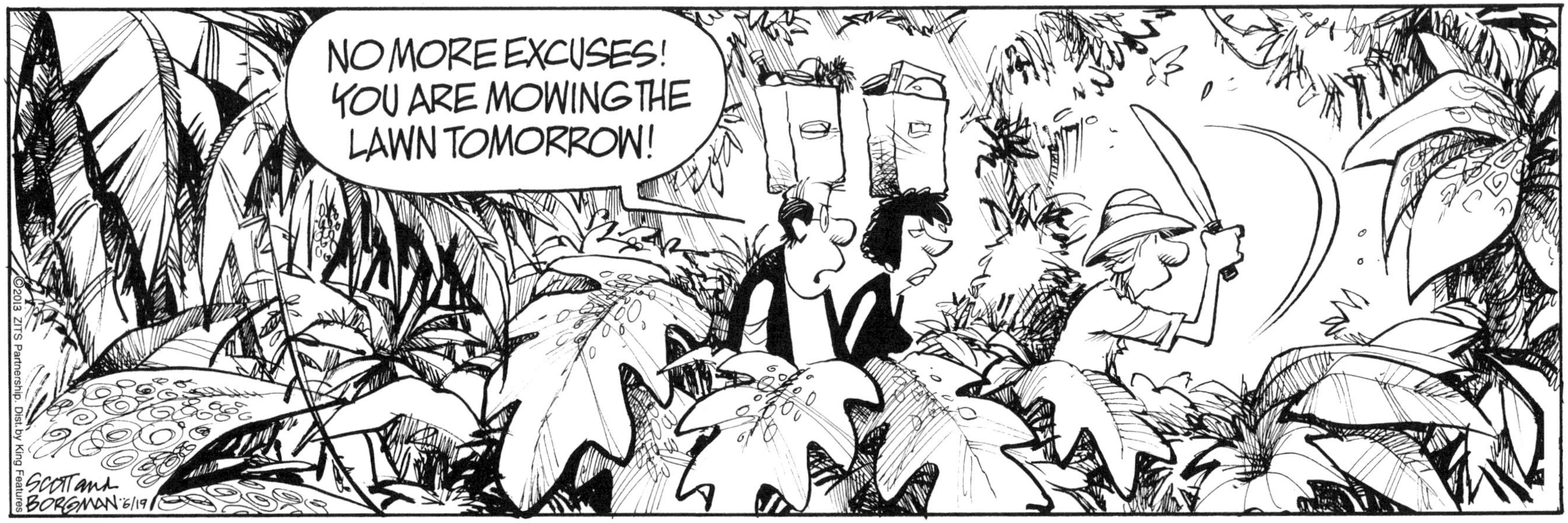
NO MORE EXCUSES! YOU ARE MOWING THE LAWN TOMORROW!
©2013 ZITS Partnership. Dist. by King Features
SCOTT and BORGMAN 6/19

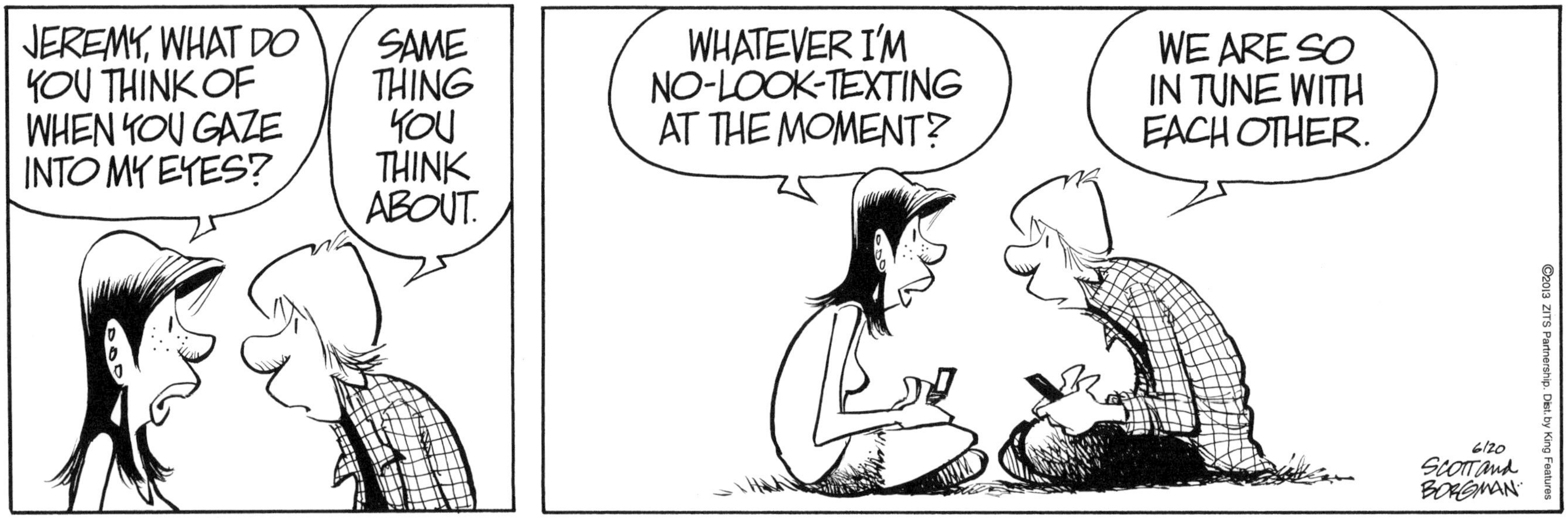
JEREMY, WHAT DO YOU THINK OF WHEN YOU GAZE INTO MY EYES?
SAME THING YOU THINK ABOUT.
WHATEVER I'M NO-LOOK-TEXTING AT THE MOMENT?
WE ARE SO IN TUNE WITH EACH OTHER.
©2013 ZITS Partnership. Dist. by King Features
6/20 SCOTT and BORGMAN

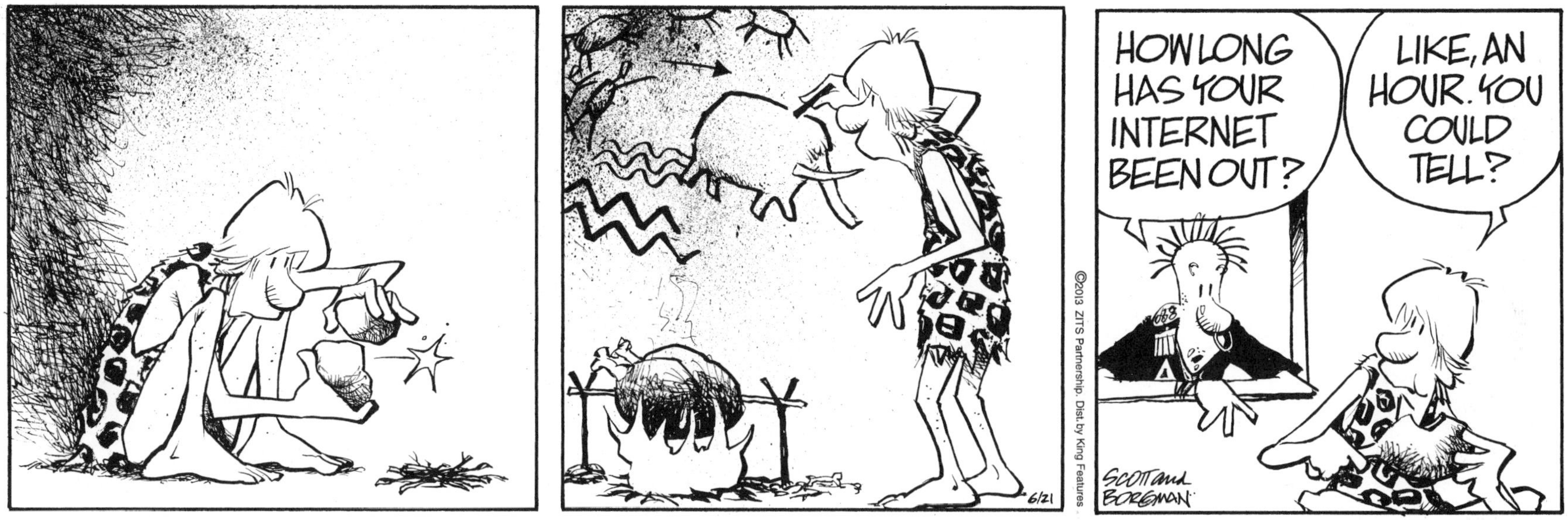
HOW LONG HAS YOUR INTERNET BEEN OUT?
LIKE, AN HOUR. YOU COULD TELL?
6/21
SCOTT and BORGMAN
©2013 ZITS Partnership. Dist. by King Features

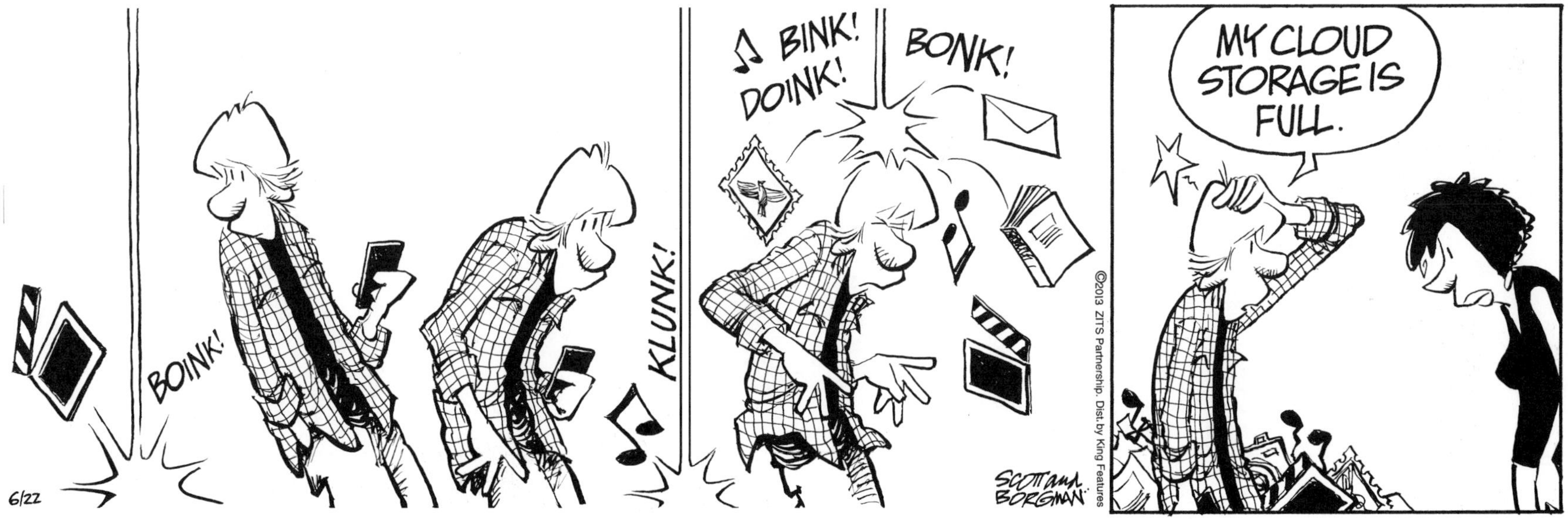
6/22
BOINK!
KLUNK!
BINK! DOINK!
BONK!
MY CLOUD STORAGE IS FULL.
SCOTT and BORGMAN
©2013 ZITS Partnership. Dist. by King Features

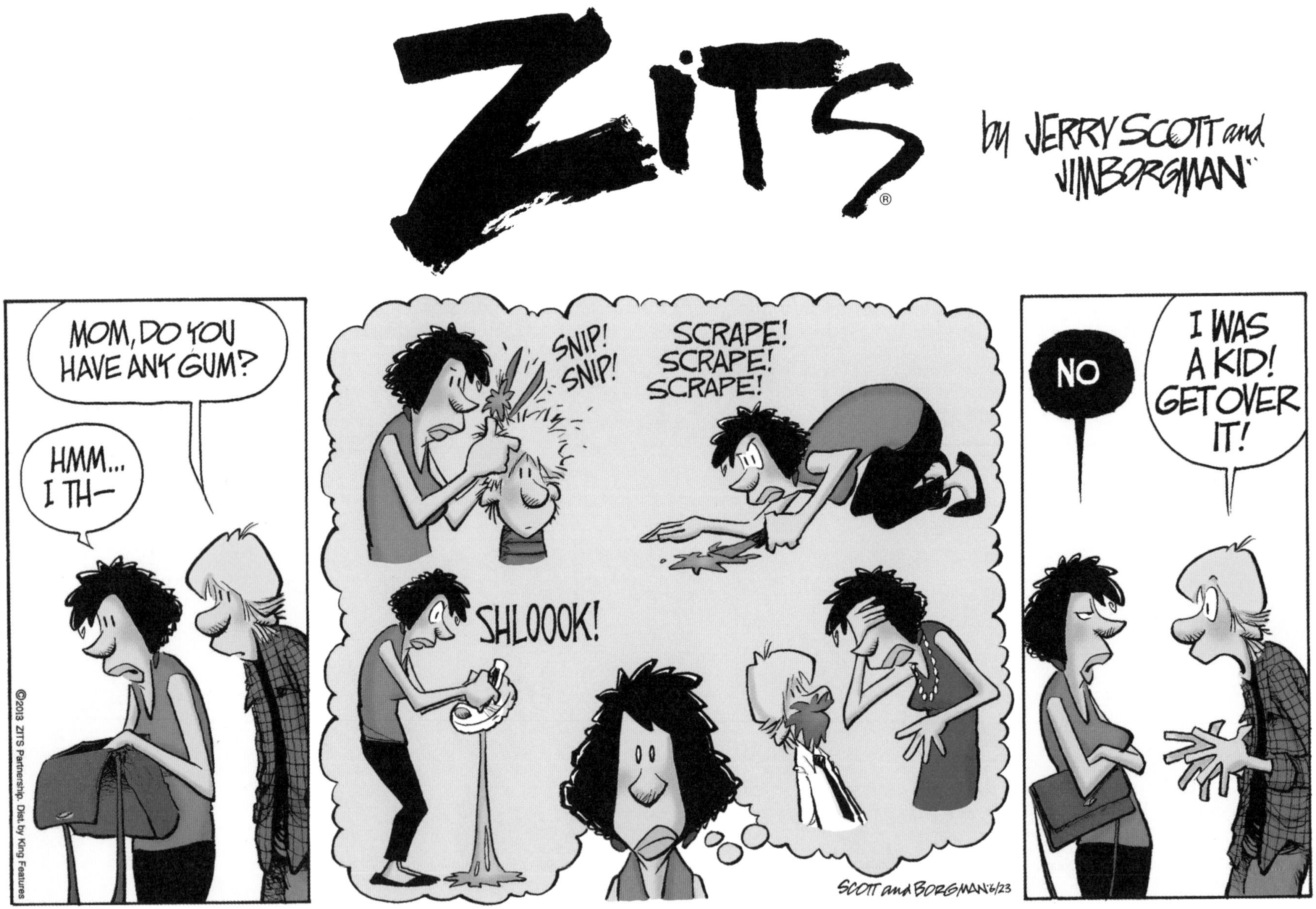
ZITS®
by JERRY SCOTT and JIM BORGMAN
MOM, DO YOU HAVE ANY GUM?
HMM... I TH—
SNIP! SNIP!
SCRAPE! SCRAPE! SCRAPE!
SHLOOOK!
NO
I WAS A KID! GET OVER IT!
SCOTT and BORGMAN 6/23
©2013 ZITS Partnership. Dist. by King Features

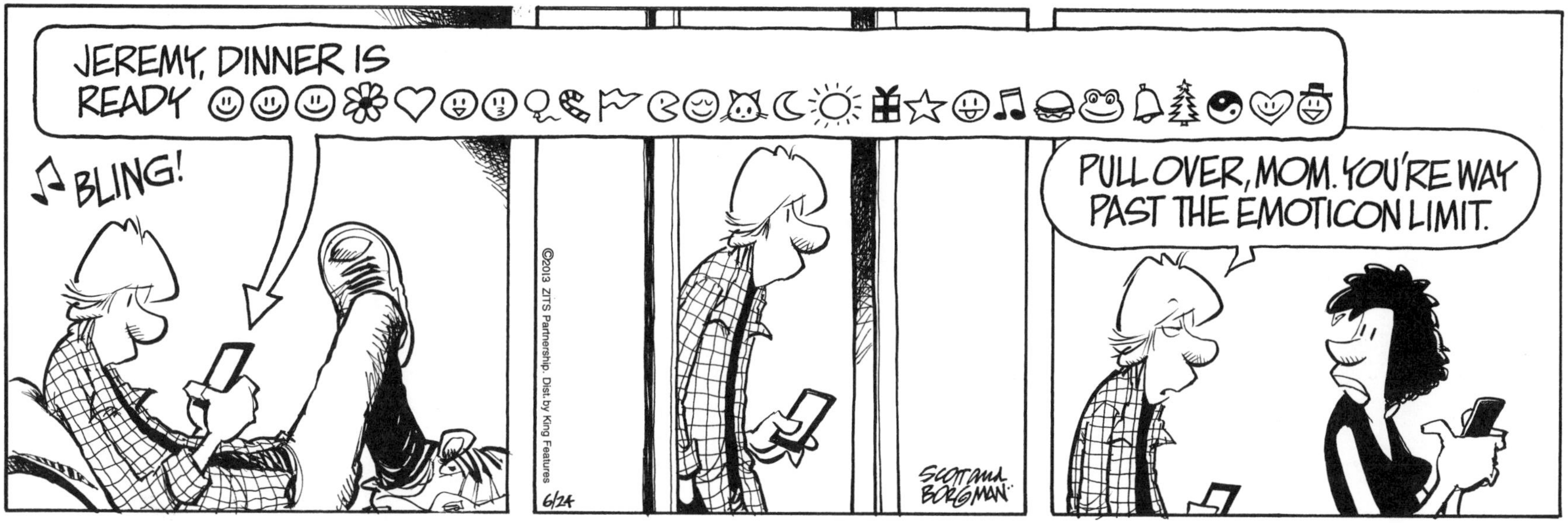
JEREMY, DINNER IS READY
BLING!
©2013 ZITS Partnership. Dist. by King Features
6/24
SCOTT and BORGMAN
PULL OVER, MOM. YOU'RE WAY PAST THE EMOTICON LIMIT.

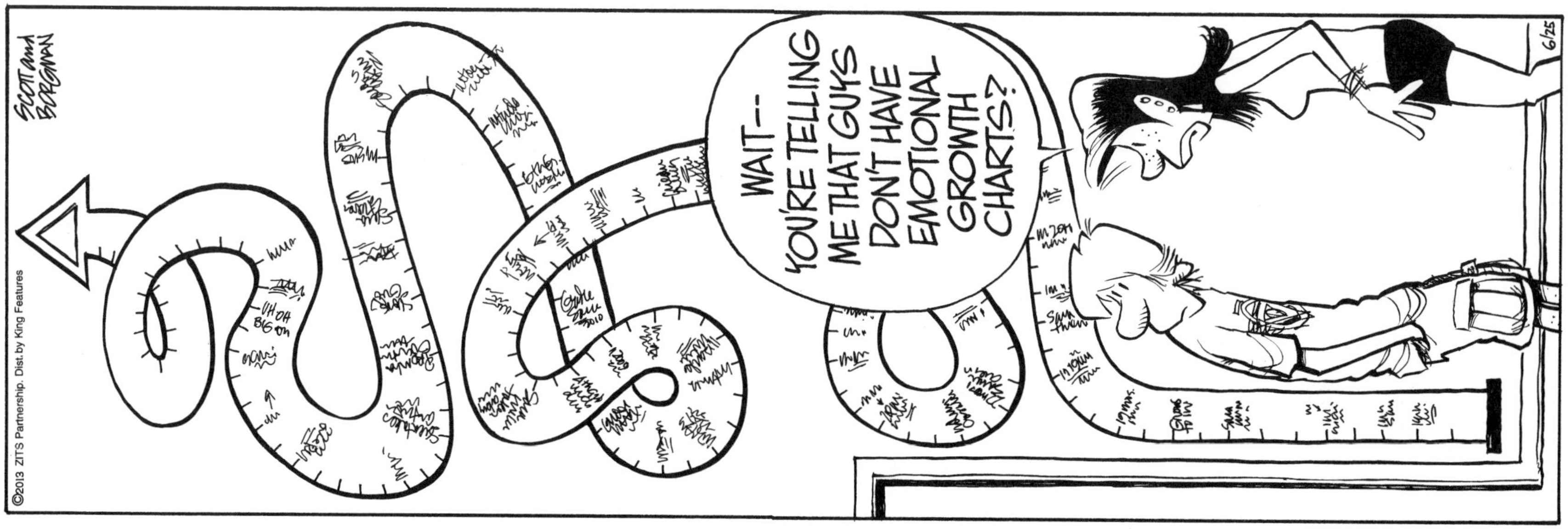
SCOTT and BORGMAN
6/25
WAIT— YOU'RE TELLING ME THAT GUYS DON'T HAVE EMOTIONAL GROWTH CHARTS?
©2013 ZITS Partnership. Dist. by King Features

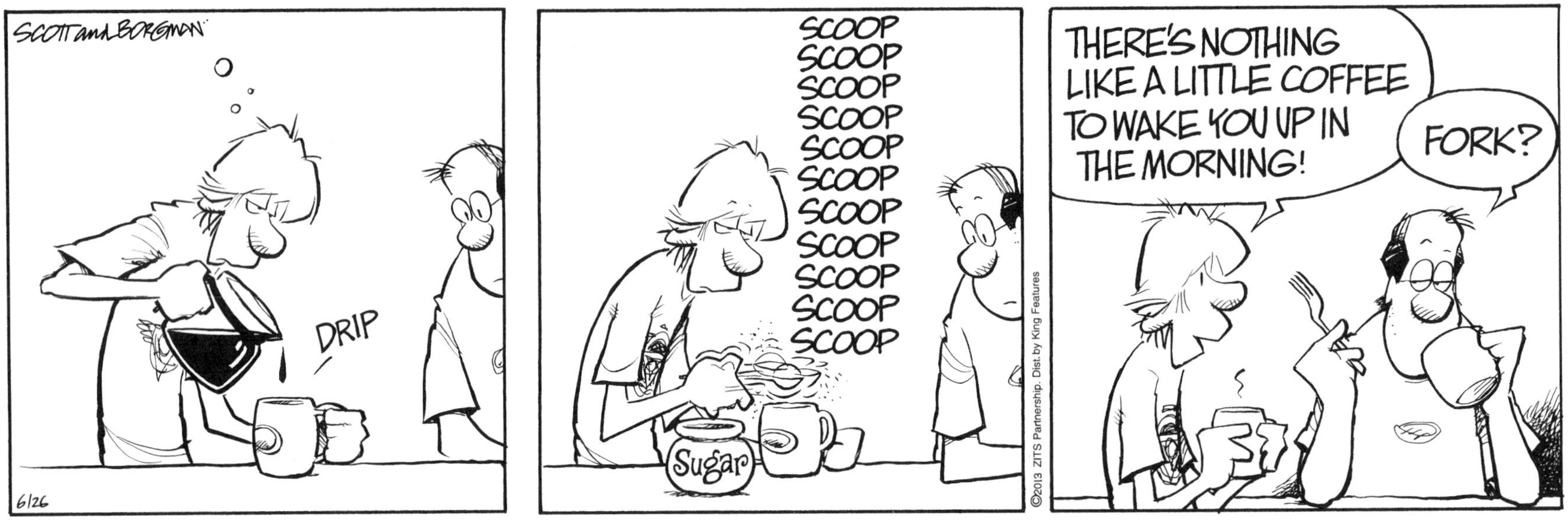
SCOTT and BORGMAN
DRIP
6/26
SCOOP SCOOP SCOOP SCOOP SCOOP SCOOP SCOOP SCOOP SCOOP SCOOP SCOOP
Sugar
©2013 ZITS Partnership. Dist. by King Features
THERE'S NOTHING LIKE A LITTLE COFFEE TO WAKE YOU UP IN THE MORNING!
FORK?

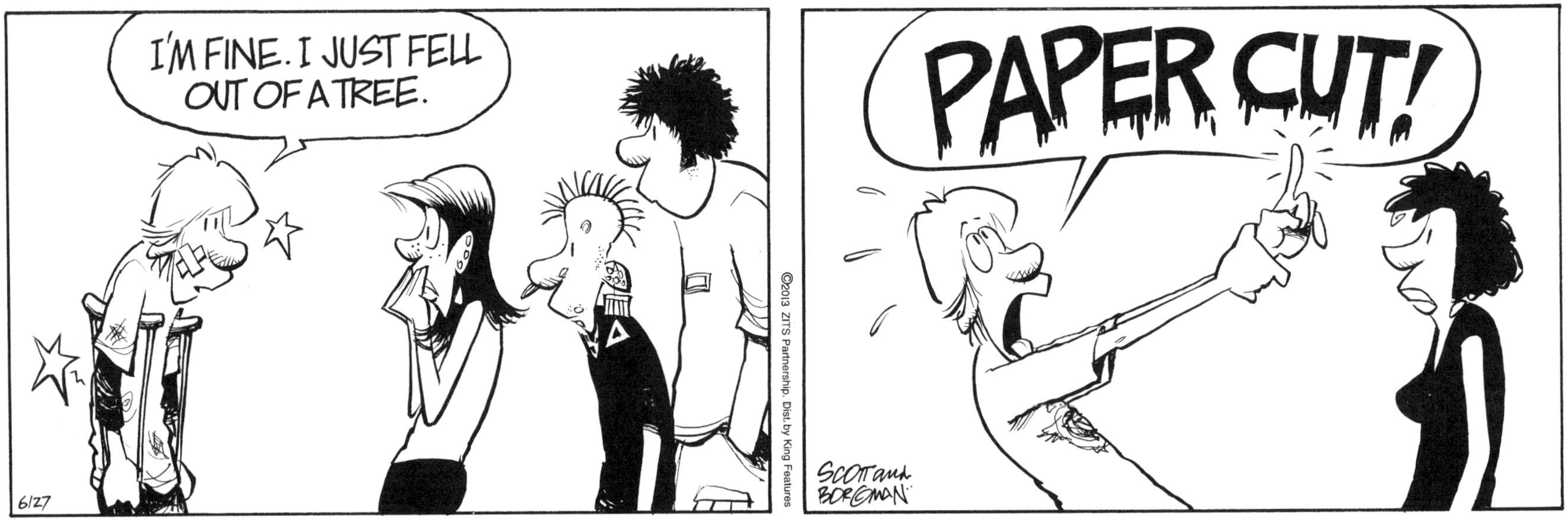
I'M FINE. I JUST FELL OUT OF A TREE.
6/27
©2013 ZITS Partnership. Dist. by King Features
PAPER CUT!
SCOTT and BORGMAN

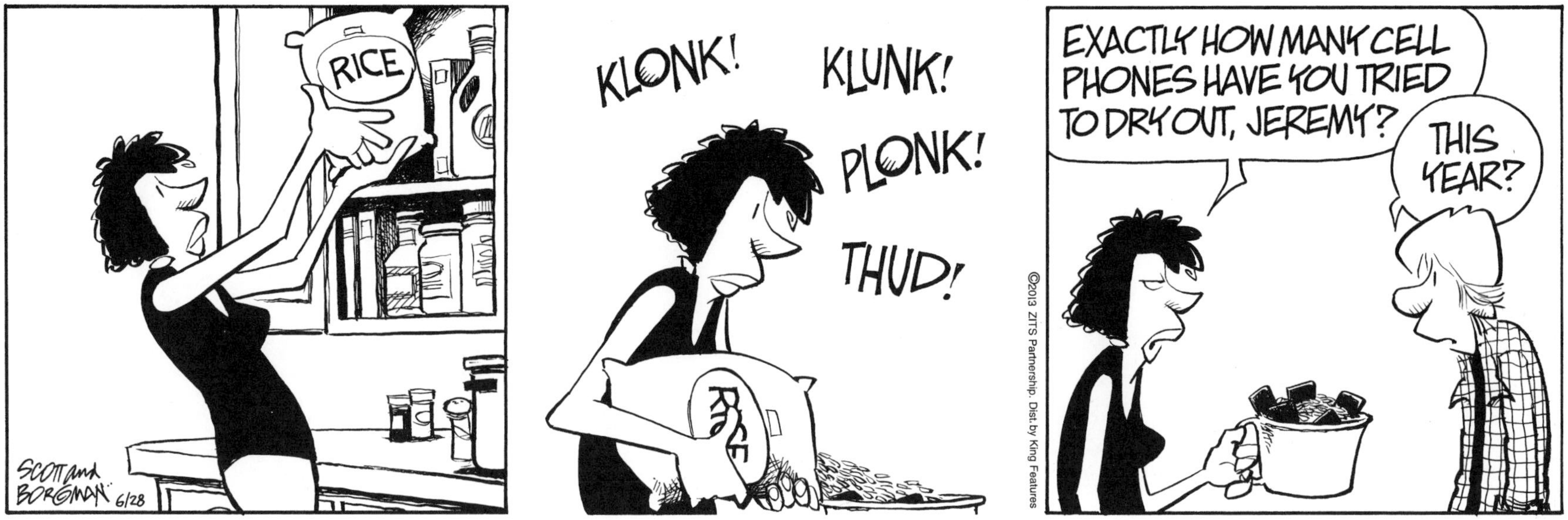
RICE
SCOTT and BORGMAN 6/28
KLONK!
KLUNK!
PLONK!
THUD!
RICE
©2013 ZITS Partnership. Dist. by King Features
EXACTLY HOW MANY CELL PHONES HAVE YOU TRIED TO DRY OUT, JEREMY?
THIS YEAR?

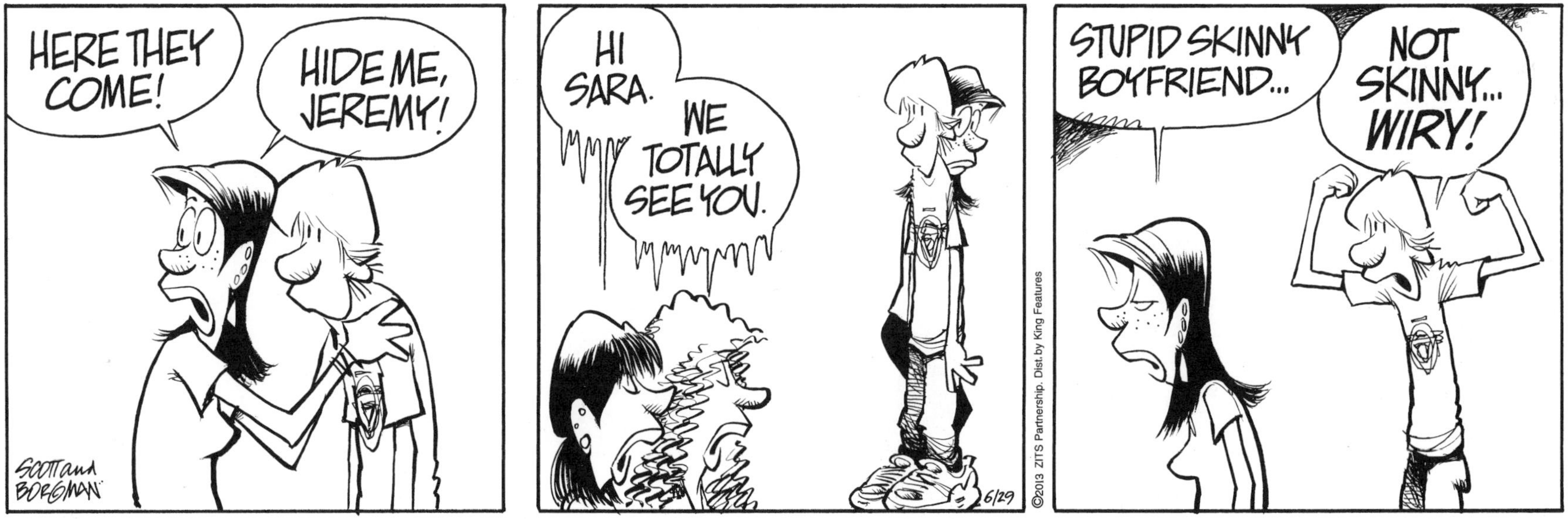
HERE THEY COME!
HIDE ME, JEREMY!
SCOTT and BORGMAN
HI SARA.
WE TOTALLY SEE YOU.
6/29
©2013 ZITS Partnership. Dist. by King Features
STUPID SKINNY BOYFRIEND...
NOT SKINNY... *WIRY!*

# ZITS

by JERRY SCOTT and JIM BORGMAN

DAD, I'M OUT OF SHAMPOO.
USE SOME OF MINE.
6/30
THANKS.
MM HMM
SCOTT and BORGMAN
CONTAINS VOLUMIZER, RIGHT?
SURE, OTHERWISE I'D LOOK BALD.

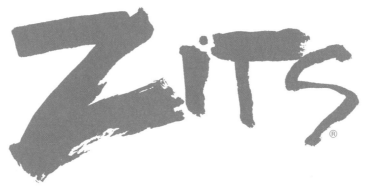

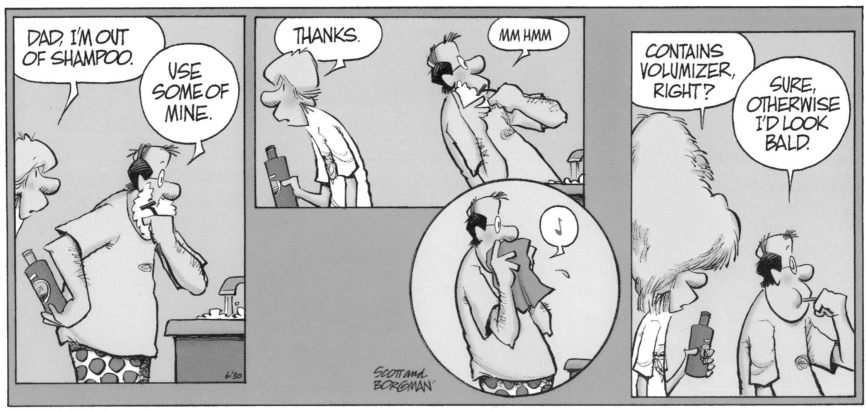

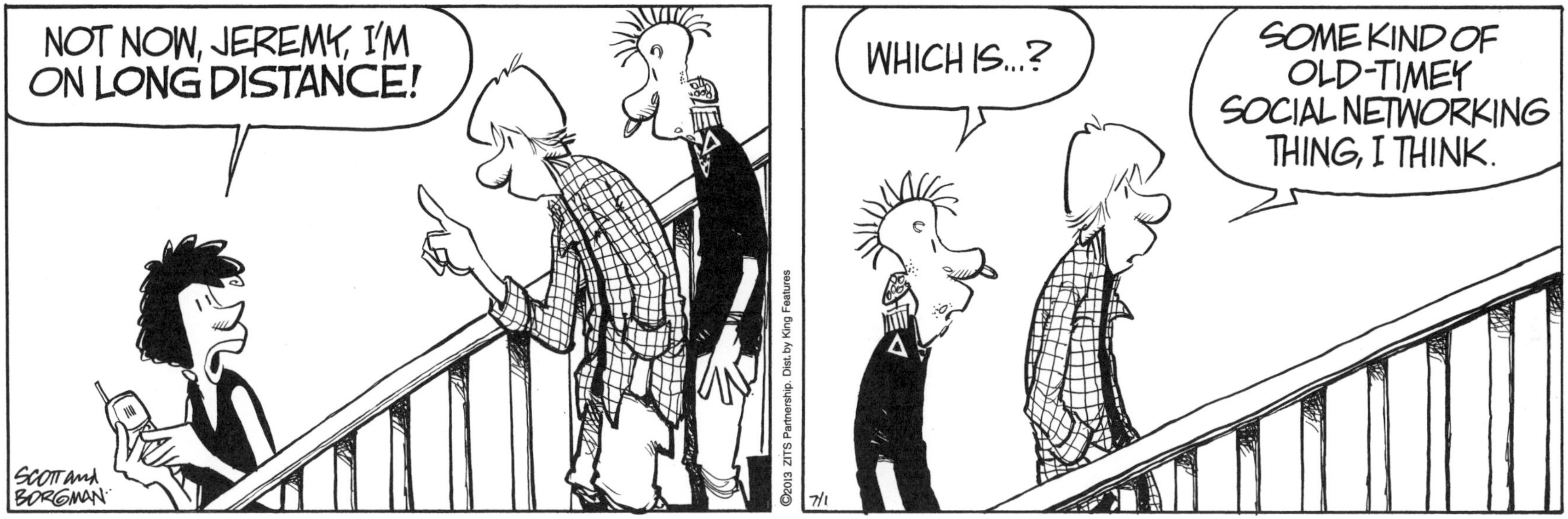
NOT NOW, JEREMY, I'M ON LONG DISTANCE!
SCOTT and BORGMAN
©2013 ZITS Partnership. Dist. by King Features
7/1
WHICH IS...?
SOME KIND OF OLD-TIMEY SOCIAL NETWORKING THING, I THINK.

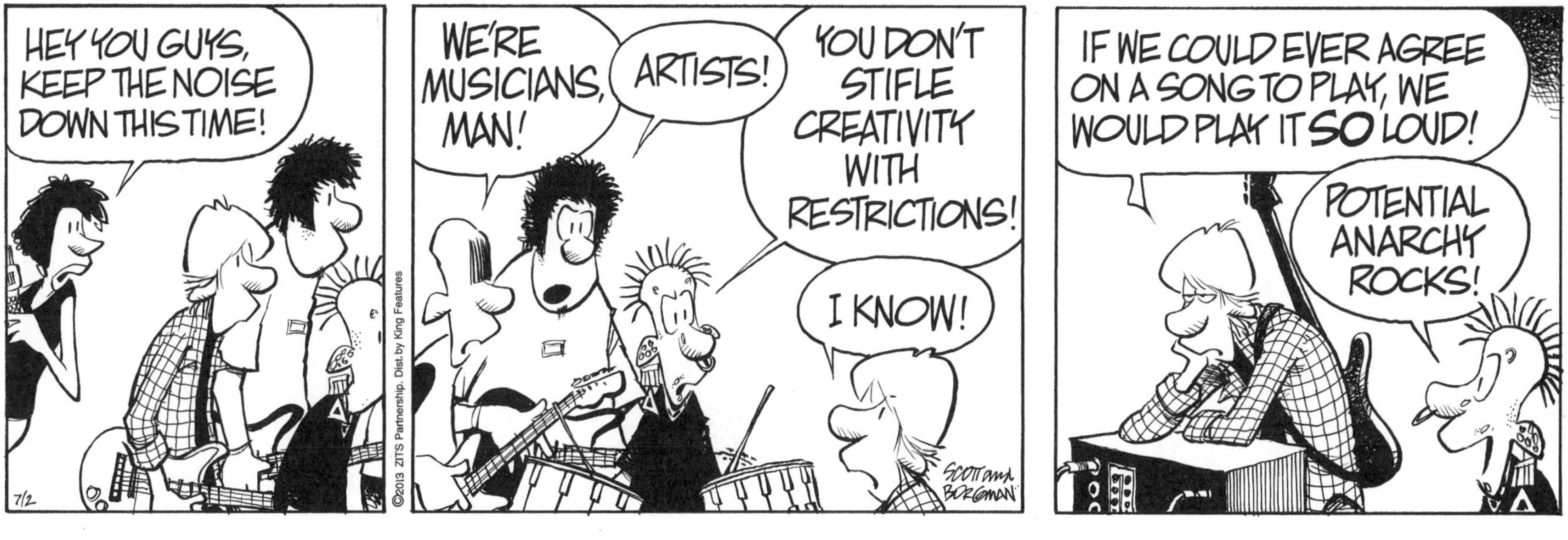
HEY YOU GUYS, KEEP THE NOISE DOWN THIS TIME!
7/2
©2013 ZITS Partnership. Dist. by King Features
WE'RE MUSICIANS, MAN!
ARTISTS!
YOU DON'T STIFLE CREATIVITY WITH RESTRICTIONS!
I KNOW!
SCOTT and BORGMAN
IF WE COULD EVER AGREE ON A SONG TO PLAY, WE WOULD PLAY IT SO LOUD!
POTENTIAL ANARCHY ROCKS!

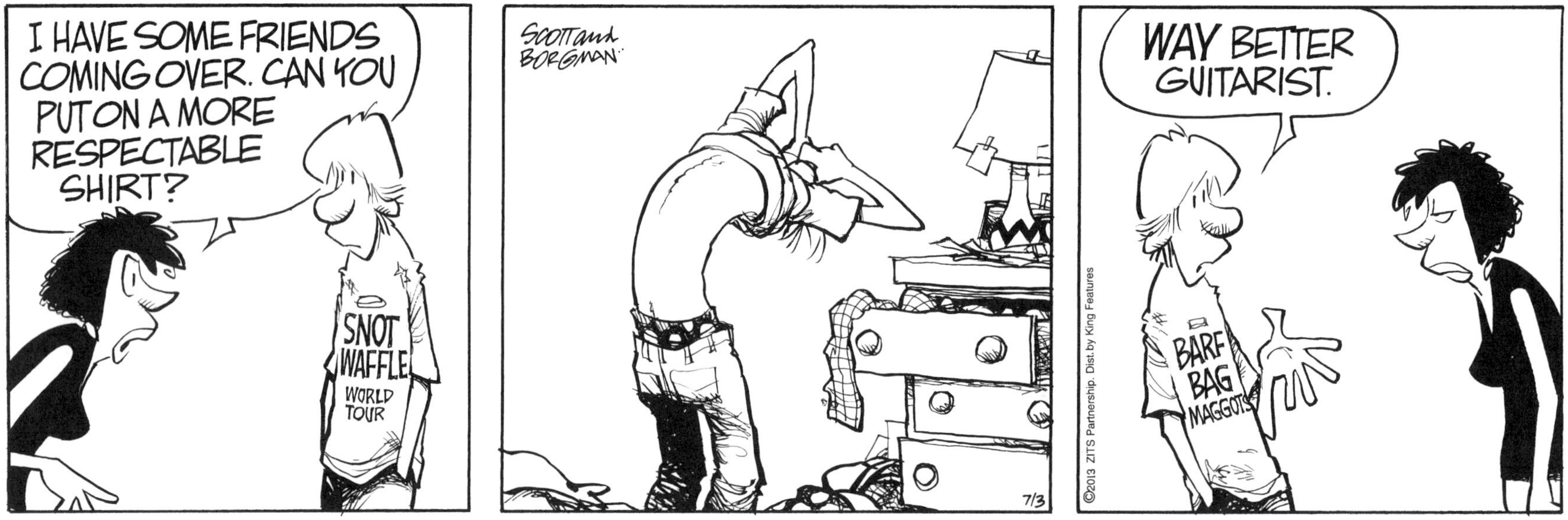
I HAVE SOME FRIENDS COMING OVER. CAN YOU PUT ON A MORE RESPECTABLE SHIRT?
SNOT WAFFLE WORLD TOUR
SCOTT and BORGMAN
7/3
WAY BETTER GUITARIST.
BARF BAG MAGGOTS
©2013 ZITS Partnership. Dist.by King Features

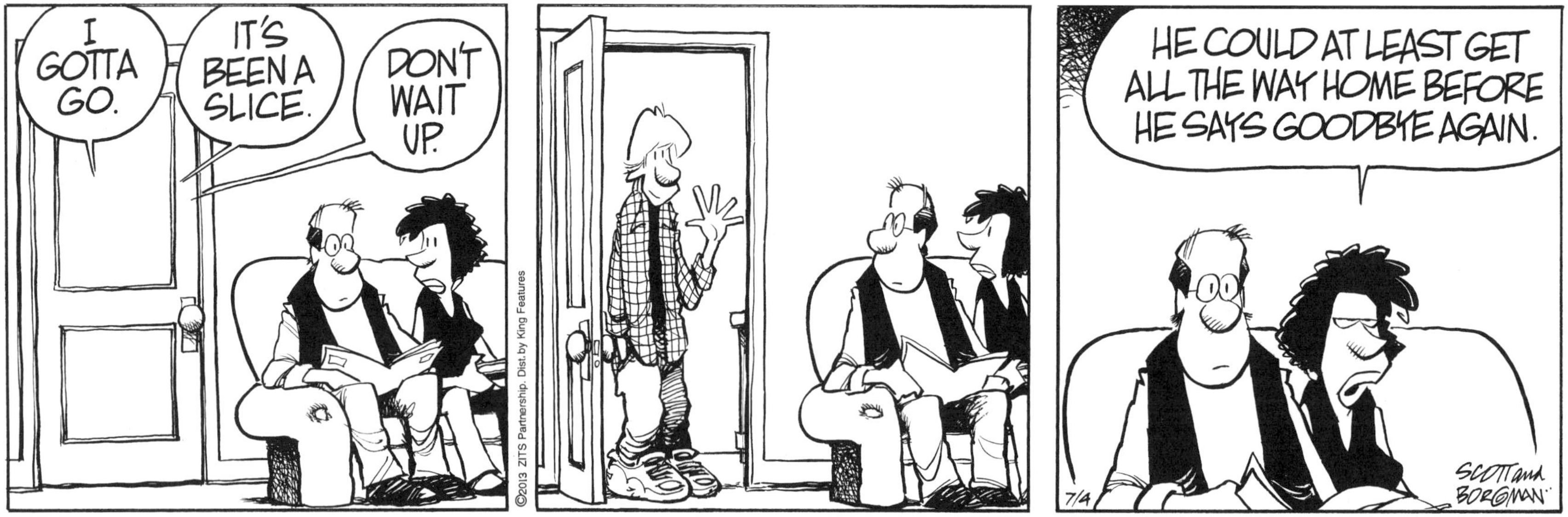
I GOTTA GO.
IT'S BEEN A SLICE.
DON'T WAIT UP.
©2013 ZITS Partnership. Dist.by King Features
HE COULD AT LEAST GET ALL THE WAY HOME BEFORE HE SAYS GOODBYE AGAIN.
7/4
SCOTT and BORGMAN

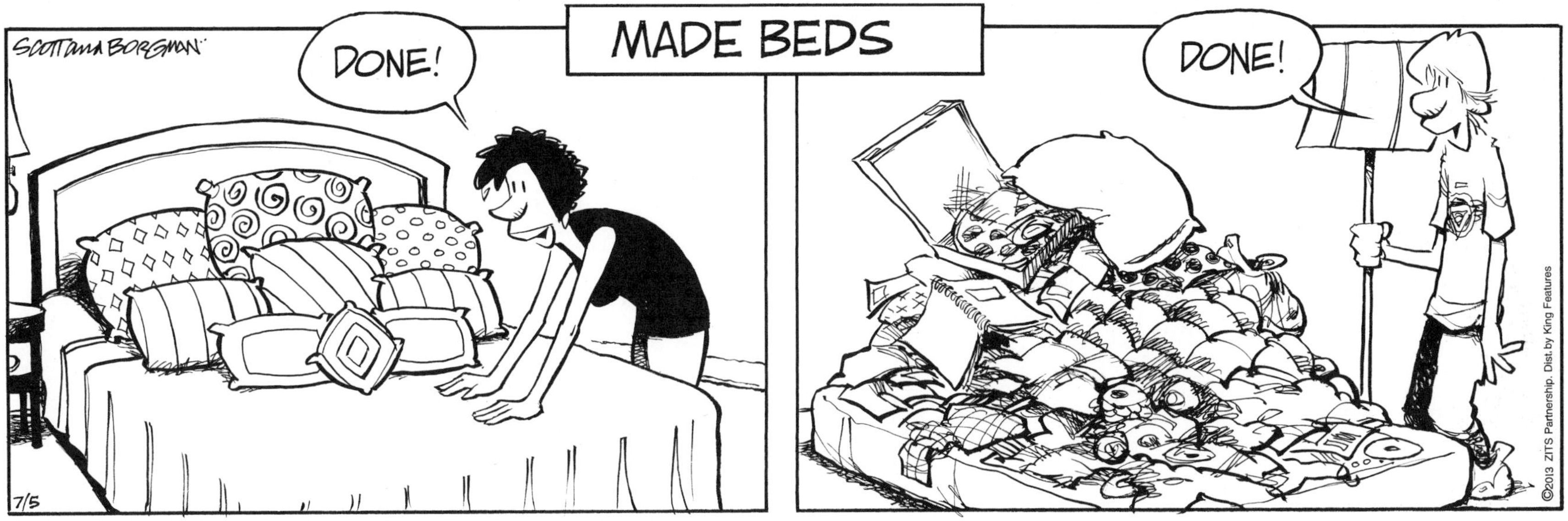
MADE BEDS
SCOTT and BORGMAN
DONE!
7/5
DONE!
©2013 ZITS Partnership. Dist. by King Features

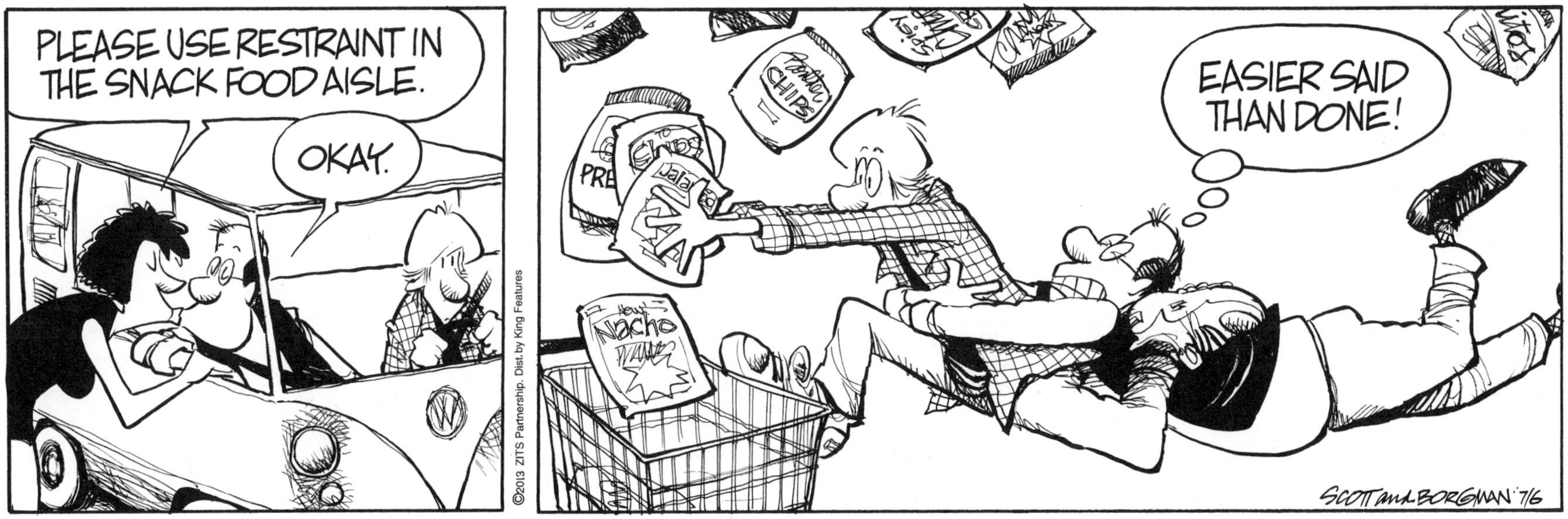
PLEASE USE RESTRAINT IN THE SNACK FOOD AISLE.
OKAY.
©2013 ZITS Partnership. Dist. by King Features
EASIER SAID THAN DONE!
SCOTT and BORGMAN 7/6

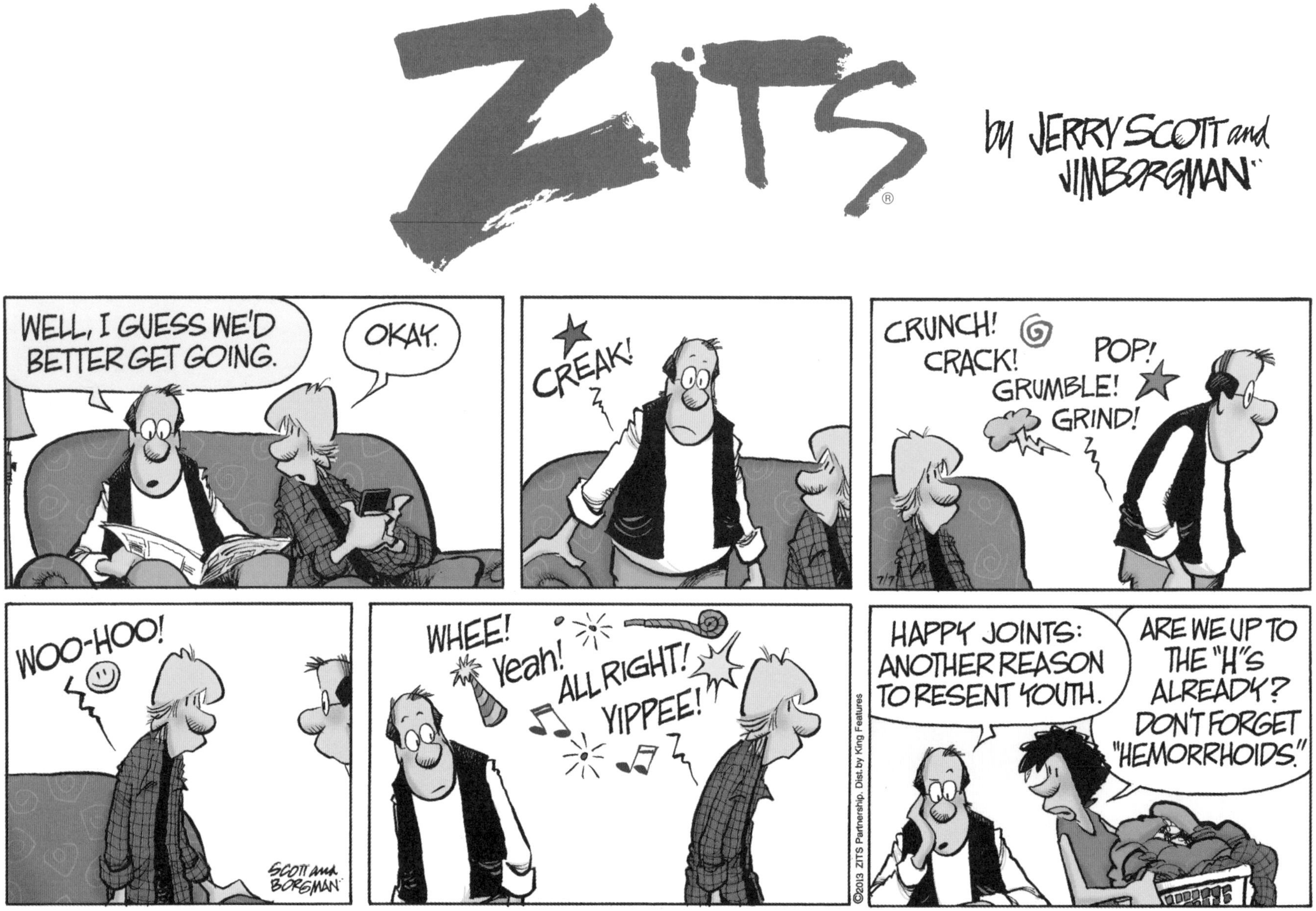
ZITS®
by JERRY SCOTT and JIM BORGMAN
WELL, I GUESS WE'D BETTER GET GOING.
OKAY.
CREAK!
CRUNCH! CRACK! POP! GRUMBLE! GRIND!
WOO-HOO!
SCOTT and BORGMAN
WHEE! Yeah! ALL RIGHT! YIPPEE!
©2013 ZITS Partnership. Dist. by King Features
HAPPY JOINTS: ANOTHER REASON TO RESENT YOUTH.
ARE WE UP TO THE "H"S ALREADY? DON'T FORGET "HEMORRHOIDS."

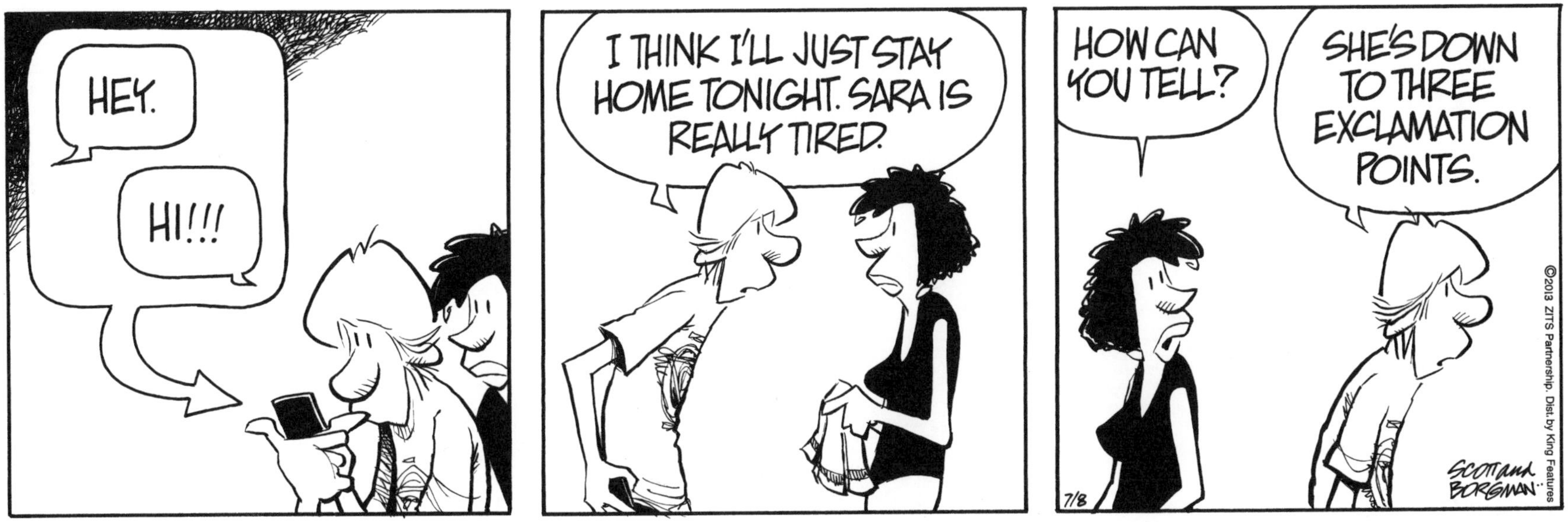
HEY.
HI!!!
I THINK I'LL JUST STAY HOME TONIGHT. SARA IS REALLY TIRED.
HOW CAN YOU TELL?
SHE'S DOWN TO THREE EXCLAMATION POINTS.
7/8
SCOTT and BORGMAN
©2013 ZITS Partnership. Dist. by King Features

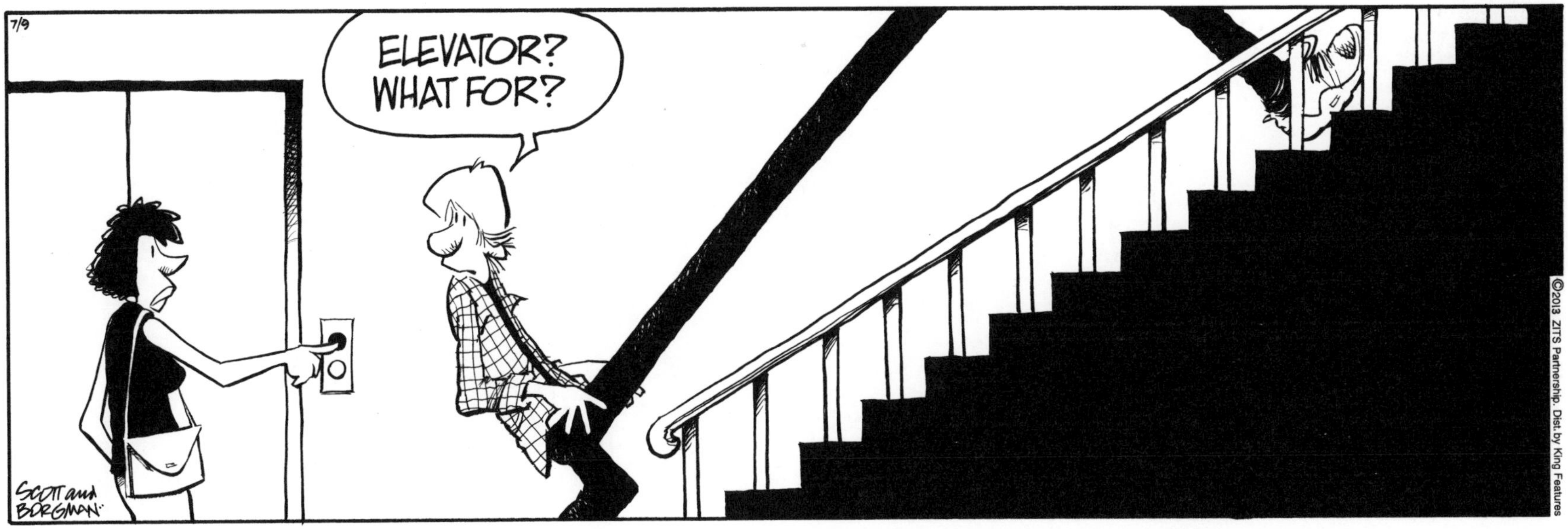
7/9
ELEVATOR? WHAT FOR?
SCOTT and BORGMAN
©2013 ZITS Partnership. Dist. by King Features

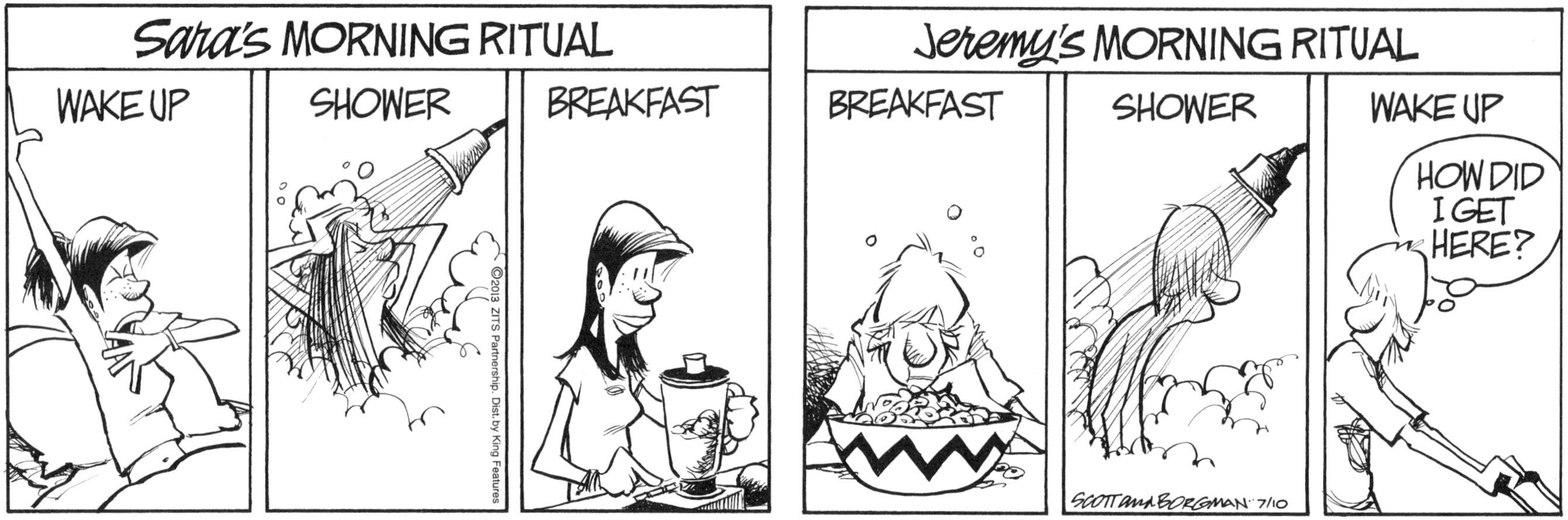
Sara's MORNING RITUAL
WAKE UP
SHOWER
BREAKFAST
Jeremy's MORNING RITUAL
BREAKFAST
SHOWER
WAKE UP
HOW DID I GET HERE?
©2013 ZITS Partnership. Dist. by King Features
SCOTT AND BORGMAN 7/10

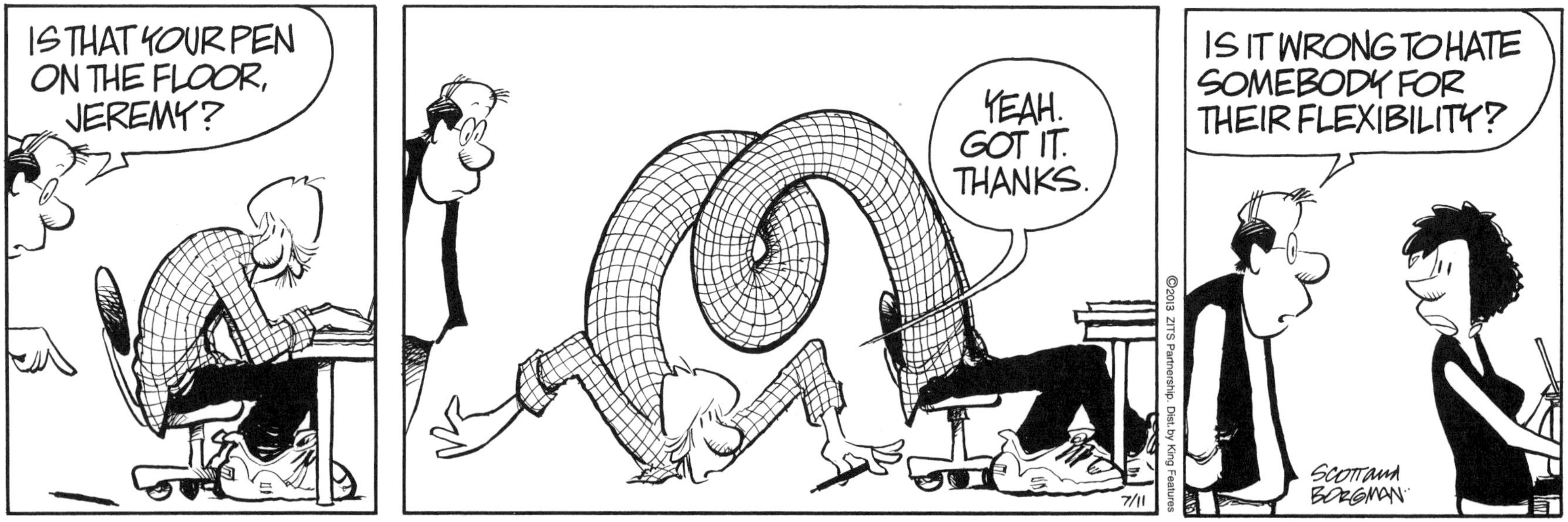
IS THAT YOUR PEN ON THE FLOOR, JEREMY?
YEAH. GOT IT. THANKS.
IS IT WRONG TO HATE SOMEBODY FOR THEIR FLEXIBILITY?
©2013 ZITS Partnership. Dist. by King Features
7/11
SCOTT AND BORGMAN

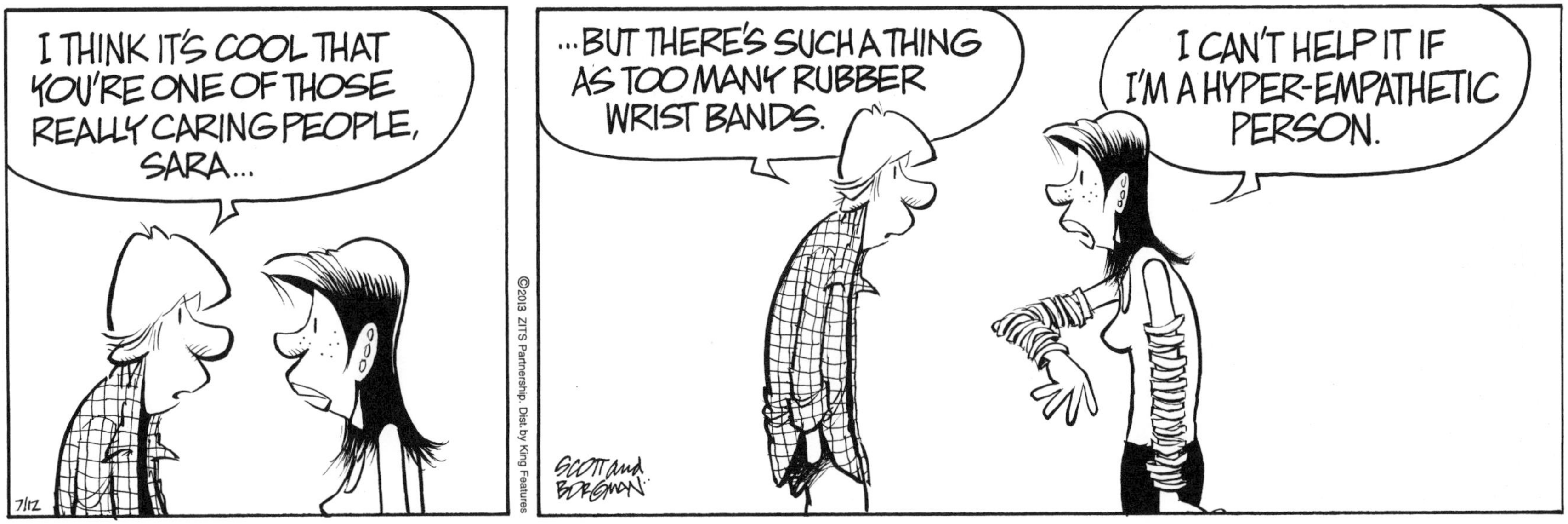
I THINK IT'S COOL THAT YOU'RE ONE OF THOSE REALLY CARING PEOPLE, SARA...
...BUT THERE'S SUCH A THING AS TOO MANY RUBBER WRIST BANDS.
I CAN'T HELP IT IF I'M A HYPER-EMPATHETIC PERSON.
7/12
©2013 ZITS Partnership. Dist. by King Features
SCOTT and BORGMAN

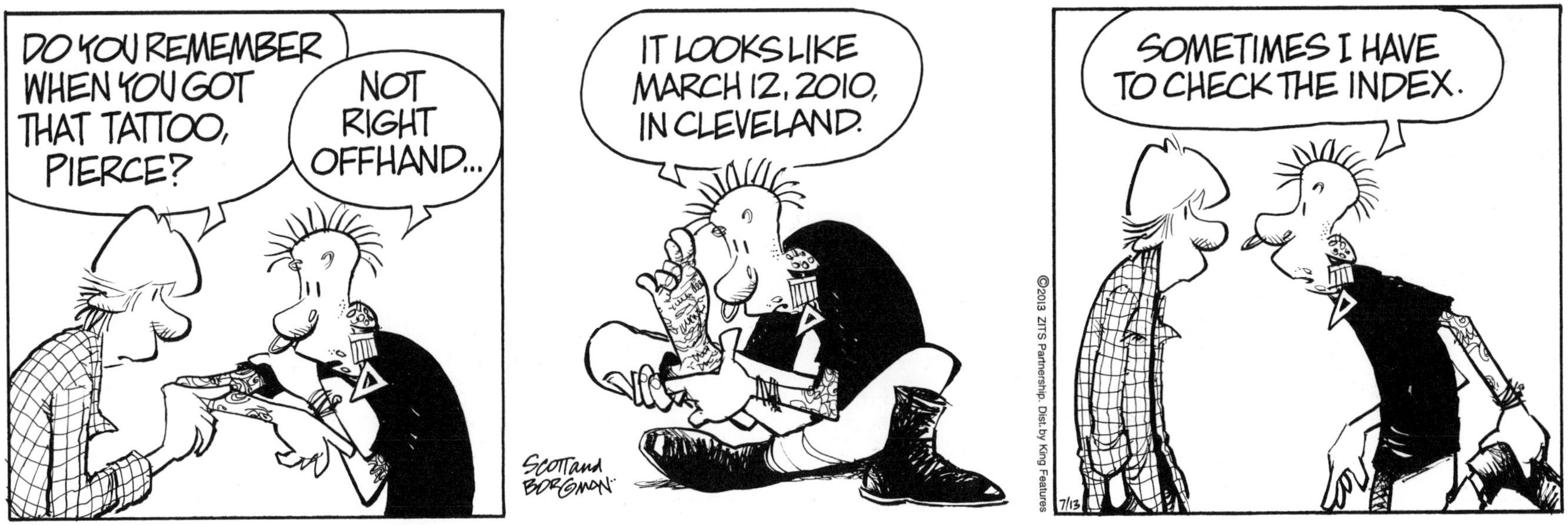
DO YOU REMEMBER WHEN YOU GOT THAT TATTOO, PIERCE?
NOT RIGHT OFFHAND...
IT LOOKS LIKE MARCH 12, 2010, IN CLEVELAND.
SOMETIMES I HAVE TO CHECK THE INDEX.
SCOTT and BORGMAN
©2013 ZITS Partnership. Dist. by King Features
7/13

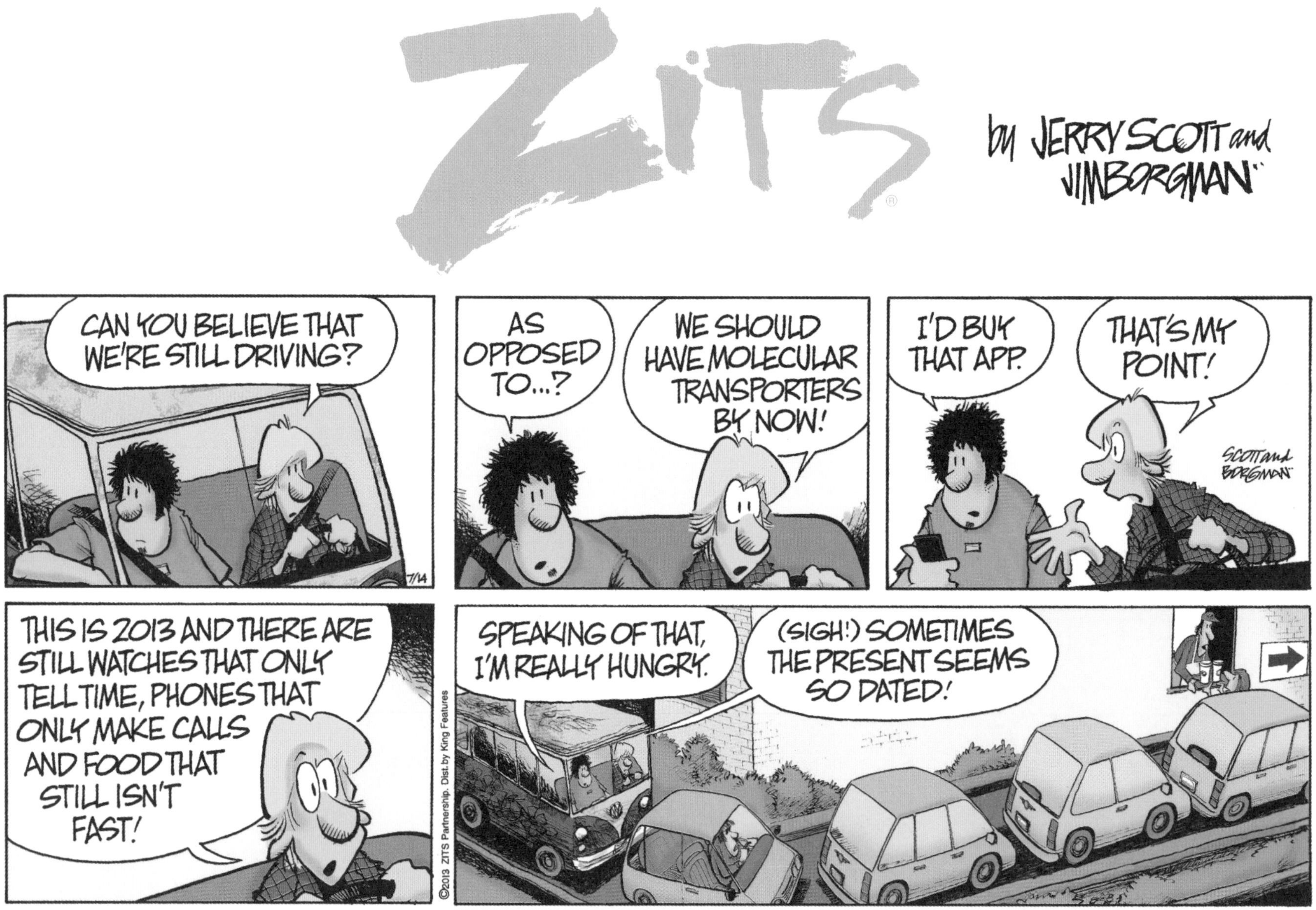
ZITS
by JERRY SCOTT and JIM BORGMAN
CAN YOU BELIEVE THAT WE'RE STILL DRIVING?
7/14
AS OPPOSED TO...?
WE SHOULD HAVE MOLECULAR TRANSPORTERS BY NOW!
I'D BUY THAT APP.
THAT'S MY POINT!
SCOTT and BORGMAN
THIS IS 2013 AND THERE ARE STILL WATCHES THAT ONLY TELL TIME, PHONES THAT ONLY MAKE CALLS AND FOOD THAT STILL ISN'T FAST!
©2013 ZITS Partnership. Dist. by King Features
SPEAKING OF THAT, I'M REALLY HUNGRY.
(SIGH!) SOMETIMES THE PRESENT SEEMS SO DATED!

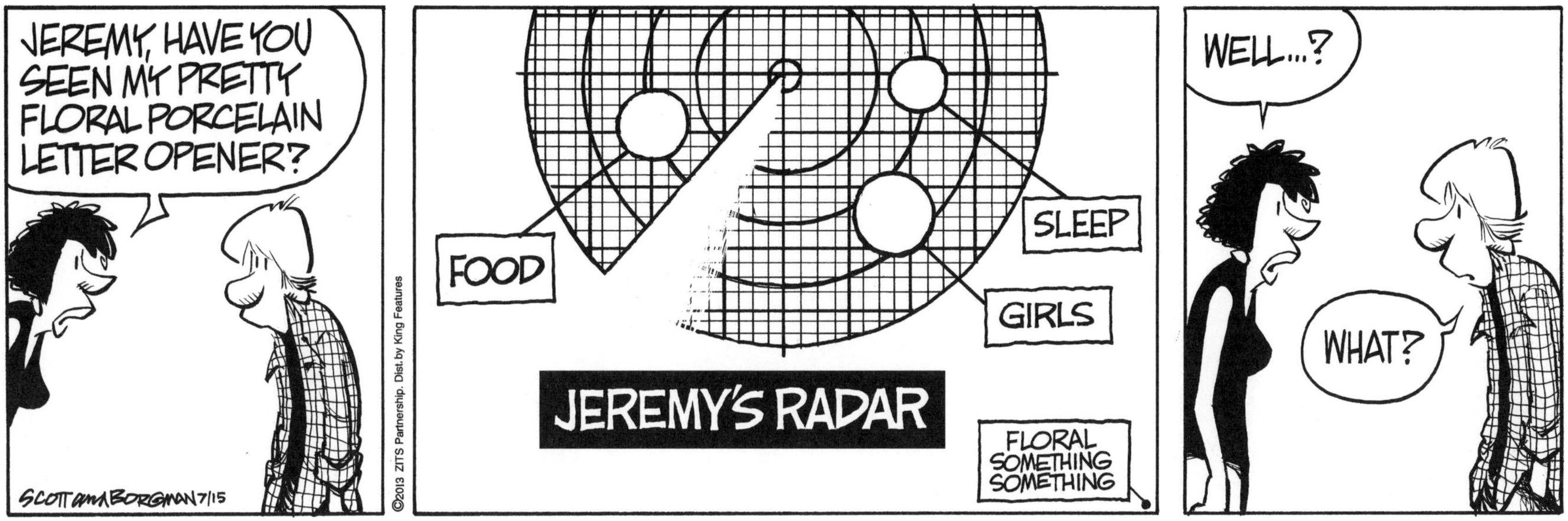

JEREMY, HAVE YOU SEEN MY PRETTY FLORAL PORCELAIN LETTER OPENER?
SCOTT and BORGMAN 7/15
©2013 ZITS Partnership. Dist. by King Features
FOOD
SLEEP
GIRLS
JEREMY'S RADAR
FLORAL SOMETHING SOMETHING
WELL...?
WHAT?


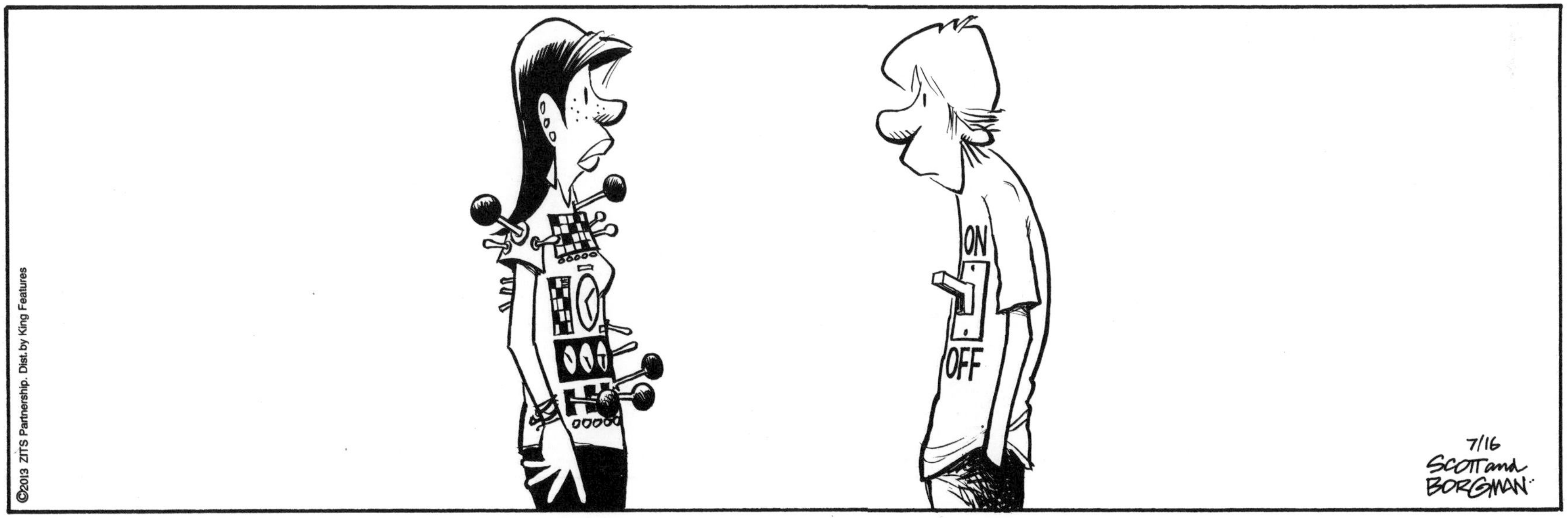

©2013 ZITS Partnership. Dist. by King Features
ON
OFF
7/16 SCOTT and BORGMAN

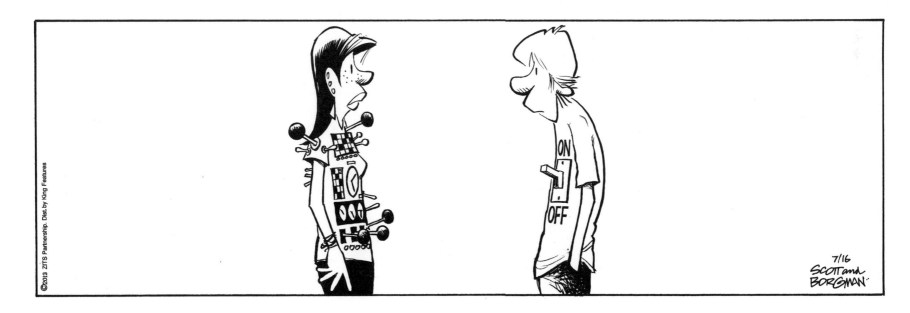

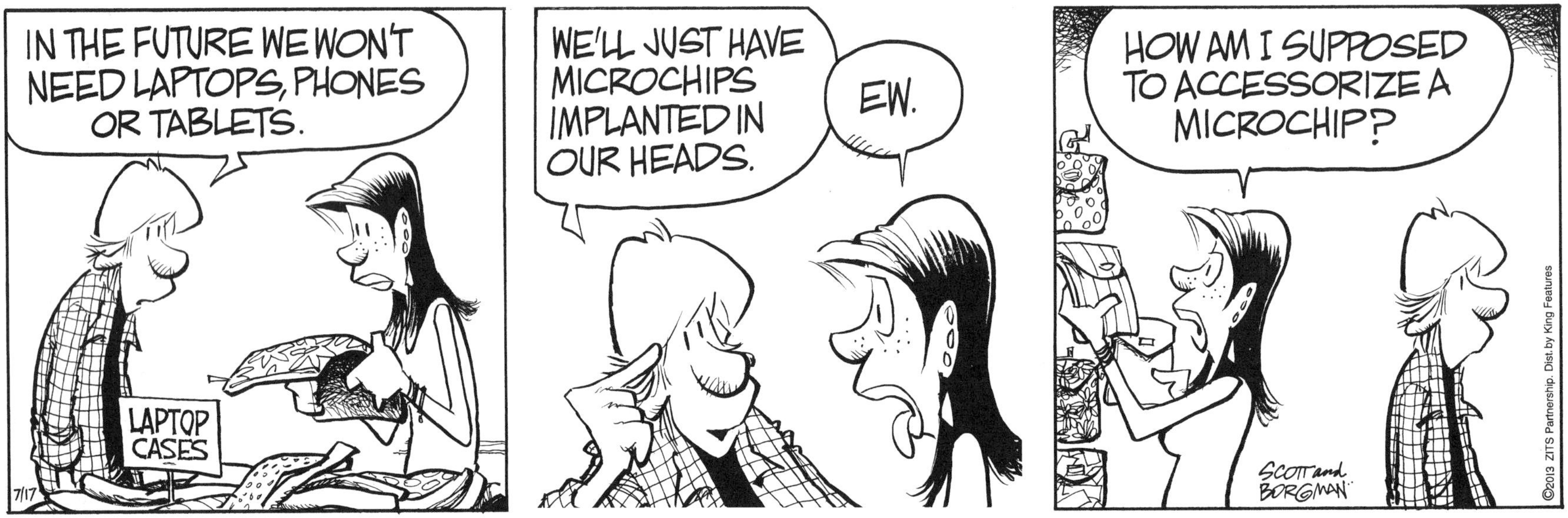
IN THE FUTURE WE WON'T NEED LAPTOPS, PHONES OR TABLETS.
LAPTOP CASES
7/17
WE'LL JUST HAVE MICROCHIPS IMPLANTED IN OUR HEADS.
EW.
HOW AM I SUPPOSED TO ACCESSORIZE A MICROCHIP?
SCOTT and BORGMAN
©2013 ZITS Partnership. Dist. by King Features

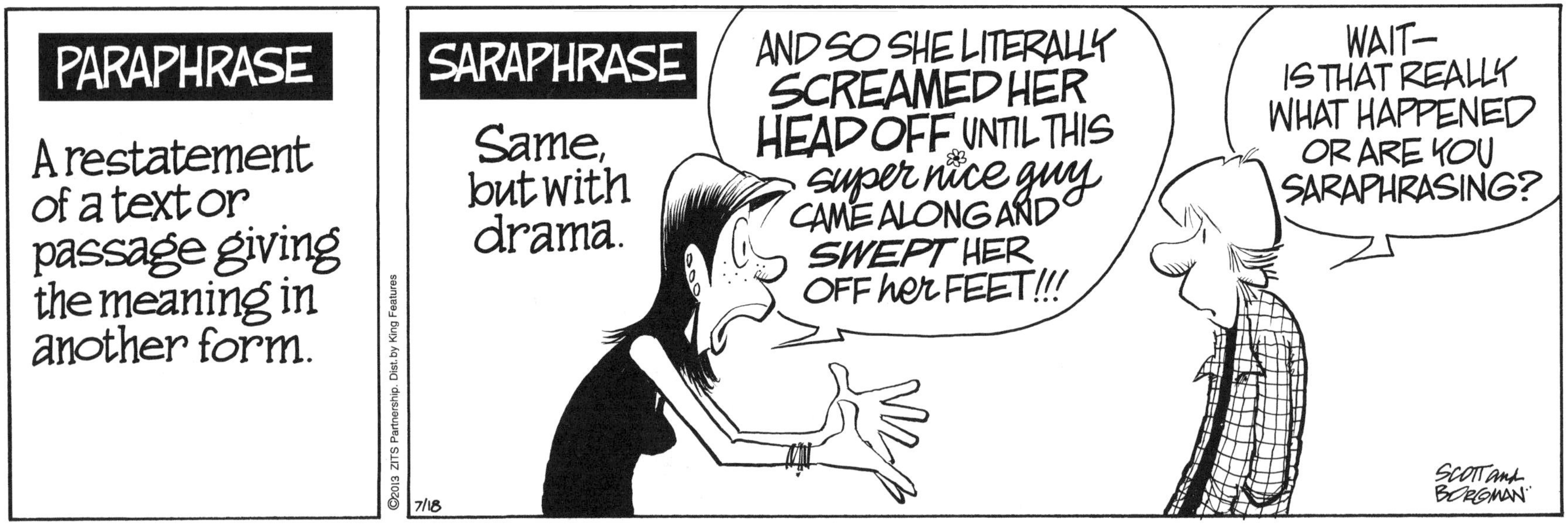
PARAPHRASE
A restatement of a text or passage giving the meaning in another form.
©2013 ZITS Partnership. Dist. by King Features
SARAPHRASE
Same, but with drama.
7/18
AND SO SHE LITERALLY SCREAMED HER HEAD OFF UNTIL THIS super nice guy CAME ALONG AND SWEPT HER OFF her FEET!!!
WAIT— IS THAT REALLY WHAT HAPPENED OR ARE YOU SARAPHRASING?
SCOTT and BORGMAN

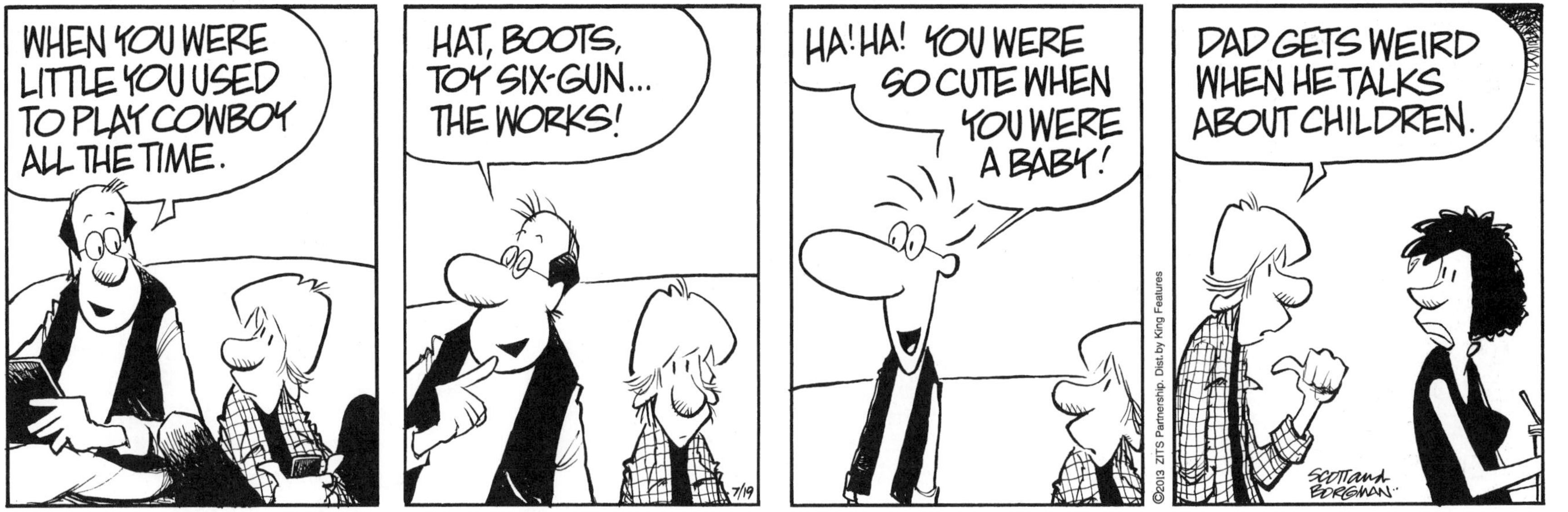
WHEN YOU WERE LITTLE YOU USED TO PLAY COWBOY ALL THE TIME.
HAT, BOOTS, TOY SIX-GUN... THE WORKS!
7/19
HA! HA! YOU WERE SO CUTE WHEN YOU WERE A BABY!
©2013 ZITS Partnership. Dist. by King Features
DAD GETS WEIRD WHEN HE TALKS ABOUT CHILDREN.
SCOTT and BORGMAN

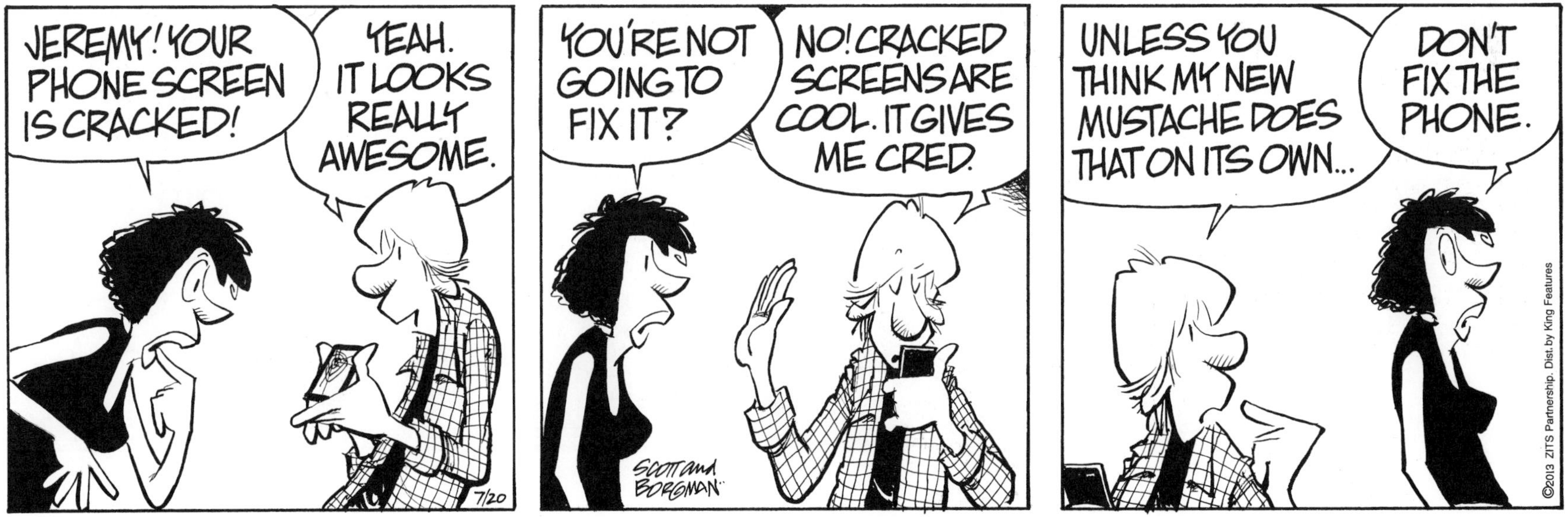
JEREMY! YOUR PHONE SCREEN IS CRACKED!
YEAH. IT LOOKS REALLY AWESOME.
7/20
YOU'RE NOT GOING TO FIX IT?
NO! CRACKED SCREENS ARE COOL. IT GIVES ME CRED.
SCOTT and BORGMAN
UNLESS YOU THINK MY NEW MUSTACHE DOES THAT ON ITS OWN...
DON'T FIX THE PHONE.
©2013 ZITS Partnership. Dist. by King Features

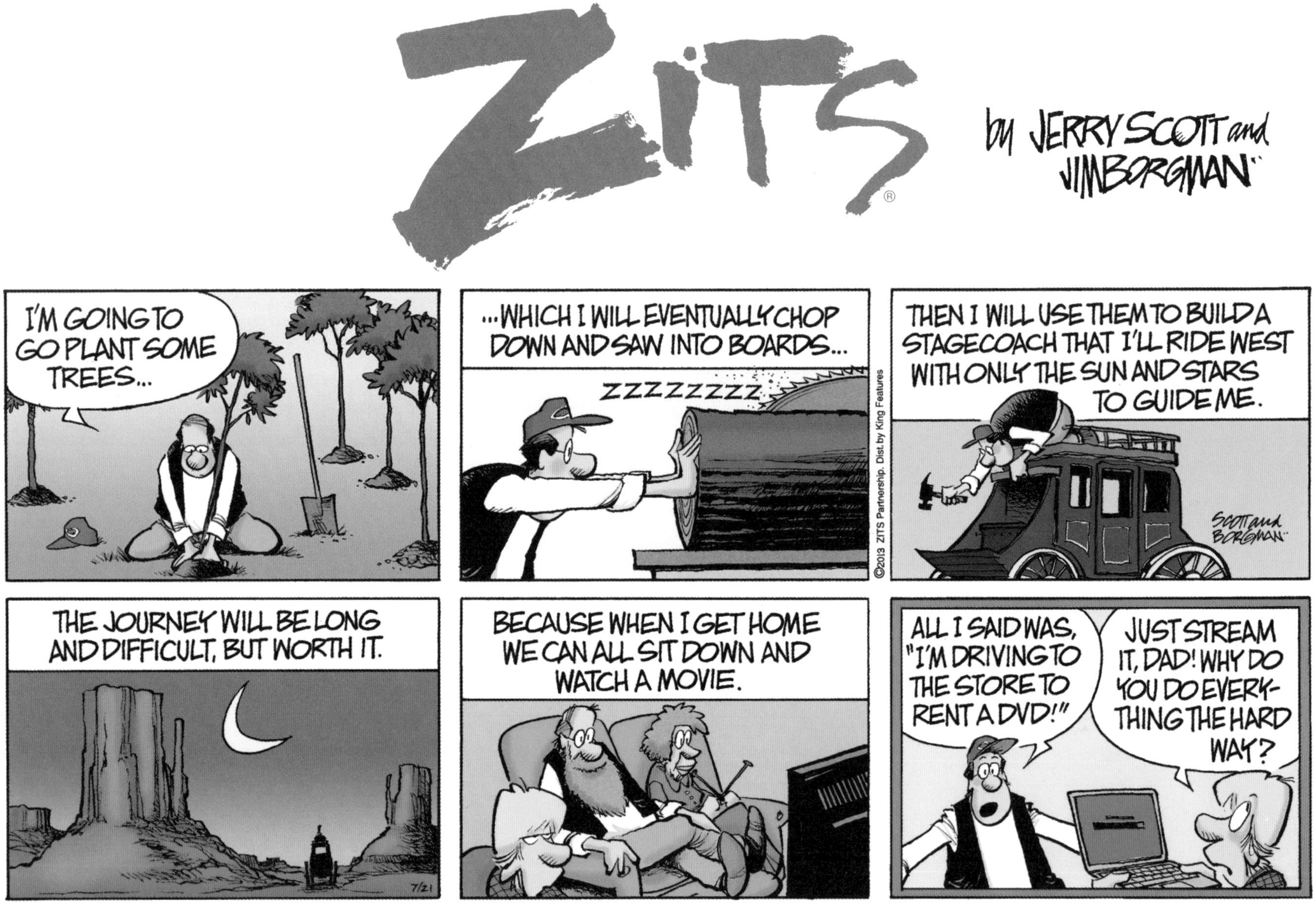
ZITS
by JERRY SCOTT and JIM BORGMAN
I'M GOING TO GO PLANT SOME TREES...
...WHICH I WILL EVENTUALLY CHOP DOWN AND SAW INTO BOARDS...
ZZZZZZZZ
©2013 ZITS Partnership. Dist. by King Features
THEN I WILL USE THEM TO BUILD A STAGECOACH THAT I'LL RIDE WEST WITH ONLY THE SUN AND STARS TO GUIDE ME.
SCOTT and BORGMAN
THE JOURNEY WILL BE LONG AND DIFFICULT, BUT WORTH IT.
7/21
BECAUSE WHEN I GET HOME WE CAN ALL SIT DOWN AND WATCH A MOVIE.
ALL I SAID WAS, "I'M DRIVING TO THE STORE TO RENT A DVD!"
JUST STREAM IT, DAD! WHY DO YOU DO EVERYTHING THE HARD WAY?

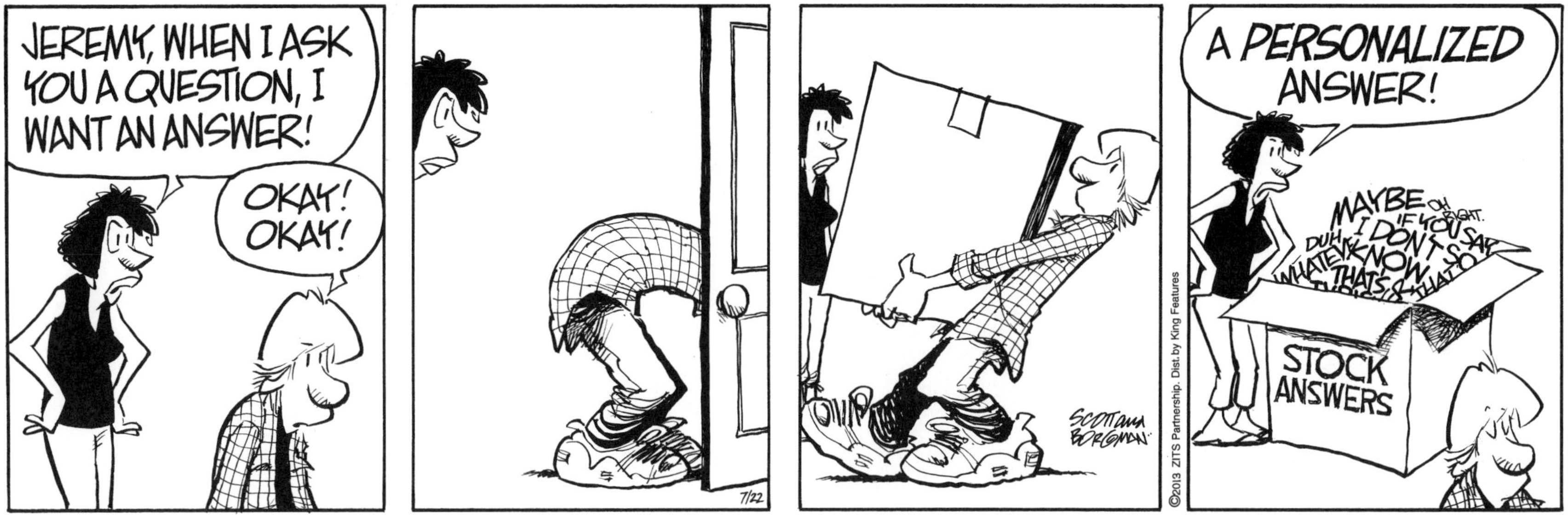

JEREMY, WHEN I ASK YOU A QUESTION, I WANT AN ANSWER!
OKAY! OKAY!
7/22
SCOTT and BORGMAN
©2013 ZITS Partnership. Dist.by King Features
A *PERSONALIZED* ANSWER!
MAYBE
DUH
STOCK ANSWERS


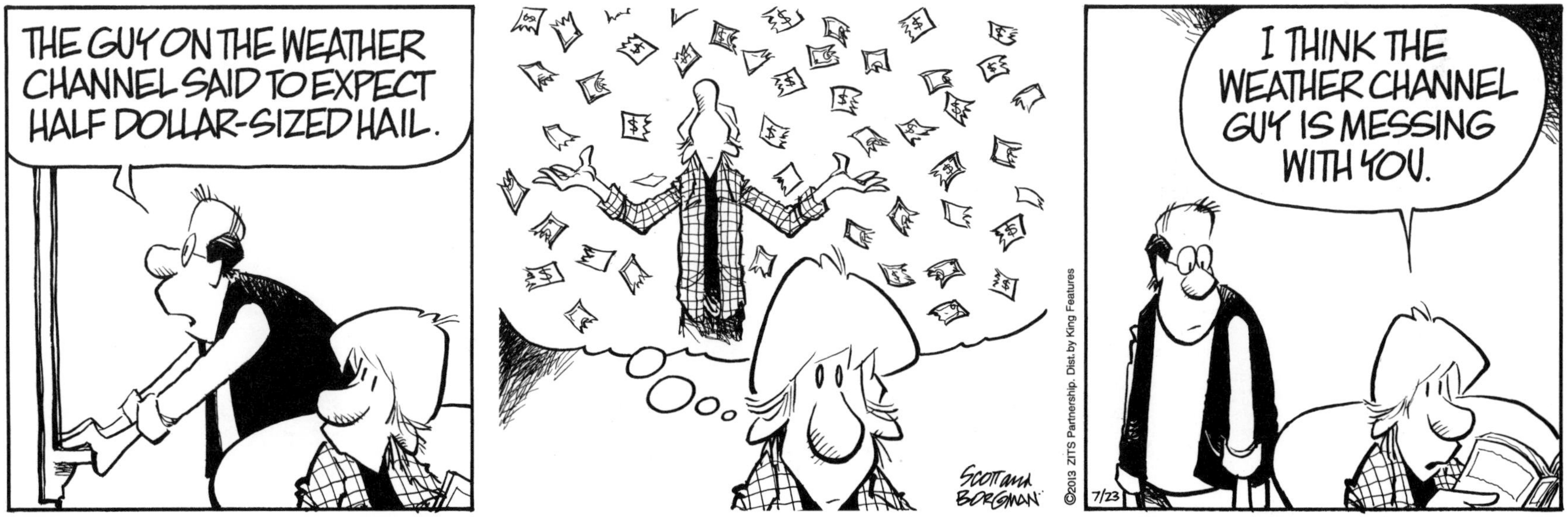

THE GUY ON THE WEATHER CHANNEL SAID TO EXPECT HALF DOLLAR-SIZED HAIL.
SCOTT and BORGMAN
©2013 ZITS Partnership. Dist.by King Features
7/23
I THINK THE WEATHER CHANNEL GUY IS MESSING WITH YOU.

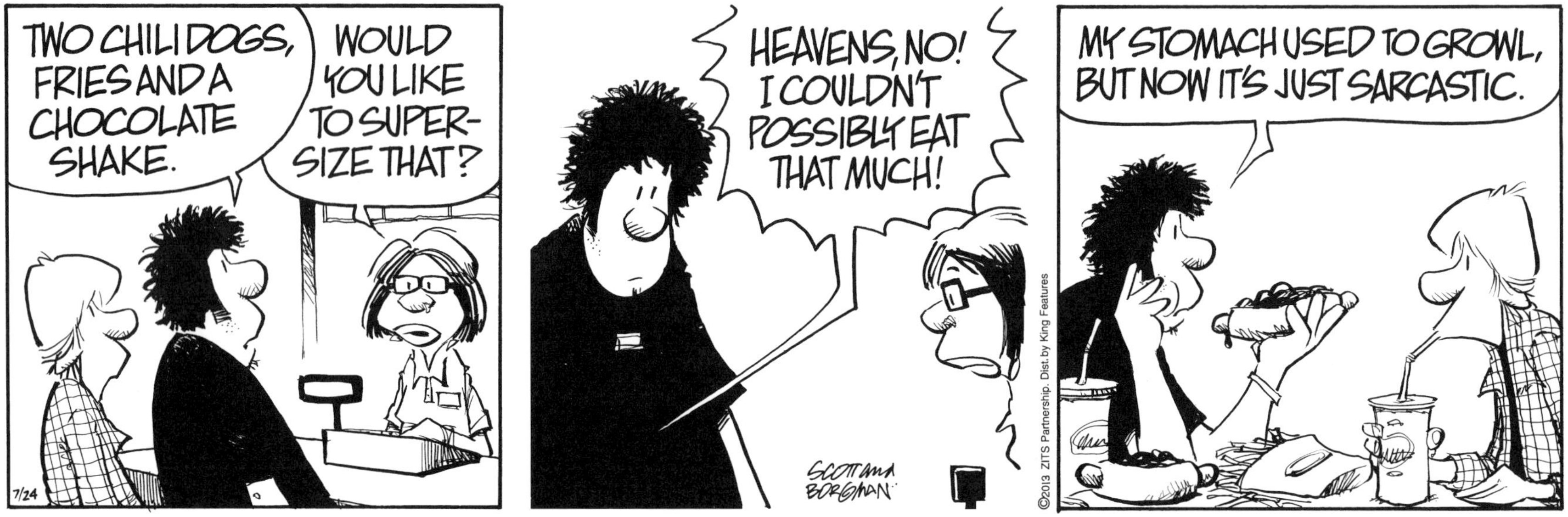
TWO CHILI DOGS, FRIES AND A CHOCOLATE SHAKE.
WOULD YOU LIKE TO SUPER-SIZE THAT?
HEAVENS, NO! I COULDN'T POSSIBLY EAT THAT MUCH!
MY STOMACH USED TO GROWL, BUT NOW IT'S JUST SARCASTIC.
7/24
SCOTT and BORGMAN
©2013 ZITS Partnership. Dist. by King Features

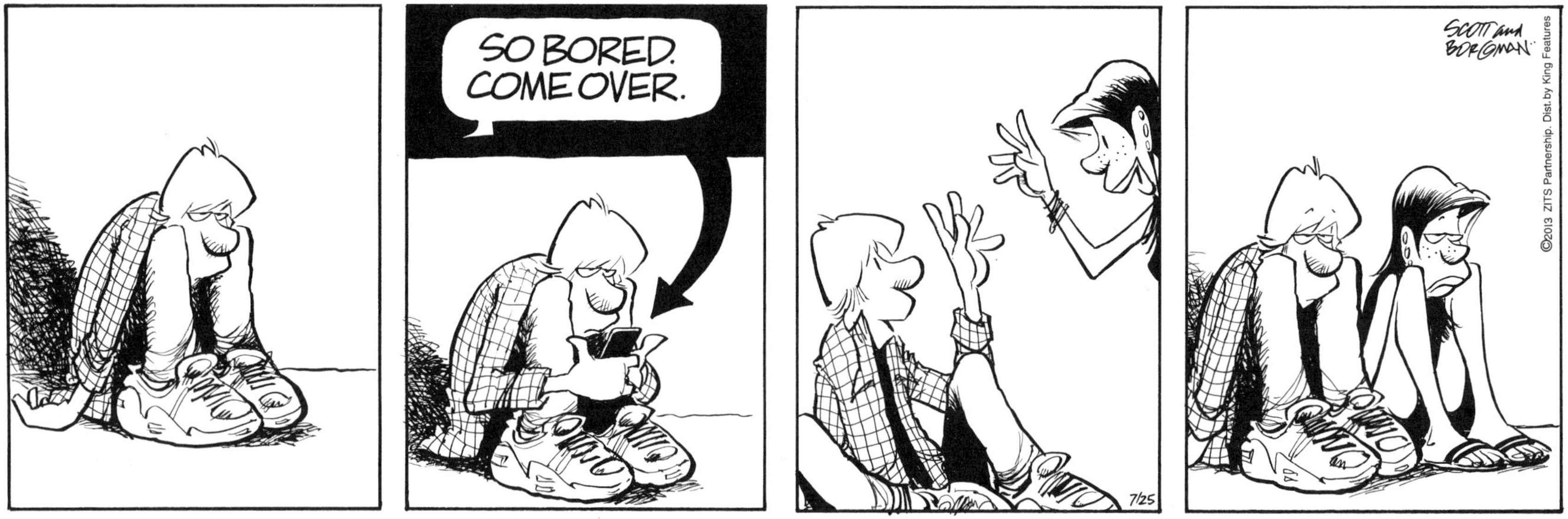
SO BORED. COME OVER.
7/25
SCOTT and BORGMAN
©2013 ZITS Partnership. Dist. by King Features

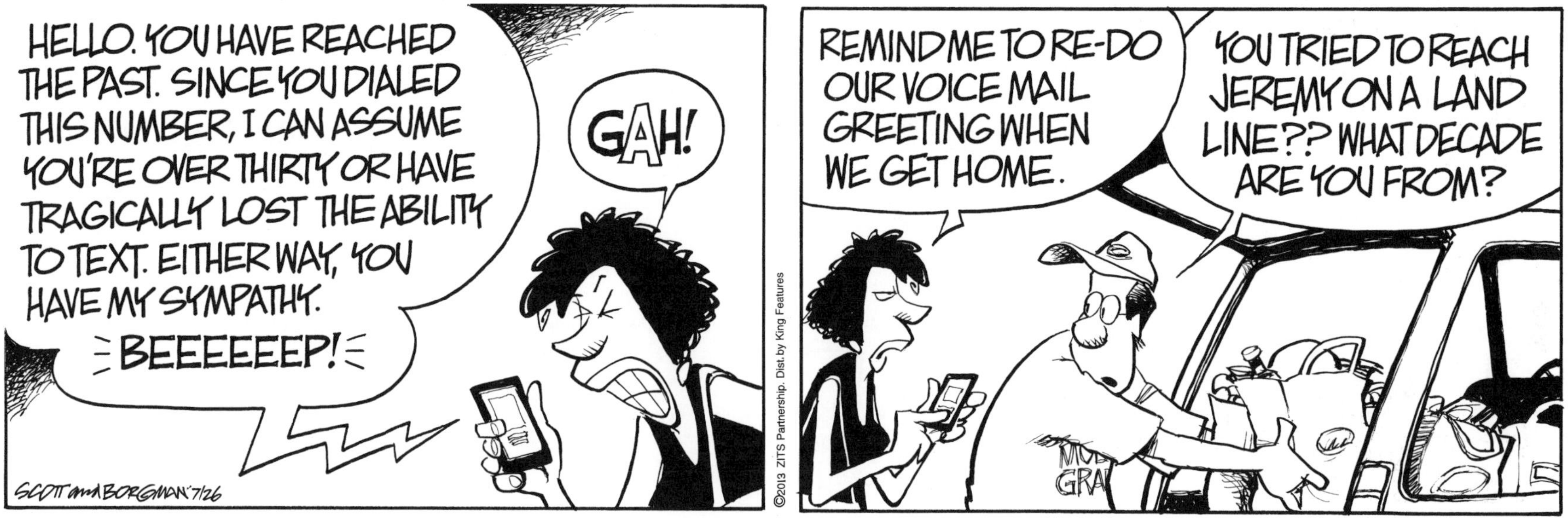
HELLO. YOU HAVE REACHED THE PAST. SINCE YOU DIALED THIS NUMBER, I CAN ASSUME YOU'RE OVER THIRTY OR HAVE TRAGICALLY LOST THE ABILITY TO TEXT. EITHER WAY, YOU HAVE MY SYMPATHY.
BEEEEEEEP!
GAH!
SCOTT and BORGMAN 7/26
REMIND ME TO RE-DO OUR VOICE MAIL GREETING WHEN WE GET HOME.
YOU TRIED TO REACH JEREMY ON A LAND LINE?? WHAT DECADE ARE YOU FROM?
©2013 ZITS Partnership. Dist. by King Features

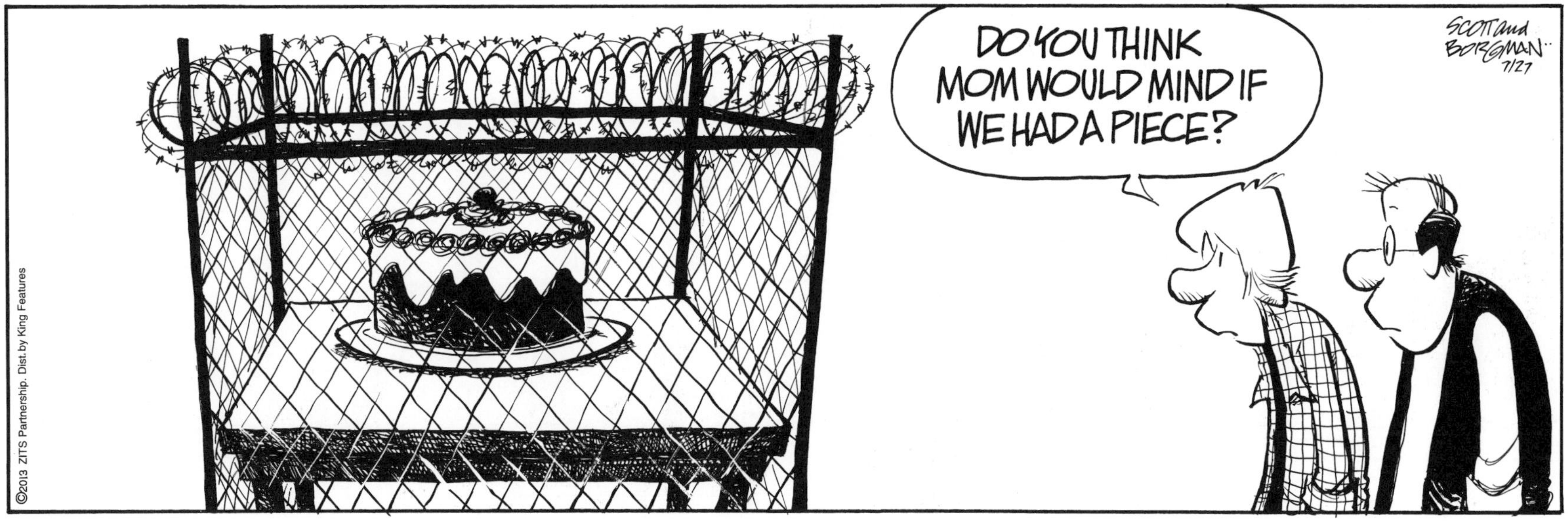
DO YOU THINK MOM WOULD MIND IF WE HAD A PIECE?
SCOTT and BORGMAN 7/27
©2013 ZITS Partnership. Dist. by King Features

# ZITS

by JERRY SCOTT and JIM BORGMAN

CARGO JEANS??
DAD!
WHAT'S WRONG WITH CARGO JEANS? THEY'RE PRACTICAL!
I CAN CARRY MY WALLET, KEYS, PHONE, YOUR MOTHER'S LIP-STICK, HER BREATH MINTS, MASCARA, PACK OF TISSUES...
7/28
...HAND SANITIZER, NAIL FILE...
YOU'RE RIGHT. I'M A BIG DENIM PURSE WITH LEGS.
IF YOU CALL THOSE LEGS.
SCOTT and BORGMAN
©2013 ZITS Partnership. Dist. by King Features

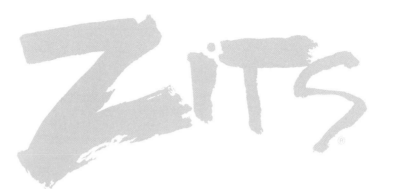

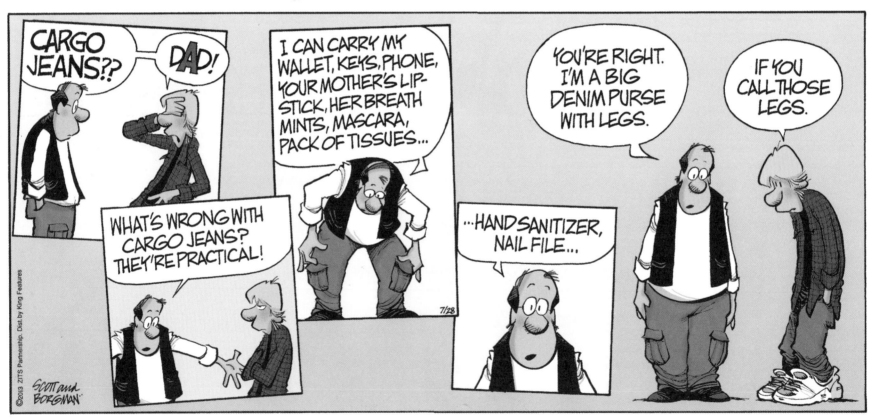

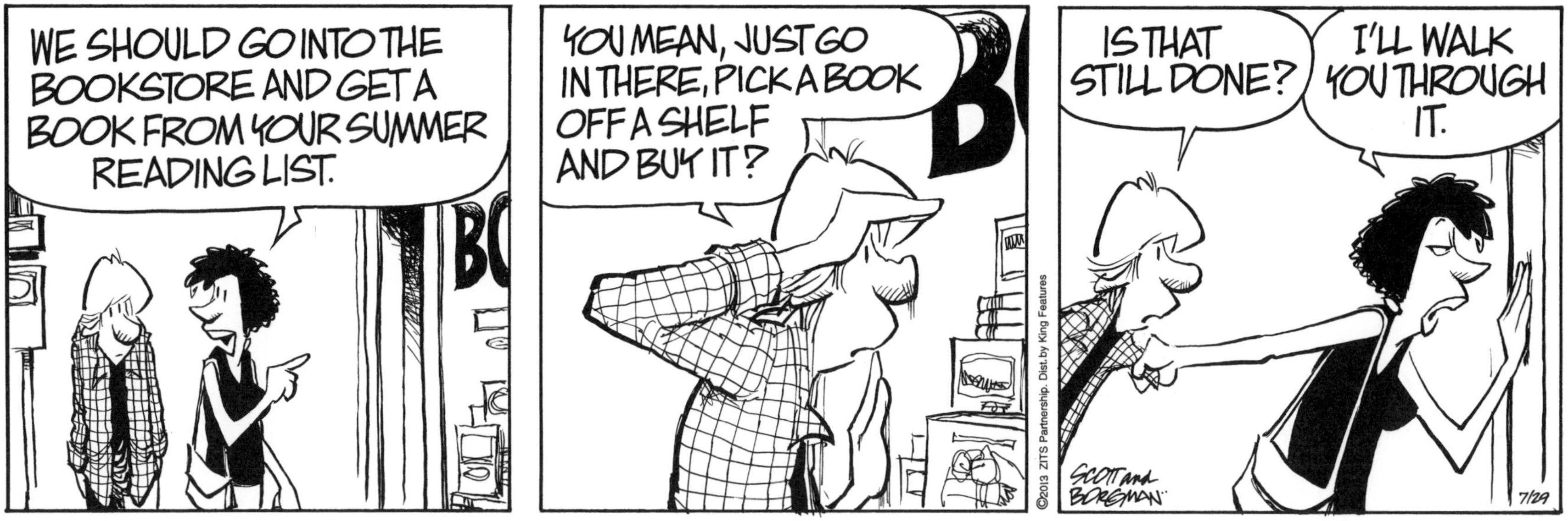
WE SHOULD GO INTO THE BOOKSTORE AND GET A BOOK FROM YOUR SUMMER READING LIST.
YOU MEAN, JUST GO IN THERE, PICK A BOOK OFF A SHELF AND BUY IT?
©2013 ZITS Partnership. Dist.by King Features
IS THAT STILL DONE?
I'LL WALK YOU THROUGH IT.
SCOTT and BORGMAN
7/29

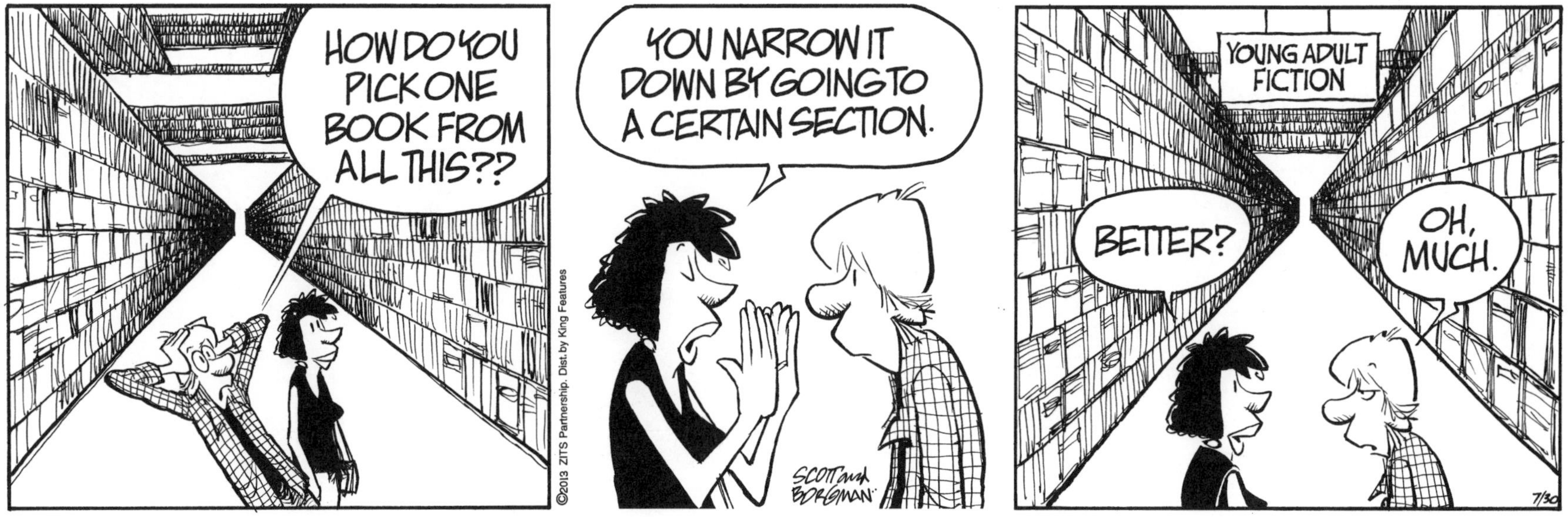
HOW DO YOU PICK ONE BOOK FROM ALL THIS??
©2013 ZITS Partnership. Dist.by King Features
YOU NARROW IT DOWN BY GOING TO A CERTAIN SECTION.
SCOTT and BORGMAN
YOUNG ADULT FICTION
BETTER?
OH, MUCH.
7/30

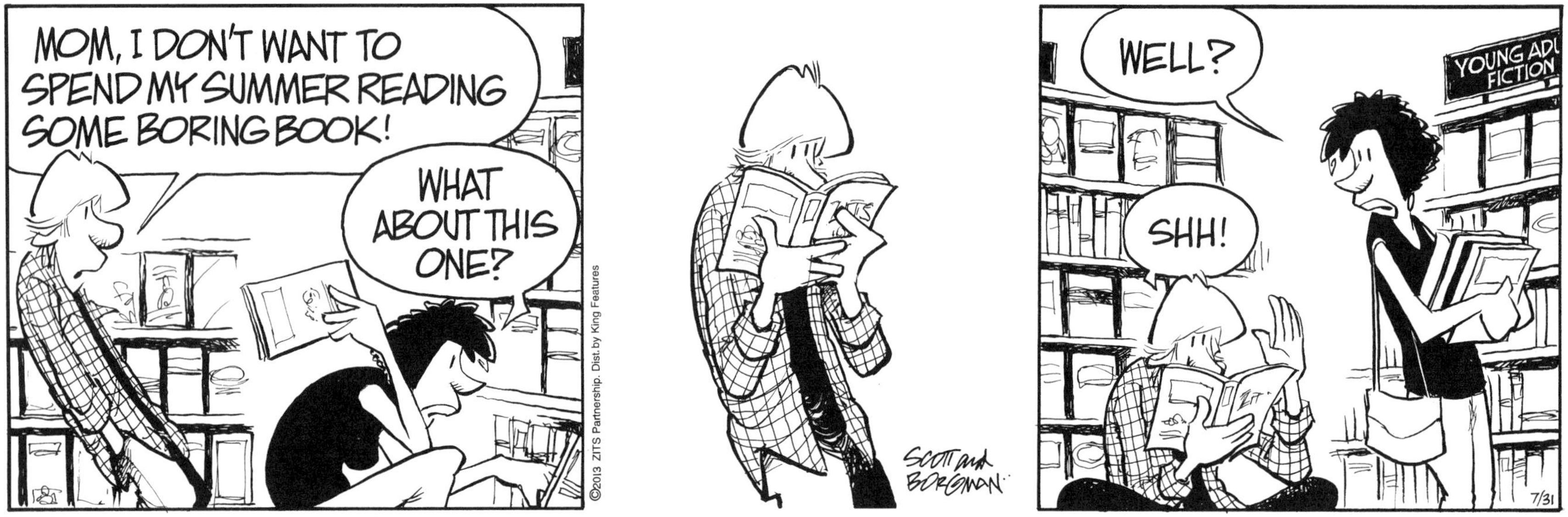
MOM, I DON'T WANT TO SPEND MY SUMMER READING SOME BORING BOOK!
WHAT ABOUT THIS ONE?
SCOTT and BORGMAN
WELL?
SHH!
YOUNG ADU FICTION
7/31
©2013 ZITS Partnership. Dist. by King Features

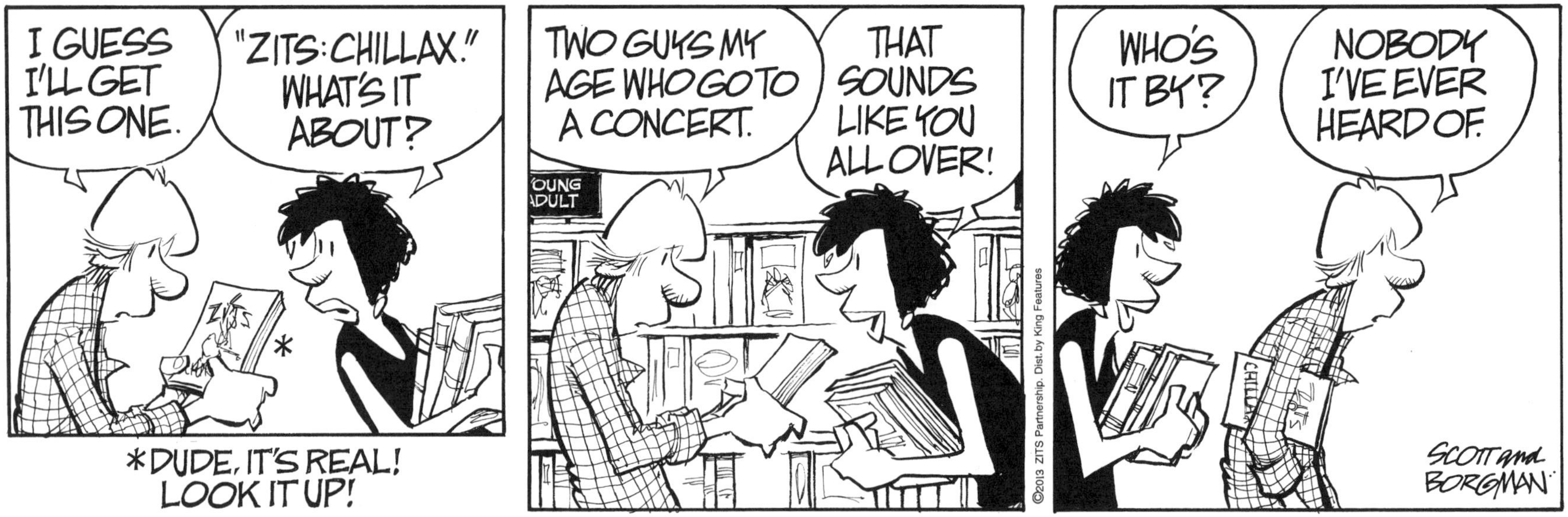
I GUESS I'LL GET THIS ONE.
"ZITS: CHILLAX." WHAT'S IT ABOUT?
*
*DUDE, IT'S REAL! LOOK IT UP!
TWO GUYS MY AGE WHO GO TO A CONCERT.
THAT SOUNDS LIKE YOU ALL OVER!
WHO'S IT BY?
NOBODY I'VE EVER HEARD OF.
SCOTT and BORGMAN
©2013 ZITS Partnership. Dist. by King Features

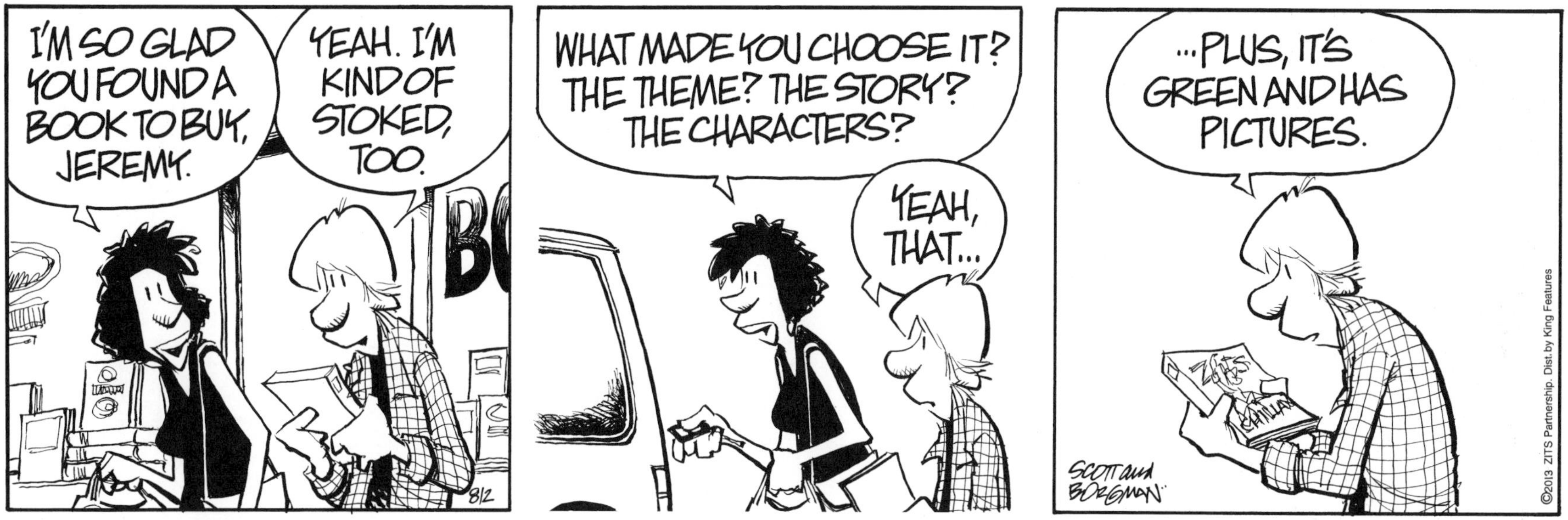
I'M SO GLAD YOU FOUND A BOOK TO BUY, JEREMY.
YEAH. I'M KIND OF STOKED, TOO.
8/2
WHAT MADE YOU CHOOSE IT? THE THEME? THE STORY? THE CHARACTERS?
YEAH, THAT...
...PLUS, IT'S GREEN AND HAS PICTURES.
SCOTT and BORGMAN
©2013 ZITS Partnership. Dist. by King Features

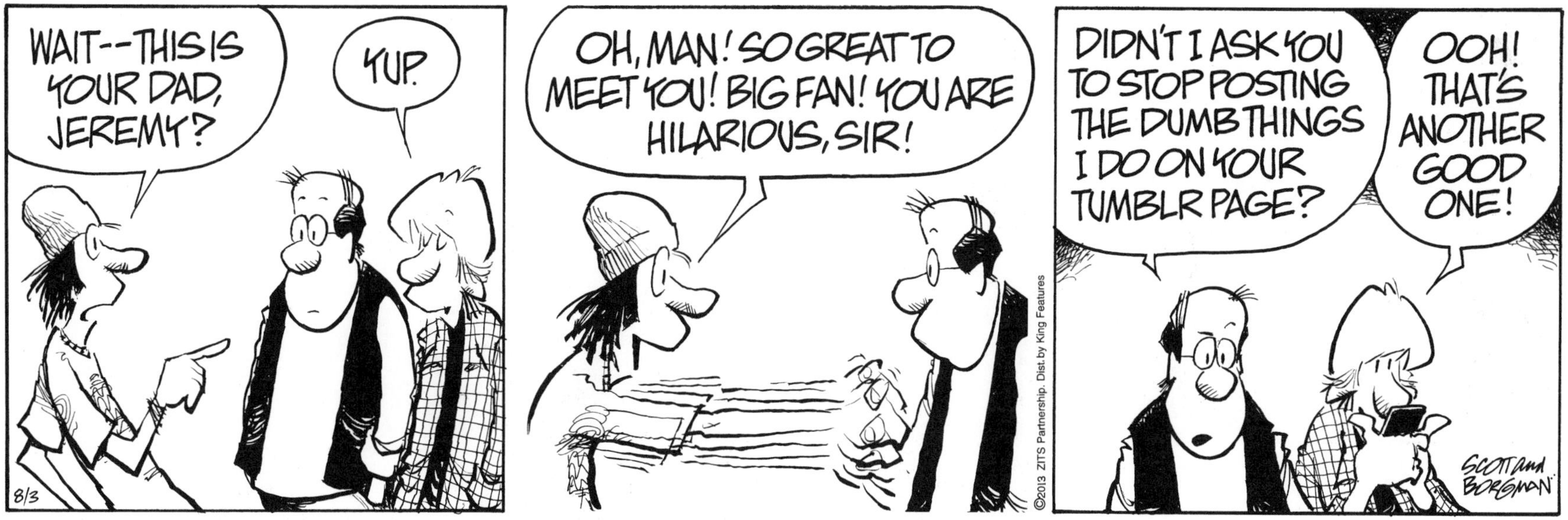
WAIT--THIS IS YOUR DAD, JEREMY?
YUP.
8/3
OH, MAN! SO GREAT TO MEET YOU! BIG FAN! YOU ARE HILARIOUS, SIR!
©2013 ZITS Partnership. Dist. by King Features
DIDN'T I ASK YOU TO STOP POSTING THE DUMB THINGS I DO ON YOUR TUMBLR PAGE?
OOH! THAT'S ANOTHER GOOD ONE!
SCOTT and BORGMAN

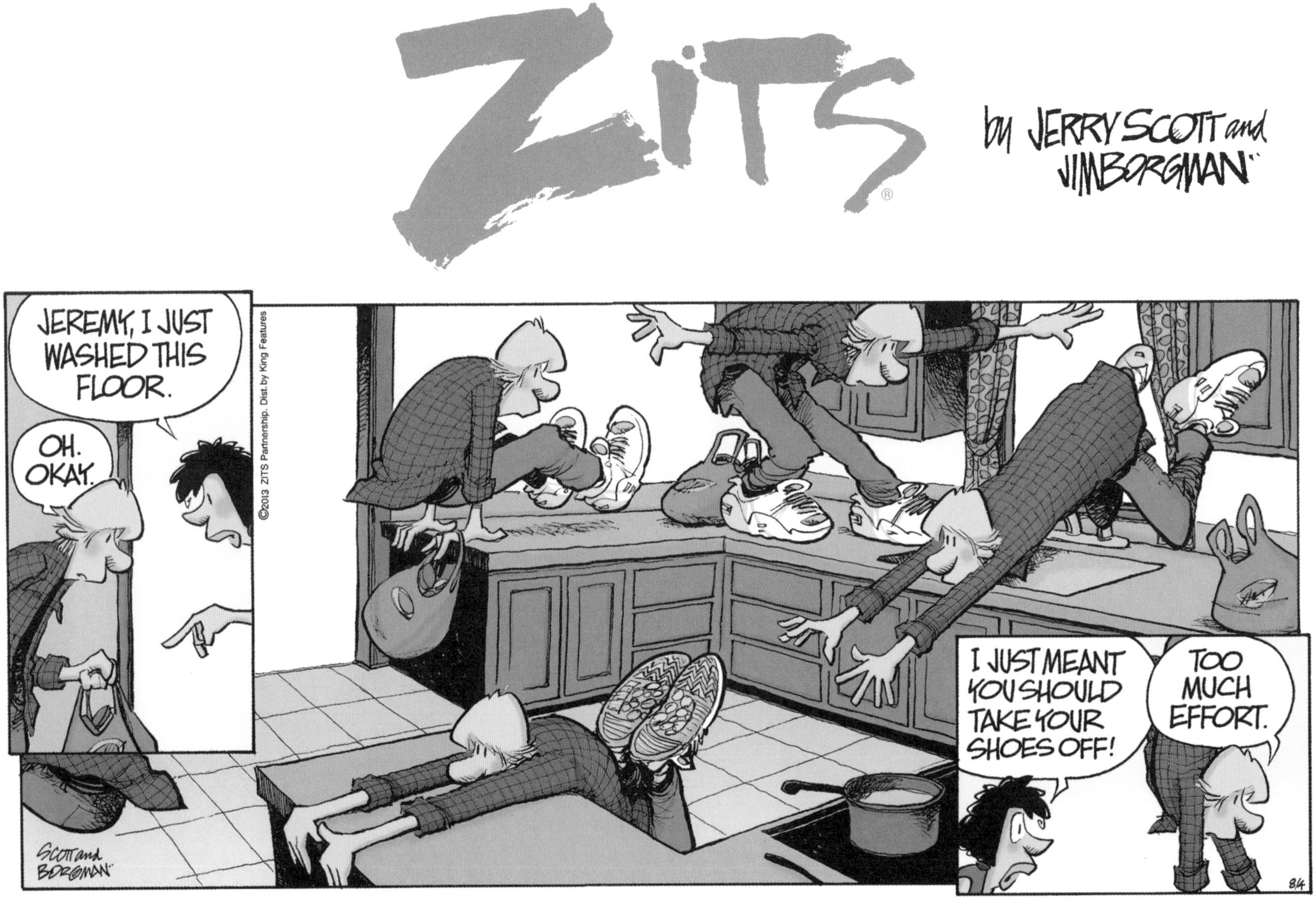
ZITS
by JERRY SCOTT and JIM BORGMAN
JEREMY, I JUST WASHED THIS FLOOR.
OH. OKAY.
©2013 ZITS Partnership. Dist. by King Features
I JUST MEANT YOU SHOULD TAKE YOUR SHOES OFF!
TOO MUCH EFFORT.
SCOTT and BORGMAN
8/4

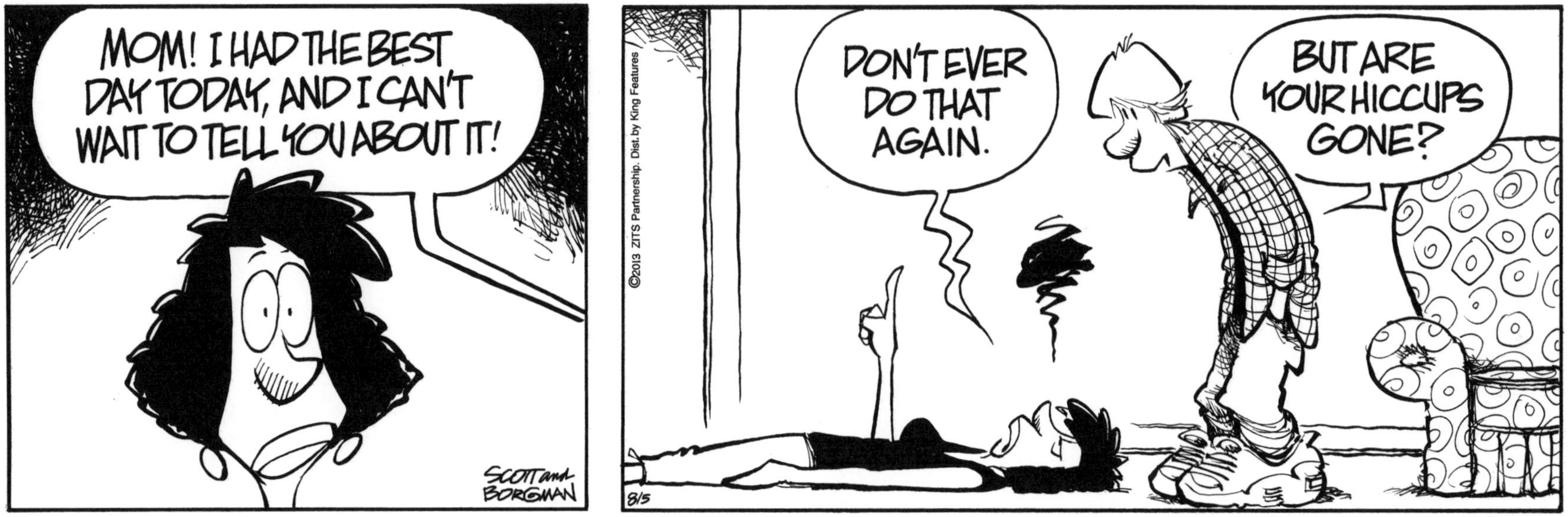
MOM! I HAD THE BEST DAY TODAY, AND I CAN'T WAIT TO TELL YOU ABOUT IT!
SCOTT and BORGMAN
©2013 ZITS Partnership. Dist. by King Features
8/5
DON'T EVER DO THAT AGAIN.
BUT ARE YOUR HICCUPS GONE?

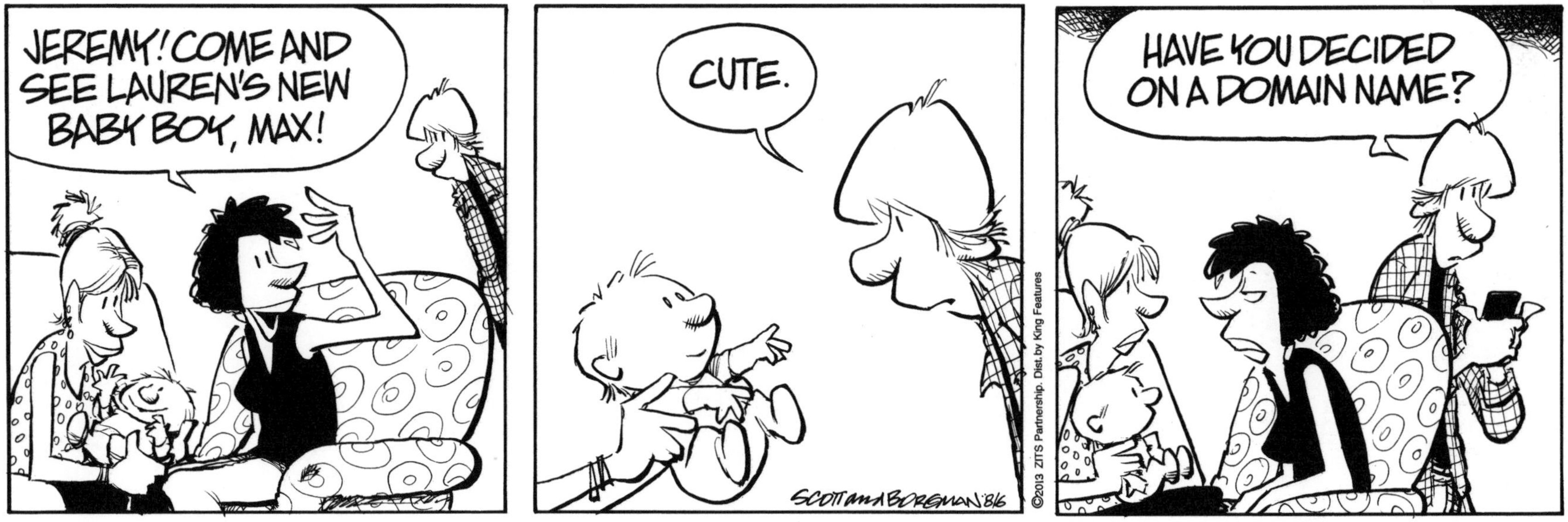
JEREMY! COME AND SEE LAUREN'S NEW BABY BOY, MAX!
CUTE.
SCOTT and BORGMAN 8/6
©2013 ZITS Partnership. Dist. by King Features
HAVE YOU DECIDED ON A DOMAIN NAME?

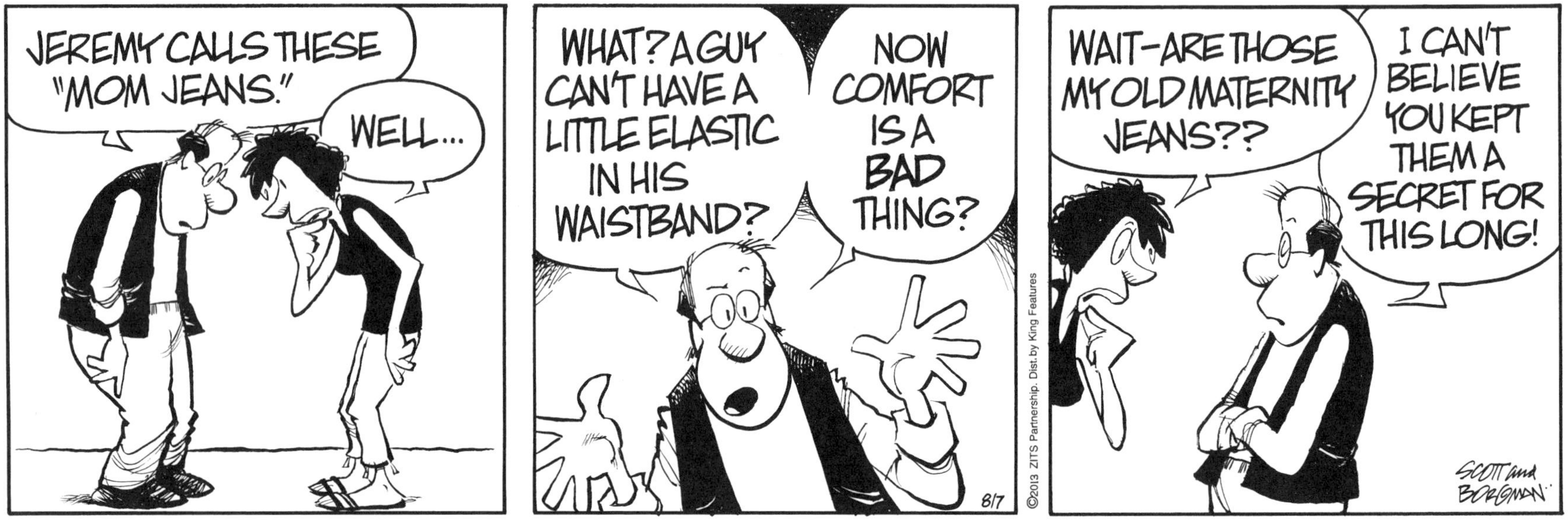
JEREMY CALLS THESE "MOM JEANS."
WELL...
WHAT? A GUY CAN'T HAVE A LITTLE ELASTIC IN HIS WAISTBAND?
NOW COMFORT IS A BAD THING?
8/7
©2013 ZITS Partnership. Dist. by King Features
WAIT-ARE THOSE MY OLD MATERNITY JEANS??
I CAN'T BELIEVE YOU KEPT THEM A SECRET FOR THIS LONG!
SCOTT and BORGMAN

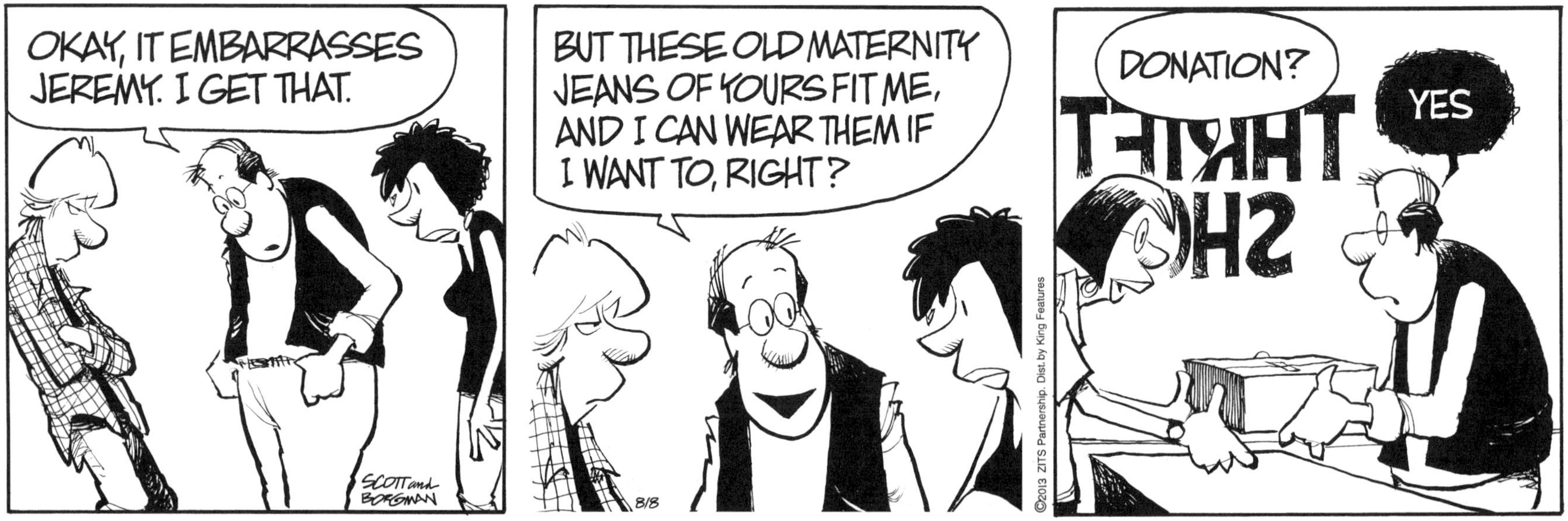
OKAY, IT EMBARRASSES JEREMY. I GET THAT.
SCOTT and BORGMAN
BUT THESE OLD MATERNITY JEANS OF YOURS FIT ME, AND I CAN WEAR THEM IF I WANT TO, RIGHT?
8/8
©2013 ZITS Partnership. Dist. by King Features
DONATION?
YES

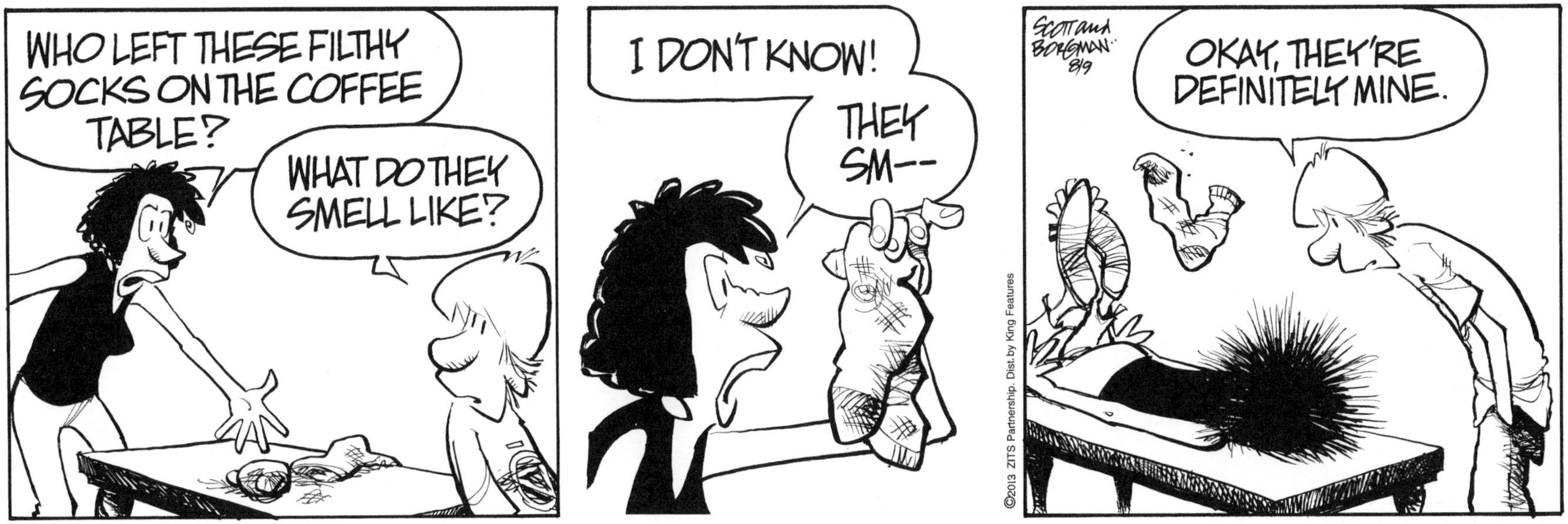
WHO LEFT THESE FILTHY SOCKS ON THE COFFEE TABLE?
WHAT DO THEY SMELL LIKE?
I DON'T KNOW!
THEY SM--
SCOTT and BORGMAN 8/9
OKAY, THEY'RE DEFINITELY MINE.
©2013 ZITS Partnership. Dist. by King Features

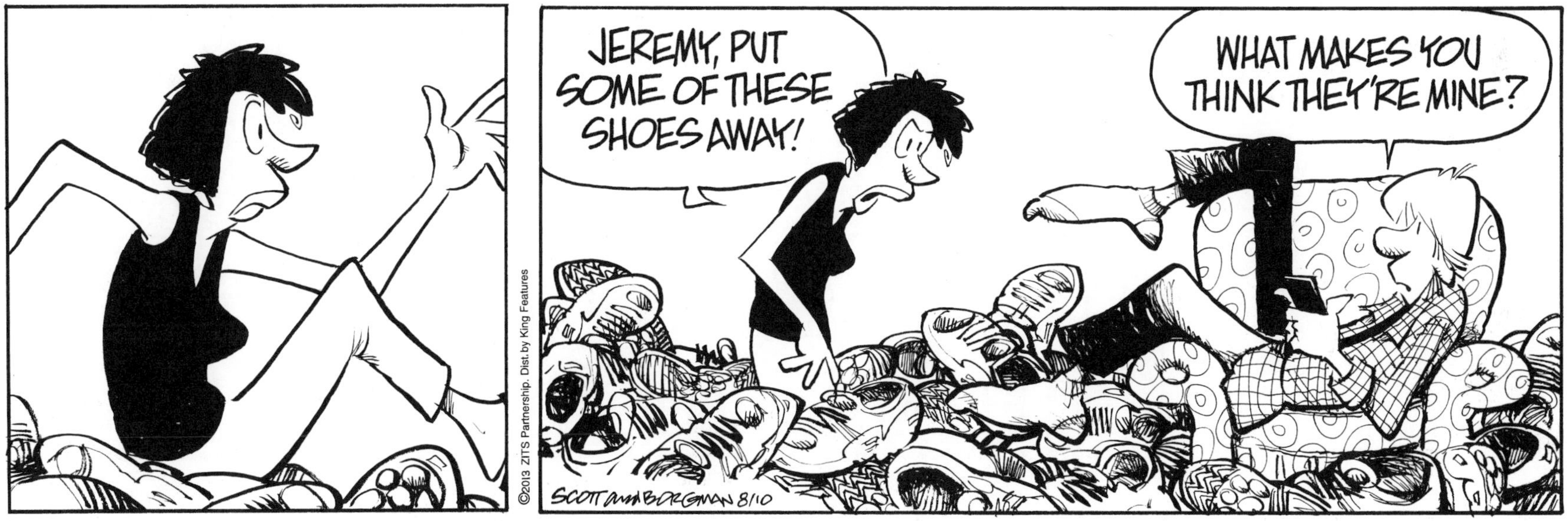
©2013 ZITS Partnership. Dist. by King Features
JEREMY, PUT SOME OF THESE SHOES AWAY!
WHAT MAKES YOU THINK THEY'RE MINE?
SCOTT and BORGMAN 8/10

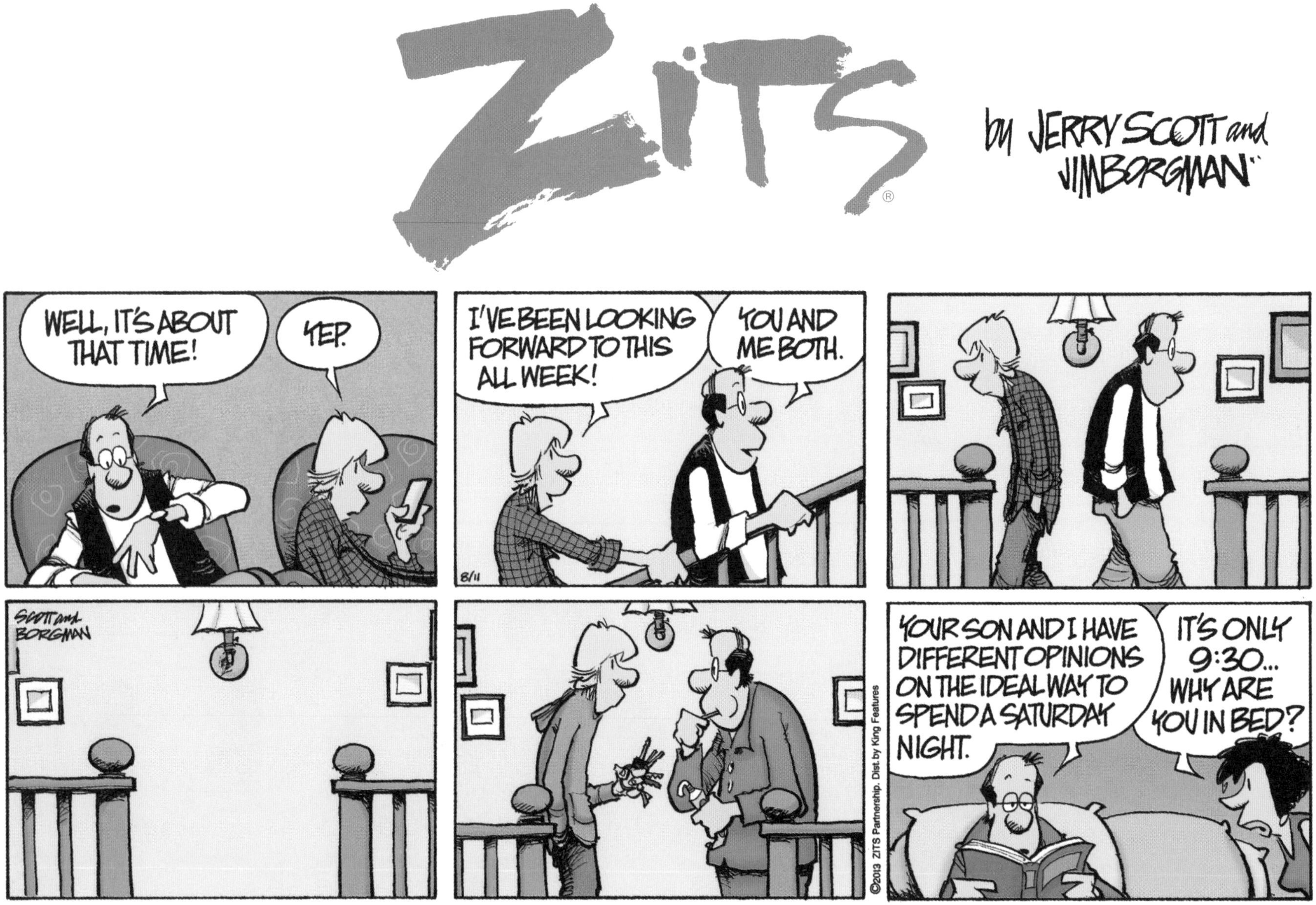
ZITS
by JERRY SCOTT and JIM BORGMAN
WELL, IT'S ABOUT THAT TIME!
YEP.
I'VE BEEN LOOKING FORWARD TO THIS ALL WEEK!
YOU AND ME BOTH.
8/11
SCOTT and BORGMAN
©2013 ZITS Partnership. Dist. by King Features
YOUR SON AND I HAVE DIFFERENT OPINIONS ON THE IDEAL WAY TO SPEND A SATURDAY NIGHT.
IT'S ONLY 9:30... WHY ARE YOU IN BED?

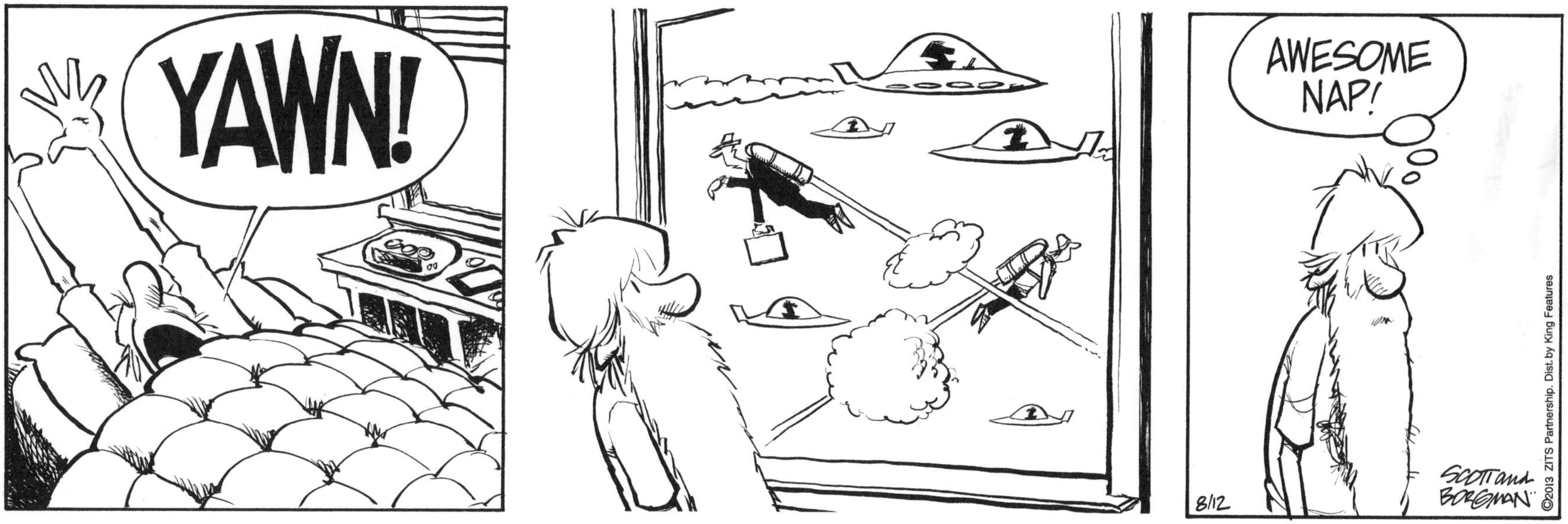
YAWN!
AWESOME NAP!
8/12
SCOTT and BORGMAN
©2013 ZITS Partnership. Dist. by King Features

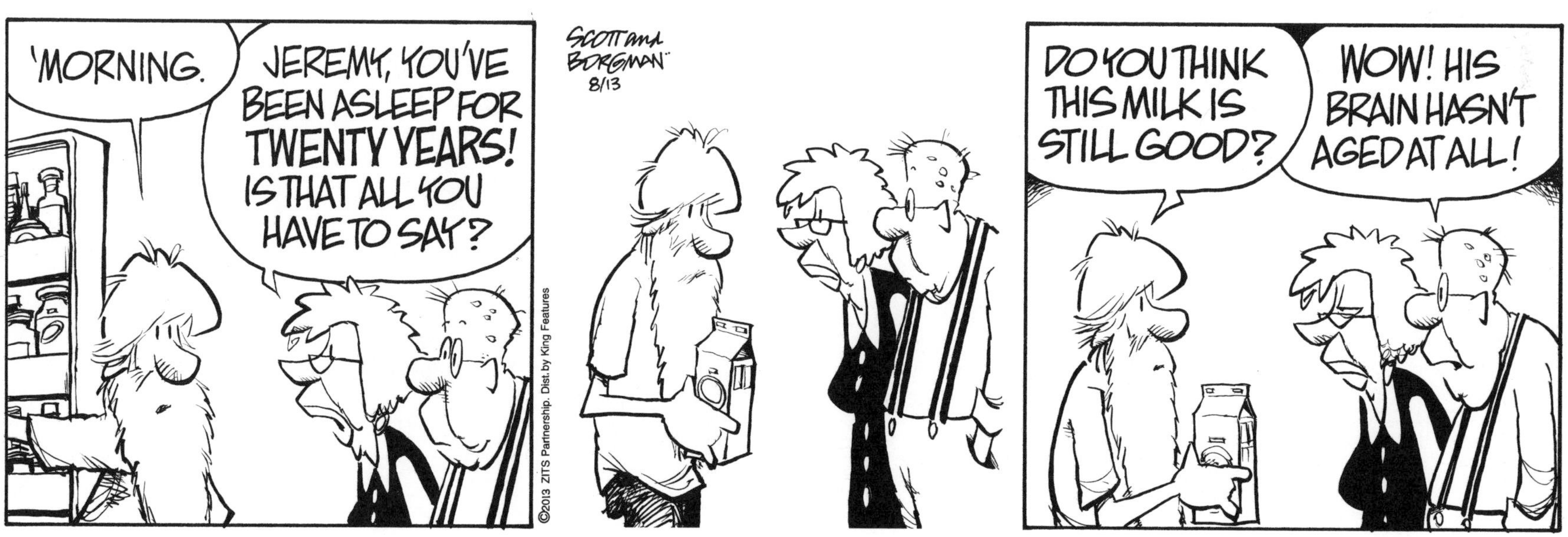
'MORNING.
JEREMY, YOU'VE BEEN ASLEEP FOR TWENTY YEARS! IS THAT ALL YOU HAVE TO SAY?
SCOTT and BORGMAN
8/13
©2013 ZITS Partnership. Dist. by King Features
DO YOU THINK THIS MILK IS STILL GOOD?
WOW! HIS BRAIN HASN'T AGED AT ALL!

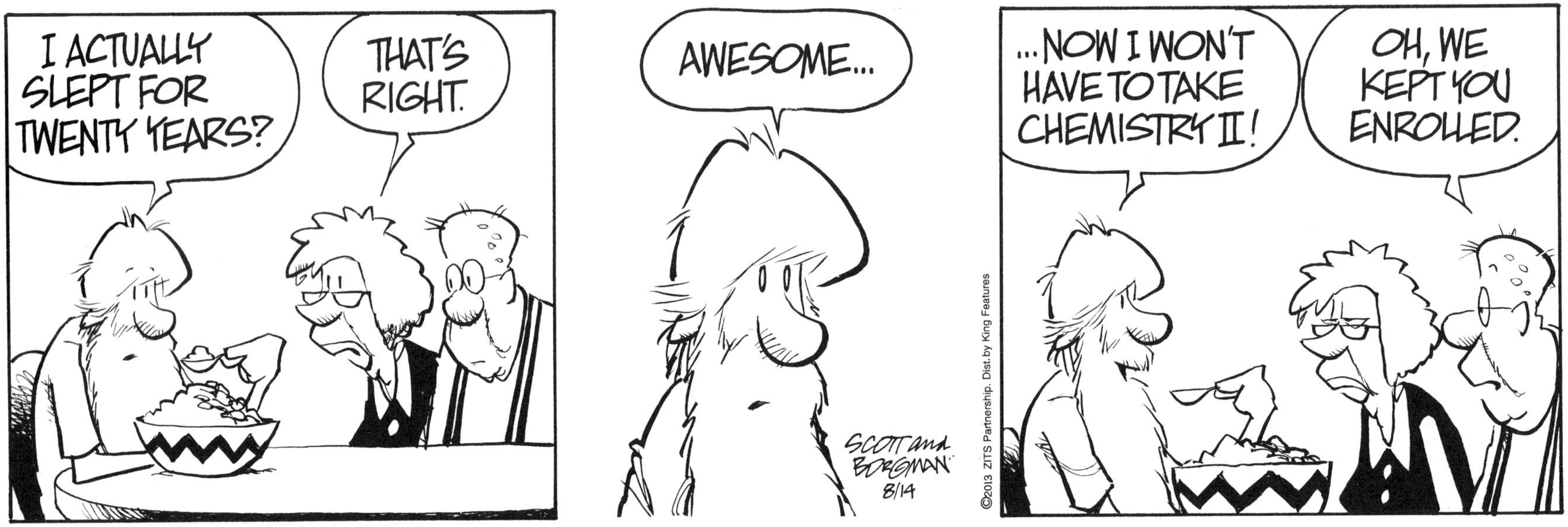
I ACTUALLY SLEPT FOR TWENTY YEARS?
THAT'S RIGHT.
AWESOME...
...NOW I WON'T HAVE TO TAKE CHEMISTRY II!
OH, WE KEPT YOU ENROLLED.
SCOTT and BORGMAN 8/14
©2013 ZITS Partnership. Dist. by King Features

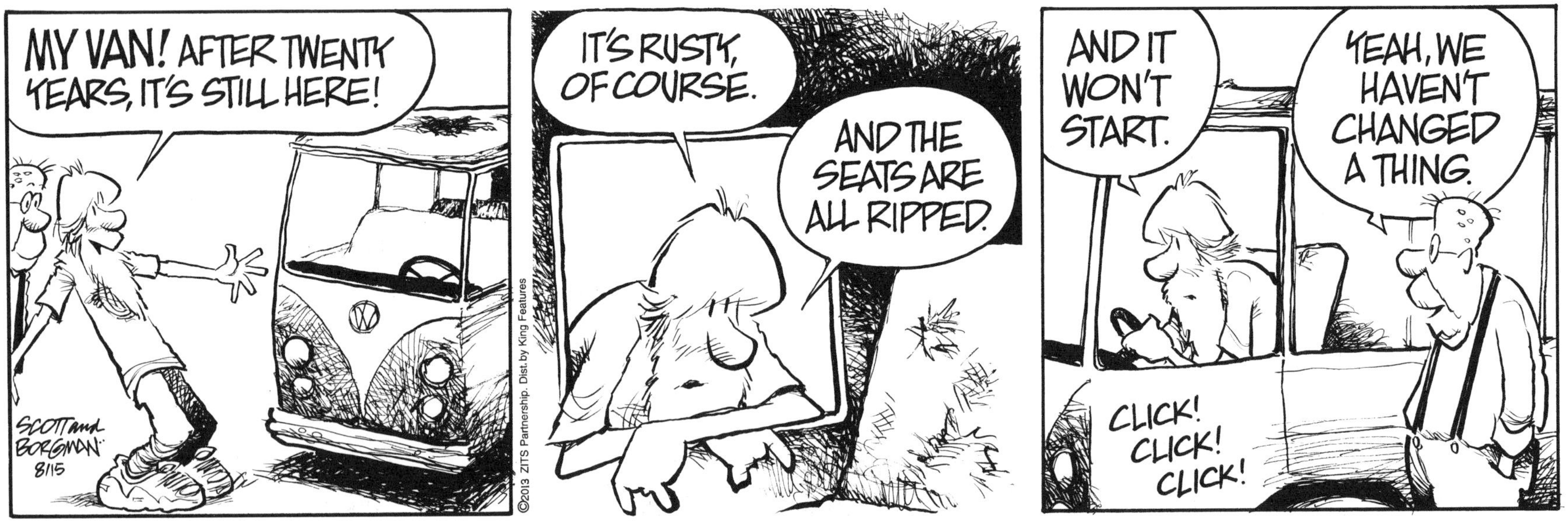
MY VAN! AFTER TWENTY YEARS, IT'S STILL HERE!
SCOTT and BORGMAN 8/15
©2013 ZITS Partnership. Dist. by King Features
IT'S RUSTY, OF COURSE.
AND THE SEATS ARE ALL RIPPED.
AND IT WON'T START.
YEAH, WE HAVEN'T CHANGED A THING.
CLICK! CLICK! CLICK!

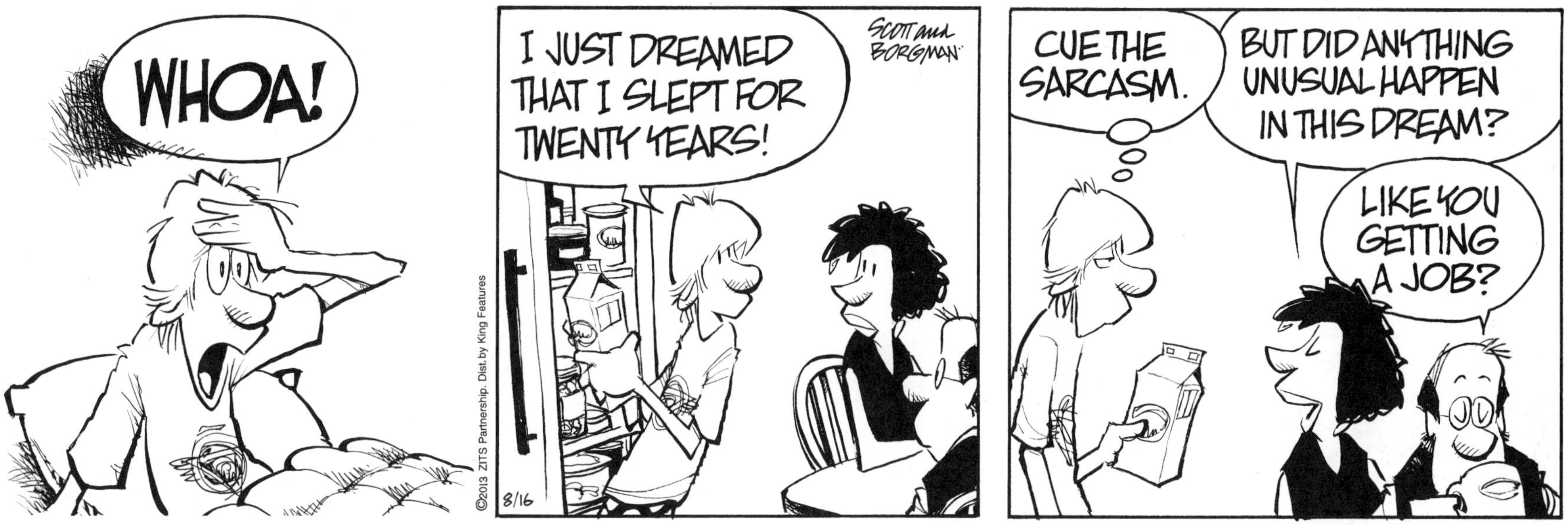
WHOA!
I JUST DREAMED THAT I SLEPT FOR TWENTY YEARS!
SCOTT and BORGMAN
©2013 ZITS Partnership. Dist. by King Features
8/16
CUE THE SARCASM.
BUT DID ANYTHING UNUSUAL HAPPEN IN THIS DREAM?
LIKE YOU GETTING A JOB?

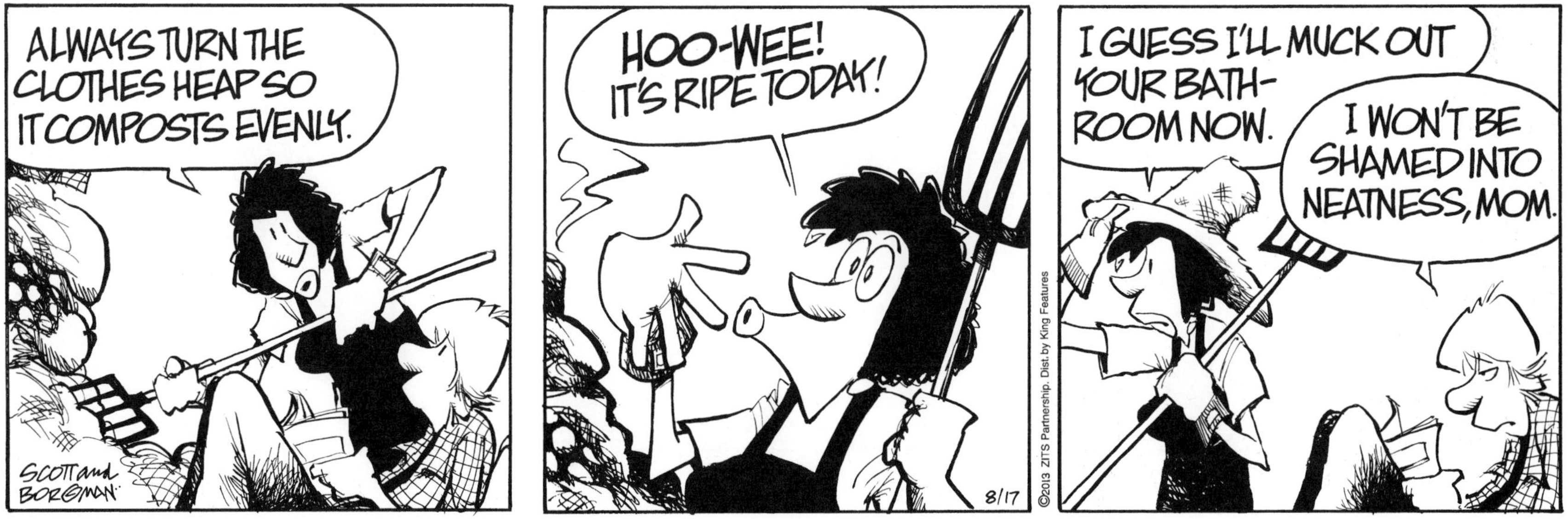
ALWAYS TURN THE CLOTHES HEAP SO IT COMPOSTS EVENLY.
SCOTT and BORGMAN
HOO-WEE! IT'S RIPE TODAY!
8/17
©2013 ZITS Partnership. Dist. by King Features
I GUESS I'LL MUCK OUT YOUR BATH-ROOM NOW.
I WON'T BE SHAMED INTO NEATNESS, MOM.

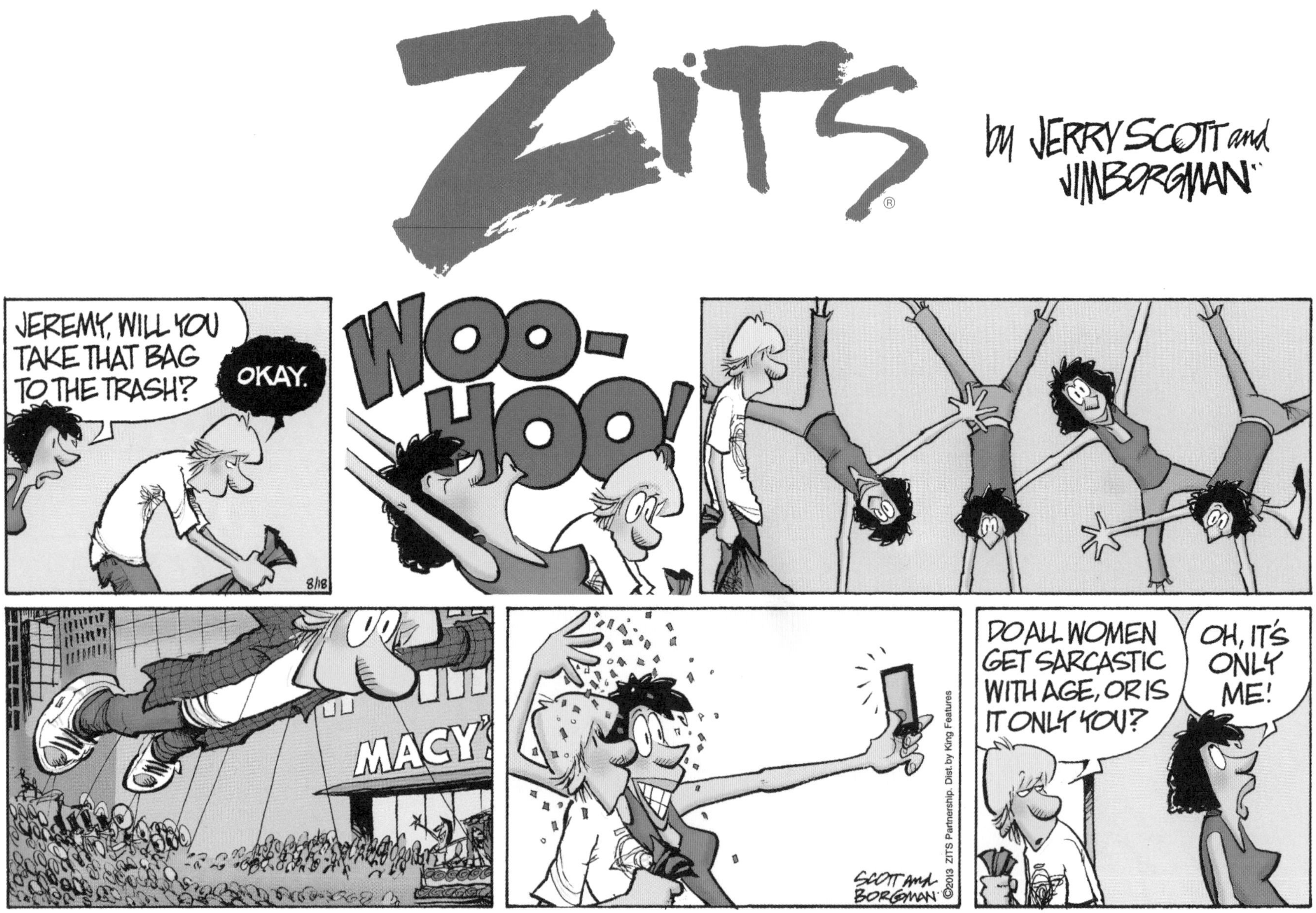
ZITS®
by JERRY SCOTT and JIM BORGMAN
JEREMY, WILL YOU TAKE THAT BAG TO THE TRASH?
OKAY.
8/18
WOO-HOO!
MACY'S
SCOTT and BORGMAN
©2013 ZITS Partnership. Dist. by King Features
DO ALL WOMEN GET SARCASTIC WITH AGE, OR IS IT ONLY YOU?
OH, IT'S ONLY ME!

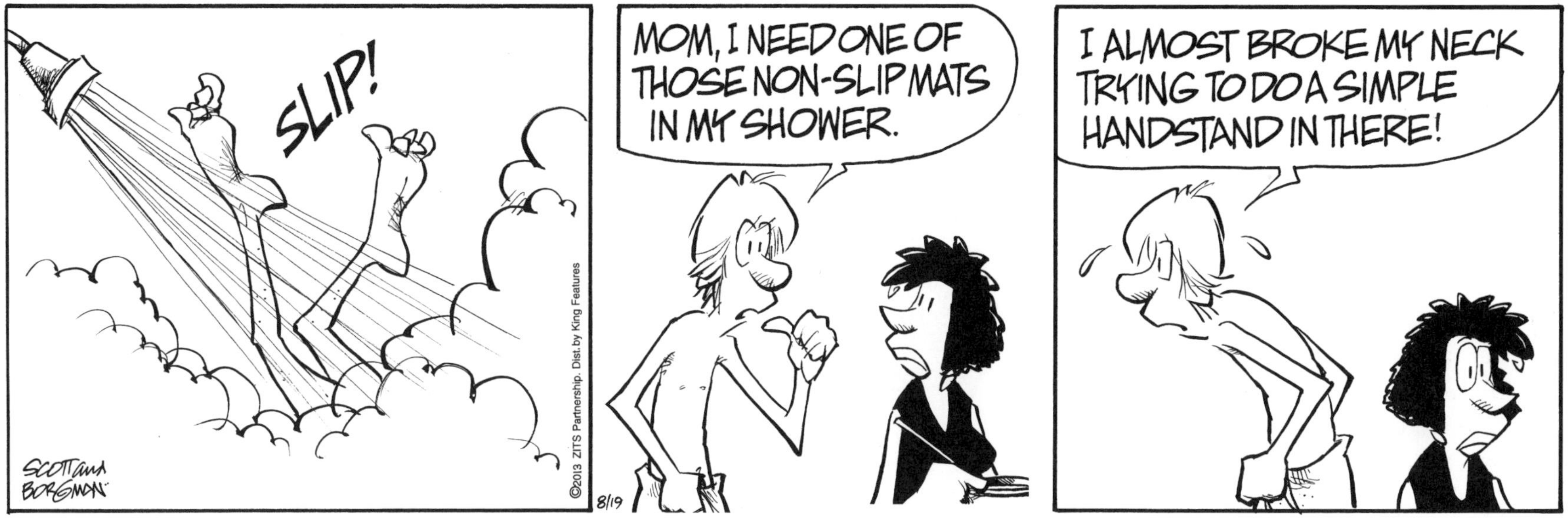
SLIP!
MOM, I NEED ONE OF THOSE NON-SLIP MATS IN MY SHOWER.
I ALMOST BROKE MY NECK TRYING TO DO A SIMPLE HANDSTAND IN THERE!
SCOTT and BORGMAN
©2013 ZITS Partnership. Dist. by King Features
8/19

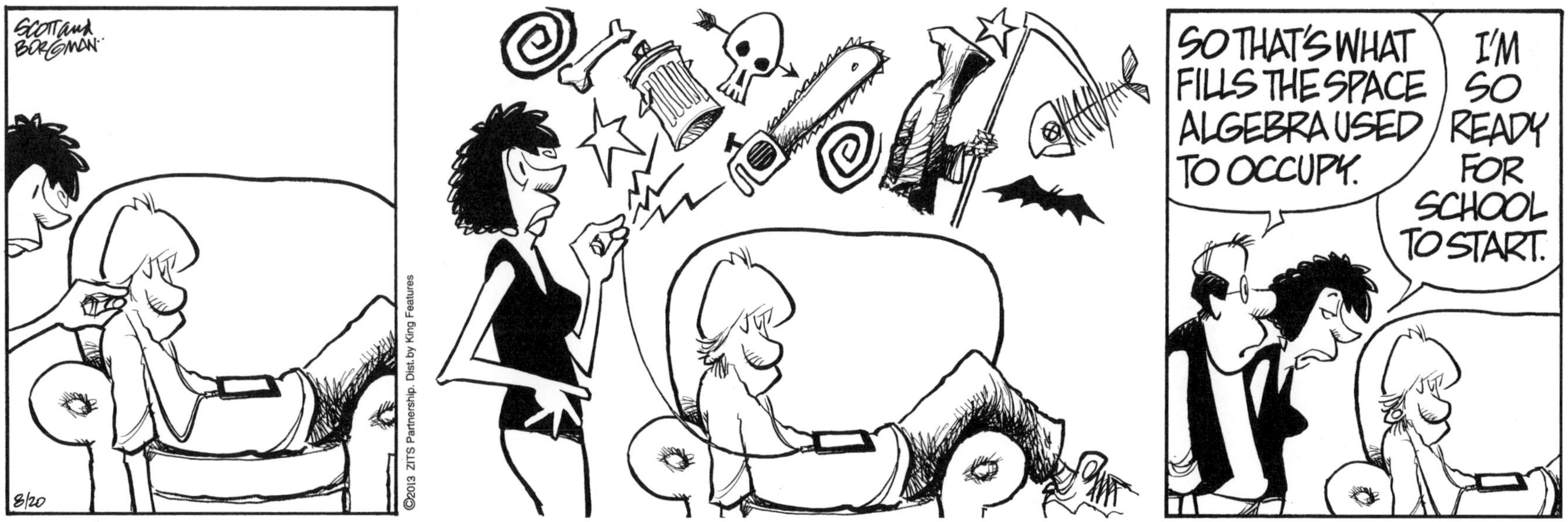
SCOTT and BORGMAN
©2013 ZITS Partnership. Dist. by King Features
8/20
SO THAT'S WHAT FILLS THE SPACE ALGEBRA USED TO OCCUPY.
I'M SO READY FOR SCHOOL TO START.

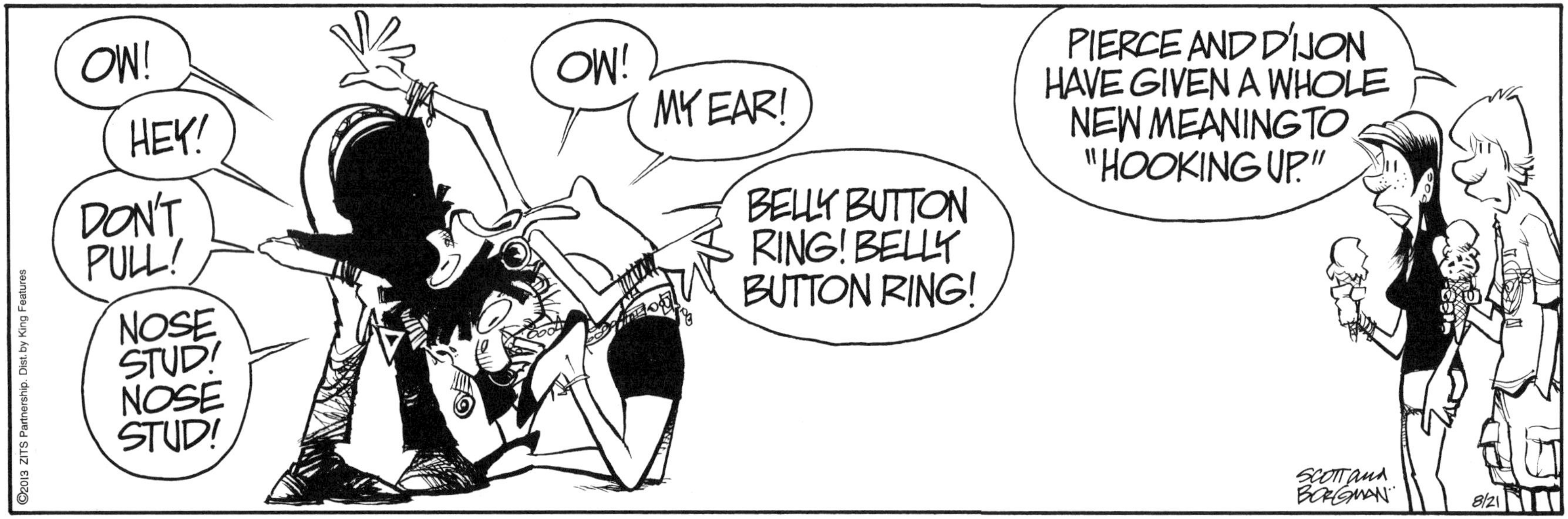
OW!
HEY!
DON'T PULL!
NOSE STUD! NOSE STUD!
OW!
MY EAR!
BELLY BUTTON RING! BELLY BUTTON RING!
PIERCE AND D'IJON HAVE GIVEN A WHOLE NEW MEANING TO "HOOKING UP."
©2013 ZITS Partnership. Dist. by King Features
SCOTT and BORGMAN
8/21

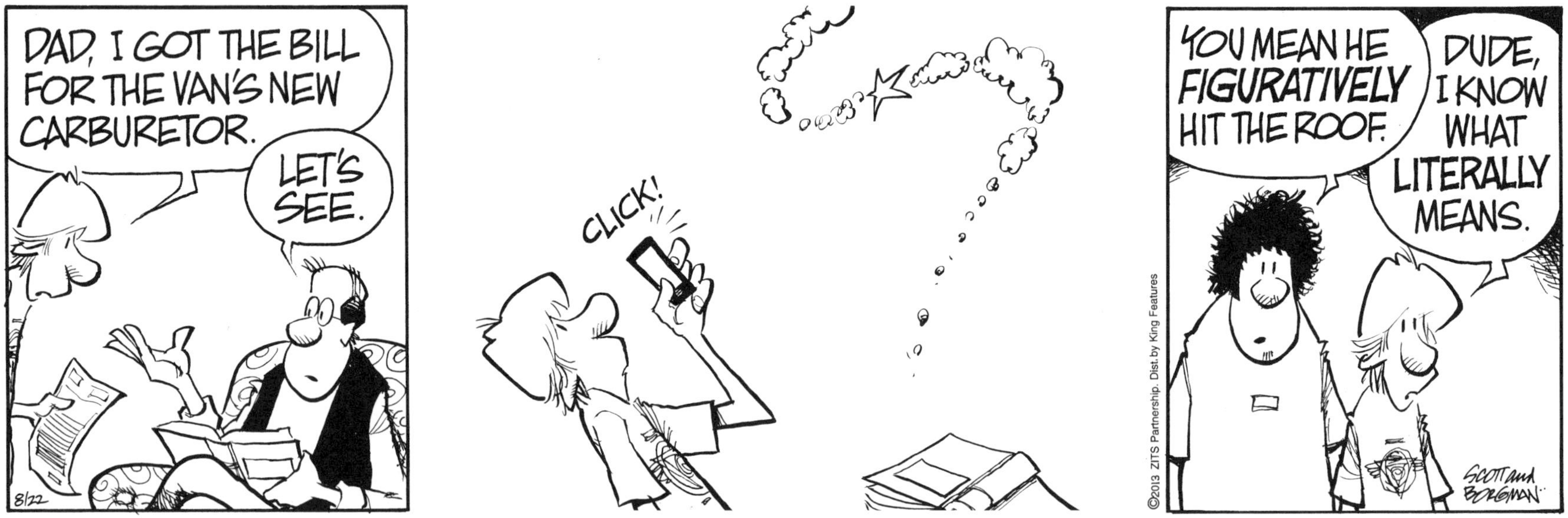
DAD, I GOT THE BILL FOR THE VAN'S NEW CARBURETOR.
LET'S SEE.
8/22
CLICK!
YOU MEAN HE *FIGURATIVELY* HIT THE ROOF.
DUDE, I KNOW WHAT **LITERALLY** MEANS.
©2013 ZITS Partnership. Dist. by King Features
SCOTT and BORGMAN

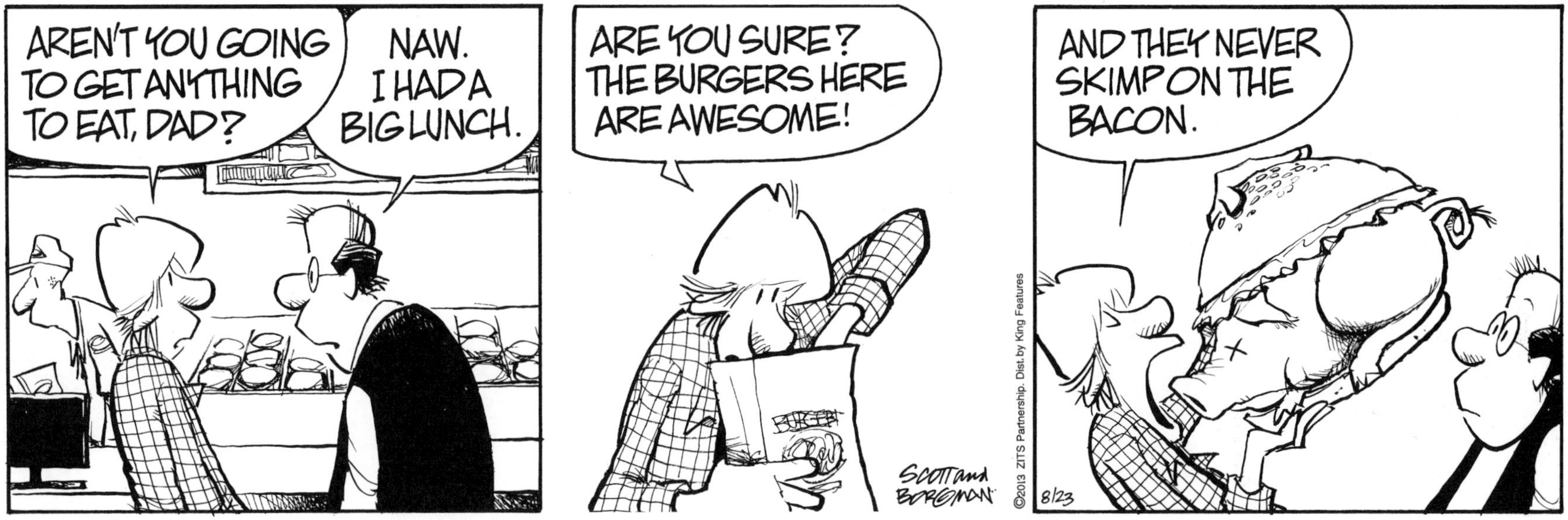
AREN'T YOU GOING TO GET ANYTHING TO EAT, DAD?
NAW. I HAD A BIG LUNCH.
ARE YOU SURE? THE BURGERS HERE ARE AWESOME!
AND THEY NEVER SKIMP ON THE BACON.
SCOTT and BORGMAN
8/23
©2013 ZITS Partnership. Dist. by King Features

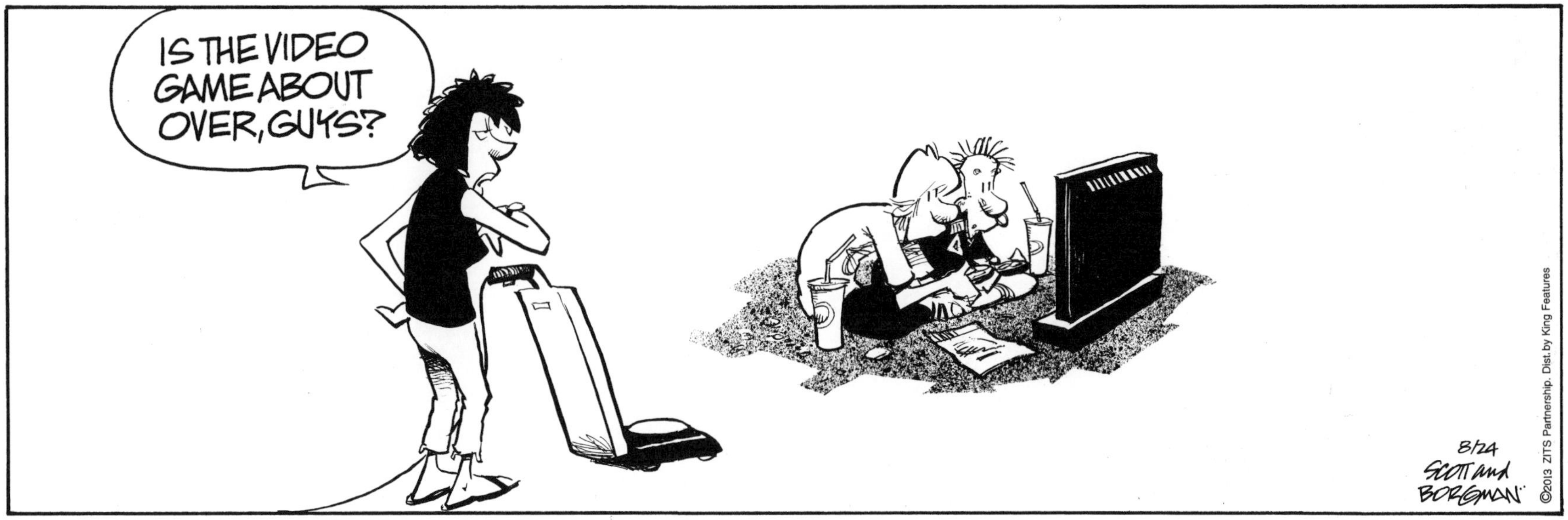
IS THE VIDEO GAME ABOUT OVER, GUYS?
8/24
SCOTT and BORGMAN
©2013 ZITS Partnership. Dist. by King Features

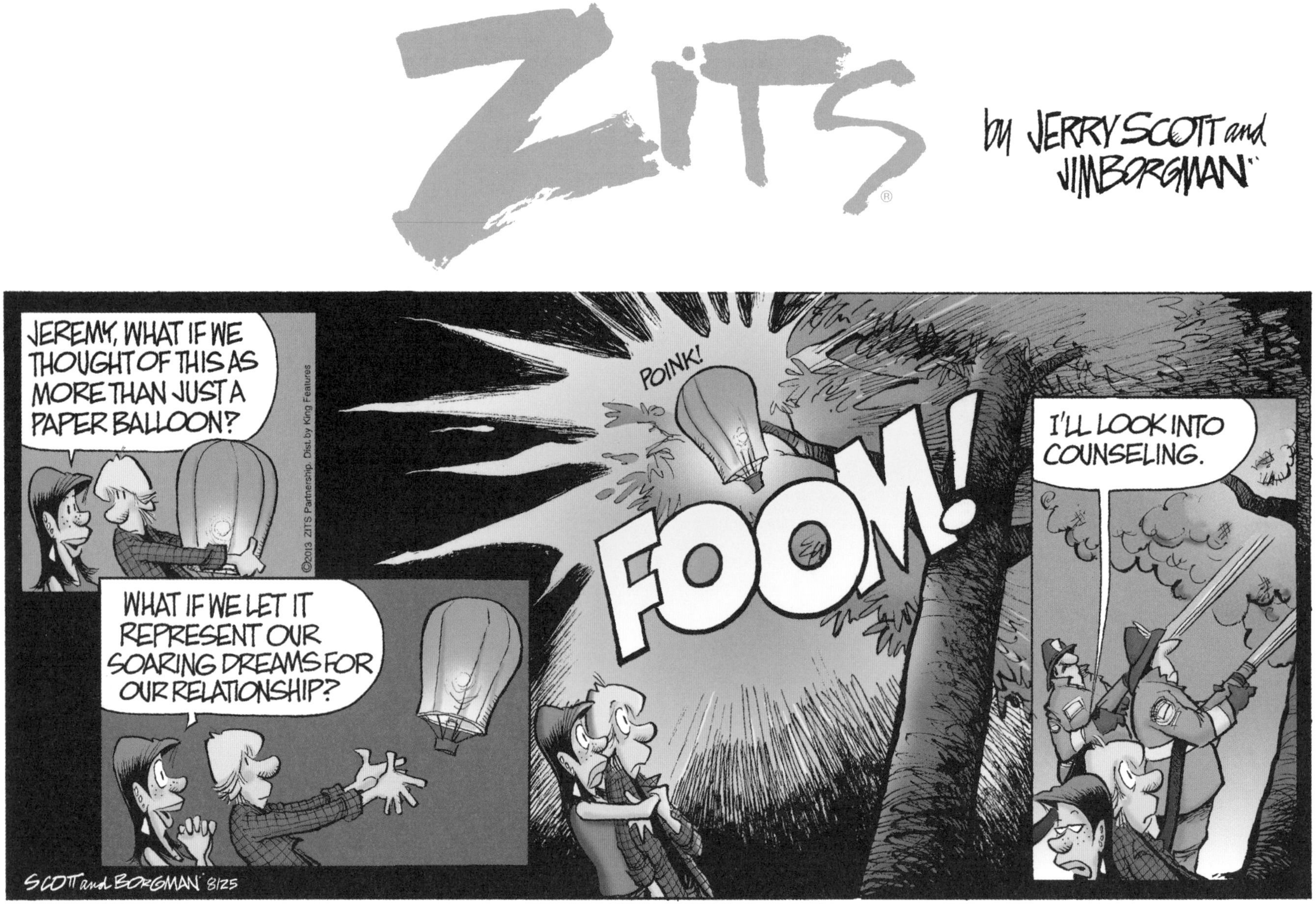
ZITS
by JERRY SCOTT and JIM BORGMAN
JEREMY, WHAT IF WE THOUGHT OF THIS AS MORE THAN JUST A PAPER BALLOON?
©2013 ZITS Partnership. Dist. by King Features
WHAT IF WE LET IT REPRESENT OUR SOARING DREAMS FOR OUR RELATIONSHIP?
SCOTT and BORGMAN 8/25
POINK!
FOOM!
I'LL LOOK INTO COUNSELING.

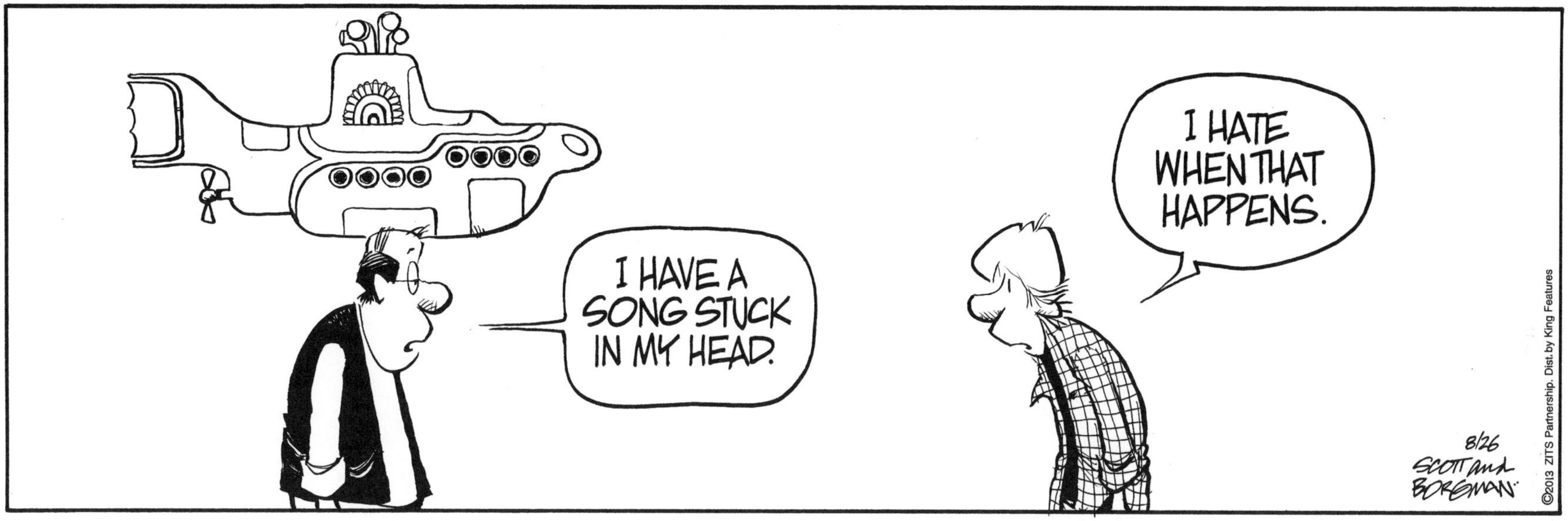
I HAVE A SONG STUCK IN MY HEAD.
I HATE WHEN THAT HAPPENS.
8/26 SCOTT and BORGMAN
©2013 ZITS Partnership. Dist. by King Features

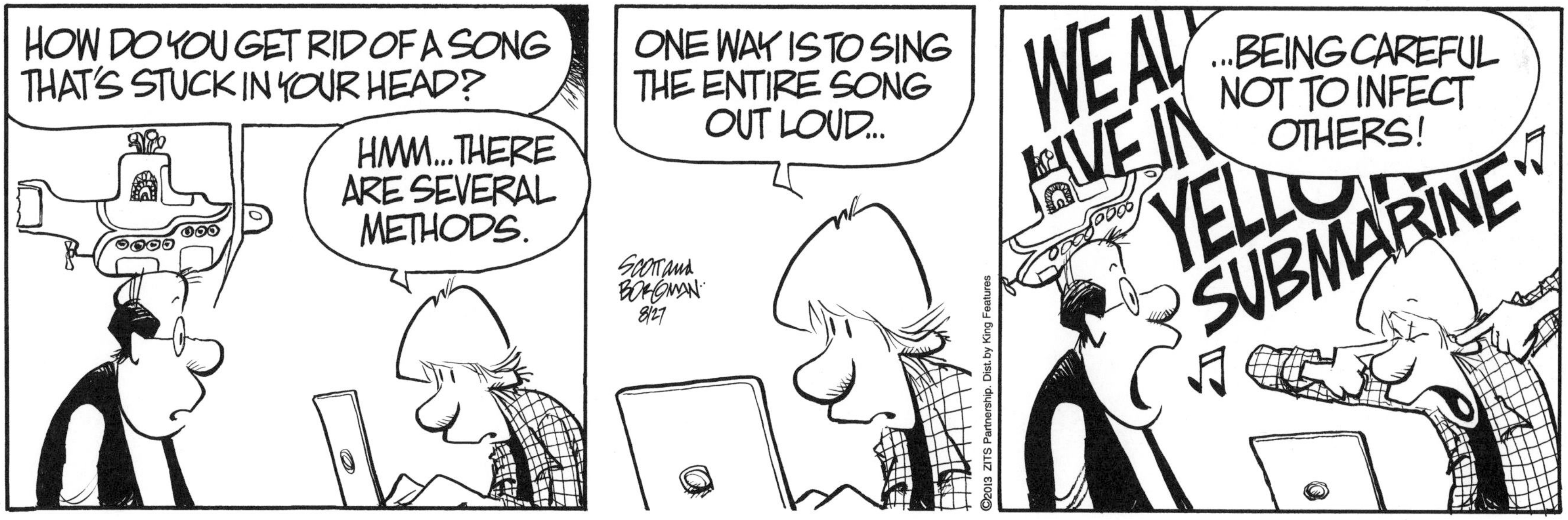
HOW DO YOU GET RID OF A SONG THAT'S STUCK IN YOUR HEAD?
HMM... THERE ARE SEVERAL METHODS.
SCOTT and BORGMAN 8/27
ONE WAY IS TO SING THE ENTIRE SONG OUT LOUD...
©2013 ZITS Partnership. Dist. by King Features
WE AL
IVE IN
YELLO
SUBMARINE
...BEING CAREFUL NOT TO INFECT OTHERS!

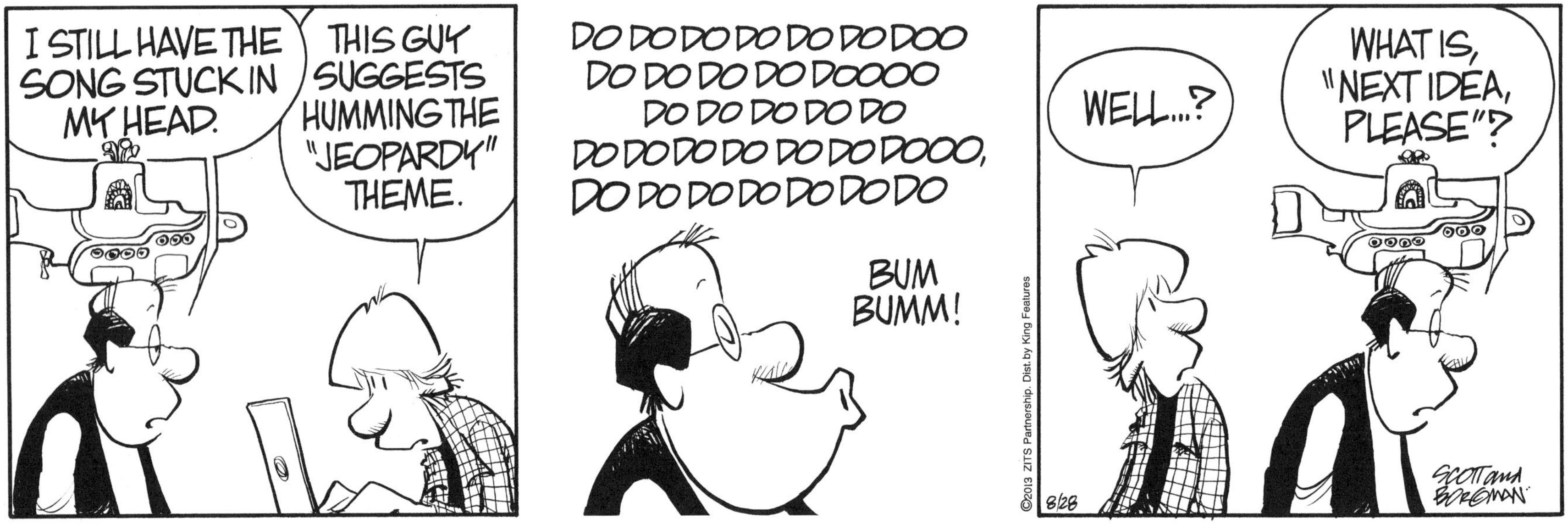
I STILL HAVE THE SONG STUCK IN MY HEAD.
THIS GUY SUGGESTS HUMMING THE "JEOPARDY" THEME.
DO DO DO DO DO DO DOO DO DO DO DO DOOOO DO DO DO DO DO DO DO DO DO DO DO DOOO, DO DO DO DO DO DO DO
BUM BUMM!
WELL...?
WHAT IS, "NEXT IDEA, PLEASE"?
©2013 ZITS Partnership. Dist. by King Features
8/28
SCOTT AND BORGMAN

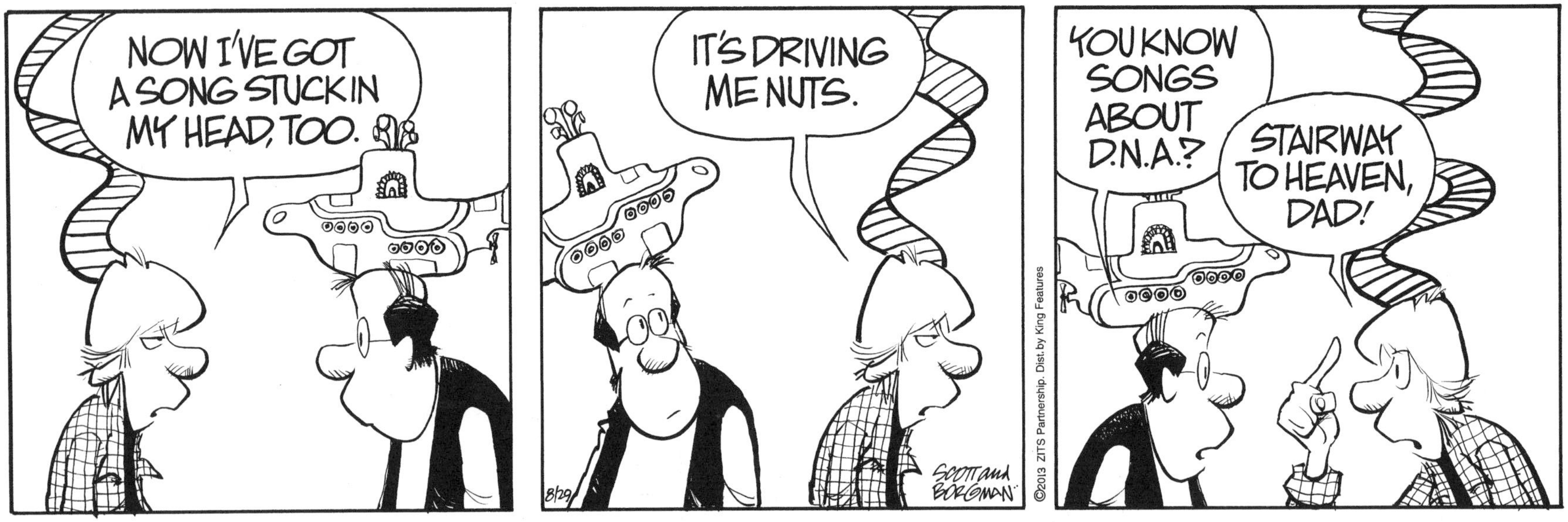
NOW I'VE GOT A SONG STUCK IN MY HEAD, TOO.
IT'S DRIVING ME NUTS.
8/29
SCOTT AND BORGMAN
YOU KNOW SONGS ABOUT D.N.A.?
STAIRWAY TO HEAVEN, DAD!
©2013 ZITS Partnership. Dist. by King Features

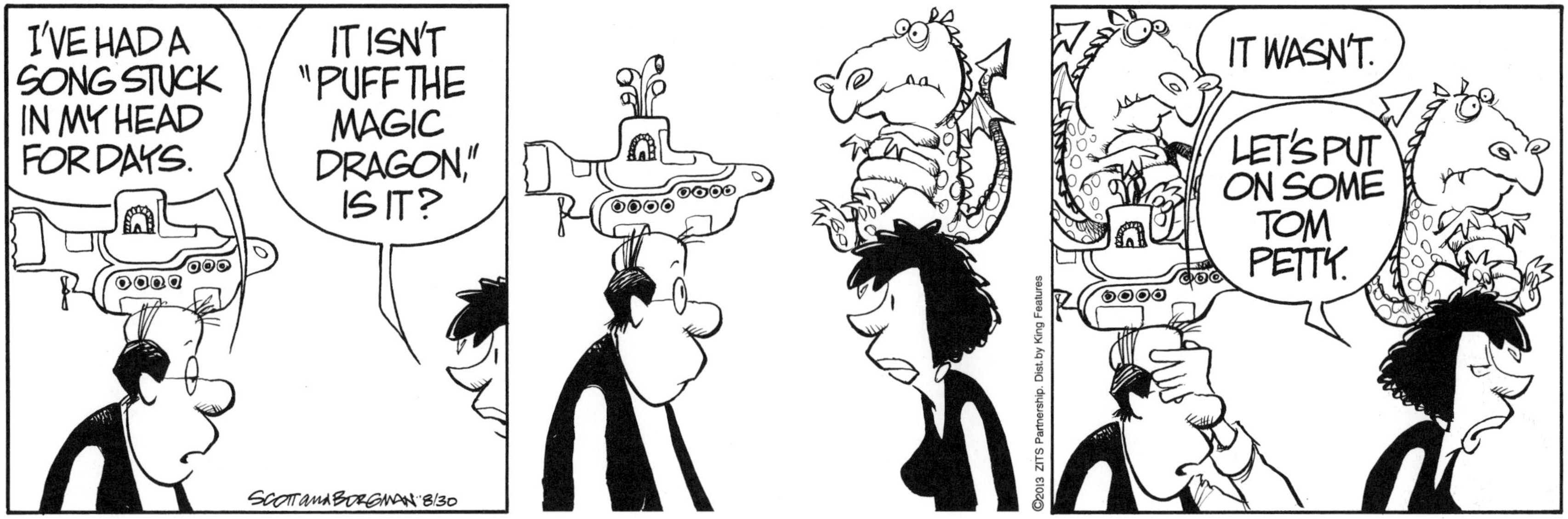
I'VE HAD A SONG STUCK IN MY HEAD FOR DAYS.
IT ISN'T "PUFF THE MAGIC DRAGON," IS IT?
IT WASN'T.
LET'S PUT ON SOME TOM PETTY.
SCOTT AND BORGMAN 8/30
©2013 ZITS Partnership. Dist. by King Features

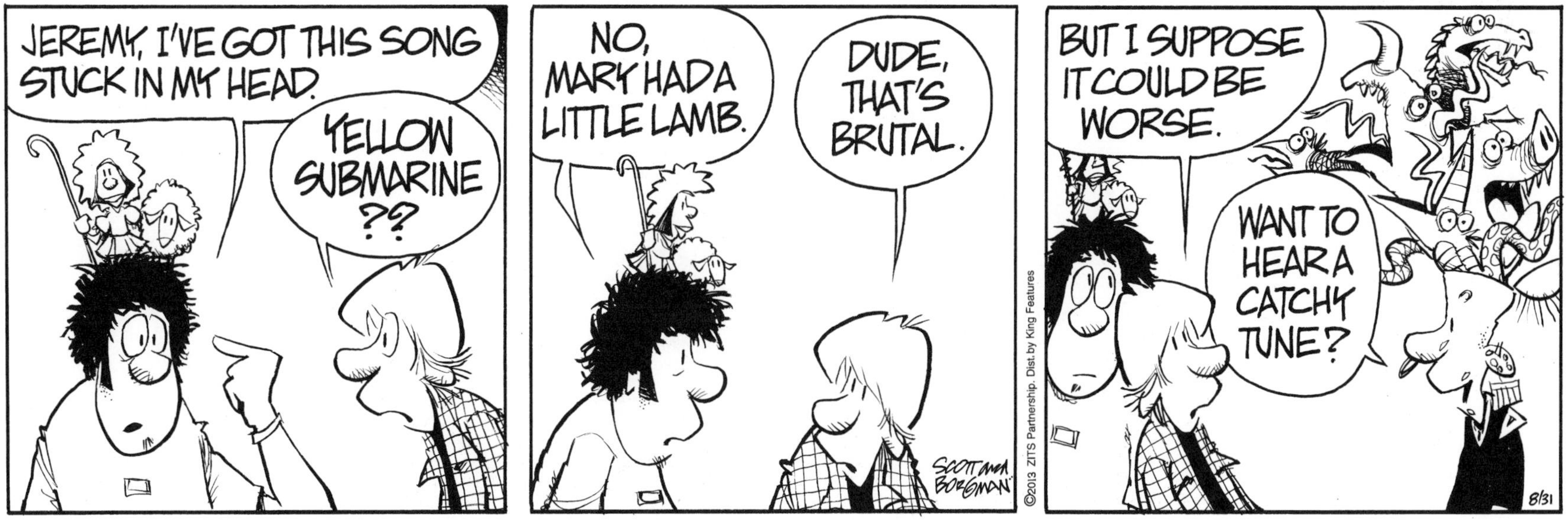
JEREMY, I'VE GOT THIS SONG STUCK IN MY HEAD.
YELLOW SUBMARINE??
NO, MARY HAD A LITTLE LAMB.
DUDE, THAT'S BRUTAL.
SCOTT AND BORGMAN
©2013 ZITS Partnership. Dist. by King Features
BUT I SUPPOSE IT COULD BE WORSE.
WANT TO HEAR A CATCHY TUNE?
8/31

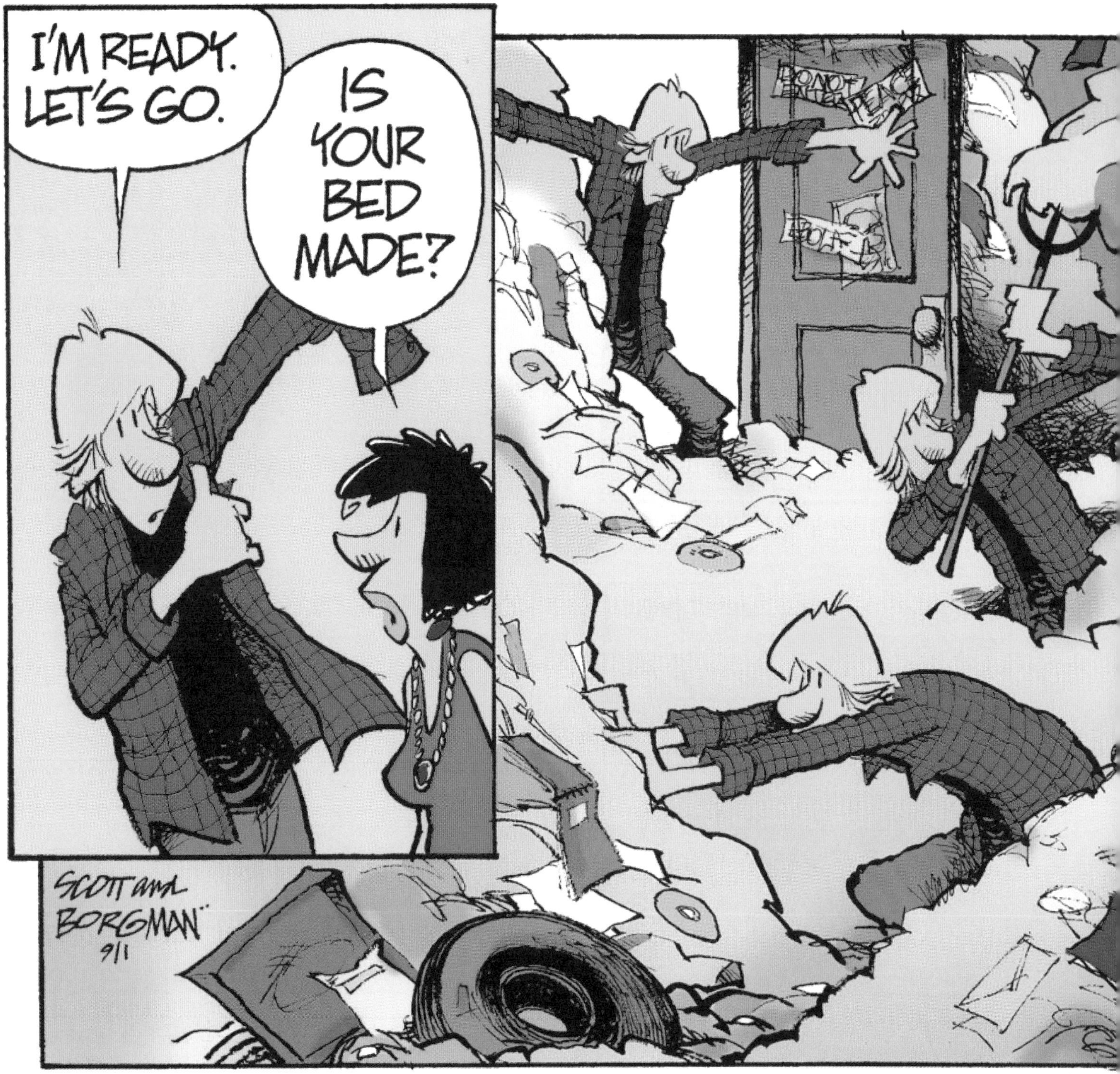
I'M READY. LET'S GO.
IS YOUR BED MADE?
DO NOT ENTER
PEACE
SCOTT and BORGMAN
9/1

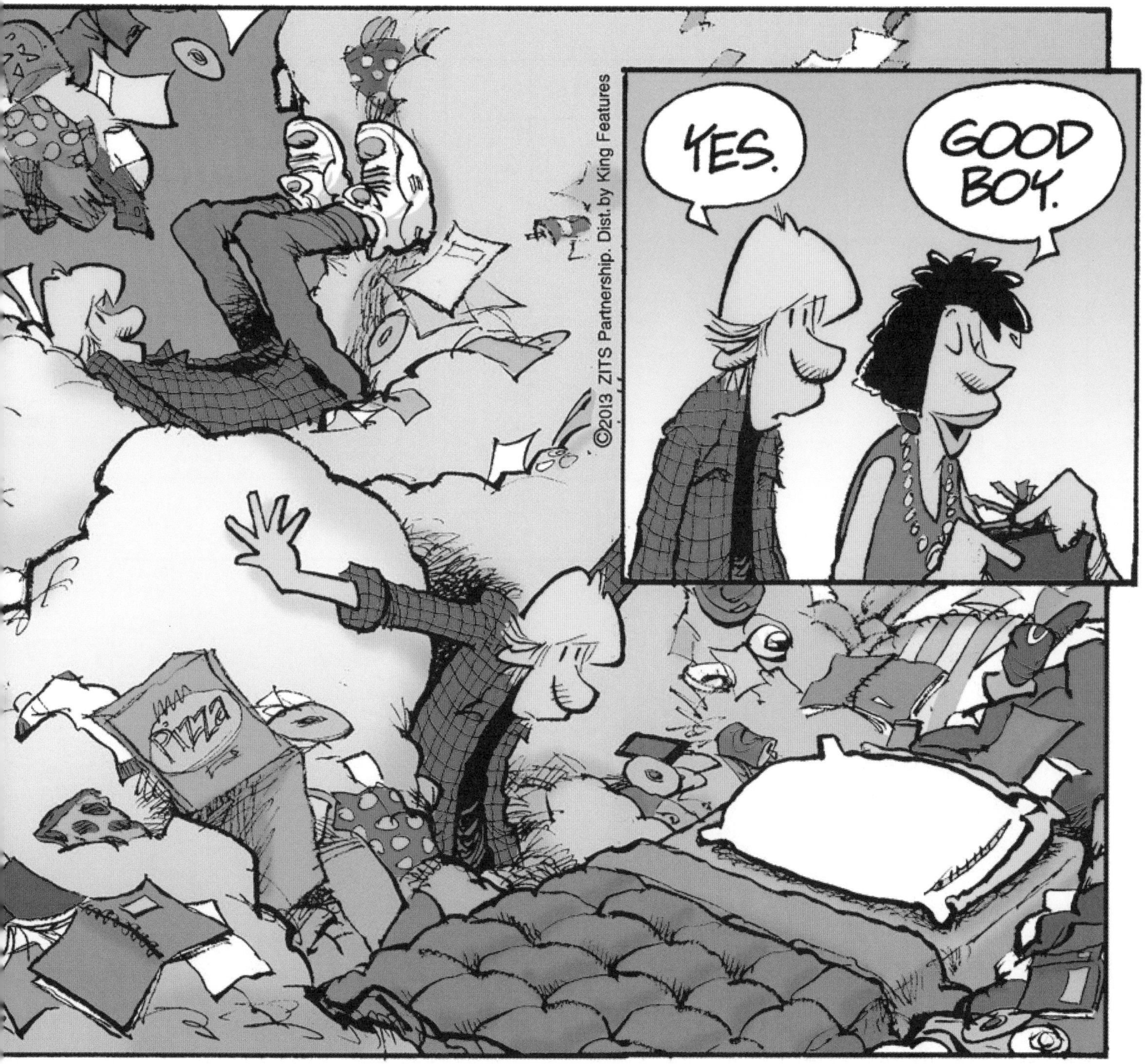
YES.
GOOD BOY.
Pizza
©2013 ZITS Partnership. Dist.by King Features

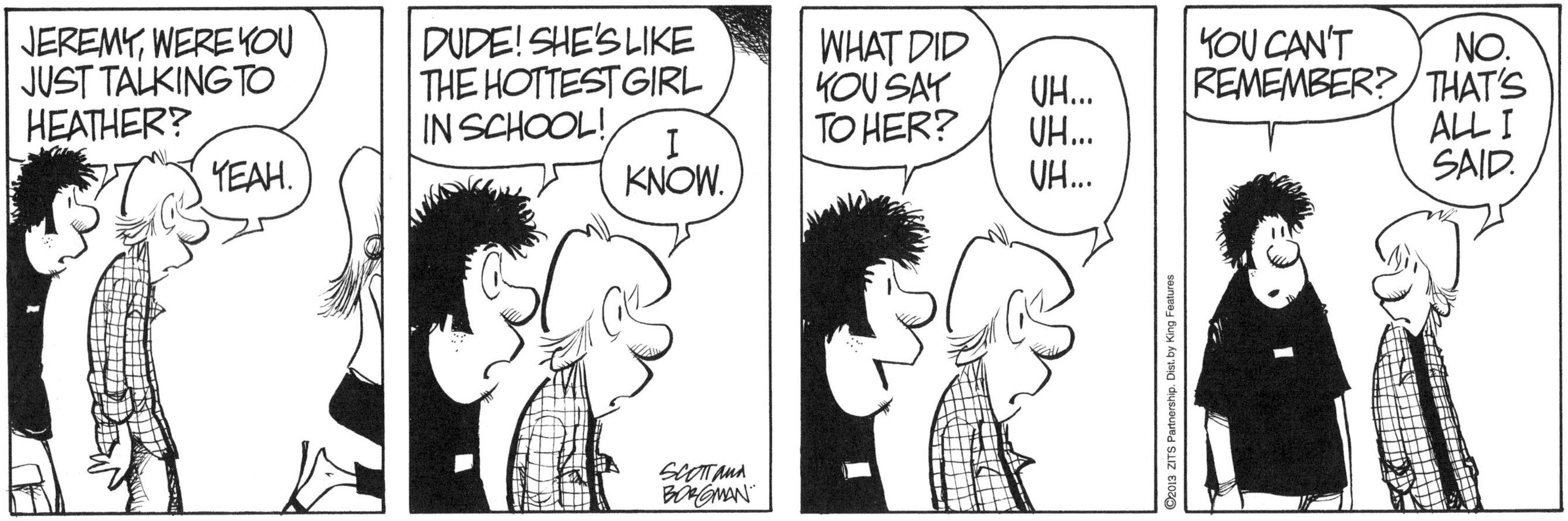
JEREMY, WERE YOU JUST TALKING TO HEATHER?
YEAH.
DUDE! SHE'S LIKE THE HOTTEST GIRL IN SCHOOL!
I KNOW.
SCOTT AND BORGMAN
WHAT DID YOU SAY TO HER?
UH... UH... UH...
YOU CAN'T REMEMBER?
NO. THAT'S ALL I SAID.



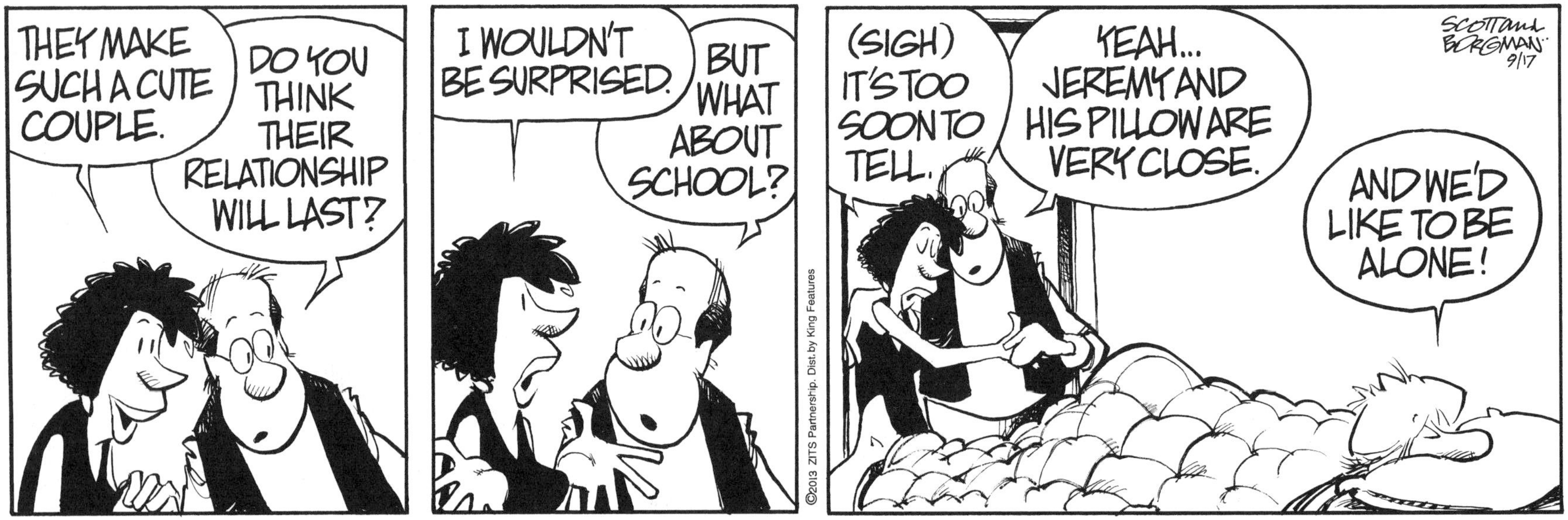
THEY MAKE SUCH A CUTE COUPLE.
DO YOU THINK THEIR RELATIONSHIP WILL LAST?
I WOULDN'T BE SURPRISED.
BUT WHAT ABOUT SCHOOL?
(SIGH) IT'S TOO SOON TO TELL.
YEAH... JEREMY AND HIS PILLOW ARE VERY CLOSE.
AND WE'D LIKE TO BE ALONE!
SCOTT AND BORGMAN 9/17

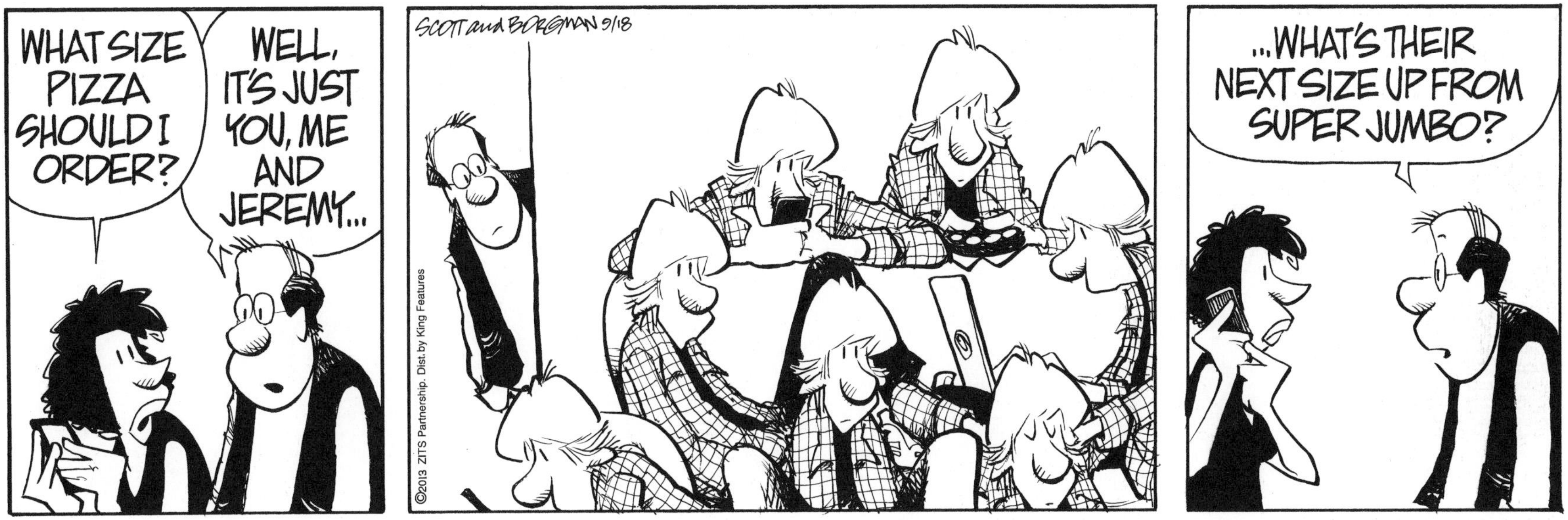
WHAT SIZE PIZZA SHOULD I ORDER?
WELL, IT'S JUST YOU, ME AND JEREMY...
SCOTT and BORGMAN 9/18
©2013 ZITS Partnership. Dist. by King Features
...WHAT'S THEIR NEXT SIZE UP FROM SUPER JUMBO?

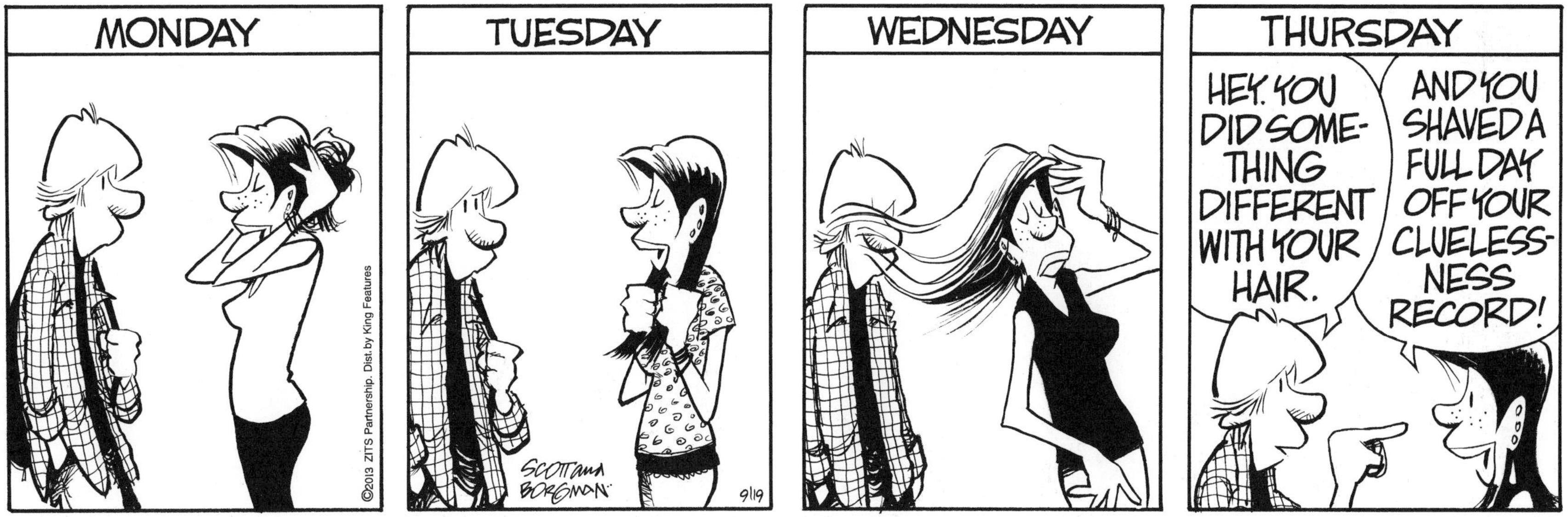
MONDAY
©2013 ZITS Partnership. Dist. by King Features
TUESDAY
SCOTT and BORGMAN
9/19
WEDNESDAY
THURSDAY
HEY. YOU DID SOME-THING DIFFERENT WITH YOUR HAIR.
AND YOU SHAVED A FULL DAY OFF YOUR CLUELESS-NESS RECORD!

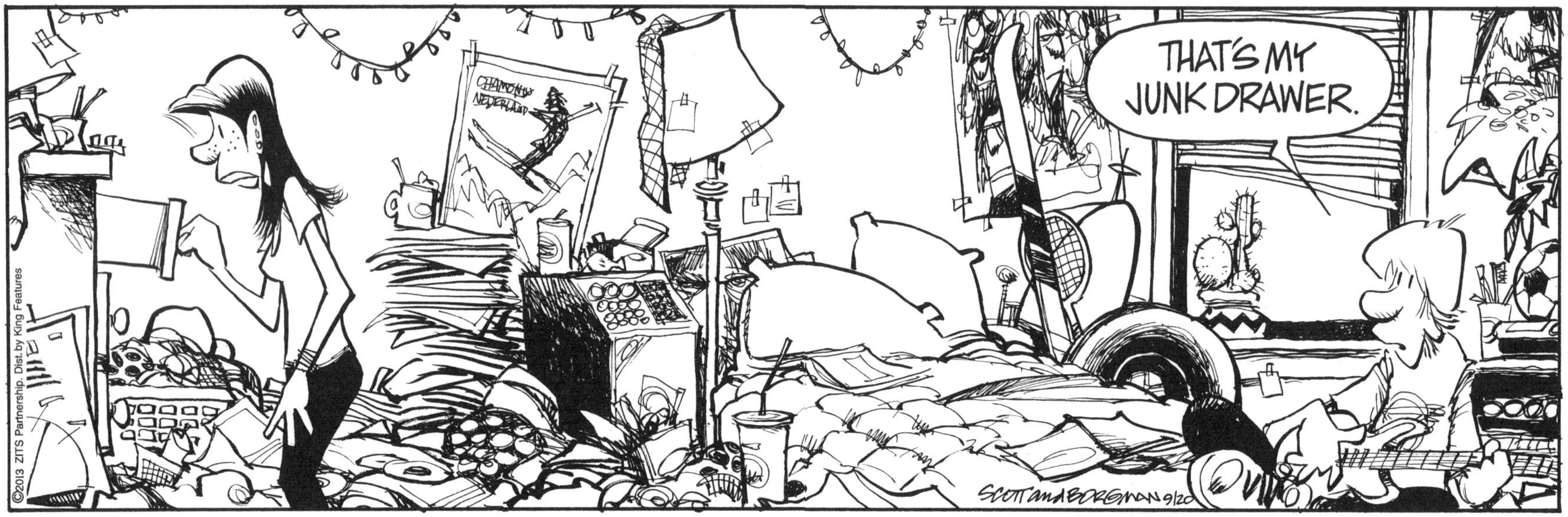
THAT'S MY JUNK DRAWER.
©2013 ZITS Partnership. Dist. by King Features
SCOTT and BORGMAN 9/20

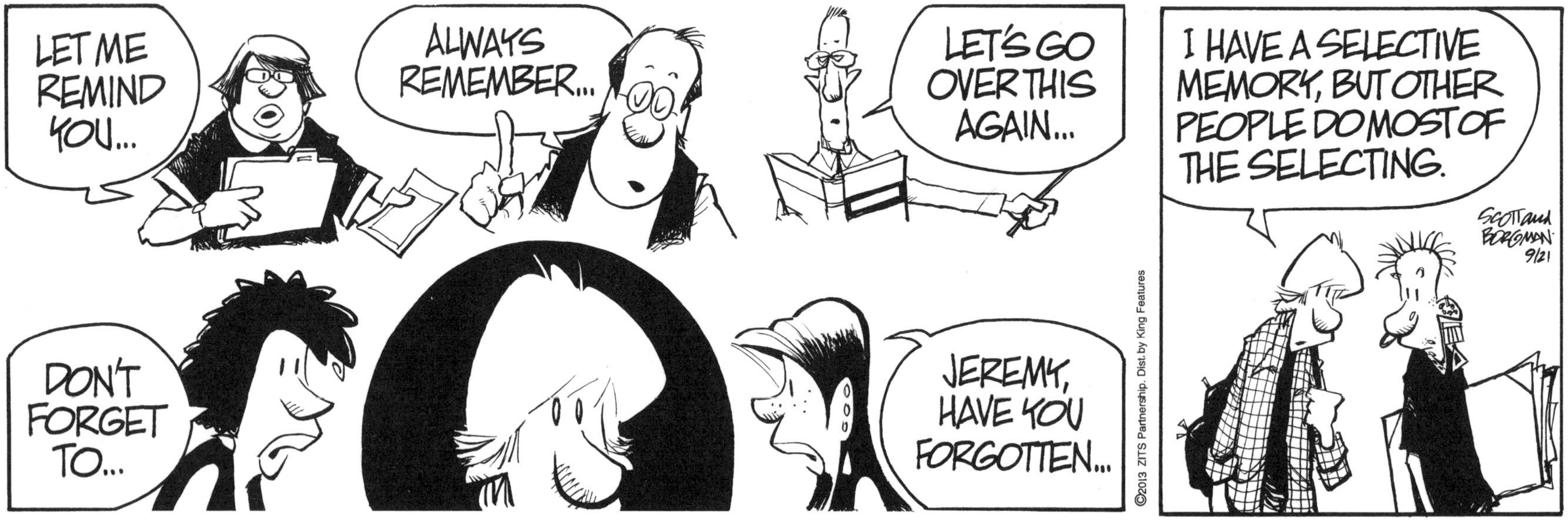
LET ME REMIND YOU...
ALWAYS REMEMBER...
LET'S GO OVER THIS AGAIN...
DON'T FORGET TO...
JEREMY, HAVE YOU FORGOTTEN...
©2013 ZITS Partnership. Dist. by King Features
I HAVE A SELECTIVE MEMORY, BUT OTHER PEOPLE DO MOST OF THE SELECTING.
SCOTT and BORGMAN 9/21

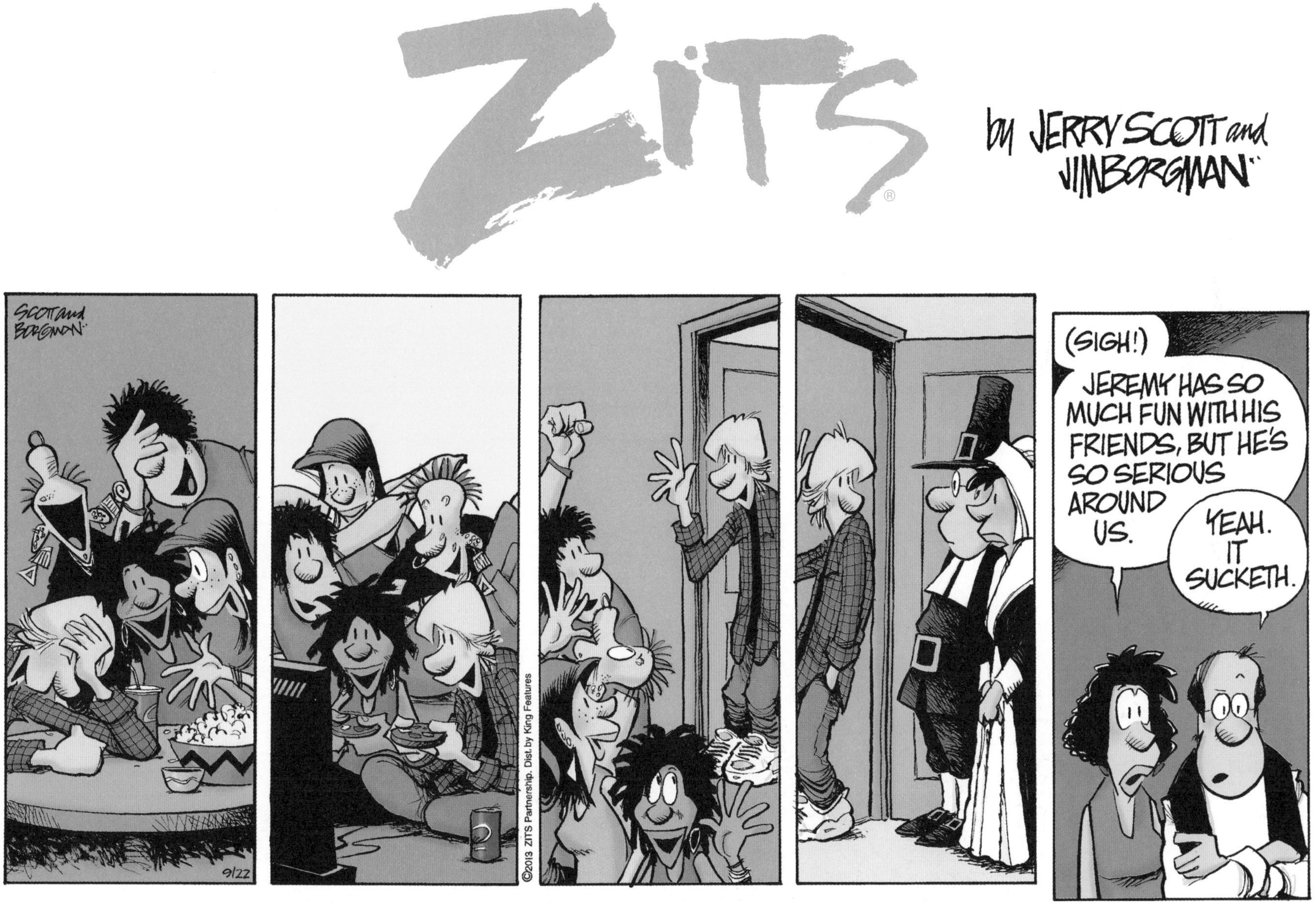
ZITS
by JERRY SCOTT and JIM BORGMAN
SCOTT and BORGMAN
9/22
©2013 ZITS Partnership. Dist. by King Features
(SIGH!)
JEREMY HAS SO MUCH FUN WITH HIS FRIENDS, BUT HE'S SO SERIOUS AROUND US.
YEAH. IT SUCKETH.

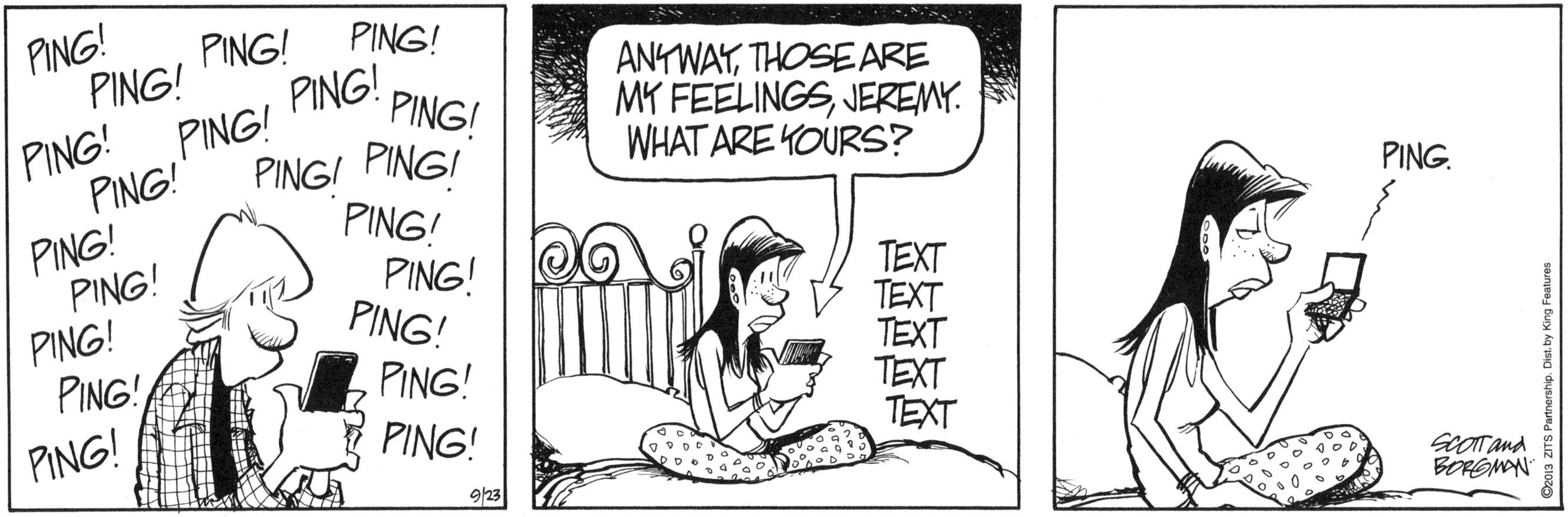
PING! PING! PING!
PING! PING! PING!
PING! PING! PING!
PING! PING! PING!
PING!
PING! PING!
PING! PING!
PING! PING!
PING! PING!
PING! PING!
9/23
ANYWAY, THOSE ARE MY FEELINGS, JEREMY. WHAT ARE YOURS?
TEXT
TEXT
TEXT
TEXT
TEXT
PING.
SCOTT and BORGMAN
©2013 ZITS Partnership. Dist.by King Features

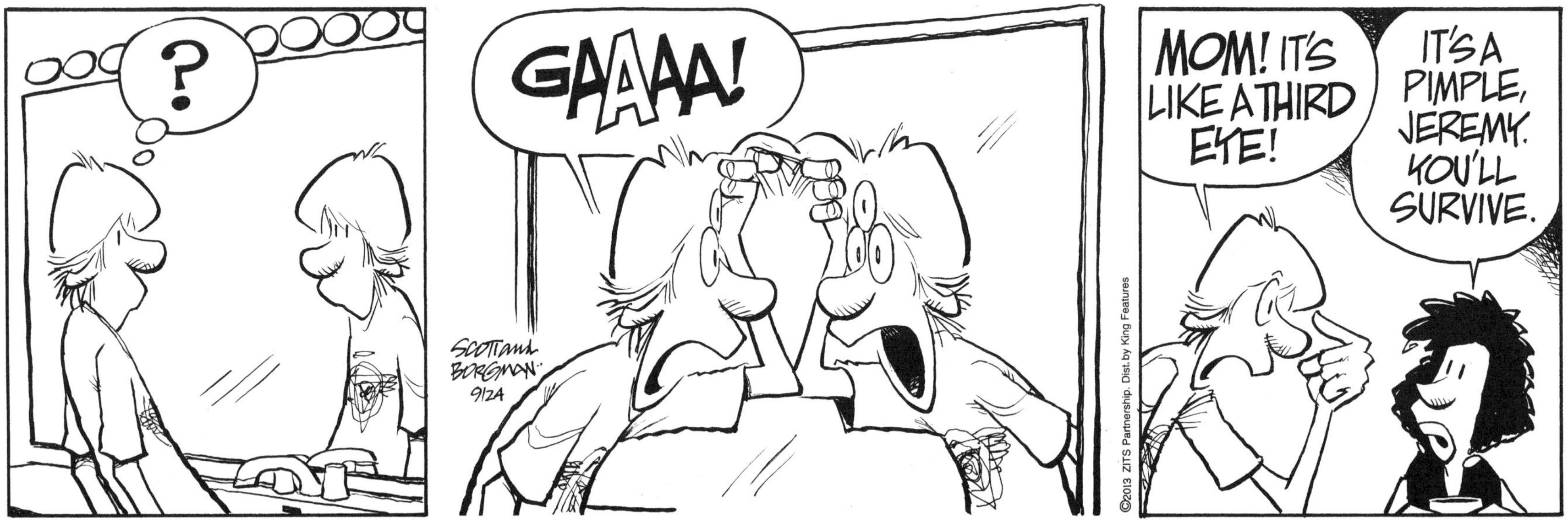
?
GAAAA!
SCOTT and BORGMAN
9/24
©2013 ZITS Partnership. Dist.by King Features
MOM! IT'S LIKE A THIRD EYE!
IT'S A PIMPLE, JEREMY. YOU'LL SURVIVE.

THANKS FOR THE CLOGGED PORE GENES, GUYS!
THE PIMPLE ISN'T THAT BIG, JEREMY. I HARDLY NOTICED IT BULGING THROUGH THE BEANIE.
THAT ISN'T HELPING.
9/25
SCOTT and BORGMAN
©2013 ZITS Partnership. Dist. by King Features

DUDE. NEW LOOK?
YEAH. I THOUGHT I SHOULD CHANGE IT UP.
STYLIN'!
REALLY? THANKS!
AND IT ALMOST COVERS THAT MAJOR ZIT.
I SHOULD HAVE WORN THE PAPER BAG.
9/26
SCOTT and BORGMAN
©2013 ZITS Partnership. Dist. by King Features

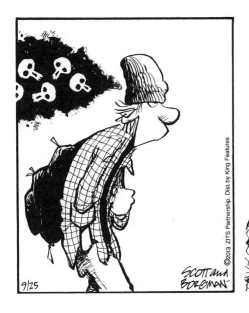

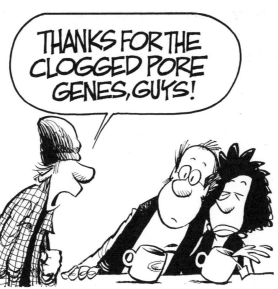

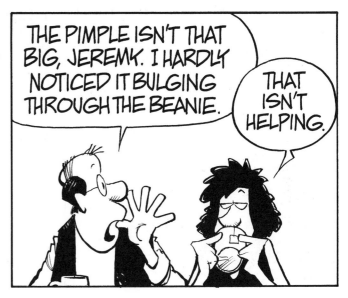

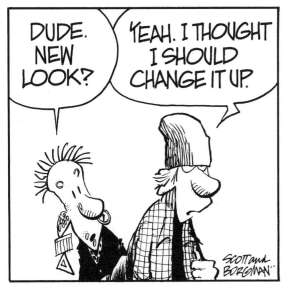

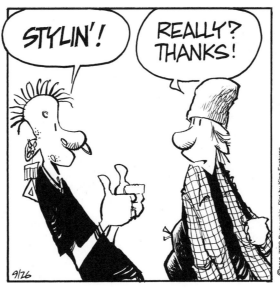

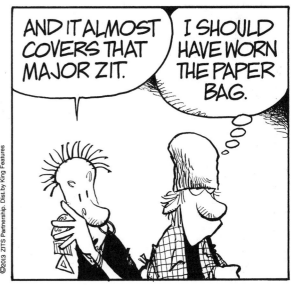

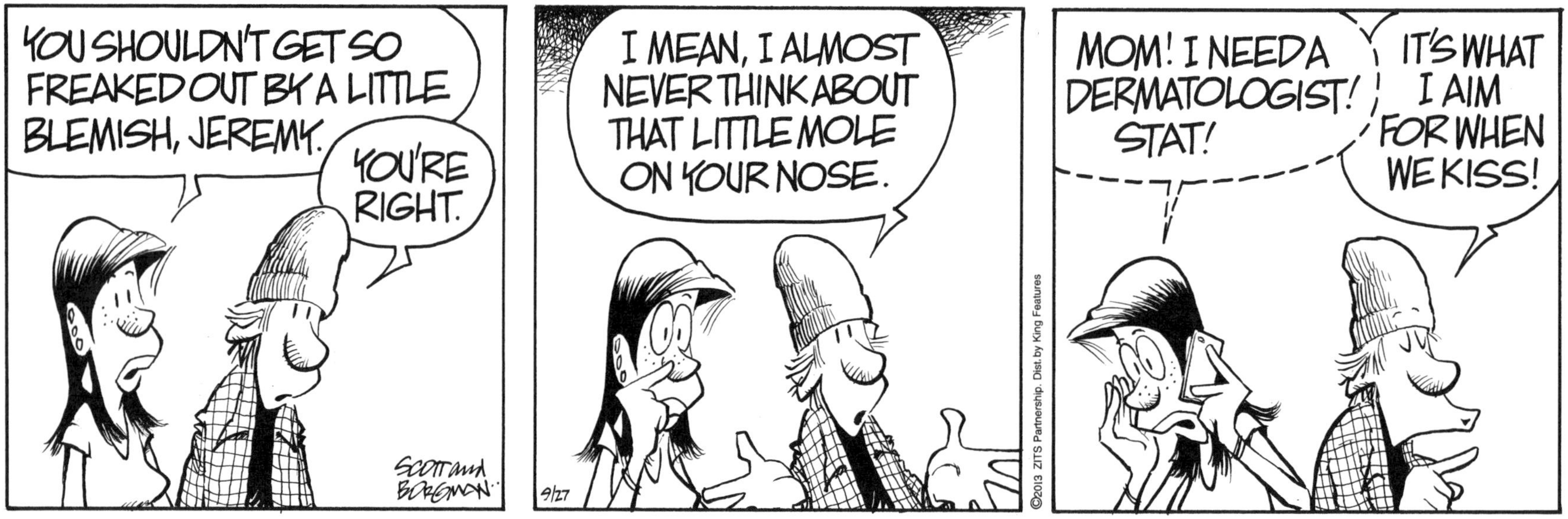
YOU SHOULDN'T GET SO FREAKED OUT BY A LITTLE BLEMISH, JEREMY.
YOU'RE RIGHT.
I MEAN, I ALMOST NEVER THINK ABOUT THAT LITTLE MOLE ON YOUR NOSE.
MOM! I NEED A DERMATOLOGIST! STAT!
IT'S WHAT I AIM FOR WHEN WE KISS!
©2013 ZITS Partnership. Dist. by King Features

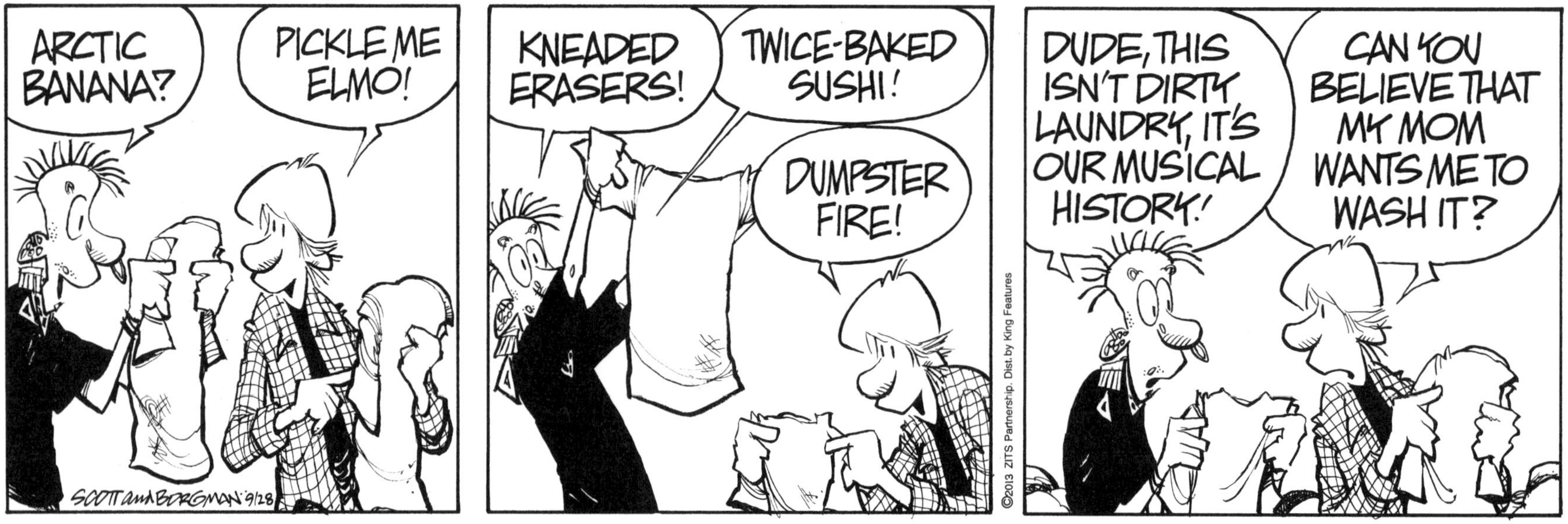
ARCTIC BANANA?
PICKLE ME ELMO!
KNEADED ERASERS!
TWICE-BAKED SUSHI!
DUMPSTER FIRE!
DUDE, THIS ISN'T DIRTY LAUNDRY, IT'S OUR MUSICAL HISTORY!
CAN YOU BELIEVE THAT MY MOM WANTS ME TO WASH IT?
©2013 ZITS Partnership. Dist. by King Features

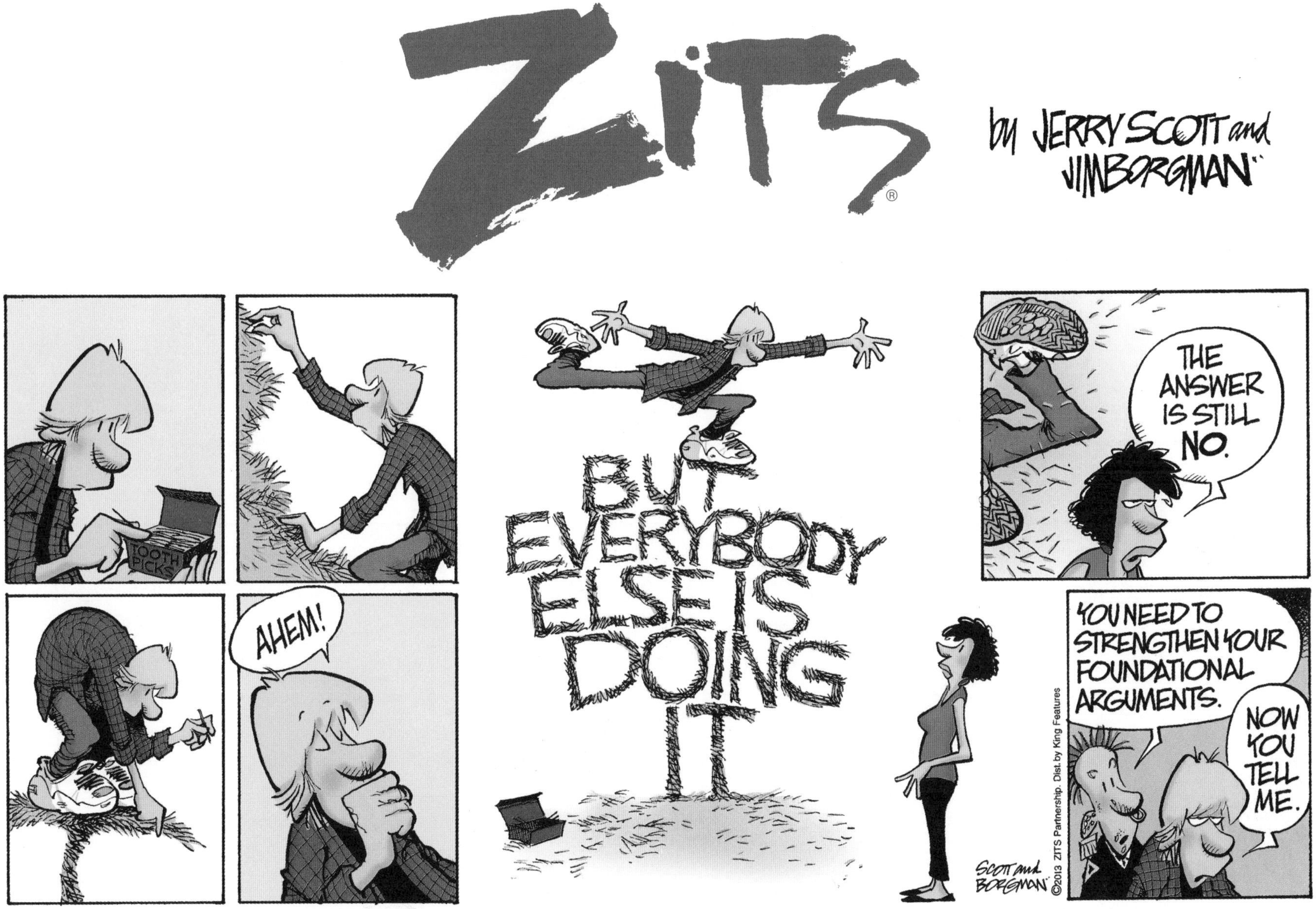
ZITS
by JERRY SCOTT and JIM BORGMAN
TOOTH PICKS
AHEM!
BUT EVERYBODY ELSE IS DOING IT
THE ANSWER IS STILL NO.
YOU NEED TO STRENGTHEN YOUR FOUNDATIONAL ARGUMENTS.
NOW YOU TELL ME.
SCOTT and BORGMAN
©2013 ZITS Partnership. Dist. by King Features

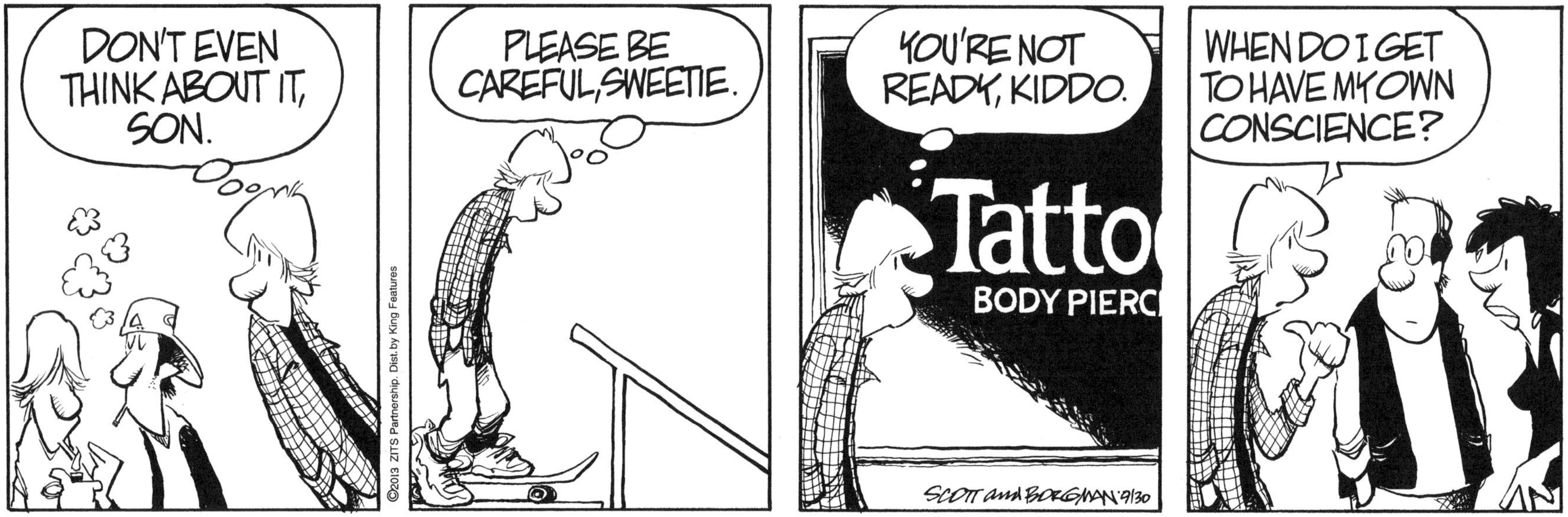
DON'T EVEN THINK ABOUT IT, SON.
PLEASE BE CAREFUL, SWEETIE.
©2013 ZITS Partnership. Dist. by King Features
YOU'RE NOT READY, KIDDO.
Tattoo
BODY PIERC
SCOTT and BORGMAN 9/30
WHEN DO I GET TO HAVE MY OWN CONSCIENCE?

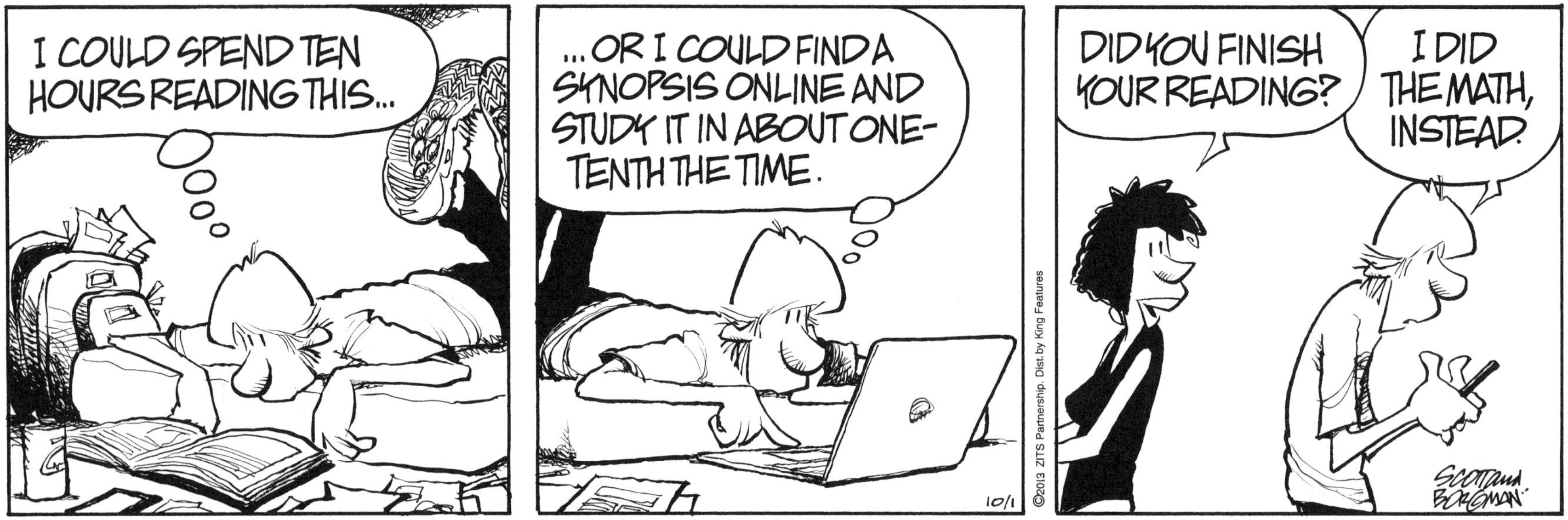
I COULD SPEND TEN HOURS READING THIS...
...OR I COULD FIND A SYNOPSIS ONLINE AND STUDY IT IN ABOUT ONE-TENTH THE TIME.
10/1
©2013 ZITS Partnership. Dist. by King Features
DID YOU FINISH YOUR READING?
I DID THE MATH, INSTEAD.
SCOTT and BORGMAN

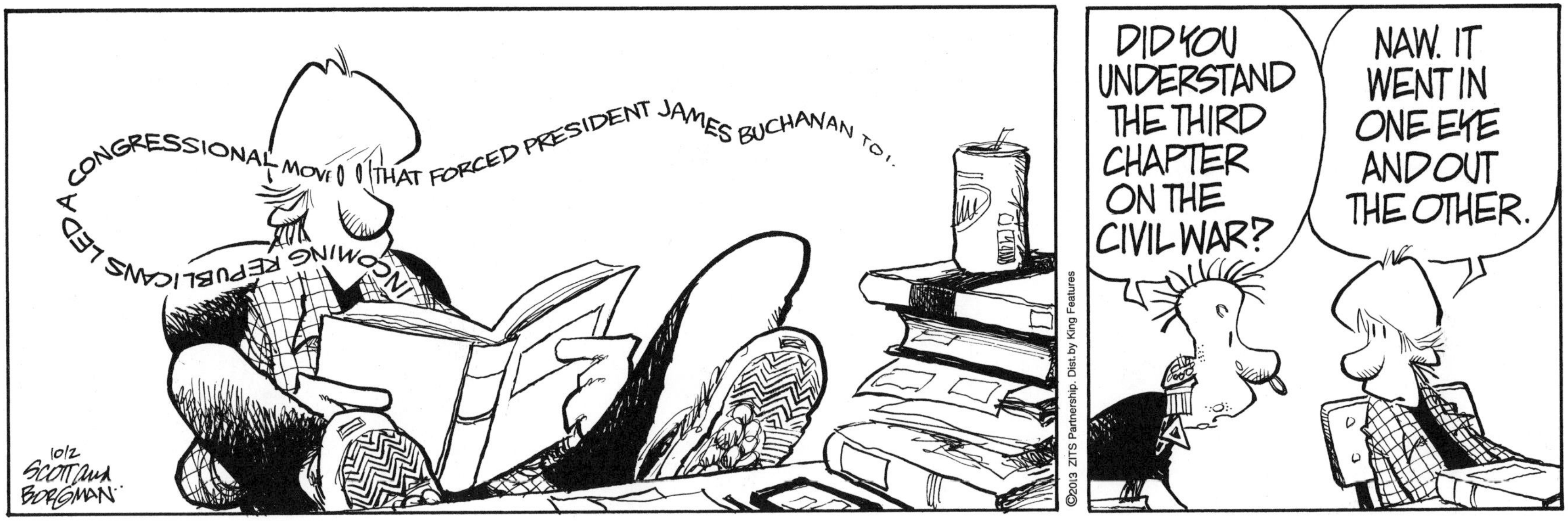
INCOMING REPUBLICANS LED A CONGRESSIONAL MOV THAT FORCED PRESIDENT JAMES BUCHANAN TO..
10/2 SCOTT and BORGMAN
DID YOU UNDERSTAND THE THIRD CHAPTER ON THE CIVIL WAR?
NAW. IT WENT IN ONE EYE AND OUT THE OTHER.
©2013 ZITS Partnership. Dist. by King Features

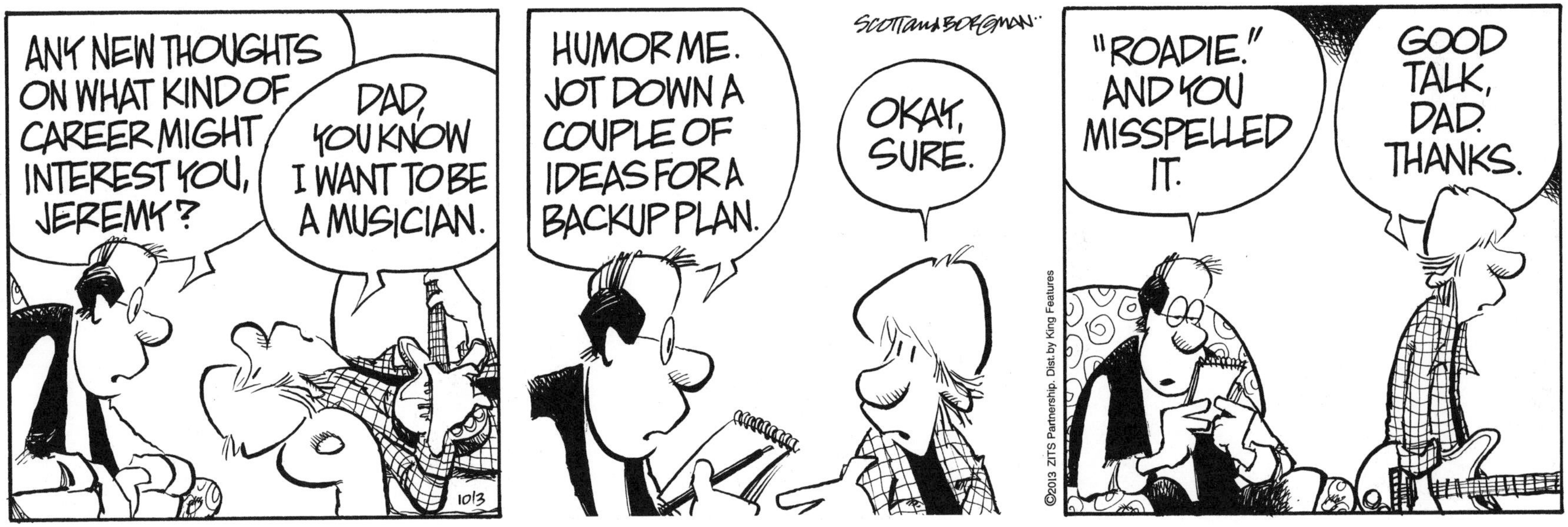
ANY NEW THOUGHTS ON WHAT KIND OF CAREER MIGHT INTEREST YOU, JEREMY?
DAD, YOU KNOW I WANT TO BE A MUSICIAN.
10/3
HUMOR ME. JOT DOWN A COUPLE OF IDEAS FOR A BACKUP PLAN.
SCOTT and BORGMAN
OKAY, SURE.
©2013 ZITS Partnership. Dist. by King Features
"ROADIE." AND YOU MISSPELLED IT.
GOOD TALK, DAD. THANKS.

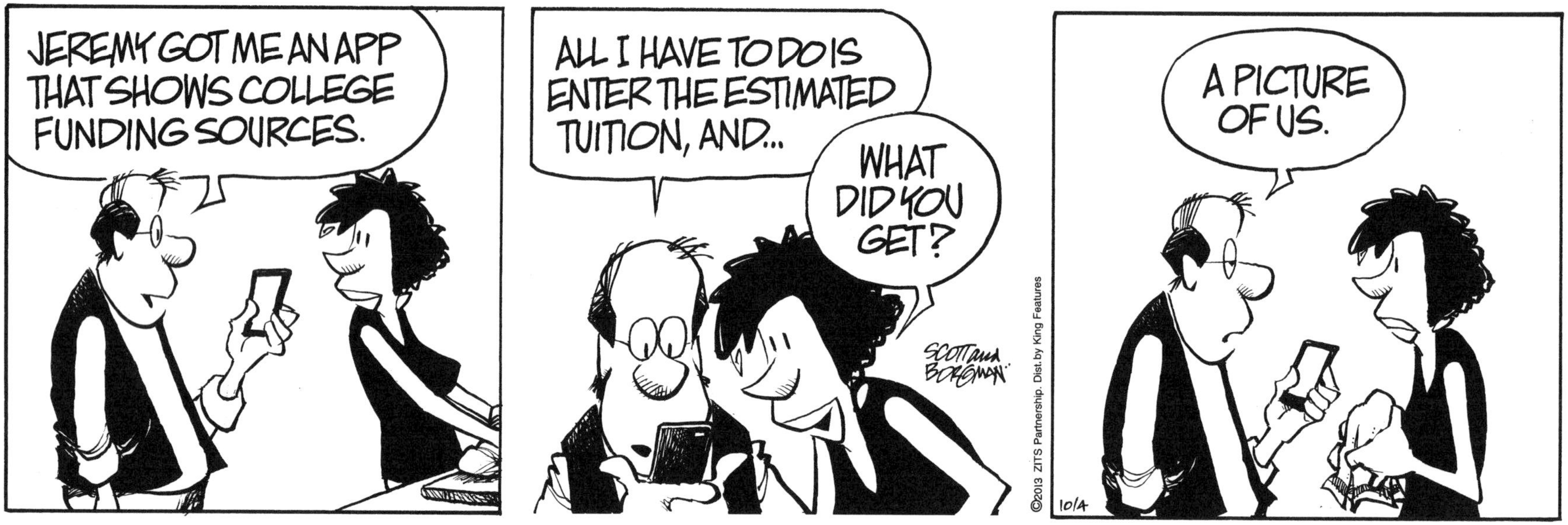
JEREMY GOT ME AN APP THAT SHOWS COLLEGE FUNDING SOURCES.
ALL I HAVE TO DO IS ENTER THE ESTIMATED TUITION, AND...
WHAT DID YOU GET?
SCOTT and BORGMAN
©2013 ZITS Partnership. Dist. by King Features
A PICTURE OF US.
10/4

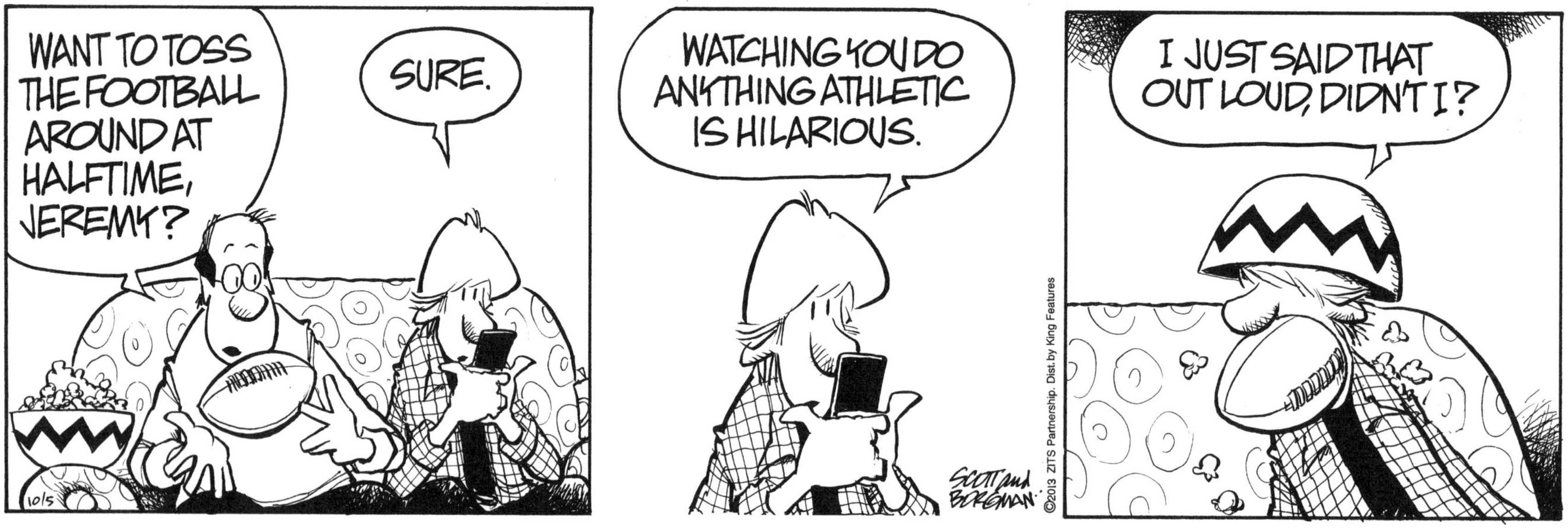
WANT TO TOSS THE FOOTBALL AROUND AT HALFTIME, JEREMY?
SURE.
10/5
WATCHING YOU DO ANYTHING ATHLETIC IS HILARIOUS.
SCOTT and BORGMAN
©2013 ZITS Partnership. Dist. by King Features
I JUST SAID THAT OUT LOUD, DIDN'T I?

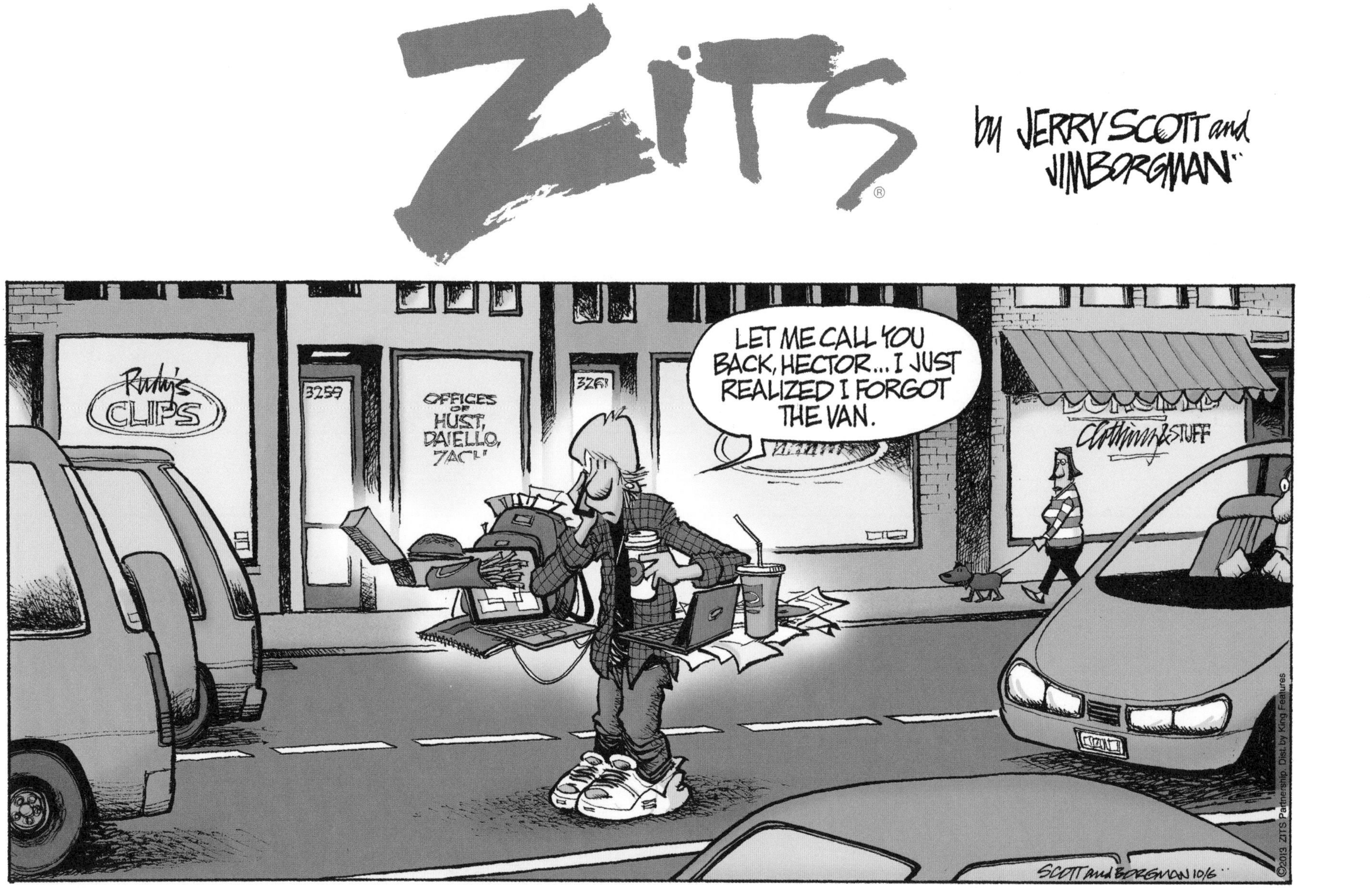
ZITS
by JERRY SCOTT and JIM BORGMAN
Rudy's CLIPS
3259
3261
Clothing & STUFF
LET ME CALL YOU BACK, HECTOR... I JUST REALIZED I FORGOT THE VAN.
SCOTT and BORGMAN 10/6
©2013 ZITS Partnership. Dist. by King Features

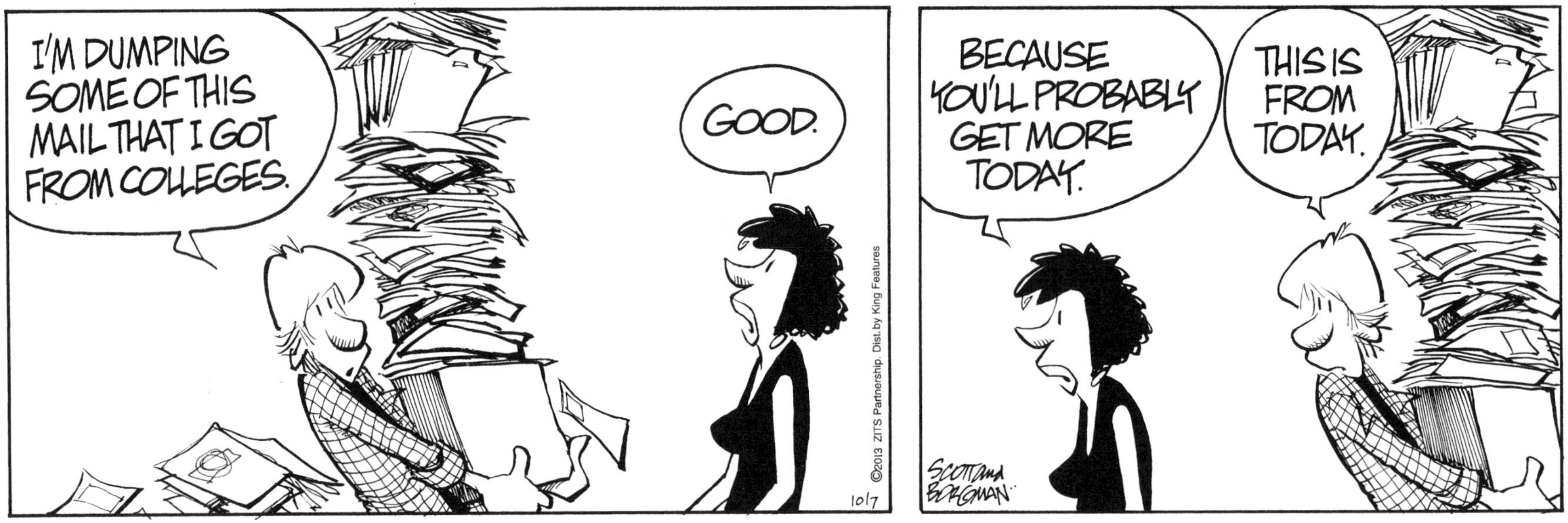
I'M DUMPING SOME OF THIS MAIL THAT I GOT FROM COLLEGES.
GOOD.
©2013 ZITS Partnership. Dist. by King Features
10/7
BECAUSE YOU'LL PROBABLY GET MORE TODAY.
THIS IS FROM TODAY.
SCOTT and BORGMAN

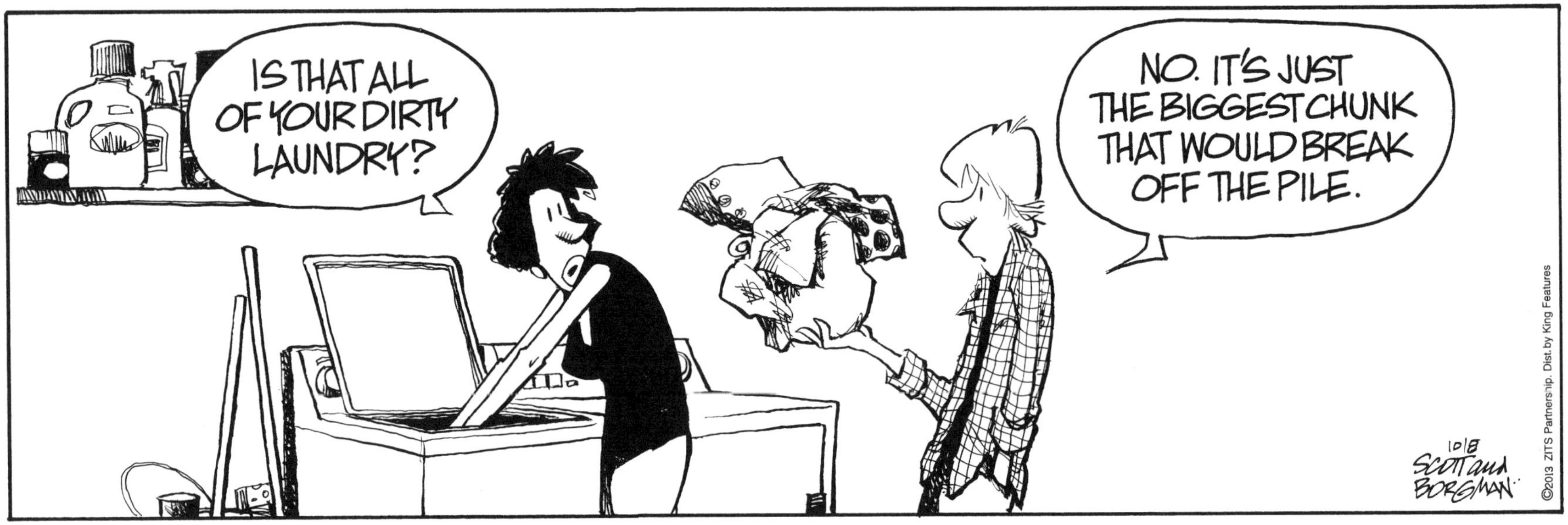
IS THAT ALL OF YOUR DIRTY LAUNDRY?
NO. IT'S JUST THE BIGGEST CHUNK THAT WOULD BREAK OFF THE PILE.
10/8
SCOTT and BORGMAN
©2013 ZITS Partnership. Dist. by King Features

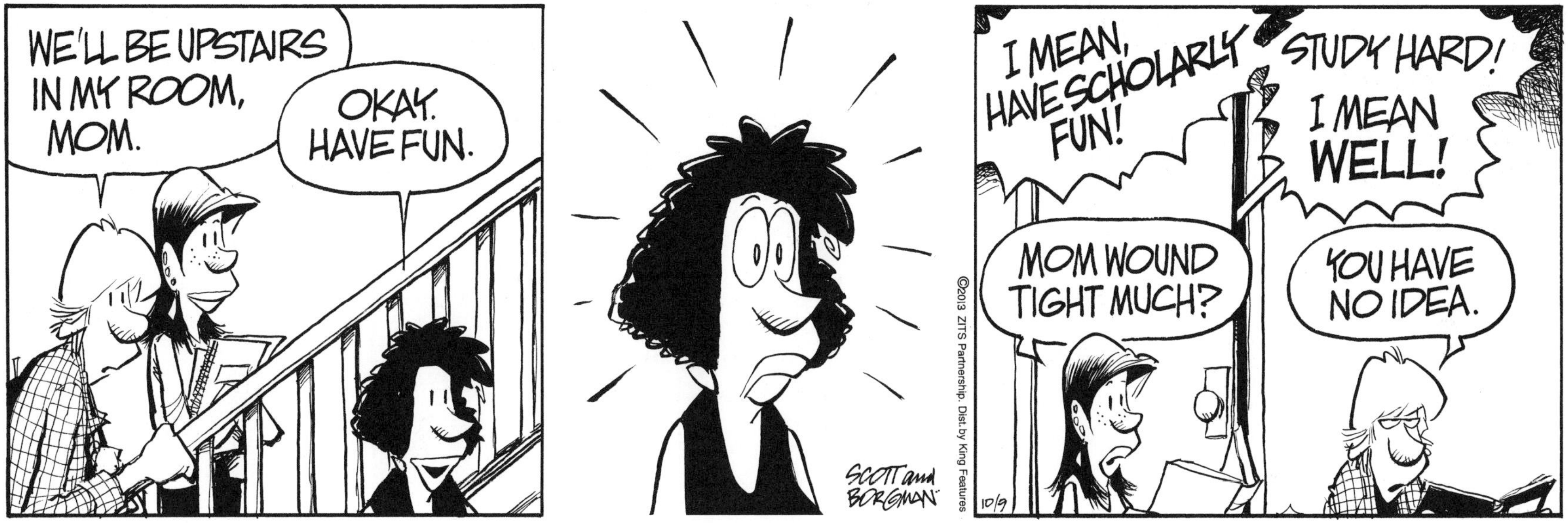
WE'LL BE UPSTAIRS IN MY ROOM, MOM.
OKAY. HAVE FUN.
SCOTT and BORGMAN
©2013 ZITS Partnership. Dist. by King Features
10/9
I MEAN, HAVE SCHOLARLY FUN!
STUDY HARD!
I MEAN WELL!
MOM WOUND TIGHT MUCH?
YOU HAVE NO IDEA.

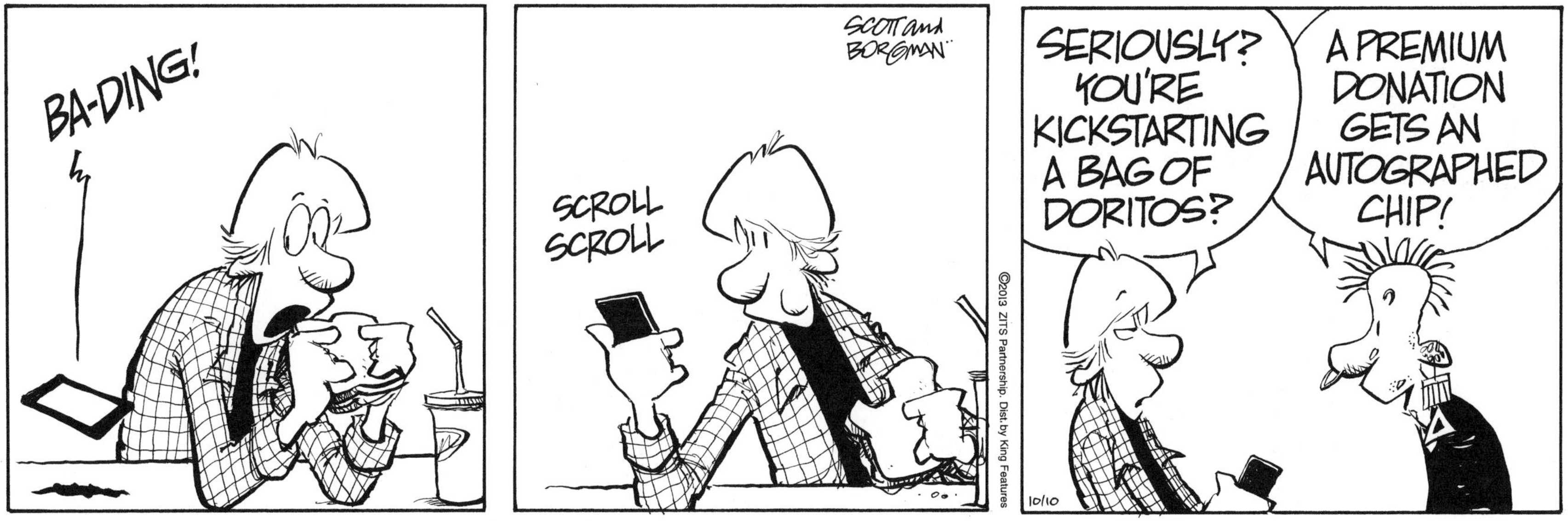
BA-DING!
SCROLL SCROLL
SCOTT and BORGMAN
©2013 ZITS Partnership. Dist. by King Features
10/10
SERIOUSLY? YOU'RE KICKSTARTING A BAG OF DORITOS?
A PREMIUM DONATION GETS AN AUTOGRAPHED CHIP!

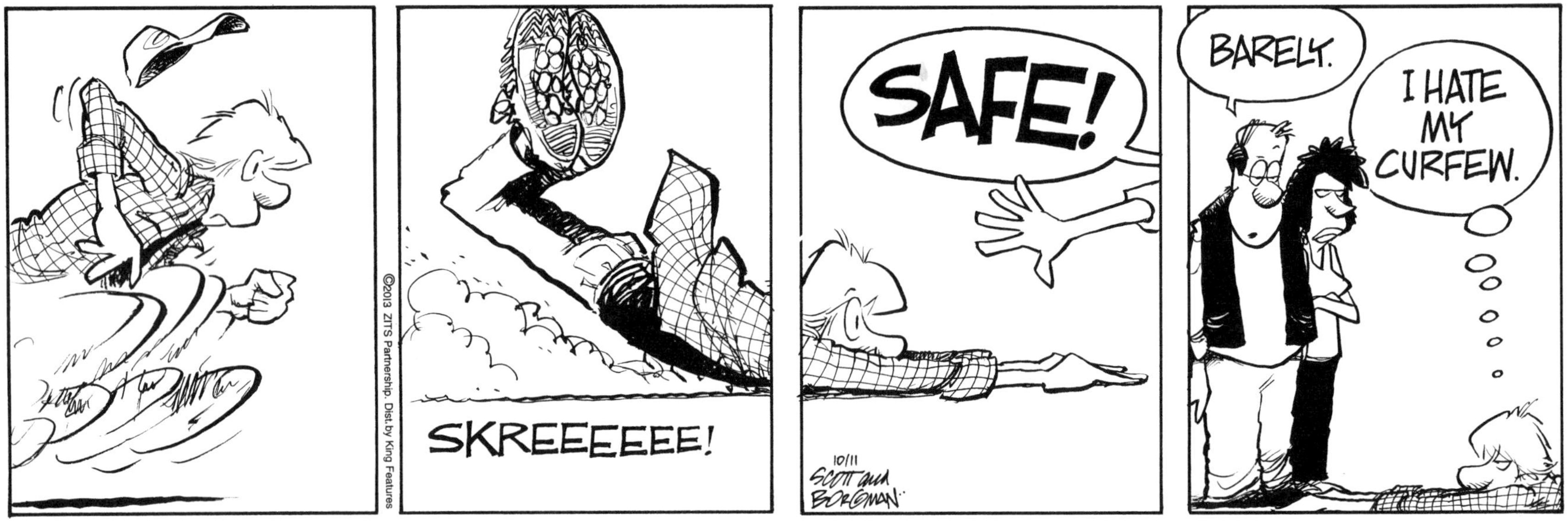
©2013 ZITS Partnership. Dist. by King Features
SKREEEEEEE!
SAFE!
10/11
SCOTT and BORGMAN
BARELY.
I HATE MY CURFEW.

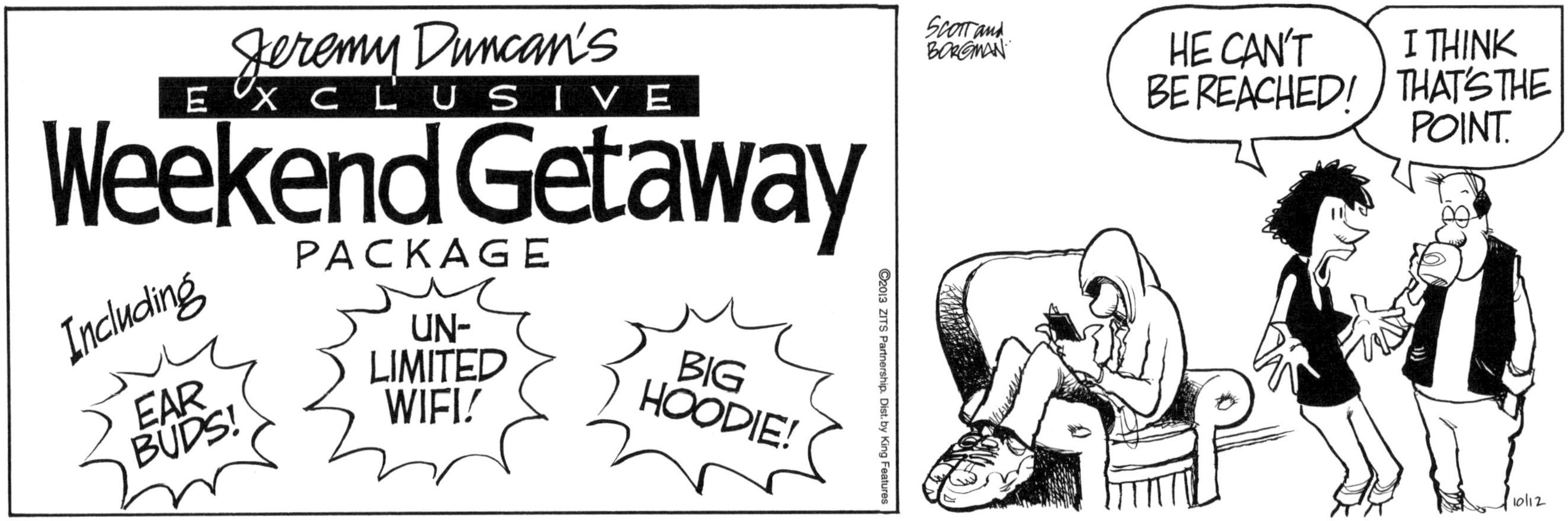
Jeremy Duncan's
EXCLUSIVE
Weekend Getaway
PACKAGE
Including
EAR BUDS!
UN-LIMITED WIFI!
BIG HOODIE!
©2013 ZITS Partnership. Dist. by King Features
SCOTT and BORGMAN
HE CAN'T BE REACHED!
I THINK THAT'S THE POINT.
10/12

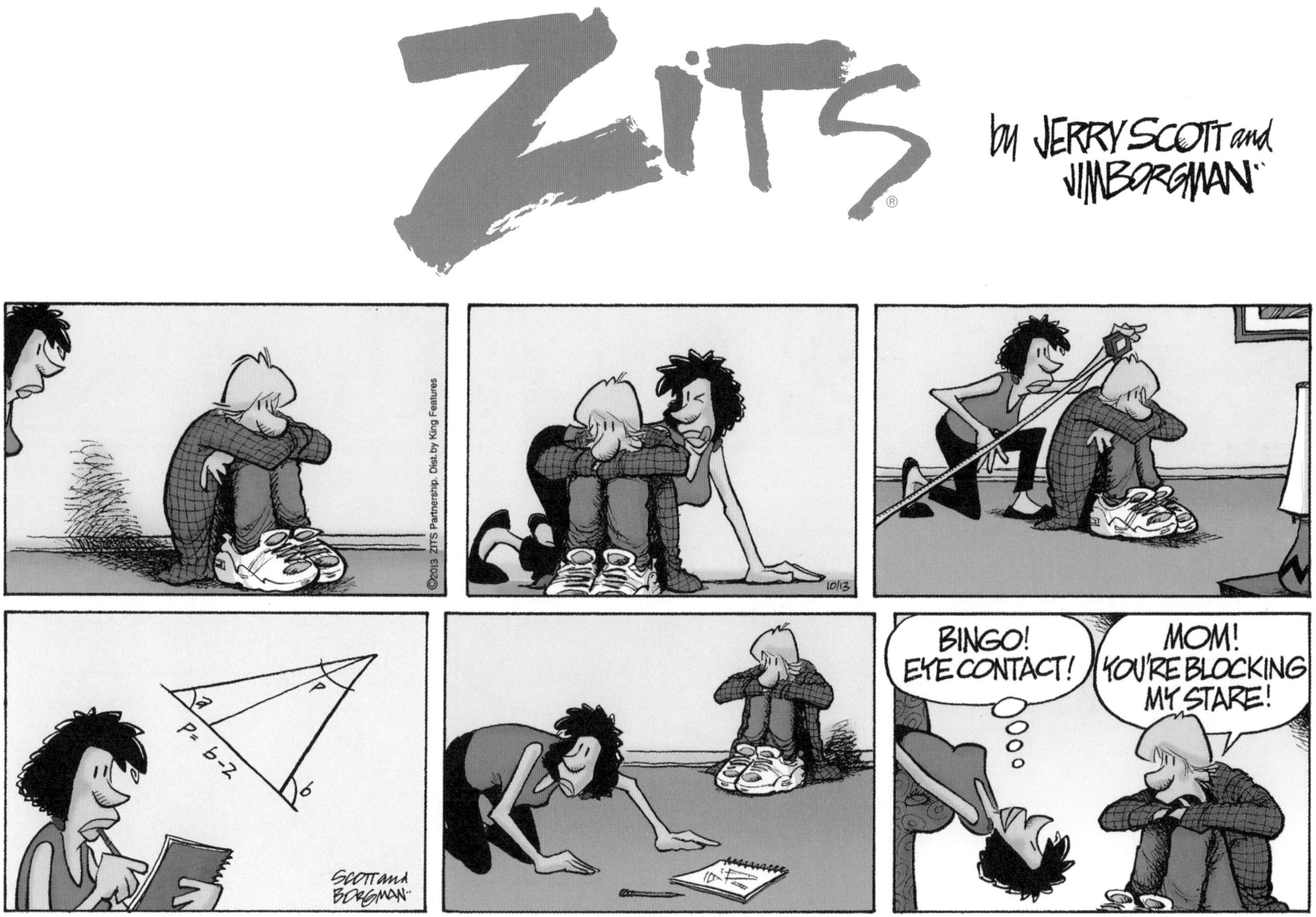
ZITS
by JERRY SCOTT and JIM BORGMAN
©2013 ZITS Partnership. Dist. by King Features
10/13
P = b-2
SCOTT and BORGMAN
BINGO! EYE CONTACT!
MOM! YOU'RE BLOCKING MY STARE!

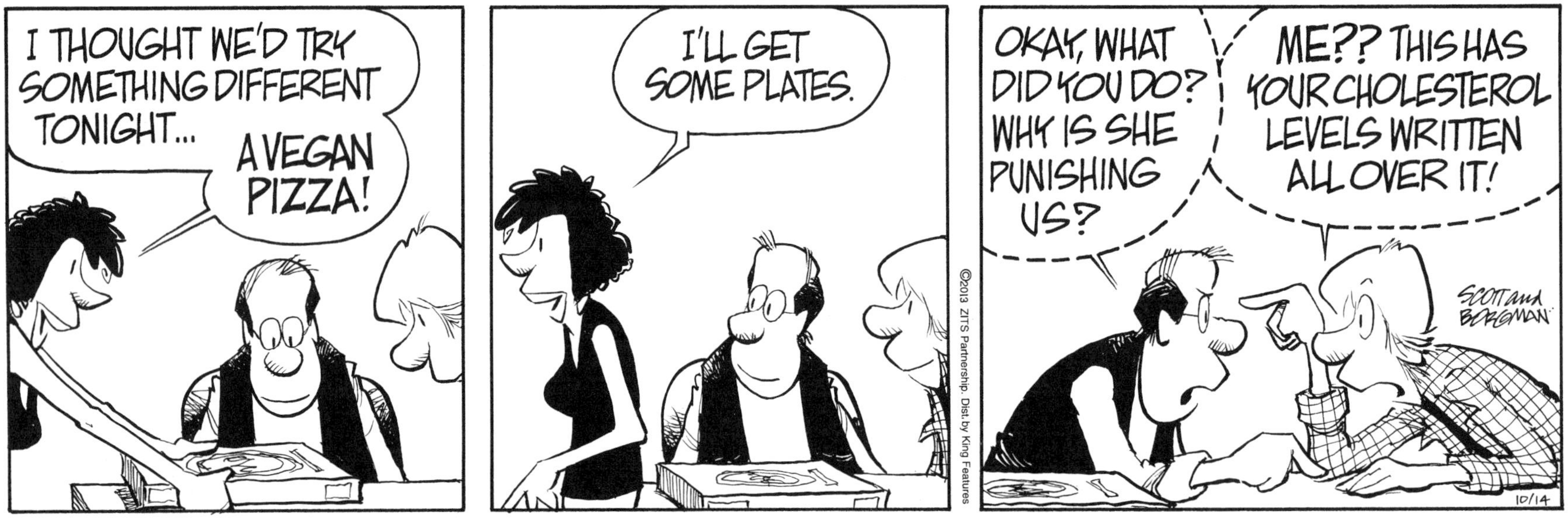
I THOUGHT WE'D TRY SOMETHING DIFFERENT TONIGHT...
A VEGAN PIZZA!
I'LL GET SOME PLATES.
©2013 ZITS Partnership. Dist. by King Features
OKAY, WHAT DID YOU DO? WHY IS SHE PUNISHING US?
ME?? THIS HAS YOUR CHOLESTEROL LEVELS WRITTEN ALL OVER IT!
SCOTT and BORGMAN
10/14

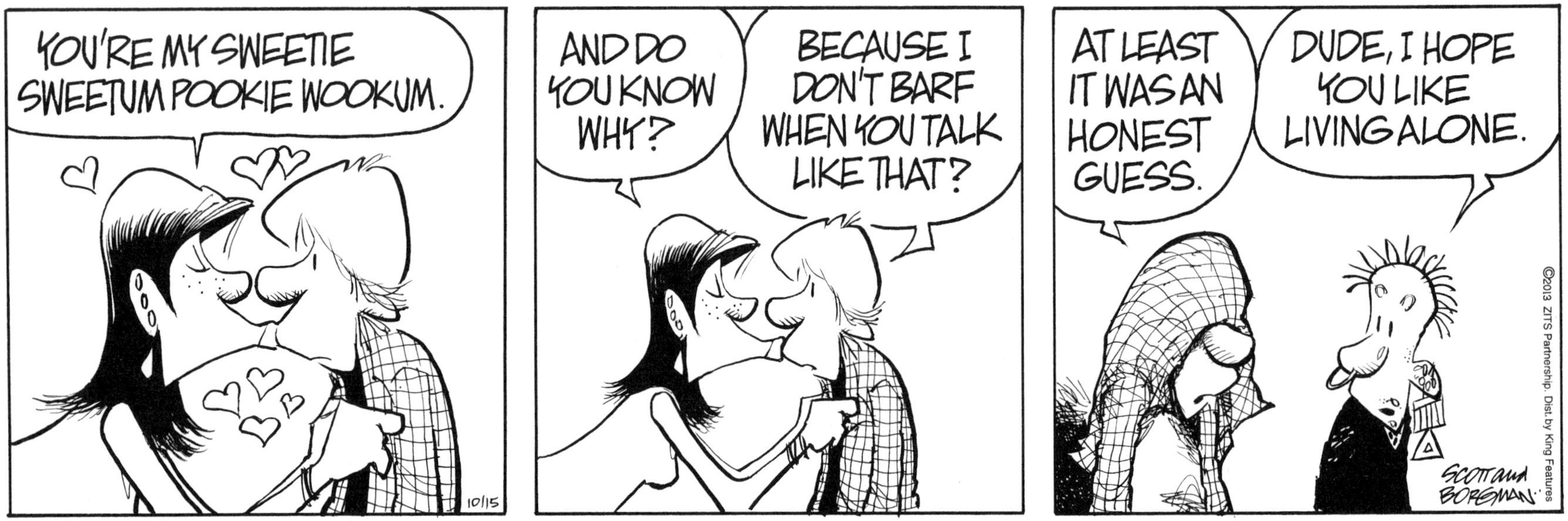
YOU'RE MY SWEETIE SWEETUM POOKIE WOOKUM.
10/15
AND DO YOU KNOW WHY?
BECAUSE I DON'T BARF WHEN YOU TALK LIKE THAT?
AT LEAST IT WAS AN HONEST GUESS.
DUDE, I HOPE YOU LIKE LIVING ALONE.
©2013 ZITS Partnership. Dist. by King Features
SCOTT and BORGMAN

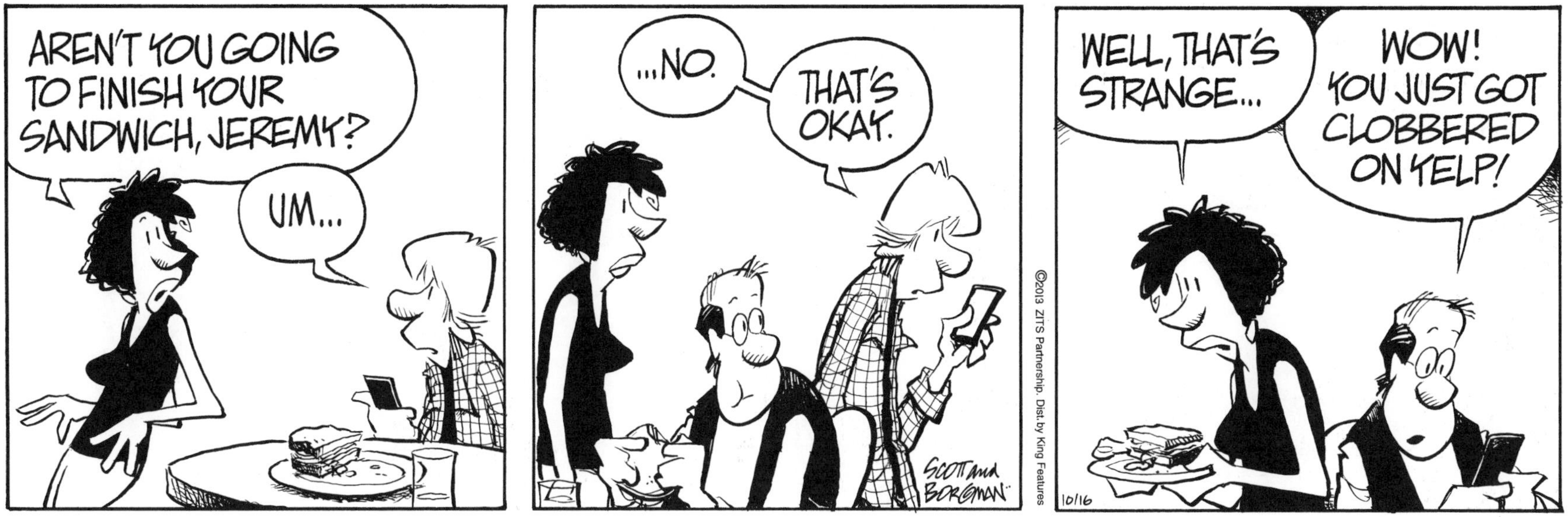
AREN'T YOU GOING TO FINISH YOUR SANDWICH, JEREMY?
UM...
...NO.
THAT'S OKAY.
WELL, THAT'S STRANGE...
WOW! YOU JUST GOT CLOBBERED ON YELP!
SCOTT AND BORGMAN
10/16
©2013 ZITS Partnership. Dist. by King Features

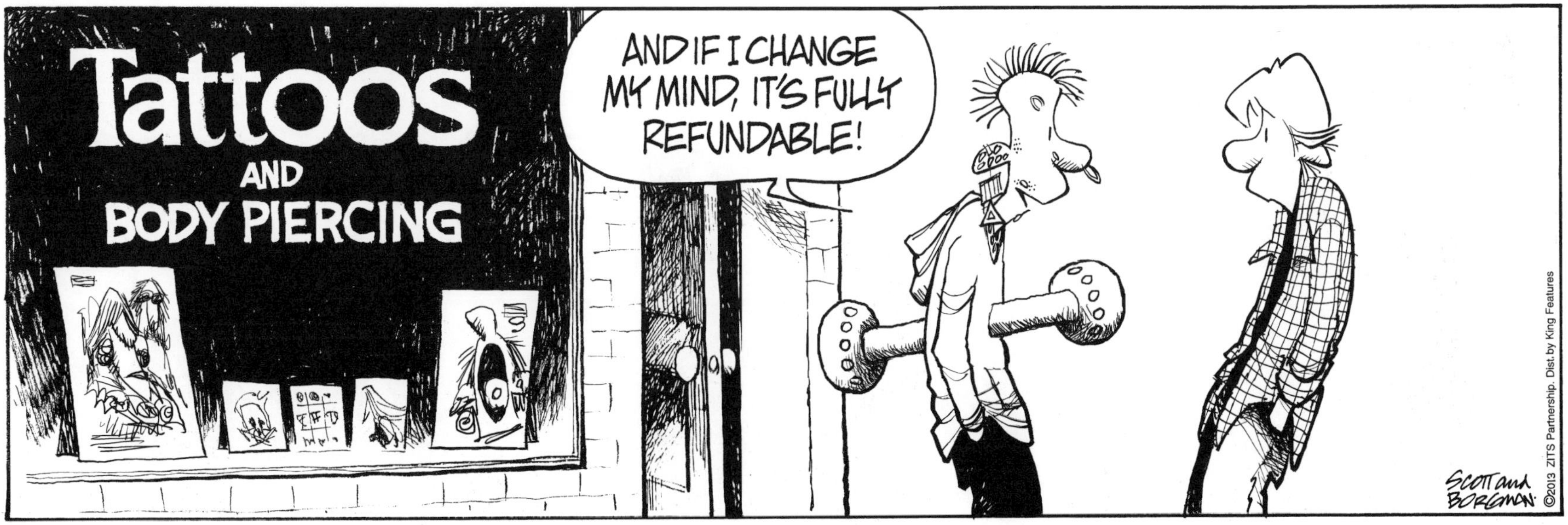
Tattoos
AND
BODY PIERCING
AND IF I CHANGE MY MIND, IT'S FULLY REFUNDABLE!
SCOTT AND BORGMAN
©2013 ZITS Partnership. Dist. by King Features

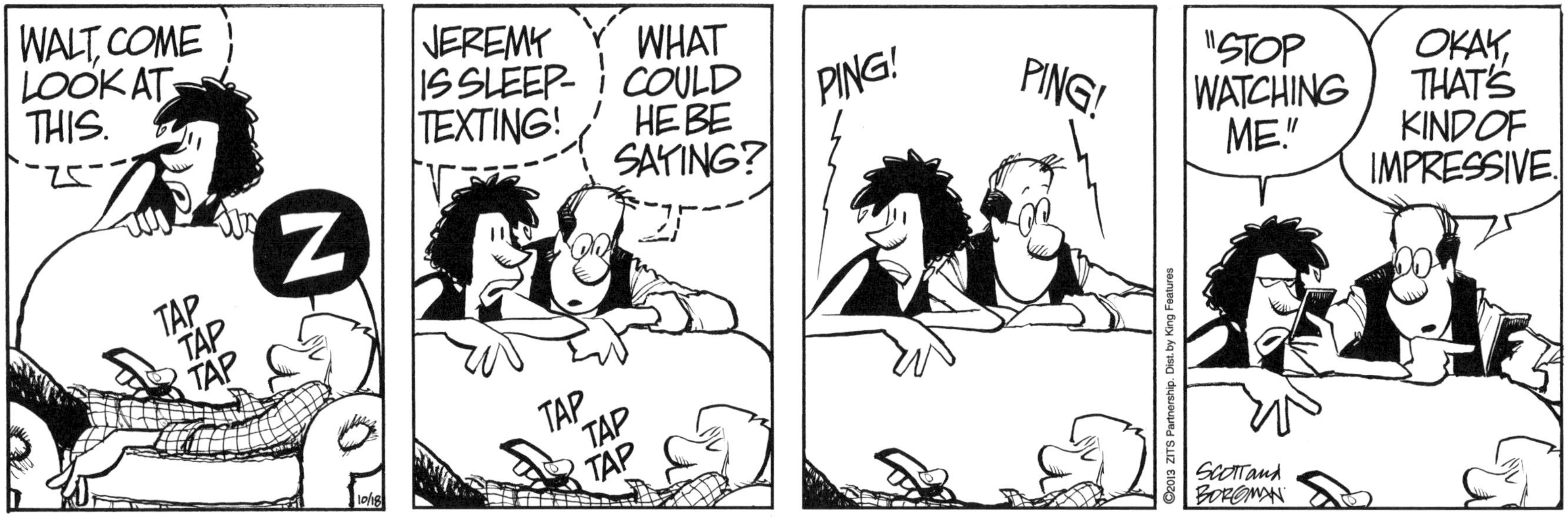
WALT, COME LOOK AT THIS.
Z
TAP TAP TAP
10/18
JEREMY IS SLEEP-TEXTING!
WHAT COULD HE BE SAYING?
TAP TAP TAP
PING!
PING!
©2013 ZITS Partnership. Dist. by King Features
"STOP WATCHING ME."
OKAY, THAT'S KIND OF IMPRESSIVE.
SCOTT and BORGMAN

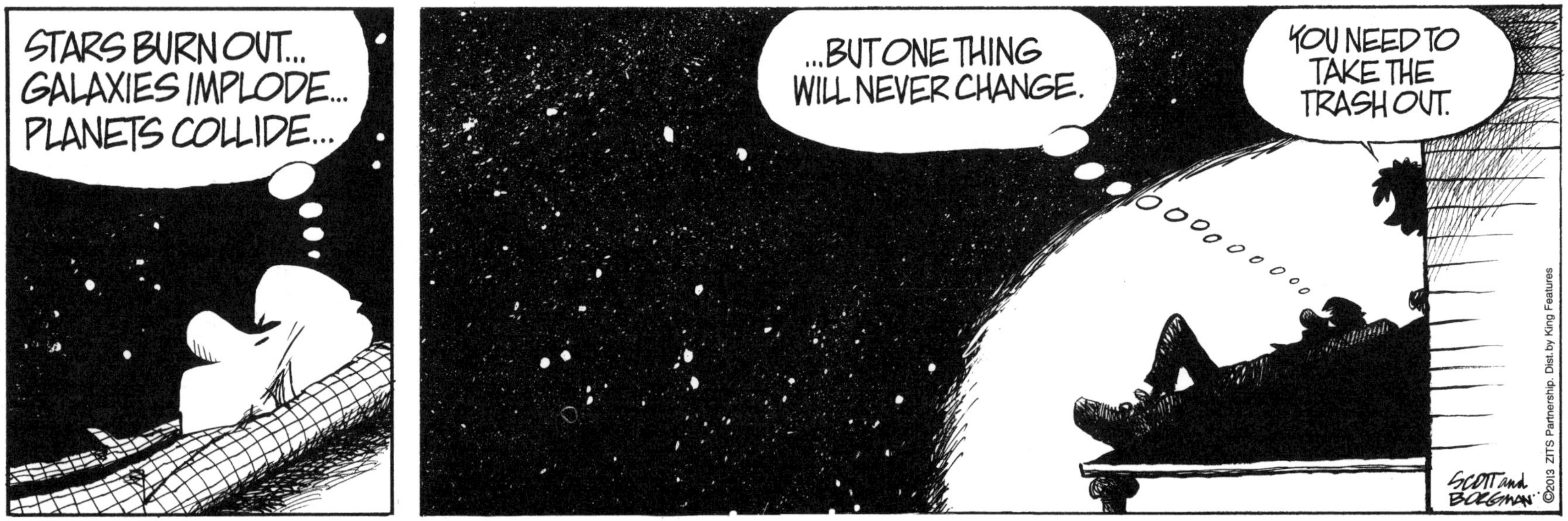
STARS BURN OUT... GALAXIES IMPLODE... PLANETS COLLIDE...
...BUT ONE THING WILL NEVER CHANGE.
YOU NEED TO TAKE THE TRASH OUT.
©2013 ZITS Partnership. Dist. by King Features
SCOTT and BORGMAN

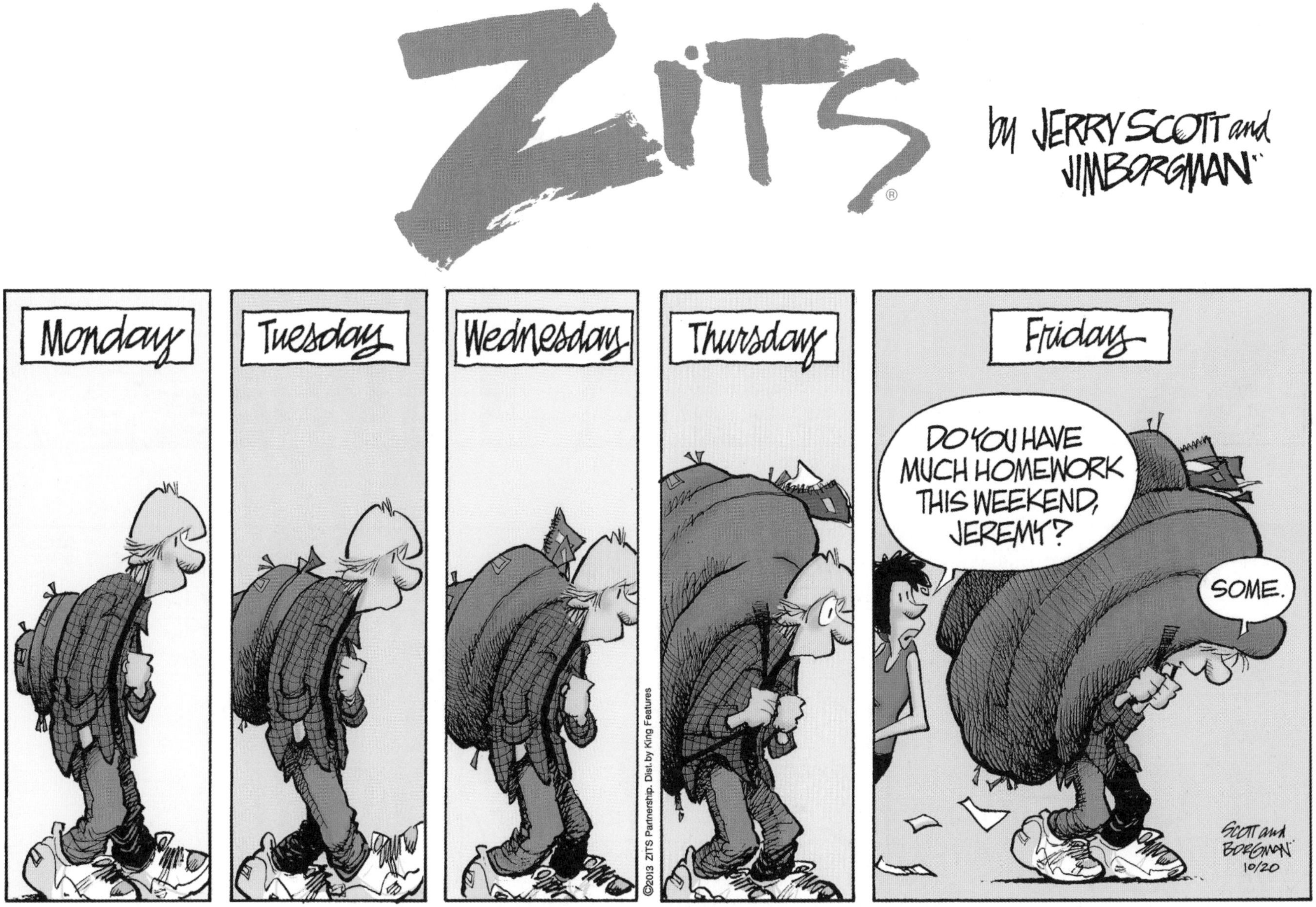
ZITS
by JERRY SCOTT and JIM BORGMAN
Monday
Tuesday
Wednesday
Thursday
Friday
DO YOU HAVE MUCH HOMEWORK THIS WEEKEND, JEREMY?
SOME.
©2013 ZITS Partnership. Dist. by King Features
SCOTT and BORGMAN 10/20

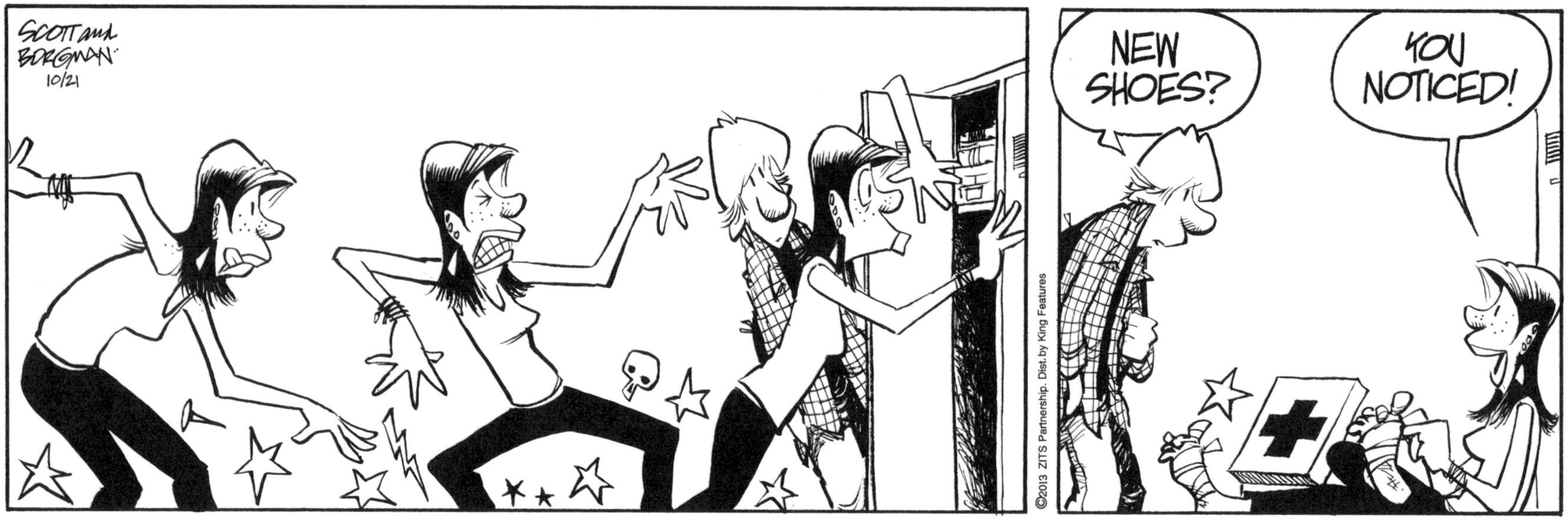
SCOTT and BORGMAN 10/21
©2013 ZITS Partnership. Dist. by King Features
NEW SHOES?
YOU NOTICED!

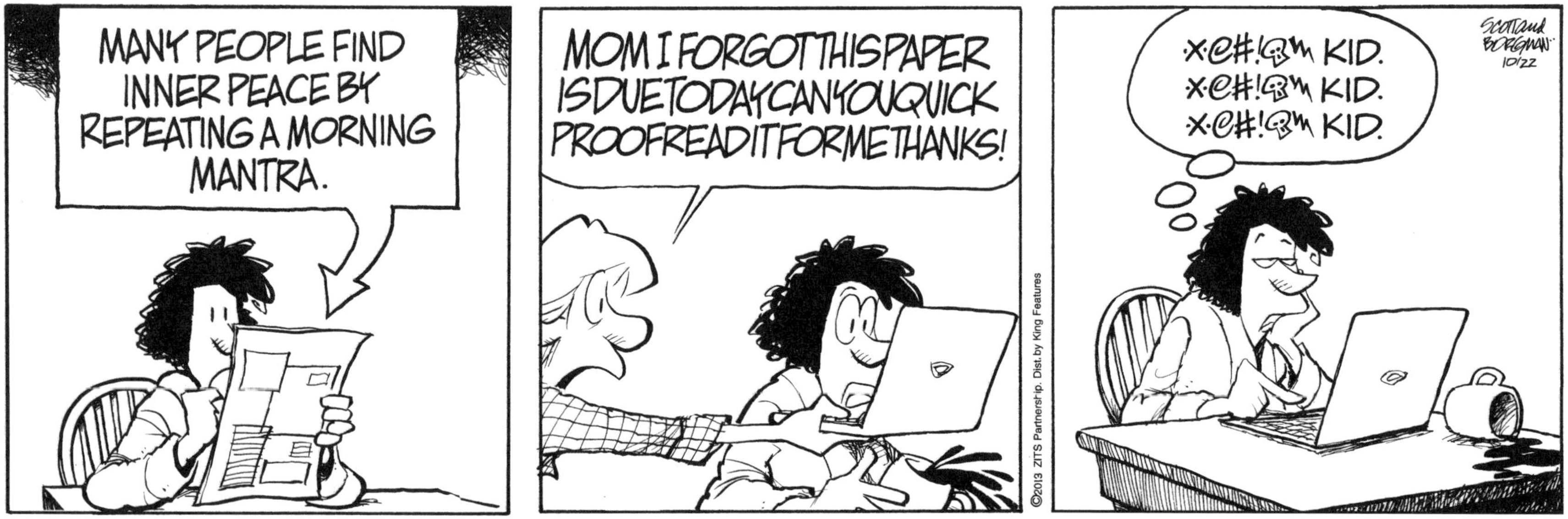
MANY PEOPLE FIND INNER PEACE BY REPEATING A MORNING MANTRA.
MOM I FORGOT THIS PAPER IS DUE TODAY CAN YOU QUICK PROOFREAD IT FOR ME THANKS!
©2013 ZITS Partnership. Dist. by King Features
SCOTT and BORGMAN 10/22
×@#! KID.
×@#! KID.
×@#! KID.

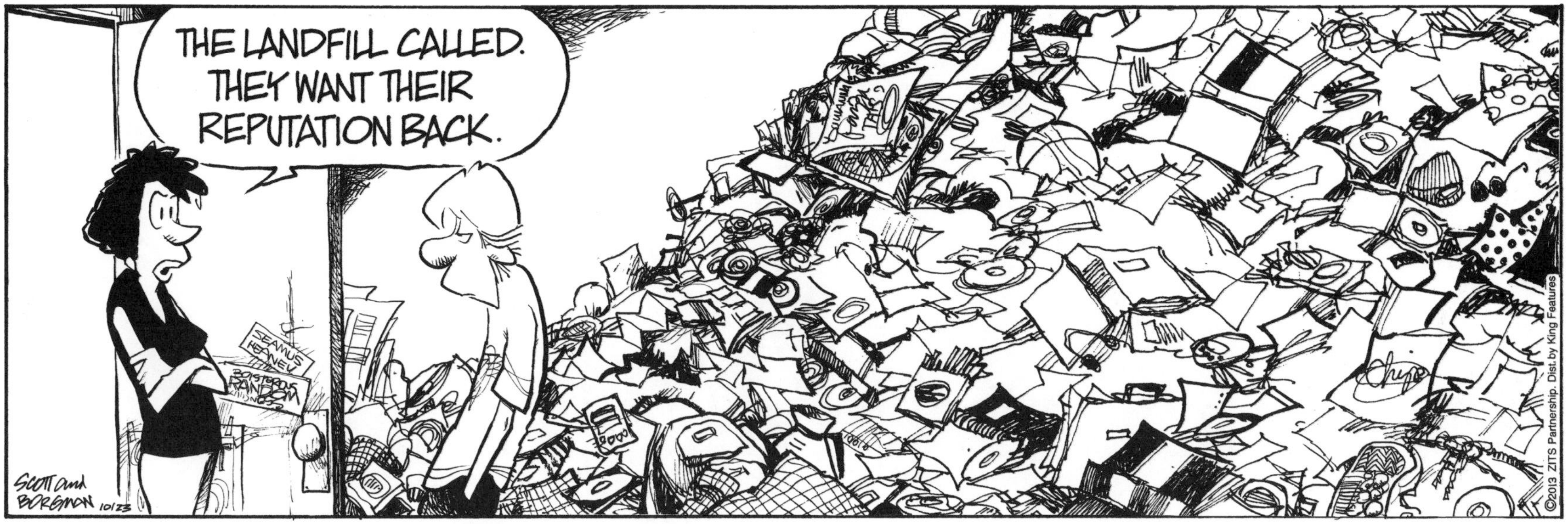
THE LANDFILL CALLED. THEY WANT THEIR REPUTATION BACK.
SCOTT and BORGMAN 10/23
©2013 ZITS Partnership. Dist. by King Features

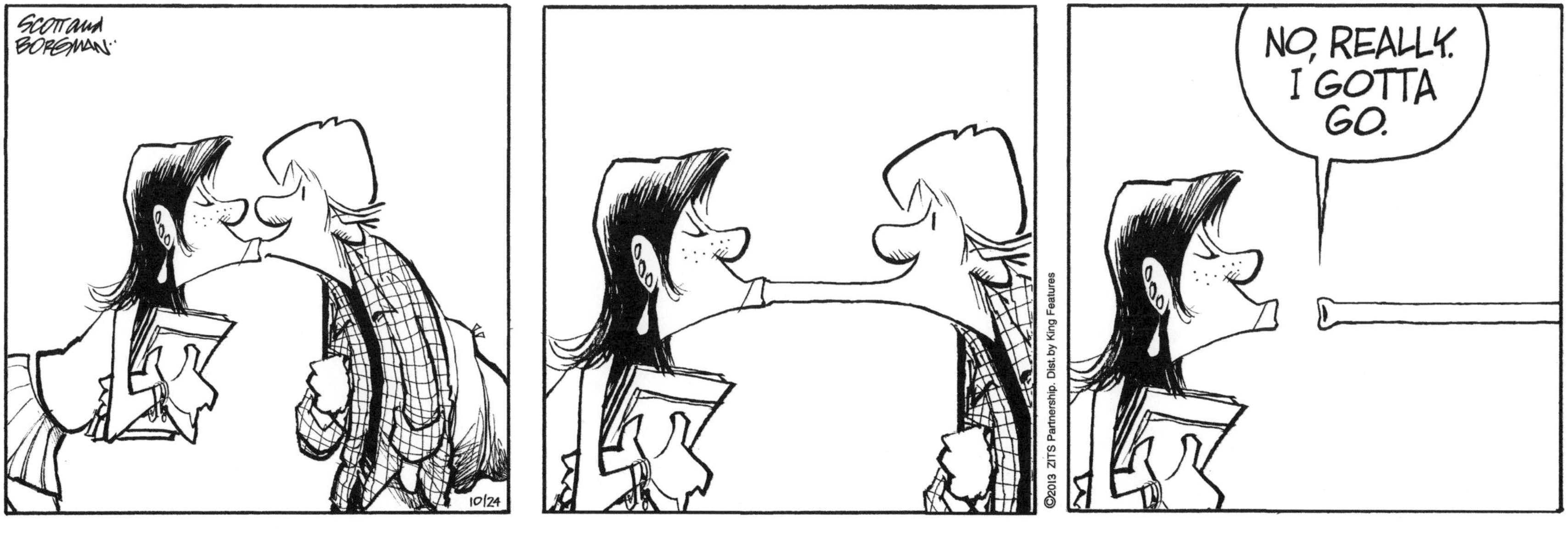
SCOTT and BORGMAN
10/24
©2013 ZITS Partnership. Dist. by King Features
NO, REALLY. I GOTTA GO.

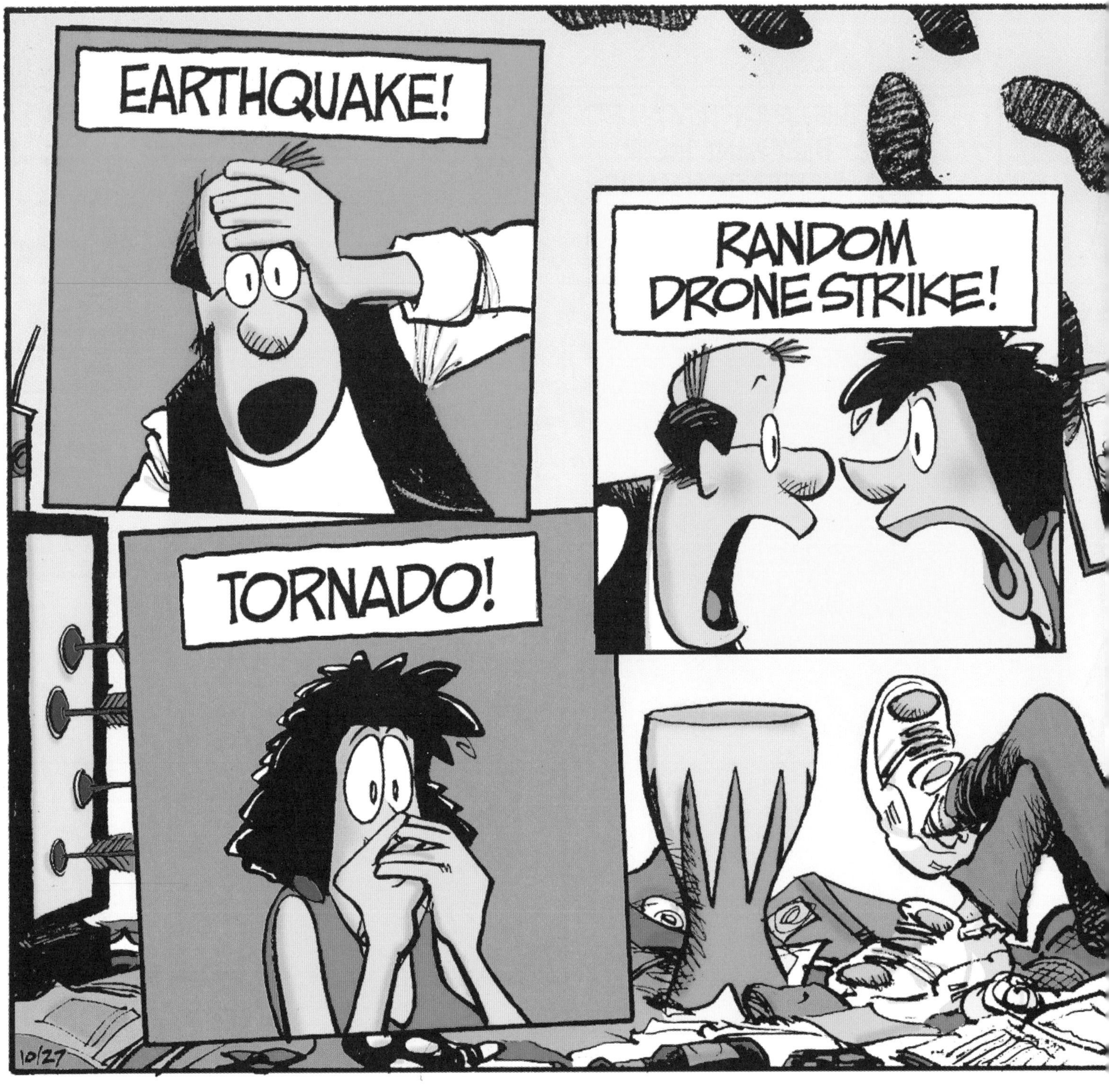
EARTHQUAKE!
RANDOM DRONE STRIKE!
TORNADO!
10/27

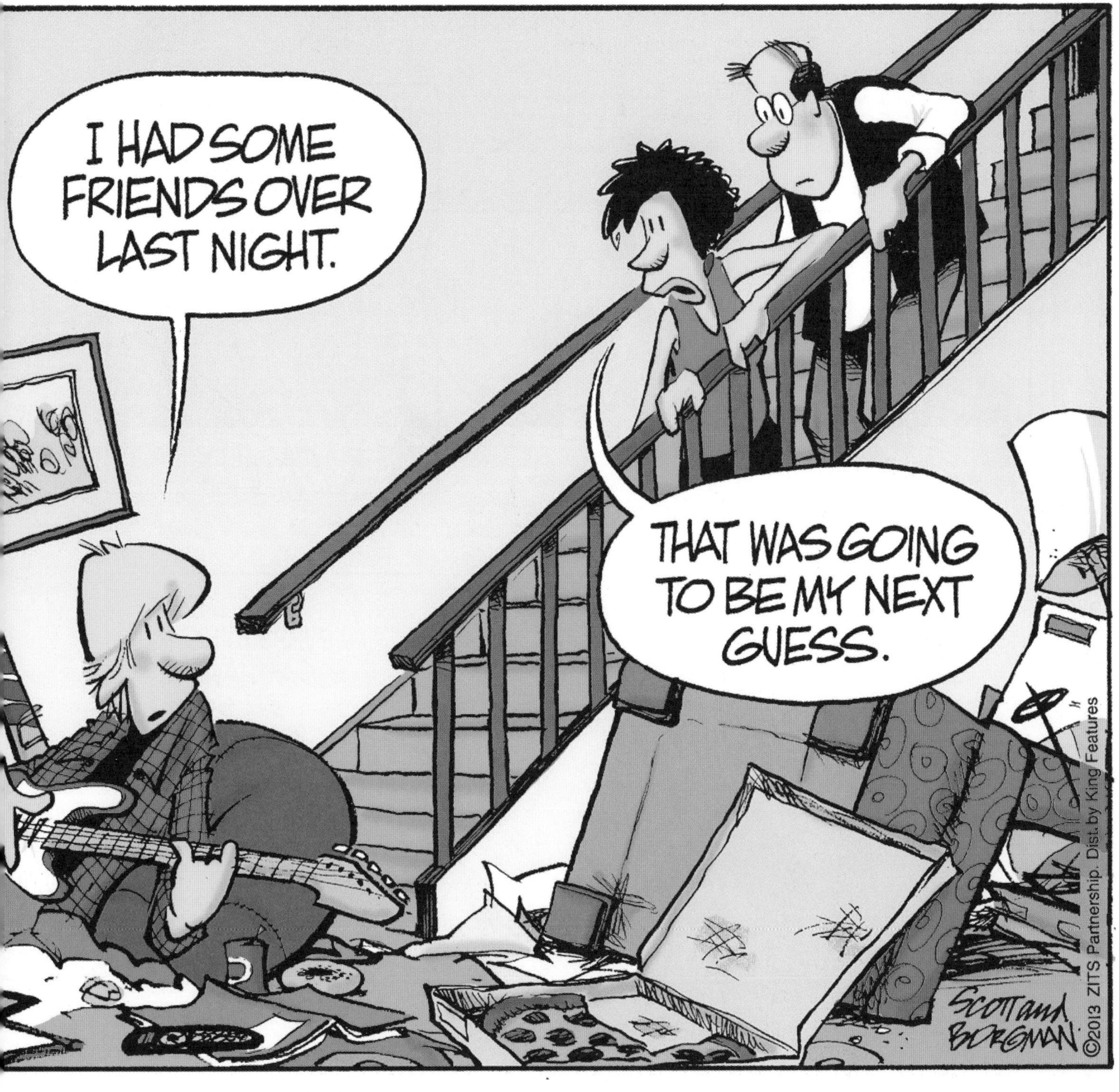
I HAD SOME FRIENDS OVER LAST NIGHT.
THAT WAS GOING TO BE MY NEXT GUESS.
SCOTT and BORGMAN
©2013 ZITS Partnership. Dist. by King Features

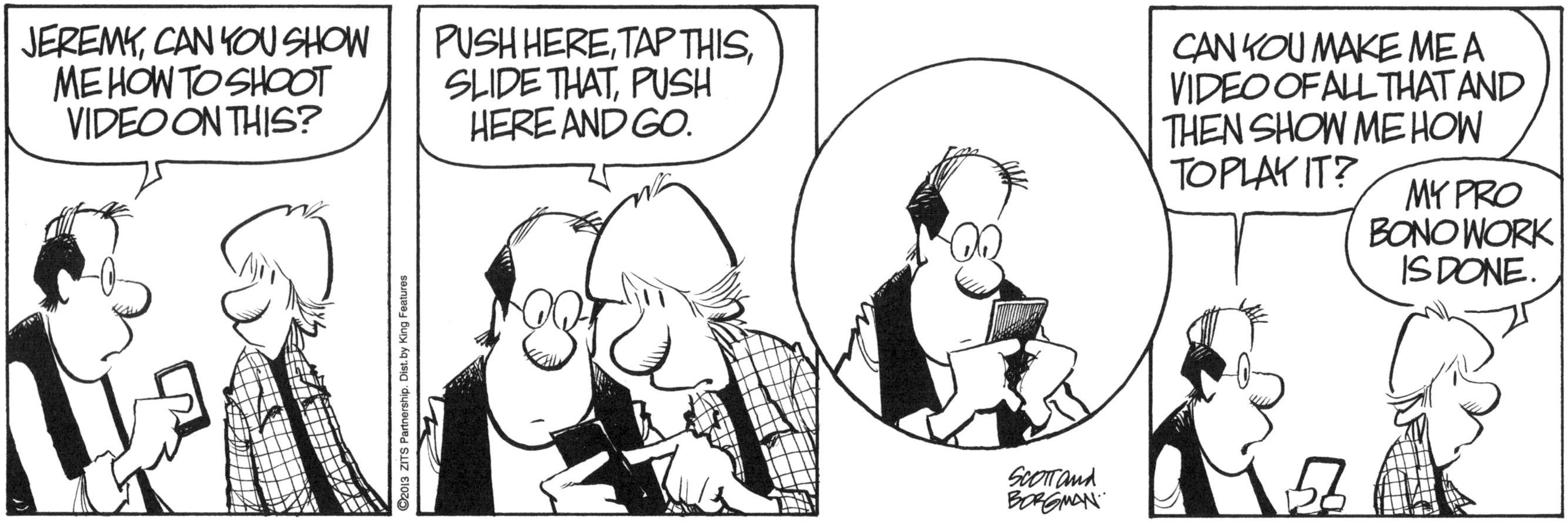
JEREMY, CAN YOU SHOW ME HOW TO SHOOT VIDEO ON THIS?
PUSH HERE, TAP THIS, SLIDE THAT, PUSH HERE AND GO.
©2013 ZITS Partnership. Dist.by King Features
CAN YOU MAKE ME A VIDEO OF ALL THAT AND THEN SHOW ME HOW TO PLAY IT?
MY PRO BONO WORK IS DONE.
SCOTT and BORGMAN

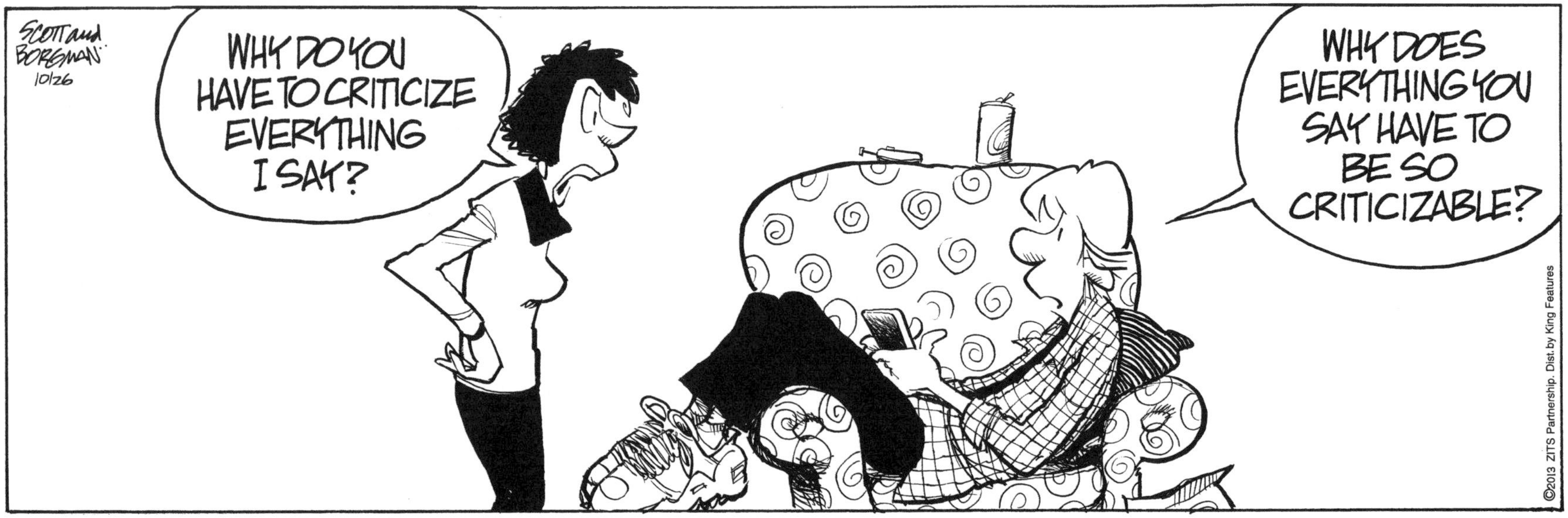
SCOTT and BORGMAN 10/26
WHY DO YOU HAVE TO CRITICIZE EVERYTHING I SAY?
WHY DOES EVERYTHING YOU SAY HAVE TO BE SO CRITICIZABLE?
©2013 ZITS Partnership. Dist.by King Features

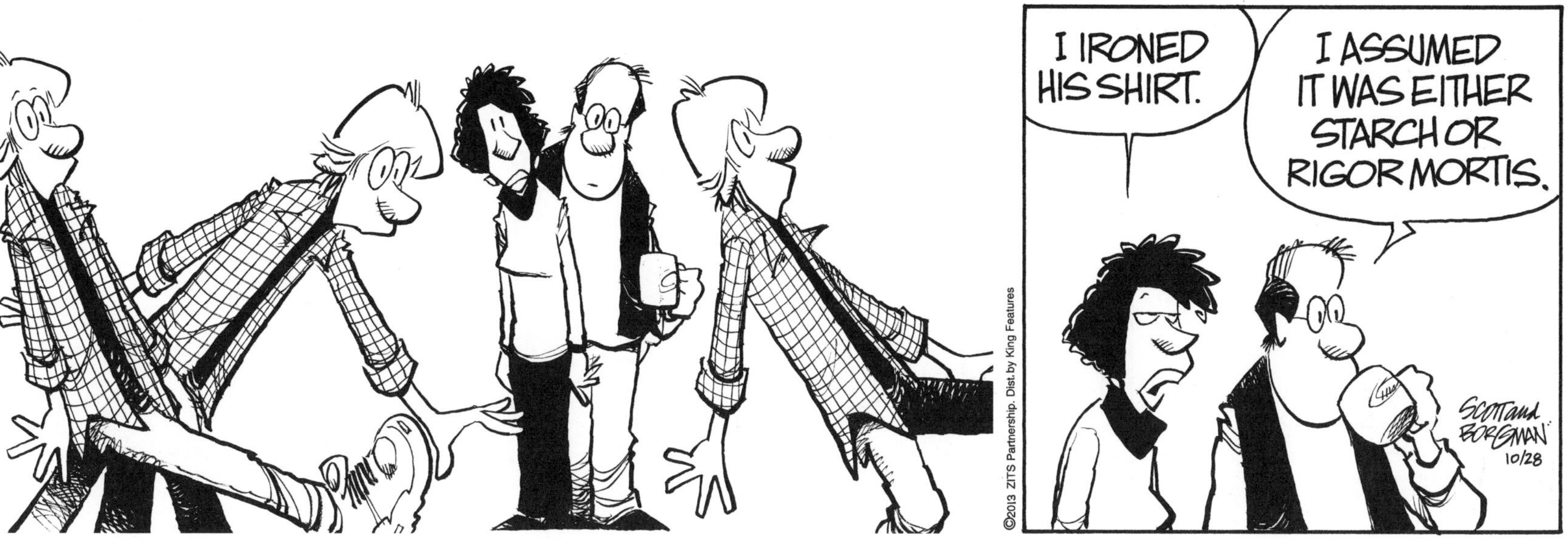
©2013 ZITS Partnership. Dist. by King Features
I IRONED HIS SHIRT.
I ASSUMED IT WAS EITHER STARCH OR RIGOR MORTIS.
SCOTT and BORGMAN
10/28

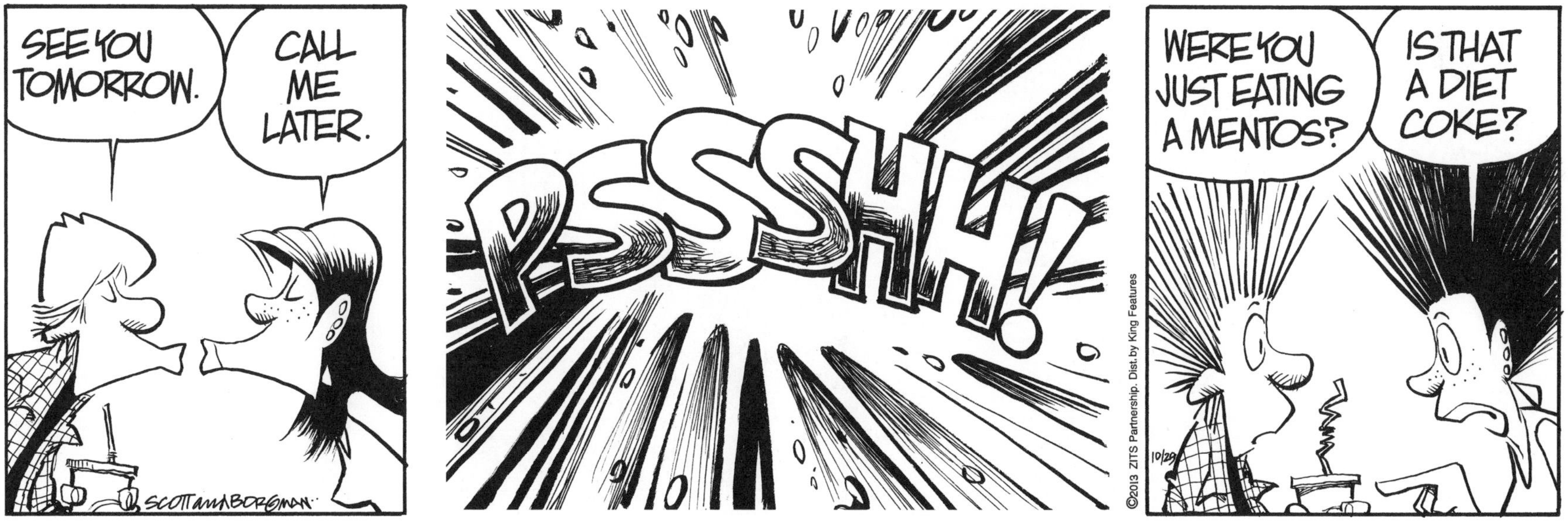
SEE YOU TOMORROW.
CALL ME LATER.
SCOTT and BORGMAN
PSSSHH!
©2013 ZITS Partnership. Dist. by King Features
WERE YOU JUST EATING A MENTOS?
IS THAT A DIET COKE?

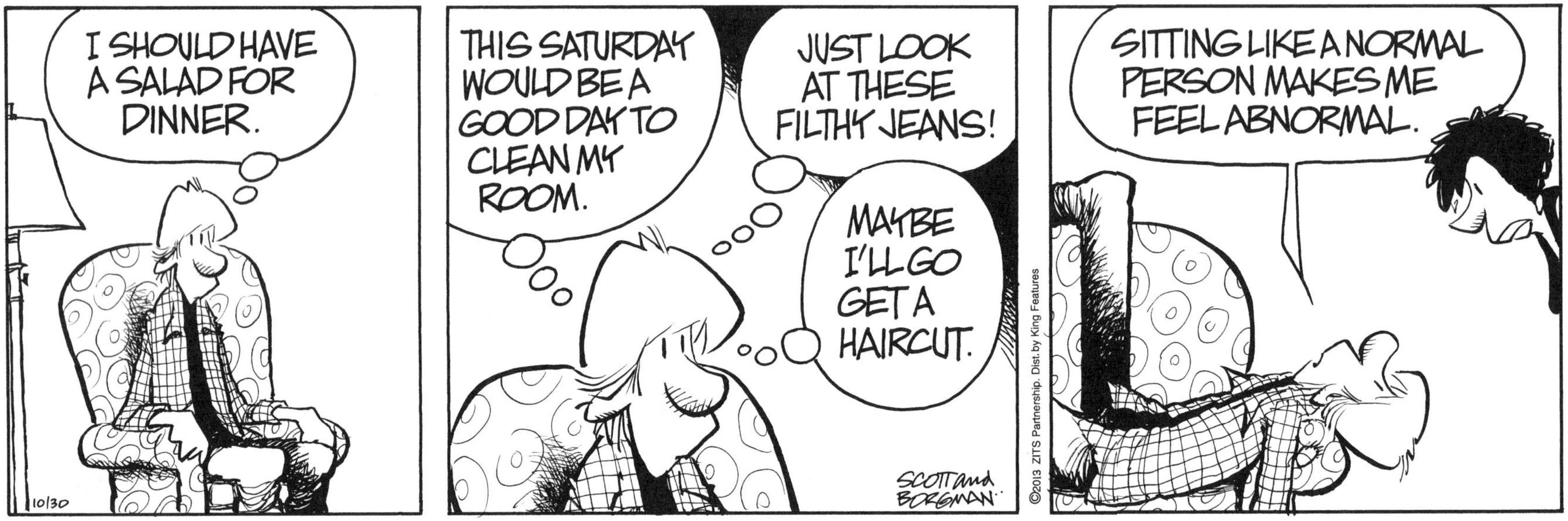
I SHOULD HAVE A SALAD FOR DINNER.
10/30
THIS SATURDAY WOULD BE A GOOD DAY TO CLEAN MY ROOM.
JUST LOOK AT THESE FILTHY JEANS!
MAYBE I'LL GO GET A HAIRCUT.
SCOTT and BORGMAN
©2013 ZITS Partnership. Dist. by King Features
SITTING LIKE A NORMAL PERSON MAKES ME FEEL ABNORMAL.

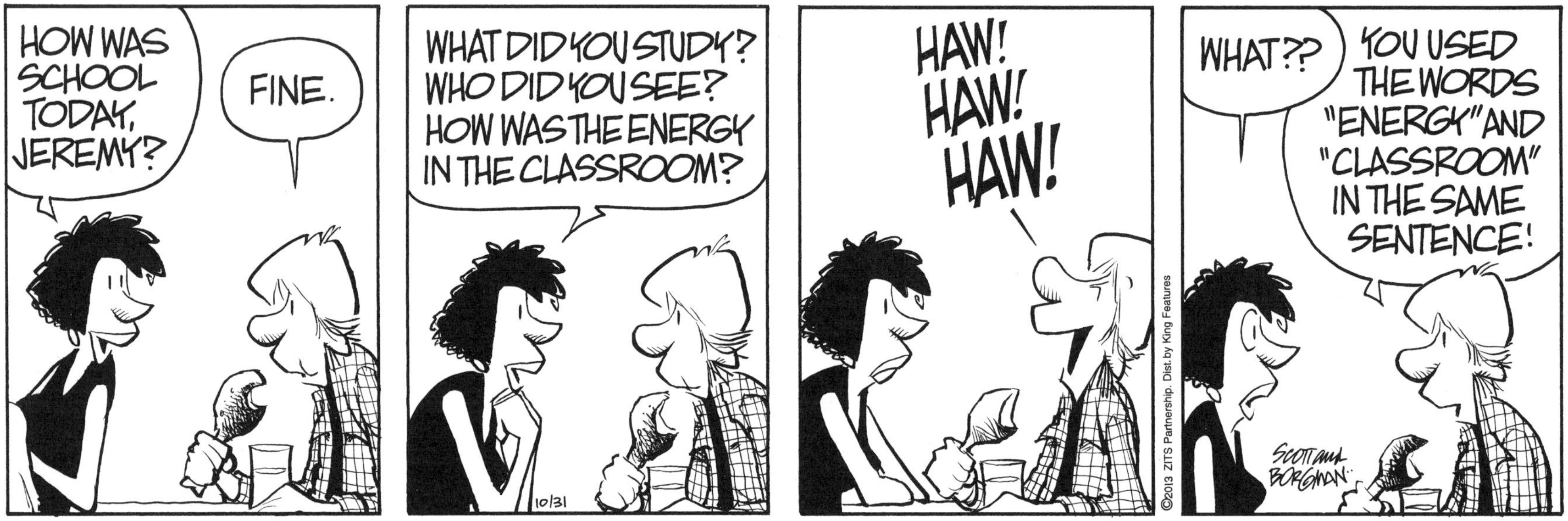
HOW WAS SCHOOL TODAY, JEREMY?
FINE.
WHAT DID YOU STUDY? WHO DID YOU SEE? HOW WAS THE ENERGY IN THE CLASSROOM?
10/31
HAW! HAW! HAW!
©2013 ZITS Partnership. Dist. by King Features
WHAT??
YOU USED THE WORDS "ENERGY" AND "CLASSROOM" IN THE SAME SENTENCE!
SCOTT and BORGMAN

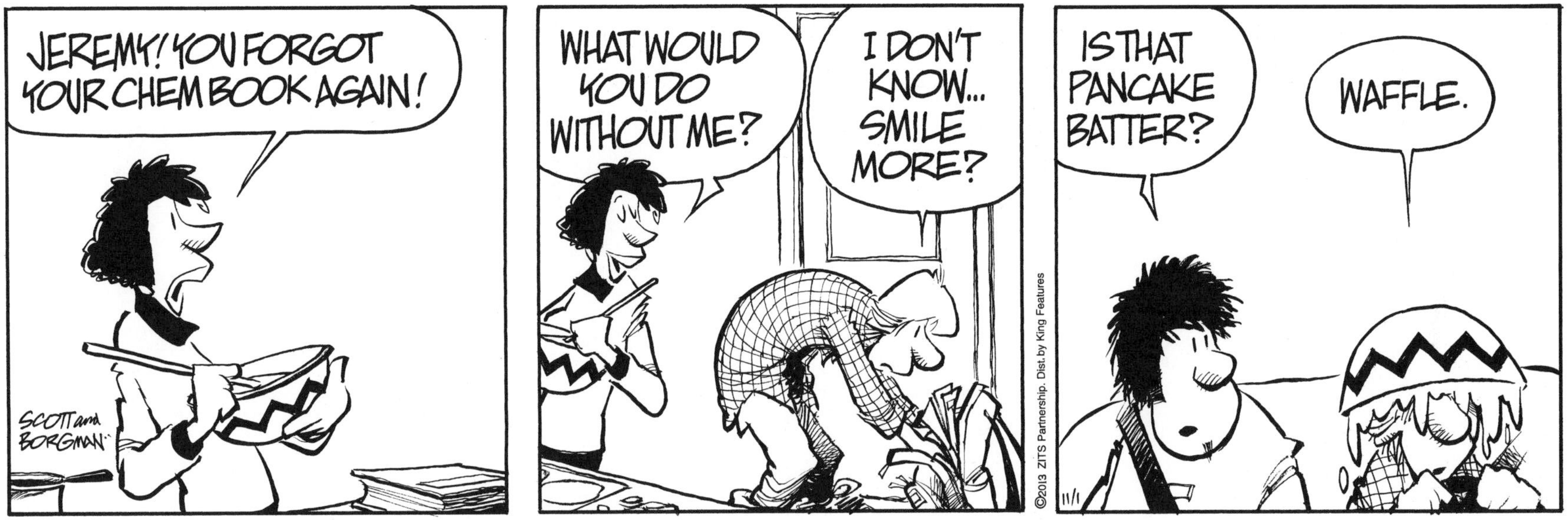
JEREMY! YOU FORGOT YOUR CHEM BOOK AGAIN!
SCOTT and BORGMAN
WHAT WOULD YOU DO WITHOUT ME?
I DON'T KNOW... SMILE MORE?
©2013 ZITS Partnership. Dist. by King Features
11/1
IS THAT PANCAKE BATTER?
WAFFLE.

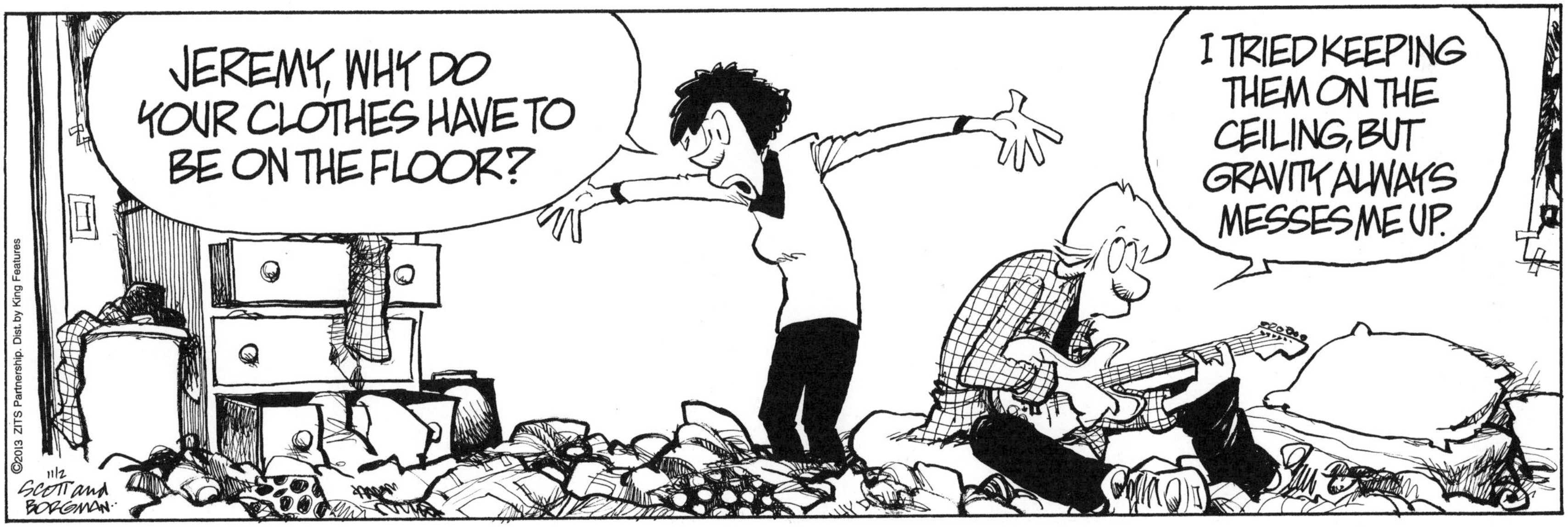
JEREMY, WHY DO YOUR CLOTHES HAVE TO BE ON THE FLOOR?
I TRIED KEEPING THEM ON THE CEILING, BUT GRAVITY ALWAYS MESSES ME UP.
©2013 ZITS Partnership. Dist. by King Features
11/2
SCOTT and BORGMAN

# ZITS

by JERRY SCOTT and JIM BORGMAN

SCOTT and BORGMAN
©2013 ZITS Partnership. Dist. by King Features
KE-RASH!
11/3
WOULD YOU GIVE ME A HEADS-UP THE NEXT TIME YOU DECIDE TO REARRANGE THE FURNITURE?

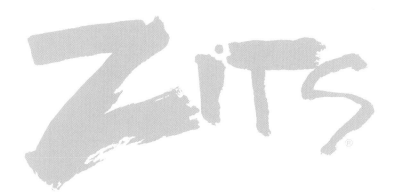

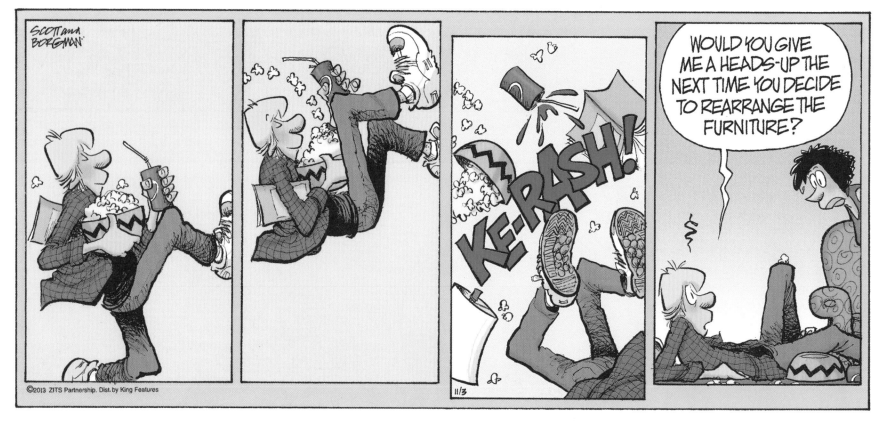

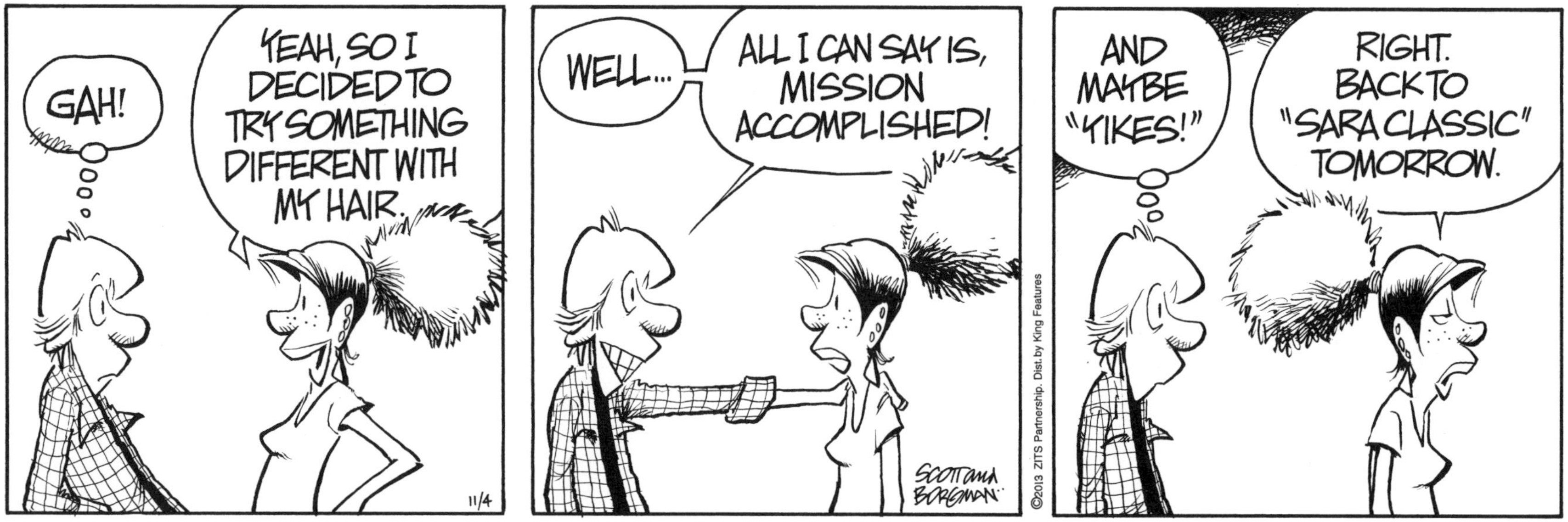
GAH!
YEAH, SO I DECIDED TO TRY SOMETHING DIFFERENT WITH MY HAIR.
11/4
WELL...
ALL I CAN SAY IS, MISSION ACCOMPLISHED!
SCOTT AND BORGMAN
©2013 ZITS Partnership. Dist. by King Features
AND MAYBE "YIKES!"
RIGHT. BACK TO "SARA CLASSIC" TOMORROW.

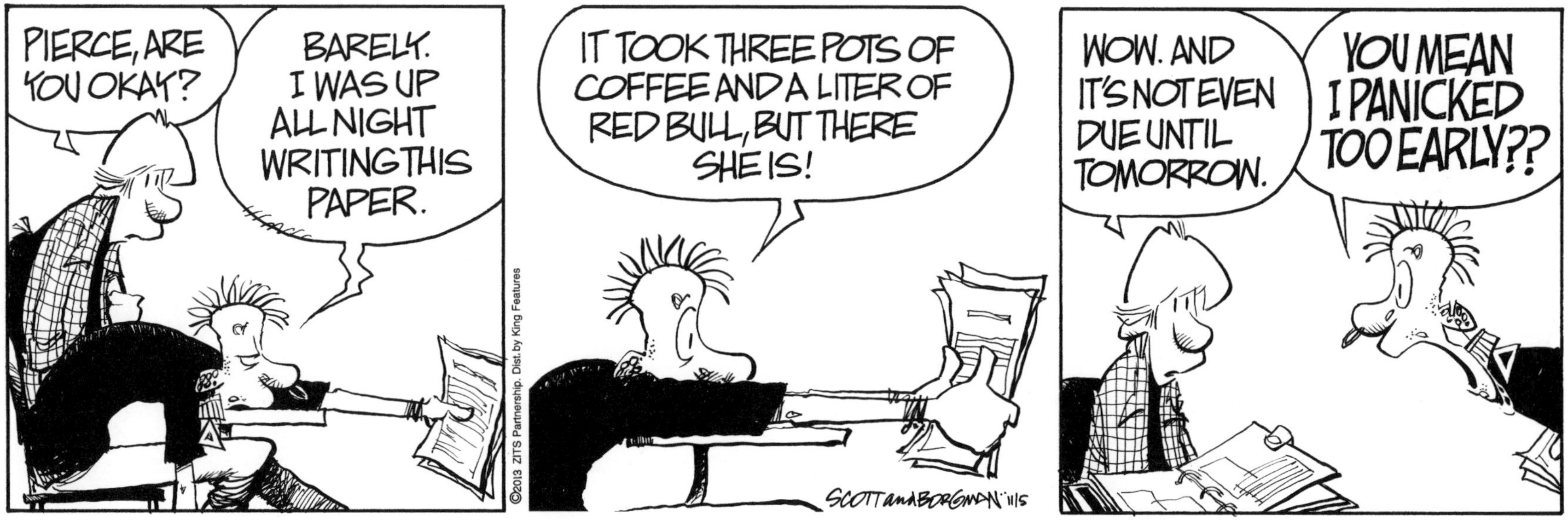
PIERCE, ARE YOU OKAY?
BARELY. I WAS UP ALL NIGHT WRITING THIS PAPER.
©2013 ZITS Partnership. Dist. by King Features
IT TOOK THREE POTS OF COFFEE AND A LITER OF RED BULL, BUT THERE SHE IS!
SCOTT AND BORGMAN 11/5
WOW. AND IT'S NOT EVEN DUE UNTIL TOMORROW.
YOU MEAN I PANICKED TOO EARLY??

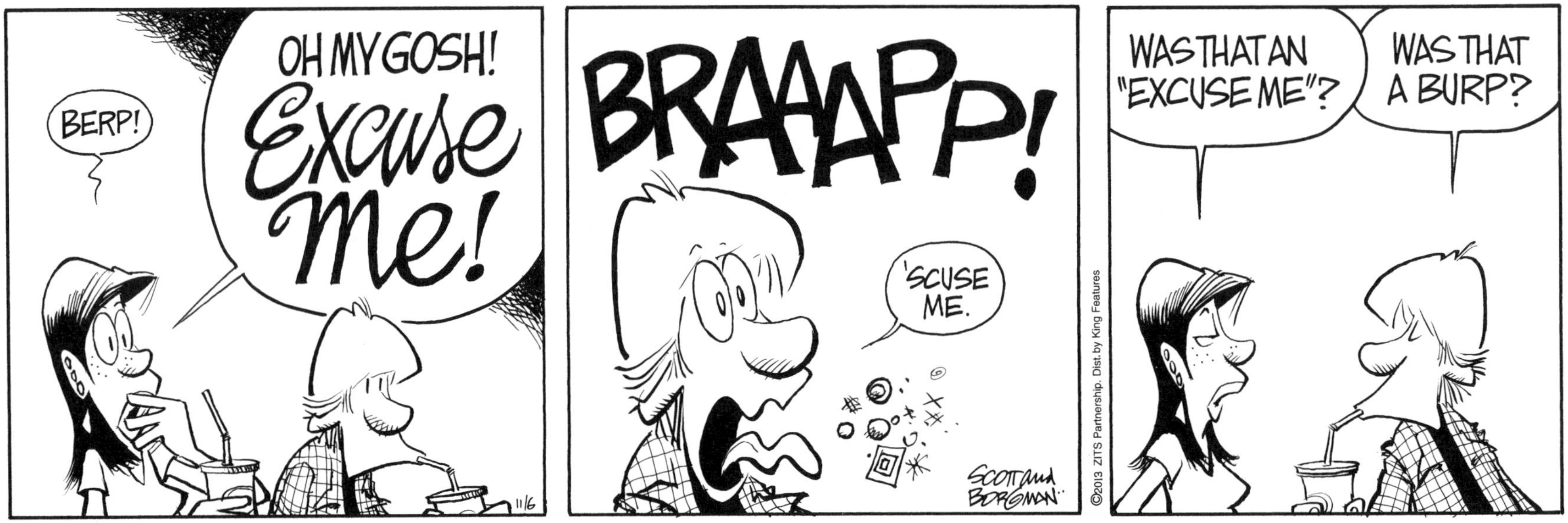
BERP!
OH MY GOSH! Excuse me!
BRAAAPP!
'SCUSE ME.
WAS THAT AN "EXCUSE ME"?
WAS THAT A BURP?
©2013 ZITS Partnership. Dist. by King Features

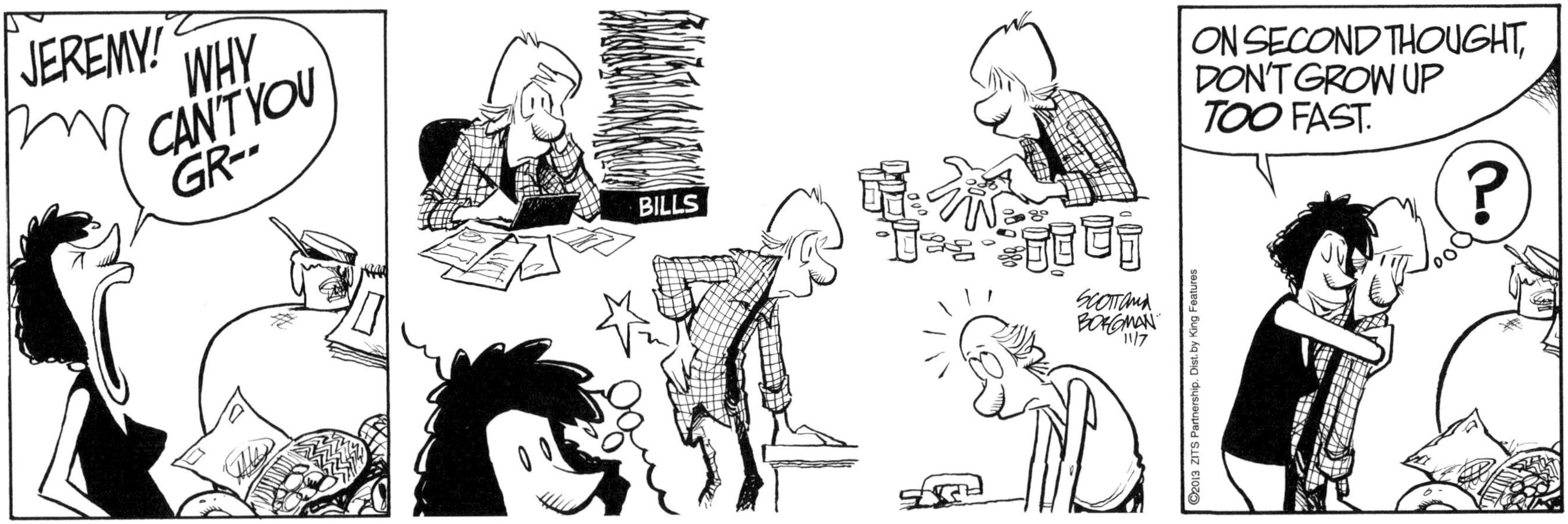
JEREMY!
WHY CAN'T YOU GR--
BILLS
ON SECOND THOUGHT, DON'T GROW UP *TOO* FAST.
?
©2013 ZITS Partnership. Dist. by King Features

ALE
DIS
11/8
©2013 ZITS Partnership. Dist. by King Features
HAVE YOU NOTICED HOW SARA BLOWS EVERYTHING I SAY OUT OF PROPORTION?
IT EVENS OUT, BECAUSE I IGNORE WHATEVER YOU TALK ABOUT.
SCOTT and BORGMAN

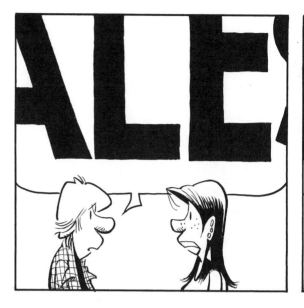

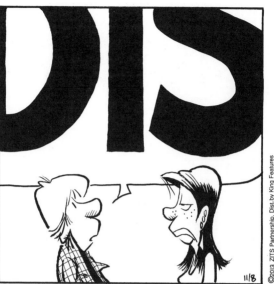

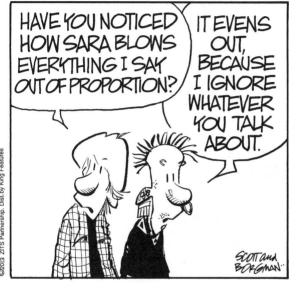

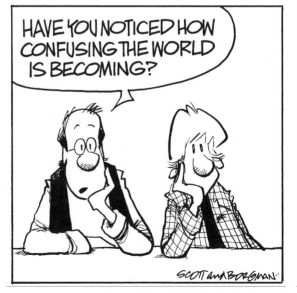

HAVE YOU NOTICED HOW CONFUSING THE WORLD IS BECOMING?
SCOTT and BORGMAN
I WAS JUST THINKING THAT I HAVE THE ANSWERS TO EVERYTHING.
11/9
YOU HAVE SO MUCH TO LEARN.
©2013 ZITS Partnership. Dist. by King Features

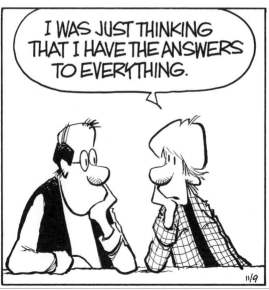

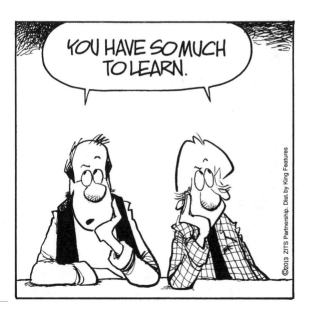

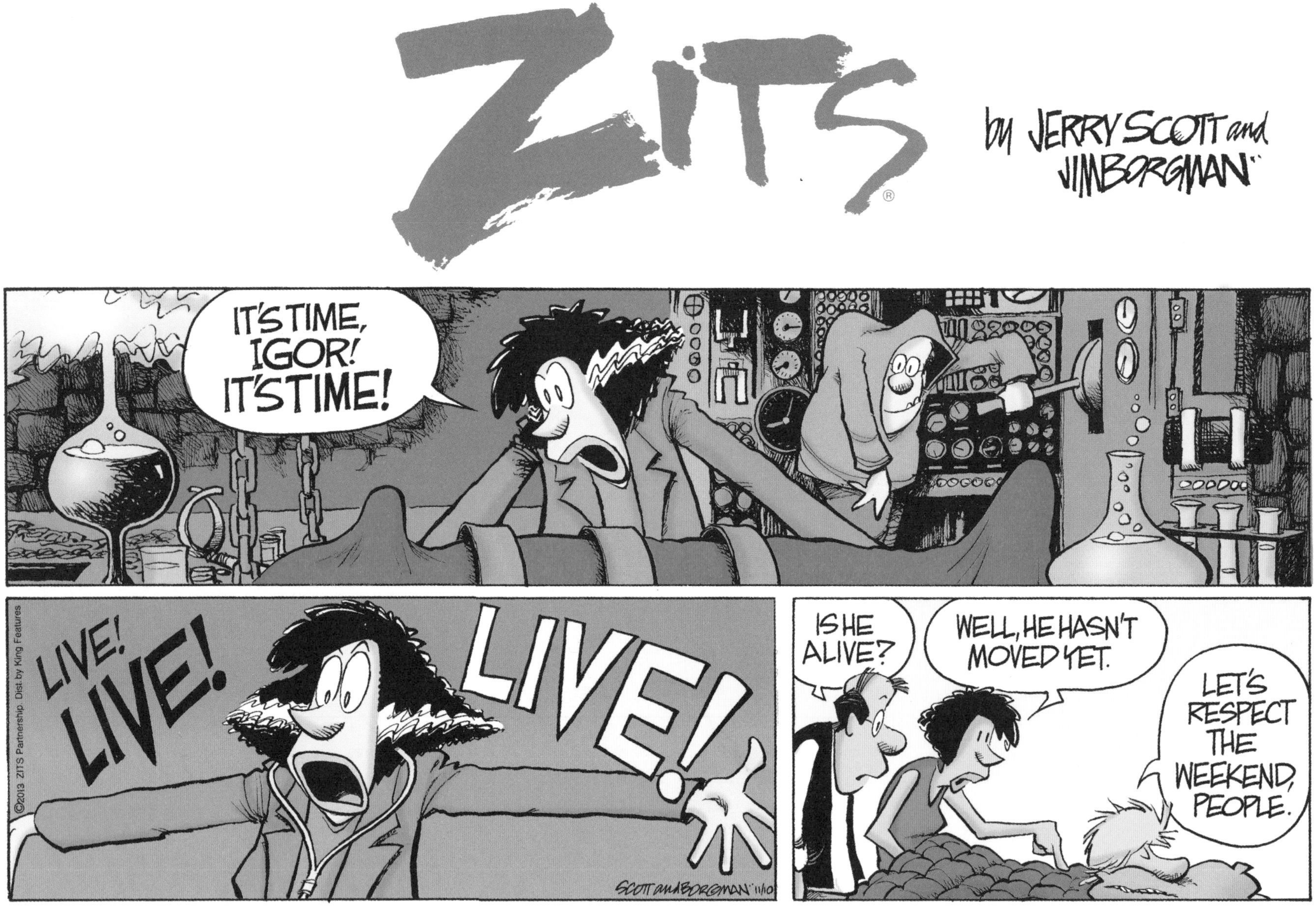
ZITS
by JERRY SCOTT and JIM BORGMAN
IT'S TIME, IGOR! IT'S TIME!
©2013 ZITS Partnership. Dist. by King Features
LIVE! LIVE! LIVE!
SCOTT and BORGMAN 11/10
IS HE ALIVE?
WELL, HE HASN'T MOVED YET.
LET'S RESPECT THE WEEKEND, PEOPLE.

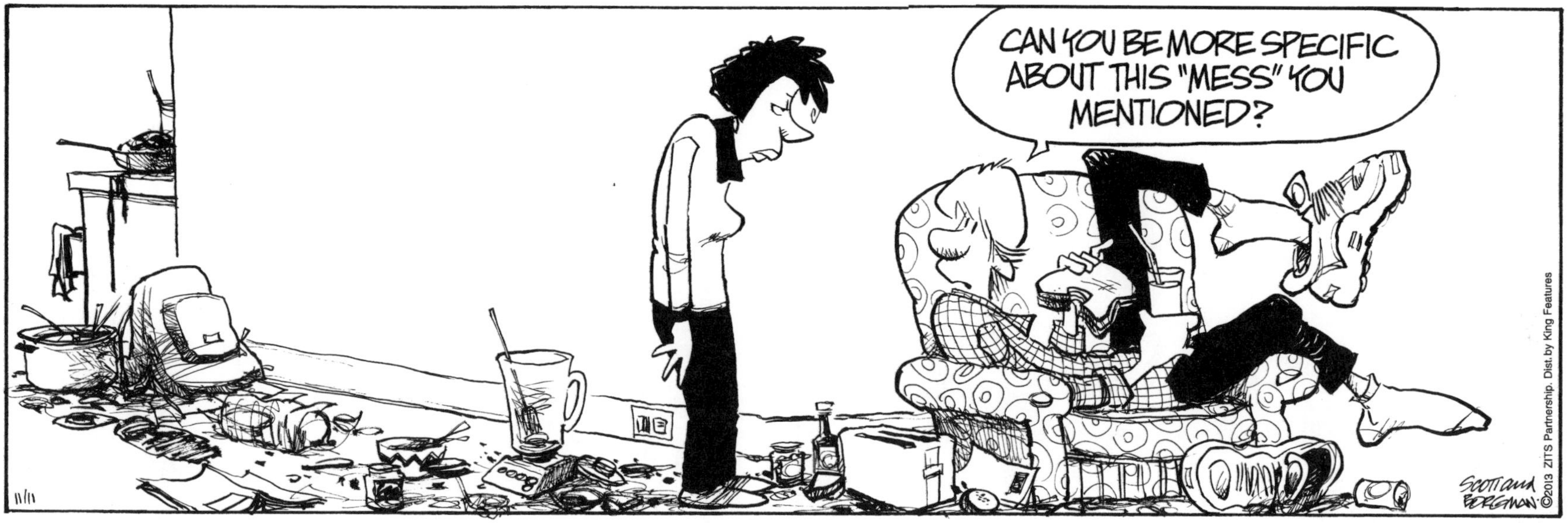
11/11
CAN YOU BE MORE SPECIFIC ABOUT THIS "MESS" YOU MENTIONED?
SCOTT and BORGMAN
©2013 ZITS Partnership. Dist. by King Features

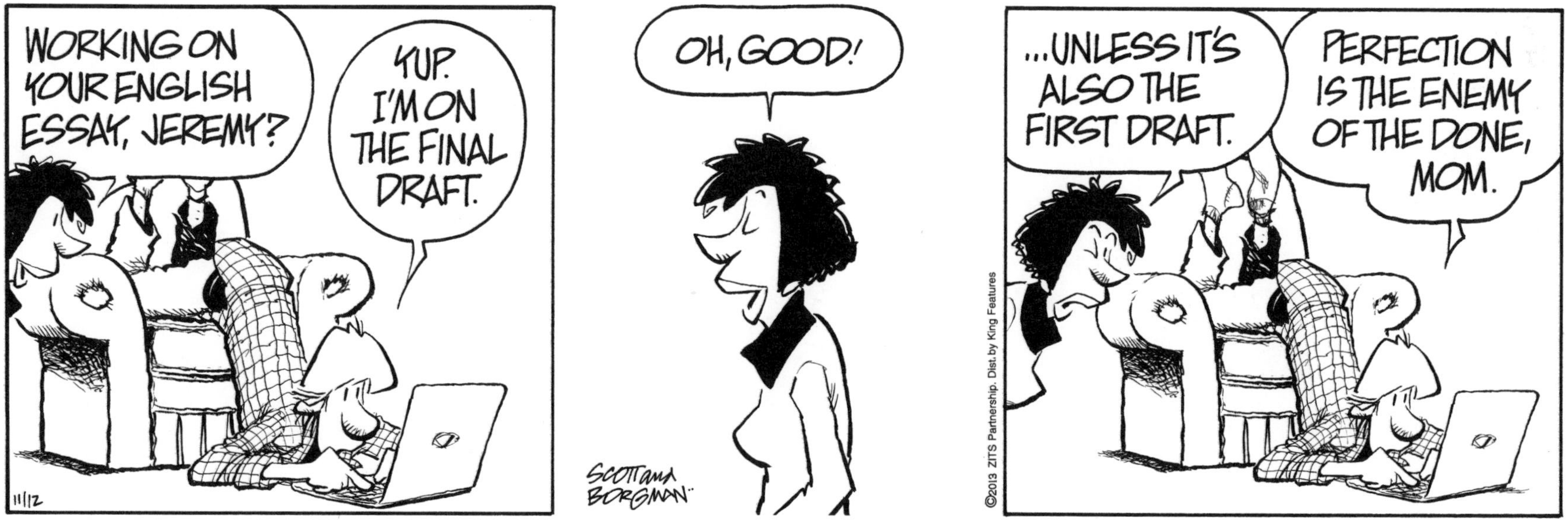
WORKING ON YOUR ENGLISH ESSAY, JEREMY?
YUP. I'M ON THE FINAL DRAFT.
11/12
OH, GOOD!
SCOTT and BORGMAN
©2013 ZITS Partnership. Dist. by King Features
...UNLESS IT'S ALSO THE FIRST DRAFT.
PERFECTION IS THE ENEMY OF THE DONE, MOM.

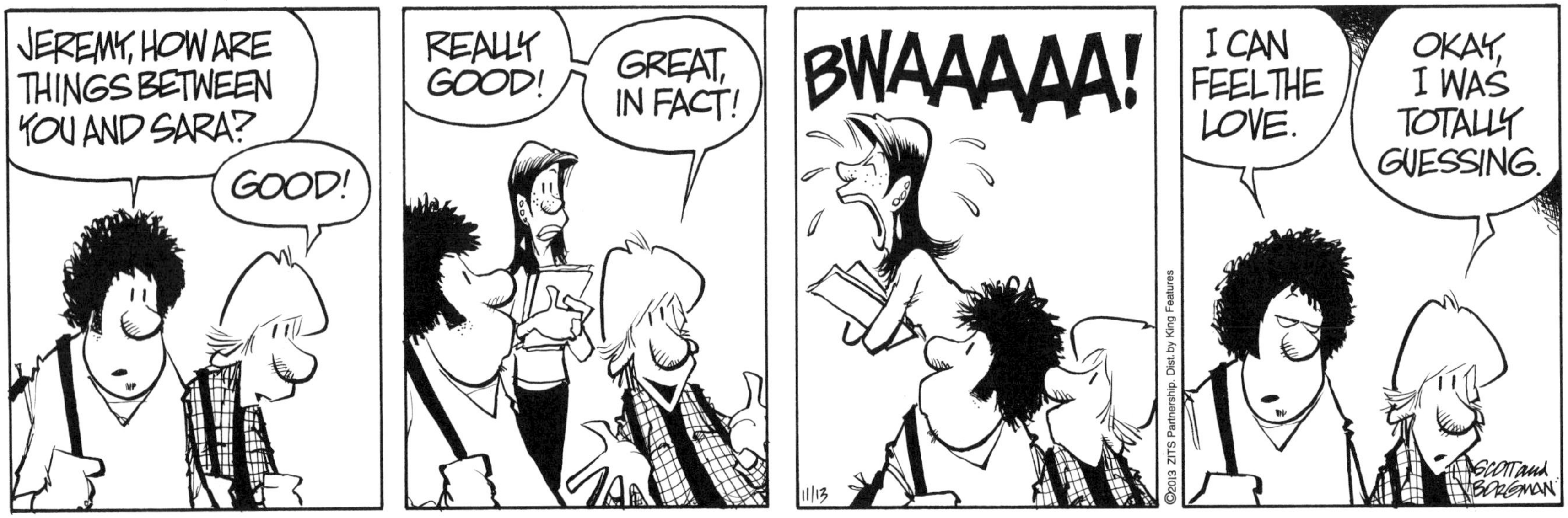
JEREMY, HOW ARE THINGS BETWEEN YOU AND SARA?
GOOD!
REALLY GOOD!
GREAT, IN FACT!
BWAAAAAA!
11/13
©2013 ZITS Partnership. Dist. by King Features
I CAN FEEL THE LOVE.
OKAY, I WAS TOTALLY GUESSING.
SCOTT and BORGMAN

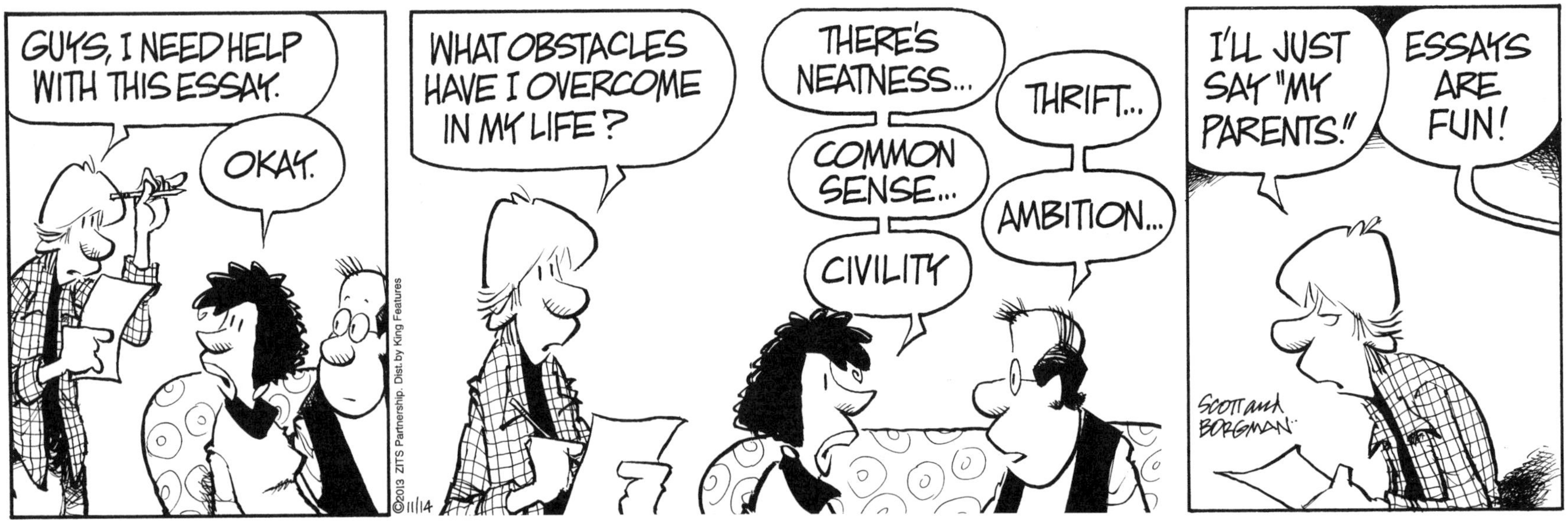
GUYS, I NEED HELP WITH THIS ESSAY.
OKAY.
©2013 ZITS Partnership. Dist. by King Features
11/14
WHAT OBSTACLES HAVE I OVERCOME IN MY LIFE?
THERE'S NEATNESS...
COMMON SENSE...
CIVILITY
THRIFT...
AMBITION...
I'LL JUST SAY "MY PARENTS."
ESSAYS ARE FUN!
SCOTT and BORGMAN

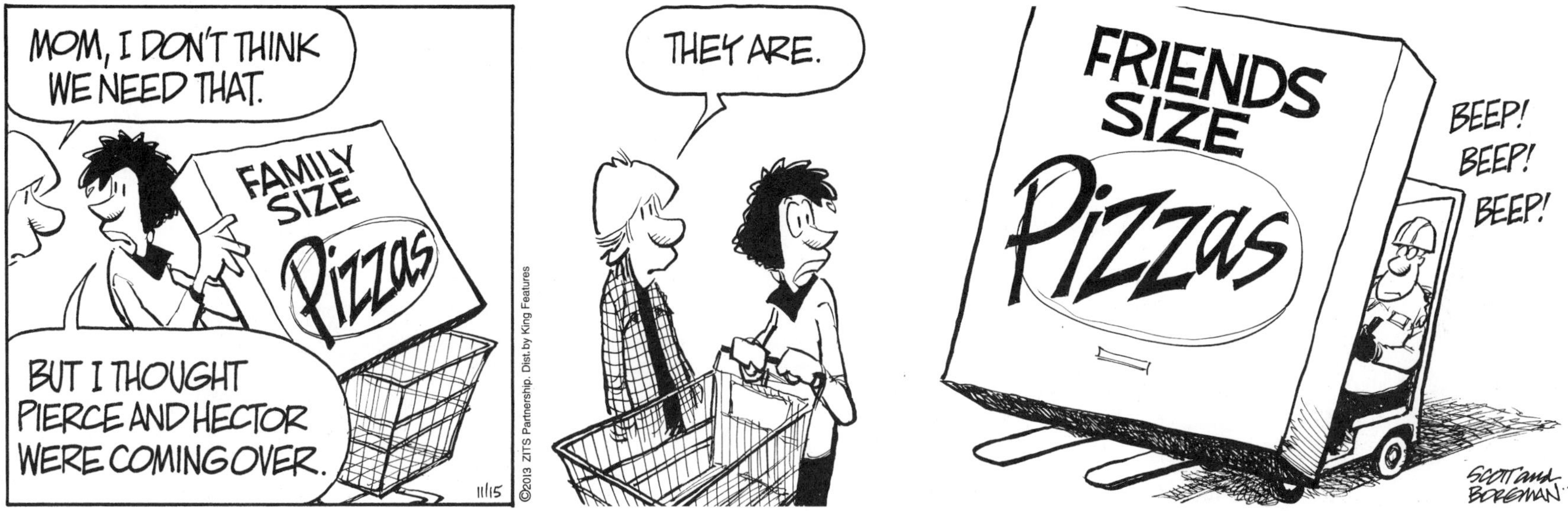
MOM, I DON'T THINK WE NEED THAT.
FAMILY SIZE Pizzas
BUT I THOUGHT PIERCE AND HECTOR WERE COMING OVER.
11/15
©2013 ZITS Partnership. Dist. by King Features
THEY ARE.
FRIENDS SIZE Pizzas
BEEP! BEEP! BEEP!
SCOTT and BORGMAN

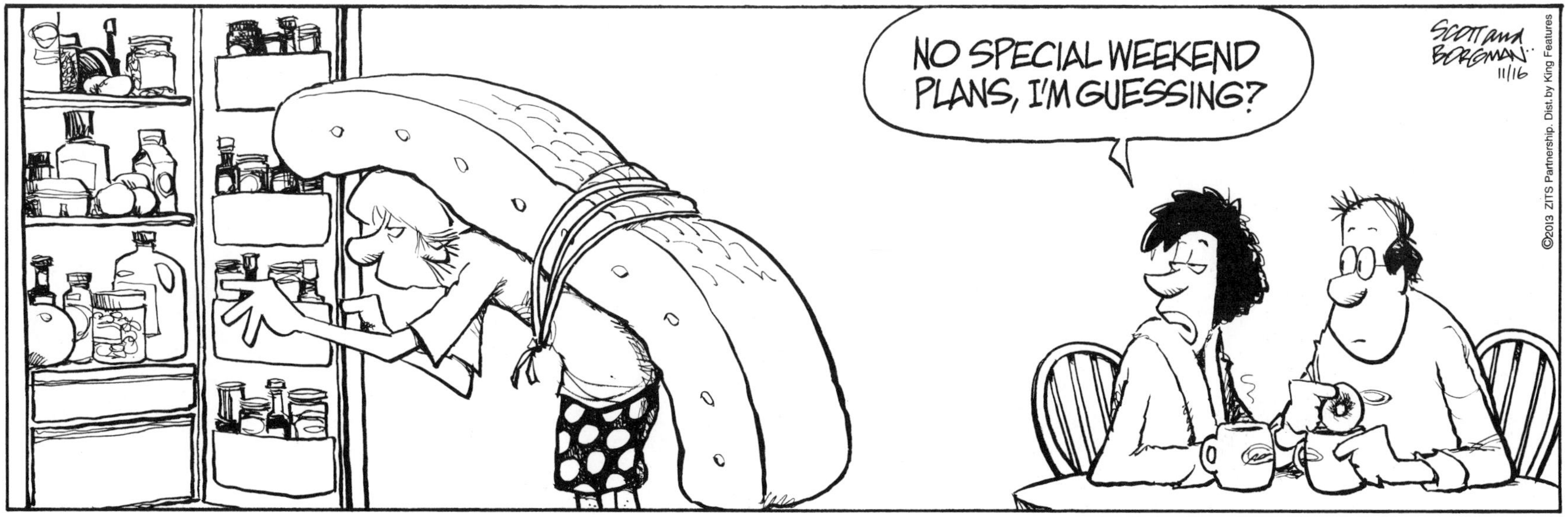
NO SPECIAL WEEKEND PLANS, I'M GUESSING?
SCOTT and BORGMAN 11/16
©2013 ZITS Partnership. Dist. by King Features

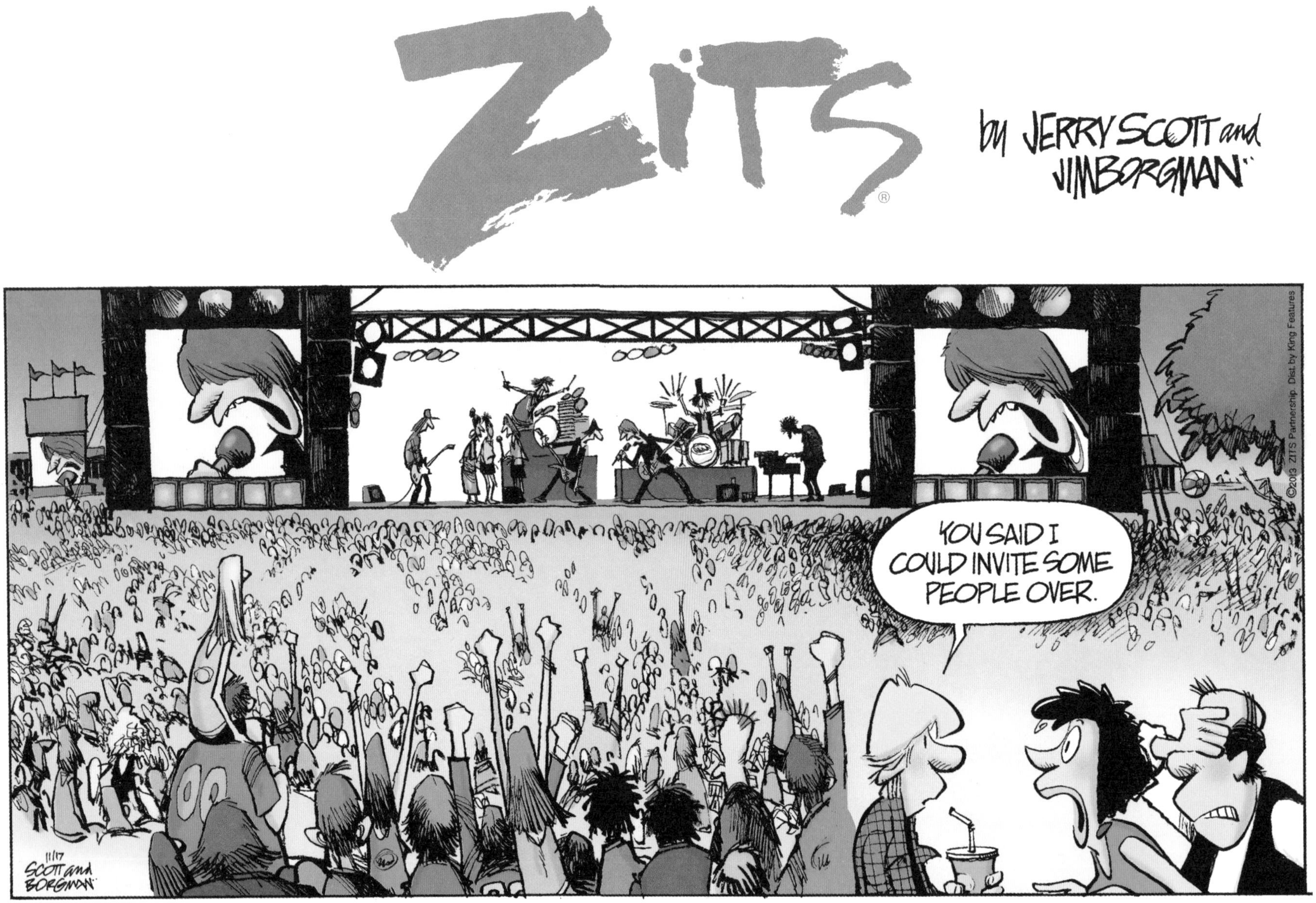
ZITS®
by JERRY SCOTT and JIM BORGMAN
YOU SAID I COULD INVITE SOME PEOPLE OVER.
©2013 ZITS Partnership. Dist by King Features
11/17 SCOTT and BORGMAN

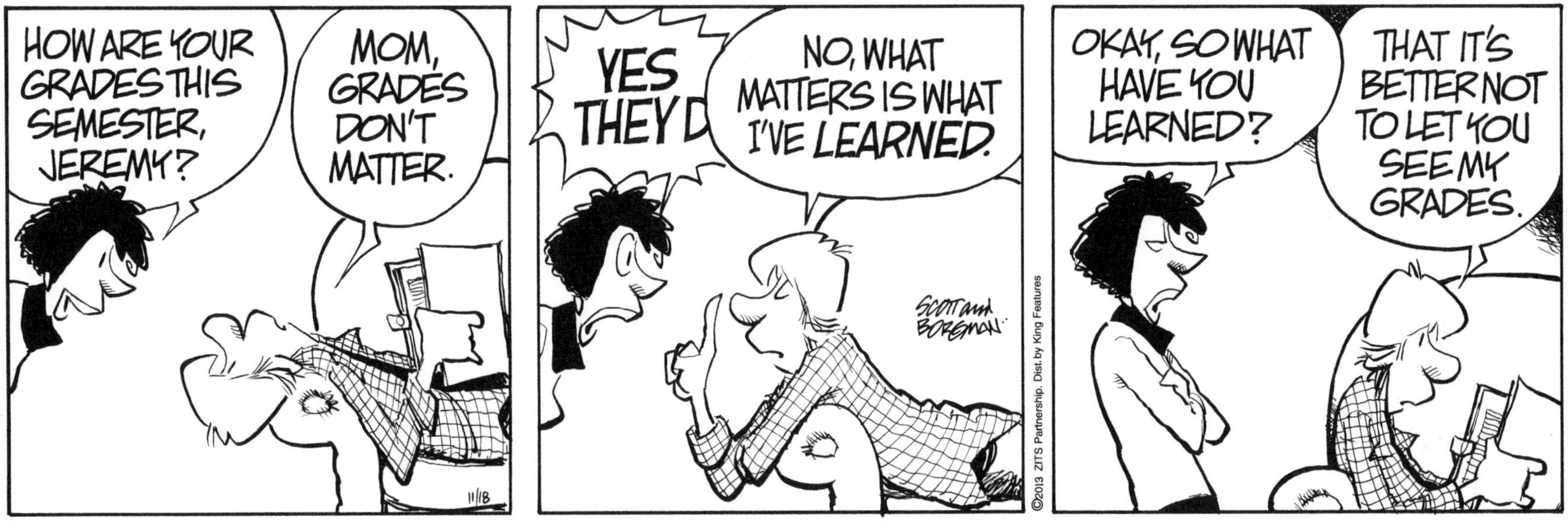
HOW ARE YOUR GRADES THIS SEMESTER, JEREMY?
MOM, GRADES DON'T MATTER.
YES THEY D
NO, WHAT MATTERS IS WHAT I'VE *LEARNED*.
OKAY, SO WHAT HAVE YOU LEARNED?
THAT IT'S BETTER NOT TO LET YOU SEE MY GRADES.
©2013 ZITS Partnership. Dist. by King Features

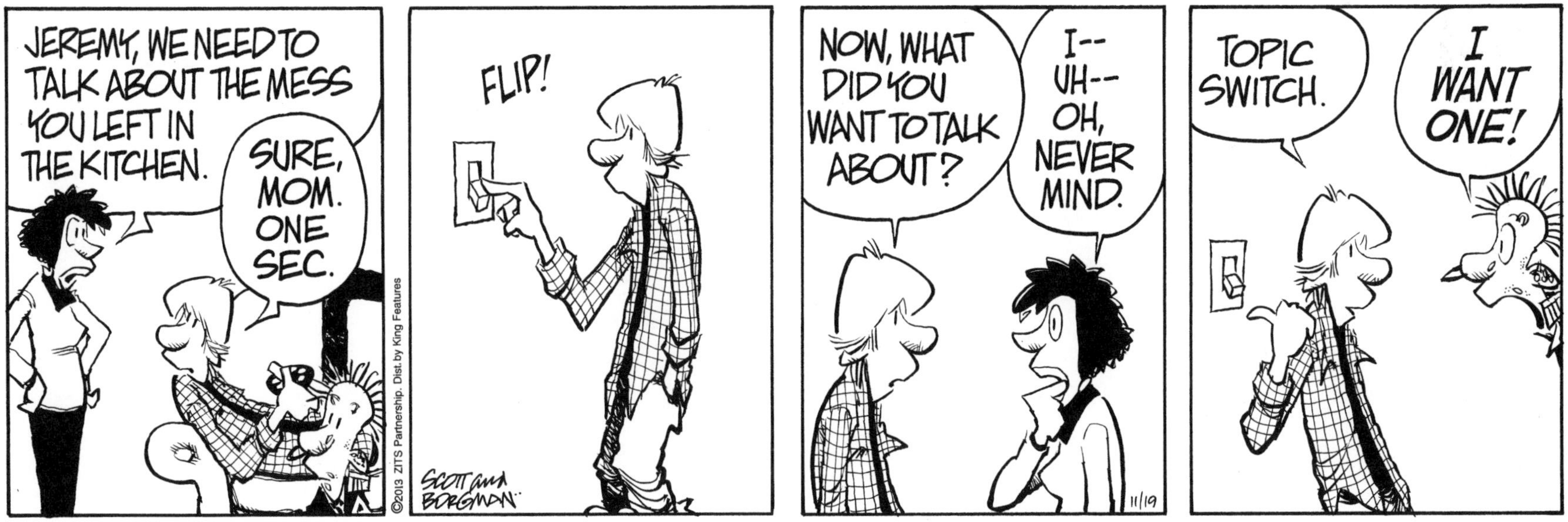
JEREMY, WE NEED TO TALK ABOUT THE MESS YOU LEFT IN THE KITCHEN.
SURE, MOM. ONE SEC.
©2013 ZITS Partnership. Dist. by King Features
FLIP!
NOW, WHAT DID YOU WANT TO TALK ABOUT?
I-- UH-- OH, NEVER MIND.
TOPIC SWITCH.
*I WANT ONE!*

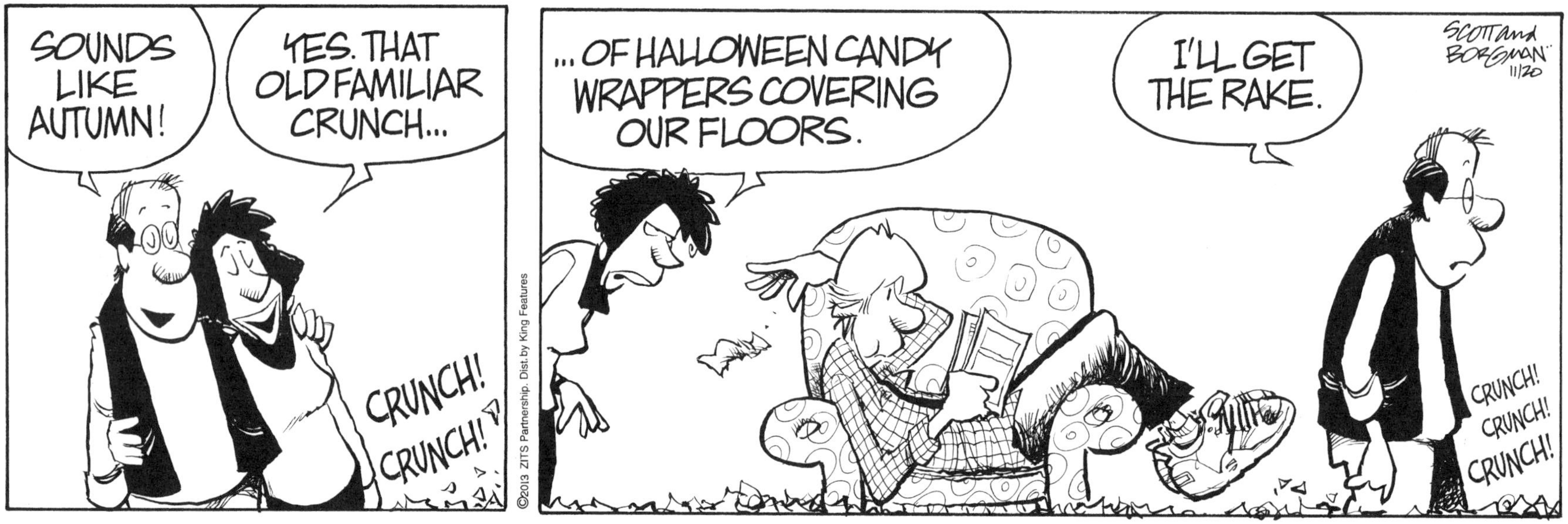
SOUNDS LIKE AUTUMN!
YES. THAT OLD FAMILIAR CRUNCH...
CRUNCH! CRUNCH!
©2013 ZITS Partnership. Dist. by King Features
...OF HALLOWEEN CANDY WRAPPERS COVERING OUR FLOORS.
I'LL GET THE RAKE.
SCOTT and BORGMAN 11/20
CRUNCH! CRUNCH! CRUNCH!

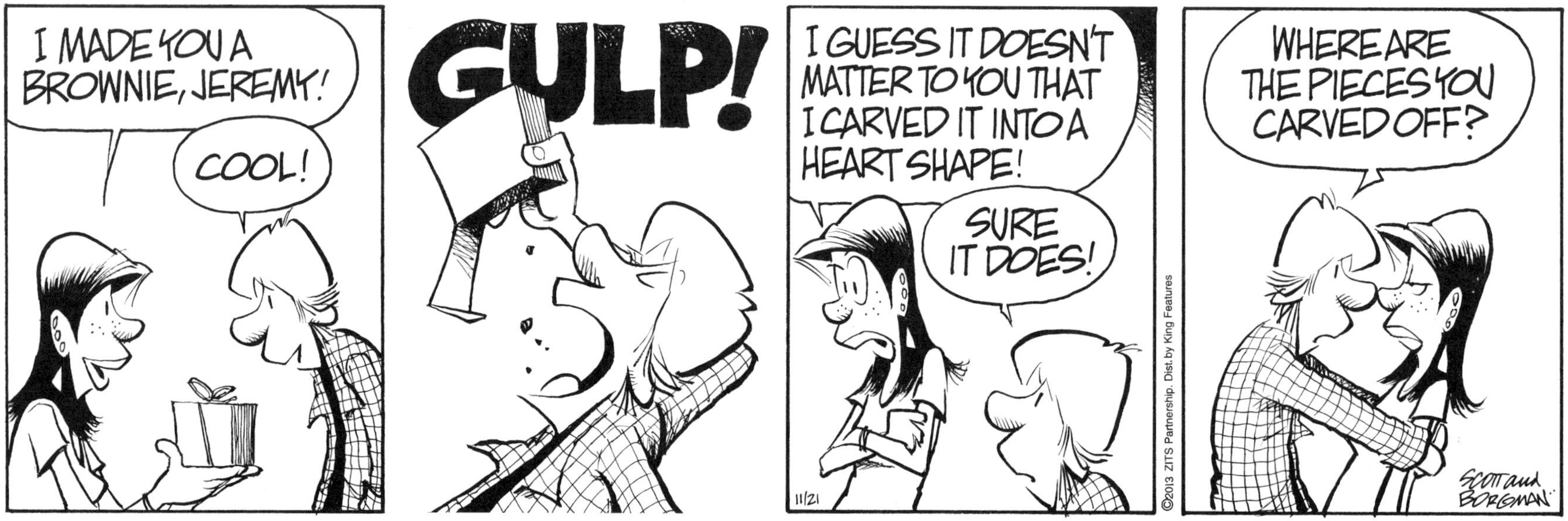
I MADE YOU A BROWNIE, JEREMY!
COOL!
GULP!
I GUESS IT DOESN'T MATTER TO YOU THAT I CARVED IT INTO A HEART SHAPE!
SURE IT DOES!
11/21
©2013 ZITS Partnership. Dist. by King Features
WHERE ARE THE PIECES YOU CARVED OFF?
SCOTT and BORGMAN

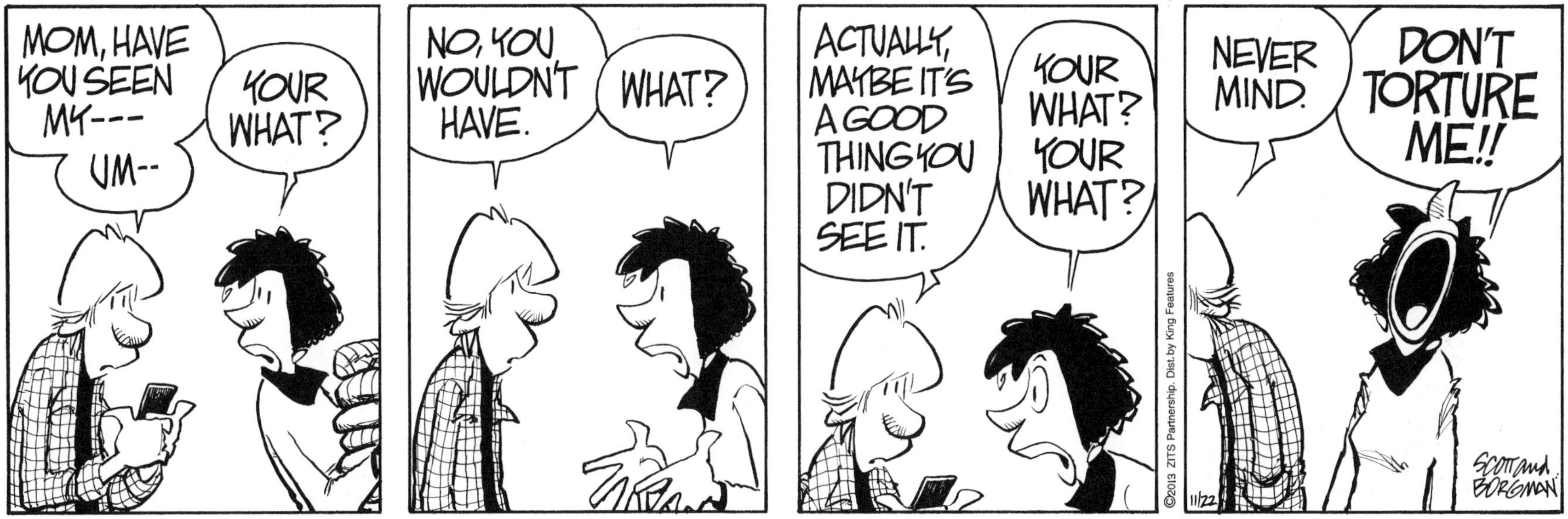
MOM, HAVE YOU SEEN MY---
UM--
YOUR WHAT?
NO, YOU WOULDN'T HAVE.
WHAT?
ACTUALLY, MAYBE IT'S A GOOD THING YOU DIDN'T SEE IT.
YOUR WHAT? YOUR WHAT?
NEVER MIND.
DON'T TORTURE ME!!
©2013 ZITS Partnership. Dist. by King Features
11/22
SCOTT and BORGMAN

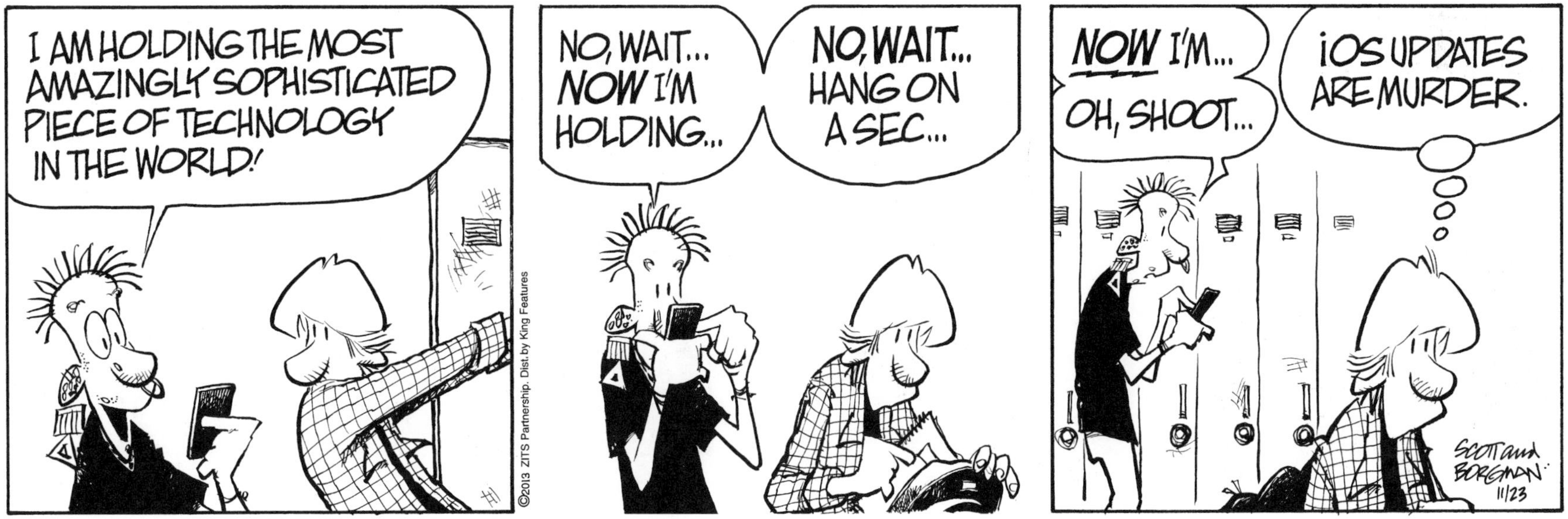
I AM HOLDING THE MOST AMAZINGLY SOPHISTICATED PIECE OF TECHNOLOGY IN THE WORLD!
©2013 ZITS Partnership. Dist. by King Features
NO, WAIT... NOW I'M HOLDING...
NO, WAIT... HANG ON A SEC...
NOW I'M...
OH, SHOOT...
iOS UPDATES ARE MURDER.
SCOTT and BORGMAN
11/23

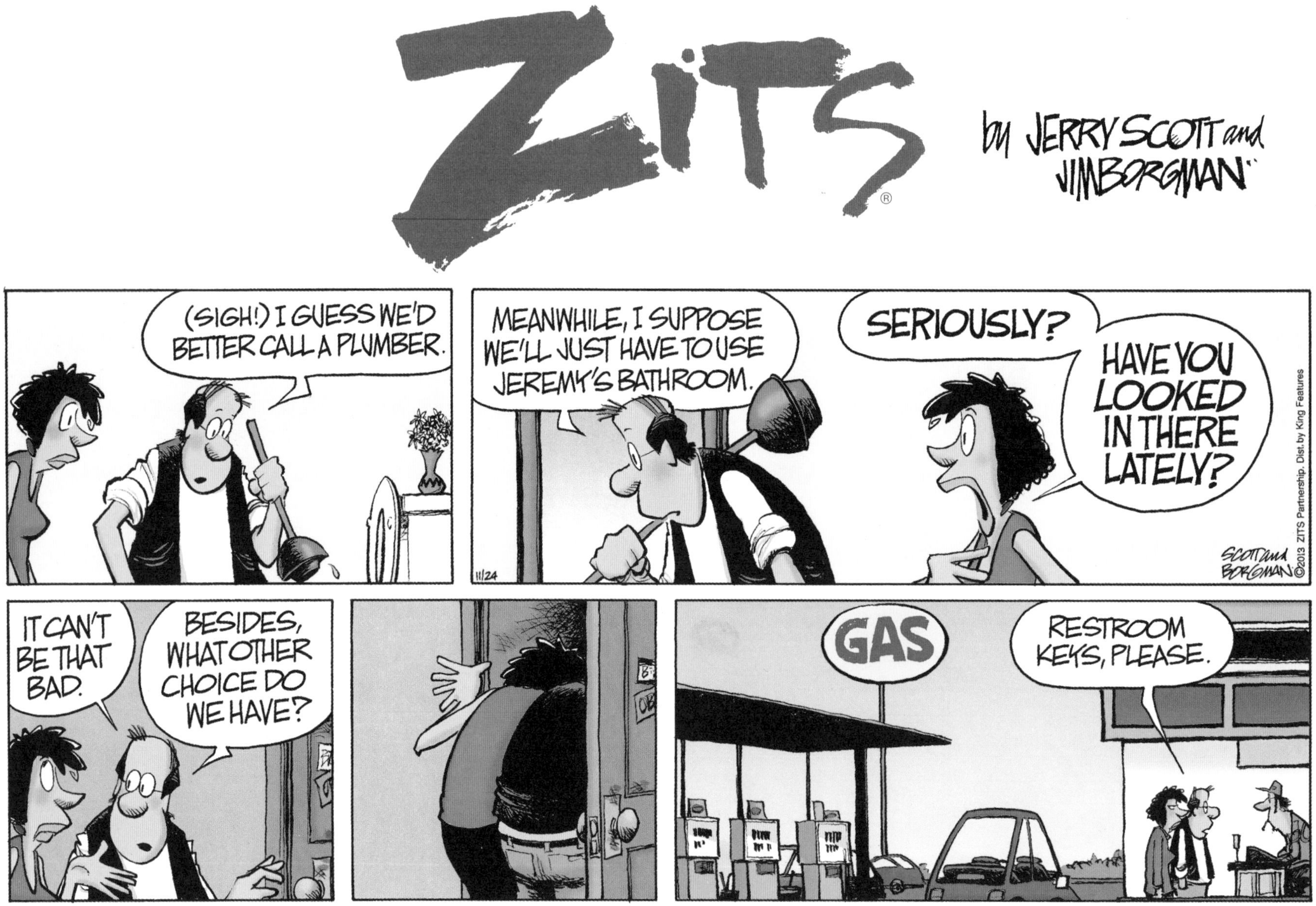
ZITS®
by JERRY SCOTT and JIM BORGMAN
(SIGH!) I GUESS WE'D BETTER CALL A PLUMBER.
MEANWHILE, I SUPPOSE WE'LL JUST HAVE TO USE JEREMY'S BATHROOM.
SERIOUSLY?
HAVE YOU LOOKED IN THERE LATELY?
©2013 ZITS Partnership. Dist. by King Features
IT CAN'T BE THAT BAD.
BESIDES, WHAT OTHER CHOICE DO WE HAVE?
GAS
RESTROOM KEYS, PLEASE.

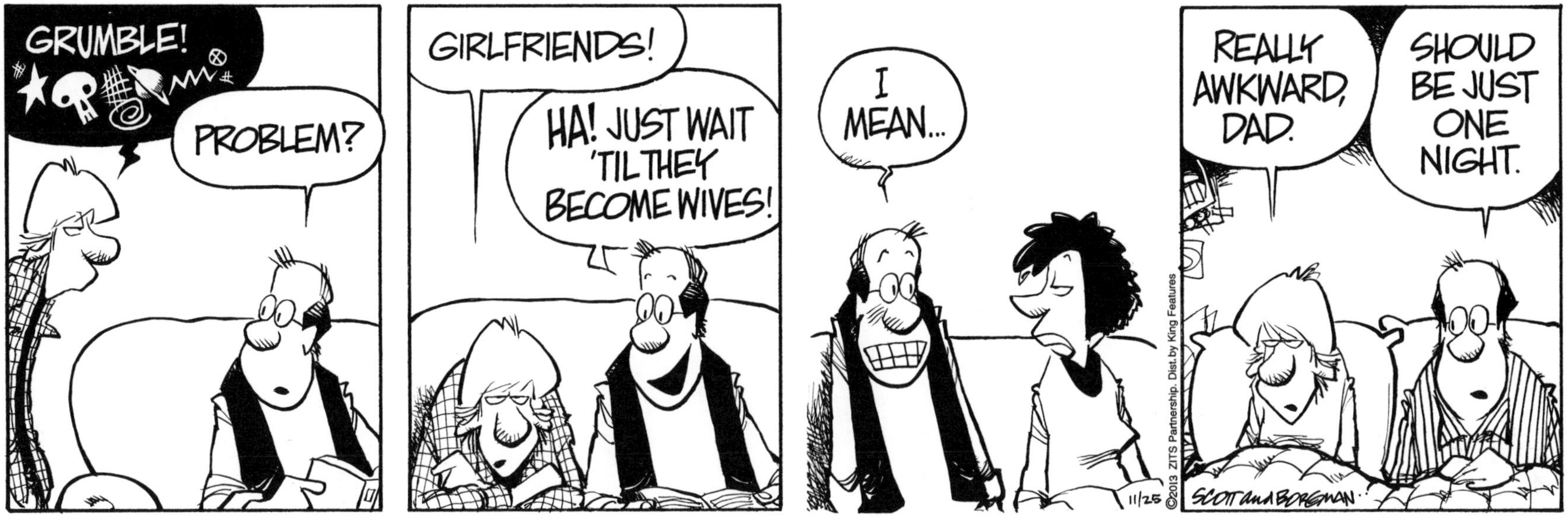
GRUMBLE!
PROBLEM?
GIRLFRIENDS!
HA! JUST WAIT 'TIL THEY BECOME WIVES!
I MEAN...
REALLY AWKWARD, DAD.
SHOULD BE JUST ONE NIGHT.
11/25
©2013 ZITS Partnership. Dist. by King Features
SCOTT and BORGMAN

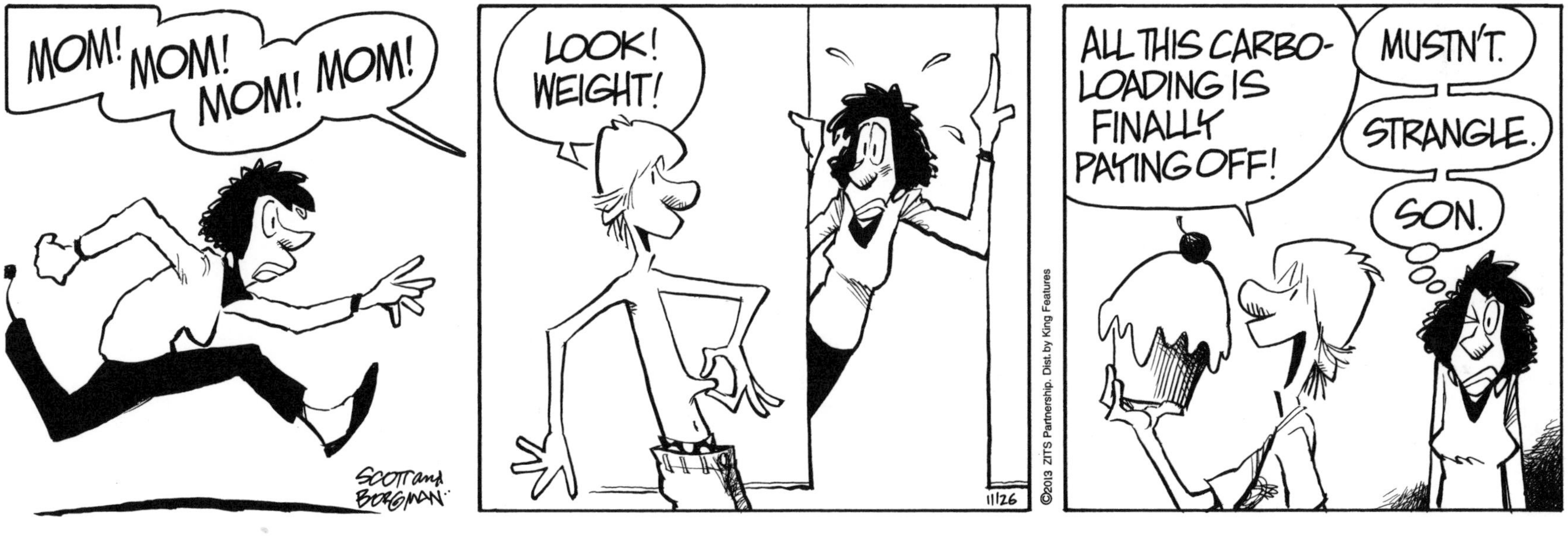
MOM! MOM! MOM! MOM!
SCOTT and BORGMAN
LOOK! WEIGHT!
11/26
©2013 ZITS Partnership. Dist. by King Features
ALL THIS CARBO-LOADING IS FINALLY PAYING OFF!
MUSTN'T.
STRANGLE.
SON.

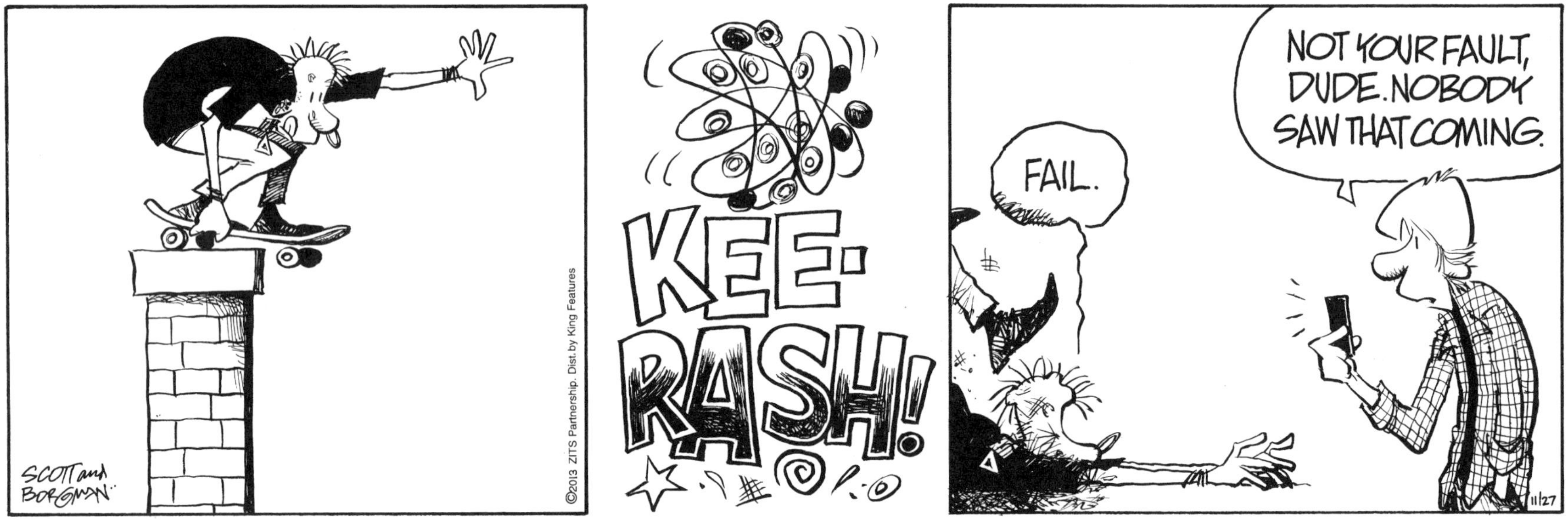
SCOTT and BORGMAN
KEE-RASH!
©2013 ZITS Partnership. Dist. by King Features
FAIL.
NOT YOUR FAULT, DUDE. NOBODY SAW THAT COMING.
11/27

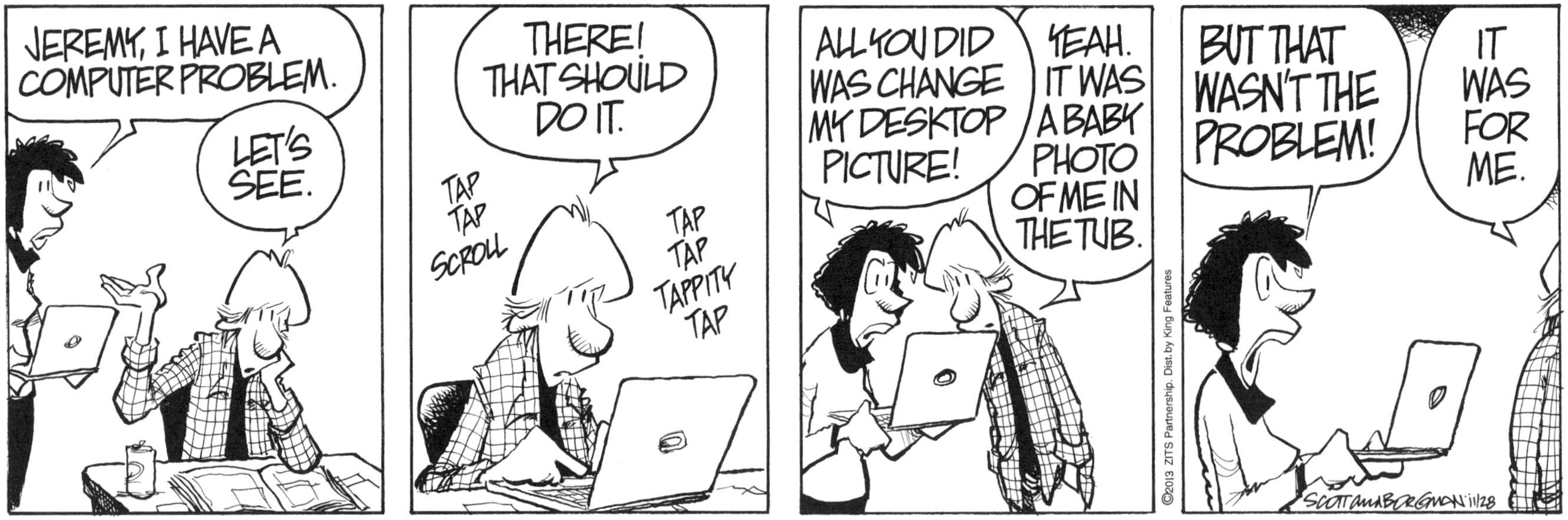
JEREMY, I HAVE A COMPUTER PROBLEM.
LET'S SEE.
TAP TAP SCROLL
THERE! THAT SHOULD DO IT.
TAP TAP TAPPITY TAP
ALL YOU DID WAS CHANGE MY DESKTOP PICTURE!
YEAH. IT WAS A BABY PHOTO OF ME IN THE TUB.
©2013 ZITS Partnership. Dist. by King Features
BUT THAT WASN'T THE PROBLEM!
IT WAS FOR ME.
SCOTT and BORGMAN 11/28

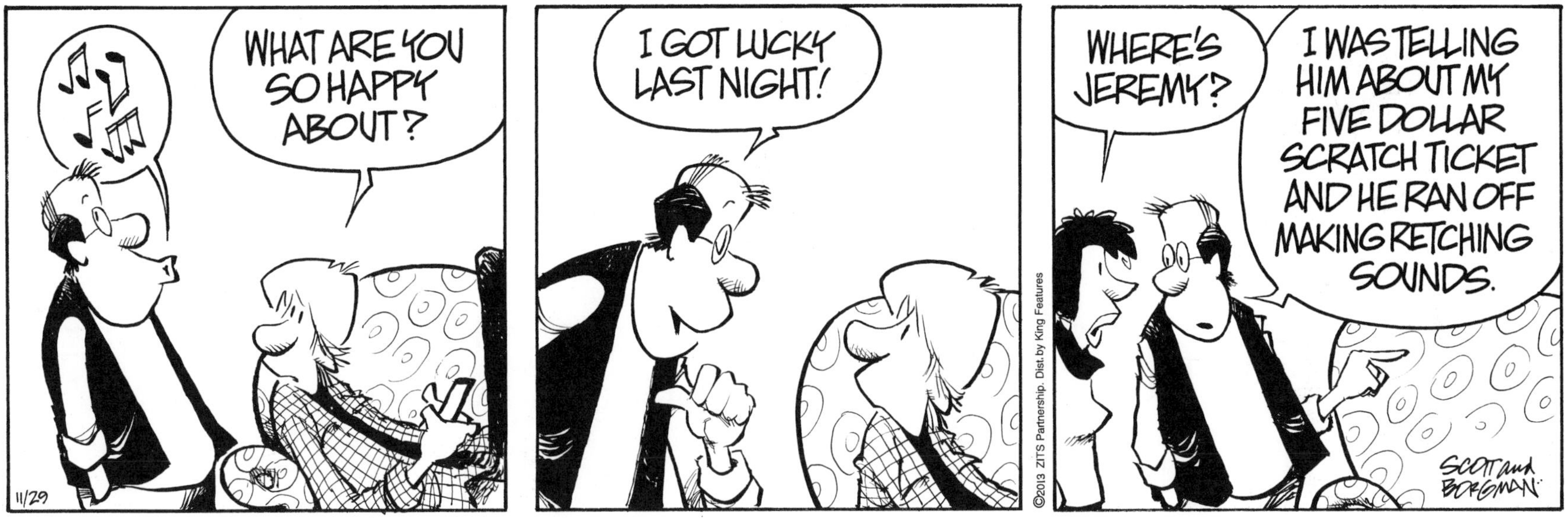
WHAT ARE YOU SO HAPPY ABOUT?
I GOT LUCKY LAST NIGHT!
WHERE'S JEREMY?
I WAS TELLING HIM ABOUT MY FIVE DOLLAR SCRATCH TICKET AND HE RAN OFF MAKING RETCHING SOUNDS.
11/29
©2013 ZITS Partnership. Dist. by King Features
SCOTT and BORGMAN

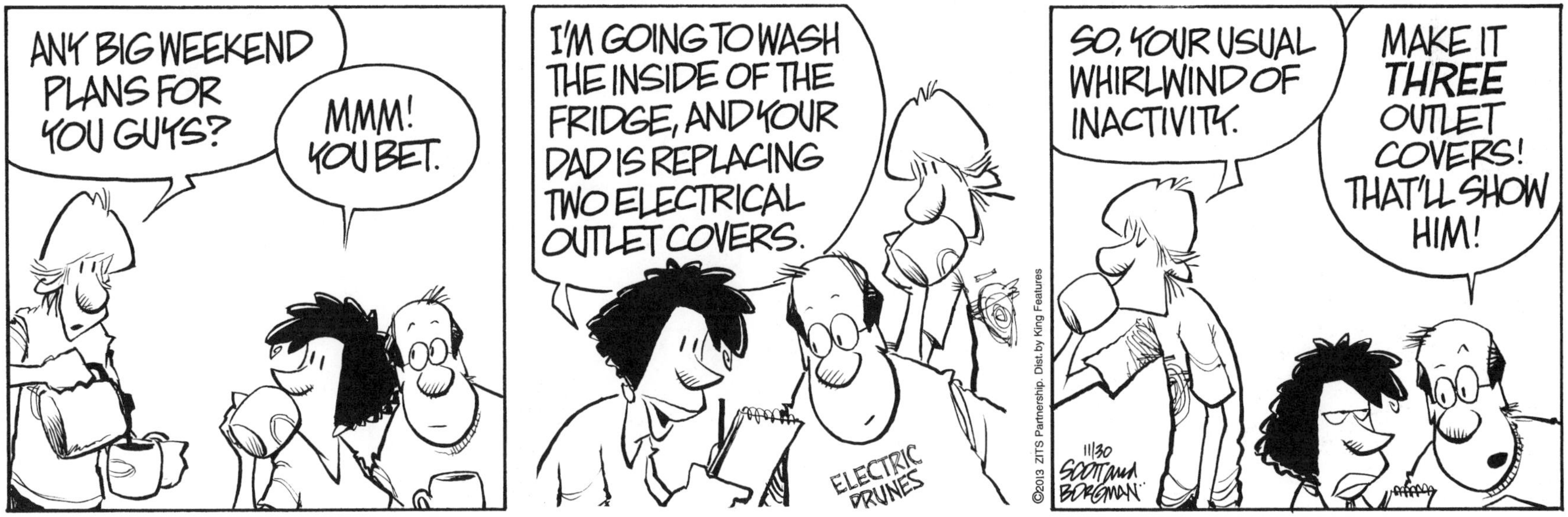
ANY BIG WEEKEND PLANS FOR YOU GUYS?
MMM! YOU BET.
I'M GOING TO WASH THE INSIDE OF THE FRIDGE, AND YOUR DAD IS REPLACING TWO ELECTRICAL OUTLET COVERS.
ELECTRIC PRUNES
SO, YOUR USUAL WHIRLWIND OF INACTIVITY.
MAKE IT THREE OUTLET COVERS! THAT'LL SHOW HIM!
11/30
©2013 ZITS Partnership. Dist. by King Features
SCOTT and BORGMAN

# ZITS

by JERRY SCOTT and JIM BORGMAN

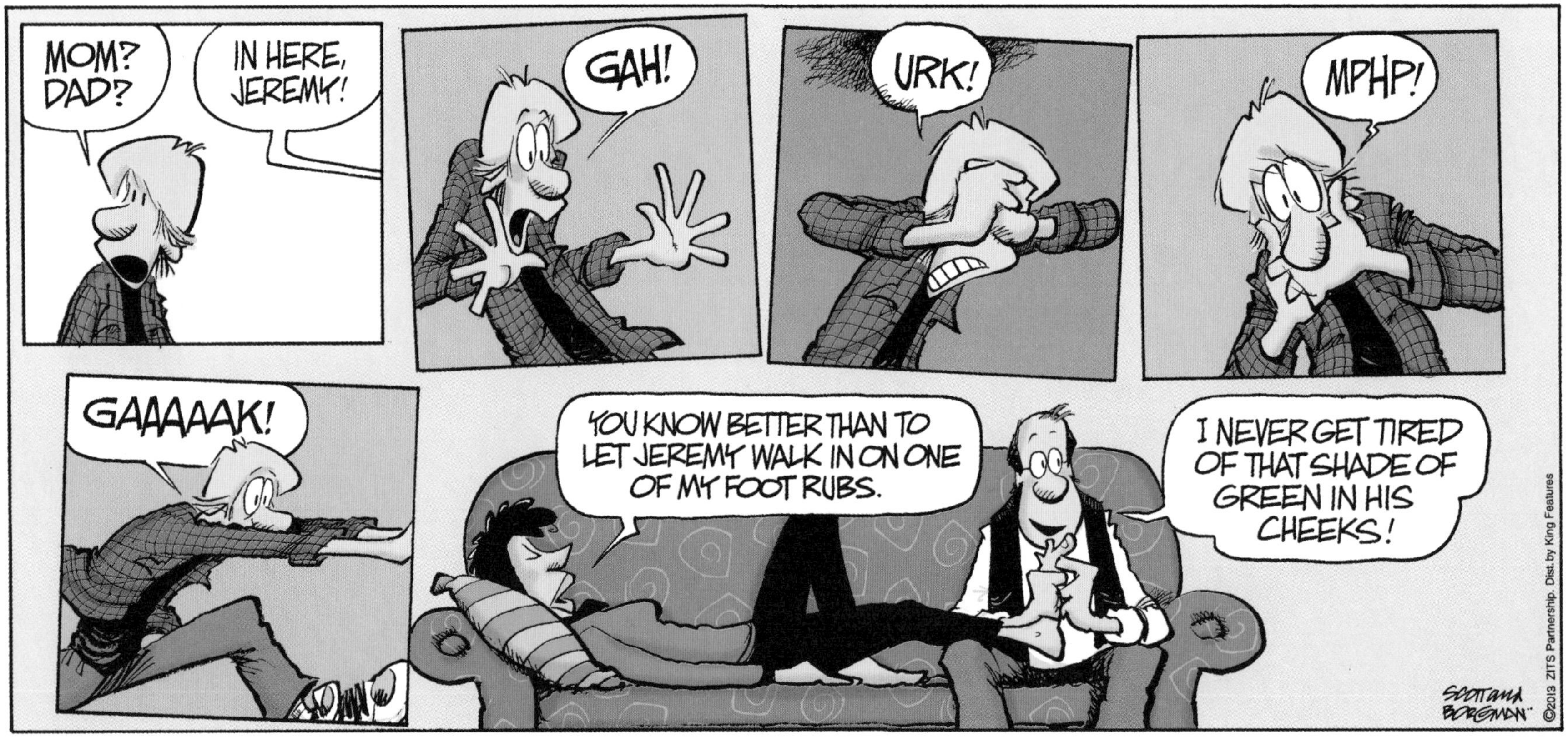
MOM? DAD?
IN HERE, JEREMY!
GAH!
URK!
MPHP!
GAAAAAK!
YOU KNOW BETTER THAN TO LET JEREMY WALK IN ON ONE OF MY FOOT RUBS.
I NEVER GET TIRED OF THAT SHADE OF GREEN IN HIS CHEEKS!
SCOTT and BORGMAN
©2013 ZITS Partnership. Dist. by King Features

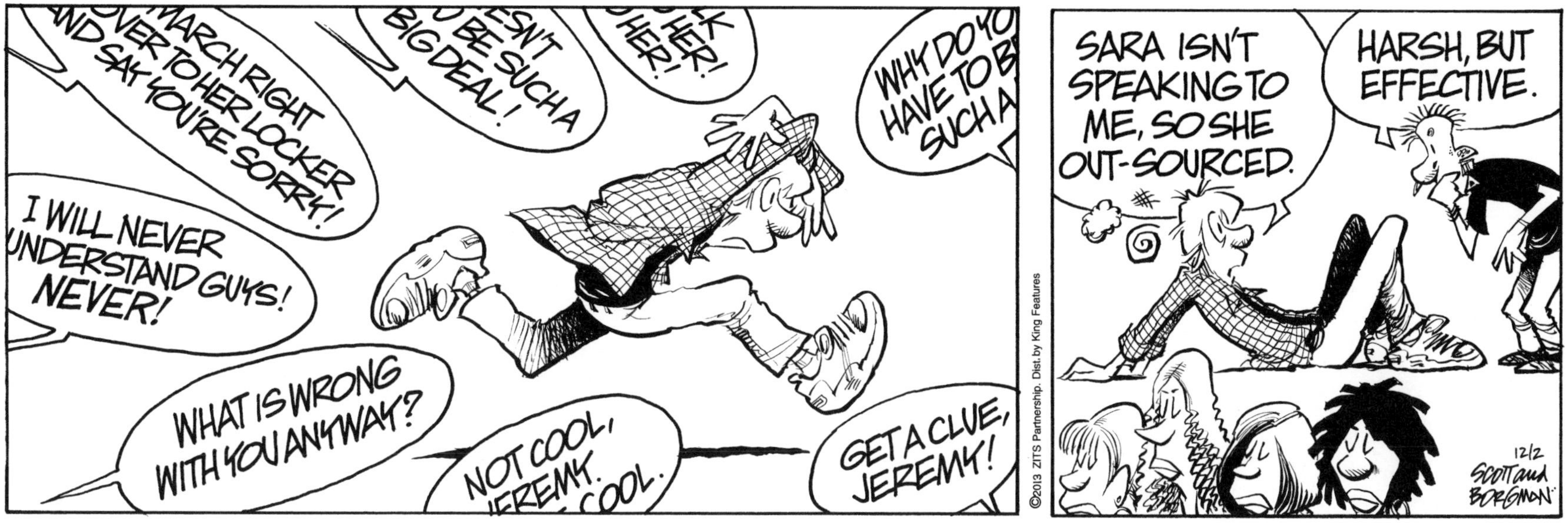
MARCH RIGHT OVER TO HER LOCKER AND SAY YOU'RE SORRY!
BIG DEAL!
I WILL NEVER UNDERSTAND GUYS! NEVER!
WHAT IS WRONG WITH YOU ANYWAY?
NOT COOL, JEREMY.
GET A CLUE, JEREMY!
©2013 ZITS Partnership. Dist. by King Features
SARA ISN'T SPEAKING TO ME, SO SHE OUT-SOURCED.
HARSH, BUT EFFECTIVE.
12/2
SCOTT and BORGMAN

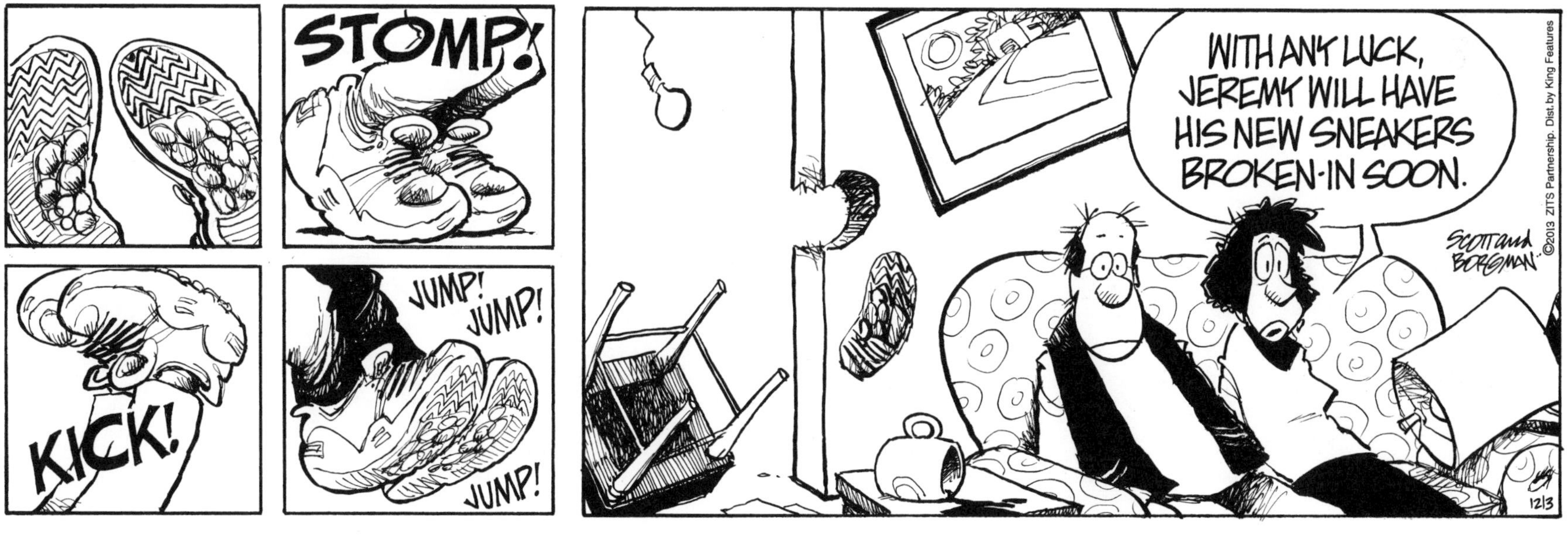
STOMP!
KICK!
JUMP! JUMP! JUMP!
WITH ANY LUCK, JEREMY WILL HAVE HIS NEW SNEAKERS BROKEN-IN SOON.
SCOTT and BORGMAN
©2013 ZITS Partnership. Dist. by King Features
12/3

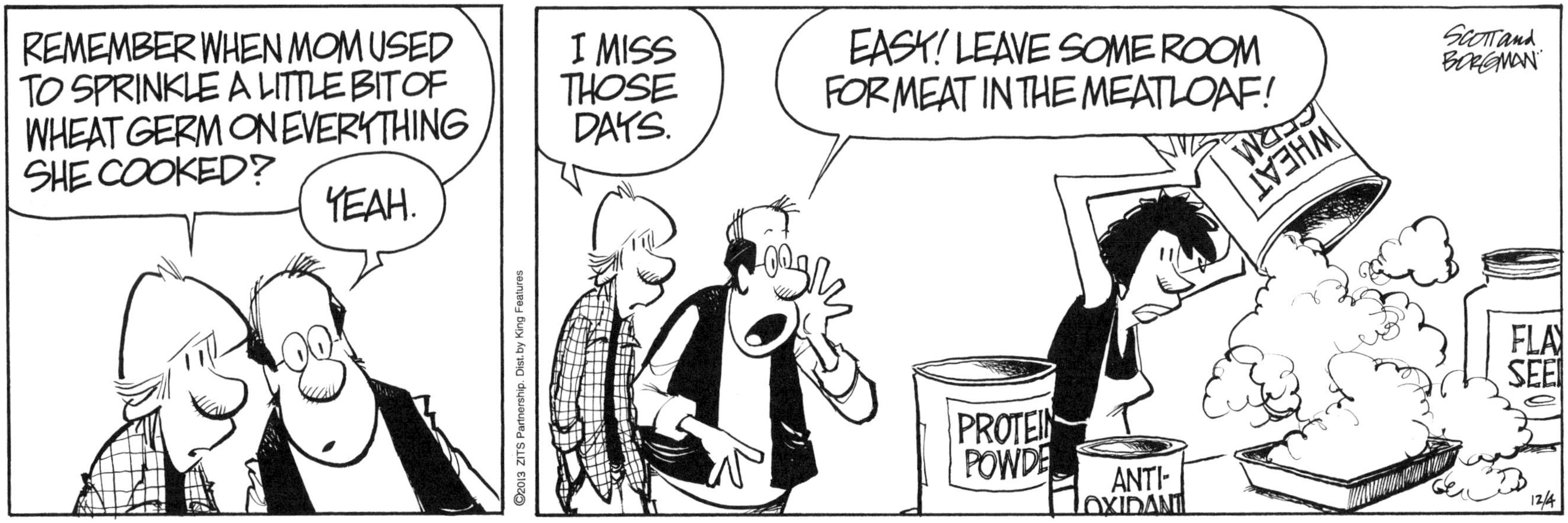
REMEMBER WHEN MOM USED TO SPRINKLE A LITTLE BIT OF WHEAT GERM ON EVERYTHING SHE COOKED?
YEAH.
©2013 ZITS Partnership. Dist. by King Features
I MISS THOSE DAYS.
EASY! LEAVE SOME ROOM FOR MEAT IN THE MEATLOAF!
SCOTT and BORGMAN
WHEAT GERM
PROTEIN POWDE
ANTI-OXIDANT
FLAX SEEI
12/4

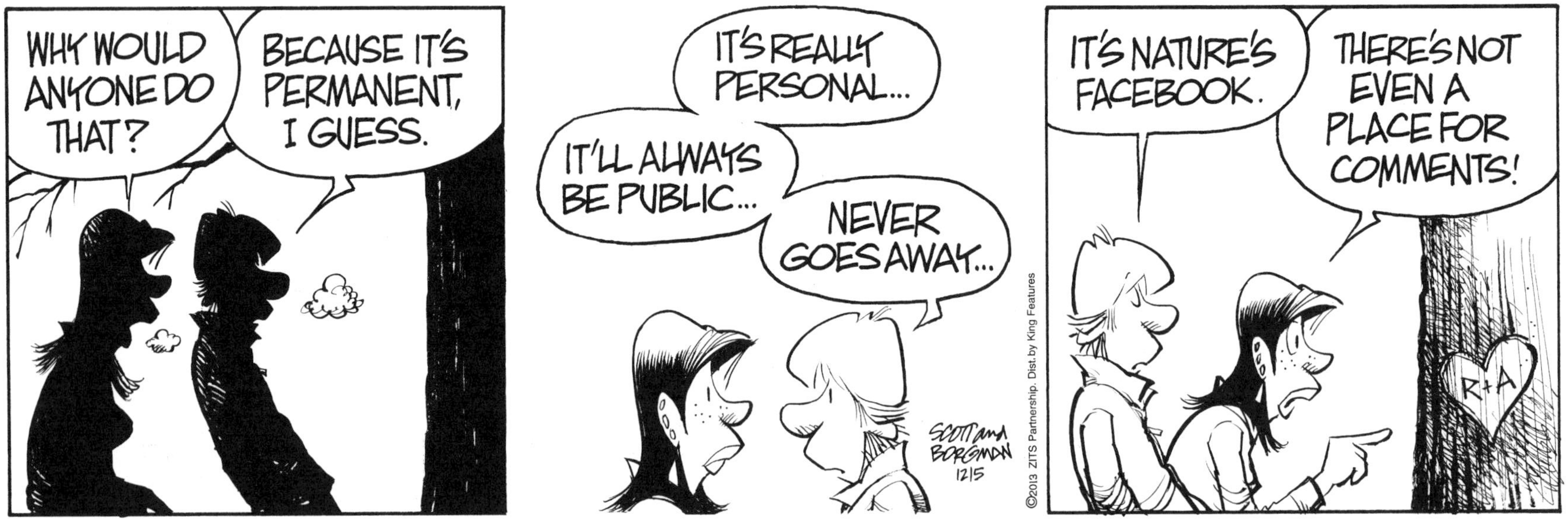
WHY WOULD ANYONE DO THAT?
BECAUSE IT'S PERMANENT, I GUESS.
IT'S REALLY PERSONAL...
IT'LL ALWAYS BE PUBLIC...
NEVER GOES AWAY...
SCOTT and BORGMAN 12/5
©2013 ZITS Partnership. Dist. by King Features
IT'S NATURE'S FACEBOOK.
THERE'S NOT EVEN A PLACE FOR COMMENTS!
R+A

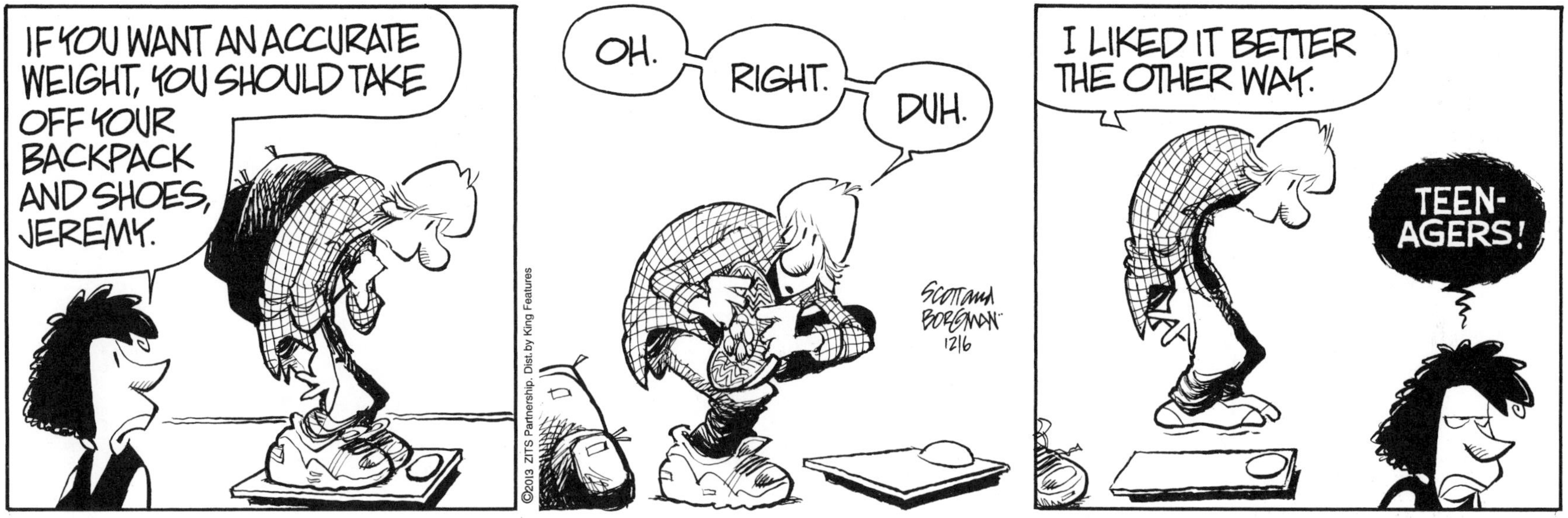
IF YOU WANT AN ACCURATE WEIGHT, YOU SHOULD TAKE OFF YOUR BACKPACK AND SHOES, JEREMY.
©2013 ZITS Partnership. Dist.by King Features
OH.
RIGHT.
DUH.
SCOTT and BORGMAN 12/6
I LIKED IT BETTER THE OTHER WAY.
TEEN-AGERS!

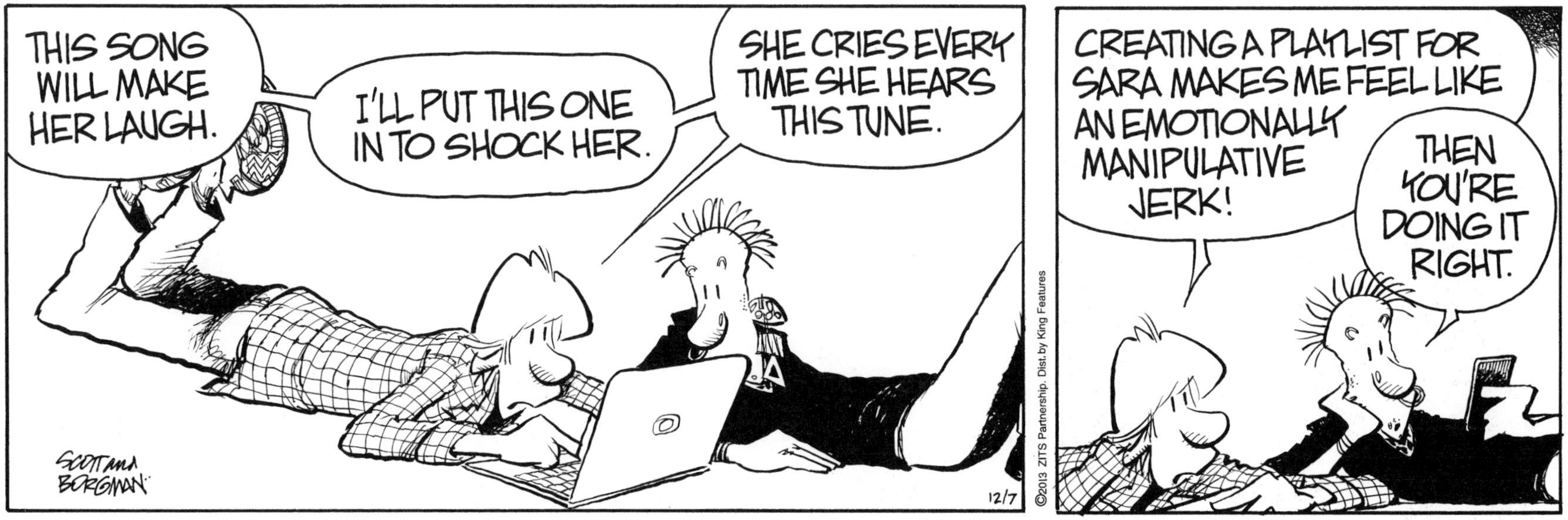
THIS SONG WILL MAKE HER LAUGH.
I'LL PUT THIS ONE IN TO SHOCK HER.
SHE CRIES EVERY TIME SHE HEARS THIS TUNE.
SCOTT and BORGMAN
12/7
©2013 ZITS Partnership. Dist.by King Features
CREATING A PLAYLIST FOR SARA MAKES ME FEEL LIKE AN EMOTIONALLY MANIPULATIVE JERK!
THEN YOU'RE DOING IT RIGHT.

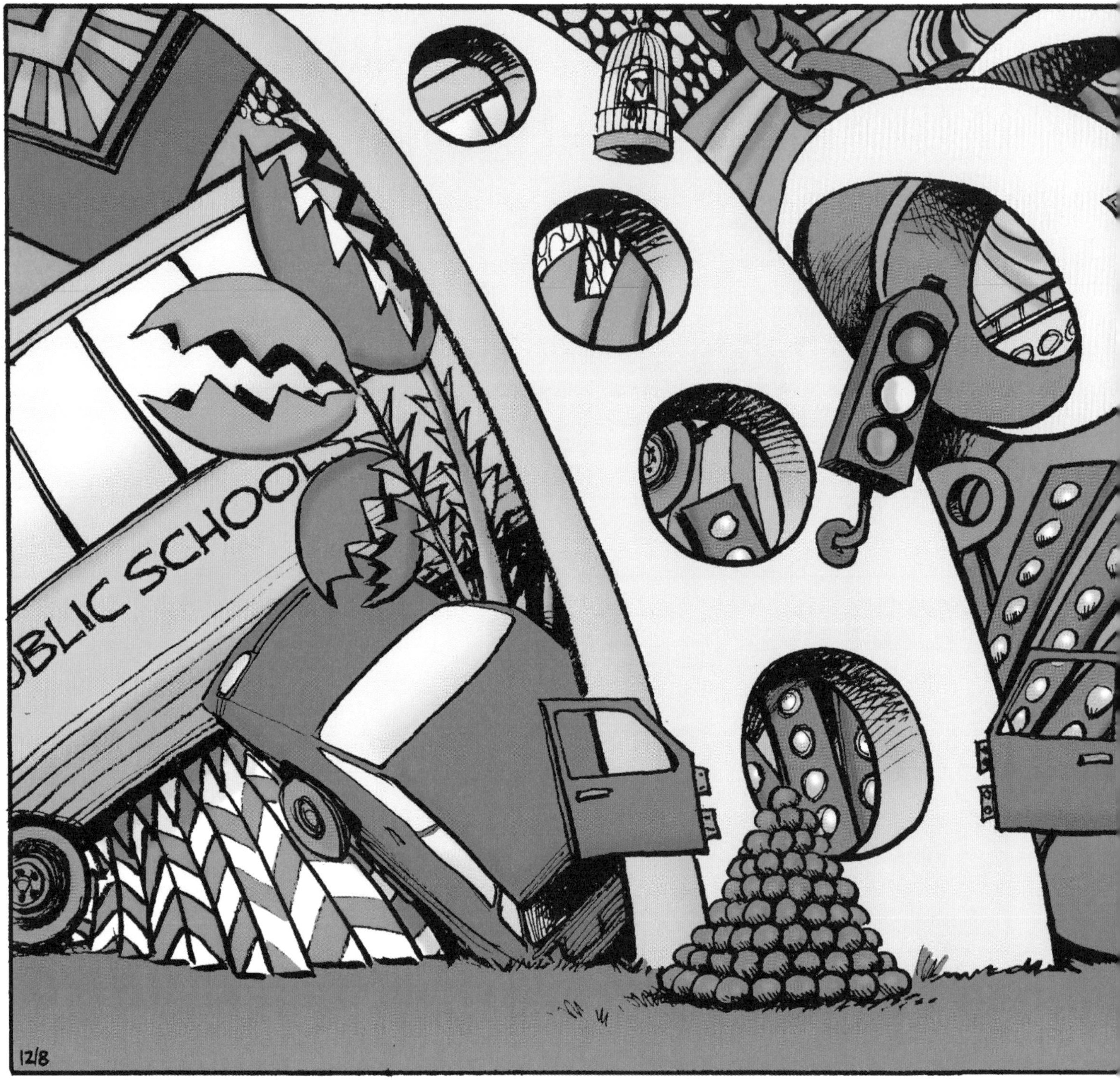
UBLIC SCHOO
12/8

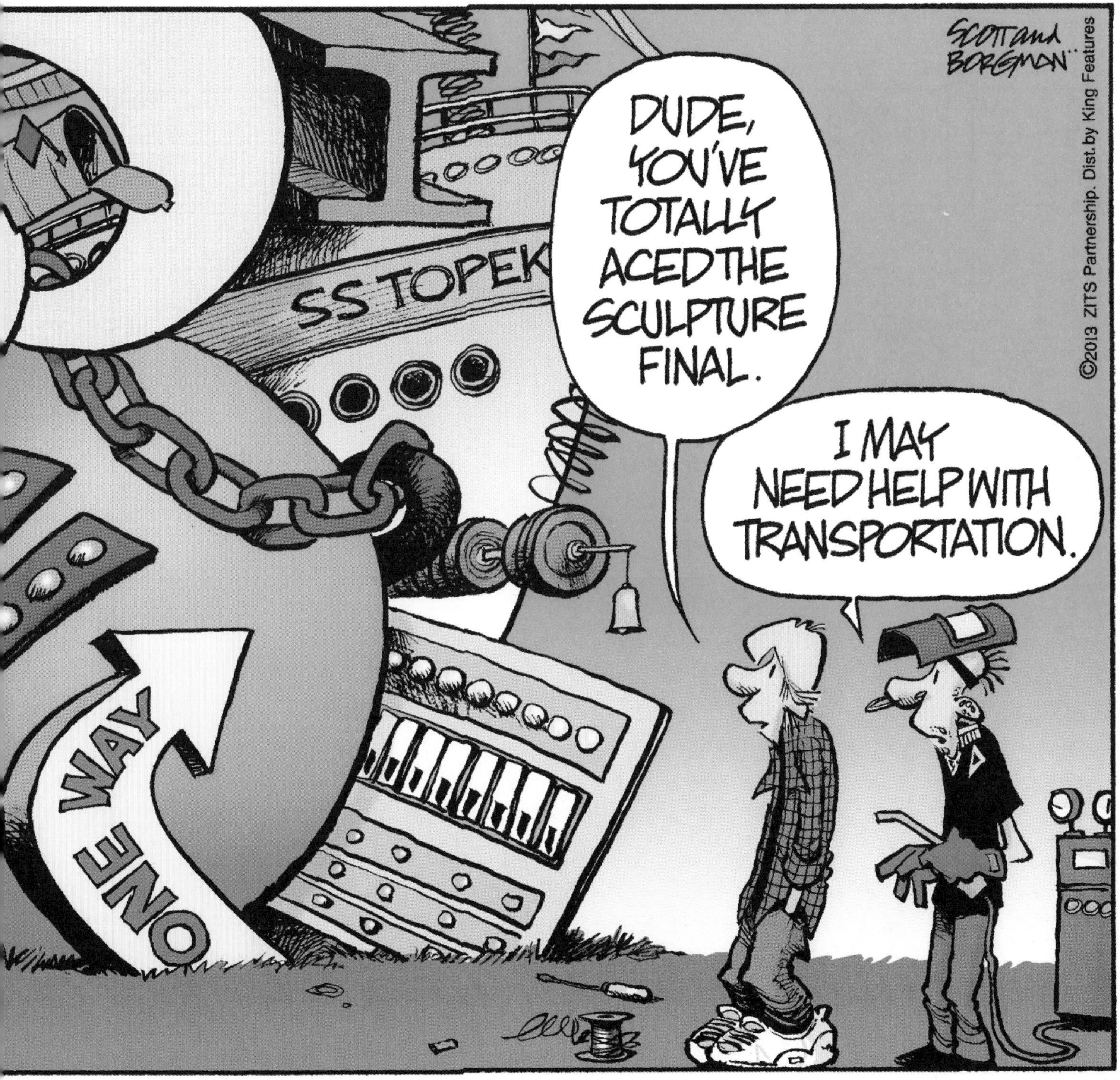
SCOTT and BORGMAN
©2013 ZITS Partnership. Dist. by King Features
SS TOPEK
DUDE, YOU'VE TOTALLY ACED THE SCULPTURE FINAL.
I MAY NEED HELP WITH TRANSPORTATION.
ONE WAY

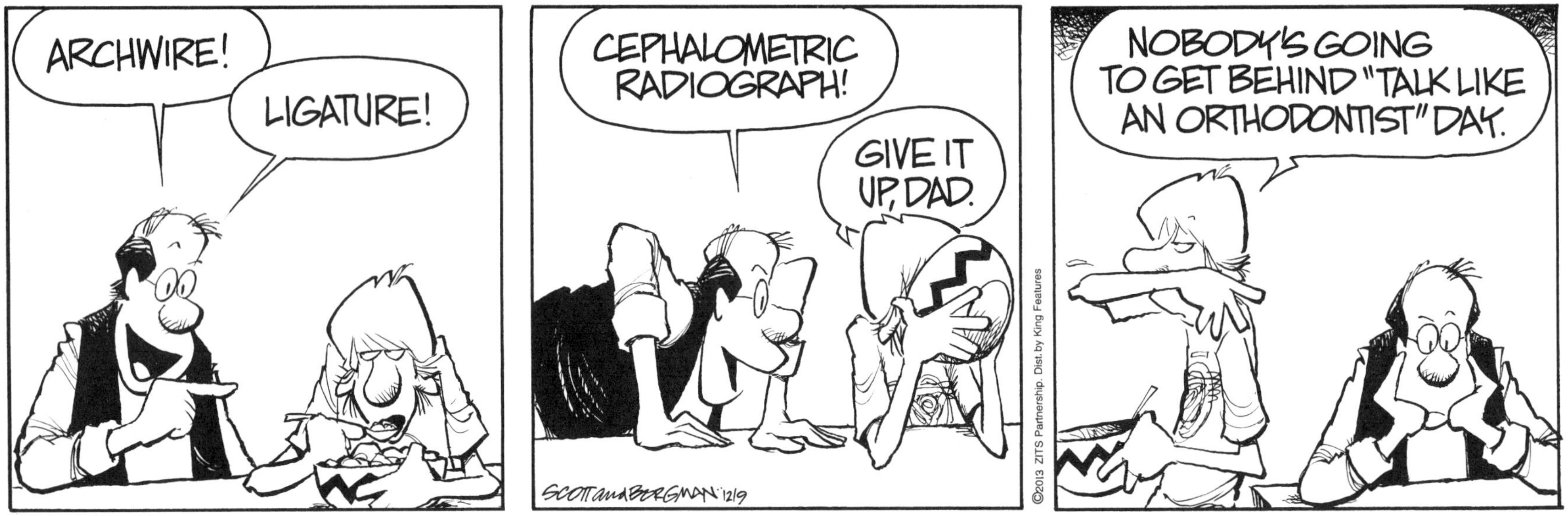
ARCHWIRE!
LIGATURE!
CEPHALOMETRIC RADIOGRAPH!
GIVE IT UP, DAD.
NOBODY'S GOING TO GET BEHIND "TALK LIKE AN ORTHODONTIST" DAY.
SCOTT and BORGMAN 12/9
©2013 ZITS Partnership. Dist. by King Features

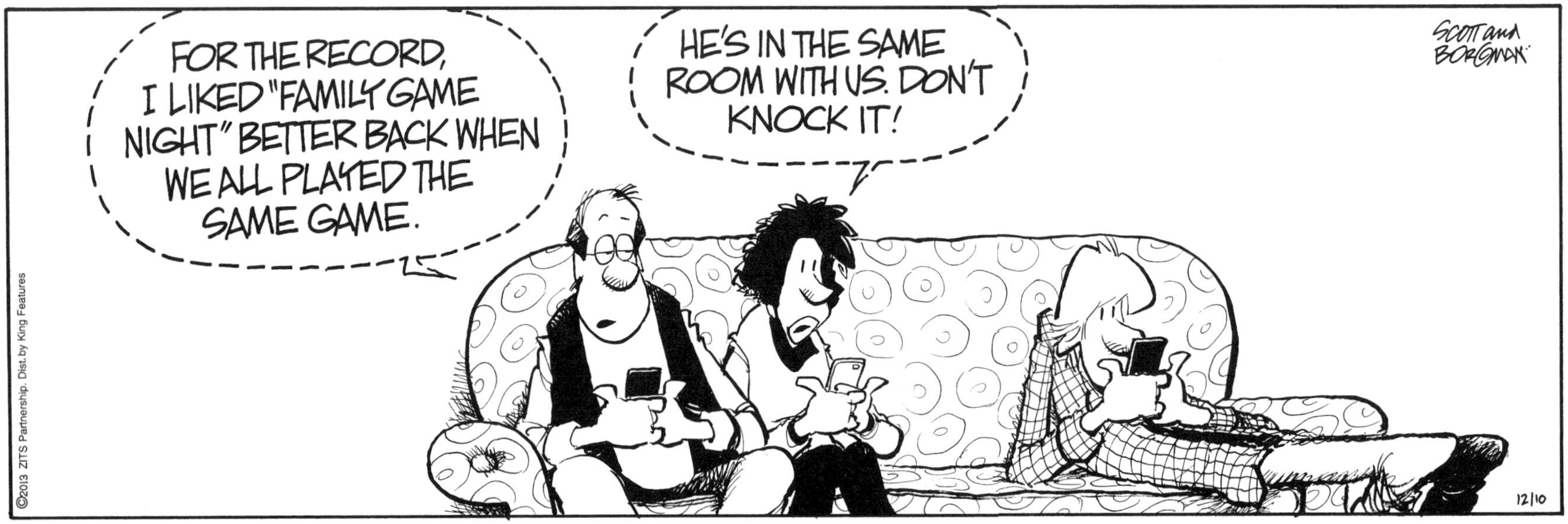
FOR THE RECORD, I LIKED "FAMILY GAME NIGHT" BETTER BACK WHEN WE ALL PLAYED THE SAME GAME.
HE'S IN THE SAME ROOM WITH US. DON'T KNOCK IT!
SCOTT and BORGMAN
12/10
©2013 ZITS Partnership. Dist. by King Features

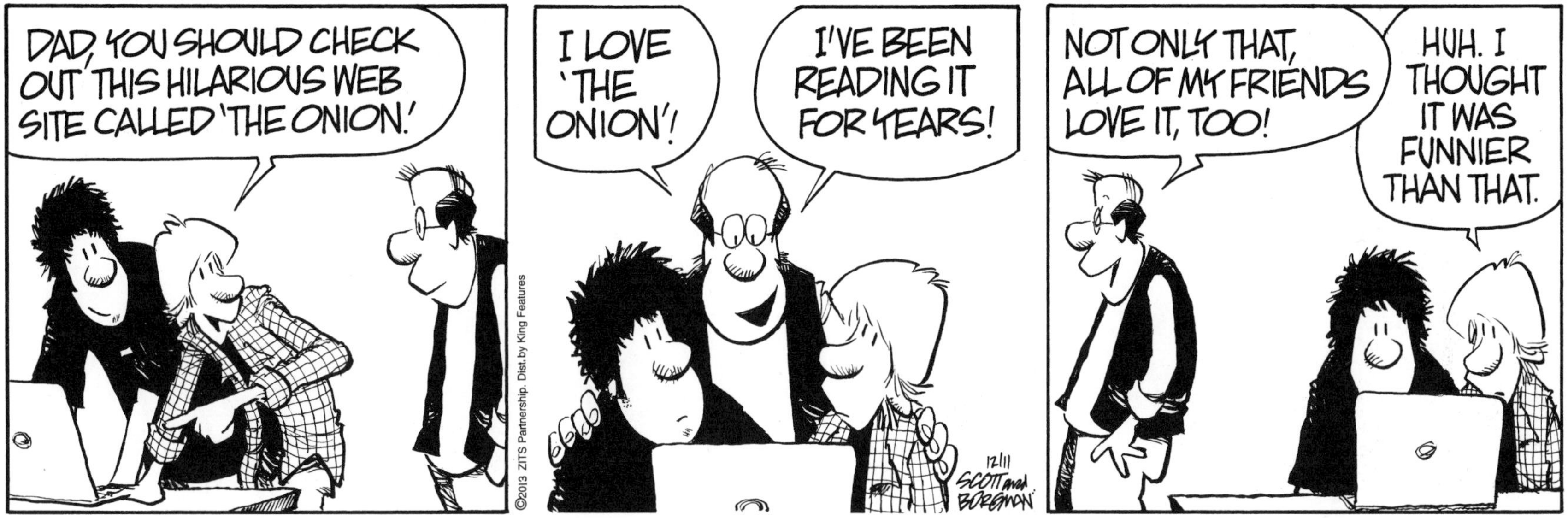
DAD, YOU SHOULD CHECK OUT THIS HILARIOUS WEB SITE CALLED 'THE ONION.'
©2013 ZITS Partnership. Dist. by King Features
I LOVE 'THE ONION'!
I'VE BEEN READING IT FOR YEARS!
12/11 SCOTT and BORGMAN
NOT ONLY THAT, ALL OF MY FRIENDS LOVE IT, TOO!
HUH. I THOUGHT IT WAS FUNNIER THAN THAT.

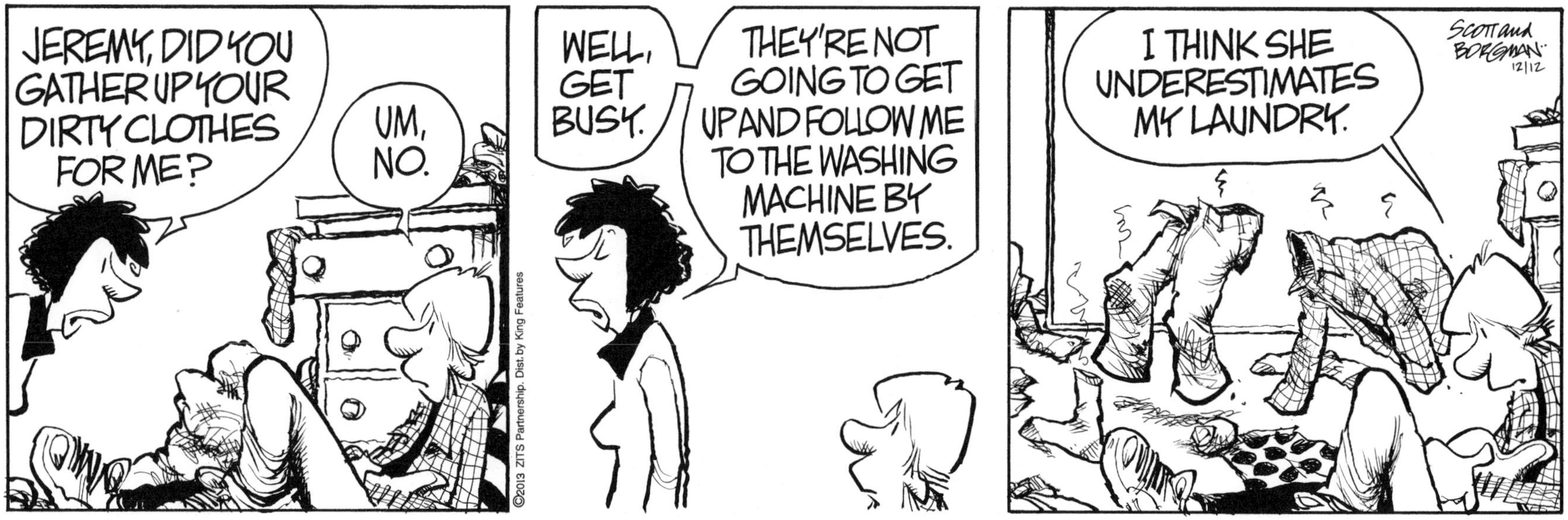
JEREMY, DID YOU GATHER UP YOUR DIRTY CLOTHES FOR ME?
UM, NO.
©2013 ZITS Partnership. Dist. by King Features
WELL, GET BUSY.
THEY'RE NOT GOING TO GET UP AND FOLLOW ME TO THE WASHING MACHINE BY THEMSELVES.
I THINK SHE UNDERESTIMATES MY LAUNDRY.
SCOTT and BORGMAN 12/12

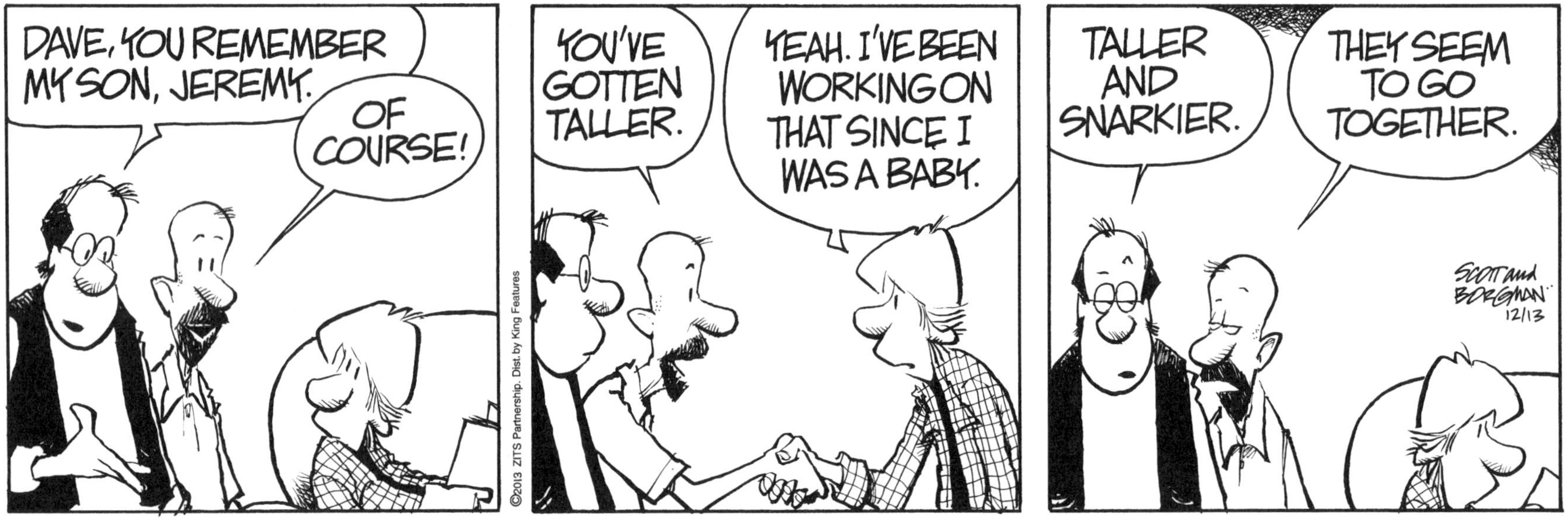
DAVE, YOU REMEMBER MY SON, JEREMY.
OF COURSE!
©2013 ZITS Partnership. Dist. by King Features
YOU'VE GOTTEN TALLER.
YEAH. I'VE BEEN WORKING ON THAT SINCE I WAS A BABY.
TALLER AND SNARKIER.
THEY SEEM TO GO TOGETHER.
SCOTT and BORGMAN 12/13

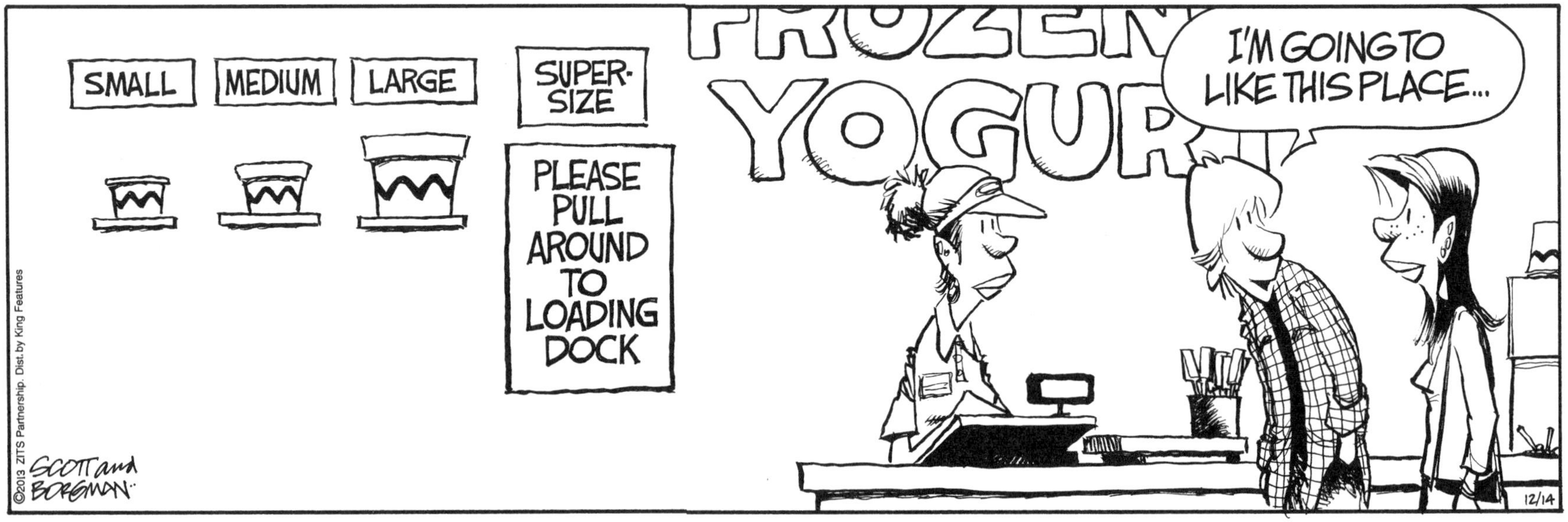
SMALL
MEDIUM
LARGE
SUPER-SIZE
PLEASE PULL AROUND TO LOADING DOCK
YOGURT
I'M GOING TO LIKE THIS PLACE...
©2013 ZITS Partnership. Dist. by King Features
SCOTT and BORGMAN
12/14

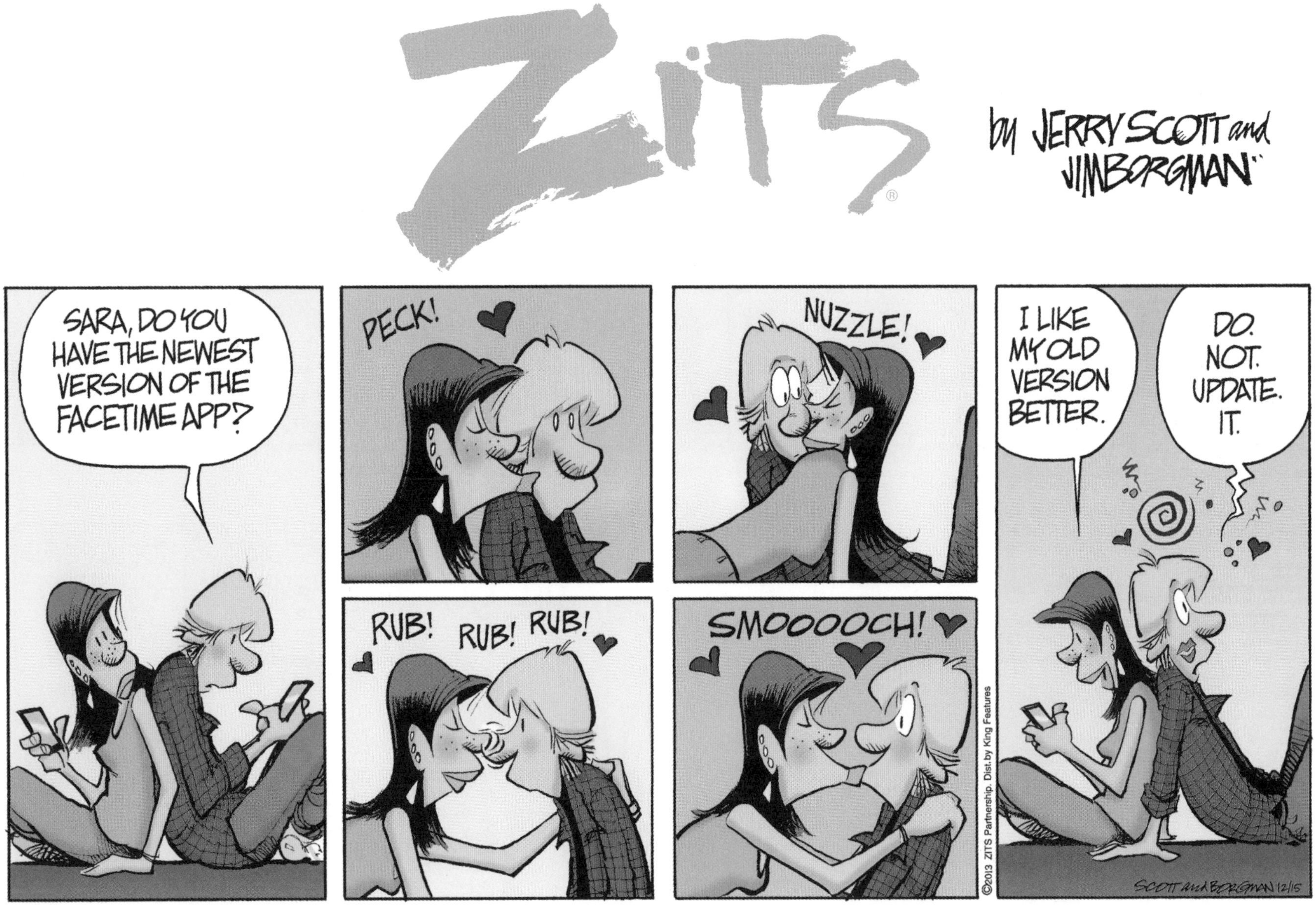
ZITS
by JERRY SCOTT and JIM BORGMAN
SARA, DO YOU HAVE THE NEWEST VERSION OF THE FACETIME APP?
PECK!
NUZZLE!
RUB! RUB! RUB!
SMOOOOCH!
©2013 ZITS Partnership. Dist. by King Features
I LIKE MY OLD VERSION BETTER.
DO. NOT. UPDATE. IT.
SCOTT and BORGMAN 12/15

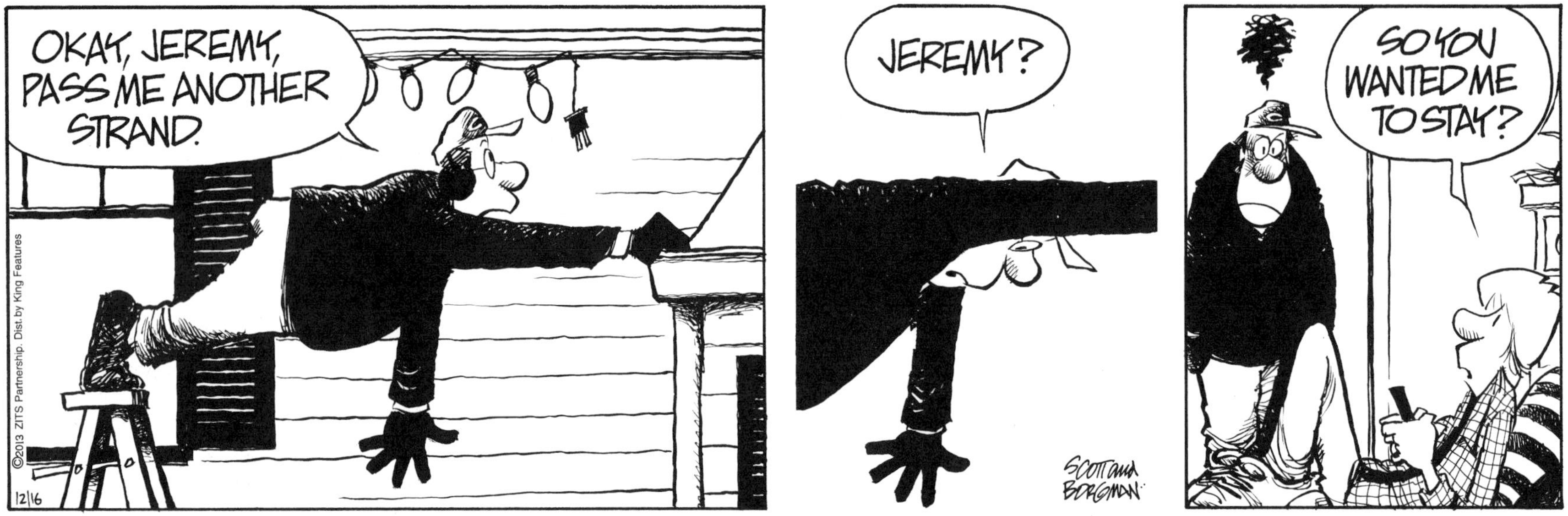
OKAY, JEREMY, PASS ME ANOTHER STRAND.
JEREMY?
SO YOU WANTED ME TO STAY?
©2013 ZITS Partnership. Dist. by King Features
12/16
SCOTT and BORGMAN

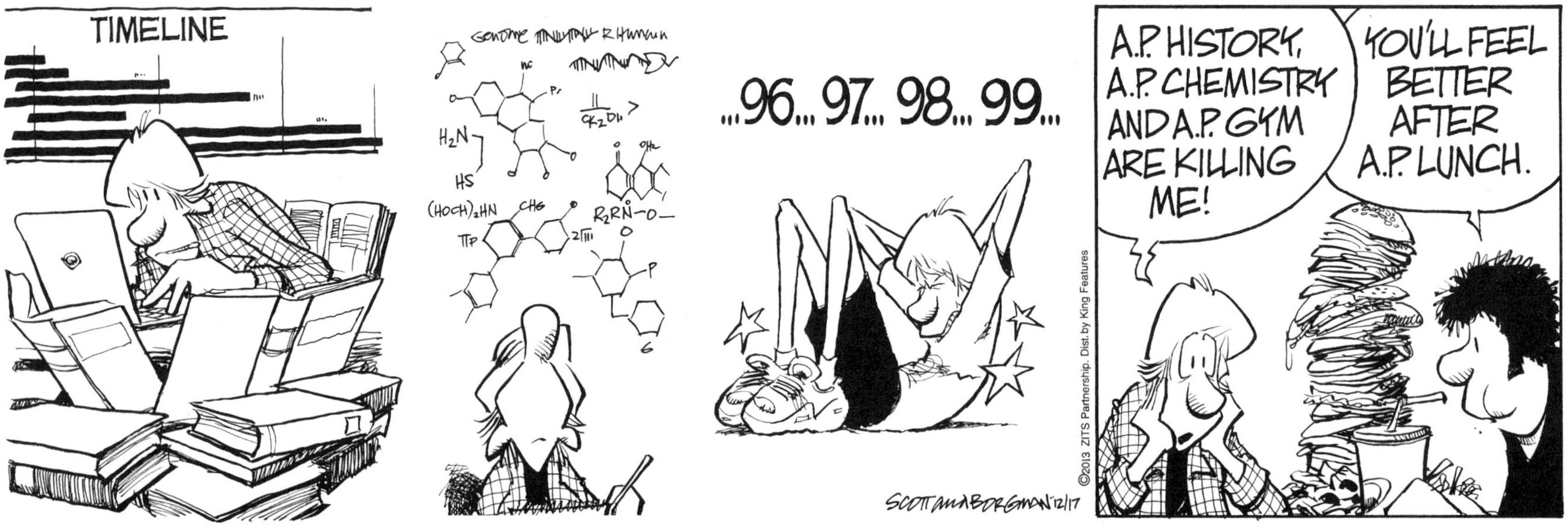
TIMELINE
...96... 97... 98... 99...
A.P. HISTORY, A.P. CHEMISTRY AND A.P. GYM ARE KILLING ME!
YOU'LL FEEL BETTER AFTER A.P. LUNCH.
©2013 ZITS Partnership. Dist. by King Features
SCOTT and BORGMAN 12/17

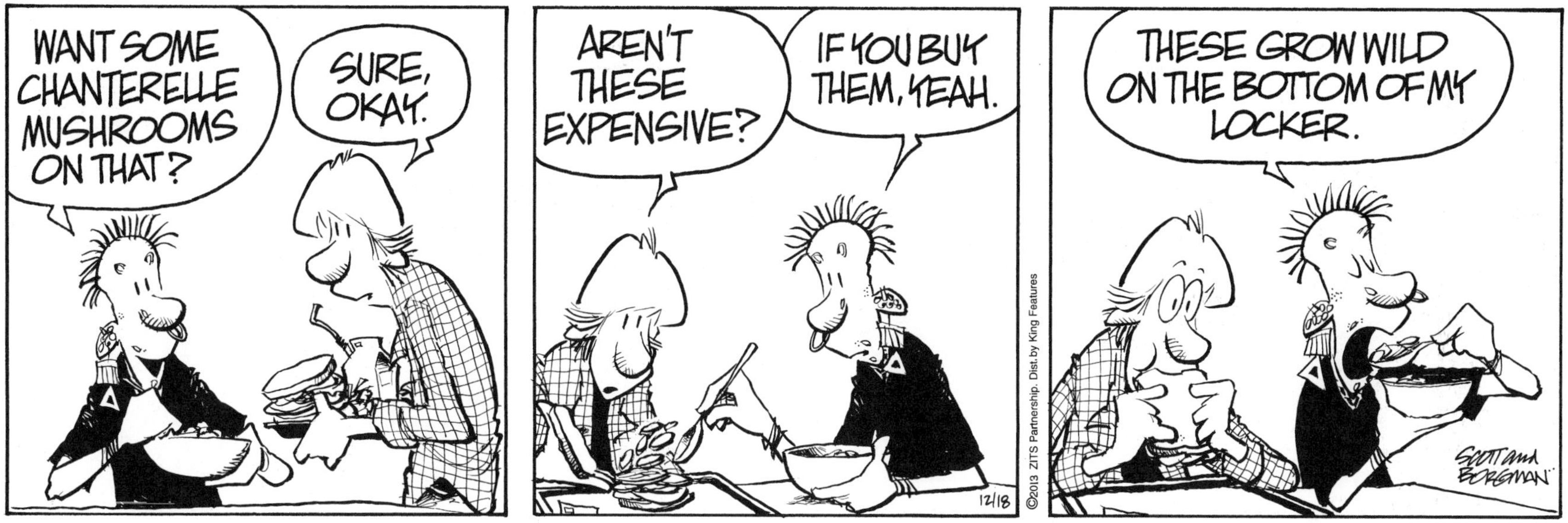
WANT SOME CHANTERELLE MUSHROOMS ON THAT?
SURE, OKAY.
AREN'T THESE EXPENSIVE?
IF YOU BUY THEM, YEAH.
THESE GROW WILD ON THE BOTTOM OF MY LOCKER.
SCOTT and BORGMAN
12/18
©2013 ZITS Partnership. Dist. by King Features

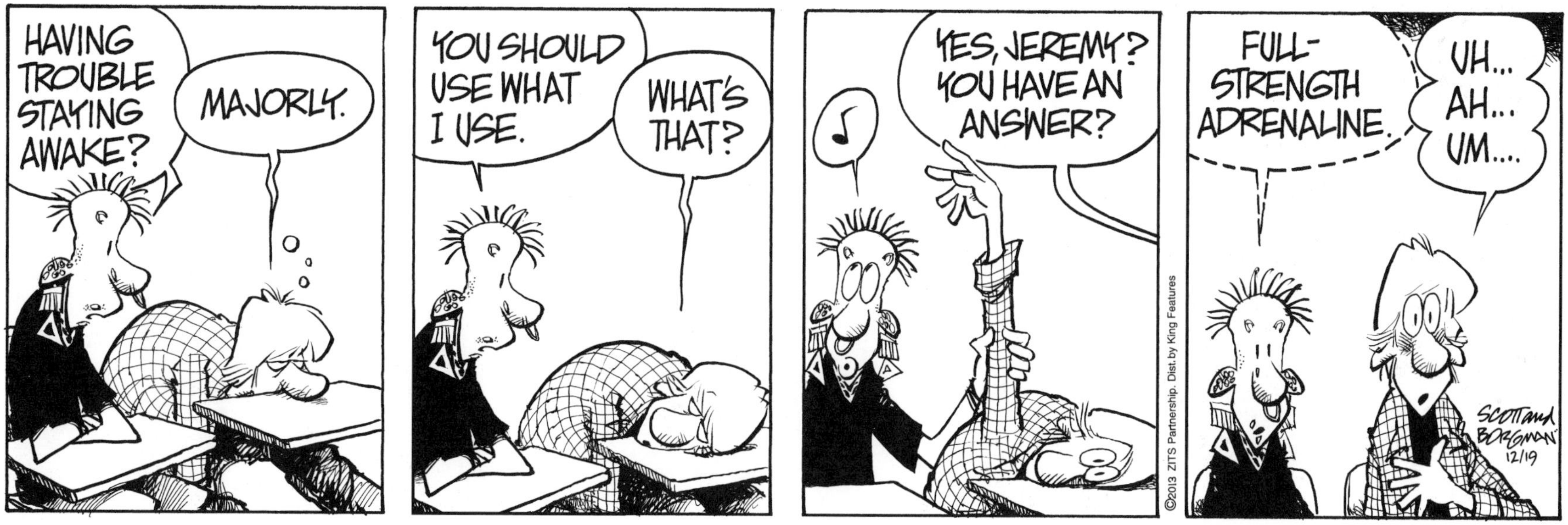
HAVING TROUBLE STAYING AWAKE?
MAJORLY.
YOU SHOULD USE WHAT I USE.
WHAT'S THAT?
♪
YES, JEREMY? YOU HAVE AN ANSWER?
FULL-STRENGTH ADRENALINE.
UH... AH... UM....
SCOTT and BORGMAN
12/19
©2013 ZITS Partnership. Dist. by King Features

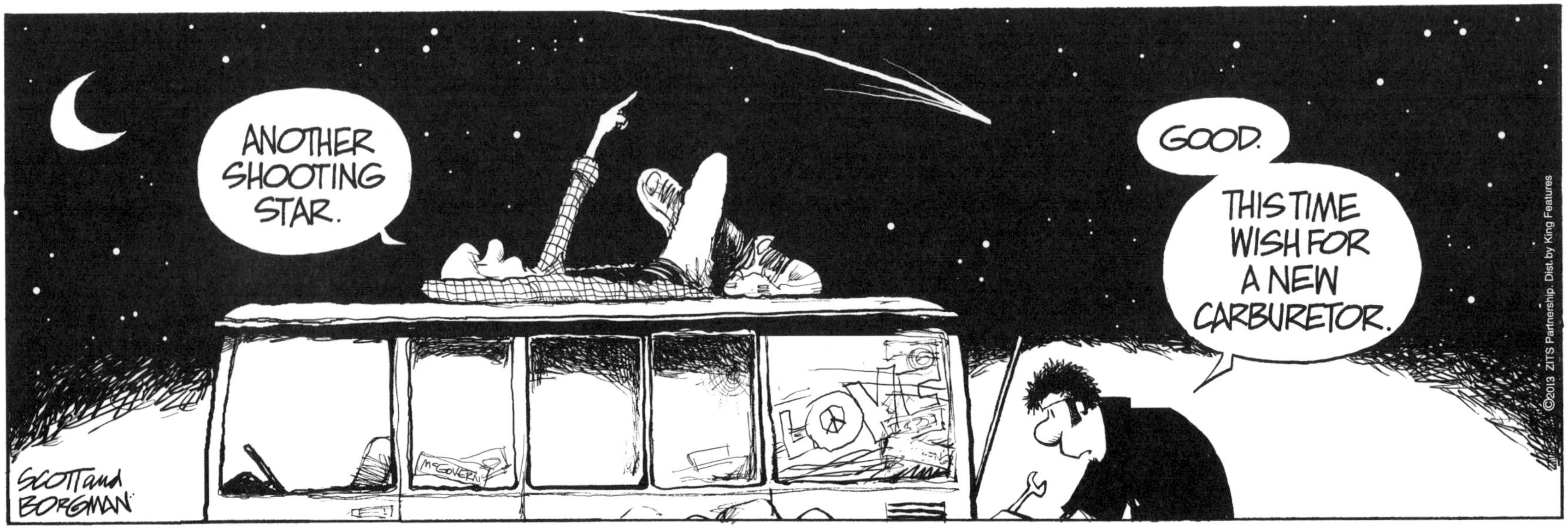
ANOTHER SHOOTING STAR.
GOOD.
THIS TIME WISH FOR A NEW CARBURETOR.
McGOVERN
LOVE
SCOTT and BORGMAN
©2013 ZITS Partnership. Dist. by King Features

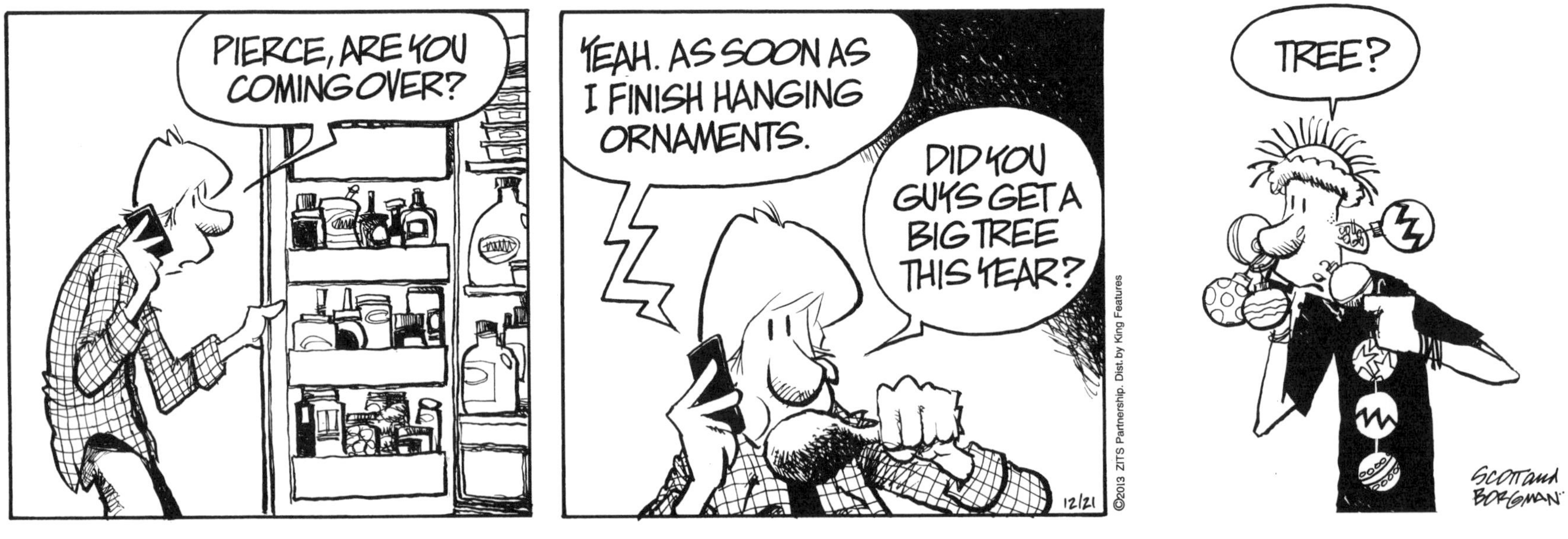
PIERCE, ARE YOU COMING OVER?
YEAH. AS SOON AS I FINISH HANGING ORNAMENTS.
DID YOU GUYS GET A BIG TREE THIS YEAR?
TREE?
12/21
©2013 ZITS Partnership. Dist. by King Features
SCOTT and BORGMAN

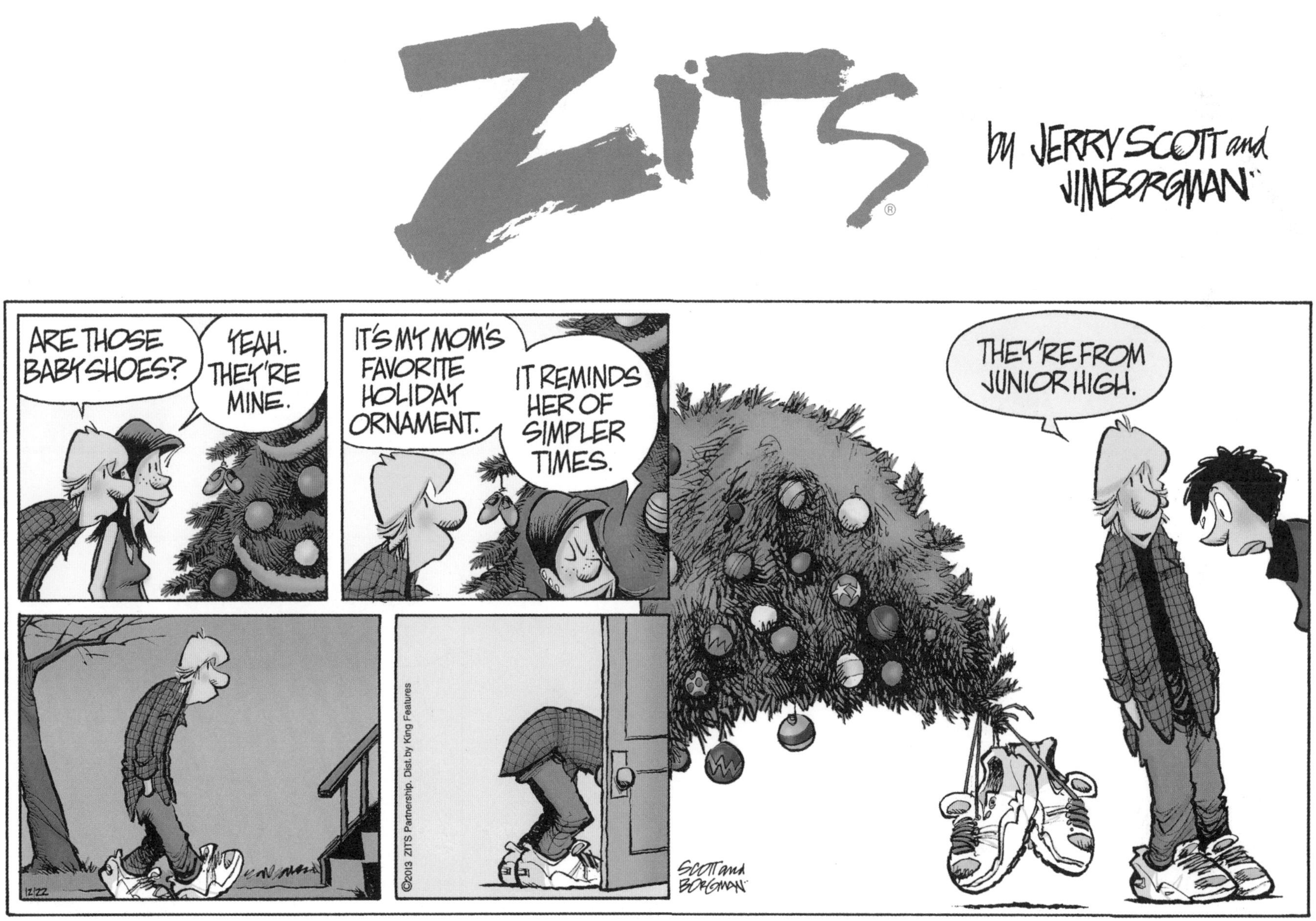
ZITS
by JERRY SCOTT and JIM BORGMAN
ARE THOSE BABY SHOES?
YEAH. THEY'RE MINE.
IT'S MY MOM'S FAVORITE HOLIDAY ORNAMENT.
IT REMINDS HER OF SIMPLER TIMES.
THEY'RE FROM JUNIOR HIGH.
12/22
©2013 ZITS Partnership. Dist. by King Features
SCOTT and BORGMAN

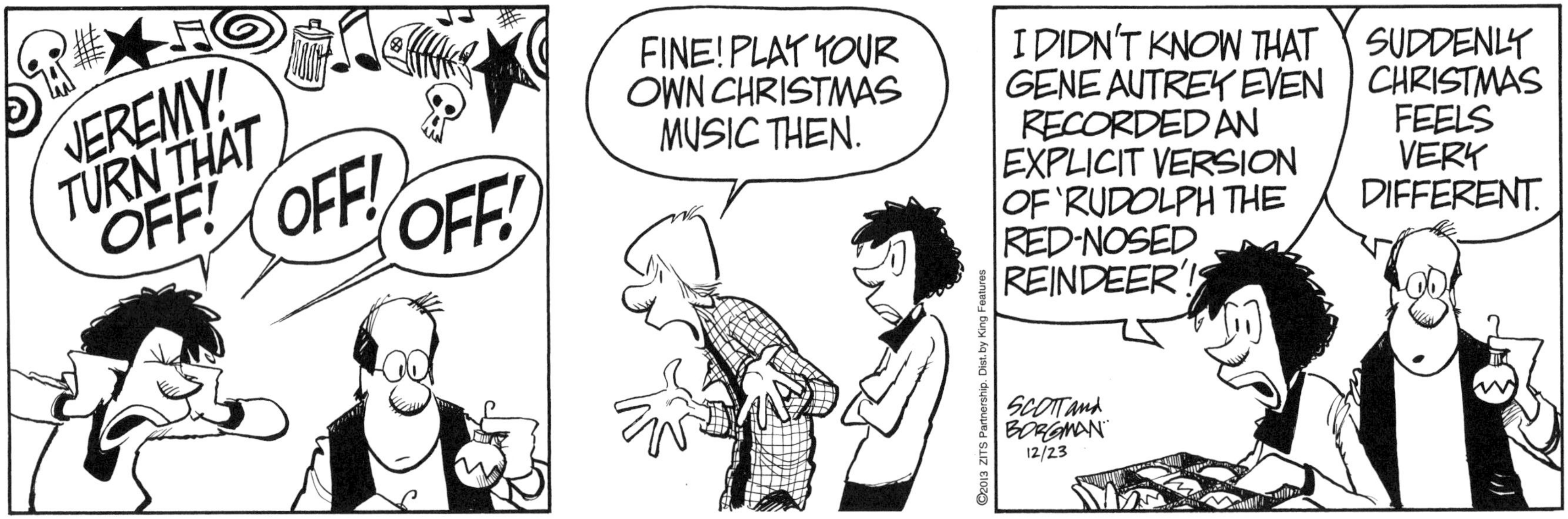
JEREMY! TURN THAT OFF!
OFF!
OFF!
FINE! PLAY YOUR OWN CHRISTMAS MUSIC THEN.
I DIDN'T KNOW THAT GENE AUTREY EVEN RECORDED AN EXPLICIT VERSION OF 'RUDOLPH THE RED-NOSED REINDEER'!
SUDDENLY CHRISTMAS FEELS VERY DIFFERENT.
SCOTT AND BORGMAN 12/23
©2013 ZITS Partnership. Dist. by King Features

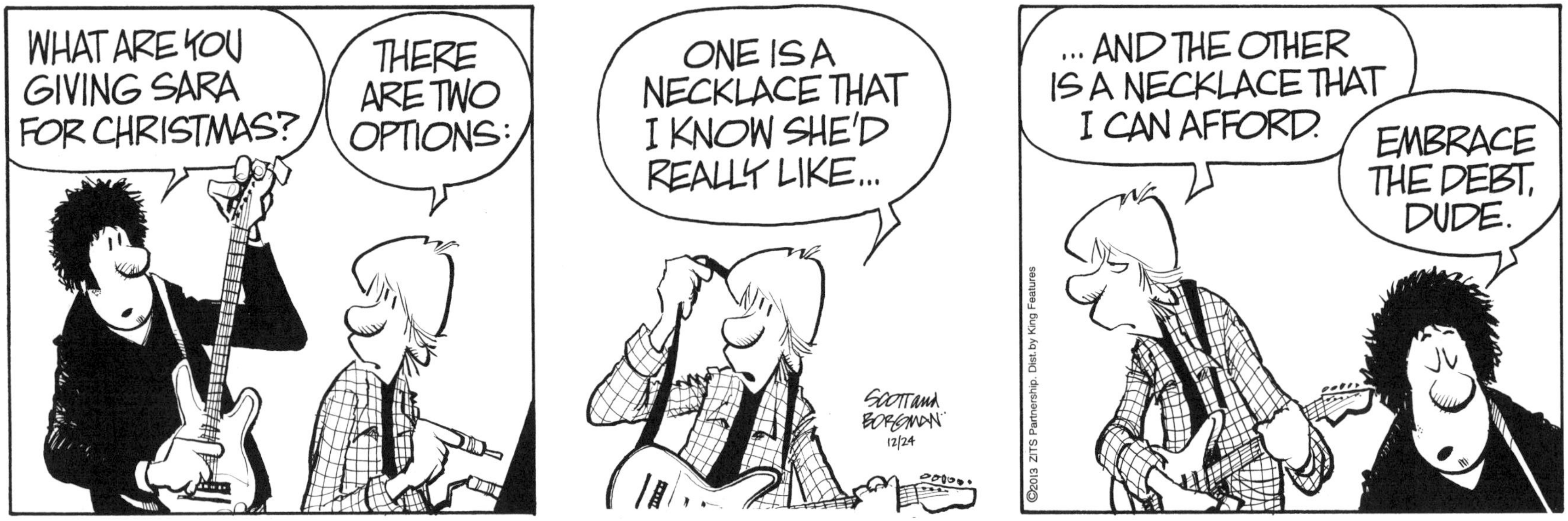
WHAT ARE YOU GIVING SARA FOR CHRISTMAS?
THERE ARE TWO OPTIONS:
ONE IS A NECKLACE THAT I KNOW SHE'D REALLY LIKE...
SCOTT AND BORGMAN 12/24
... AND THE OTHER IS A NECKLACE THAT I CAN AFFORD.
EMBRACE THE DEBT, DUDE.
©2013 ZITS Partnership. Dist. by King Features

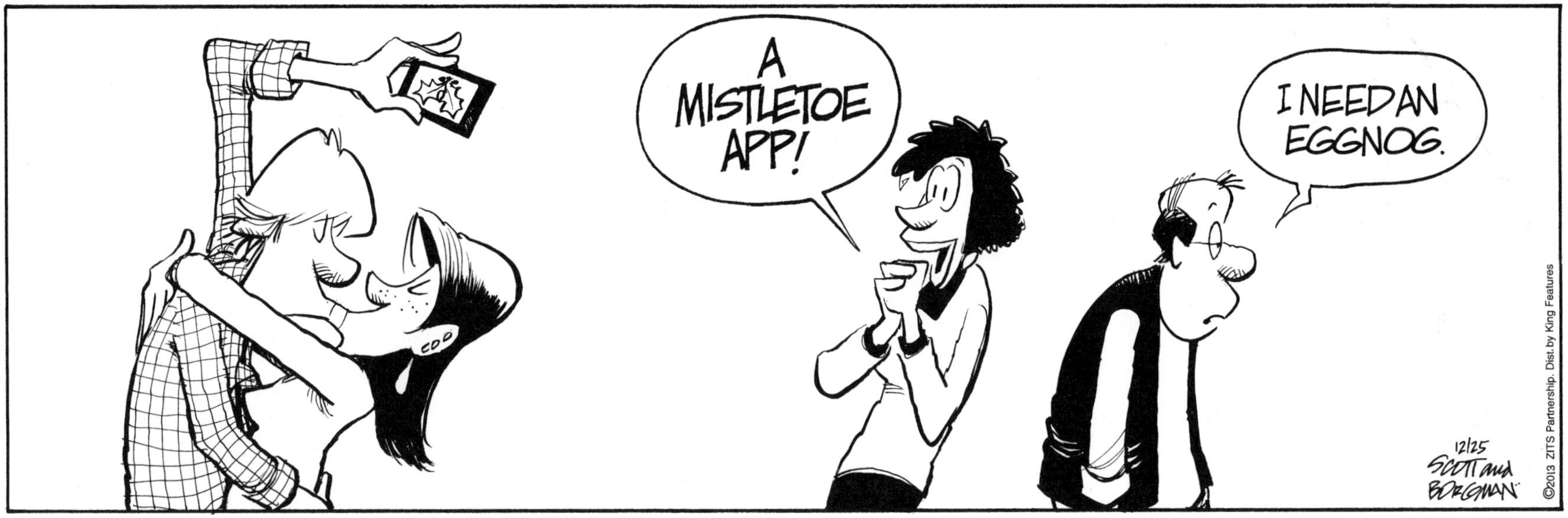
A MISTLETOE APP!
I NEED AN EGGNOG.
12/25 SCOTT and BORGMAN
©2013 ZITS Partnership. Dist. by King Features

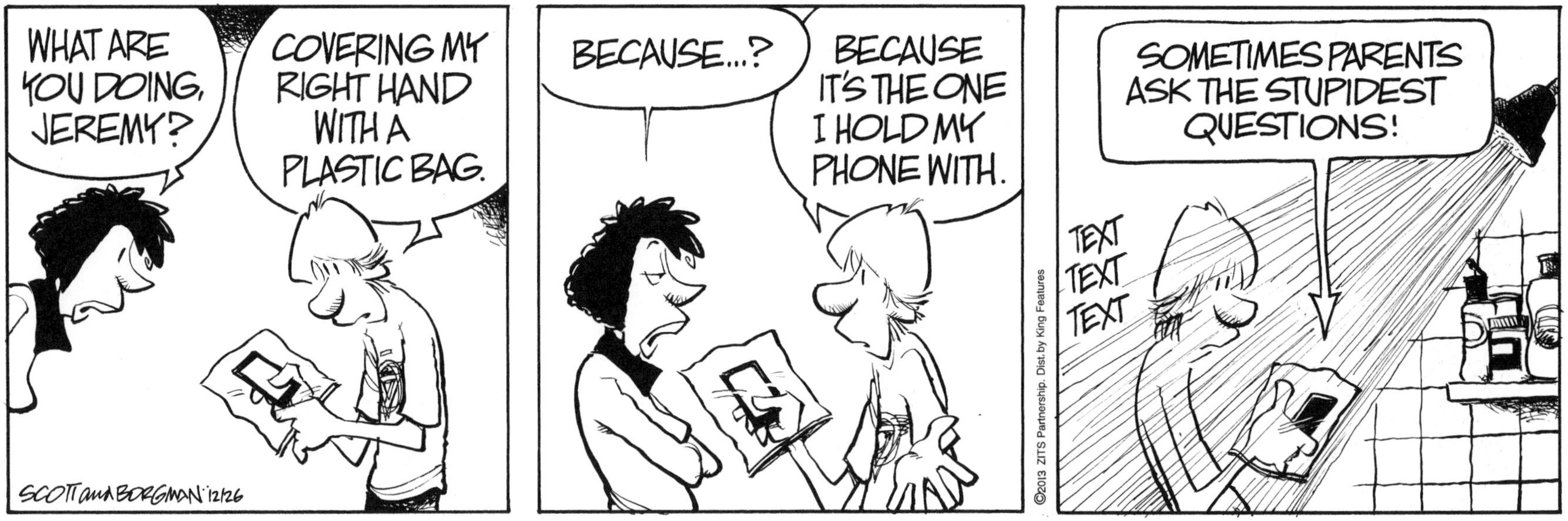
WHAT ARE YOU DOING, JEREMY?
COVERING MY RIGHT HAND WITH A PLASTIC BAG.
SCOTT and BORGMAN 12/26
BECAUSE...?
BECAUSE IT'S THE ONE I HOLD MY PHONE WITH.
©2013 ZITS Partnership. Dist. by King Features
SOMETIMES PARENTS ASK THE STUPIDEST QUESTIONS!
TEXT TEXT TEXT

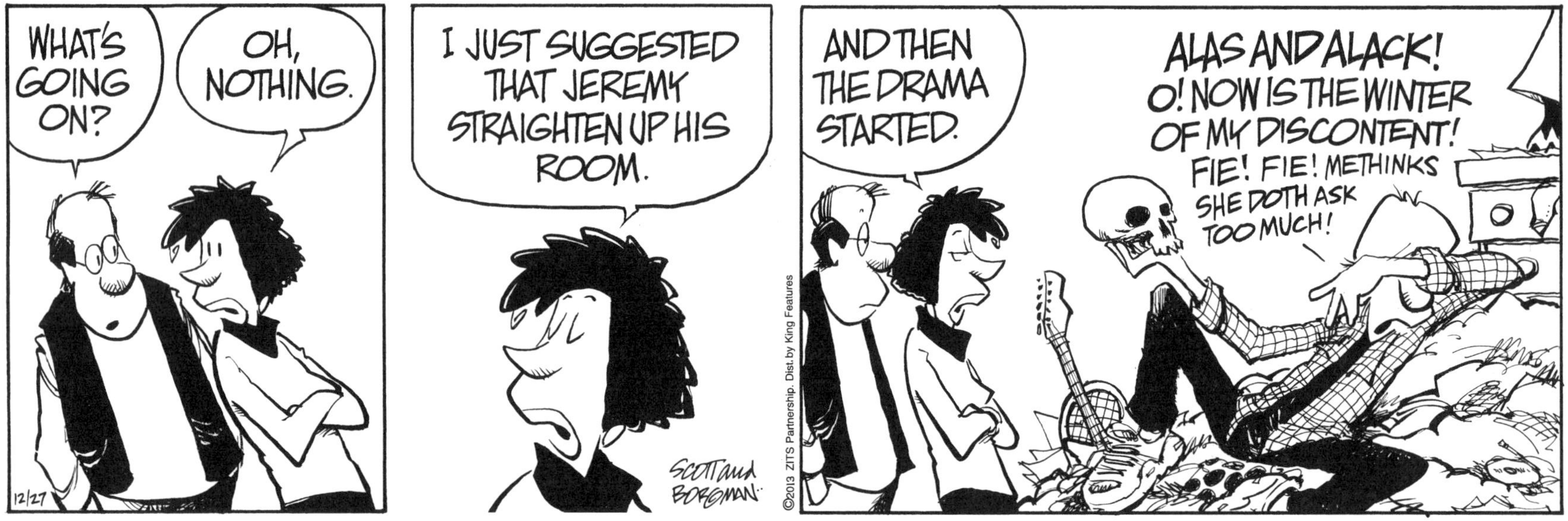
WHAT'S GOING ON?
OH, NOTHING.
12/27
I JUST SUGGESTED THAT JEREMY STRAIGHTEN UP HIS ROOM.
SCOTT and BORGMAN
©2013 ZITS Partnership. Dist. by King Features
AND THEN THE DRAMA STARTED.
ALAS AND ALACK!
O! NOW IS THE WINTER OF MY DISCONTENT!
FIE! FIE! METHINKS SHE DOTH ASK TOO MUCH!

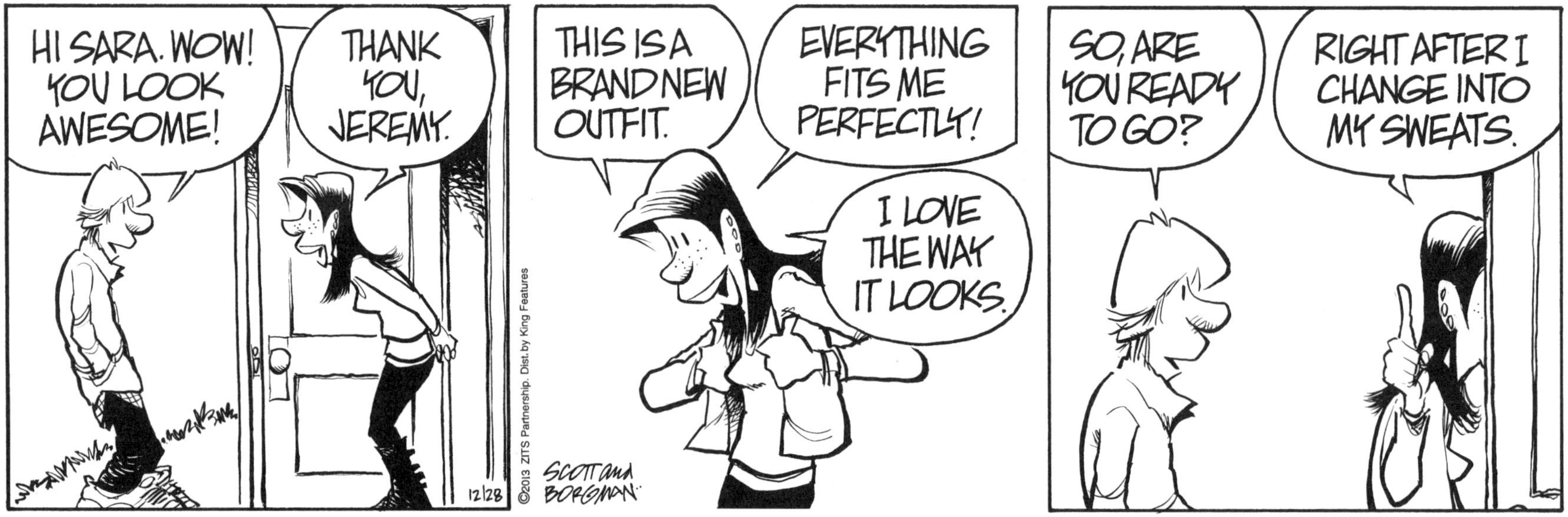
HI SARA. WOW! YOU LOOK AWESOME!
THANK YOU, JEREMY.
12/28
©2013 ZITS Partnership. Dist. by King Features
SCOTT and BORGMAN
THIS IS A BRAND NEW OUTFIT.
EVERYTHING FITS ME PERFECTLY!
I LOVE THE WAY IT LOOKS.
SO, ARE YOU READY TO GO?
RIGHT AFTER I CHANGE INTO MY SWEATS.

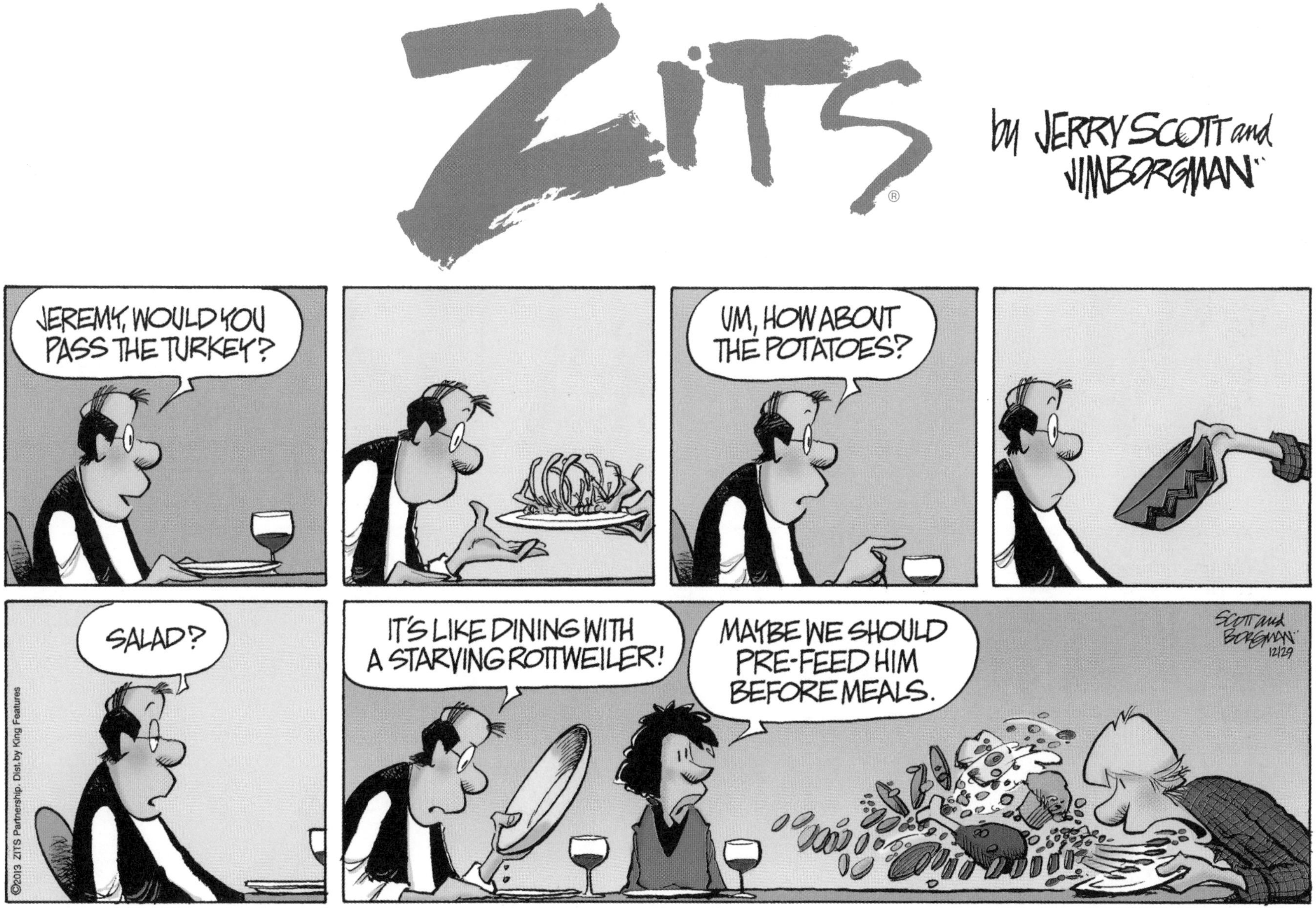
ZITS
by JERRY SCOTT and JIM BORGMAN
JEREMY, WOULD YOU PASS THE TURKEY?
UM, HOW ABOUT THE POTATOES?
SALAD?
IT'S LIKE DINING WITH A STARVING ROTTWEILER!
MAYBE WE SHOULD PRE-FEED HIM BEFORE MEALS.
SCOTT and BORGMAN 12/29
©2013 ZITS Partnership. Dist. by King Features

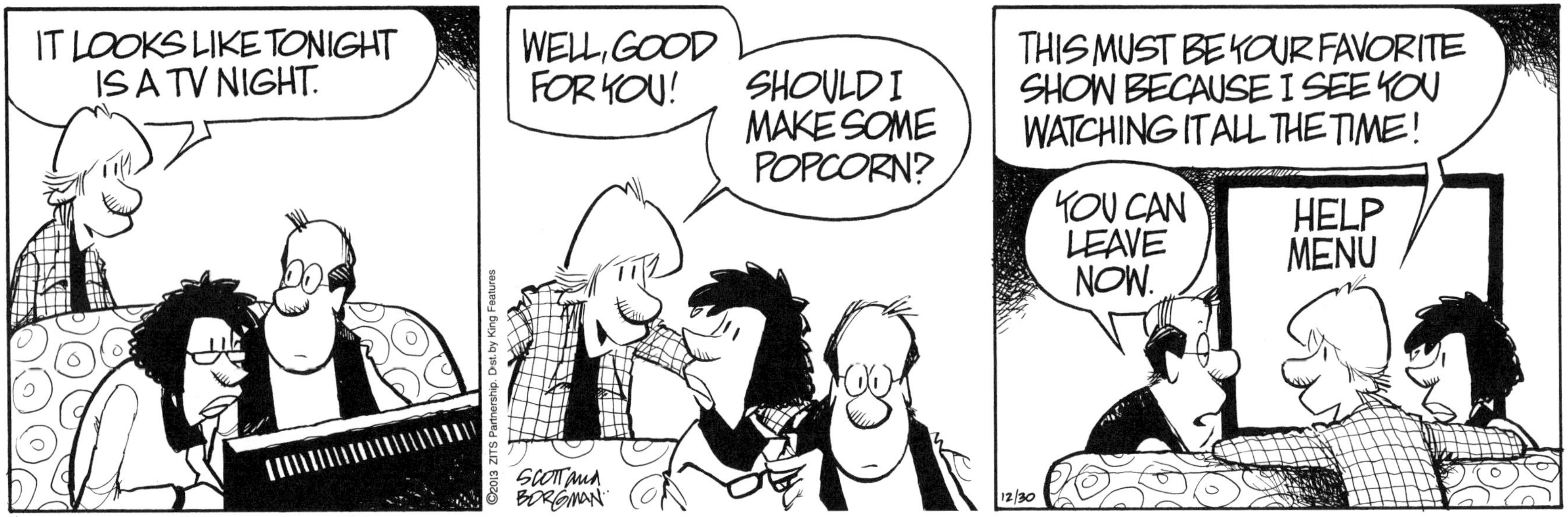
IT LOOKS LIKE TONIGHT IS A TV NIGHT.
WELL, GOOD FOR YOU!
SHOULD I MAKE SOME POPCORN?
THIS MUST BE YOUR FAVORITE SHOW BECAUSE I SEE YOU WATCHING IT ALL THE TIME!
YOU CAN LEAVE NOW.
HELP MENU
SCOTT AND BORGMAN
©2013 ZITS Partnership. Dist. by King Features
12/30

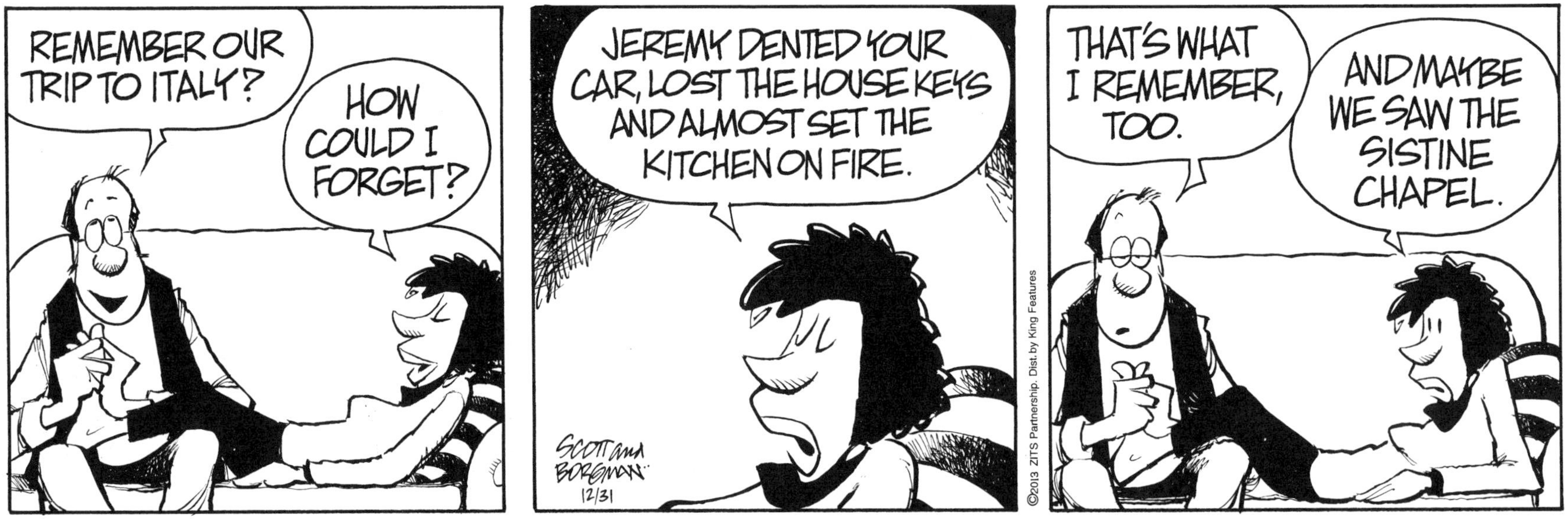
REMEMBER OUR TRIP TO ITALY?
HOW COULD I FORGET?
JEREMY DENTED YOUR CAR, LOST THE HOUSE KEYS AND ALMOST SET THE KITCHEN ON FIRE.
SCOTT AND BORGMAN
12/31
THAT'S WHAT I REMEMBER, TOO.
AND MAYBE WE SAW THE SISTINE CHAPEL.
©2013 ZITS Partnership. Dist. by King Features

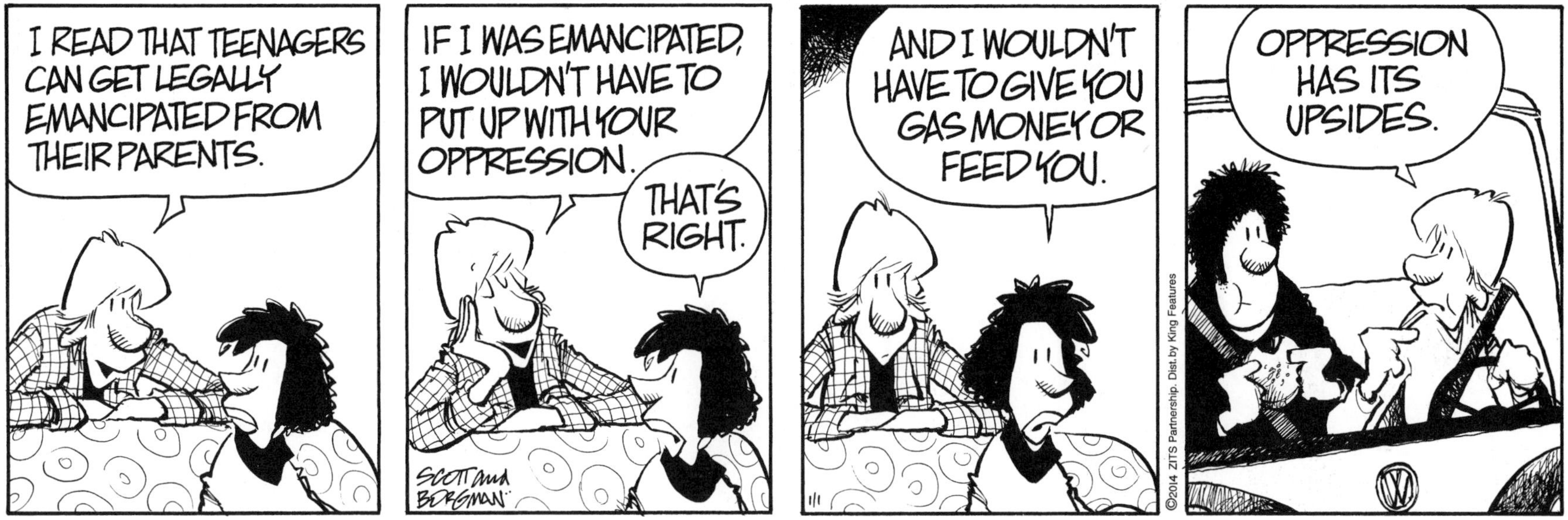
I READ THAT TEENAGERS CAN GET LEGALLY EMANCIPATED FROM THEIR PARENTS.
IF I WAS EMANCIPATED, I WOULDN'T HAVE TO PUT UP WITH YOUR OPPRESSION.
THAT'S RIGHT.
SCOTT and BORGMAN
AND I WOULDN'T HAVE TO GIVE YOU GAS MONEY OR FEED YOU.
1/1
©2014 ZITS Partnership. Dist. by King Features
OPPRESSION HAS ITS UPSIDES.

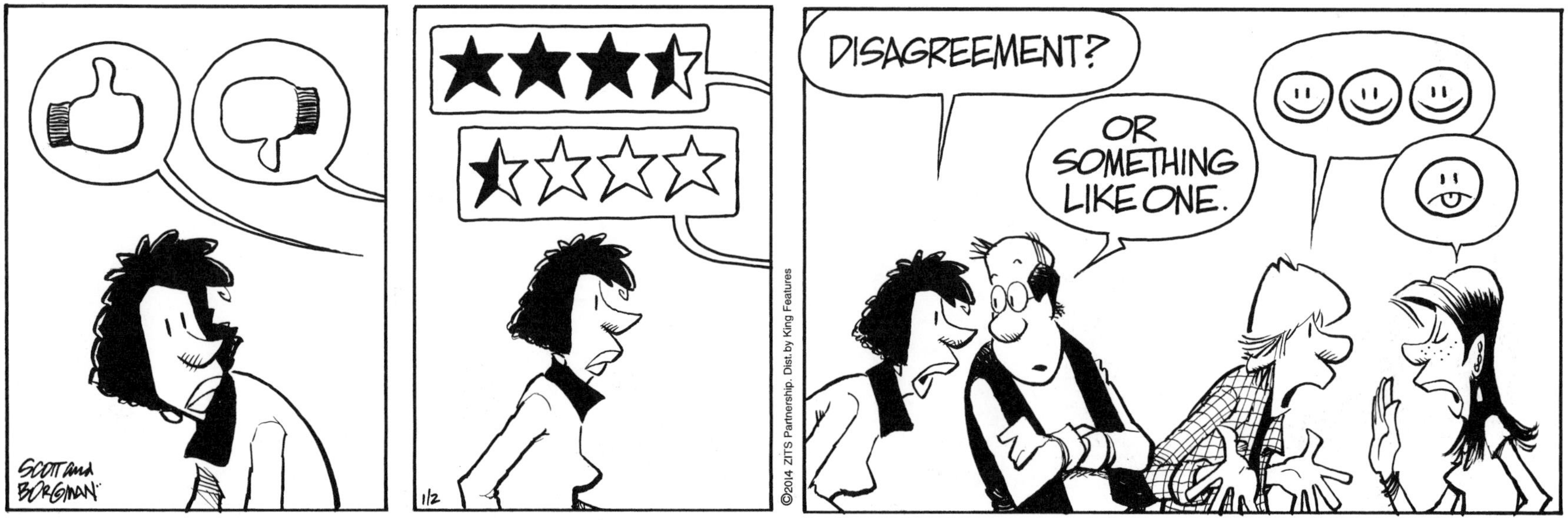
SCOTT and BORGMAN
1/2
©2014 ZITS Partnership. Dist. by King Features
DISAGREEMENT?
OR SOMETHING LIKE ONE.

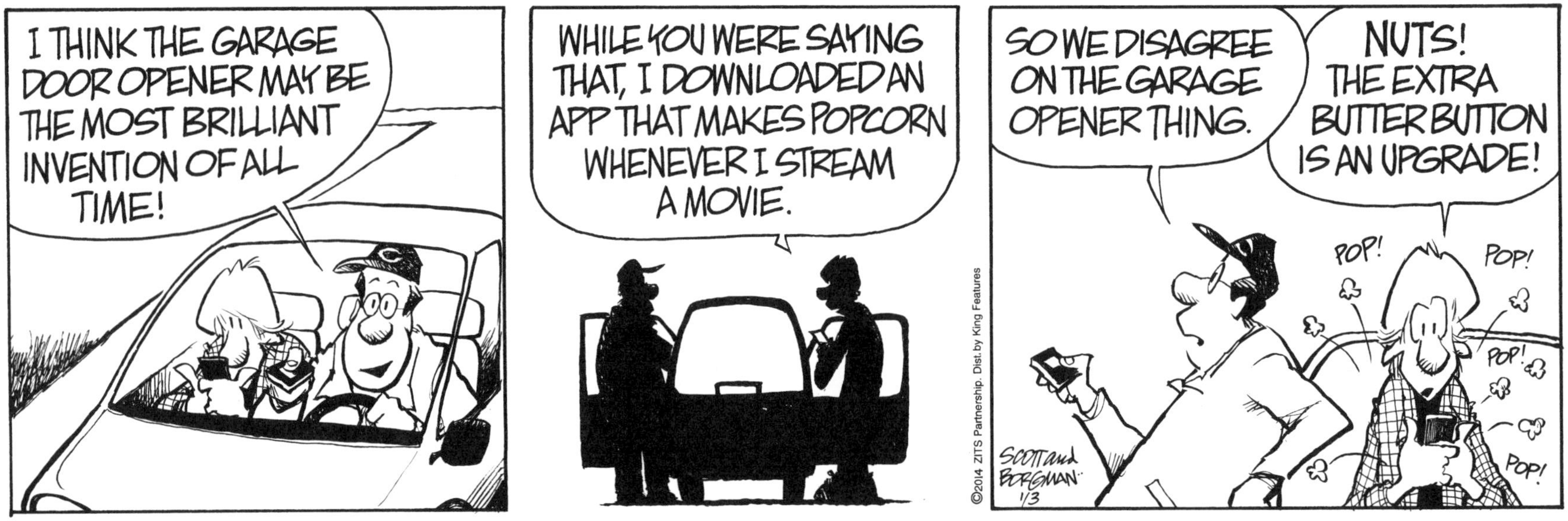
I THINK THE GARAGE DOOR OPENER MAY BE THE MOST BRILLIANT INVENTION OF ALL TIME!
WHILE YOU WERE SAYING THAT, I DOWNLOADED AN APP THAT MAKES POPCORN WHENEVER I STREAM A MOVIE.
©2014 ZITS Partnership. Dist. by King Features
SO WE DISAGREE ON THE GARAGE OPENER THING.
NUTS! THE EXTRA BUTTER BUTTON IS AN UPGRADE!
POP!
POP!
POP!
POP!
SCOTT and BORGMAN 1/3

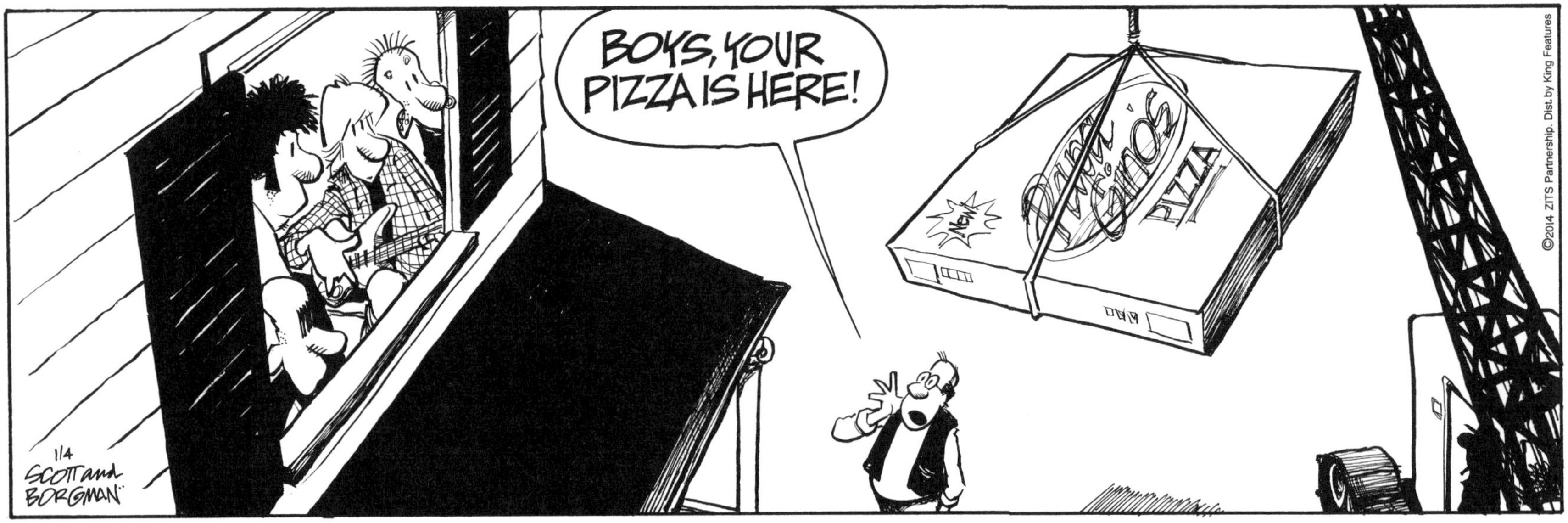
BOYS, YOUR PIZZA IS HERE!
©2014 ZITS Partnership. Dist. by King Features
1/4 SCOTT and BORGMAN

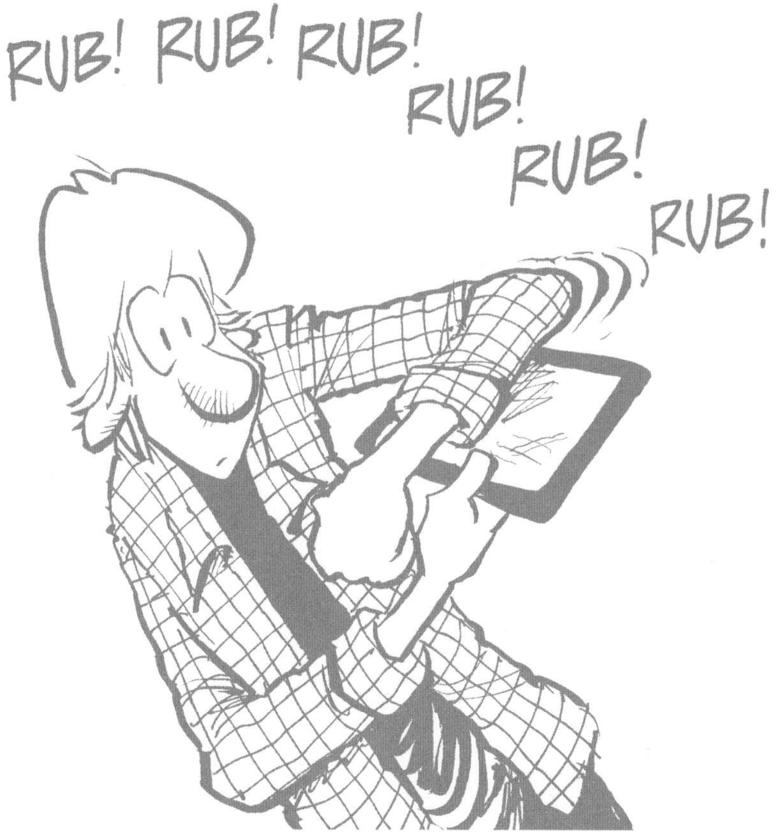
RUB! RUB! RUB!
RUB!
RUB!
RUB!

*Zits*® is syndicated internationally by King Features Syndicate, Inc. For information, write
King Features Syndicate, Inc., 300 West Fifty-Seventh Street, New York, New York 10019.

Andrews McMeel Publishing, LLC
an Andrews McMeel Universal company
1130 Walnut Street, Kansas City, Missouri 64106
www.andrewsmcmeel.com

14 15 16 17 18 SDB 10 9 8 7 6 5 4 3 2 1

ISBN: 978-1-4494-5867-6

Library of Congress Control Number: 2014935608

ATTENTION: SCHOOLS AND BUSINESSES
Andrews McMeel books are available at quantity discounts with bulk purchase for
educational, business, or sales promotional use. For information, please e-mail the
Andrews McMeel Publishing Special Sales Department: specialsales@amuniversal.com.

zitscomics.com • facebook.com/zitscomics • twitter.com/therealzits • rockgod99.tumblr.com